Benefits of Leisure

Benefits of Leisure

Edited by

B. L. Driver
Perry J. Brown
George L. Peterson

Venture Publishing, Inc.
State College, Pennsylvania

Cover Design: Sikorski Design
Cover Illustration: Pam Heidtmann
Production: Bonnie Godbey
Printing and Binding: BookCrafters, Chelsea, MI

Library of Congress Catalogue Card Number 91-67118
ISBN 0-910251-48-7

TABLE OF CONTENTS

III. RESPONSES FROM DISCIPLINARY PERSPECTIVES

IV. SUMMARY

V. APPENDIX:

PREFACE

The benefits of leisure are measured in two ways for different purposes. One type of measure is used by economists for tests of economic efficiency in benefit-cost analyses. The other type—where benefits are viewed as improved or desired conditions of individuals, groups, and society—is used to define and quantify the magnitudes of the positive impacts from production and use of leisure services. There is an extensive and rich literature on the "economic efficiency" benefits of leisure. Considerably less documentation exists on "benefits as desirable consequences." This text helps fill that information gap.

As indicated by the *Table of Contents*, the text has 35 chapters: 5 are introductory; 21 are state-of-knowledge, generally about a specific type of benefit; 8 represent responses from different disciplines and have a strong methodological or epistemological orientation; and there is one summary/integrative chapter. The purposes of the text are to explain the need for systematic information on the benefits of leisure, document what is known, and recommend future directions for study and analysis.

All of the 57 authors, from the 6 countries represented, were commissioned to prepare their chapters. However, the monetary commissions offered generally covered only the travel costs to attend a workshop in Snowbird, Utah, at which preliminary and previously circulated drafts were previewed to provide feedback to the authors. Thus, the first note of appreciation from us, must be to each author for the considerable time and effort contributed to this text. We are pleased with the results and trust that the reader will share our belief that the chapters are of high quality. Secondly, we thank Charles Loveless and Gregory Super, of the USDA Forest Service, for their help at the workshop. A simple thanks seems inadequate to recognize the contributions of Joyce Hart for her typing and other clerical assistance and Jan Shepard Cottier for her fine job of editing. Lastly, but significantly, production of this text would not have been possible without the financial assistance of the Rocky Mountain Forest and Range Experiment Station of the USDA Forest Service; the College of Forestry of Oregon State University; the Recreation Management Staff of the USDA Forest Service in Washington, DC; the Natural Resources Management Branch of the U.S. Army Corps of Engineers; the Economic Analysis and Research Branch of the U.S. Environmental Protection Agency; and Venture Publishing, Inc.

The text should be of interest to all leisure professionals, in the many specialties of that field; to professionals in related fields; and to the lay reader. The authors hope that graduate students, particularly, will find the chapters to be of value to them and stimulate many master's theses and doctoral dissertations on the benefits of leisure.

B.L.D.
P. J. B.
G. L. P.

I.

INTRODUCTORY CHAPTERS

Research on Leisure Benefits: An Introduction to This Volume

B. L. Driver
Rocky Mountain Forest and Range Experiment Station
USDA Forest Service
Fort Collins, Colorado

Perry J. Brown
College of Forestry
Oregon State University
Corvallis, Oregon

George L. Peterson
Rocky Mountain Forest and Range Experiment Station
USDA Forest Service
Fort Collins, Colorado

This volume comprises 35 chapters on the benefits of leisure that were written by 57 well-known experts from six countries. Preliminary drafts of these chapters were reviewed at a meeting of the authors in Snowbird, Utah in May, 1989, and those drafts were revised to incorporate feedback received. This introductory chapter sets the stage for those that follow. It establishes some definitions and the organization of this volume, and explains our purposes and philosophical/conceptual orientation.

DEFINITIONS

Benefits and Values

It is well established that decisionmakers who allocate resources need valid and reliable information on the beneficial and detrimental consequences of alternative uses. They use information on monetary value, for example, to compute internal rates of return on alternative investments and to make benefit/cost analyses. Monetary valuation answers only some of the many questions facing decisionmakers, however, so they need other kinds of information as well—information that describes and explains the consequences in other than monetary terms.

Although these informational needs exist for all allocation decisions, the decisions of concern here are those dealing with the creation and maintenance of leisure opportunities. This topic is timely because as leisure expenditures and demands continue to grow, the methods for specifying and measuring the "good" and "bad" consequences of maintaining and using leisure resources remain inadequate, as do methods for appraising the value of these consequences to individuals, groups, and society.

Confounding the tasks of describing consequences and estimating worth are semantic problems and myopic disciplinary perspectives. Different people use the words "values," "benefits," and "costs" in different ways, and as Boulding (1956) has stated more generally, "One wonders sometimes if science will not grind to a stop in an assemblage of walled-in hermits, each mumbling to himself in a private language that only he can understand."

To help establish some definitions, we will describe the approach we adopted for this volume (as discussed in several recent papers by P. Brown 1984, Driver and Peterson 1986, Driver and Burch 1988, Peterson et al. 1990). Figure 1 shows the basic schema which employs a production process perspective to valuation.

Figure 1 shows all the analytical tasks required for comprehensive evaluations of the good and bad impacts of a proposed investment alternative and measurement of the

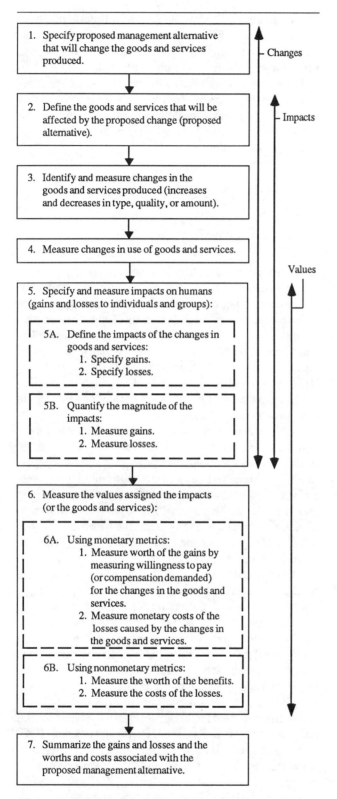

Figure 1. Analytical tasks required to evaluate and value impacts of a proposed resource allocation decision.

relative worth and costs of these impacts. A basic assumption underlying the logic of the Figure 1 paradigm is that decisionmakers need to know what are the good and bad impacts, as well as what are their relative worth and costs.

Boxes (tasks) 1-4 are self-explanatory except perhaps for differences between Boxes 3 and 4; the goods and services produced in Box 3 might not be used, which is indicated by Box 4. Thus, both measures are needed for efficient, responsive, and effective allocations. Our concern here is with Boxes 5 and 6 which address evaluating gains (benefits) and losses, and estimating the values assigned either the gains and losses or the leisure services that produced them. We will refer to these two boxes to define the way the word benefit is used in this volume.

Two uses of the word "benefit" are common in the resource allocation literature. One is the economists' use of the word to mean an economic gain, measured in monetary terms (or, as strictly defined, a "potential Pareto improvement," see Randall 1984a). Box 6A in Figure 1 captures this definition. Economic valuation is an important information input to benefit/cost analysis and economic impact analysis of resource management alternatives (see chapters in this volume by Kealy and by Johnson and Brown). Benefit/cost analysis is an information system that addresses the economic efficiency objective (Randall 1984b), and economic impact analysis addresses the equity objective by providing information about the distribution of economic costs and benefits. This volume does not focus on economic benefits of leisure because the economists' approach is well covered elsewhere (Peterson and Randall 1984, Cummings et al. 1986, Peterson et al. 1988).

The second concept of benefit, and the focus of this volume, is the one of everyday usage reflected by how the word "benefit" is defined in most dictionaries. That usage is indicated by the word "gain" in Box 5 of Figure 1. Within this context, the word "benefit" refers to a *change* that is viewed to be advantageous—an improvement in condition, or a gain to an individual, a group, to society, or to another entity (as discussed in this volume by Rolston). The economists' "benefit" is simply a monetary valuation of that gain as indicated in Box 6A1.

This concept of benefit as an improved condition is really synonymous with the idea of utility in consumer economics. The difference is that utility is generally viewed as an unquantifiable abstraction, while benefit as a specific type of gain is definable and quantifiable. Benefits defined as gains or advantageous changes are thus directly subject to predictive modeling and to testing for cause and effect relationships, as suggested in Figure 2 by the very general flow model of leisure choice and impact (including beneficence), which was adopted with modification from Harris et al. (1984).

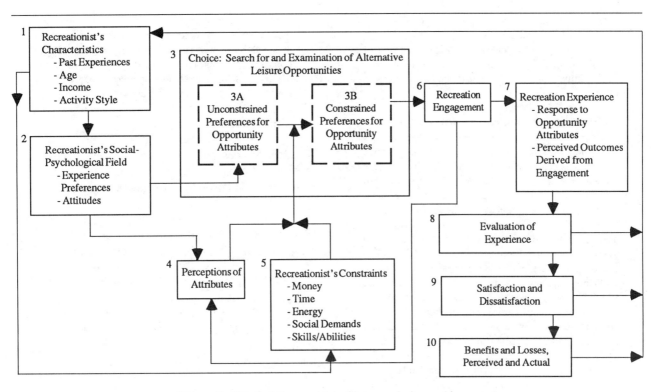

Figure 2. General flow model of leisure choice and impact.

Elsewhere (Driver and Peterson 1986, Driver and Burch 1988, Schreyer and Driver 1989), these two concepts of benefits have been called "monetary" and "nonmonetary" measures to emphasize differences in measurement methodology and the purposes served by each. More recently, we have referred to these two measures as "economic efficiency" and "benefit-as-improved-condition" measures, because economic metrics can be used to quantify improved conditions. A Driver and Peterson paper (1986: 3-5 of Values Section) summarized the differences between, and needs for, these two types of measures as follows:

> The economic [efficiency] way of measuring the value of outdoor recreation benefits has seldom attempted to identify or describe the specific beneficial functions (e.g., improved conditions) provided by a unit of recreation opportunity. Rather, it simply shows how much money one is willing to give up to use the opportunity as an instrument to obtaining the beneficial function(s). That amount of money will change with context, so the context needs to be specified. Thus, benefits in economic studies are indexed by the consumers' willingness to pay to obtain a good or service or the compensation demanded to forego or give up a possessed good or service. Some economic studies have looked at the attributes of a good or service that is required for the realization of

particular beneficial functions, but those functions are seldom if ever specified by the analyst...

The economic efficiency measures are used to determine the relative degree to which particular public investments, or changes in such, add to or detract from national economic welfare. These changes in economic welfare are expressed as aggregate net national economic benefits and are indexed by prices that sovereign consumers voluntarily are willing to pay, minus the costs of providing the goods and services. Put simply, the most economically efficient allocations are those that increase net willingness to pay the most; they contribute more to aggregate economic welfare than alternative allocations that do not provide the same "benefits" per public dollar involved.

These efficiency analyses serve as a valuable input to resource allocation decisions by helping prevent wasteful allocations of scarce national resources. They are especially useful because all measures of benefits and costs are in commensurate metrics, usually dollars. Also, the measures overcome the need to undertake the difficult...tasks of identifying and quantifying what the actual beneficial functions are (say of the spiritual values of natural areas), including gaining consensus about the context within which a particular consequence can or cannot be considered a benefit and to whom. They also record directly the values of sovereign individuals (e.g., as expressed by their revealed choices in markets) rather than the values of others (elected representatives, etc.) who attempt to interpret values for individuals and groups of such.

The noneconomic [benefit-as-improved-condition] measures are needed to help define better what recreation is and is not. That basic information is helpful in public allocation decisions but even more so in advancing the body of professional knowledge about recreation—just as cause and effect relationships needed to be documented to improve the effectiveness of the medical professions. Results from the noneconomic measures are needed also to supplement the economic efficiency measures in public resource allocation decisions. Because of multiple public and private objectives, the efficiency measures are important but not sufficient (Randall 1984b). Two equally efficient options can have very different distributional consequences, so it is important to expose how the gains and losses are divided up among the people. It is true also that two equally efficient options can produce very different kinds of beneficial consequences, irrespective of distributional differences. Most people would say that a hundred dollars worth of education is more valuable than a hundred dollars worth of candy (assuming equal public costs), though the economic efficiency criterion assigns them equal economic value. Public decisionmakers desire to know what type and amount of benefits are being produced as well as their dollar worth. In fact, the primary role of elected representatives is conflict resolution, which is usually achieved by making reasonable compromises. Information on benefits is needed to understand the competing interests and demands involved.

The noneconomic measures also help policymakers understand better those benefits not indexed by the economic measures, such as any spin-off (merit good or external) benefits to nonusers or to society at large, preservation/environmental benefits that might be realized in the future but are outside the sovereign consumers' economic decision calculus, and benefits of sustained yield management not attributable directly to flows of goods and services over a particular planning period. In addition, the noneconomic measures are useful in recreation resource management. For example, by employing the tenet from public finance that the beneficiaries should pay, information on how and on which types of users benefit could help guide fee policies. The benefits information could also help decide when constraints should and should not be set in mathematical planning models (e.g., linear programming) to assure that certain types of goods and services will be delivered. Lastly, the noneconomic measures can help increase the

wisdom of the sovereign consumers (who derive most of their information from sources outside themselves) about what purchases and activities will and will not be beneficial (e.g., benefits of not eating food high in cholesterol, of persistent aerobic exercise, of stress management, of not smoking, of avoiding drug abuse, etc.). This information will increase the validity of the economic efficiency measures.

These and other uses of the economic efficiency and benefit-as-improved-condition measures are discussed in more detail in Schreyer and Driver (1989) and Driver (1990).

To summarize, benefits are improved conditions, and an economic "benefit" is the monetary worth of the improvements as measured by the prices that people are willing to pay for the goods, services, and conditions that comprise the improvements. This is reflected by Boxes 5 and 6 of Figure 1. Specifically, Peterson et al. (1990) collapsed the analytical tasks defined by those two boxes into the following three phases of evaluation. Although attention was directed to evaluating the benefits and values of public amenities, the following logic applies to evaluating the losses, too.

1. *Qualitative Analysis*:
   A. Specify the beneficial change(s) being studied.
   B. Select variables (and their parameters) that will be used in Phase 2 to quantify the scope and magnitude of the specified benefit(s).
   C. Select variables (and their parameters) that will be used in the Phase 3 valuations.

2. *Quantitative Analysis*: Quantify the scope and magnitude of the benefit(s).

3. *Valuation*: Measure the worth assigned the benefits, and/or the goods and services that produce them, using economic and other metrics.

An example might help. Suppose that one is interested in the benefits of an exercise trail, and that as a part of the qualitative analysis, reduction of hypertension has been specified as a possible benefit. To perform the Phase 1 analysis, one could select changes in systolic and diastolic blood pressure as the variable to be used with readings above 140/90 selected as indicators of hypertension. Then, one could select willingness to pay for use of the exercise trail, reduced health cost, or other measures to use in the Phase 3 valuation stage to estimate the value assigned that benefit. During the Phase 2 quantification stage an experimental design could be used to measure how much systolic and diastolic pressure changed with and without use of the trail and with different levels of use. Then, during Phase 3 Valuation, the worth of any benefits documented would be estimated.

While we recognize that Boxes 5 and 6 of Figure 1 call for evaluating the losses and costs of investments in amenity and other resources, our attention is limited to benefits in this volume.

Leisure And Recreation

In the preliminary draft of this chapter, we stated we would use the words "leisure" and "recreation" synonymously. However, there was much discussion at the meeting in Snowbird, and in many of the chapters in this volume, about the problems caused by the lack of a clear and widely accepted definition of the word "leisure" and poor differentiation of the words "leisure" and "recreation"—especially within the context of specifying, measuring, and valuing the benefits of leisure. This problem is not resolved by the chapters in this volume, nor do we expect it will be soon.

Generally, the authors agree that recreation refers to behaviors that are engaged in voluntarily for their intrinsic rewards during times when one is not committed to meeting basic survival and comfort needs, attaining material possessions, or meeting on-going social obligations. "Obligations" is a key word as there is consensus that recreation occurs during nonwork time and is accompanied by a relatively high level of perceived personal freedom (lack of outside control) and a low sense of being time-bound.

While some of the authors view leisure in the same way as recreation, others hold the view that leisure itself denotes a desirable state, such as the state of flow (see chapter by Csikszentmihalyi and Kleiber). Within that context, leisure as a good (or higher) state, condition, or experience is a benefit. Had we adopted that perspective, we would have titled this volume *Leisure and Other Benefits of Recreation*. We didn't because we do not know what that state of leisure is. Also, we doubt if there is a specific human response that can be called leisure. This position reflects our opinion that there are no theories of leisure behavior, only theories of human behavior that help explain leisure behaviors as rather generic human behaviors. Can a particular response be called a state of leisure when many people respond to some types of work and nonwork, nonleisure stimuli the same as they do to nonwork, leisure stimuli?

We are thus left with varied definitions and orientations. We do not see this as a serious problem because of the rather commonly held intuitions and understandings of what leisure and recreation are which seem to differ more in nuance than substance and which seem to serve rather specific purposes for different people. Or put differently, if the disparity were all that great, we should be able to converge on the essential dimensions of our disagreements and come up with more explicit differentiation of the differing dimensions of recreation and leisure. But leisure professionals have not been able to do that after several decades of deliberating these "differences."

WHY THIS VOLUME?

Because leisure behavior is commonly considered to be intrinsically rewarding, it is almost tautological to say it is beneficial. Recreationists voluntarily behave in ways they deem rewarding and beneficial. If it is not self-evident that beneficial consequences exist, there are other indicators. The most recent National Outdoor Recreation Household Survey (USDI National Park Service 1986) showed that 89 percent of the respondents (aged 12 and over) engaged at least once in outdoor recreation activities the previous year. Other studies show that billions of dollars are spent each year on leisure and that the users would be willing to pay even more, if need be. It seems reasonable to presume that these data reflect sizable benefits, even if some of the recreationists engaged in behaviors that are not beneficial.

The issue then is not whether leisure activities produce beneficial consequences. The questions are: What are those consequences? Who benefits? What are the magnitudes of the beneficial consequences? What type of pursuits and environments produce which benefits? How dependent are specific beneficial consequences on particular recreational settings and environments and, if not highly dependent, are there strong preferences that specific benefits be realized from particular leisure behaviors in particular settings? What are the attributes of those settings necessary for benefit production? What is the value—or relative worth—of the beneficial consequences? How do we apply information on these benefits in leisure policy analysis and in the delivery of leisure services?

Practically all of the chapters in this volume point out that too little information exists to answer the above questions. Some reasons for that deficiency follow.

- A "work ethic" still nurtures the perspective that recreation is something relatively unimportant or unproductive for which a right must be earned. Fortunately, this concept is losing strength, but it has served to reduce the systematic study of the benefits of leisure.
- Recreation opportunities are frequently provided as public goods because of the consensus that

they are needed and "good" for people and for society in general. This perspective has deterred systematic evaluation of the specific dimensions of these benefits, because recreation has already been defined as socially good.

- Unlike other services, there has been no united interest group(s) to push the merits of recreation in the public policy arena. The groups that exist frequently display conflicting interests. Other social services (e.g., national defense, public education, housing, transportation, medicine, communication, sanitation, defense, food production) have been given higher research priority, in part because of this lack of united recreation pressure groups.
- Until recently, research on leisure has lagged, so few empirically supported theories have been developed, and methods for quantifying the beneficial consequences have remained embryonic.
- Many public agencies have been slow to develop professional career ladders to reward recreation expertise in line and staff positions. The leisure professions have not had equal status and emphasis. Highly talented people frequently found other employment, rather than promote leisure and leisure research within those unsupportive institutions.
- Because of the complexity of the subject, deficiencies in research funding, and lack of expertise, little research using nonmonetary measures has been done on leisure benefits.

Since about 1970, the situation has changed drastically:

- Interest in leisure has grown greatly. That growth can in part be attributed to changing life styles, better integration of outdoor recreation in multiple-use management by federal and state agencies, increased income, more leisure time, earlier retirement, better health, and improved equipment.
- The quality of professional expertise has increased significantly, with leisure scientists gaining considerable recognition in many disciplines, and recreation managers receiving more consideration within the public agencies.
- There is a growing awareness of the need for better information about the beneficial consequences of leisure. For example, the last three national reports on outdoor recreation research needs rated measurement of benefits as high to highest priority.

- Most importantly, there is increasing institutional and financial support for the necessary research, and there is a rapidly growing cadre of extremely well-qualified experts in many disciplines that want to get involved.

This volume arose from the deficiencies stated above, the current situation of leisure studies, and because the time is right. Its specific purposes are to:

- Explain the needs for research on the beneficial consequences of leisure activities.
- Document what scientific evidence exists about specific types of beneficial consequences of leisure behavior.
- Establish the scientific credibility of research on the beneficial consequences and encourage research on those benefits.
- Demonstrate the feasibility of such research, describe methods that have been and can be used, and give direction to future research.

SCOPE OF THIS VOLUME

The fundamental problem associated with the concept of benefit as improved condition is one of determining who decides that a particular change is beneficial or not; drug addicts apparently perceive they gain from getting "high," and designation of a land area as wilderness under provisions of the 1964 Wilderness Act (PL 88-577) would be seen as beneficial by some people (e.g., members of the Wilderness Society), while others (e.g., owners of a company that had planned to mine that designated area) might perceive losses. Thus, the context is important (Brown and Slovic 1988); a person who once perceived benefits from jogging might no longer after sustaining a knee injury from that activity. This issue has been considered in other recent papers, such as one by Driver and Burch (1988: 35-36) who stated:

> ...To answer the question "What are the gains and losses that will occur?" we need to know who gains and who loses and how. Qualitative analyses [Peterson et al. 1990] are needed to help answer these questions, because saying that an impact is a gain or loss involves a valuation by the gainers and losers or by those who represent them. Those judgments reflect the gainers' and losers' held values (or preferential judgments), and they vary from one context to another (T. Brown 1984)...

At some stage, gainers and losers should be involved in defining the gains and losses to protect the sovereignty of those whom the proposed allocation will impact. Those impacted must definitely be involved directly in defining any gains and losses that are not yet well specified. Such involvement might, for example, include members of an Indian tribe claiming sacred significance of a land area, recreationists desiring use of the same area, or a mining company seeking profit from mineral extraction. On the other hand, less involvement is...needed where good definitions exist for certain impacts, such as the cardiovascular benefits of using an area for exercise...or the losses associated with wildfires caused by recreationists.

Despite these needed qualifications, we did not find the question of what constitutes a benefit of leisure to be a serious problem when organizing this volume simply because there was considerable consensus about what is or is not beneficial. For example, before requesting the authors to write their chapters, we asked over 100 of our professional associates to recommend types of benefits that should be considered. There was wide consensus that led to our selecting the 21 types or classes of benefits discussed in the 21 state-of-knowledge chapters in this volume.

Retrospectively, we know of no type or category of benefit of leisure that was omitted, except perhaps gaining a sense of perceived personal freedom or control. But we do not know if that is a benefit, a dimension of leisure which facilitates the realization of benefits, or both. Thus, we believe this volume comprehensively covers all the known and highly probable beneficial consequences of leisure activity. These activities refer to any recreational engagement (including play) in any type of environment or setting. Attention is not limited to a particular topical area such as outdoor recreation. We believe that all likely benefits should be identified before they are attributed to particular recreation activities or settings.

We did experience some problems in avoiding overlap because one improved condition can facilitate another until some "ultimate" beneficial state is attained. For example, recreation-related *mental or physical relaxation* might promote *higher productivity at work*, which could lead to increased *economic security*, which has been identified as an important contributor to *life satisfaction* (Campbell 1981). This problem is elaborated in the chapter by Driver, Tinsley, and Manfredo. Because current knowledge does not permit identification of the links in many of these "chains of benefit causality," this volume does not attempt to focus on ultimate benefits. Thus, some of the chapters focus on several links in the same chain, which causes some overlap.

Several of the authors stated at the meeting at Snowbird—and a few in their chapters in this volume—that they epistemologically object to our position that the analyst should specify a consequence of leisure activity as a gain or loss during the qualitative phase of inquiry (Box 5A of Figure 1). Their position was that someone other than the scientist should make these value judgments. We understand and respect that position but stick by our recommendation because: 1) the survey of over 100 of our professional peers made prior to the workshop showed there was considerable consensus that the consequences considered in the 21 state-of-knowledge chapters are in fact benefits; 2) we believe the benefit being researched will be defined more explicitly following our approach; 3) readers of the research reports will be better prepared to know whether they agree or disagree with the definitions given, they will then be better able to articulate their differences in opinion, and these disagreements will serve to tighten subsequent variable specification; 4) we do not fear that the research will be tainted or the results misinterpreted to prove that hypothesized benefits do exist, and even if this did happen, it would soon be discovered within the basic "error detection" nature of science and scientific review.

In our attempt to be comprehensive, we wished to include consideration of all measures of the benefits of leisure. As we see it, there are two basic measures of the beneficial consequences of leisure—measures of beneficial changes in behavior and introspective measures. Measures based on behavioral (performance) change include improvements in the physical health, increased productivity, family solidarity, etc., of people or of physically defined environmental entities. The introspective measures comprise two classes, those that focus *directly* on benefits as improved conditions (say, perceived increased productivity at work) and *indirect* introspective measures. The indirect measures do not focus on improved conditions but on a construct (such as exercising, being with one's family, experiencing challenge, or exploring) from which inferences can be made about probable beneficial consequences (i.e., health, family solidarity, skill development, and learning). This volume covers all known measures—physiological, psychological, social, and economic. Both "quantitative" and "qualitative" approaches for evaluating the benefits are considered.

The contributors were invited to author or coauthor one of the following four types of papers that reflect the four major sections of this volume:

- Introductory chapters (5) that set the stage by describing trends in leisure activity and in philosophies about leisure, and identify needs for information on the benefits.

- Chapters (21) that describe the state of knowledge about a particular type (or class) of benefit(s) of leisure activity.
- Chapters (8) that represent responses from different disciplinary perspectives which take a strong methodological orientation.
- The integrative summary chapter.

The 21 state-of-knowledge papers have been grouped into the following areas that reflect different disciplinary perspectives and/or types of measures used:

- Physiological and psychophysiological measures.
- Psychological measures.
- Sociological measures.
- Economic and environmental measures (grouped together because there were only two papers).

The authors of the state-of-knowledge papers were requested to address the following "content areas" in their chapters:

- *Specification*: How well specified is the beneficial consequence addressed by the paper? Is it a fairly well identified, defined, and documented benefit, such as the cardiovascular advantages of persistent aerobic exercise, or is it more a proposition or hypothesis such as increased productivity at work?
- *Measurement of magnitude*: What is known from systematic research about the magnitude of the beneficial consequence? What methods were used to make those measures and how adequate are they?
- *Relative importance or worth*: What is known about the relative importance of the beneficial consequence, including monetary measures of that assigned value? A large beneficial change might have less value than a different beneficial change of smaller magnitude.
- *What additional research is needed*? What needs to be done, and what methods should be used? Special attention should be given to past methods used and improvements needed in methods.
- *Feasible research designs*: Each author of a state-of-knowledge paper also was asked to outline at least two research designs that could be implemented, if funding were available, to measure the type of beneficial consequence considered in the paper.

The reader will notice that some authors followed these instructions more closely than others.

Because of the paucity of research on some types of probable beneficial consequences, several of the state-of-knowledge papers focus more on presenting a rigorous definition of the probable benefit(s) being considered and on the problems of measuring the targeted beneficial consequence(s) than on reporting findings of past empirical studies.

The last chapter by Mannell and Stynes provides an excellent integrative summary of the works in this volume. Therefore, it would be redundant for us to give a brief description of the content of each chapter as is commonly done in introductions. That content is indicated generally in the table of contents.

We are pleased with the chapters that were prepared. We are sure this volume will encourage more and better research on the benefits of leisure, which will help advance the leisure professions.

LITERATURE CITED

Boulding, K. E. 1956. General systems theory—the skeleton of science. Management Science. 2: 197-208.

Brown, P. J. 1984. Benefits of outdoor recreation and some ideas for valuing recreation opportunities. In: Peterson, G. L.; Randall, A., eds. Valuation of wildland resource benefits. Boulder, CO: Westview Press: 209-220.

Brown, T. C. 1984. The concept of value in resource allocation. Land Economics. 60: 231-246.

Brown, T. C.; Slovic, P. 1988. Effects of context on economic measures of value. In: Peterson, G. L.; Driver, B. L.; Gregory, R., eds. Amenity resource valuation: Integrating economics with other disciplines. State College, PA: Venture Publishing, Inc.: 23-30.

Campbell, A. 1981. The sense of well-being in America: Recent patterns and trends. New York, NY: McGraw Hill.

Cummings, R. G.; Brookshire, D. S.; Schulze, W. D. 1986. Valuing environmental goods: Assessment of the contingent valuation method. New York, NY: Rowman and Allenheld.

Driver, B. L.; Peterson, G. L. 1986. The values and benefits of outdoor recreation. An integrative overview. In: A Literature Review. President's Commission on Americans Outdoors. Washington, DC: Government Printing Office: 1-9 of Values Section.

Driver, B. L.; Burch, W. R., Jr. 1988. A framework for more comprehensive valuations of public amenity goods and services. In: Peterson, G. L.; Driver, B. L.; Gregory, R., eds. Amenity resource valuation: Integrating economics with other disciplines. State College, PA: Venture Publishing, Inc.: 31-45.

Driver, B. L. 1990. The North American experience in measuring the benefits of leisure. In: Hamilton-Smith, E., ed. Proceedings of a workshop on measurement of recreation benefits. Bundoora, Victoria, Australia: Phillips Institute.

Harris, C. C.; Driver, B. L.; Bergersen, E. P. 1984. Do choices of sport fisheries reflect angler preferences for site attributes? In: Proceedings, Symposium on recreation choice behavior. Gen. Tech. Rep. INT-184. Ogden, UT: USDA Forest Service Intermountain Forest and Range Experiment Station: 46-54.

Peterson, G. L.; Randall, A. 1984. Valuation of wildland resource benefits. Boulder, CO: Westview Press.

Peterson, G. L.; Driver, B. L.; Gregory, R., eds. 1988. Amenity resource valuation: Integrating economics with other disciplines. State College, Pennsylvania: Venture Publishing, Inc.

Peterson, G. L.; Driver, B. L.; Brown, P. J. 1990. The benefits of recreation: Dollars and sense. In: Johnson, R. L.; Johnson, G. V., eds. Economic valuation of natural resources: Issue, theory and applications. Boulder, CO: Westview Press: 7-24.

Randall, A. 1984a. The conceptual basis of benefit cost analysis. In: Peterson, G. L.; Randall, A., eds. Valuation of wildland resource benefits. Boulder, CO: Westview Press: 53-63.

Randall, A. 1984b. Benefit cost analysis as an information system. In: Peterson, G. L.; Randall, A., eds. Valuation of wildland resource benefits. Boulder, CO: Westview Press: 65-75.

Schreyer, R.; Driver, B. L. 1989. The benefits of leisure: Needs for more study of cause and effect. In: Jackson, E. L.; Burton, T. L., eds. Understanding leisure and recreation: Mapping the past, charting the future. State College, PA: Venture Publishing, Inc.: 385-419.

USDI National Park Service. 1986. 1982-1983 Nationwide recreation survey. Washington, DC: Government Printing Office.

Needs for Information on Leisure Benefits in the Legislative Process

George H. Siehl
Natural Resources Division
Congressional Research Service
Library of Congress
Washington,
District of Columbia

Peter H. Kostmayer
Member of Congress, 8th District of Pennsylvania
U.S. House of Representatives
Washington,
District of Columbia

The views presented here are those of the authors and do not necessarily reflect those of CRS or the Library of Congress.

INTRODUCTION

This assessment of needs for information about the benefits of leisure activities is based on the operations and operating environment of the United States Congress. Some requirements or circumstances are unique to that body, but with some tailoring, much of this assessment also applies to state legislatures. While several specific topical information needs are suggested, the focus of the discussion is on how certain characteristics of legislative bodies determine both the need for information and the way in which the information will be processed and used. Some of these characteristics result in what some observers consider less than optimal use of available information.

Ours is a time when greater amounts and wider varieties of information are available than ever before. Through technology, more diverse means of providing information have become available—television, cable, cassette, computers and modems, video conferences, and facsimile machines—but time and opportunity for consuming and contemplating this bounteous harvest seem to shrink. Legislators and their staffs are particularly pressed for time and simply do not have the ability to absorb and ponder all the information they are presented.

While it would be easy to say that legislators need better information, not more information, that would be as fallacious as it is facile—the truth is, the more we know, the more we need to know. This information equation is made more difficult because more people in legislative and other policymaking positions need to know the same information at about the same time.

What Congress needs to know about the benefits of leisure and recreation could fill a book—perhaps that is this book.

However, the information needs of Congress are also partly unknown, specialized, and made more difficult to present in a useful fashion because of the structure and nature of the legislative process. That structure and process are described below so that those who have, or who develop the needed information might more easily make it available to legislators and staff.

THE LEGISLATIVE ENVIRONMENT

This description of the legislative environment is based on the United States Congress, but the setting is one which many state legislators should find familiar. State legislatures may differ from this description largely in the specifics of organization, length of the legislative session, and the resources (especially staff) available to carry out the legislative function.

Tensions of Time

Time constraints are being cited more frequently by observers such as Peter Morrison who said, "The scarcest resource people have is not money but time" (Bradley 1987), and legislators are not about to disagree. There are two aspects to the temporal tension felt by the legislator: the first is the feeling that there is not enough time to do the job before the session expires or the next election arrives; the second is the underlying worry that long-term needs and the implications of decisions may be ignored (or inadequately considered) as action is taken to solve immediate problems. Obviously, Congress is not alone in this vexatious situation. It is similar to concerns about American corporate managers who place more emphasis on quarterly results than on the long-term interests of their corporations.

Corporate America faces a deadline of sorts in its quarterly reporting requirements, faced with the expectation of showing increased profitability or growth along a continuing time path. Congress, on the other hand, "self-destructs" every two years after all House Members and one-third of the Senators must stand for election. Any bills not enacted by the end of a Congress must return to "square one," and begin the entire legislative cycle again in the new Congress. Continuity may suffer as a result.

Within each 2-year Congress, there are two complete budget cycles to be dealt with on a tight schedule set by law. Funds for the operation of all federal programs are normally dependent on the timely completion of the budget/appropriations cycle, although in recent years, several departments or independent agencies of government have been funded through continuing resolutions rather than individual agency appropriation bills. Difficulties with the budget/appropriations process, apart from time pressures, are discussed later. While the budget/appropriations process is under way, committees with authorizing and oversight responsibilities are examining existing programs and considering measures to modify existing programs or create new ones.

Congress, as a representative body, also finds a need to respond to the inquiries, requests, and needs of constituents. Members, as politicians, travel back to their districts frequently, as well as make appearances in the nation's Capitol and around the country to speak, to listen, to be seen and evaluated, and to raise campaign funds.

Each of these activities, plus considering new legislation and participating in the budget and appropriations process, consumes available time and sharpens the need for succinct and pertinent information.

Constituencies and Special Interest Clusters

Legislators most directly represent those who are eligible to vote for or against them, but they have other constituencies as well. These added constituencies include all those people represented by the legislative body, but outside the individual Member's district. The Member's political party is also a constituency of sorts, one which provides guidance and suggestions on some issues, and which may help to influence Members' decisions on votes and on matters deserving more attention.

While constituencies are well understood, special interest "clusters" are not. As used here, the term refers to the grouping of interests—for and against—around a legislative issue or topic. Positions taken by interests in a cluster may reflect viewpoints ranging from calm, rational analysis to raw emotion. Political scientists have referred to the typical clustering as a Washington "iron triangle" of interests surrounding an issue, consisting of a federal agency, the relevant congressional oversight committee, and outside interest groups concerned with the agency's programs. A Member of Congress working on a committee, faces the task of representing varied home constituencies, while balancing the other diverse interests concerned with the issues.

Issues cannot always be decided on their own merits, particularly when dollars or other limited resources are being allocated. Each such issue must also be weighed in relation to competing demands for the available resources. Any federal budget deficit ranging well above $100 billion will likely remain a check against federal largess for all but the most crucial programs. However, in such situations, broad, united coalitions may be able to gain legislative support for a program not generally considered crucial.

Against this backdrop of interest groups and relatively weighted issues, those trying to provide information which is not immediately recognized as relevant face two overriding considerations—the committee structure and the budget process of the Congress. Committee structure complicates the flow of information because of fragmentation and subsequent compartmentalization of subject matter. The budget process largely precludes the counting of noneconomic benefits. (Even economic benefits may be ignored for budget accounting purposes if the benefits fall in another committee's jurisdiction.) Despite their seemingly cumbersome nature, both of these elements, or something similar to them, seem essential to the legislative process at this time. The contributions and limitations of the committee system and the budget process are noted below.

Committee Structure

Committee structure provides the means for delegating the initial authority and responsibility for dealing with groups of issues. The committee system allows for sharing the work to be done, and for development of expertise by legislators on specific topics. This expertise and responsibility are among the reasons why jurisdiction over an issue is carefully monitored by committees and any perceived incursions are challenged.

It was such a challenge by the leadership of the House Appropriations Committee that led Mr. Udall to withdraw his American Heritage Trust Act (H.R. 4127) from consideration by the House Rules Committee in the closing days of the 100th Congress.

Weighed against the benefit of expertise developed by a committee system is a social cost stemming from the inability to deal with programs or issues in their entirety. The general preference is to cut legislative proposals to fit the jurisdiction of a single committee. Such tailoring can help to speed passage because only one House and one Senate committee have to work the bill into their schedules for hearings, mark-up and reporting. A bill which is more comprehensively drawn may invite unwanted attention from other committees which believe a part of the bill's content falls within their jurisdiction. Referral to more than one committee will generally cause delay, and may doom the bill to a lingering death from inaction. And the second committee might alter the bill enough to undercut or destroy the original intent.

Legislatures may function efficiently in compartments, but life does not. There are many associations which deal with leisure activities—many are represented in this volume. These associations are concerned with issues which transcend much of the committee structure of the Congress. Thus, there are many fertile fields in which to plant the seeds of information, and the challenge lies in determining which committees can provide the fullest (or any) yield. The options include those committees which exercise either authorization, oversight, appropriations, or budget functions. They may also include the legislative support organizations which are not committees of the Congress, but serve as information sources and clearinghouses for Members interested in a particular topic such as the environment, tourism, future studies, a geographic region, or an industry. In the House of Representatives, these options may focus on the Committee on Interior and Insular Affairs and its subcommittees on Oversight, Investigations, and National Parks and Public Lands; or the Subcommittee on Interior and Related Agencies of the Appropriations Committee. The committees on Agriculture and Small Business are also important as

Congress shows interest in using amenity resources to stimulate rural economics. Individual Members, who, apart from their committee or constituency ties, may have an interest or expertise in a particular issue are another option. Committee and personal staff are often important as conduits to the elected official for ideas and information and as subsequent significant actors in the legislative process.

The Budget Process

The other overriding consideration, the current budget process, is newer than the committee system, having been established by Congress in the Congressional Budget and Impoundment Control Act of 1974 (P.L. 93-344) and significantly modified by the Balanced Budget and Emergency Deficit Control Act of 1985 (P.L. 99-177) or, as more commonly known, the Gramm-Rudman-Hollings Act. The budget process can be important. It has been criticized by some, especially House committee chairmen, as having too much control over legislative action within the committee system itself. A number of committee chairs have tried, with little success, to lessen the constraints imposed on their committees by the budget process (Cohen 1982, Dewar 1983). That many Members are still unhappy with the constraints of the budget process on the authorizing committees has been illustrated by Haas (1988). He quotes one senior House Member, who said, "The focus on the budget and the timetables, or delays in resolving budget issues, constrain the authorizing committees in terms of their ability to report out bills." Another Member told him, "There is such a latent anger regarding the thrashing of the authorization process that it really threatens to overwhelm this place."

One might contend that the appropriations committees and the budget process provide means for integrating the disparate, constrained legislative efforts and establishing a more holistic programmatic view. At this time, however, the reality of the budget deficit and the constraints which it imposes largely drive the appropriations/budget process. If, in a post-deficit era, such integration did become a dominant force in federal legislative efforts, there would be a tremendous increase in the need for information to secure the desired integration. It is likely, however, that two problems would hamper such an effort: authorizing committee chairs would doubtless struggle to regain the control they said they have already lost to the budget process, and the time limitations inherent in passing annual appropriation bills would allow little opportunity for extensive additional committee work in an already tight schedule. Neither of these problems are insurmountable; negotiation and compromise between authorizing and appropriating committees could establish a new procedure, and appropriations could be passed for multi-year periods (as has often been the case in the past), thus building more time for review into each appropriation cycle.

Unmet requests for facilities, programs, and services in all areas of federal activity, a continuing high budget deficit, the continuing operation of conflicting programs, and the inability to cooperate (through lack of authority or funds) with public and private parties to achieve desired ends can be, and have been, documented. The needs of legislators for information and ideas on these and other topics are, arguably, more pressing than ever before, but the above described restraints on the full flow of information remain.

INFORMATION IN THE LEGISLATIVE ENVIRONMENT

Anyone who doubts the possible emergence of an information-based economy would probably drop those doubts after watching Congress function over a week or more. Data, information, knowledge, and wisdom daily cross thousands of Capitol Hill desks and minds, and yet, there is more to follow. Every user has an individual mix and weighting of sources for their information. The information comes solicited and unsolicited, its arrival eagerly awaited or dreaded, and the content warmly embraced or flatly rejected. On Capitol Hill and throughout Washington—information comes in a tide which sometimes slows, but may never stop to reverse itself until the end of a Congress. From this tide, what kinds of information, and what sources, are most important in the eyes of Congress?

Legislators maintain an array of trusted, independent sources of information and, because information from such sources reaches the legislator, that information has the potential to be acted upon, and thus can be very important. However, staff of committees or a Member's personal office, as noted above, can also play a key role in determining what is important because they control part of the flow, and hence the visibility of information to the Member. They are delegated the responsibility for much of the screening, handling, and dissemination of information directed to the elected official.

Burson-Marsteller, a government relations firm, funded research by the Institute for Government Public Information Research (Institute 1981) to determine the relative importance to congressional staff of various information sources on different kinds of issues. One finding from the report seems particularly relevant for leisure benefit researchers, and it is a point that will be noted again below. The report said:

It is worth noting that government information resources far outranked scholarly publications and studies. This could reflect a genuine preference for official data or simply the time pressures which congressional staff face, making it difficult for them to read long technical papers or reports.

Participating staff were asked to rank the visibility of 96 types of communications typically reaching congressional offices, scoring "1" for types seen very frequently and ranging to a score of "5" for those never seen. The procedure was repeated three times to assess the impact on issues of district or state importance, on issues for which the member had responsibility, and on issues of general importance. The report presented a cumulative ranking showing the 30 highest ranking types of communications and the 11 lowest ranking. Scholarly publications or reports did not make either list, so they rank somewhere from 31st to 85th on the list. The 10 highest ranking sources from the cumulative list are shown in Table 1.

Table 1. Highest ranking types of communications.

Method	Average Rank
1. Spontaneous letters from constituents	1.67
2. Telephone calls from constituents	3.67
3. Congressional Research Service	4.00
4. Articles in major daily newspapers	5.00
5. Editorials in major daily newspapers	7.00
6. Visits from constituents	7.67
7. Articles in district daily newspapers	7.67
8. Congressional Record	8.33
9. Editorials in district daily newspapers	8.67
10. Government publications	11.67

When the results on visibility of communication types were ranked by source, those coming from constituents placed first, followed by government, print media, broadcast media, special interests, and miscellaneous, the category which includes nongovernment research studies and reports.

A final excerpt from the Institute's report is found in Table 2, in which the 10 highest visibility sources are shown for three types of issues: general, those in which the member has oversight or other responsibility, and those of local or state importance.

Apart from communicating as a constituent or through government reports, individuals may wish to consider the use of articles in major newspapers (which show a relatively high ranking) as a medium for reaching a congressional audience.

Table 2. Highest ranking types of communications by issue.

General	Oversight	Local
1	2	2
4	3	4
3	1	8
2	6	7
5	5	11
8	9	6
14	8	1
7	4	14
13	10	3
12	7	16

RIDING THE TIDE

This volume is a part of the tide of information flowing into Congress and other legislative chambers; information of considerable breadth and, in many cases, subtlety. The scope of leisure benefits has been outlined in some detail (Driver 1988). One purpose of this volume is to determine how that information can be channeled to inform the Congress or other legislators so as to enhance the support and delivery of leisure services, despite the constraints imposed by committee structure and the budget process. The achievement of that goal is a complex task, the particulars of which will vary with individual cases. There are three elements, however, that seem worth considering in all cases: good science, good writing, and awareness of trends.

Good Science and Good Writing

The need for good science is obvious to the research community, and it is the very least that decisionmakers deserve. No more needs to be said about this element. The science is not sufficient in and of itself, however, and here the need for good writing becomes clear. Few legislators have academic backgrounds in resource management or a field of science; more often than not they are lawyers or businessmen. They can, and do, master issues of considerable complexity, but they do not have time to acquire an entire new formal education. Therefore, communicate with them—write what can be read and understood by an intelligent nonspecialist. Provide the legislators with well-founded recommendations and the best available estimates of the consequences of implementing (and not implementing) those recommendations.

In *The Last Intellectuals,* Jacoby (1987) notes the demise of scholars willing and able to write on matters of public concern in a manner that stimulates informed public consideration and debate on those issues. Those scholars largely have been replaced, he contends, by new academics who consider ever smaller topics in terms comprehensible only by a narrow circle of fellow academics. He wrote, "As intellectuals became academics, they had no need to write in a public prose; they did not, and finally they could not."

In his view, informed public discourse on issues is suffering, if not disappearing, as a result; instead, slogans and catch-phrases become the currency of public discourse.

It is worth noting, perhaps, that Jacoby addresses an example of the kind of nonconventional relationships which this volume is examining. He discusses land use, particularly the destruction of inexpensive bohemias by urban renewal in the 1960s and 1970s, as an important factor in the decline of broad, interactive clusters of intellectuals, a fateful step toward the specialist academic circles he decries.

Awareness of Trends

The final element noted above, awareness of trends, refers not to changes in leisure and related subject areas, but to changes in the legislative environment. Briefly, some of the most important of these include:

- Less time for legislators to consider individual issues;
- More concerns with budget deficits or their likelihood;
- More interest in local effects of policy decisions;
- Increased responsibility of states in decision-making;
- Party shifts in legislatures after redistricting in 1991; and
- More use of new technology in presentation of information.

These trends offer both opportunities and challenges in showing the broad range of noneconomic benefits of leisure and recreation activities. The state legislatures, because of their increasing responsibility but generally more limited research and analytical resources, may be particularly open to a new assessment of the myriad benefits of leisure. As state governments expand or reorganize to deal with their expanded responsibilities, some legislatures may also adjust their structures or processes. If information and suggestions are at hand, some changes to provide for more comprehensive consideration of leisure and recreation benefits might be achieved.

AREAS OF OPPORTUNITY

The topics under discussion in this volume suggest many possible avenues of research, information gathering, and communication to Congress in order to build a better understanding of the various beneficial consequences of leisure and recreation activities. Two sets of relationships which could be of interest to the Congress at this time are those melding leisure activities with environmental stability and with community stability.

Public opinion polls, ballot questions, and newspaper and magazine coverage all show that Americans have a high degree of concern with the protection of their environment. They seem to be particularly concerned with the issues of growth management and environmental threats to personal health. An examination of the ties between leisure and environmental stability might include:

- The role and impact of volunteer activities such as clean-up campaigns, bird-banding, habitat expansion, and erosion control;
- The environmentally beneficial consequences of dedicating areas of land and water for leisure and recreation activities; and
- The ethical and educational gains derived from nature-based activity.

Outdoor recreation and other land-based activities are being identified as one means of providing jobs and income to rural communities in which agriculture, forestry, mining, or energy recovery have dropped rapidly in importance. The stabilization which might result from the substitution of leisure-related pursuits is foremost an economic benefit. The secondary benefits, however, are more attuned to the themes of this volume. Among those possible secondary benefits to be examined are:

- The preservation of rural lifestyles;
- The continuation of families living in proximity to the land;
- The maintenance of social diversity;

- The reduction of population drifts to urban areas simply because there is no economic alternative; and
- The avoidance of the social and economic costs of unemployment.

Some additional suggestions for multidisciplinary research on leisure and recreation at the policy level have been raised previously (Siehl 1988). These suggestions range from better identification of user motivations and recreation interests to determining if migrants to nonmetropolitan areas become involved in nearby public land management planning efforts. Through such information, legislators and other policymakers can authorize and fund most appropriately, and can better evaluate the advice they receive from many quarters.

SUMMARY

The breadth of the context for leisure essayed by this volume, deserves full consideration by decisionmakers—and demands clear articulation by supporters. However, neither history nor current practice give much encouragement toward achieving these goals. Congress and other legislative bodies can seldom consider—let alone treat—any subject in all its manifestations. The constraints of time are compounded by organizational structures which set rather precise jurisdictional boundaries, and by the budgeting and funding processes which may limit the financial resources available for legislative programs.

A related matter, although not discussed in this paper, is that Congress frequently hears from advocacy groups about natural resource considerations and federally managed lands, but seldom hears about the related individual and social considerations.

If a broader agenda, based on the full array of beneficial consequences of leisure is to be set by Congress and the state legislatures, a new effort seems necessary. Information on those consequences must be developed through good science, and the information must be presented in a manner easily comprehendible by legislators. Those who would present this information should be aware of the several avenues into the Congress or state legislatures—and the barriers which often block those avenues.

LITERATURE CITED

Bradley, B. 1987. Knowing tastes, needs of baby-boom generation is a marketing challenge. Christian Science Monitor. June 8, 1987.

Cohen, R. E. 1982. House braces for showdown over how it should package its annual budget. National Journal. Nov. 27, 1982: 2024-2026.

Dewar, H. 1983. House committee chairmen proposing changes to recoup their budget power. Washington Post. A21, April 27, 1983.

Driver, B. L. 1988. What are they, how big are they, and what are they worth: some ideas on recreation benefits. In: McDonald, B. and McDonald, C., conference director and editor. Southeastern recreation research conference: Proceedings of a technical conference; 1988 February; Asheville, NC. Athens, GA: University of Georgia Institute for Behavioral Research:7-20.

Haas, L. J. 1988. Unauthorized action. National Journal. Jan. 2, 1988: 17-21.

Institute for Government Public Information Research, American University. 1981. A study of the exposure of federal legislative offices to various information vehicles. Available from Burson-Marsteller, Washington, DC. 32 p.

Jacoby, R. 1987. The last intellectuals. New York: Basic Books. 290 p.

Siehl, G. H. 1988. A policy analyst's views on some relevant research topics. In: McDonald, B. and McDonald, C., conference director and editor. Southeastern recreation research conference: Proceedings of a technical conference; 1988 February; Asheville, NC. Athens, GA: University of Georgia Institute for Behavioral Research:32-43.

Managerial Needs for Information on Benefits of Leisure

Darrell E. Lewis
Natural Resources Management Branch
U.S. Army Corps of Engineers
Washington,
District of Columbia

H. Fred Kaiser
Forest Inventory, Economics, and Recreation
Research Division
USDA Forest Service
Washington,
District of Columbia

Managers responsible for providing recreation opportunities to the public need to have an understanding of how leisure benefits individuals and society. Competition for scarce resources makes it no longer sufficient for managers to simply carry out the mission of providing recreation opportunities without more sophisticated information. This is particularly true when decisionmakers are thought to be biased towards commodity-oriented options, where benefits are more readily identified and quantified.

Managers need both economic and noneconomic measures of leisure benefits. In the past, application of evaluation concepts by land managers has been primarily informal and intuitive, particularly where conflicts over resource allocations have not been intense. For many years, the success of judgmental planning methods was measured by continuing political support and relative lack of controversy over land use policies.

The situation has changed as pressures have mounted for maximizing net public benefits. The environmental movement led to federal legislation, regulations, and executive orders that required increased attention to economic and environmental consequences of federal natural resource management actions. For example, the 1974 Forest and Range Land Renewable Resources Planning Act (RPA) directs the Forest Service to identify management needs, opportunities, and alternative programs and to analyze their long-term costs and benefits. The 1976 Federal Land Policy and Management Act requires the Bureau of Land Management to develop multiple-use management plans for lands under its administration and to inventory the resource values of these lands to identify changes and emerging resource needs. The Principles and Guidelines for Water Resources Development direct the U. S. Army Corps of Engineers, Bureau of Reclamation, and Soil Conservation Service to identify the national economic development benefits of their projects.

These legislative and administrative guidelines have stimulated a major need for identification of recreation and other leisure benefits. For example, the National Forest System is now guided by Section 6 of the Forest and Range Land Renewable Resource Act, which requires formulation of a detailed planning system for program coordination. Some key characteristics of this system are:

- allocation of resource production targets based on the resource capability of each administrative unit and on the relative efficiency of production;
- use of national assessment and program planning findings by regional foresters to prepare

regional plans which show how targets are distributed among national forests within each region; and
- use of the assigned regional targets and local information on capabilities to prepare a multi-resource plan for each national forest.

As the Forest Service and other agencies have discovered, resource planning and evaluation are complex processes. Public land management covers a wide range of activities and the use of diverse combinations of natural resource management facilities. Identification and measurement of leisure benefits from public lands can create major challenges because some of the outputs from these lands lack a conventional pricing mechanism.

WHAT DO MANAGERS DO?

To provide perspective, we need to review just what a manager does before we go any further. Managers have a complex task, with requirements frequently outnumbering capabilities. It's the manager's job to allocate funds and personnel to the highest priority work and assure that scarce resources are utilized effectively and efficiently. There is no cookbook! Managers have a broad latitude, but must produce defendable programs. The key is that, with all this latitude, the manager is accountable.

Mission

Managers start with a mission, or in most cases, multiple missions. In the public sector, missions are found in laws. Broad legislative mandates are digested into policies and regulations that the field manager implements with the resources provided through a budgetary process. Missions are frequently broad with inherent conflicts between missions.

Plans

After the mission is understood and documented, the manager must analyze the resources within his or her area of responsibility. A plan is developed which spells out what will be done and what resources will be required. The necessary information is gathered and analyzed. A public involvement process frequently introduces numerous conflicting views. Taking all of this into account, the manager decides on a course of action. The final plan is approved. The original plan is periodically reevaluated for validity in relation to current conditions.

Implementation

The manager now allocates personnel and funds to the accomplishment of the plan. Facilities are constructed. Personnel are recruited, hired, trained, and equipped. Operation and maintenance activities commence.

Operations and Maintenance

The manager continues to monitor operations and maintenance activities to assure the program is consistent with the original mission. In each budget cycle, the manager must justify the utilization of resources at current levels.

WHY DO MANAGERS NEED BENEFITS INFORMATION?

The manager is always in need of more information about all aspects of his or her program, but at levels of detail comparable to that available for competing issues. Although it can be tempting for public managers and analysts to ignore leisure benefits, they must be considered in making adequate resource evaluations and in justifying programs. Simply, leisure benefits are too important to too many people to ignore their magnitude and value when justifying programs and budgets, formulating and analyzing policies, and making investment decisions. If leisure benefits are ignored, interested publics will take the administrators to task and challenge their decisions, sometimes in court.

Obviously, public administrators need information on the benefits of leisure to help evaluate the merits of leisure service programs against competing program needs. Administrators can use information on leisure benefits to communicate how they view the value of these resources, and legislators can respond based on their perception of values. At a minimum, stating the magnitude and value of leisure benefits enables the opening of a dialogue about these resources relative to other resources. Such a dialogue has proven valuable when legislators are interested in how resource administrators justify their program and budget requests.

Policymakers, in particular, need to have a complete understanding of the relative merits of competing programs. This is significant where the noneconomic nature of the benefits of leisure programs dampen the priority level of these programs. Managers need information on the benefits of leisure programs to assist in the difficult task of allocating scarce resources (funds and personnel) efficiently. This is particularly important given today's climate of declining resources and ever increasing demands. Unfortunately, economic benefits dominate this decisionmaking process. The noneconomic benefits are too often left to the manager to assess through "common sense." The manager is forced to rely on intuition to incorporate the noneconomic aspects of the issue into the decision process. This leaves the manager vulnerable to competitors' versions of the "common sense" aspects of the issue.

The issue of below-cost timber sales on national forests is a case where leisure values are proving to be an important part of the debate. Concern is expressed by conservation and forest industry groups, forest and economic professionals, and Congress about whether or not some national forest timber sales fail to recover the costs of offering them, or involve expenditures that are not cost-effective. This interest has intensified the discussion of leisure benefits currently being used by the Forest Service to justify these sales. Questions concern whether or not these values are properly identified and defined and if proper measurement techniques have been used to establish estimates of benefits.

The same kinds of issues arise when administrators propose programs and budgets to Office of Management and Budget (OMB) staff. The reasonableness and precision of leisure benefit estimates are often important issues because OMB staff want to know precisely what benefits will be produced for what costs. The OMB, like Congress, is interested in the tradeoffs among programs between and within agencies. Reliable value estimates enable credible assessment of such tradeoffs.

Reliable estimates of leisure benefits are also needed for managerial decisions within public agencies. They also are useful for program and budget justification and are needed for budget allocation, land management planning, resolution of policy conflicts, and project investment analysis. In making managerial decisions, benefit estimates can be used to conduct tradeoff and benefit-cost analyses, and build the value of management outputs into estimates of present net worth. Without objective benefit estimates for leisure resources, these values are entered subjectively as constraints in the planning analyses and then limit the production of other outputs. In this case, we usually have a difficult time transmitting the meaning of these constraints to all decision-makers and we do not know what these constraints are worth; we just impose them.

Estimates of leisure values, similar to those of commodity resources, are needed for investment analysis. If one is considering wildlife habitat management, construction of a trail, or forest preservation for scenic and wildlife maintenance, one needs benefit estimates of the outputs to assess whether the projects are financially sound.

Finally, leisure benefits are useful for dealing with the public. They communicate to the public how agencies value different benefits by making it clear that the value of leisure benefits is neither zero nor infinity. They also provide a reference so that the public can counter agency values. For example, when agencies display to the public the value of flat water recreation with a dam and the value of wild river recreation without the dam, tradeoffs become readily apparent. Also, if the value of recreation opportunities is used to justify below-cost timber sales or any other management activity, the public can assess the reasonableness of the justification if explicit benefits are given.

WHAT DOES THE MANAGER NEED?

While there is probably no limit to the needs of managers for better information on benefits of leisure programs, there are several specific areas where managers could use some help.

Fees

The issue of fees for recreation continues to be open for debate. In recent times, budget constraints have swung the pendulum towards self-sufficiency of recreation programs. Rather than continue a public subsidy of recreation areas, many think that managers should recover costs from the user wherever possible. A clearer understanding of the benefits of these programs would help resolve this issue. Are the individual users the primary beneficiaries? What about the value of access to public recreation opportunities by all segments of the population? Are there benefits to society at large? If so, can they be quantified and documented? Do particular types of users benefit more than others from participation in certain recreation activities? These and similar facts would clearly assist both policymakers and managers.

Substitutability

Managers are frequently involved in a process of resolution of issues through compromise. We know that some leisure activities can be substituted for rather easily and others cannot. Managers need to know where flexibility exists and where it doesn't. They need to know when and if benefits are lost by proposed substitutions. This information would be invaluable to the manager in resolving conflicts between recreation activities.

It's also important that any measures used be accepted at policy levels where resource allocations are made. Field and middle management people tend to apply an intuitive approach that attempts to recognize both economic and noneconomic measures of benefits of leisure. However, higher levels of management tend to rely more heavily on economic measures. Leisure or recreation programs have traditionally fared poorly when this occurs.

Consumer Knowledge

When informed, the public is capable of expressing its views in a number of ways: through their political representatives, through public involvement processes, and even more specifically through their decisions on what leisure activities to engage in. A public that is better informed about leisure benefits will provide more valid input for overall missions, policies, plans, and other aspects of public management.

Interrelationships

What influence does the availability of leisure opportunities have on other public programs and social objectives? Are societal costs reduced by the availability of leisure opportunities? Intuitively, we think crime rates are reduced, law enforcement costs are reduced, social program costs are lowered, etc. If this is so, managers at all levels need to be able to document this in their justifications for resource allocations. They would be able to justify expenditures based on *net costs or benefits* to society. Leisure programs would be partially justified as preventive programs based on projected reductions in costs of other programs. This alone would dramatically change the way leisure programs are viewed in most policy and resource allocation processes today.

Professionalism

Managers need verified measures of benefits of leisure for a variety of professional reasons. Managers need help in either supporting or clarifying their intuitive understandings of the benefits of leisure. Confirmation of their intuitive opinions on the benefits of leisure would boost their personal satisfaction and self-esteem in their role as professionals in providing leisure opportunities. More significantly, this improved professionalism would enhance their recognition and support by society. The profession of providing recreation opportunities could only benefit from this enhanced public credibility.

SUMMARY

Anticipated increases in human population and needs for economic development will continue to exert pressures to exploit our lands for timber, livestock, and other industrial products. At the same time, needs to provide leisure opportunities will increase. Balancing the competing demand for commodities and leisure will require thoughtful and rigorous evaluation of alternatives. Significant progress has been made in theoretical and applied aspects of leisure benefits. However, much work remains to be done.

Empirical work is needed to define relevant leisure benefits, estimate production possibilities, and define social values. Studies on the various relationships between resource inputs and outputs are needed. These dynamic interactions are presently only partially understood. In addition, studies involving different accounting stances should be pursued. Analysis will not replace resource decisionmaking, but refinements in theory and application will continue to enhance the usefulness of analysis.

Values of leisure need to be estimated. They are useful for program and budget justification at Congressional, OMB, department, and agency levels; for policy formulation and analysis; and for investment decisions at all levels. The task before us is to develop valuation methods to the point of acceptability to land managers, policymakers, Congress, and ultimately the public, who must be convinced both of the credibility of a method of valuing extra-market resources and of its practicality. We have made much progress with theory and method in recent years; the challenge is for development and application to proceed. We must know when and when not to use information about leisure benefits, and we must know how to improve our techniques to ensure meeting tests of credibility, validity, reliability, and practicality.

Managers in the field of leisure services *do* need better information on the benefits of leisure activities. They are facing greater fiscal and personnel constraints each year. They need better information to justify their very existence and to do a better job of managing with limited resources. Issues like the role of leisure in increasing national productivity and competitiveness in the world labor market need to be woven into the basic understanding of the very fiber of this Nation! While there is some understanding at the individual or corporate level, to date, little attention has been given to the aggregate importance of leisure activities to productivity at the *national* level. As this Nation's leaders struggle with the monumental (and immediate) task of keeping the United States competitive in the emerging global market, it is imperative that they not be handicapped by ignorance or misinformation regarding the fundamental role of leisure in the modern world.

Philosophical Perspectives on Leisure in English-Speaking Countries

Thomas L. Goodale
Department of Health, Sport, and Leisure Studies
George Mason University
Fairfax, Virginia

Wes Cooper
Department of Philosophy
University of Alberta
Alberta, Edmonton,
Canada

We aim to shed some light on the benefits of leisure from a philosophical point of view, with particular reference to English-speaking countries. Before turning to that, however, we would like to indulge in some reflections on the affinity between leisure and philosophy. This connection may not be obvious in our own time, due to the specialization and professionalization of leisure theory; but this is all the more reason to remind ourselves of it. Earlier in our century the link between philosophy and leisure was affirmed by two modern classics of leisure theory: Josef Pieper's (1963) *Leisure, the Basis of Culture* first published in 1947; and Sebastian de Grazia's (1962) *Of Time, Work, and Leisure.* Both works are rich in allusion to the philosophical tradition of Western civilization, especially the philosophy of ancient Greece and of Christianity. To some extent, in de Grazia and particularly in Pieper, one gets the sense that leisure theory, at least at its most fundamental levels, *is* philosophy. Only in the last two decades has leisure theory effectively declared its independence from "the queen of the sciences," as philosophy has been called. Following in the footsteps of the natural sciences and the other social sciences, leisure theory is distinguishing itself from general philosophical reflection.

Socrates was perhaps the first conspicuous consumer of leisure, aggravating his fellow Athenians by discussing philosophy with his students and the citizens he chanced to meet in the streets. They put him to death for worshiping false gods and corrupting the youth, but their harsh judgment of him may also have been an anticipation of the Puritan disdain for idleness. Socrates was, however, asking himself and prodding those around him to ask, "How ought I to lead my life?" This is the fundamental philosophical question, for without an answer to it there is the ultimate danger that one's life is not worth living: the unexamined life is not worth living, as Socrates tells us in Plato's *Crito*. And so his leisure was devoted to an examination of life which would show his fellow Athenians how to lead worthwhile lives.

Socrates' way of life is pursued systematically by the so-called guardians of Plato's ideal city (as described in *The Republic*); they are freed of the toil which falls on the soldiering and working classes in order that they might attain knowledge of the Good and derivative values. Plato's student Aristotle, in turn, discovered a remarkable convergence between leisure and philosophy, because leisure, or at least the most serious use of leisure, is what one does for its own sake, quite apart from any practical or instrumental value it might have. And philosophy—contemplation of eternal truths—turns out to be the only thing that is truly worth doing for its own sake. At the same time it is totally useless for any practical purpose. So Aristotle concluded in the *Nicomachean Ethics* that philosophy excels in the serious use of leisure. Jumping to the seventeenth century for a final example, we observe that Descartes laid the foundations for modern philosophy in his *Meditations* by indulging, and insisting that his readers indulge, in the utmost leisure so that, entirely freed of mundane cares and responsibilities, they might for a time become pure enquirers into whether knowledge is possible. This is a deep connection between leisure and knowledge, or at least between a conception of leisure which contrasts it with work and a conception of knowledge which is Cartesian; knowledge is not essentially related to instrumental action, as the American pragmatists would later affirm, but on the contrary, it is best revealed in a state of leisure in which one is entirely detached from the need for action.

Among our social institutions it is the educational system, and especially the universities, which give pronounced expression to the affinity between philosophy and leisure. Many chroniclers of Western civilization have suggested that the ideal of a liberal education can be traced back to the educational program that Plato laid out in *The Republic,* an ideal in which the leisure of the philosophical "guardians" figures prominently. So it is plausible to suppose that the impact of philosophy on leisure will be underestimated if the large part that education plays in our lives is overlooked.

On the other hand, education does not always play such a large part in the life of a society. It has not always done so in America, for instance. The society that Tocqueville characterized in 1840 had much less prominent educational institutions than contemporary America, and we will observe shortly how this difference calls for some qualifications of his insights. It is enough now to affirm that the greatest institutions of leisure in our societies are our schools and universities. Other, perhaps more stereotypical leisure activities—even television viewing!—pale into relative insignificance by comparision with schooling, both in terms of time and money spent on it, and in terms of the value we place upon it. This amounts to the single most important social triumph of the historical friendship between leisure and philosophy. Although English-speaking countries are in various ways practically-oriented, that practicality takes place against an enormous backdrop of leisure spent in learning. Even that great spokesman for pragmatism and "cash value," William James, was a life-long academic, and a Harvard philosopher to boot! Though the direct connection between leisure and philosophy is severed in contemporary life—few of us philosophize in our leisure time—the connection is preserved indirectly in our commitment to liberal education.

Our universities can be traced to less remote antecedents than Plato: to the professional schools of theology, law, medicine, etc., which emerged around the tenth century. Defenders of the liberal arts tradition reasonably view these preparation-for-work schools as tarnishing the ideal of a liberal education. To the extent that our educational system reflects these antecedents, it provides training for a place in the nation's work force but does not promote education as an end in itself or even as a preparation for citizenship or discriminating choice. It may be, as John Dewey (1916) argued, that the oldest antithesis in education is the conflict between the "professional" and the "Platonic" ideal of education.

In what follows we briefly note some commonalities in leisure perspectives among the major English-speaking countries, then review some schools of philosophical thought which have influenced those perspectives, and finally we comment on some recent trends in leisure theory and venture some speculations about the future.

THE ENGLISH-SPEAKING COUNTRIES: SIMILARITIES AND DIFFERENCES

There are, all things considered, about 60 countries in which the English language is used to a considerable extent. In countries like Israel, Egypt, Jordan, and Syria, and in Sri Lanka, Bangladesh, and Pakistan, English is neither an offical nor the majority language but is used extensively in business and government affairs. Although a minority language, English is an official language in South Africa and Singapore, and also the Philippines, Lesotho, Botswana, Nigeria, and Tanzania, and about 20 other countries. In addition, there are about 20 countries in which English is the majority language, Belize and Granada among them. Yet we tend to think mainly of five countries as the "English-speaking" countries: England, the United States, Canada, Australia, and New Zealand. Of the countries in which English is the majority language, these five make up an overwhelming proportion in land area, population, and material wealth. The United States, indeed, has twice the number of English-speaking inhabitants as all the other countries combined.

There are good reasons, then, for our tendency to focus on these five countries and on the United States in particular. These countries share other important characteristics. They are, for example, highly urbanized, technologically sophisticated, relatively affluent, and highly literate. It would be reasonable therefore to infer that patterns of leisure activity in these countries will vary systematically from patterns in countries which lack these characteristics. The leisure of the English-speaking world, accordingly, will tend to be distinctively the leisure of the city, taking advantage of the forms of interaction made possible by the concentration of people in a small area. The fast pace and variety of city life can be expected to influence the institutions and instruments of leisure, which will tend to be ever-changing and innovative. It will tend to be technological or technologically dependent leisure; television viewing, for example, is technological leisure, and visiting far-off destinations is technologically dependent leisure—dependent, that is, on the technology of air travel. It will tend to be leisure of the affluent, requiring rather large expenditures such as those incurred in taking a skiing holiday or a child's being equipped for participation in a hockey league. It will tend to be leisure which calls upon sophisticated skills and talents, such as literacy of the ordinary kind, or "computer literacy," or some such talent which flourishes in an urban, affluent, technological milieu. This context makes intelligible a pattern noted by observers from each of the five countries: the growth of travel and tourism and fitness activities, increasing commercialization of recreation and particularly sport, and participation as consumers of entertainment and the products of popular culture (Rojek 1985, Stoddart 1986, Yenken and Cushman 1987).

These countries are also predominantly Christian—Protestant or Anglican in particular. But in the absence of an unlikely wave of theocratic fervor such as the Middle East is experiencing, it is not to be expected that religion will be a salient category within which people tend to think of their free time; at any rate there is nothing like the salience that religion had only two centuries ago. Race may be more salient, to the extent that these societies fail to avoid creating racially characterizable under-classes of citizens who lack the wealth and education to participate in the leisure activities of the more fortunate. But there are many prominent dimensions of leisure activity, corresponding to subcultures which center around age, gender, employment, income, ethnicity, geography, etc. These subcultures are so diverse that one would find it easier to cross any of the five nations' boundaries, moving to a comparable subculture, than to cross subcultures in one's own country. For this reason we are inclined to say that differences amongst the five countries appear to be more of degree than of kind. This is not to deny that the relative isolation of Australia and New Zealand compared to Britain's proximity to continental Europe and Canada's sharing more than 2,000 miles of border with the United States; differences in climate, land area, and natural resources; and other local conditions shape behaviors and also perspectives particularly with reference to leisure in the respective populations. On the other hand, the historical influence of Britain is stamped upon all of them, although the decline of this influence has been more rapid in the United States than in Canada, Australia, and New Zealand. The United States appears to differ from the four Commonwealth countries in the balance between capitalism and socialism,

the U.S. for instance being the only one of the five without a comprehensive national program for medical care. It is not altogether implausible to relate this difference to the relatively warm reception of Herbert Spencer's Social Darwinism in the U.S.

Similarities among these countries appear to outweigh differences and perhaps differentiate them from other countries. For example, as of 1986, average work hours per year totaled 1,938 among the British and 1,924 among Americans. The Japanese totaled 2,150, or more than five 40-hour weeks more, while West Germans and the French averaged 1,655 and 1,643, respectively, or about seven 40-hour weeks less than the British-American average (The Washington Post 1989). The similarities are so great, in fact, that Canada, for example, is often preoccupied with developing and maintaining a cultural identity separate from that of the United States and guarding itself from further assimilation by its neighbor to the south. In Australia and New Zealand, too, questions are raised about national and local cultures separate from, and some fear inferior to, British culture. We are inclined to preach that political encouragement of multiculturalism, as in Canada, is on the right track for most of the five countries, essentially for the reasons given by John Stuart Mill in his classic essay, *On Liberty*. These societies are sufficiently advanced to benefit from the diverse experiments in living, including experiments in use of leisure, which encouragement of cultural diversity promotes. New possibilities for human development and happiness should be revealed, and this should happen quickly in response to the influences of urban life, affluence, technological sophistication, and literacy, as described above.

Favorite free time activities of Australians parallel those of North Americans, with television leading other activities which tend to be home-based, passive, and informal (Australia Department of Sport, Recreation and Tourism 1985). Leisure spending is led by home entertainment products. We expect this trend to continue, although it will be influenced by the special characteristics of the five countries. Technological sophistication, for instance, is leading towards less passivity in home-based leisure. Even television is becoming "interactive," allowing children to play games with television programs using sophisticated (and expensive!) accessories, allowing adults to shop or do banking, etc.

The nihilistic elements of the drug culture infect English-speaking Oceania (Fiske et al. 1987) as they do North America (Bloom 1987) and elsewhere, and reveal subcultures with which the five nations must come to terms. It would be a mistake to ignore or play down the role of drugs and alcohol in the leisure activity of the five countries, and it will take great wisdom to define that role properly in the future.

Leisure is often equated with free time in the English-speaking countries, contrasted with work, and negatively valued (Elias and Duning 1986) in comparison to work, presumably because of an association drawn between "leisure hedonism" and the decline of the work ethic. Leisure is conceived as a time for consumption, in correlation with work as a time for production (Fiske et al. 1987). We suspect that this attitude will change as the nature of work in our societies changes as the result of improved working conditions, flexible work hours, and more meaningful work creating a sense of professionalism, etc. The changes will bring about more "leisurely" work, in the sense of work that one enjoys for its own sake as well as wanting it so as to "make a living."

DERIVING PHILOSOPHICAL PERSPECTIVES FROM CONDUCT

It is impossible to isolate a single philosophy of leisure which is common to the five countries. Philosophical perspectives on leisure are not independent of philosophical perspectives on religion, politics, society, economy, psychology, etc., and these display a bewildering variety. Furthermore, a philosophy of leisure is likely to be implicit in a person's outlook rather than being consciously acknowledged. While most people may be able to characterize themselves as optimistic or pessimistic, ascetic or hedonistic, elitist or egalitarian, liberal or conservative, they would have difficulty articulating their philosophy of leisure. Supplying such articulations seems to us a priority for the theoretical side of leisure studies.

Nineteenth century Americans, it has been observed, knew little of and paid little attention to the abstruse theories and speculations of British and Continental philosophies. Relying on common sense, they regarded philosophy as the resort and consolation of the bewildered and unhappy, and most Americans considered themselves neither (Commager 1950: 8,9). Yet, however poorly articulated and however distant from philosophy in any formal sense, philosophy was expressed daily in the conduct of life. Tocqueville made the point very well in his classic 1840 study, *Democracy in America,* and he is worth quoting at length, in order to remind ourselves of the possibility of retrieving a philosophy from conduct.

I think that in no country in the civilized world is less attention paid to philosophy than in the United States. The Americans have no philosophical schools of their own; and they care little for all the philosophical schools into which Europe is divided, the very names of which are scarcely known to them. Yet it is easy to perceive that almost all of the inhabitants of the United States conduct their understanding in the same manner, and govern it by the same rules; that is to say, without ever having taken the trouble to define the rules, they have a philosophical method common to the whole people. To evade the bondage of system and habit, of family maxims, class opinions, and, in some degree, of national prejudices; to accept tradition only as a means of information, and existing facts only as a lesson to be used in doing otherwise and doing better, to seek the reason of things for one's self, and in one's self alone; to tend to the results without being bound to means, and to aim at the substance through the form; such are the principle characteristics of what I call the philosophical method of the Americans. But, if I go further, and seek amongst these characteristics the principle one which includes most all the rest, I discover that, in most of the operations of the mind, each American appeals only to the individual effort of his own understanding…America is therefore one of the countries where the precepts of Descartes are the least studied, and are best applied (Tocqueville 1945: 3,4).

Much has changed since Tocqueville wrote, including the emergence of pragmatism later in the nineteenth century as a distinctly American philosophy, and in the twentieth century the emergence of a large and sophisticated philosophical community. But despite these changes, Tocqueville's characterization continues to have the ring of truth. This is so also when he writes on matters more closely related to leisure, such as the particularly churning, innovative character of Americans' pursuit of gratification, a phenomenon we remarked upon earlier.

The greater part of men who constitute these nations are extremely eager in the pursuit of actual and physical gratification. As they are always dissatisfied with the position which the occupy, and are always free to leave it, they think of nothing but the means of changing their fortune, or increasing it. To minds thus predisposed, every new method which leads by a shorter road to wealth, every machine which spares labor, every instrument which diminishes the cost of production, every discovery which facilitates pleasures or augments them, seems to be the grandest effort of the human intellect. It is chiefly from these motives that a democratic people addict itself to scientific pursuits… (Tocqueville 1945: 46).

And in the following passage Toqueville draws out the individualistic, rather than collectivist or communitarian self-conception of Americans.

As social conditions become more equal, the number of persons increases who, although they are neither rich nor powerful enough to exercise any great influence over their fellows, have nevertheless acquired or retained sufficient education and fortune to satisfy their own wants. They owe nothing to any man, they expect nothing from any man; they acquire the habit of always considering themselves as standing alone, and they are apt to imagine that their whole destiny is in their own hands.

Thus not only does democracy make every man forget his ancestors, but it hides his descendants and separates his contemporaries from him; it throws him back forever upon himself alone, and threatens in the end to confine him entirely within the solitude of his own heart (Tocqueville 1945: 105,106).

Surely these words serve as a warning to us even today, as the rapidity of change initiated by science and actualized in technology tempts us to suppose that the insights and wisdom of earlier centuries are antiquated.

This excursion into *Democracy in America* serves to indicate how a student of leisure might tease out a people's philosophy of leisure from acute observation of their conduct. Perhaps Tocqueville's portrait was overdrawn, and of course it would be less accurate viewed as a representation of contemporary America. But Tocqueville's words echo in Linder's (1970) depiction in *The Harried Leisure Class* and in Goodale and Godbey's (1988) suggestion that wanderlust has supplanted leisure. That potpourri of contemporary mini-portraits, *Harper's Magazine* (1988), also reports that among Americans earning less than $15,000 per year, 5% say they have achieved the American dream; of those earning over $50,000, 6% say this. Has not Tocqueville extracted the meaning of these statistics when he says,

In America I saw the freest and most enlightened men placed in the happiest circumstances that the world affords; it seemed to me as if a cloud hung upon their brow, and I thought them serious and almost sad in their pleasures...(they) are forever brooding over advantages they do not possess. It is strange to see with what feverish ardor the Americans pursue their own welfare, and to watch the vague dread that constantly torments them lest they should not have chosen the shortest path which may lead to it (Tocqueville 1945: 144).

Plus ça change?

PHILOSOPHIES SHAPING PERSPECTIVES ON LEISURE

Most inquiries into the history of thinking about leisure begin with classical Greek philosophy, and with Aristotle in particular. It is salutary to reflect that no one may have thought more deeply about leisure than Aristotle did over 2,400 years ago. Since his thinking instructs by contrast with many current philosophical perspectives on leisure, a very brief outline of his thinking introduces this account of the principal schools of thought which have shaped current perspectives.

Aristotle's Perspective

Aristotle distinguished leisure sharply from mere amusement or relaxation, which are valuable only for their instrumental value in preparing one for serious activity. Leisure properly so called is not instrumental at all, but rather it is concerned with things that are intrinsically good, that is, such goods as an excellent man would choose for their own sake. Leisure is the occasion for the cultivation of many intermediate goods, such as friendship, in the Aristotelian hierarchy of goods, and also for the highest good of all, which is "study" or contemplative understanding of eternal and divine first principles.

So leisure activities are constitutive of happiness or "Eudamonia" in many fundamental ways. Leisure for Aristotle can also be characterized negatively, as freedom from the necessity of being occupied. Only this freedom affords the opportunity for becoming virtuous, by permitting one to learn to use one's intelligence in choosing the "golden mean" of moderation between excess and defect, too much and too little. If one's conduct were constantly driven by necessity, then although one might do the right thing by luck or even habit, the element of decision guided by intelligence would be lacking, and so virtue would be lacking. Leisure offers freedom from such necessity, and consequently it is the foundation of virtue. So happiness is not only *made up* in large measure of leisure activities such as friendship and study, but it is also *dependent* on leisure during periods of character formation, since virtue is dependent on leisure and happiness is impossible without virtue. The importance of leisure is not measured by its preparing one for work, or by the fleeting pleasures it brings, but rather by its multidimensional contribution to a well-lived life.

Aristotle's conception of leisure is very different from the one which is most influential in English-speaking countries today, according to which leisure is "free time," especially time in which one is free from the demands of work. But there is a lingering sense, which Aristotle's vision serves to articulate, that leisure has an important part to play in a life, transcending its value as a time-filler in off-work periods.

Rationalism and Empiricism

These philosophies address domains seemingly remote from leisure's roots in ethical and religious reflection, addressing more directly the philosophical domain of metaphysics and epistemology. The rationalist tradition, in which reason as a source of knowledge is more fundamental than sense-experience, can be traced back to Plato's view that philosphers' reason can put them in contact with realities beyond the empirical world; and the empiricist tradition, in which sense-experience of the empirical world is fundamental, can be traced back to Aristotle. But the great spokesmen for empiricism were the British Empiricists of the seventeenth and eighteenth centuries—Locke, Berkeley, and Hume.

Volumes of criticism have been addressed at the spread of empiricist thought to the spiritual spheres of life. Santayana's observation (1968: 37) that without play, "we should have remained eternally empiricists, or (to use a shorter Greek word) idiots," is among the more caustic commentaries. But we venture the generalization that the cultures of the English-speaking countries tend to have an empiricist spirit, and that this extends to the ways they think about leisure. The tendency in these societies to equate leisure with free time, for instance, is useful for an empirically oriented social science of leisure. It suggests ways of studying leisure quantitatively, of framing and testing hypotheses with empirical content, and of conforming in other ways to canons of empiricist methodology. A second instance of our generalization is the "this-worldly" orientation that Tocqueville remarked upon:

> A native of the United States clings to this world's goods as if he were certain never to die; and he is so hasty in grasping at all within his reach that one would suppose he was constantly afraid of not living long enough to enjoy them. He clutches at everything, he holds nothing fast, but soon loosens his grasp to pursue fresh gratifications (Tocqueville 1945: 144).

Calvin's Protestantism

The Christian traditions of the five countries have influenced their philosophies profoundly. One important case in point is the Protestant work ethic. Predestination, a belief that salvation was exclusively a matter of God's grace, paradoxically led to diligence, perseverance, thrift, punctuality, and other Protestant ethic virtues. This was because, as Calvin explained, whatever work one does and good works one produces, whatever success one has, and whatever one's profit and material gain, all is attributable to God alone. So good works and success were interpreted as a sign of grace and, although they did not assure salvation, they gave reason for hope. Thus the Protestant work ethic provided religious motivation for the pursuit of secular material gain. The material self-interest which some found justified by Calvin's theology was reinforced, two centuries later, in Adam Smith's capitalist economic philosophy. The "invisible hand" of providence and natural law produced the greatest well-being for all out of the self-interested pursuits of each individual.

Although the religious motivation has dwindled in the five countries by now, the secular outlook has come to be second nature in them. And the Calvinist association of leisure with time not working, and so with idleness, and consequently with vice and sin—unless it is justified as a way of preparing for further work—can still be found today in the implication of triviality that is often suggested by the equation of leisure with free time.

Utilitarianism

If the English-speaking countries tend to be empiricist in their metaphysical and epistemological presuppositions, then they are utilitarian in their moral theory. Utilitarianism singles out pleasure or happiness as what is good, and pain as what is bad, and it says that the right thing to do is to maximize the good by promoting the greatest balance of pleasure over pain. The Utilitarian movement that Bentham and the Philosophical Radicals began in the eighteenth century has helped to direct our legislators and social engineers towards making provision for pleasure-breeding or distress-reducing institutions of leisure, such as holidays, social security or social insurance provision for the leisure of retirement, and schools; and for constraints on work such as prohibition of slavery, curtailment of child labor, and limitations on the working day. The Marxist movement must also be mentioned in this regard, as well as the vigorous feminist movement in contemporary philosophy. The influence of these philosophies on our lives, in helping to expand the opportunities for leisure for so many of us, has come to be taken for granted and thus overlooked. The child who is going to school instead of a sweat shop does not appreciate his debt to philosophy, and to utilitarian social criticism in particular. The same may be said of the woman who is pursuing an education and a career rather than being consigned to the "basement" of social life, or the worker who is protected by unions and legislation from poverty or slavery. So a large gap should be expected between the acknowledged influence of philosophy on a typical person's life and the actual influence.

On the negative side of the utilitarian tradition, is the criticism that it does not take rights seriously. Bentham dismissed talk of rights as nonsense, and natural rights as "nonsense on stilts." Utilitarianism is prepared to sacrifice the welfare of a few in order to achieve "the greatest good for the greatest number," and one may detect the influence of this doctrine, when racism isn't the required explanation, in the way that native peoples or minorities are sometimes treated in some of the five countries.

Utilitarianism tends also to be too demanding on our capacities for calculation and for being concerned with promoting happiness wherever it might occur. What will maximize the good in the long run and in the final analysis is often entirely problematic, and utilitarianism seems to fight human psychology in implying that each of us should be as concerned with the happiness of far-off strangers as with our own. Utilitarianism can demand a level of self-sacrifice, then, which would eliminate the part which leisure plays in the lives of the citizens of the five countries. Our obligation to relieve distress would be so overwhelming that free time would be an immoral luxury. It would seem that Utilitarianism and Calvinism, for rather different reasons, arrive at the same dim view of leisure!

Utilitarianism is easily misunderstood. It can be taken to imply concern for what is useful for some limited purpose. Then concern about utility comes to be about means to these limited ends, rather than the philosophical end of happiness or pleasure. For example, someone might demand an accounting of the "utility" of leisure, presupposing a limited purpose or end, to which leisure should serve as means. This might be restoration of energies for work, say, or improving one's fitness, etc. But if utility is merely happiness or pleasure wherever it is found, as Utilitarianism implies when it is correctly understood, then leisure may have high utility in and of itself, quite apart from its having any further "utility" in some limited sense. Indeed a strenuous concern to make one's leisure instrumentally beneficial can compromise the quality of the leisure (Mullett 1988). We suspect that the fitness boom has had this effect on jogging which can come to be viewed by the jogger more and more as a means to fitness (or virtue!), and less and less as something intrinsically worth doing. We do not mean to imply that it is a mistake to inquire into the benefits of leisure in an instrumental sense, however. In the spirit of utilitarianism one will be interested in these, but also in the benefits which are internal to leisure activity per se.

Social Darwinism

Although its roots were British, Herbert Spencer's adaptation of Darwin's evolutionary biology was more influential in the United States than anywhere else. It provided seemingly solid, scientific evidence that the rugged and ruthless capitalists were only acting according to laws of nature. Economic and other social institutions were construed as subject to the same laws as evolutionary biology; then in a cruel twist of fallacious logic, the plight of the poor, ill, and disabled was compared to the plight of a species which is biologically unfit to survive. Charity was viewed as wasteful and dangerous, either delaying or tampering with the process of natural selection which yields the survival of the fittest. The basic mistake of Social Darwinism was to lose sight of the specific theoretical meaning of "fitness" in evolutionary theory. Since that conception has to do with reproductive success, a capitalist's financial victories in a laissez-faire market have no special connection to Darwinian fitness. And they certainly do not imply that he is more "deserving" to reproduce, because he is somehow "better." This normative vocabulary is totally alien to evolutionary theory, and by cloaking it in the mantle of Darwin's legitimacy, Social Darwinism begs the question of how our social institutions should be designed.

In the precarious political balance between liberty and equality, Social Darwinism weighted the scales in favor of liberty. Among the residuals of Social Darwinism may be the low tax rates and high poverty rates from which the U.S. suffers in comparison to other English-speaking countries. Leisure theorists can take pride that Spencer's appropriation of Darwin was found bankrupt by their forebears (who were prominent among those who sought reform of the conditions of industrialism, urbanization, and exploitive capitalism) in the playground and community center movements which included leisure facilities addressing the special needs of the poor. Recognizing the extent and gravity of the problem of poverty, they encouraged extensive government involvement in the economy during the great depression of the 1930s, marking the political rejection of Social Darwinism.

Pragmatism

Pragmatism is a distinctly American philosophy associated with the names of Charles Pierce, William James, and John Dewey. It opposed the abstraction and aridity of traditional philosophical systems, and favored "getting down to brass tacks" (to use an American idiom) with the ideas we use, by showing how those ideas work and what practical difference they make. In leisure theory a pragmatic attitude would prompt us to ask whether thinking of leisure in Aristotle's way or Calvin's way would make a difference in our lives, or whether they just amount to different conceptualizations of lives which will run their courses in a certain way regardless of our Aristotelian or Calvinist beliefs. Knowing the work that an idea should do and understanding its function is essential to assessing its truth, according to a pragmatist. For instance, the function of science is to predict and thereby control, and so the truth of a scientific hypothesis is judged by its capacity to generate true predictions.

But religion has a different function, of answering the human need for hope, and therefore religious statements should be judged by how well they satisfy that need. One implication of this pragmatist view of different functions is that it would be a mistake to treat belief in God like belief in a scientific hypothesis. Similarly, if leisure "works," so to speak, when it is contributing toward going for the best on the whole, as Aristotle implies, then one will assess leisure differently than one would if its function were to prepare someone for the demands of the job or to fill up empty moments of free time. One would make different judgments about whether a person was using his leisure wisely, for instance.

Pragmatism can easily be misunderstood, and was misunderstood, causing William James to lament, "The pragmatism that lives inside of me is so different from that I succeed in waking inside of other people, that their's makes me feel like cursing God and dying" (Commager 1950: 101). Commager notes that "the transition from the principle that truth is to be discovered in the practical consequences of conduct to the notion that whatever works is necessarily true was dangerously easy," and the danger is compounded by the vulgar error of interpreting the "work" that beliefs perform as necessarily having to do with expedience, giving rise to a pseudo-pragmatic ideology of "capitalism, opportunism, and smugness" (White 1962: 564).

Existentialism

Understood as the articulation of an attitude, a mood, or an emotional state, existentialism is a highly introspective, inward-looking philosophy, preoccupied with feelings like anxiety, boredom, aloneness, and dread. But understood as a philosophical system, its basic tenets are that existence precedes essence and that we are utterly free to make of our lives what we will. According to both the Christian and Aristotelian traditions, essence precedes existence in the sense that there is a plan or purpose—God's plan in Christianity, the purpose of normal human development in Aristotle—by which to judge how one's life should go. But existentialism assumes that there is no such guidance, hence its expression of feelings of anxiety and aloneness. Moreover, we are free to make anything of our lives. The course of a lifetime is not etched predeterminedly by God as Calvinists supposed, but rather is a clear slate upon which each of us existentially etches our own being.

From an existential perspective leisure is an opportunity for the self-definition which comes from our making choices about what is worth doing. If I choose to spend my leisure in writing, and perhaps to make that a focal point of my life, I am creating myself thereby, bringing a writer into existence who was not predetermined to exist. Existentialism in leisure theory is bound to be critical of the popular mindset according to which one's life lies before one in an alternating pattern of work and free time. One's choice to acquiesce in this pattern, and perhaps to consume the prepackaged leisure products that advertisers have found to possess mass appeal, is itself a fateful self-defining choice. There is no antecedent Ego which unproblematically floats through leisure; rather, I am constructing myself through my leisure. With this insight, the existential sense of dread at the prospect of utter freedom to make irretrievably fateful decisions about one's identity extends to leisure.

Existentialism can be viewed as having a good deal in common with the "perceived freedom" conception of leisure which has gained currency in academic leisure theory. Leisure as activity in which one perceives oneself as free is not limited to free time, but is equally possible at work. It may be that the influence of existentialism has contributed towards a shift from primarily sociological to primarily psychological perspectives on leisure in scholarly studies.

This completes our brief and highly selective overview of philosophical perspectives on leisure. Other philosophical perspectives might be mentioned as well, but we have tried to be illustrative rather than comprehensive. We hope to have said enough to suggest that further investigations of philosophical perspectives would show how each sheds a unique light on the phenomenon of leisure. We recommend such investigations to the reader.

LEISURE COMMONLY UNDERSTOOD

There is little to suggest the flourishing of the Aristotelian, Calvinistic, or Pieperian notions of leisure in contemporary English-speaking countries. The most widely shared conception of leisure equates leisure with free time, and this is most often conceived as time free from work, obligation, or any other necessary activity. Leisure in this sense is generally thought of as earned by effort, work, discipline, denial, sacrifice, and the like. It is not a gift of grace, like Pieper's notion of leisure as an effortless acquiescence in one's own being and festive celebration with the Gods. Gifts are usually received with some sense of duty to appreciate, use wisely or as the giver might wish, etc. But this sense is diminished in earned leisure, which is like "discretionary" money that one can spend as one pleases. Yet our leisure tends to look beyond itself. It may take the form of work towards some further end: to earn money or to save it; to reduce stress; to rest for the work to come; to improve one's health or appearance; to find oneself; to make oneself useful and of some account, etc. What one wants to do can take the form of escape, usually from one's daily routine and milieu. Tourism, vacation resorts, theme parks, television and movies, and various other activities and services respond to this desire. Alcohol and other drugs, high risk and adventure pursuits, also provide temporary escapes in different ways.

We tend to perceive freedom as doing what one wants to do, and we tend also to attempt to realize this freedom, not by trimming our wants to our abilities, but by expanding our abilities so that we can do as we want. There are many avenues for this expansion, depending on what ability or resource is lacking. Time-saving devices are intended to increase our time, which we perceive as a scarce commodity. Lacking money, we work more and perhaps save more, or more likely borrow money. We may take assertiveness training or take courses designed to increase our ability to do what we want. Tocqueville's portrait in the following passage has faded little:

> Their [the Americans'] taste for physical gratification must be regarded as the original source of that secret disquietude which the actions of the Americans betray and of that inconstancy of which they daily afford fresh examples. He who has set his heart exclusively upon the pursuit of worldly welfare is always in a hurry, for he has but a limited time at his disposal to reach, to grasp, and to enjoy it. The recollection of the shortness of life is a constant spur to him. Besides the good things he possesses, he every instant fancies a thousand others that death will prevent him from trying if he does not try them soon (1945: 145).

More recently, Godbey (1985) has argued that a good deal of recreation spending—a larger house or lot for entertaining or gardening, a second car or van or motor home, a vacation, etc.—reflects a form of greed in which, faced with a choice due to resource limits, one chooses everything instead and goes into debt.

The ancient Stoic strategy of truncating one's wants so as to align them with one's abilities and resources is not congenial to our temperaments for the most part, although there are some who seek freedom in this way. We tend to think that the truncating strategy is wrongheaded, despite the dangers that Godbey reminds us of, because the pruning of desire that it involves seems tantamount to an abnegation of one's personality—a kind of self-mutilation. So, in the spirit of the existentialist perspective, we counsel that the freedom of leisure should make possible the fullest exploration of personality. Leisure ought to encourage the accomplishment of ambitious projects, not complacent acceptance of the path of least resistance. Though it is a good idea to stay out of debt!

Time, in English-speaking countries, is perceived as a scarce commodity. The fact that we measure it in increasingly small amounts—now nanoseconds—testifies to this. We experience time as monochronic, unidimensional, and inexorable. The experience of time as rythmic and cyclical is being lost. So, for example, experiencing a season as a season—as recurring and in that sense plentiful—and not a temporal step towards some remote goal or terminus, is psychologically more difficult for us than it was for our ancestors, who were closer to nature than to the clock. There is so much to do: "So many pedestrians, so little time," as the bumper sticker says; or "Death to down time," as the high tech slogan goes.

Rifkin's *Time Wars* (1987) plausibly suggests that time, rather than territory or wealth, is the battlefield of the future, in which the combatants will struggle for the power to dictate the experience of time by others. The contemporary sense of time-famine contributes to the level of stress in our societies, and to leisure remedies such as consumption of alcohol and drugs which offer a temporary haven from the push of time. More satisfactory havens are being explored by Csikszentmihalyi and his colleagues, who study the escape from time in the experience of "flow," a calm sense of timelessness, in athletes and others who accomplish demanding but not overwhelming tasks (Csikszentimihalyi 1975).

Solutions to the problem of time-famine are desperately needed. Recent polls report that balancing time and energy among various priorities is, among Americans at least, the principle concern (Barrett 1988: 4). Recent studies in Canada indicate that one-third of those employed full-time would prefer shorter hours and the proportionate reduction in income that would mean. A 1975 study in Sweden found that 76 percent of respondents thought the standard of living was too high and a substantial majority preferred limiting income and careerism, and preferred a life that was simpler and calmer, with little material affluence beyond a necessary minimum (Gorz 1982: 121). Polls in Europe taken in the late 1970s revealed that more than one-half the workers, given the choice between more work or more free time, chose more free time (Gorz 1982: 140).

SPECULATIONS ABOUT FUTURE PERSPECTIVES

We began our discussion of philosophy and leisure noting their affinity in both classical and sometimes also contemporary conceptualizations of leisure. Noted, too, was the central role of education both as the opportunity provided by freedom from the necessity of being occupied and as the basis for choosing wisely how leisure is to be occupied. Some of that education, for which the English-speaking countries (among others) have made extensive arrangements, comes about through formal training whch includes both the liberal arts and career training. Some of that education is acquired in other less formal and institutional ways. It is not particularly bold to speculate that the educational dimension of leisure will grow as explosively in the next century as it has in the past one. Global competition in science and technology and industries dependent upon them, the rapid spread of an information network over the world, increased years of schooling for children, and many other factors point in this direction.

Time-famine for those pursuing careers, underemployment for many in economies that are demanding less labor, the clear and present danger of the consequences of environmental degradation, increasingly sophisticated and well-informed populations—all suggest a markedly different future. We predict that solutions to environmental degradation may be the fundamental force for change in leisure behavior, dovetailing with less fundamental but still important forces, such as the ones just mentioned, to create the leisure patterns of the future. Advocates of slow growth, smaller cities, less reliance on the automobile, cleaner energy, intermediate technology, soft energy sources, voluntary simplicity, etc., can all be viewed as responding to these dovetailing forces. They are saying that the Earth is under threat, and that our societies must begin to practice ways of living that can promise a sustainable future. These ways of living must appeal to citizens who cannot be left in the dark or be cynically manipulated because of new high levels of education, communication, and community organization.

Under these conditions we see a more central place for rewarding leisure, both in the sense of leisure as free time and leisure as leisurely work. Those in careers will tend to professionalize and humanize their work and working conditions, and those who choose underemployment of one form or other will increasingly define themselves in terms of valuable leisure activities. The personal, social and environmental costs of work will become more evident, and the costs will be reduced. Free time for increasingly sophisticated people will produce leisure patterns of greater depth and quality.

We expect to see more creative activity in leisure, more time for reflection and deepening of relationships with family and friends, more resistance to the passive and mindless forms of leisure that the phrase "couch potato" conjures up. As work-centered lifestyles give way to leisure-centered lifestyles, and as work itself becomes more self-expressive, socially conscious, and environmentally sensitive, we expect to see more pluralistic and richly diverse societies, flourishing in a sustainable future. We expect the individualism that Toqueville commented upon, insofar as its vestiges still remain, to disappear. It is a conceit we can no longer afford. It will be replaced by a new sense of human community and a new sense of our relationship to the Earth.

LITERATURE CITED

Aristotle. 1985. Nicomachean ethics. Indianapolis, IN: Hackett.

Australia Department of Sport, Recreation and Tourism. 1985. Recreation and tourism study. Canberra: Australia Department of Sport, Recreation and Tourism.

Barrett, M. E. 1988. Balance: the new buzzword. USA Weekend: October 21-23, 1988: 4-5.

Bloom, A. 1987. The closing of the American mind. New York, NY: Simon and Schuster.

Commager, H. S. 1950. The American mind. New Haven, CT: Yale University Press.

Csikszentmihalyi, M. 1975. Beyond boredom and anxiety. San Francisco, CA: Jossey-Bass.

de Grazia, S. 1962. Of time, work and leisure. New York, NY: The Twentieth Century Fund.

Descartes, R. 1986. Meditations on first philosophy. New York, NY: Cambridge University Press.

Dewey, J. 1916. Democracy and education. New York, NY: The Macmillan Company.

Elias, N.; Dunning, E. 1986. Quest for excitement: sport and leisure in the civilizing process. Oxford: Basil Blackwell.

Fiske, J.; Hodge, B.; Turner, G. 1987. Myths of Oz: reading Australian popular culture. Sydney: Allen and Unwin.

Godbey, G. 1985. Planning for leisure in a pluralistic society. In: Recreation and leisure: issues in an era of changes. State College, PA: Venture Publishing, Inc.

Goodale, T. L.; Godbey, G. C. 1988. The evolution of leisure: historical and philosophical perspectives. State College, PA: Venture Publishing, Inc.

Gorz, A. 1982. Farewell to the working class: an essay on post-industrial socialism. London: Pluto Press.

Harper's Magazine. 1988. Harper's index. Harper's Magazine: Oct. 15, 1988.

Linder, S. B. 1970. The harried leisure class. Irvington, NY: Columbia University Press.

Mill, J. S. 1983. On liberty. Indianapolis, IN: Hackett.

Mullett, S. 1988. Leisure and consumption: incompatible concepts? Leisure Studies. 7(3): 241-253.

Pieper, J. 1963. Leisure, the basis of culture. New York, NY: Mentor Books.

Plato. 1961. Crito. In: Kaplan, J. D., ed. Dialogues of Plato. New York, NY: Washington Square Press: 41-62.

Plato. 1981. The republic. Indianapolis, IN: Hackett.

Rifkin, J. 1987. Time wars: the primary conflict in human history. New York, NY: Henry Holt and Company.

Rojek, C. 1985. Capitalism and leisure theory. London: Tavistock Publications.

Santayana, G. 1968. The soul at play. In: The birth of reason and other essays. Irvington, NY: Columbia University Press: 34-45.

Stoddart, B. 1986. Saturday afternoon fever: sport in the Australian culture. North Ryde, Australia: Angus and Robertson.

Tocqueville, A. 1945. Democracy in America. Vol. II. New York, NY: Random House-Vintage.

The Washington Post. 1989. Digest: January 12, 1989: E1.

White, M., ed. 1962. The age of analysis. Boston, MA: Houghton Mifflin.

Yenken, D.; Cushman, G. 1987. Leisure, culture, and the environment. World Leisure and Recreation. XXIX(3) (Fall): 26-31.

Relations Between the Development of Culture and Philosophies of Leisure

Geoffrey C. Godbey
Department of Leisure Studies
The Pennsylvania State University
University Park, Pennsylvania

Bohdan Jung
Research Institute for Developing Countries
Central School of Planning and Statistics
Warsaw, Poland

THE MEANING OF CULTURAL DEVELOPMENT

To understand leisure in cross-cultural perspective, we must first understand the development of culture and the extent to which such development occurs in identifiable stages.

As UNESCO proclaimed the years 1988-1997 to be the World Decade for Cultural Development, the term "cultural development" gained wide publicity, yet remained far from being unambiguous. This ambiguity stems from different understandings of both "culture" and "development" elements of the term. In its broadest anthropological sense, culture makes human beings unique and different from other animals. As a consequence of this opposition between culture and nature, all forms of human activity and their products are an expression of culture, and all forms of culture reflect human development (Benham 1981). The understanding of cultural development may also be limited to the arts and creative skills, which narrows it to participation in cultural activities (Kloskowska 1983). While considerations of leisure tend to embrace the narrower meaning of cultural participation, a cross-cultural perspective requires us to study the wider cultural context of leisure found in social and individual ways of living and being, perceptions of existence, behavior patterns, value systems, and beliefs (Kelly 1987).

Development theory tends to view culture as one of the neglected dimensions of development (Ki-Zerbo 1976). People who do not take part in the process of economic and social changes or scientific progress, because they perceive the process as irrelevant to their own identity and the specificity of their culture, feel alienated from the advantages of development, such as the enjoyment of leisure (McHenry 1981, Rascallon 1983). The important elements of cultural development needed to eliminate this form of alienation should therefore include:

- acknowledging the cultural dimension in development;
- asserting and enhancing cultural identities uprooted in the process of development, including preservation of the national cultural heritage;
- broadening participation in the cultural life; and
- promoting exchange and understanding (as well as tolerance) between cultures.

These elements, all interrelated with leisure activities, also correspond to UNESCO's Plan of Action for the World Decade for Cultural Development (UNESCO 1987).

Do Cultures Develop in Identifiable Stages?

As there is no universally accepted definition of "better" or "worse" culture, the identifiable stages of a culture's development are not necessarily synonymous with its moral worth. The link between cultural development and the evolution of societies and their economies is most often established through the extent of industrialization and urbanization (Rezsohazy 1969). Working in industry and living in the city demands strict observance of time schedules, norms of punctuality, etc., associated with "clock" (mechanical) time, which is not necessary in rural societies living on "cyclical" time (natural time). We would thus have a succession of traditional (i.e., preindustrial, predominantly rural), modern and post-industrial culture in statu nascendi. However, this sequence of cultural development is challenged by new patterns which emerge in individual countries, such as urbanization without industrialization (developing countries) (de Lima-Camargo 1984), rapid transition from traditional to modern societies without elimination of preindustrial structures or the rise of individualism (e.g., Japan, the newly industrialized countries of Southeast Asia), or the return (temporary?) to some form of ethical fundamentalism in many "modernized" countries. The vision of post-industrial society also fades away as overdevelopment and underdevelopment exist in close proximity in the world's richest countries.

The second line of thought is the identification of stages of cultural development in relation to the scope of cultural participation, with emphasis on the shift from elitist to mass cultures.[1] Beside the alleged drop in the artistic quality of culture, the emergence of mass culture is associated with the commodification and commercialization of culture, the resulting transformation of cultural participation into cultural consumption, the opening of global culture markets, and mass leisure (Scardigli 1983).

Spatial criteria allow us to define three subsystems of culture: informal contacts (with family and friends), local cultural institutions, and national (soon global) mass media (Wnuk-Lipinski 1981). The historical evolution consists of the transition from informal contacts dominant in traditional societies through popularity of local cultural institutions at intermediate levels of development to supranational media. The identification of subsystems of culture leads to a relatively undisputed classification based on forms of cultural expression: from oral cultures through print on to the image, with more and more information being sorted in digital form and transmitted with the help of computers (Kobayashi 1986).

Efforts have also been made to refine and update the above classification to take into account the competition within the media: after the age of books and the press, there came the age of the radio, the cinema, then the age of the television with its further expansion into the video and satellite variants. On the international level, this was integrated with the international life cycle hypothesis for cultural goods (i.e., the time gap in peak popularity of the movies in the developed Western countries, in Eastern Europe and in the developing countries).

Finally, the identification of stages in cultural development can be studied in its international and ideological dimension of relations between local and global culture, as well as the related problem of the role played in this field by state policy and strategies of development. The identification of stages is, in this case, a much more controversial issue. The intellectual appeal of "national culture" is diminishing as it is increasingly seen as an expression of official state ideology, with its implied totalitarian and autocratic character. However, there is also a substantial argument in favor of protecting local peripheral cultures from the European or Western-biased domination (cultural imperialism of core countries) through a New World Cultural Order. Analyzing the problem of cultural diffusion, a distinction is made between spontaneous inter-cultural communications (a dialogue between cultures) and official international cultural exchanges subject to state policy, yet no guidelines can be offered for optimal proportions between these two.

The above outline of identifiable stages of cultural development suggests that there is general agreement on the sequence in which the various forms and means of cultural expression succeed each other, but there is no consensus as to the meaning of these changes and their impact on the content which these cultures convey. In the European tradition, historical periods could be identified through prevailing cultural styles (Middle Ages, Renaissance, Romantisicm, etc.) and their impact on works of art. Today, it is the newly invented "cultural products" which create cultural styles and give names to the quickly changing substages of the media era. Oral traditional cultures jump into the TV and video age as these become present in the Third World. One can no longer speak of a classical international life cycle for cultural products, which instantly become global. At worst, this cycle is shortened from decades to years. It seems that the development and diffusion of new mass communication techniques and media, as well as international tourism, do not so much challenge the hitherto used stages of cultural development, as make their relevance purely historical. The global, media-dominated and largely mass (in the sense of its target population) culture is now present both in urban and rural, industrial and agricultural, as well as traditional and modern societies.

ARE CULTURE AND CULTURAL DEVELOPMENT SYSTEMATICALLY RELATED TO LEISURE AND LEISURE IDEALS?

While the term "leisure" may apply more to a limited range of meanings within Western cultures, it would appear that the meaning, use, and incidence of "free time" varies systematically with various aspects of culture and with stages of cultural development.

Industrialization and Urbanization

It would appear that the level of industrialization is systematically related to free time. While industrialization and urbanization need not occur simultaneously in the development of a culture (or sometimes do not occur at all), the notions of Gemeinschaft and Gesellschaft are useful in examining changes in free time. Gemeinschaft, according to Tonies, referred to "a society characterized by the predominance of intimate primary relationships and by emphasis upon tradition, consensus, informality, and kinship. This pattern of society is most closely approximated by rural-agricultural societies" (Theodorsen and Theodorsen 1969: 170).

Gesellschaft referred to "a type of society in which secondary relations predominate, that is, in which social relationships are formal, contractual, expedient, impersonal and specialized" (Theodorsen and Theodorsen 1969: 173).

Gesellschaft has many of the aspects of "modernism" which increasingly characterize our world. Modernism, according to MacCannell, is identifiable by "advanced urbanization, expanded literacy, generalized health care, rationalized work arrangements, geographical and economic mobility, and the emergence of the nation-state as the most important sociopolitical unit" (MacCannell 1976: 7). These, however, are secondary in importance, MacCannell believed, to the overall totality of modern life which sets modern societies in opposition to both their own past and to less developed nations. "No other major social structure distinction (certainly not that between the classes) has received such massive reinforcement as the ideological separation of the modern from the nonmodern world" (MacCannell 1976: 8). Modernism is documented by the giving of foreign aid and the sending of "development" teams to other nations which wish, themselves, to "develop." Along with the previous conditions mentioned which characterize modernity, there is also the pervasive feeling among those in modern nations that less modern cultures are somehow more "authentic" or that reality is occurring elsewhere. Thus, while the emerging conditions of modernism become more and more pervasive, the feeling of inauthenticity is also more prevalent.

The extent to which the world is modernizing is related to free time in numerous ways. Kaplan (1960) believed that the transformation from Gemeinschaft to Gesellschaft resulted in systematic changes in leisure from conservative to faddish, body-centered to mind-centered, spontaneous to organized, utilitarian to cultural orientation, generalized to specialized activities, few choices to many choices, group-centered to individual-centered, noncommercial to commercial, participation to observation, and outdoor to indoor. This typology, however, is itself subject to challenge since within both Gemeinschaft and Gesellschaft cultures there are stages of cultural development which may contradict the logic of this typology. Religious holidays, for instance, may have been much more highly organized in Gemeinschaft cultures than such holidays in Gesellschaft cultures. As this change takes place, modernism results not in the disappearance of the nonmodern world but its artificial preservation and reconstruction within modern society.

> The separation of nonmodern cultural traits from their original contexts and their distribution as modern playthings are evident in the various social movements toward naturalism, so much a feature of modern societies; cults of folk music and medicine, adornment and behavior, peasant dress, Early American decor, efforts, in short, to museum the premodern (MacCannell 1976).

Such efforts are not confined to cultural artifacts but extend also to the existing regional or ethnic cultural traditions which don't conform to emerging images of modernity.

Cultural Pluralism

A related notion is that of cultural pluralism—"cultural heterogeneity, with ethnic and other minority groups maintaining their identity within a society" (Theodorsen and Theodorsen 1969)—which appears to be systematically related to free time. In the modern era, however, pluralism must be thought of as the extent to which different ethnic and minority groups pervade a culture, whether or not they reside in the culture. Thus, for example, the urban areas of Brazil are becoming more pluralistic not only because of resident ethnic groups such as Japanese, Italians, and Germans, but also because of the great influence of North American television and popular music which is pervasive in Rio de Janeiro and Sao Paulo. Cultural pluralism, whether due to ethnically diverse groups in the culture or due to their presence in the mass media and other cultural outlets, may shape leisure or free time (Godbey 1985: 115) as shown in Table 1.

Democratization

Free time in a culture is also systematically shaped by the extent to which culture becomes democratized. Certainly this notion may have several different meanings. As Zuzanek (n.d.) observed, democratization of culture may refer to: a lessening of the distance between intellectual elite groups and other sectors of society, a broadening of the audience for the arts and profound changes in its composition, mass distribution of products of high culture at prices within reach of all and at places where they were never available before, and the right to culture as a basic human right. More specifically, in regard to leisure or free time, democratization of a culture may mean the decline of a "leisure class." According to Galbraith (1958: 25),

> Nearly all societies at nearly all times have had a leisure class—a class of persons who were exempt from toil. In modern times and especially in the United States, the leisure class, at least in any identifiable phenomenon, has disappeared. To be idle is no longer considered rewarding or even entirely respectable.

In North America, as elsewhere, democratization of culture has led to the decline of a leisure class which is replaced by a larger class for whom work is no longer very painful.

Concepts of Time

Free time, we have argued, is directly linked to stages of cultural development, as is the concept of time itself. It is not to argue that given cultures have a single concept of time, but rather that one concept comes to predominate. The 2.6 billion Hindus in the world, for example, have a wide variety of beliefs and practices, but tend to share a belief in inborn duty, virtue, and destiny (Dharma); a belief in a cosmic law of credits and debits for good and evil acts (Kharma); a belief in the transmigration of souls and their eventual release from time (Moksha); and a belief in the ultimate ground of reality (Brahama). The Vedas, sacred hymns, describe the world as one in which creation and destruction pursue their relentless labor simultaneously, hand in hand. As a defense against such a world, they advocate belief in the insignificance of time's passage. Time, while real enough for daily chores, is judged unimportant in the economy of the universe (Fraser 1987: 17).

The Chinese have historically had a preference for organic naturalism in which time and nature are viewed as aspects of dynamic, living systems which, having an affective dimension, must be qualitatively explored. Both the Hindu judgment of time as important and the Chinese preference for thinking of time in natural, qualitative terms are systematically changed as a culture develops toward the prevailing conditions of modernism. The Hebrew tradition, and then Christianity, changed thinking about time. "History ceased to be just one thing after another and became, instead, an intricately interwoven series of events that progressed from a well defined beginning to an appointed goal. This history is known as salvation history, and with it, the idea of linear time was born" (Fraser 1987: 21). In modern cultures, time is quantitatively conceptualized as linear and is, eventually, viewed as the ultimate scarce resource. Scheuch (1972) noted in analyzing results from a massive study of the use of time undertaken in 12 countries, "the more a person is part of an industrial society with a very high density of communication, and the more educated the person, the more he is likely to do a number of activities simultaneously." In quantitative terms, those who reside in modern cultures wish to increase the "yield" on time as they do on money.

IS THE CONCEPT OF LEISURE RELEVANT TO ALL CULTURES AND STAGES OF CULTURAL DEVELOPMENT?

The Aristotelian idea of leisure which, for the Western world is where the concept was created, would today not be amenable to either the Western or the Eastern world. It was a concept designed for males only, was in opposition to materialism, assumed a rigid hierarchy among humans, and stressed the obligation to participate in civic activities as part of the proper use of leisure. It can be argued that most subsequent definitions of leisure originated in Western or European-based civilizations and are intellectual products of that culture. Those definitions, therefore, stress the meaning of leisure applicable to the present stages of industrial and urban civilizations. The exclusion, for instance, of semi-obligations from leisure may seriously deform the image of life after work in many developing countries where celebrations and festivities of religious types are an essential element of culture. The distinction between work and nonwork obligations varies from one Western country to another, not to mention comparison between different cultures. The same is true of the validity of comparisons between such

Table 1. Leisure in singular and plural culture societies.

	Plural Culture Society	Single Culture Society
Concept	Leisure is anything the individual chooses to do which he/she finds pleasurable; leisure is unlimited, an end in itself.	Leisure is a set of identifiable experiences which the individual is taught to enjoy; leisure is limited, a means to an end.
Variation in Behavior	Range of acceptable behavior wide.	Range of acceptable behavior narrow.
Standards	Laws set limits; no universally accepted mores by which to judge leisure behavior.	Mores and folkways set limits of behavior; universal standards for leisure based upon perceived cultural necessity.
Role	Individual and subcultural identity linked to leisure behavior.	Tribal, local or national identity linked to leisure behavior.
Role Problems	Difficult to judge leisure ethically; dispute over leisure values; lack of meaning.	Lack of experimentation or alternatives; persecution of that which is foreign; easy to use leisure as a means of social control.
Government's Role	Identification of recreation needs difficult; may provide only selected kinds of services or serve certain subcultures or groups disproportionately.	Identification of recreation needs easy; may provide services which act as a common denominator.
Commercial Organization's Role	Commercial sector has more diverse opportunities; can cater to individual or subculture tastes; easier to create needs.	Commercial sector has more limited opportunities; more difficult to create needs or cater to individual or subculture tastes.

criteria as psychological state of being, attitude, pleasure, or personal autonomy. The idea of leisure as a time freed from work and subsistence constraints through gains in the productivity of labor, struggles of the trade unions, work legislation, and improvement in the living standards (access to time-saving services and products, discretionary income) is applicable to the Western world and, at best, parts of urban areas elsewhere in the world. In developing countries the scope and participation in activities considered as "culture and recreation" is expanding without substantial gains in productivity, efficient pressure from trade unions, and the existence of many modern amenities.

This suggests that the conceptualization of leisure has been limited to elements typical of the Western, urban-industrial civilization, instead of making references to more universal features which are present in the more flexible and culturally unbiased term "free time." Even this term, however, must be operationalized within the context of a specific culture. The forces which make time "free" may have to do with weather, work role, politics, gender, or a sign from the gods.

MODERNISM AND A MORE HOMOGENEOUS WORLD PHILOSOPHY OF LEISURE

The consequences of the spread of modernism on cultural diversity is critical in terms of emergent leisure patterns and philosophies.

Do Modern Cultures Become More Like Each Other?

While it would be a mistake to assume that modern nations ever fully assimilate into indistinguishable cultural units, a number of strong forces within modern cultures both encourage homogeneity among modern nations and draw nonmodern nations into the modern world. Among such forces are phenomena as diverse as television, computers, tourism, and the emergent world economy (see Figure 1).

Computers in all countries work basically the same. All input for such machines is a zero or a one. "Bureaucracies and computers have much in common: both must work reliably by fixed laws and without ambiguity. Because they share these talents, computing machines and bureaucratic people can easily be combined" (Fraser 1987: 327). Within finance, computers have become the essential international bookkeepers, transferring over $300 billion daily among banks on five continents. Within social policy, the huge population explosion, the increasing homogenization of needs, and the near uniformity in systems of production and distribution have meant that "statistics must replace individual attention in public administration" (Fraser 1987: 328). Not only do computers produce more information than any organization can digest, they have also brought about a greater tendency to test for facts in mass educational institutions, which favors rote memorization. Critical analysis, interpretation, inference, and application are increasingly the province of an elite group of "think tank" intelligentsia. Computers make everything happen faster.

Television, also, has contributed to the homogenization of modern cultures. In this area, the program capacity of the United States, which far surpasses the rest of the world, has meant that American television content, production, and distribution methods are emulated in both modern and modernizing countries. Such TV content, which stresses the centrality of style, gratuitous sex and violence, and the reduction of complex or ambiguous political or social issues to overly simple dimensions, can be seen in Jakarta, Mexico City, or Melbourne. Television further hastens the homogenization of needs and definitions of success and happiness.

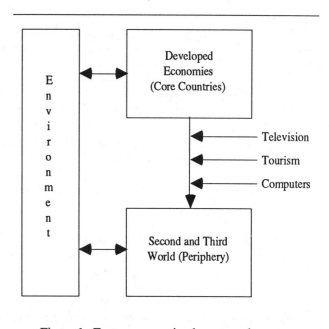

Figure 1. Factors promoting homogeneity among nations.

It also, of course, defines and shows models for the successful use of leisure. Both television content and computer communications increasingly leak across borders. Controlling computer use puts individual nation-states further behind in competition in the emergent world economy; allowing free access to them diminishes the power and the uniqueness of individual nation-states.

Perhaps a similar case may be made for tourism. Machlis and Burch (1983) argued that tourism may be understood as relations among strangers, and for tourism situations in which the guest strangers are from modern nations and the host strangers are from developing nations, a cycle of involvement is created which includes a gradual reshaping of everyday life to suit the tourist. "Tourism, above all, is a means to confront strangers and strange settings in an orderly and normative way that confirms the rightness of our daily life" (Machlis and Burch 1983: 688). Gradually, the definition of everyday life preferred by the tourist will be forced upon the host. Further, individuals in such host cultures may develop a distorted view of the tourist's everyday life since the tourist presents a picture of temporary overconsumption not related to his or her usual style of life.

The internationalization of the economies of modern nations and, increasingly, of developing nations has also had a profound homogenizing effect. Not only is industry within various nations increasingly interdependent, but such interdependence includes a vast range of technological issues, such as the production and distribution of microchips, weapons, and medical machinery. It also includes environmental issues. The impact of the depletion of the ozone layer will be as profound or more so for small Caribbean islands than for Canada, even though Canada and the United States contribute far more to the depletion of the ozone layer than do such islands.

While a fundamentalist backlash against many aspects of modernism may be seen in some countries and among members of some sects or branches of faiths such as Islam and Christianity, the larger trend is toward the blunting of ideology and an economic pragmatism to facilitate economic advance. Such a trend is evident in China, the Union of Soviet Socialist Republics, Israel, the United States, and elsewhere. While the nations of the world remain distinct, the nation-state makes less and less sense in geopolitical terms. Communication, pollution, weapons systems, transportation systems, and human beings permeate borders with greater ease.

Will a World Philosophy of Leisure Emerge?

If nations are in the process, essentially, of becoming more and more alike, it may be assumed that the cultural values attributed to leisure as well as the use of leisure itself will become more similar. If modern nations shape developing nations more than vice-versa, it might be assumed that the leisure of developing nations would come to resemble more and more the leisure values and behaviors of modern ones. While this assumption might seem logical, there are several factors which argue against its occurrence.

As presently undertaken, leisure in modern nations is dependent upon a vast array of material goods and services which cannot be duplicated throughout the world due to economic constraints. Even if such models could be duplicated, the environmental consequences of doing so would be catastrophic. If the Chinese owned automobiles (the sine qua non of many leisure experiences for those in modern nations) at the same rate of ownership as, say, North Americans, the polar ice caps would melt. Tourism and pleasure travel among Third World nations, if undertaken at the rate of those in modern nations, would produce immense problems to both Third World societies and their natural and person-made environments.

Perhaps North America, Western Europe, Japan, and other modern nations cannot serve as a model for the rest of the world in regard to leisure even if the rest of the world wants the leisure values and behaviors those in modern nations practice. Just as the North American diet is not an appropriate model for developing nations, neither is the hugely consumptive, individualistic model of leisure. North America, with 6% of the world's population, consumes 40% of the world's energy, 40% of the world's illegal drugs, and almost one-half of the world's commercial airliners (Godbey 1989). The exceedingly open-ended quality of leisure in modern nations, the narcissism, and the degree of commodification mean such a concept cannot be transported to developing nations without immense cultural and environmental harm being done.

Nevertheless, the leisure styles of modern nations, particularly North America, have about them a series of qualities which are widely desired among developing nations. The sense of individual freedom, mobility, style, and relative independence from church, state, and family are widely admired. Additionally, the opportunity to consume vast amounts of material goods during leisure is not only admired by developing nations but also emulated whenever possible, often with a flair surpassing Veblen's worst expectations. There is, we would argue, a strength of leisure culture in modern nations which is greater than the strength of leisure culture in developing nations. This is not to argue that the "goodness" of such culture is greater in modern nations, merely that, having been exposed to the leisure choices associated with modernity, individuals from developing nations will, ultimately, trade their own leisure styles for those of modern nations. Doing this, as we have previously stated, would likely produce an environmental, economic, and cultural catastrophe. Developing nations cannot emulate the extraordinarily consumptive model of leisure which modern nations exhibit. They cannot own all-terrain vehicles at the same rate, cannot visit international vacation spots at the same rate, cannot consume drugs, food, books, or a myriad of leisure equipment as do their counterparts in the modern world. The world's population, lest we forget, is in the historically unprecedented process of doubling or even tripling over the next four decades and almost none of that growth will come from modern nations. It would be the height of folly to assume that a highly materialistic lifestyle can be provided for them. It is also folly to assume that modern nations can seal themselves off from the consequences of this huge growth. Not only do developing nations control strategic natural resources vital to the well-being of developed nations, but they may also use the threat of switching political alliances to obtain economic and political concessions. The economy has been internationalized, terrorism has become the atom bomb of the developing nations and the computer, television, and mass tourism let those in developing nations know about life elsewhere. Those in villages in India see rich Texans on television, nomads see the vapor trails of the jet planes overhead.

Given this situation, there will likely be a desire on the part of those in many developing nations to emulate the leisure habits of modern ones. As modern nations become increasingly aware of the consequences of this happening, they will view it with increasing alarm. While there may now be enthusiasm in some quarters that the People's Republic of China is headed, with great uncertainty, toward more materialism and capitalism in their culture, the practical consequences of this on the environment, already jeopardized by the behavior of modern nations, may cause modern nations to seek to intervene to slow such change.

Modern nations, because they serve increasingly as a model of leisure use for developing ones to whom they are increasingly visible, will have no choice but to modify their own styles of life if they expect developing nations to follow. Doing this will require restricting some forms of personal freedom, taxing consumption, and taking a philosophical approach to leisure and, indeed, to the rest of life which might be called pragmatic—that is, the philosophical assumption that the goodness of an idea can be determined by the extent to which it works. Pragmatism will likely dictate a less consumptive model of leisure experience on a global basis. While sudden technological advances such as the perfection of nuclear fusion might in some ways lessen the need to limit consumption, in other ways it would not. Imagine, for a moment, tourists from the People's Republic of China visiting London or Paris in June at the same rate that North Americans or Japanese do, even if they traveled there by nonpolluting means.

If we establish a ratio between material resources in the world and population and then imagine the population doubling, current resources are cut in half except for the impact of technology and redistribution. While both these influences are powerful and unknown (who, for instance, could have predicted that Japan would become the most powerful economic power in the world?), it seems likely that leisure viewed as open-ended consumption will have to change, and the modern nations who increasingly provide the models of leisure to which many developing nations aspire will have to lead by example. They will likely do so with great reluctance but will, nevertheless, if only from pragmatic considerations. Unless they do, the developing world may seek to follow—with disastrous results.

If we come to the conclusion that a major reorientation of leisure patterns must take place in developed countries in order for the global frame of reference constituted by these patterns to become viable for the rest of the world, then we may have to analyze the factors which will help to bring about or inhibit this transformation. One factor which in the short- and medium-range future may have a detrimental effect on the global awareness of the need to change leisure patterns would be the growing struggle for cultural hegemony between the United States and a newly-united Western

Europe which, after the post-war era of strong American cultural domination, has high expectations concerning the development of its own cultural model and its impact on Europe's former colonies and spheres of cultural influence. Another factor which could inhibit the reorientation of leisure patterns could come from a regional grouping of the Pacific countries under the supremacy of Japan, which could help to diffuse leisure-related durables to mass consumers throughout Southeast Asia on a previously unheard of scale.

On the other hand, in the poorest of the world's countries, there exists a phenomenon which halts the spread of leisure patterns associated with high consumption of material goods. This phenomenon, known as high leisure preference at low levels of income, consists basically of keeping material needs low and converting most of the surplus the economy is able to produce into nonconsumptive free time (mainly passive resting, but also talks with neighbors and family members, plays, walks, etc.) (Sahlins 1976). Such a development would likely be supported by developed nations as long as it was coupled with lowering birth rates.

Stressing the need for a new global philosophy of leisure and a global reorientation of leisure patterns, we may speculate on three possible scenarios of change. The first one, which could be labeled as mutual adjustment, would imply that both developed and developing countries realize the constraints of the common reference model used for leisure and decide to alter it drastically, both with respect to leisure practices in developed countries and expectations in developing countries. The second hypothesis, which is perhaps the most probable one, is that of cultural barter. In exchange for the developing countries' agreement not to copy the most consumptive forms of leisure practiced in the West, they would be provided with various types of widely-conceived cultural assistance, such as free access to satellite television, to music and video tapes, various forms of cultural exchange, assistance in preservation of cultural and historical heritage, free technological transfers, and/or joint production of consumer durables serving leisure needs, with emphasis on collective, rather than individual forms of "consuming" leisure. Additionally, developed nations would give tangible evidence of their willingness to reorient their highly consumptive leisure patterns.

The third scenario, hopefully the least probable one, would be that of mutual hostility (real or pretended), under which the developing countries would try to reshape their leisure models by sealing themselves off from outside cultural influence, controlling the flow of information, and glorifying national cultures and virtues to the point of becoming xenophobic.

The problem of reorientation adjustment must also be viewed from the perspective of development strategies and development praxis in the Third World. The historical experience of the developing countries and of East Europe has taught us that while some of the ideas behind these strategies become an element of these countries' social and economic policies, their consistent implementation leaves much to be desired. This raises the question of whether any profound restructuring of social needs in these countries is possible without a very tangible threat brought about by either a military, economic, or environmental crisis. A reorientation in leisure patterns among both developed and developing nations is dependent, therefore, upon establishing a more common view of social, economic, and ecological ideals based upon an increasing recognition of interdependence. Such a recognition could constitute the first step toward a philosophy of leisure appropriate to nations in vastly different circumstances.

ENDNOTES

[1] In this section abstraction is made of such elements of cultural dynamics as the struggle between avant-garde and Establishment culture, incorporation of counter-culture and youth culture into mainstream culture, etc.

LITERATURE CITED

Benham, D. 1981. Reflections sur les dimensions culturelles du developpement. Paris: UNESCO.

de Lima-Camargo, O. 1984. Temps libre et culture des aires urbaines dans les societes en voie de developpement — Le cas du Bresil. Revue Tiers Monde. No. 97:1-23.

Fraser, J. T. 1987. Time—the familiar stranger. Redmond, WA: Tempus Books.

Galbraith, J. K. 1958. The affluent society. New York, NY: Mentor Books.

Godbey, G. 1989. The future of leisure services: thriving on change. State College, PA: Venture Publishing, Inc.

Godbey, G. 1985. Leisure in your life: an exploration. 2nd ed. State College, PA: Venture Publishing, Inc.

Kaplan, M. 1960. Leisure in America: a social inquiry. New York, NY: John Wiley and Sons.

Kelly, J. 1987. Freedom to be: a new sociology of leisure. New York, NY: Macmillan.

Ki-Zerbo, J. 1976. Culture et development. Geneva: IIES.

Kloskowska, A. 1983. Sociology of culture. Warszawa: PWN. (In Polish).

Kobayashi, K. 1986. Computers and communications. Cambridge, MA: MIT Press.

MacCannell, D. 1976. The tourist—a new theory of the leisure class. New York, NY: Schocken Books.

Machlis, G.; Burch, W. 1983. Relations among strangers: cycles of structure and meaning in tourist systems. Sociological Review. 31:666-689.

McHenry, M. P. 1981. Culture: the forgotten dimension. Development: The Seeds of Change. No. 34:1-78.

Rascallon, P. 1983. Le developpment culturel et les pays du Tiers-Monde. Revue Tiers Monde. No. 95, Juillet-Septembre.

Rezsohazy, R. 1969. Temps sociaux et developpement, la renaissance. Bruxelles: du Livre.

Sahlins, M. 1976. Stone age economics. Chicago, IL: Aldine Publishing Co.

Scardigli, V. 1983. La consommation: culture du quotidien. Paris: PUF.

Scheuch, E. 1972. The time budget interview. In: Szalai, A., ed. The use of time-daily activities of urban and suburban populations. The Hague, Netherlands: Mouton. 77 p.

Theodorsen, G. A.; Theodorsen, A. G. 1969. Modern dictionary of sociology. New York, NY: Thomas Y. Growell.

UNESCO. 1987. A practical guide to the world decade for cultural development. Paris: UNESCO.

Wnuk-Lipinski, E. 1981. Time budget—social structure—social policy. Wroclaw: Ossolineum. (In Polish).

Zuzanek, J. [no date]. Democratization of culture in a sociological perspective. Ontario, Canada: University of Waterloo.

II.

STATE-OF-KNOWLEDGE CHAPTERS

II.

STATE-OF-KNOWLEDGE CHAPTERS

A. Physiological and Psychophysiological Measures

Health Benefits of Physical Activity

Ralph S. Paffenbarger, Jr., M.D.
Division of Epidemiology
Stanford University School of Medicine
Stanford, California

Robert T. Hyde
Division of Epidemiology
Stanford University School of Medicine
Stanford, California

Ann Dow
Tahoe National Forest
Nevada City Ranger District
USDA Forest Service
Nevada City, California

Supported by grants from the National Heart, Lung and Blood Institute (HL 34174) and the National Cancer Institute (CA 44854). Report number XL in a series on chronic disease in former college students.

INTRODUCTION

Much information on health promotion and disease prevention has been obtainable only by using the methods of epidemiology. This is especially true of studies of the relationships of physical activity or exercise to health and longevity. Although the virtues of vigorous lifestyle have been discussed for centuries, the real importance of physical exertion to vitality and survival has been appreciated only since the middle of our 20th century. As workaday jobs have become increasingly sedentary, often denying opportunities for physical activity at work, the need for leisure-time sports play and other physical energy output has become painfully evident. Also the issues and processes involved have proven to be highly complex, ranging from heredity, lifestyle patterns, and environment to matters of physiology, chronic disease, and aging.

Investigations of physical activity and health soon encounter problems of confounding or interaction with eating behavior, tobacco use, other social habits, and a host of personal characteristics. These influences on health are not mutually exclusive, nor do they operate independently. Rather, they blend, amplifying or diminishing the effects of one another. Their busy traffic is a two-way street where we must differentiate the benefits of exercise from the hazards of sedentariness, the defenses of physical fitness from the assaults of aging, the avoidable accidents of disease from the inevitable count-downs of becoming old.

The list of personal and environmental influences involved is sufficient to guarantee that almost any set of observations will have to take into account a complex array of their interactions even if only the most important are to be analyzed for their effects on health. The key techniques are comparison and contrast, using study procedures that must be designed to meet rigorous epidemiological principles. These include the demonstration of significant statistical association between presumed causes and observed effects. And there should be appropriate consistency, persistence, independence, dose-response relationship, specificity, alterability, repeatability, and confirmation of findings. Differences between groups under contrast often require adjustments for age and other influences (Paffenbarger 1988). Fortunately the electronic era we live in has greatly enhanced the potential caliber of epidemiological research and has opened many new doors toward better understanding of the problems we seek to solve. Nevertheless, the physical activity studies dealing with physical fitness, health, and longevity remain among the most complex and most important that we are being expected to deal with today (Bouchard et al. 1990).

DEFINITIONS

Some approaches have defined physical activity or exercise as bodily movement accomplished by muscle power and the expenditure of energy. Physical fitness is then taken to be a set of attributes that represent the capacity to perform the physical activity. Health is not merely the presence or absence of disease but a continuum representing all levels of bodily vitality from the utmost to the lowest endpoint (euphoria to death?). But levels of physical activity and physical fitness also extend over a considerable range that would seem to parallel in many respects the concept of health as a continuum. So do quality of life and longevity, which is postponement of death.

Characterization of physical activity to derive methods of evaluation, and to establish standards of prescription for individuals, and intervention for groups, must address a series of questions. Minimal, optimal, and detrimental levels of physical activity need to be identified. Among the most salient questions are the following. What types of physical activity are involved—endurance, weight-bearing, strength-inducing, flexibility, balance, psychologically oriented, individual, team, competitive, therapeutic, palliative, meditative? How much activity—assessed by its frequency, duration, and constancy? How intense is the exercise—by level of energy expenditure in time increments, or by percentage of maximal work capacity? By whom is the activity performed, or for whom planned—considering age, sex, health status, health purpose, and personal goal? Given these differences, it is likely that any given level of effort might be low for one individual yet too much for another.

FINDINGS FROM RESEARCH

Epidemiological evidence supports the concept that sedentary living habits are directly and causally related to the incidence of hypertensive-atherosclerotic diseases, especially coronary heart disease, sudden cardiac death, and stroke. The relationship of regular physical activity in reducing risk of coronary heart disease, and in reducing its recurrence, is plausible as a natural physiological process. The relationship is temporally sequenced, consistent, persistent, independent, biologically graded, and coherent with existing knowledge on the pathogenesis of these diseases (Caspersen 1989, Fentem and Turnbull 1987, Paffenbarger et al. 1990, Powell et al. 1987).

Habitual physical activity leads to a reduced resting heart rate and lower blood pressure levels. Vigorous exercise reduces the incidence of hypertension and among established hypertensives, it lowers both systolic and diastolic blood pressure levels (Paffenbarger et al. 1983, Seals and Hagberg 1984).

Exercise reduces blood glucose levels, increases the effectiveness of endogenous insulin and holds promise of decreasing the incidence or delaying the development of noninsulin-dependent diabetes mellitus (Helmrich and Paffenbarger[1]). It is a basic component of effective therapy for the type of delayed-onset (adult) diabetes. Exercise also is recommended in treatment of insulin-dependent (juvenile onset) diabetes although there is no evidence that exercise prevents its occurrence and there is some concern that it may worsen diabetic consequences, especially eye complications (Gyntelberg et al. 1977; Holloszy et al. 1977, 1987; Vranic et al. 1986).

Sustained physical activity leads to a decrease in fat body mass and an increase in lean body mass, with resultant increased basal metabolism and a lower risk of obesity. Together with recommendations concerning prudent dietary measures, a physical activity regimen is recommended for immediate and long-term control of obesity (Bray 1989, Siscovick et al. 1985).

In childhood and adolescence, habitual physical activity, as opposed to a sedentary lifestyle, leads to increased bone mass and bone strength. A gradual and sustained loss of bone mass begins in the third to fourth decade of life and continues unrelentingly in all subsequent decades. Physical activity, particularly weight-bearing and strength-building activities, help sustain bone mass and reduce the incidence of trauma-induced fractures. Thus physical activity helps prevent osteoporosis and its consequences, and is recommended in the rehabilitation of the osteoporotic subject (Aloia et al. 1978, Holloszy and Coyle 1984, Holloszy et al. 1971, Smith and Raab 1985).

Habitual physical activities increase muscle strength and improve the structure and function of connective tissues (ligaments, tendons, cartilage) and joints. Hence physical activity may prevent the complex of conditions leading to chronic back pain syndrome and the extensive debility associated with it (Tipton et al. 1986).

The role of physical activity in preventing various types of arthritis is uncertain; however, increased muscle strength, bone density, and connective tissue offer promise of a preventive effect. While exercise can be underused and overused, moderate nonweight-bearing exercise may be beneficial for the patient with osteoarthritis (Lane et al. 1986).

Regular bouts of moderate physical activity reduce the symptoms of mild or moderate depression and anxiety neuroses by improving self-image, social skills, mental health, perhaps cognitive functions, and total well-being (Taylor et al. 1985).

Mortality from all causes and longevity are influenced by exercise, fitness, and other considerations of lifestyle. Pekkanen et al. (1987) studied the influence of high physical activity on incidence of premature death from any cause among 636 healthy Finnish men aged 45-64 at entry, who were followed for 20 years, 1964-1984. There were 287 deaths, 106 due to coronary heart disease, but the men who had been most active lived 2.1 years longer than men less active (Table 1), mainly because of differences in coronary heart disease risk.

Table 1. Age effects, death from all causes by gradients of physical activity in 636 Finnish men, 1964-1984.

Physical activity at baseline	No. of men at baseline	Mean age at baseline	Mean age at death (year)			
			First 10% dead	First 20% dead	First 30% dead	All men dead
Low	386	54.9	60.3	62.6	64.5	67.4
High	250	55.2	62.5	64.6	66.8	69.1
Added years of life from high activity[1]			1.4	2.0	2.4	2.1
P =			0.006	<0.001	<0.001	0.002

[1]Adjusted for differences in age, blood pressure, serum cholesterol, and cigarette smoking.

Source: Pekkanen et al. 1987

Thus the benefit was in avoidance of premature death, and the survival curves of high actives and low actives converged in the last five years of follow-up. Those who died differed more in fitness elements, such as levels of body-mass index than those who survived, but the differences seemed too small to account for the survival advantage associated with the more active men. In fact, low body-mass index was an adverse characteristic relative to all-cause mortality, even though obesity tends to promote coronary heart disease risk. The converging survival curves of the high and low activity groups might reflect converging levels of activity, or altered influences of activity with aging, or both. All in all, however, the results show that the longevity benefits ascribed to high activity or vigorous exercise were appreciable. Their relationships to characteristics of fitness remain to be clarified. The investigators interpreted the survival patterns as showing that physical activity tends to promote longevity by avoidance of premature death but is unlikely to extend the natural life span of man.

The Finland longevity study invites a number of comparisons to reports on physical activity and longevity among Harvard alumni (Paffenbarger et al. 1984, 1986). The Finnish men were a smaller study population followed over a longer interval and represented a higher percentage of deaths, so their analyses did not have to rely on actuarial projections and estimates of survival such as were needed in the Harvard alumni study. Therefore, the more literal Finnish observations substantiate the Harvard findings. Despite what would seem to be obvious difference in lifestyles, the results of the two studies show remarkable agreement in most respects.

We have studied large cohorts of former students who had attended Harvard University, 1916-1950, and reported on their health habits and health status in post-college years. A total of 16,936 men had been followed from 1962 through 1978 for rate and cause of death in an attempt to identify personal and lifestyle characteristics, including various modes of physical activity, that were related to these outcomes. Extensive data on these men had been gathered from university archives recorded in their student days, from successive questionnaires completed by the alumni in their middle life or old age, and from official death certificates of those who had died. Analyses of these data have identified host and environmental precursors of cardiovascular diseases, cancers, other natural causes of disease and death, and traumatic deaths.

In 16 years of follow-up (1962-1978), representing 213,716 man-years of observation, 1,413 deaths from all causes were recorded. Alumni reported habitual physical activities in 1962 as walking, stair-climbing, and recreational endeavors such as sports play and work around the garden and home. The energy used for these activities was expressed in kilocalories (kcal) per week as an indicator of energy expenditure. Index increments of less than 500, 500 to 1,999 and 2,000 or more kcal per week represented 15%, 46%, and 39% of the man-years of observation.

Other personal and lifestyle characteristics (hypertension, body-weight extremes or changes, genetic or familial tendencies, cigarette smoking) were assessed as potential confounders or interactive elements with physical activity as it influenced health. Table 2 gives total and cause-specific rates of death by three levels of physical activity after adjustment for the other lifestyle characteristics mentioned. There is a strong inverse relationship between level and death from all causes, total cardiovascular diseases (including both coronary heart disease and stroke), and total respiratory diseases. The trend is similar but less strong for total cancers, and weak for other natural and unnatural causes.

Table 2. Cause-specific death rates per 10,000 man-years of observation[1]
among 16,936 Harvard alumni, 1962-1978, by physical activity index.

Cause of Death	Physical Activity Index (kcal/week)			One-Tail Test for Trend, P
	<500	500-1,999	2,000+	
All causes (n=1,413)	84.8	66.0	52.1	0.001
Total Cardiovascular Diseases (n=640)	39.5	30.8	21.4	0.001
Coronary heart disease (n=441)	25.7	21.2	16.4	0.002
Stroke (n=103)	6.5	5.2	2.4	0.001
Total Respiratory Diseases (n=60)	6.0	3.2	1.5	0.001
Total Cancers (n=446)	25.7	19.2	19.0	0.026
Lung (n=89)	6.2	3.7	4.0	0.116
Colorectal (n=58)	2.2	2.3	3.5	0.091[2]
Pancreas (n=41)	1.8	2.4	1.0	0.085
Prostate (n=36)	2.2	1.5	1.6	0.359
Total Unnatural Causes (n=146)	8.7	7.1	5.9	0.032
Accidents (n=78)	3.6	3.9	3.0	0.147
Suicides (n=68)	5.1	3.2	2.9	0.049

[1]Adjusted for differences in age, cigarette smoking, and hypertension.
[2]Opposite trend.

Since individuals may choose sedentary habits because of illness, death rates were recomputed for major causes of death after omitting the first 2 of the 16 years of follow-up. In this truncated analysis there remained a strong relationship between sedentary habits and death from total cardiovascular, and respiratory causes, but an insignificant relationship to death from all cancers and other causes. This testifies to the specificity of the association for cardiovascular-respiratory illnesses, although physical inactivity may predispose to colon and perhaps certain other cancers.

What specific types of physical activity might influence rates of death from all and specific causes? Table 3 addresses this question for cardiovascular mortality. It lists the age-adjusted death rates and relative risks of death from cardiovascular disease associated with specified levels and combinations of three types of physical activity assessed per week: walking six or more miles, stair-climbing up and down 36 or more floors (or stories), and actively playing sports of any type or amount.

Among men denying participation in all 3 activities (16% of the man-years), there were 41 deaths per 10,000 man-years. Using this rate as a standard for comparison, relative risks less than 1.00 were observed with the presence

of any activity or combination of activities, ranging from 0.80 for any single activity to 0.62 for any two, and to 0.53 for all three activities.

Sports play was the most influential in leading to decreased mortality in this 16-year follow-up interval, followed closely by walking and stair-climbing as about equal in importance. Although intensity and persistence of these activities were not measured and are not considered in this analysis, it is likely that sports play generally was more vigorous and sustained than walking and stair-climbing.

Ultimately, the study of exercise, fitness, and lifestyle is likely to reveal some of their potential beneficial impact on the well-being of individuals. Part of the answer may be seen in longevity estimates. A further approach is to consider the implications of attributable risk estimates.

Relative and attributable risks of death, derived from a multivariate analysis and contrasting the presence and absence of five adverse personal characteristics, with adjustment for age and each of the other four characteristics, are given in Table 4. Note that in this analysis we begin with a condition of sedentariness and then show what effect conversion to a level of adequate physical activity might be expected to have on health status. The levels of the other

Table 3.   Rates and relative risks of death from cardiovascular diseases (CVD) among 16,936 Harvard alumni, 1962-1978, by types of weekly physical activity.

	Weekly Physical Activity			Prevalence in Man-Years %	CVD Death Rate per 10,000 Man-Years[1]	Relative Risk of CVD Death
	Walk 6+ Miles	Climb 36+ Floors	Sports Play			
No activity	-	-	-	16	41	1.00
One out	-	-	+	17	28 ⎤	0.69 ⎤
of three	-	+	-	7	30 ⎬ 33	0.72 ⎬ .80
activities	+	-	-	14	38 ⎦	0.93 ⎦
Two out	-	+	+	8	27 ⎤	0.66 ⎤
of three	+	-	+	16	19 ⎬ 26	0.48 ⎬ .62
activities	+	+	-	10	34 ⎦	0.82 ⎦
All three activities	+	+	+	12	22	0.53

[1]Adjusted for age differences.

characteristics, such as cigarette smoking, are likewise shifted from adverse to favorable health implications. First, the relative risk estimates are used to describe the respective levels, in this case referring to a 16-year follow-up in the Harvard alumni study.

Men with a sedentary lifestyle, that is those expending fewer than 2,000 kcal per week, were at 31% higher risk of death during the follow-up interval than more active men; cigarette smokers had a 73% higher risk than nonsmokers; hypertensive men a 76% higher risk than normotensive men; men with a net weight gain of less than 7 kilograms after college were at 33% greater risk than men who had gained more; and men who had lost one or both parents before the age of 65 were at 15% greater risk than men whose parents survived to age 65 or beyond. Alumni with one or more of these adverse characteristics were at 94% greater risk of death from any cause than classmates with none of the characteristics.

Clinical attributable risks shown in the table give estimates of potential percentage reductions in the risk of death for persons who might exchange an adverse characteristic for its more healthful counterpart. Sedentary men who become more active might reduce their risk of death by 24%.

Reformed cigarette smokers might have 43% lower mortality experience; and hypertensive men who achieved normal blood pressures might have 42% lower mortality. Men with low net weight gain since college might have 25% lower risk of death if they had gained more; men with history of early parental mortality might have experienced a 13% reduced death risk if both parents had lived longer. If an alumnus with one or more of these adverse characteristics could have avoided all of them, his risk of death from any cause during the follow-up interval might have been reduced by 48% over the experience of classmates who had one or more of the adverse characteristics.

Community attributable risks estimate the potential reductions in death rates in a population or group of people whose unfavorable characteristics were converted to more healthful features. These estimates take the prevalence of the characteristics into account. As seen in the table, the risk of death might have been reduced among the Harvard alumni by 16% if every man had expended 2,000 or more kcal per week in walking, stair-climbing, and recreational activities. Total abstinence from cigarettes might have cut the community death rate by 22%; abolition of hypertension, by 6% (relatively small because of its low prevalence); a

Table 4.   Relative and attributable risks[1] of death from all causes among
16,936 Harvard alumni (1962-1978), by selected adverse characteristics.

Adverse Characteristic	Prevalence in Man-Years (%)	Relative Risk of Death	Clinical Attributable Risk (%)	Community Attributable Risk (%)
Sedentary lifestyle[2]	62.0	1.31	23.6	16.1
Cigarette smoking[3]	38.2	1.73	43.2	22.5
Hypertension[4]	9.4	1.76	42.1	6.4
Low net weight gain[5]	35.1	1.33	24.6	10.3
Early parental death[6]	33.3	1.15	13.1	4.8
One or more of the above[7]	90.5	1.94	47.7	45.3

[1]Adjusted for differences in age and each of the other characteristics listed.

[2]Energy expenditure of less than 2,000 kcal/week in walking, climbing stairs, and playing sports.

[3]Any amount.

[4]Physician-diagnosed.

[5]Net gain in body-mass index of less than 3 English units since college (not more than 7 kg or 15 lb).

[6]One or both parents dead before the age of 65.

[7]Adjusted for differences in age only.

greater weight gain, by 10%; and survival of both parents to age 65 or older, by 5%. If all five adverse characteristics had been completely eliminated from the Harvard community, the death rate from all causes might have been reduced by nearly one-half (45%).

In discussing the longevity patterns of the alumni, we may consider their rates and relative risks of all-cause mortality by gradients of physical activity assessed by their physical activity index. As in other analyses the breakpoint between low and high physical activity index is taken at 2,000 kcal per week, and death rates are expressed per 10,000 man-years. The more active of the 16,936 alumni had 28% lower risk of death from any cause during the 16 years of follow-up than the less active men. The gradient showed a steady decline as activity levels increase from less than 500 to an optimum level of 3,500 kcal per week, and the trend is highly significant (P<0.0001).

From the all-cause mortality data in the Harvard alumni study, it is possible to estimate an individual's added years of life to be gained by having the benefits of favorable lifestyle elements, including the habit of adequate contemporary physical activity, here a physical activity index of 2,000 or more kcal per week (Table 5).

The bottom line of the table shows that the greatest gain would be achieved by avoiding hypertension, the next by not smoking cigarettes, and the third by exercising enough to have a high index, i.e., for men with these specific adverse characteristics. Since the influence of physical activity is partly independent of the other characteristics, and their contributions are also partly cumulative, a lifestyle that combined several of these virtues might be expected to gain more years of added life than from any single item alone. We have already seen that exercise promotes longevity mainly by avoiding premature death from coronary heart disease. Appropriate exercise seems to have a similar influence in staving off hypertension, which is highly predictive of increased coronary heart disease risk and shortened survival (Paffenbarger et al. 1983).

Cigarette smoking is associated with death from lung cancer and other afflictions, as well as promoting coronary heart disease: therefore avoidance of cigarette smoking might be expected to postpone mortality in several ways, which may account for its larger benefit. Nonsmokers might be reducing their risk of premature death from coronary heart disease, and from lung cancer, etc., whether or not they were vigorous exercisers; if they were exercisers, so much the better their chances for extended longevity.

Table 5. Added years of life from favorable lifestyle patterns[1] in men up to
the age of 80, as estimated from Harvard mortality experiences, 1962-1978.

Age at Entry (year)	Physical Activity Index 2,000+ vs. <2,000 kcal/week	Cigarette Nonsmoking vs. Smoking	Normotensive vs. Hypertensive	Net Weight Gain of 7+ vs. <7 kg	Parental Longevity 65+ vs. <65 yrs.
35-39	1.50	2.68	3.48	1.22	1.15
40-44	1.39	2.62	3.31	1.16	0.98
45-49	1.10	2.38	2.60	1.05	0.76
50-54	1.20	2.23	2.20	1.03	0.76
55-59	1.13	2.00	1.84	1.14	0.45
60-64	0.93	1.64	1.51	1.01	0.22
65-69	0.67	0.98	1.20	0.59	0.09
70-74	0.44	0.51	0.37	0.34	0.06
75-79	0.30	0.03	0.18	-0.04	0.04
Average[2]	1.25	2.26	2.72	1.09	0.81

[1]Each lifestyle pattern is adjusted for differences in all of the other patterns listed.

[2]Weighted average adjusted for differences in age and all of the other patterns listed.

Net weight gain since college may have somewhat conflicting implications as high weight gain tends to predict coronary heart disease and low weight gain predicts other fatal diseases such as cancer, the ravages of alcoholism, etc. The table shows it is better to gain seven or more kilograms than less, which appears to be a low-end cutpoint hinting at the latter causes of death. If we also had an upper cutpoint relating to coronary heart disease, the table would be offering us a mid-range or scope within which weight gain would be most likely to enhance longevity. Then the years gained by optimum weight control might be somewhat increased over the present numbers in that column. The differing implications for coronary heart disease and all-cause mortality may help explain why obesity is often found to be weak or ambivalent as an element of health risk. Individuals who weigh the same may be quite different in their body composition, one fat and the other muscular (and it is likely that they will differ also in their habits of physical activity, which influence body composition). Therefore, some combined assessment of physical activity and weight gain might reveal even more pertinent implications for longevity than the separate columns tabulated here.

Controlling for the influence of physical activity versus other elements of lifestyle or physiology is complicated by the fact that physical activity is usually a positive or beneficial influence that modifies the impact of the other characteristics, such as obesity or cigarette smoking, the influences of which are adverse. The suggestion has often been made that much of the benefit of vigorous exercise or physical activity may consist of countering adverse influences of unwise habits (smoking, alcohol) or unfortunate characteristics (hypertension, heredity). We need to sort out the mechanisms by which physical activity promotes good health and longevity, both short-term and long-term, whether by cardiovascular modifications, metabolic processes, or other physiological considerations. By exploring the elements of fitness we ought to arrive at a clearer picture of the most important and pivotal aspects of influences of physical activity on the various systems of the body and the processes by which these influences determine our health status and longevity. As yet there have been few studies designed to reveal influences of physical fitness on longevity. Where does fitness fit in? Some might approach that topic by looking at the lifestyles and health patterns of athletes. But athleticism may not be a satisfactory equivalent for physical fitness, since one might be considered fit without being an athlete. What observations can we make about fitness and longevity from earlier studies of British civil servants, San Francisco longshoremen, the Harvard alumni, Los Angeles safety workers, or groups of Norwegians and Finns (Caspersen 1989, Fentem and Turnbull 1987, Powell et al. 1987)? Although the epidemiological patterns of fitness can be expected to parallel those of physical activity, it is obvious that we need much more epidemiological study of fitness in order to apply and extend the information so far obtained from clinical studies.

RESEARCH NEEDS

In considering research needs, we are concerned here principally with leisure-time activities requiring energy expenditure and their type, frequency, duration, and intensity. We accept outright the recognition that physical activity is beneficial and *indeed essential* to health and survival. Research on types of physical activity should focus on what kinds are most likely to be, or become, available from the USDA Forest Service or comparable recreational resources, actual or potential. Such studies should attempt to categorize these activities according to facilities available or necessary, relative levels of patronage expected, seasonal characteristics, accessibility, appropriateness as to objectives or expected results, and locale, i.e., natural advantages at hand.

We need to address considerations of *quality of life,* which, in the context of physical activity, refers especially to matters of *good health* or *well-being* in the most literal sense. Quite apart from any of its economic implications, a lifelong state of well-being, i.e., a high and promising quality of life, is something to be desired in and of itself, for its own sake. No one should presume to set a price on this. But quality of life still needs a great deal of study before we can claim to have achieved its best definition and realization. Here the folk proverb has been all too true, so far, that "we grow too soon old and too late smart." Today, almost everyone agrees that our world has got to begin giving more consideration to quality of life than it has ever been given before.

Patronage translates into a need to know what sorts of physical activity are being considered for whom—the young, the athletic, the untrained, the middle-aged, the elderly, the aged, the disabled, the handicapped, the restricted, the minority, the male, the female, individually and in combination. Each locale and recreational resource will have its different set of opportunities for patrons in these categories, none of whom should be left out if they might be included.

Competing ventures should also be assessed as these, too, might well determine what the needs and patronage of any proposed new recreational facility might be. On the other hand, the existence of one facility, such as a ski slope or ski lift, might facilitate the provision of additional recreational ventures such as hang gliding, rock climbing, or even some unique opportunities for picnics or hiking or a water slide.

Studies of accessibility are likely to find that mere proximity is not always a prime requirement. People travel hundreds of miles to reach their favorite recreational areas. Nevertheless, studies are needed to determine what the requirements are for such patronage to develop, e.g., lodging for overnight or extended periods, ample parking, easy vehicular access, suitable general transportion (such as a ski train or bus service), etc. These considerations need to be addressed in planning any recreational facilities. A special study might well be mounted concerning the elderly as a population subgroup of special interest to recreational planning.

ENDNOTES

[1] S.P. Helmrich and R.S. Paffenbarger, Jr., in paper on physical inactivity and other predictors of insulin-dependent diabetes mellitus, in preparation.

LITERATURE CITED

Aloia, J. F.; Cohn, S. H.; Ostuni, J., et al. 1978. Prevention of involutional bone loss by exercise. Annals of Internal Medicine. 89: 356-358.

Bouchard, C.; Shephard, R.; Stephens, T., et al., eds. 1990. Exercise, fitness and health. Champaign, IL: Human Kinetics.

Bray, G. A. 1989. Exercise and obesity. In: Bouchard, C.; Shephard, R.; Stephens, T., et al., eds. Exercise, fitness and health. Chapter 41. Champaign, IL: Human Kinetics.

Caspersen, C. I. 1989. Physical activity epidemiology: concepts, methods, and applications to exercise science. In: Pandolf, K.B., ed. Exercise sports sciences reviews. Volume 17, Chapter 12: 423-473.

Fentem, P.; Turnbull, N. 1987. Benefits of exercise for heart health: a report on the scientific basis. In: Exercise-heart-health. London: The Coronary Prevention Group: 110-125.

Gyntelberg, F.; Rennie, M. J.; Hickson, R. C.; Holloszy, J. O. 1977. Effect of training on the response of plasma glucagon to exercise. Journal of Applied Physiology: Respiratory and Environmental Exercise Physiolology. 43: 302-305.

Holloszy J. O.; Coyle, E. F. 1984. Adaptations of skeletal muscle to endurance exercise and their metabolic consequences. Journal of Applied Physiology: Respiratory and Environmental Exercise Physiology. 56 (4): 831-838.

Holloszy, J. O.; Oscai, L. B.; Mole, P. A.; Don, I. J. 1971. Biochemical adaptations to endurance exercise in skeletal muscle. In: Pernow, B.; Saltin, B., eds. Muscle metabolism during exercise. New York, NY: Plenum Press: 51-61.

Holloszy, J. O.; Rennie, M. J.; Hickson, R. C., et al. 1977. Physiological consequences of the biochemical adaptations to endurance exercise. Annals of the New York Academy of Sciences. 301: 440-450.

Holloszy, J. O.; Schultz, J.; Kusnierkiewicz, J., et al. 1987. Effects of exercise on glucose tolerance and insulin resistance. Acta Medica Scandinavica Supplement. 711: 55-65.

Lane, N. E.; Block, D. A.; Jones, H. H., et al. 1986. Longdistance running, bone density, and osteoarthritis. Journal of the American Medical Association. 9: 1147-1151.

Paffenbarger, R. S., Jr. 1988. Contributions of epidemiology to exercise science and cardiovascular health. Medicine and Science in Sports and Exercise. 20: 426-438.

Paffenbarger, R. S., Jr.; Hyde, R. T.; Wing, A. L. 1990. Physical activity and physical fitness as determinants of health and longevity. In: Bouchard, C.; Shepard, R.; Stephens, T., et al., eds. Exercise, fitness, and health. Champaign, IL: Human Kinetics Books: 33-48.

Paffenbarger, R. S., Jr.; Hyde, R. T.; Wing, A. L.; Hsieh, C.-c. 1986. Physical activity, all-cause mortality, and longevity of college alumni. New England Journal of Medicine. 314: 605-613, and 315: 399-401.

Paffenbarger, R. S., Jr.; Hyde, R. T.; Wing, A. L.; Steinmetz, C. H. 1984. A natural history of athleticism and cardiovascular health. Journal of the American Medical Association. 252: 491-495.

Paffenbarger, R. S., Jr.; Wing, A. L.; Hyde, R. T.; Jung, D. L. 1983. Physical activity and incidence of hypertension in college alumni. American Journal of Epidemiology. 117: 245-257.

Pekkanen, J.; Marti, B.; Nissinen, A.; Tuomilehto, J. 1987. Reduction of premature mortality by high physical activity: a 20-year follow-up of middle-aged Finnish men. Lancet. 1: 1473-1477.

Powell, K. E.; Thompson, P. D.; Caspersen, C. J.; Kendrick, J. S. 1987. Physical activity and the incidence of coronary heart disease. Annual Review of Public Health. 8: 253-287.

Seals, D. R.; Hagberg, J. M. 1984. The effect of exercise training on human hypertension: a review. Medicine and Science in Sports and Exercise. 16: 207-215.

Siscovick, D. S.; Laporte, R. E.; Newman, J. F. 1985. The disease-specific benefits and risks of physical activity and exercise. Public Health Reports. 100: 180-188.

Smith, E. L.; Raab, D. M. 1985. Osteoporosis and physical activity. Acta Medica Scandinavica Supplement. 711: 149-156.

Taylor, C. B.; Sallis, J. F.; Needle, R. 1985. The relation of physical activity and exercise to mental health. Public Health Reports. 100: 195-202.

Tipton, C. M.; Vailas, A. C.; Matthes, R. D. 1986. Experimental studies on the influences of physical activity on ligaments, tendons and joints: a brief review. Acta Medica Scandinavica Supplement. 711: 157-168.

Vranic, M.; Lickley, H. L. A.; Davidson, J. K. 1986 Exercise and stress in diabetes mellitus. In: Davidson, J. K., ed. Clinical diabetes mellitus. New York, NY: Thieme-Stratton. Chapter 15.

Cardiovascular Benefits of Physical Activity

Victor F. Froelicher, M.D.
Long Beach Veterans' Administration Medical Center
and
University of California Medical School
Irvine, California

Erika Sivarajan Froelicher
Los Angeles County Department of Health Services
Los Angeles, California

PREFACE

Animal Studies

Animal studies have consistently shown increased heart strength, heart size, and vascularity in wild animals compared to domestic animals or animals exercised regularly. The key question has been can blood flow to the heart muscle be increased? This is important since the major heart disease in modern countries is atherosclerosis. Atherosclerosis results in fatty deposits that block blood flow through the coronary arteries. The coronary arteries carry blood to the heart muscle to deliver oxygen and nutrients. When these arteries are blocked, chest pain called angina pectoris occurs as well as heart attacks and death. Exercise itself does not prevent the fatty deposits from forming. The fatty deposits are stopped from forming by changes in diet (decrease in cholesterol and saturated fats), avoidance of cigarettes, and control of high blood pressure. However, exercise makes the heart better able to deal with these blocks. The coronary arteries are larger and there are more side channels called collateral vessels for blood to reach the heart muscle due to exercise.

Human Studies

The benefits of exercise have been documented by morphological studies, hemodynamic studies, epidemiological studies, and clinical trials. These will be discussed in order, but first it is important to understand that the cardiovascular benefits are limited to dynamic exercise. Dynamic exercise involves the motion of large muscle groups. This contrasts with isometric exercise such as weight lifting.

Morphologic Benefits

The morphological changes in the heart have been documented by echocardiography. This is a noninvasive technique utilizing sound waves that bounce off the heart muscle to measure the thickness, size, and function of the heart. Echocardiographic studies have documented in man the changes noted in animals.

Hemodynamic Benefits

A regular dynamic exercise program results in a decrease in resting heart rate, a drop in heart rate and systolic blood pressure at submaximal workloads, an increase in maximal ventilatory capacity, and an increase in the capacity to do dynamic work. These hemodynamic changes are brought about by an exercise prescription that considers intensity, mode, duration, and frequency. The mode must be dynamic exercise such as walking, running, jogging, bicycling, swimming, or cross country skiing. The intensity should be over 50% of the current maximal capacity, duration should be at least 30 minutes per exercise session, and the frequency should be at least 3 times during the week spread out evenly. This is a means for optimizing the hemodynamic changes mentioned above also called the "training effect."

Epidemiological Studies

Epidemiology is the study of the distribution of disease and factors that effect this distribution in populations. In well people, the inverse association of physical activity and cardiovascular disease has been definitely demonstrated. Many studies support a lifestyle of physical activity as being protected from death due to cardiovascular disease. Often leisure time was assessed because of the relative inactivity at work. Individuals physically active during leisure time have a lower death rate due to coronary heart disease (CHD). How much physical activity is protective? In a causal sense, physical inactivity is not as important as diet, blood pressure control, or cigarette smoking; however, it is more prevalent. Less than half of the population in the USA or Canada obtain 20 minutes of exercise 3 times a week. The studies suggest that mild increases in physical activity are protective. It is not necessary to follow the prescription for hemodynamic effects mentioned previously. Vigorous walking appears to be all that is necessary.

Clinical Trials

In over 10 randomized trials of exercise training in patients who have survived a myocardial infarction (MI), it has been shown that there is a lower death rate in those who have participated in the exercise program.

Conclusion

A mild to moderate exercise program is very safe in the healthy population without symptoms. Though the risk increases with the intensity of exercise, the risk is largely only a concern in those with known heart disease. Mild to moderate walking, however, is a sane and safe recommendation for the general population including those with heart disease.

A consensus of the medical profession is that mild to moderate exercise or physical activity during leisure time is a wise personal choice for achieving and maintaining cardiovascular health.

The purpose of this chapter is to describe the cardiovascular benefits of physical fitness. The chapter begins with a review of animal studies, next are physiological studies in man evaluating cardiac changes, followed by epidemiological studies regarding physical activity during leisure time, an overview of exercise as treatment for heart disease, and then conclusions.

ANIMAL STUDIES RELATING CHRONIC EXERCISE TO CARDIAC CHANGES

Animal studies provide some of the strongest evidence for the health benefits of regular exercise. Studies have included:

- myocardial hypertrophy;
- myocardial microcirculatory changes;
- coronary artery size changes;
- coronary artery vasomotor tone;
- coronary collateral circulation;
- cardiac mechanical and metabolic performance;
- myocardial mitochondria and respiratory enzymes; and
- effects on atherosclerosis and risk factors.

Many effects have been demonstrated in the various studies, and a review of some of these follows.

Myocardial hypertrophy.—Numerous studies have demonstrated that vigorous exercise can induce cardiac hypertrophy in animals. Heart/body ratios are invariably larger in wild animals as compared with the domestic form of an animal species. Heart hypertrophy is due to exercise in young rats, whereas in older rats, exercise causes a decline in heart weight due to a loss of myocardial fibers or a decrease in fiber mass.

Myocardial microcirulatory changes.—In comparing tame and wild animals, the density of muscle cells and capillaries was found to be much greater in the more active wild animals. In young animals, cardiac hypertrophy is secondary to fiber hyperplasia, whereas in older animals, it is secondary to cellular hypertrophy. The capillary bed responds most markedly to growth stimuli when applied at an early age.

There is an age-related response of the ventricular capillary bed and myocardial fiber width in rats. At autopsy, the myocardial fiber width is constant, whereas the capillary/fiber ratio is increased in the exercised rats over the controls in all age groups. The capillary density decreases with age and is increased over the controls only in young exercised rats.

Experiments have been performed to study the effects of chronic exercise on the heart at different ages in rats. Age groups were subdivided into a control group, a group that swam for 1 hour daily, and a group that swam for 1 hour 2 days a week. After 10 weeks, the animals were sacrificed. Although the response of the rat heart to chronic exercise varied with age, the capillary/fiber ratio increased at all ages.

An exercise-induced reduction in myocardial infarction size after coronary artery occlusion in the rat has been reported. Exercise training resulted in a 30% reduction of myocardial infarct size after coronary artery occlusion, most likely due to increased vascularity. The effects of exercise on myocardial infarction in young versus old rats revealed that exercise improved survival of the old rats. In addition, the exercised old rats manifested cardiac hypertrophy, reduced infarction enzyme levels, and less evidence of arrhythmias or ECG changes.

Coronary artery size changes.—The effects of exercise on the coronary tree of rats has been studied by the corrosion-cast technique. After the animals were sacrificed, their hearts were weighed, then the coronary arteries were injected with vinyl acetate. In the rat, forced exercise caused a greater increase in the coronary tree size than cardiac weight increase, provided the exercise was not too strenuous or frequent. Swimming in rats resulted in an increased luminal cross-sectional area of the main coronary arteries in the young and strenuously exercised adult rats that experienced an increase in ventricular weight.

Coronary artery vasomotor tone.—The effects of exercise on large coronary artery vasoreactivity was studied in dogs trained by treadmill running for 8 weeks. The blunted constrictor response in the trained animals suggested that exercise reduces epicardial coronary vasoconstriction.

Coronary collateral circulation.—Eckstein (1957) performed the classic study of the effect of exercise and coronary artery narrowing on coronary collateral circulation. He surgically induced a constriction in the circumflex artery in approximately 100 dogs during a thoracotomy. Various degrees of narrowing were induced, but only dogs that developed ECG changes were included in the study. After 1 week of rest, the dogs were put into 2 groups. One group was exercised on a treadmill 1 hour a day, 5 days a week, for 6 to 8 weeks. The other group remained at rest in cages. The extent of arterial anastomoses to the circumflex artery was then determined. A second thoracotomy was performed, and blood pressure was stabilized mechanically. The circumflex artery was isolated and divided beyond the surgical constriction. The flow rate through the constriction

and the flow rate from the distal end of the artery were measured. When these values were plotted against one another, the less the antegrade flow (or the greater the constriction), the greater the retrograde or collateral flow. Also, the exercised dogs had a greater value for retrograde flow than did the rested dogs for any degree of constriction. Moderate and severe arterial narrowing resulted in collateral development proportional to the degree of narrowing. Exercise led to even greater coronary anastomosis.

The effects of endurance exercise on coronary collateral blood flow has been studied in miniature swine (Bloor et al. 1984). Coronary collateral blood flow was measured in 10 sedentary control pigs and in 7 pigs that ran 20 miles a week for 10 months. Radioisotope labeled microspheres were injected into the left atrium during each of three conditions: control, total occlusion of the left circumflex artery, and total occlusion plus mechanically elevated aortic pressure. Ten months of endurance exercise training did not have an effect on the development of coronary collaterals as assessed by microsphere blood flow measurements in the left ventricle of the pigs. When this was repeated after causing artificial partial occlusions in the coronary arteries of the pigs (i.e., ischemia present), exercise enhanced myocardial perfusion.

Cardiac mechanical and metabolic performance.—The effects of physical training on the mechanical and metabolic performance of the isolated rat heart has been studied. In exercised rats, the function of the heart as a pump was improved and this effect was at least partially due to improved oxygen delivery. Other studies support the concept that the exercise-hypertrophied heart is functionally superior to the normal heart. Under controlled loading conditions, hearts of chronically exercised rats continued to perform better during ischemia than did hearts of sedentary controls.

Myocardial contractility and adenosine triphosphatase activity of cardiac contractile proteins before and after exercise training has been studied using chronically instrumented dogs. After training, maximal contractility was within normal limits at rest, but significantly elevated by submaximal exercise.

Effects of risk factors on atherosclerosis.—Kramsch et al. (1981) randomly allocated 27 young adult male monkeys into 3 groups. Two groups were studied for 36 months and 1 group was studied for 42 months. Of the groups studied for 36 months, one was fed a vegetarian diet for the entire study whereas the other was fed the vegetarian diet for 12 months and then an isocaloric atherogenic diet for 24 months. Both were designated as sedentary because their physical activity was limited to a single cage. The third group was fed the vegetarian diet for 18 months and then the atherogenic diet for 24 months. This group exercised regularly on a treadmill for the entire 42 months. ST-segment depression, angiographic size of coronary artery narrowing, and sudden death were observed only in the sedentary monkeys fed the atherogenic diet. In addition, post-mortem examination revealed marked coronary atherosclerosis and stenosis in this group. Exercise was associated with substantially reduced overall atherogenic involvement, lesion size, and collagen accumulation. These results demonstrate that exercise in young adult monkeys increases heart size, left ventricular mass, and the diameter of coronary arteries. Also, the subsequent experimental atherosclerosis, induced by the atherogenic diet given for 2 years, was substantially reduced. Exercise before exposure to the atherogenic diet delayed the development of the manifestation of coronary heart disease. The important question this study raises is, "At what point comparable to the human lifespan were these studies initiated and what percentage of that lifespan was represented by the 3 years of observation?"

Studies in rats and dogs have found increased resistance to ventricular fibrillation after regular running, possibly through mechanisms involving cyclic adenosine monophosphate and the slow calcium channel.

HUMAN STUDIES SUPPORTING MORPHOLOGIC CHANGES

Echocardiography before and after an exercise.—Ehsani et al. (1978) reported rapid changes in left ventricular (LV) dimensions and mass in response to physical conditioning and deconditioning. Two groups of healthy young subjects were studied. The training group consisted of 8 competitive swimmers who were studied serially for 9 weeks. Exercise training induced rapid adaptive changes in LV dimensions and mimicked the pattern of chronic volume overload, and modest degrees of exercise-induced LV enlargement were reversible. Surprisingly, changes in LV dimension occurred early during endurance training, but there was no significant increase in measured LV posterior wall thickness until the fifth week of training. Estimated LV mass significantly increased after the first week of training.

DeMaria et al. (1978) reported the results of M-mode echocardiography in 24 young normal subjects before and after 11 weeks of endurance exercise training. The subjects were participating in a program of endurance physical conditioning as part of police training and ranged in age from 20 to 34 years. After training, they exhibited an increased LV end-diastolic dimension, a decreased end-systolic dimension, and both an increased stroke volume and shortening fraction. An increase in mean fiber shortening velocity was observed, as were increases in LV wall thickness, ECG voltage, and LV mass.

Adams et al. (1981) noninvasively studied the effects of an aerobic training program on the heart of healthy college-age men. Compared with the control group, echocardiography after training showed an increase in LV end-diastolic dimension, but no change in wall thickness or in ejection fraction. Although there was no change in myocardial wall thickness, the increase in end-diastolic dimension resulted in a calculated increase in LV mass.

Landry et al. (1985) evaluated 20 sedentary subjects and 10 pairs of monozygotic twins submitted to a 20-week endurance exercise program. Results indicate that cardiac dimensions are amenable to significant modifications under controlled endurance training conditions and that the extent and variability of the response of cardiac structures to training are perhaps genotype dependent.

Studies in patients with heart disease.—Ehsani et al. (1981) reported their results after 12 months of intense exercise in a highly selected group of 10 patients with coronary heart disease. All 10 had asymptomatic exercise-induced ST-segment depression. Eight comparable men were considered as controls. After 3 months of exercise training at a level of 50% to 70% of maximal oxygen consumption, the level of training increased to 70% to 80%, with two to three intervals at 80% to 90% interspersed throughout the exercise session.

The maximal amount of exercise-induced ST-segment depression was lessened. A weight loss from a mean of 79 kg to 74 kg occurred. The sum of the ECG voltage representing heart mass increased by 15%. Both LV end-diastolic dimension and posterior wall thickness were significantly increased after training.

If applied to most patients with coronary disease, this intensity certainly could lead to a high incidence of orthopedic and cardiac complications. Rehabilitation patients with exercise-induced ST-segment depression who exceed standard exercise prescriptions are at increased risk of cardiac events.

Ditchey et al. (1981) obtained echocardiograms on 14 coronary patients before and after an average of 7 months of supervised arm and leg exercise. Exercise training led to improvement; however, this was not accompanied by any significant change in LV end-diastolic diameter or wall thickness. Likewise, an index of LV mass did not change significantly after training by any measurement convention.

Exercise electrocardiographic studies.—Since abnormal ST-segment shifts in coronary patients are most likely secondary to ischemia, lessening of such shifts would be consistent with improved myocardial perfusion. For purposes of comparison, only similar myocardial oxygen demands can be considered; therefore, only ST-segment measurements at matched double products should be compared. The studies of the effect of an exercise program on the exercise electrocardiogram are summarized in Table 1. In all of the studies, training produced a lowering of heart rate for all submaximal exercise levels, permitting performance of more work before the onset of angina or ST-segment depression (which occurred at the same heart rate before and after training) or both.

Controversy now exists whether or not cardiac changes can occur in patients with heart disease and if they do, whether these changes require high intensity exercise. If high intensity exercise is needed, the risk to people with heart disease must be considered, and exercise cannot be advocated as a public health measure during leisure time without medical supervision and the availability of medications and instrumentation for defibrillation.

EPIDEMIOLOGICAL STUDIES RELATING PHYSICAL ACTIVITY TO CARDIAC EVENTS

Since most animal, clinical, and pathologic studies have not shown exercise to be directly related to the atherosclerotic process, it is reasonable to conclude that physical inactivity does not have a direct effect on atherosclerosis. Instead, the effects of regular exercise enable the body to better tolerate ischemia and lessen the manifestations of coronary heart disease. In addition, it can possibly alter other risk factors for atherosclerosis. The potential beneficial actions of regular exercise are multifactorial which makes physical inactivity a complex risk factor to assess. Some of the difficulties in studying physical inactivity as a risk factor will be discussed along with many of the studies that have been performed.

Does exercise protect from coronary artery disease rather than select out those with less disease who are better able to tolerate being physically active? Exercise can be related to other risk factors or risk markers, and often studies have not considered the selection of these factors. Particularly in a modern, mechanized society, there is usually only a small gradient of activity difference between various jobs. An important consideration is that people often leave active jobs with onset of the first symptoms of heart disease, even without realizing the cause of the symptoms. There may be a premorbid transfer from an active job to a less active job, biasing the relationship of inactivity to coronary heart disease. Also, individuals are often selected for active jobs or for lifestyles of physical activity. There are other difficulties in studying this question, including the uncertainty of what type and quantity of exercise is protective.

Although the most accurate way of assessing the physiologic effect of an activity level would be an exercise test, few studies have had this luxury. Job title or class has often been used as a proxy variable for occupational energy expenditure and, in some instances, has been quite accurate. However, consideration of off-the-job activity, i.e., leisure time, is important. Questionnaires have been used, but their reproducibility and accuracy are often doubtful. Parameters such as vital capacity, handgrip strength, and dietary assays have obvious limitations.

Many different types of populations have been used for epidemiologic studies. There are three basic types of epidemiologic studies: retrospective, cross-sectional, and prospective studies. Retrospective studies involve populations in which data has been obtained in the past, not specifically for epidemiologic purposes. Prevalence, or cross-sectional studies consist of screening a population for the current manifestations of a disease. Prospective, or longitudinal, studies involve a cohort of individuals specifically chosen and studied for the purpose of following them over a period of time for the development of disease.

Physical fitness vs. physical activity.—The question remains whether activity level or actual maximal oxygen uptake best predicts the risk for coronary heart disease. Leon et al. (1981) have shown that in healthy men, the results of resting measurements and a questionnaire correlate highly with treadmill time using a multivariate equation.

Retrospective studies of physical inactivity.—The retrospective studies include large population studies that have utilized death certificate and population data from an entire city, state, or country. Activity level was judged from the occupation listed on the death certificate, and the end point was coronary artery disease listed on death certificates. For brevity, only the classic studies of Morris will be reviewed here.

Morris has presented the data from the occupational-mortality records in England and Wales, interpreting the information as support for the hypothesis that occupational physical inactivity is a risk factor for coronary artery disease (Morris and Crawford 1958). The level of activity was based on the independent evaluation of the occupations by several industrial experts. The activity level of the last job held was found to be inversely related to the mortality from coronary artery disease, as determined from death certificates.

Morris (1975) presented data from a sequence of epidemiologic studies to support the hypothesis that: "Men in physically active jobs have a lower incidence of coronary heart disease than men in physically inactive jobs. More important, the disease is not so severe in physically active workers, tending to present first in them as angina pectoris and other relatively benign forms and to have a smaller early case fatality and a lower early mortality rate."

Table 1.   Studies performed with exercise electrocardiographic analysis before and after an exercise program.

Principal Investigator	Number Trained	Number of Controls	Length of Exercise Program	ECG Lead(s) Monitored	Description of Subjects	Exercise ECG Results
Costill	24	____	3 mos	CM_s	Three groups: ST depression; CHD and ST depression; Low fitness, no ST depression	No change in ST-segment response
Salzma	100	None	33 mos	C_1V, CH_6	MI, angina, and/or abnormal exercise ECG	ST-segment changes correlated to changes in functional capacity
Kattus	13	15	5 mos	CA_s	Asymptomatic abnormal exercise ECG	Similar ST-segment improvement rate in control subjects
Detry	14	None	3 mos	CB_s	MI and/or angina	No change in computerized ST-segment measurements at matched DP
Raffo	12	12	6 mos	CM_s	Angina with abnormal exercise ECG	Higher heart rate for same amount of ST depression
Watanabe	14	None	6 mos	XYZ	Mixed coronary disease	Changes only in spatial analysis
Ehsani	10	8	12 mos	V_{4-6}	9 post-MI>4 mos 1 with 3-VD; all with asymptomatic ST depression	Less ST-segment depression at matched DP and at maximal exercise; higher DP at ischemic ST threshold (0.1 mV flat)
PERFEXT[1]	48	59	12 mos	XYZ	MI, stable exertional angina pectoris, coronary artery bypass surgery	No significant difference at matched DP

MI = myocardial infarction; DP = double product (SBP x HR); VD = vessel disease; ECG = electrocardiogram.

[1] PERFusion, PERFormance, EXercise Trial, University of California, San Diego.

Source: Froelicher 1987a: 377.

The first study dealt with the drivers and conductors of the London transport system. Thirty-one thousand white males, 35 to 64 years of age, were included for analysis over a period of 18 months from 1949 to 1950. The end points were coronary insufficiency, myocardial infarction, and angina as reported on sickleave records, and listing of coronary artery disease on death certificates. The age-adjusted total incidence was 1.5 times higher in the driver group as compared with the conductor group and the sudden and three-month mortality was two times higher.

Morris subtitled a paper "The Epidemiology of Uniforms," which reported that the drivers had greater girth (i.e., larger uniform sizes were considered since weight was not recorded) than the conductors. In 1966, Morris also showed that the drivers had higher serum cholesterols and higher blood pressures than did the conductors. Also, a study by Oliver documented that for some unknown reason, even the recruits for the two jobs differed in lipid level and in weight (Oliver 1967). These differences put the drivers at increased risk to coronary artery disease for reasons other than an approximated difference in physical activity.

Prospective studies of physical inactivity.—In 1958, Stamler et al. (1960) began a prospective study of 1,241 apparently healthy male employees of the Peoples Gas Company in Chicago. By 1965, there were 39 deaths due to coronary disease among the groups. They found that the coronary disease mortality was higher in blue-collar workers (37 deaths per 1,000 men) who had an estimated higher habitual activity at work than in the white-collar workers (20 deaths per 1,000).

From 1956 to 1960, 687 healthy London busmen were examined for risk factors and coronary disease. In 1965, they were re-examined and 47 cases of coronary heart disease were diagnosed, including sudden deaths, MI, ECG changes, and angina. Incidence rates per 100 men over 5 years were 4.7 for conductors and 8.5 for drivers. However, the drivers were found to have significantly higher blood pressure and serum cholesterol than the conductors—this potential confounding effect between the association of physical activity and CHD was not evaluated.

Epstein and colleagues studied the relationship of vigorous exercise during leisure time to cardiac events in approximately 17,000 middle-aged male executive civil servants. On a randomly selected Monday morning they recorded their leisure time activities over the previous weekend (Morris 1975). Their work was sedentary. An 8-1/2 year follow-up of this population demonstrated a 50% lower incidence of coronary events in those maintaining rigorous activity on the weekend. Morris and colleagues reported the results of following 337 healthy middle-aged Englishmen. During 1956 to 1966, these men participated

in a 7-day dietary survey. Men with a high-caloric intake, as assessed by diet, had a lower rate of disease. A high-caloric intake can be considered to be directly related to physical activity.

Paffenbarger et al. (1970) reported numerous analyses of epidemiologic data from San Francisco longshoremen. Paffenbarger concluded that physical activity is protective. The threshold of 5 kcal/min seemed to hold for strenuous bursts rather than for sustained activity.

Paffenbarger also studied 36,000 Harvard University alumni who entered college between 1916 and 1950 (Paffenbarger et al. 1981). Three high-risk characteristics were identified in this study: low physical activity index (less than 2,000 kcal/wk), cigarette smoking, and hypertension. Presence of any one characteristic was accompanied by a 50% increase in risk, and the presence of two characteristics tripled risk. Maintenance of a high physical activity index could possibly have reduced heart attack risk by 26%.

In Framingham, Massachusetts, approximately 5,000 men and women, 30 to 62 years old and free of clinical evidence of coronary disease at the onset, have been examined regularly since 1949 (Kannel et al. 1986). Coronary disease mortality was subsequently found to be higher in cohorts with indices or measurements consistent with a sedentary lifestyle. However, physical inactivity did not have the predictive power of the three cardinal risk factors. Kannel and Sorlie re-analyzed the Framingham data for the effects of physical activity on overall mortality and cardiovascular disease mortality. The effect on mortality of being sedentary was rather modest compared with the other risk factors, but persisted when these other factors were taken into account. A low correlation was noted between physical activity level and the major risk factors.

A prospective study by Peters et al. (1983) suggests that poor physical work capacity, as measured by bicycle ergometry in apparently healthy Los Angeles County workers is related to subsequent MIs. This is one of the few follow-up studies to measure exercise capacity directly rather than to estimate activity level. An adjusted relative risk of 2.2 was found only in men with certain other risk factors present; namely, above-median cholesterol, smoking, above-median systolic blood pressure, or a combination of these. Similar findings were demonstrated by data from the Lipid Research Clinic with exercise capacity measured by treadmill testing.

Buring et al. (1987) evaluated data on a series of 568 married men who died of coronary heart disease and an equal number of controls matched for age, sex, and neighborhood of residence. Information was collected from the wives of both cases and controls on a large number of variables including usual occupation, job-related and leisure time physical activity, medical history, and lifestyle. Usual occupation was dichotomized into blue-collar and white-collar work. White-collar workers had a statistically significant 30% decreased risk of fatal coronary heart disease compared with blue-collar workers once the effects of reported coronary risk factors were considered. These data suggest that occupation is significantly associated with fatal coronary heart disease.

The relation of self-selected leisure time physical activity (LTPA) to first major coronary disease events and overall mortality was studied in 12,138 middle-aged men participating in the Multiple Risk Factor Intervention Trial (Leon et al. 1987). Total LTPA over the preceding year was quantitated in mean minutes per day at baseline by questionnaire, with subjects classified into tertiles (low, moderate, and high LTPA). During 7 years of follow-up, moderate LTPA was associated with 63% as many fatal CHD events and sudden deaths, and 70% as many total deaths as low LTPA. Mortality rates with high LTPA were similar to those in moderate LTPA; however, combined fatal and nonfatal major CHD events were 20% lower with high as compared with low LTPA. LTPA had a modest inverse relation to CHD and overall mortality in middle-aged men at high risk for CHD.

The relationship of leisure time physical activity to mortality was investigated in 3,043 white US railroad workers followed for 20 years. The Minnesota Leisure Time Physical Activity Questionnaire was used and the risk estimate for coronary heart disease deaths was 1.39 after adjusting for age for sedentary men who expended 40 kcal/week compared with active men who expended 3,632 kcal/week. This risk remained when adjusted for other risk factors.

In the most extensive review to date, Powell et al. (1986) reviewed 43 such studies and concluded that an inverse relationship between physical activity and the incidence of CHD was observed in over two-thirds of the studies. Also, the relationship was strongest in those studies that best measured physical activity.

Intervention in healthy individuals.—Bly et al. (1986) investigated the relationship between exposure to a comprehensive worksite health promotion program and health care costs and utilization. The experience of two groups of Johnson & Johnson employees (N=5,192 and N=3,259) exposed to Live for Life, a comprehensive program of health screenings, lifestyle improvement programs, and worksite changes to support healthier lifestyles, was compared with that of a control group (N=2,955) over a 5-year period. Changes in maximal oxygen consumption were inversely associated with changes in risk factors.

As part of the multifactorial 6-year randomized trial of risk factor intervention, 60,881 men in 80 factories located in Belgium, Italy, Poland and the UK, aged 40 to 59 were randomized (Kovat 1986). The treatment group received advice regarding diet, smoking, weight, blood pressure, and exercise. The intervention group had a 6.9% reduction in fatal CHD, 14.8 % nonfatal MI, and 10.2% total CHD. These benefits were related to risk factor change and sustenance.

EXERCISE INTERVENTION IN PATIENTS WITH HEART DISEASE

Cardiac rehabilitation has been defined as the process concerned with the full development of each persons' physical, mental, and social potential after a cardiac event. The following objectives should be achieved through cardiac rehabilitation: reversal of the effects of deconditioning; education of the individual and family regarding risk factors for heart disease; assistance in returning to activities that are important to him/her; reduction of psychological disorders; reduction of the cost of health care by shortening treatment time and reducing medications; prevention of premature disability; and lessening of the need for institutional care of elderly patients.

Contraindications to exercise training.—Absolute contraindications are known or suspected conditions that prevent the patient from participating in exercise programs. Some of the absolute contraindications are unstable angina pectoris, dissecting aortic aneurysm, complete heart block, uncontrolled hypertension, congestive heart failure or dysrhythmias, thrombophlebitis, and other complicating illnesses. In some conditions, contraindications are relative; the benefits outweigh the risks involved if the patient exercises cautiously. The relative contraindications include frequent premature ventricular contractions, controlled dysrhythmias, intermittent claudication, metabolic disorders, and moderate anemia or pulmonary disease. If these contraindications are observed closely, studies show that the incidence of exertion-related cardiac arrest in cardiac rehabilitation programs is small, and because of the availability of rapid defibrillation, death rarely occurs.

Rehabilitation programs.—A post-hospital rehabilitation program should be physician prescribed and can vary greatly from patient to patient. Most patients, following a cardiovascular event, will not require formal rehabilitation services to restore them to their previous level. Only a small percentage of patients will require supervised continuous ECG-monitored exercise programs in addition to the counseling services. The major expense of rehabilitation programs is the supervised ECG-monitored exercise portion which requires trained personnel and expensive equipment. However, programs can take various forms. The program can be informal, involving patient counseling by the primary physician or a specialist with or without an exercise prescription to be carried out without supervision at home or in a health facility. Formal programs can include patient counseling by a primary physician, or counseling services plus a supervised exercise prescription without continuous ECG monitoring, or they can include counseling plus supervised continuous ECG-monitored exercise. Exercise training should be based on a dynamic rather than uniform prescription and may be subject to change.

Duration of program.—The exercise prescription and education programs can usually be achieved over a 12-week period, and are based on 3 sessions per week, for 25-30 minutes per session, at an appropriate intensity. Those identified as high risk patients should be supervised and/or monitored as prescribed by the physician.

The exercise prescription.—Stationary cycling is of equal value to a walking and jogging program. Usually, stationary cycling can be initially tolerated at 100-300 kpm/min. If one workload cannot be tolerated for the required time span, then the interval training method should be used. For patients with low fitness levels, this may include some zero-resistance pedaling.

Along with the range of motion exercises, strength training can also be emphasized at this stage of recovery. The strength training recommended should be dynamic, with as little isometric exercise as possible, and should use large muscle groups (arms, legs, shoulders and back). Activities such as push-ups and sit-ups that have a large isometric component are not recommended.

Cardiac changes in CHD patients.—Many favorable physiological changes have been documented in patients with coronary heart disease who have undertaken an aerobic exercise program. These include lower submaximal and resting heart rate, decreased symptoms and increased maximal oxygen consumption for a given workload. Peripheral adaptations are at least partially responsible for these changes, and controversy exists as to the effects of chronic exercise on the heart. However, it is unclear if these changes actually increase perfusion or protect the heart during ischemia.

Nuclear medicine procedures to noninvasively assess myocardial perfusion and performance were employed before and after exercise training in a year long trial called PER-FEXT (PERFusion, PERFormance, EXercise Trial) (Froelicher 1987b). There was no significant difference at rest, during the three stages of exercise, or in the percent change from rest to exercise between the control and trained group, at one year, in ejection fraction, end-diastolic volume, stroke volume, or cardiac output. An improvement in the thallium scores, particularly in the angina patients, was consistent with animal studies suggesting that ischemia is the best

inducer of collateral flow and that exercise can increase this stimulus. Changes in ST-segment depression did not occur. One of the only changes in ventricular function or volume was the significantly lower percent change end-systolic volume in the exercise intervention patients. It appears that the trained heart has to use the Frank Starling mechanism less than the untrained heart probably due to lessened ischemia and/or improved contractility.

Intervention studies with a follow-up.—Kallio et al. (1979) were part of a project coordinated by the World Health Organization. The study included 375 consecutive patients under 65 years of age treated for acute MI from 2 urban areas in Finland between 1973 and 1975. On discharge, the patients were randomly allocated, both groups were followed for 3 years. The program for the intervention group was started 2 weeks after hospital discharge. The cumulative coronary mortality was significantly less in the intervention group than in the controls (18.6% versus 29.4%). This difference was mainly due to a reduction of sudden deaths in the intervention group (5.8% versus 14.4%).

Kentala (1972) studied 298 consecutive males less than 65 years of age admitted to the University of Helsinki Hospital in 1969 with a diagnosis of acute MI. They were divided into two groups by the year of birth: controls were from odd-numbered years and exercisers were from even-numbered years. Eighty-one controls and 77 exercisers were accepted for the study. The training group was also urged to increase daily home activities after the exercise program, especially walking. There were 2 training sessions weekly, later increased to 3 per week, with 20-minute warm-up and 20-minute exertion (bicycle, rowing, stairs), followed by a cool down phase. The exercise heart rate was optimally set at 10 beats less than the maximal heart rate recorded from exercise testing.

Wilhelmsen's study included patients born in 1913 or later and hospitalized for an MI between 1968 and 1970 in Göteborg, Sweden (Wilhelmsen et al. 1975). Patients were randomized to a control group (n=157) or an exercise group (n=158). The exercise group trained 3 times a week for 30 minutes a session. Calisthenics, cycling, and running were performed at 80% of the maximal age-predicted heart rate. After one year, the exercise group showed increased work capacity, lower blood pressure, but no difference in blood lipids.

The National Exercise and Heart Disease Project (NEHPD) included 651 men post-MI enrolled in five centers in the United States (Shaw 1981). It was a randomized three-year clinical trial of the effects of a prescribed supervised exercise program starting 2 to 36 months after an MI (80% were more than 8 months post-infarction). In this study 323 randomly selected patients performed exercise 3 times a week that was designed to increase their heart rate to 85% of their individual maximal heart rate achieved during treadmill testing, and 328 patients served as controls.

The 3-year mortality rate was 7.3% (24 deaths) in the control group versus 4.6% (15 deaths) in the exercise group. Deaths from all cardiovascular causes (acute MI, sudden death, arrhythmias, congestive heart failure, cardiogenic shock, and stroke) for the 3-year follow-up were 6.1% (20 deaths) in the control group versus 4.3% (14 deaths) in the exercise group. Neither difference was statistically significant. However, when deaths due to acute MI were considered as a separate category, the exercise group had a significantly lower rate: one acute fatal MI per 3 years (0.3%) in the exercise group versus 8 fatal MIs (2.4%) in the control group. The rate of all recurrent MIs per 3 years, fatal and nonfatal, did not significantly differ between groups. The number of rehospitalizations for reasons other than MI were identical in the two groups. The need for coronary artery surgery was also equal in both groups—16 controls and 17 exercisers underwent surgery in the 3-year period. The patients in the exercise group who suffered a reinfarction had a lower mortality rate, suggesting that an exercise program increases an individual's ability to survive an MI.

The Ontario Study randomized 733 males to either a high intensity group or a low intensity exercise group (Rechnitzer et al. 1983). The high intensity group trained by walking or jogging at 65% to 85% of their maximal oxygen consumption twice a week for 1 hour each session. This continued for 8 weeks after which they trained 4 times a week on their own. The low intensity group trained once a week with relaxation exercises, volleyball, bowling, or swimming for 1 hour. Both groups were encouraged to stop smoking and control their weight. Less than 5% of the low intensity group exercised vigorously and regularly. The dropout rate was 47%. The rate of reinfarction in the high intensity group was 14% and 13% in the low intensity group. They found that the high intensity exercise program had similar results to one designed to produce a minimal training effect and did not reduce the risk of reinfarction.

May and colleagues (1983) have presented an excellent review of the long-term trials in secondary prevention after MI. Trials reported prior to November 1981 were considered in which both intervention and follow-up were carried out beyond the time of hospital discharge. Random assignment and a minimum sample size of 100 were required. Total mortality was used whenever possible, in order to minimize bias. All patients randomized were included in the mortality estimates to reduce the bias of differential withdrawal. A number of intervention studies are summarized in Table 2.

For those of us who recognize the clinical value of exercise and cardiac rehabilitation, the effectiveness of the exercise programs, as measured by the percent reduction in deaths that would have occurred if the intervention had been applied to the control group, is quite encouraging. It appears that exercise is as safe and effective as the other available means of secondary prevention.

Oldridge et al. (1988) have reported a meta-analysis of these studies which supports the conclusion that an exercise program decreases mortality in patients post-MI.

Interventions not yet properly studied include cigarette smoking, bypass surgery, percutaneous transluminal angioplasty, blood pressure reduction, fibrinolytic agents, calcium antagonists, inotropics, and afterload reduction.

CONCLUSION

Animal studies have provided substantial evidence of the cardiovascular benefits of regular physical activity. Improved coronary circulation has been demonstrated in exercise-trained animals by increased coronary artery size, greater capillary density, reduced myocardial infarction size, and maintenance of coronary flow in response to hypoxia. Whether changes in myocardial collateralization improves perfusion remains controversial, but exercise probably improves perfusion when ischemia is present. Studies utilizing various animal models have reported improvement in cardiac function secondary to exercise training. Improved intrinsic contractility, faster relaxation, enzymatic alterations, calcium availability and enhanced autonomic and hormonal control of function have all been implicated.

Compelling studies in experimental animals which clearly demonstrate increased myocardial capillary growth and enlargement of extramural vessels in response to chronic physical exercise, continue to stimulate the search for proof that exercise programs in man will increase myocardial vascularity and develop coronary collaterals. Perhaps the beneficial effects of exercise would be more apparent in humans if we were as compliant to an exercise program as animals.

Animal studies add considerable data to our knowledge of the effects of chronic exercise on the heart. They demonstrate that there are morphologic and metabolic changes that make the cardiovascular system better able to withstand stress, possibly even that imposed by atherosclerosis. These favorable adaptations are more marked in young animals than in older animals. The data regarding beneficial effects of chronic exercise on the atherosclerotic process or on serum cholesterol levels are only suggestive, however, and

Table 2. Summary of the randomized trials of cardiac rehabilitation.

Investigator	Year	Population Randomized					Mean No. Months Entry Post MI	Mean Age	Years FU	Dropouts (%)		Returned to Work (%)		RE-MI (%)		Percent Mortality					
		Total	Controls	Exercised	Exclusions	% Women				Cntrl.	Exer.	Cntrl.	Exer.	Cntrl.	Exer.	Sudden (%)		Cardiac (%)		Total (%)	
																Cntrl.	Exer.	Cntrl.	Exer.	Cntrl.	Exer.
Kentala	72	158	81	77	150		2	53	1			5	8							22	17
Palatsi	76	380	200	180	>65	19.0	2.5	52	2.5		35	33	36	15	12	3	6	14	10	14	10
Wilhelmsen	77	313	157	158	27%>57	10.0	3	51	4		46					18	16			22	18
Kallio	79	375	187	183	>65	19.0	3	55	3					13	20	14	6	29	19	30	22
NEHDP	81	651	328	323	280	0	14	52	3	31	23			7	5			6	4	7	5
Ontario	82	733	354	379	28,>54	0	6	48	4	45	46			13	14					7	10
Bengtsson	83	171	90	81	45,>65	0	1.5	56	1	6	17	73	75	4	2					7	10
Carson	83	303	152	151	>70	0	1.5	51	3.5			81	81	7	7					14	8
Vermeulen	83	98	51	47		0	1.5	49	5	4	4			18	9	7	4	10	4	10	4
Roman	83	193	100	93		10.0	2	55	9					5	4			5	3	6	4
Mayou	83	129	42	44	>60	0	1	51	1.5	25	25	30	57								
Froelicher	84	146	74	76		0	4	53	1	14	17			1	1					0	1
Hedback	85	297	154	143	>65	15.0	1.5	57	1		45	59	66	16.2	5.4			7.8	8.4	7.8	9.1
Averages										21	29	47	54	10	8	11	8	12	8	12	10

Source: Froelicher 1987a: 442.

better studies are required to confirm this effect. The study by Kramsch et al. (1981) provides the strongest evidence for a favorable impact of exercise on the primary prevention of coronary disease. In this study, exercise lessened ischemic manifestations, but only diet stopped progression of coronary atherosclerosis. Nevertheless, the therapeutic and preventive use of exercise is supported by animal studies, but such efforts should be adjunctive to modification of the risk factors that have a well-demonstrated influence on the atherosclerotic process.

Animal studies strongly support the benefits of regular exercise on the heart. Myocardial ischemia is a necessary stimulus for the development of collateral vessels, but exercise appears to enhance their development. Exercise does not affect the atherosclerotic process, but lesions are less of a threat to myocardium supplied by coronary arteries enlarged by exercise.

M-mode echocardiography has been utilized to evaluate cardiac adaptations to exercise training in both cross-sectional and longitudinal studies. Reported cardiac changes secondary to endurance training in young subjects have included increased ventricular mass, wall thickness, volume, and function. The echocardiographic studies have failed to yield consistent and conclusive results, probably because of problems with reproducibilities of echocardiographic measurements. However, increases in left ventricular mass may not occur in younger subjects unless higher levels of exercise are used and may never occur in older subjects.

An exercise program can not be said to lessen exercise-induced ischemia as assessed indirectly by ST-segment depression in most cardiac patients. If cardiac patients are pushed to higher levels of exercise than usually accomplished or tolerated by middle-aged individuals, perhaps more dramatic cardiac changes can be induced. However, patients with exercise-induced ST-segment depression who exceed their usually prescribed exercise limits are known to be at higher risk of cardiac events during and immediately after bouts of exercise.

The association between physical inactivity and the underlying atherosclerotic process is modest compared with other factors such as serum cholesterol, cigarette smoking, and hypertension. An inversely proportional association between the level of activity and degree of atherosclerosis has not been demonstrated. Physical inactivity does not necessarily precede the atherosclerotic process. However, the relationship between physical inactivity and cardiac events is strong.

Epidemiologists now are emphasizing the differences between the level of exercise to lessen the risk of cardiovascular disease and the level to obtain the hemodynamic and morphologic changes secondary to training. The latter requires careful attention to the following components of the exercise prescription; intensity, duration, frequency, and mode. The prescription for good health however, can be less vigorous. In fact, vigorous walking for one-half hour, 4 to 5 times per week, is probably sufficient to obtain health benefits. The point is that the epidemiological studies have demonstrated that levels much less intense than the usual exercise prescription for fitness are adequate for a protective effect. Interestingly, activity surveys have demonstrated that more than 50% of the population exercises less than 20 minutes 3 times a week. This makes inactivity a very prevalent risk factor.

Recent studies of primary prevention support the lifestyle of regular physical activity. Regular exercise most likely decreases one's risk for coronary heart disease and helps to decrease other risk factors. The inclusion of regular moderate exercise in one's lifestyle makes good sense for many reasons. It can improve the quality of life by lessening fatigue and by increasing physical performance. The recommendation of a moderate exercise habit can help people pay attention to their health and make the changes necessary to lessen coronary risk factors. The most significant advances in public health have been in the prevention, not the treatment, of disease. The current public interest in physical fitness may be (embarrassingly) more effective than the influence of the medical profession in making the public take responsibility for maintaining health.

There is controversy regarding the effect of exercise on the hearts of patients with established coronary heart disease. High level exercise may result in cardiac changes but the normally prescribed programs result in only modest changes. High level exercise prescriptions also have resulted in a high complication rate in patients similar to those reported as benefiting the most. Meta-analysis of the controlled trials of cardiac rehabilitation demonstrates a 20% reduction in mortality in patients after an MI who are in an exercise program.

LITERATURE CITED

Adams, T. D.; Yanowitz, F. G.; Fischer, A. G., et al. 1981. Noninvasive evaluation of exercise training in college-age men. Circulation. 64: 958.

Bengtsson, K. 1983. Rehabilitation after myocardial infarction. Scand. J. Rehabil. Med. 15: 1-90.

Bloor, C. M.; White, F. C.; Sanders, T. M. 1984. Effects of exercise on collateral development in myocardial ischemia in pigs. Journal of Applied Physiology: Respiratory and Environmental Exercise Physiology. 56: 656-665.

Bly, J. L.; Jones, R. C.; Richardson, J. E. 1986. Impact of worksite health promotion of health care costs and utilization. Journal of American Medical Association. 256: 3235-3240.

Buring, J. E.; Evans, D. A.; Fiore, M., et al. 1987. Occupation and risk of death from coronary heart disease. Journal of American Medical Association. 258(6): 791-792.

Carson, P.; Phillips, R.; Lloyd, M., et al. 1982. Exercise after myocardial infarction: a controlled trial. J. R. Coll. Physician Land. 16: 147-151.

Costill, D. L.; Branam, G. E.; Moore, J. C., et al. 1974. Effects of physical training in men with coronary heart disease. Med. Sci. Sports. 6: 95.

DeMaria, A. N.; Neumann, A.; Lee, G., et al. 1978. Alterations in ventricular mass and performance induced by exercise training in man evaluated by echocardiography. Circulation. 57: 237-244.

Detry, J.; Bruce, R. A. 1971. Effects of physical training on exertional ST segment depression in coronary heart disease. Circulation. 44:390-397.

Ditchey, R. V.; Watkins, J.; McKirnan, M. D., et al. 1981. Effects of exercise training on left ventricular mass in patients with ischemic heart disease. American Heart Journal. 101: 701-706.

Eckstein, R. W. 1957. Effect of exercise and coronary artery narrowing on coronary collateral circulation. Circ. Res. 5: 230.

Ehsani, A. A.; Hagberg, J. M.; Hickson, R. C. 1978. Rapid changes in left ventricular dimensions and mass in response to physical conditioning and deconditioning. American Journal of Cardiology. 42: 52.

Ehsani, A. A.; Heath, G. W.; Hagberg, J. M., et al. 1981. Effects of 12 months of intense exercise training on ischemic ST-segment depression in patients with coronary artery disease. Circulation. 64: 1116-1124.

Froelicher, V. F. F. 1987a. Exercise and the heart: Clinical concepts. 2d ed. Year Book Medical Publishers.

Froelicher, V. F. F. 1987b. The effect of exercise on myocardial perfusion and function in patients with coronary heart disease. European Heart Journal. 8: 1-8.

Hedback, B.; Perk, J.; Perski, A. 1985. Effect of a post-myocardial infarction rehabilitation program on mortality, morbidity, and risk factors. J. Cardiopulmonary Rehabil. 5: 576-583.

Kallio, V.; Hamalainen, H.; Hakkila, J., et al. 1979. Reduction in sudden deaths by a multifactorial intervention programme after acute myocardial infarction. Lancet. 2: 1091-1094.

Kannel, W. B.; Belanger, A.; D'Agostino, R., et al. 1986. Physical activity and physical demand on the job and risk of CH disease and death: The Framingham Study. American Heart Journal. 112: 820-825.

Kattus, A. A.; Jorgenson, C. R.; Worden, R. E., et al. 1972. ST-segment depression with near-maximal exercise: its modification by physical conditioning. Chest. 62:678.

Kentala, E. 1972. Physical fitness and feasibility of physical rehabilitation after myocardial infarction in men of working age. Ann. Clin. Res. 4.

Kovat, R. 1986. Prevention of CHD (WHO Multicenter Project). Lancet.

Kramsch, D. M.; Aspen, A. J.; Abramowitz, B. M., et al. 1981. Reduction of coronary atherosclerosis by moderate conditioning exercise in monkeys on an atherogenic diet. New England Journal of Medicine. 305: 1483-1489.

Landry, F.; Bouchard, C.; Dumesnil, J. 1985. Cardiac dimension changes with endurance training. Journal of American Medicial Association. 254: 77-80.

Leon, A. S.; Jacobs, D. R.; DeBacker, G., et al. 1981. Relationship of physical characteristics of life habits to treadmill exercise capacity. Am. J. Epidemiol. 653-660.

Leon, A. S; Connett, J.; Jacobs, D. R.; Rauramaa, R. 1987. Leisure-time physical activity levels and risk of coronary heart disease and death. Journal of American Medical Associaton. 258(17): 2388-2395.

May, G. S.; Furberg, C. D.; Eberlein, K. A.; Geraci, B. J. 1983. Secondary prevention after myocardial infarction: A review of short-term acute phase trials. Prog. Cardiovascular Disease. 25: 335-359.

Mayou, R. A. 1983. A controlled trial of early rehabilitation after myocardial infarction. Cardiac Rehabilitation. 3: 397-402.

Morris, H. J. N. 1975. Uses of epidemiology. New York, NY: Churchill Livingston, Inc.

Morris, H. J. N.; Crawford, M. D. 1958. Coronary heart disease and physical activity of work. Br. Med. J. 2: 1485.

Oldridge, N., et al. 1988. A meta-analysis of cardiac rehabilitation and cardiac mortality. J. Am. Med. Assoc.

Oliver, R. M. 1967. Physique and serum lipids of young London busmen in relation to ischemic heart disease. Br. J. Intern. Med. 24: 181.

Paffenbarger, R. S.; Laughlin, M. E.; Gima, A. S., et al. 1970. Work activity of longshoremen as related to death from coronary heart disease and stroke. New England Journal of Medicine. 282: 1109.

Paffenbarger, R. S.; Wing, A. L.; Hyde, R. T. 1981. Chronic disease in former college students: Physical activity as an index of heart attack risk in college alumni. American Journal of Epidemiology. 108: 161-175.

Palatsi, I. 1976. Feasibility of physical training after myocardial infarction and its effect on return to work, morbidity, and mortality. Acta Medica Scandinavia Supplement. 599.

Peters, R. K.; Cady, L. D.; Bischoff, D. P., et al. 1983. Physical fitness and subsequent myocardial infarction in healthy workers. Journal of American Medical Association. 249: 3052-3056.

Powell, K. E.; Spain, K. G.; Christenson, G. M.; Mollenkamp, M. P. 1986. The status of 1990 objectives for physical fitness and exercise. Public Health Reports. 101: 15-22.

Raffo, J. A.; Luksic, I. Y.; Kappagoda, C. T., et al. 1980. Effects of physical training on myocardial ischemia in patients with coronary artery disease. Br. Heart Journal. 43: 262.

Rechnitzer, P. A.; Cunningham, D. A.; Andrew, G. M., et al. 1983. Relation of exercise to the recurrence rate of myocardial infarction in men. American Journal of Cardiology. 51: 65-69.

Roman, O.; Gutierrez, M.; Luksic, I., et al. 1983. Cardiac rehabilitation after acute myocardial infarction. Cardiology. 70: 223-231.

Salzman, S. H.; Hellerstein, H. K.; Radke, J. D., et al. 1969. Quantitative effects of physical conditioning on the exercise electrocardiogram of middle-aged subjects with arteriosclerotic heart disease. Measurements in Exercise ECG. 1969:388.

Shaw, L. W. 1981. Effects of a prescribed supervised exercise program on mortality and cardiovascular morbidity in patients after a myocardial infarction. American Journal of Cardiology. 48: 39-46.

Stamler, J.; Kjelsberg, M.; Hall, Y. 1960. Epidemiologic studies on cardiovascular-renal diseases: Analysis of mortality by age-race-sex-occupation. J. Chronic. Dis. 12: 440.

Vermeulen, A.; Liew, K. I.; Durrer, D. 1983. Effects of cardiac rehabilitation after myocardial infarction: Changes in coronary risk factors and long-term prognosis. American Heart Journal. 105: 798-801.

Watanabe, K.; Bhargara, B.; Froelicher, V. F. 1982. A computerized approach to evaluating rest and exercise-induced ECG/VCG changes after cardiac rehabilitation. Clin. Cardiol. 5:27-34.

Wilhelmsen, L.; Sanne, H.; Elmfeldt, D., et al. 1975. A controlled trial of physical training after myocardial infarction. Prev. Med. 4: 491-508.

Psychophysiological Indicators of Leisure Benefits

Roger S. Ulrich
College of Architecture
Texas A & M University
College Station, Texas

Ulf Dimberg
Department of Psychology
Uppsala University
Uppsala, Sweden

B. L. Driver
Rocky Mountain Forest and Range Experiment Station
USDA Forest Service
Fort Collins, Colorado

INTRODUCTION

Different authors prefer to distinguish between the concepts "leisure," "recreation," and "play," but for the purposes of this chapter such distinctions are not necessary. Specifically, our main objectives include examining: 1) the use of psychophysiological methods for investigating consequences of leisure experiences; 2) the role of leisure activities and leisure environments, particularly natural environments, in helping people cope with various types of stressors; and 3) the possibilities and challenges for future research. In a nutshell, our primary interest is the application of psychophysiological approaches to the issue of restorative influences of leisure activities and settings—how they facilitate coping with everyday annoyances and stresses. "Psychophysiological" refers to research approaches that are concerned with the measurement of physiological responses as they relate to human emotions, cognition, stress, and behavior.

Physiological measures are being used increasingly in leisure research to investigate important health-related benefits derived from physical exercise, such as improved cardiovascular performance (see chapters in this volume by Froelicher and Froelicher; and Paffenbarger, Hyde, and Dow). Apart from exercise benefits, physiological methods have great promise for contributing to the identification and measurement of such positive consequences of passive leisure experiences as recovery from stress. More generally, physiological measures can be used effectively to assess important consequences for well-being that are not tied directly to physical exertion. Most of the discussion in this paper is concerned with psychophysiological approaches for investigating restorative benefits, not related directly to exercise, of leisure experiences in natural environments.

The next section overviews physiological measures used in psychophysiology that potentially can be applied in investigating a wide range of responses and beneficial effects associated with leisure experiences. Examples of findings from psychophysiological studies are described that relate to leisure and recreation issues. Psychophysiological methods are discussed from the standpoint of their capabilities, advantages, and limitations for leisure research. The discussion then shifts to stress-reducing consequences of leisure encounters with natural environments. Conceptual notions regarding stress are discussed, and findings from verbally based approaches, and then psychophysiological methods are surveyed that relate to restorative influences of nature. Subsequent sections describe research needs and summarize the major points of the chapter.

PHYSIOLOGICAL MEASURES IN PSYCHOPHYSIOLOGY

For decades, physiological measures have been used extensively as indicators of human responses to emotional, stressful, and arousal-increasing stimulation. In psychophysiology, physiological activity is typically detected from aspects or levels of four major bodily response systems: 1) electrocortical, 2) autonomic, 3) skeleto-muscular, and 4) endocrine. Measurements of activity in the first three bodily systems are usually made with skin surface electrodes, whereas endocrine excretions are assessed using biochemical methods. Important indicators of *electrocortical* activity are the rhythmic brain potentials (e.g., alpha waves, beta waves), measured by the electroencephalograph (EEG), and cortical-evoked potentials. The *autonomic* nervous system controls glands, internal organs, and involuntary muscles. Major autonomic response parameters include cardiovascular activity (e.g., heart rate, blood pressure, blood volume), and sweat gland activity which typically is measured as electrical skin conductance in the hands. Responses from the *skeleto-muscular* system, such as muscle tension, can be measured by recording electromyographic (EMG) activity with skin electrodes attached over specific muscle regions. Assessment of *endocrine* activity involves biochemical measurement of various stress hormones, such as epinephrine and norepinephrine levels in blood and urine samples.

In general, these various physiological measures have been used to indicate different degrees of attention, arousal, and stress-related reactions, as well as cognitive processing and specific emotional states. For instance, a stress response in contrast to relaxation is associated with increased physiological activity evident in autonomic responses such as heart rate, blood pressure, and skin conductance, as well as with muscle tension and blocking of alpha EEG activity. There is considerable evidence that different emotional reactions or states—which constitute an important component of human well-being—are associated with differential bodily reactions. For example, a stimulus that elicits feelings of fear usually induces a physiological reaction of increased heart rate and skin conductance activity. General categories of stimuli that elicit bodily responses include social stimuli, task-related stimuli, cognitive/internal stimuli, and visual or auditory environmental stimuli (e.g., Grings and Dawson 1978). As an example of responsiveness to simple environmental stimuli, a low intensity auditory stimulus such as a tone evokes a momentary cluster of physiological reactions (e.g., short-term or phasic heart rate deceleration and increased skin conductance) that is called an "orienting" response, which typically diminishes or habituates with repeated exposures or presentations. An intense or aversive environmental stimulus, on the other hand, evokes a defensive reaction characterized by phasic heart rate acceleration and nonhabituating skin conductance responses. (For a recent survey of physiological responses to environments see Weiss and Baum 1987.)

Autonomic activity has considerable relevance for leisure research because autonomic measures can be used to assess, for instance, stress as well as perceptual sensitivity to environmental stimuli. An important issue concerning autonomic activity has been whether specific emotional states are reflected by distinct patterns of autonomic responses. This has been demonstrated in a study by Ekman, Levenson, and Friesen (1983); they recorded several autonomic indicators and found that the autonomic nervous system differentiated between positive and different negative emotions. It has also been shown that the evoked autonomic reactions are consistent with reactions in other emotional response levels or systems such as the muscular-expressive (facial) and experiential/cognitive (e.g., Dimberg 1987a).

An alternative method developed in recent years for measuring emotional responses is the facial electromyographic (EMG) technique. This method is based on the proposition that human facial muscles constitute a biologically preprogrammed output system for emotional reactions (Darwin 1872). Thus, emotional activity can be detected by attaching small skin electrodes over specific facial muscles which form the basis for displaying specific facial expressions of emotion (e.g., happiness, fear, anger). Several studies have demonstrated that the facial EMG technique is sensitive and can detect different emotional responses to a broad range of visual and auditory stimuli (e.g., Dimberg 1986). There is limited evidence that facial EMG can differentiate attitudinal responses, perhaps especially when attitudes have a salient emotional component (Petty and Cacioppo 1983). Facial EMG response patterns are also congruent with responses evoked in the cognitive/experiential and the autonomic systems. (For a review of research on facial EMG see Dimberg 1990).

Returning to the concern for the applicability of psychophysiology to recreation and leisure issues, the following section describes research examples that illustrate how measurements of autonomic activity, facial EMG, and electrocortical activity can detect bodily reactions to environmental stimuli such as landscape scenes. These examples relate to perceptual intake and emotional responses in contexts where stress is not an issue. Later sections focus on research concerning stress.

Research Examples: Physiological Responses to Environmental Stimuli

In psychophysiology, one important way of defining human-environmental interactions has been in terms of perceptual intake and rejection (Coles 1984, Lacey 1967). Environmental intake (attention to external stimuli or events) is characterized by phasic or short-term heart rate deceleration, whereas perceptual rejection of environmental stimuli is associated with heart rate acceleration or slight deceleration. From this perspective it can be predicted that environmental stimuli which are experienced as interesting should elicit an attentional response followed by an autonomic response pattern characterized by distinct heart rate deceleration. By contrast, environmental stimuli that are comparatively less interesting should not evoke a large heart rate deceleration.

This prediction was investigated by Dimberg and Ulrich[1] who exposed subjects to color slides of both interesting and pleasant natural scenes (unspectacular high depth or spatially open settings) and less interesting and preferred natural views (low depth or spatially enclosed settings). Heart rate was monitored while subjects were seated in a laboratory and were repeatedly exposed to the different slides with a stimulus duration of 8 seconds. The results for heart rate responses are illustrated in Figure 1. As predicted, the high depth scenes evoked a distinct phasic heart rate deceleration that was larger than the response to the less interesting low depth slides. These data support the notion that interesting and preferred natural environments spontaneously elicit a physiological response indicating sensory intake/attention.

Other research has demonstrated that the facial EMG technique can sensitively detect different physiological reactions to simple environmental stimuli such as tones of low intensity (75 dB) and high intensity (95 dB) (Dimberg 1987b). High intensity auditory stimuli evoke a response dominated by increased corrugator muscle activity (the corrugator muscle is used when frowning in negative emotional expressions). Some subjects appraise a low intensity tone as unpleasant whereas others perceive the tone as neutral in terms of pleasantness. Those individuals who appraise such sounds as unpleasant react with clearly higher corrugator muscle response. These findings are paralleled by results from a pilot study by Dimberg and Ulrich who measured facial EMG while subjects were exposed to slides of natural landscapes that varied in rated preference levels. It was found that the overall preference scores were negatively correlated with the overall evoked corrugator responses. In other words, scenes rated lower in preference elicited higher corrugator activity indicating a comparatively negative emotional reaction.

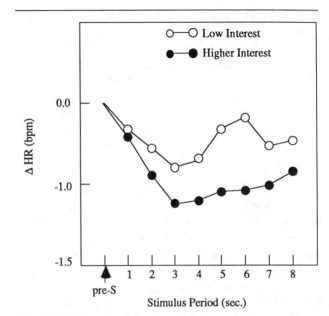

Figure 1. Mean phasic heart rate change expressed in beats per minute (bpm) form the pre-stimulus level for subjects exposed to slides of spatially open landscapes (higher interest) and spatially restricted environments (lower interest). (From Dimberg and Ulrich[1])

Responses to visual landscapes have also been investigated using measurements of electrocortical activity (Ulrich 1981). Recordings were made of brain wave activity in the alpha frequency range while subjects viewed lengthy slide presentations of either natural or urban scenes. In general, higher levels of alpha activity are associated with lower levels of physiological arousal and with feelings of wakeful relaxation. Findings showed that alpha amplitudes were higher during the natural rather than urban exposures, which suggest that individuals were more wakefully relaxed when viewing nature. Likewise, self-ratings of affective states indicated that subjects had more positively-toned feeling states when viewing the natural scenes.

Advantages of Physiological Measures

Much research in the leisure benefits area has been based on verbal measures such as attitudinal scales or self-ratings. Compared to verbal indicators, the physiological measures used in psychophysiology can offer certain important advantages. Many of the physiological responses described earlier can be recorded continuously during leisure experiences, thereby yielding insights concerning the temporal character or duration of effects, as well as the magnitude of consequences. Importantly, physiological methods can identify certain influences on well-being that probably are outside the conscious awareness of leisure participants, and therefore may not be identified or assessed with validity using verbal measures (Ulrich 1988). In this regard, only physiological procedures are suited to identifying and measuring such physiological consequences as reductions in blood pressure associated with recovery from stress (Ulrich and Simons 1986). The use of physiological measures in leisure research will likely contribute to uncovering numerous important beneficial consequences that would otherwise remain hidden to investigators.

Another point in favor of psychophysiological approaches is that physiological findings tend to have scientific credibility. Also, considerable importance is often assigned to physiological data relating to well-being by courts and decisionmakers, and in some legislative situations. An indication of the credibility of physiological measures, and of the widespread acceptance of physiological well-being as an important societal value, is that findings regarding many physiological effects (e.g., blood pressure) usually are considered permissible data by courts (Ulrich 1988). For instance, if physiological findings are presented regarding beneficial leisure consequences linked to a particular natural environment, courts would probably be more likely to decide that these benefits must be considered in assessing the social value of the environment, often regardless of whether economic values can be assigned. Finally, physiological evidence of benefits, especially relating to consequences for physiological well-being, may carry weight in environmental impact statements.

In the case of most physiological measures, there are usually considerable advantages in using them in designs that combine physiological and verbal methods. Research approaches that obtain data from different response modes (physiological, verbal, and sometimes behavioral)—compared to studies that assess responses in only one mode, or employ a single type of measure—yield a broader range of inferences or conclusions. Because one important indication of validity is the extent of consistency among results obtained from different measures and modes, psychophysiological approaches can offer the major advantage of allowing assessment of convergent validity. For instance, if findings from a study indicated a pattern of agreement among physiological and verbal indicators, this would suggest convergent validity and imply that the results justified confidence. Although verbal measures alone may be sufficient for investigating benefits in many situations, it should be noted that verbal methods should never be used alone to assess *detrimental* consequences associated with long-term environmental stressors or risks. For assessing negative consequences over a period of weeks or months, the validity

of verbally based indicators is exceedingly problematic (Ulrich 1988). Validity considerations in stress research often dictate the use of multi-measure research approaches that combine physiological, verbal, and often behavioral indicators (Baum et al. 1985, Evans and Cohen 1987).

Limitations of Physiological Measures

As with all methods, psychophysiological procedures have limitations or disadvantages which must be considered before undertaking research. Perhaps the main drawback is that these methods tend to be time consuming and expensive, especially compared to verbal measures. Most physiological procedures necessitate the recording of data from subjects on an individual basis, often over an extended time period, which raises obstacles to the study of large samples. High quality equipment for psychophysiology is expensive, and its use and maintenance requires technical expertise. Certain physiological measures can be perceived by subjects as invasive, and may therefore require a lengthy baseline or habituation period combined with a long data collection session which may produce undesirable effects on subjects such as irritability or fatigue. Also, the procedural requirements of physiological measures often constrain the activity of subjects. At the extreme, some physiological recordings are so sensitive to movement artifacts (e.g., brain wave activity) that subjects must be instructed to sit motionless in a comfortable chair during the data collection. Because of these constraints, several measures are difficult and awkward to use in field studies, and are more appropriate in laboratory research. However, some psychophysiological methods are well suited to field conditions, and hold great promise for advancing our understanding of leisure benefits. Also, rapid advances in electronics miniaturization are creating new opportunities for applying physiological measures in field settings. Lightweight, noninvasive, battery powered units worn by subjects can record or transmit important physiological responses such as heart rate and skin conductance.

Having overviewed physiological measures in terms of their capabilities, advantages, and limitations, the discussion now shifts to stress, and then to survey findings from physiological methods regarding stress-reducing consequences of leisure in natural environments.

STRESS AND LEISURE EXPERIENCES

Stress: Conceptual Notions

A stress reaction is the process whereby a person responds physiologically, psychologically, and often with behaviors, to a situation that threatens well-being (Baum et al. 1982). The physiological component consists of many responses in different bodily systems, such as the autonomic and neuro-endocrine, which mobilize the individual for coping with the situation. Although stress is construed primarily as a delete-rious phenomenon, certain short-term stressful situations can improve human performance in nonleisure and leisure behaviors (Evans and Cohen 1987). A related point is that many so-called "adventure recreation" programs are prem-ised on the notion that exposure to stressfully challenging situations can have beneficial consequences related to self-development (Ewert 1988). Nevertheless, we will mainly use the word "stress" in a negative sense to refer to an unde-sirable state or condition that needs to be mitigated over time to prevent decrements in human performance and well-being, including illness.

Several influential theoretical perspectives on human-environment interactions converge in predicting that if indi-viduals are stressed, leisure encounters with most natural settings will have stress-reducing influences—while expo-sures to many urban environments may hamper recuperation (Ulrich et al., in press). For instance, *cultural* and other learning-based perspectives suggest that Western cultures condition their inhabitants to prefer nature and dislike cities. *Overload* perspectives suggest that urban environments, compared to most natural settings, tend to have higher levels of complexity and other stimulation that place taxing proc-essing demands that should slow or hamper restoration from stress (Cohen 1978, Milgrams 1970). As another example, *evolutionary* perspectives premise that because humans evolved over millions of years in natural environments, we are to some degree physiologically and psychologically adapted to natural rather than urban settings. Authors who adopt the evolutionary position often contend that humans have an unlearned predisposition to attend and respond positively to natural content such as vegetation and water (e.g., Driver and Green 1977, Kaplan and Kaplan 1982, Stainbrook 1968, Ulrich 1983). Because we lack evolution-ary tuning for urban or built environments, experiences with such settings place greater demands on processing resources, and may require more coping or adaptation effort (Stainbrook 1968). If an individual is stressed, these de-mands should hamper recuperation.

In sum, all of these perspectives, and others not dis-cussed here (e.g., arousal theory), imply that leisure encoun-ters with unthreatening natural environments, compared to the influences of most urban settings, should tend to foster greater recovery from stress. Accordingly, leisure environ-ments, especially those which are predominately natural, may help prevent certain types of stress or reduce their levels, particularly when the source is in the physical envi-ronment. Also, if the stressor is not tied to the physical environment (e.g., illness), even brief exposures to natural content may be positively distracting, producing positive feelings and blocking or reducing stressful thoughts (Ulrich 1979, 1981). This implies that therapeutic natural settings or content are not restricted to wilderness environments; they might be areas that can be used readily, such as a park or parkway, or natural content or spaces that might be inte-grated with living and work places (Kaplan and Kaplan 1989, Ulrich 1979). We are speaking generally; some urban settings are comforting and restorative, and certain encoun-ters with "nature" can be quite stressful.

A concept relevant to coping with stress during leisure is that of "temporary escape" (e.g., Driver and Knopf 1976). This escape might be passive or mental only, such as through meditation, daydreaming about a favorite recreation area, or just gazing out a window at a pleasant natural view. Or the temporary escape might reflect active coping with a stressor, as when an individual actually travels to a recreation site or area. Kaplan and Talbot (1983) use the phrase "being away" in a manner which appears largely the same as temporary escape, in the context of restoration that involves distancing oneself from negative distractions, or from one's day-to-day work. They also postulate that restorative influences of recreation in natural environments are fostered by attention-holding properties of nature, by coherent properties of nature that facilitate comprehension and confidence, and by compatibility between the recreationist's purposes and the actions or demands imposed by the setting. It seems likely that many situations involving temporary escape are stress-reducing partly because the recreationist achieves some sense of control with respect to the stressor. Many studies on environmental stress have found that achieving control tends to reduce the negative effects of stressors (Evans and Cohen 1987). In sum, leisure experiences in natural envi-ronments probably reduce stress through a combination of mechanisms, including achieving control through active coping or escape, through physical exercise, and therapeutic effects of exposures to natural content which may have both learned and biological origins.

Stress-Reducing Influences of Leisure Activities: Findings from Verbal Methods

There has been considerable research on the perceived therapeutic benefits of leisure activities in helping people cope with various stresses through temporary escape. The great majority of studies have employed questionnaires or self-report methods to evaluate the relative importance of particular leisure activities and settings in helping different types of recreationists cope with stress. Perhaps the best known is the work of Tinsley and his associates (e.g., Tinsley and Kaas 1979), and Driver and his associates (e.g., Driver and Knopf 1976). Tinsley and Driver, working separately and together, have developed two similar but different sets of psychometric instruments for identifying and measuring the motivational bases of recreation choice, some of which are clearly stress-related. Findings from the many applications of these instruments, in several different locations and for different types of leisure activities, document rather convincingly the importance of leisure for stress mitigation. Some examples of typical results from this work are discussed below. (For a more detailed discussion of methods and findings, see the chapter in this volume by Driver, Tinsley, and Manfredo.)

Tinsley and his associates identified 27 leisure activity-specific needs; these needs were quantified by using "Paragraphs about Leisure" methodology (Tinsley and Kaas 1979). Several of the 27 scales (e.g., compensation, catharsis, and independence) explicitly or implicitly tap leisure motivations related to coping with stress. Results of studies that have applied these scales to different types of recreationists participating in various activities in different locations show that leisure activities are important for helping people cope with stress as well as for meeting other non-stress-related needs (Tinsley et al. 1985). Recently, Tinsley used factor analysis to reduce the 27 scales to 8 "psychological benefits of leisure" (Tinsley and Tinsley 1988). Although this resulted in reduced specificity, the theme of stress mitigation remains, such as in the benefit labeled "compensation."

While the work of Driver and his associates is theoretically similar to that of Tinsley and his colleagues, it differs considerably in orientation and methods. Specifically, the purposes are to define and measure the psychological bases of recreation demand (primarily for outdoor recreation opportunities) by quantifying the relative importance of specific persistent-over-time reasons for deciding to engage in chosen activities. In recent years, the conceptual foundation of the work has been shifted to the expectancy-valence model of choice in social psychology, as Fishbein and Ajzen

perfected their theory of reasoned action (see Ajzen 1985 and his chapter in this volume). After more than 50 empirical studies, the measurement instrument has evolved to contain 43 "Recreation Experience Preference" (REP) scales that assess specific types of experiences desired and expected from leisure activities. These scales are shown in Table 1, along with the 19 more general recreation experience preference domains into which the 43 REP scales can be logically and empirically grouped. The REP scales were developed to facilitate management of recreation areas using an "experience-based" approach which requires targeting management objectives and prescriptions toward the provision of specified types of recreation experience opportunities identified by the REP scales (Manfredo et al. 1983).

Several of the REP scales explicitly tap the theme of temporary escape from stress. (See especially domains 3 and 4 in Table 1 and also domains 7, 9, and 12). Considerable data have been obtained for these stress-related scales from over 100 empirical studies carried out by Driver, his associates, and others who have used the REP scales. For example, Table 2 shows the mean scores and rank order (RO) of the mean scores (within an activity) for seven outdoor recreation activities studied in northeastern Pennsylvania (Driver and Cooksey 1980). Scales 1, 2, 4, 5, 7, and 9 are explicitly related to stress mediation, and others (12, 14, 15, 18, 20) have some relation to stress. One can notice from the mean scores, and more quickly from the rank order by activity, that various stress mediation/temporary escape items consistently fall in the top 5 or 6 most highly ranked experience preferences for each of the 7 recreation activities.

Table 3 shows results for an early version of the REP scales that was administered to recreational users of the Au Sable River in Michigan (Driver 1975). The data are displayed differently than in Table 2 to show the percentages of the three types of recreationists studied (canoeists, fishermen, and stream-bank owners of homes and cottages) who rated single item "expected consequences" (an early name for the REP scales) either Extremely Important or Very Important as a reason for using the river on the day when they were interviewed on site. Items 2, 3, 5, 6, 7, 8, and 10 are explicitly stress-related, with the first several being rated of high importance by large percentages of the respondents.

Table 4 shows findings from a study by Davis (1973) that used selected REP scales to evaluate motivations of users of the large Belle Isle Park, which is near downtown Detroit and is used by a high percentage of middle- to very low-income people. The table contains the mean scores for the 10 most highly rated scale items of the 40 included in the study. The results strongly suggest that stress reduction or temporary escape have considerable importance for these primarily inner-city recreationists.

Table 1. Recreation experience preference (REP) scales making up the recreation experience preference domains. [1]

1. Enjoy nature
   A. Scenery
   B. General nature experience

2. Physical fitness

3. Reduce tension
   A. Tension release
   B. Slow down mentally
   C. Escape role overloads
   D. Escape daily routines

4. Escape physical stressors
   A. Tranquility/solitude
   B. Privacy
   C. Escape crowds
   D. Escape noise

5. Outdoor learning
   A. General learning
   B. Exploration
   C. Learn geography of area
   D. Learn about nature

6. Share similar values
   A. Be with friends
   B. Be with people having similar values

7. Independence
   A. Independence
   B. Autonomy
   C. Being in control

8. Family relations
   A. Family kinship
   B. Escape family

9. Introspection
   A. Spiritual
   B. Personal values

10. Be with considerate people (social security)

11. Achievement/stimulation
    A. Reinforcing self-confidence
    B. Social recognition
    C. Skill development
    D. Competence testing
    E. Seeking excitement
    F. Endurance
    G. Telling others

12. Physical rest

13. Teach/lead others
    A. Teaching/sharing skills
    B. Leading others

14. Risk taking

15. Risk reduction
    A. Risk moderation
    B. Risk prevention

16. Meet new people
    A. Meet new people
    B. Observe other people

17. Creativity

18. Nostalgia

19. Agreeable temperatures

[1] Individual REP scales are under each domain if there are more than one scale per domain and listed by the name given the domain when there is only one scale per domain

Data from scores of other studies that have used Tinsley's, Driver's, or related scales could also be presented that would disclose patterns of findings similar to those in Tables 1-4. But that seems unnecessary for drawing this conclusion: the conventional wisdom that recreation is important not only for growth and development but also for restoration through stress mediation is strongly supported by the many studies on the motivational bases of leisure choice (Knopf 1983). This research consistently shows that temporary escape benefits are perceived by the recreationists studied to be of high importance. This literature also indicates that leisure can have a wide variety of other stress-mediating functions, and that different activities vary with respect to stress-reducing benefits.

STRESS-REDUCING INFLUENCES OF LEISURE EXPERIENCES: PHYSIOLOGICAL FINDINGS

To date, a very small amount of leisure-related research has used physiological procedures to investigate stress reduction benefits. Although a few studies have examined stress-reducing influences of *passive* recreation experiences, there is a shortage of studies concerning stress-mitigating consequences of active recreation. At this early stage in the use of physiological procedures, there is also a shortage of studies that relate verbally expressed benefits such as temporary escape to physiological measurements of stress mitigation.

A limited amount of work has produced findings suggesting that passive leisure experiences can have significant positive psychophysiological consequences. For example, Heywood (1978) induced stress in subjects with a period of

Table 2. Mean scores on preferred psychological outcome scales by participants in seven activities in Pennsylvania.[1] (RO) designates rank order of mean scores, with tied scores given the same rank. Standard deviations are in parentheses.

Psychological Outcome	Camping			Picnicking			Lake Swimming			Pool Swimming			Motor Boating			Lake Fishing			Stream Fishing			Max. Diff. in $\bar{x}$'s [2]
	RO	$\bar{x}$	(sd)	RO	$\bar{x}$	(sd)	RO	$\bar{x}$	(sd)	RO	$\bar{x}$	(sd)	RO	$\bar{x}$	(sd)	RO	$\bar{x}$	(sd)	RO	$\bar{x}$	(sd)	
1. Escape daily routine	3	3.9	(1.2)	4	3.1	(1.7)	3	3.6	(1.1)	1	3.5	(1.4)	1	4.5	(1.3)	1	4.3	(1.3)	2	4.0	(1.3)	1.4
2. Physical rest [3]													4	3.9	(1.5)	1	4.3	(1.5)	2	4.0	(1.4)	
3. Enjoy nature	1	4.4	(1.2)	1	3.7	(1.3)	1	4.0	(1.2)	1	3.5	(1.5)	6	3.6	(1.2)	4	3.8	(1.4)	2	4.0	(1.2)	0.9
4. Escape physical pressures	7	3.3	(1.4)	8	2.6	(1.6)	6	3.2	(1.1)	9	2.5	(1.3)	2	4.2	(1.5)	2	4.1	(1.7)	1	4.1	(1.3)	1.7
5. Tranquility - privacy	1	4.4	(1.2)	1	3.7	(1.2)	2	3.8	(1.3)	4	3.2	(1.4)	7	3.5	(1.3)	3	3.9	(1.3)	3	3.7	(1.0)	1.2
6. Be with other people	4	3.8	(1.3)	2	3.6	(1.3)	2	3.8	(1.2)	3	3.3	(1.4)	3	4.0	(1.1)	6	3.4	(1.4)	8	2.9	(1.1)	1.1
7. Slow down mentally	6	3.4	(1.4)	6	2.9	(1.8)	5	3.3	(1.1)	5	3.1	(1.5)	9	3.2	(1.4)	5	3.5	(1.4)	5	3.4	(1.2)	
8. Exercise - physical fitness	8	3.2	(1.4)	8	2.6	(1.6)	4	3.4	(1.2)	1	3.5	(1.6)	8	3.4	(1.4)	7	3.1	(1.5)	4	3.5	(1.3)	0.9
9. Escape role overloads	5	3.7	(1.5)	5	3.0	(1.8)	3	3.6	(1.2)	2	3.4	(1.5)	7	3.5	(1.5)	6	3.4	(1.6)	6	3.3	(1.5)	0.7
10. Family togetherness	2	4.0	(1.6)	3	3.4	(1.9)	6	3.2	(1.3)	1	3.5	(1.7)	5	3.7	(1.3)	8	3.0	(1.7)	10	2.7	(1.2)	1.3
11. Learning - discovery	8	3.2	(1.2)	5	3.0	(1.3)	6	3.2	(1.2)	8	2.6	(1.3)	8	3.4	(1.3)	9	2.8	(1.4)	7	3.2	(1.1)	0.8
12. Security	8	3.2	(1.3)	8	2.6	(1.6)	7	3.1	(1.2)	7	2.8	(1.3)	10	3.0	(1.5)	10	2.7	(1.5)	11	2.6	(1.3)	
13. Nostalgia	8	3.2	(1.4)	7	2.7	(1.7)	8	3.0	(1.2)	8	2.6	(1.4)	12	2.8	(1.4)	8	3.0	(1.6)	8	2.9	(1.4)	
14. Independence - autonomy	9	2.7	(1.3)	10	2.3	(1.5)	8	3.0	(1.2)	9	2.5	(1.4)	13	2.7	(1.3)	11	2.6	(1.3)	9	2.8	(1.1)	
15. Agreeable temperatures													12	2.8	(1.6)	12	2.5	(1.5)	8	2.9	(1.4)	
16. Teaching - sharing skills	11	2.4	(1.2)	9	2.5	(1.2)	11	2.7	(1.2)	10	2.2	(1.3)	13	2.7	(1.5)	12	2.5	(1.5)	11	2.6	(1.2)	
17. Meet/observe other people	9	2.7	(1.3)	8	2.6	(1.2)	9	2.9	(1.4)	6	3.0	(1.4)	11	2.9	(1.2)	12	2.5	(1.3)	13	2.4	(1.2)	
18. Introspection	10	2.5	(1.2)	8	2.6	(1.4)	10	2.8	(1.2)	10	2.2	(1.3)	15	2.3	(1.4)	13	2.4	(1.5)	13	2.4	(1.3)	
19. Achievement	11	2.4	(1.1)	9	2.5	(1.2)	10	2.8	(1.2)	10	2.2	(1.2)	14	2.5	(1.3)	14	2.2	(1.2)	12	2.5	(1.1)	
20. Seek stimulation													17	1.9	(0.8)	15	2.0	(1.1)	13	2.4	(1.1)	
21. Creativity	10	2.5	(1.1)	8	2.6	(1.2)	10	2.8	(1.2)	10	2.2	(1.1)	18	1.8	(1.1)	15	2.0	(1.3)	13	2.4	(1.3)	1.0
22. Spiritual	12	2.2	(1.2)	10	2.3	(1.2)	12	2.5	(1.2)	11	1.8	(1.0)	16	2.0	(1.3)	15	2.0	(1.3)	14	2.2	(1.3)	0.7
23. Social recognition													18	1.8	(1.1)	16	1.6	(1.1)	15	2.1	(1.3)	
24. Risk taking	13	1.7	(0.9)	11	2.1	(1.1)	12	2.5	(1.3)	11	1.8	(1.0)	19	1.6	(0.8)	17	1.4	(0.8)	16	2.0	(1.2)	1.1
Sample Size	535			406			241			268			100			122			104			

1 Rating was done on a 6-point Likert-type response format on which 1 designated "not important" and 6 designated "extremely important."

2 This column shows the maximum difference in mean scores across activities when means differed at least 0.7.

3 A blank cell indicates that the row scale was not included in the questionnaire for the column activity.

Source: Driver and Cooksey 1980.

Table 3. Percent of Au Sable River (Michigan) users who reported selected expected consequences as either extremely or very important.

Abbreviated Wording of Expected Consequences	Percent of Respondents Checking the Extremely or Very Important Response[1]
1. To enjoy the out-of-doors	
Canoeists and Fishermen	80
Residents-Cottage Owners	87
2. Chance to escape city	
Canoeists and Fishermen	59
Residents-Cottage Owners	85
3. Restful environment	
Canoeists and Fishermen	79
Residents-Cottage Owners	73
4. Enjoy natural surroundings	
Canoeists and Fishermen	67
Residents-Cottage Owners	78
5. Breathe fresh air	
Canoeists and Fishermen	65
Residents-Cottage Owners	84
6. Escape city noise	
Canoeists and Fishermen	62
Residents-Cottage Owners	82
7. Change from the routine	
Canoeists and Fishermen	65
Residents-Cottage Owners	73
8. To feel free	
Canoeists and Fishermen	54
Residents-Cottage Owners	64
9. Be together as family	
Canoeists and Fishermen	50
Residents-Cottage Owners	70
10. Change from busy job	
Canoeists and Fishermen	45
Residents-Cottage Owners	67

[1] Responses were to a 9-point response format that ranged from extremely to not at all important.

Table 4. Rank-order mean scores for top 10 of 40 items used in Belle Isle, Michigan study (N = 300).

REP Scale Items	Overall Mean Scores[1]
1. Find it relaxing	7.9
2. Can take it easy	7.3
3. Get away from hustle and bustle	7.3
4. Gives my mind a rest	7.1
5. Is welcome change of pace	7.1
6. Pleasant change from my job	7.1
7. Chance to relieve tensions	6.9
8. Chance to be with friends	6.9
9. Escape pressures of work	6.7
10. Get family together for awhile	6.6

[1]Score of 9 indicated item was extremely important and 1 indicated it was not at all important.

frustrating mental arithmetic, and then monitored stress recovery using a battery of physiological measures while the individuals had access to a variety of passive distractions— e.g., watching television, reading, and listening to music. Findings suggested that if individuals perceived the distraction as potentially positive or enjoyable, significant stress recovery was observed as indicated by reductions in heart rate, skin conductance, upper back muscle tension, and respiration. However, when the potentially recreative experience was perceived as nonrecreative or unenjoyable, less recovery occurred. The findings suggest that even a few minutes of passive leisure, if appraised positively by participants, can produce substantial stress recuperation that is clearly evident in different bodily systems.

As discussed in an earlier section, various theoretical perspectives converge in predicting that if people are stressed, passive leisure encounters with most natural environments will have stress-reducing influences, whereas many urban environments will hamper recovery. In a test of this notion, 120 subjects first viewed a stressful movie, and then were exposed to 10-minute color/sound videotapes of different natural and urban settings (Ulrich and Simons 1986; Ulrich et al., in press). Data concerning stress recovery during the environmental presentations were obtained from self-ratings of feeling states and from four physiological measures: heart rate, skin conductance, muscle tension, and pulse transit time (a noninvasive measure that correlates with systolic blood pressure). Findings from all measures, verbal and physiological, were consistent in indicating that recuperation from stress was much faster and more complete when individuals were exposed to natural rather than urban environments. In the case of the physiological stress indicators, greater recovery influences of the natural settings were suggested by lower levels of skin conductance fluctuations, lower blood pressure (i.e., longer pulse transit times), and greater reductions in muscle tension (Figures 2-4). Likewise, results from affective self-ratings suggested that much more recuperation in the psychological component of stress was produced by the natural environments. In contrast to the urban environments, the natural settings produced greater reductions in feelings of fear and anger/aggression, and were associated with far higher scores for positive feelings such as "elated or pleased." The pattern of convergence across data from different response modes, physiological and verbal, suggests that the main conclusion regarding greater stress-reducing effects of the natural environments justifies confidence.

In the same study, heart rate data revealed directionally different responses during stress recovery to the natural versus urban environments; heart rate following onset of the nature presentations decelerated, whereas acceleration occurred during the urban exposures. As discussed in an earlier

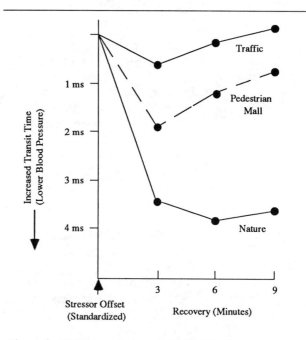

Figure 2. Pulse transit time (systolic blood pressure correlate) during recovery from stress. (From Ulrich and Simons 1986)

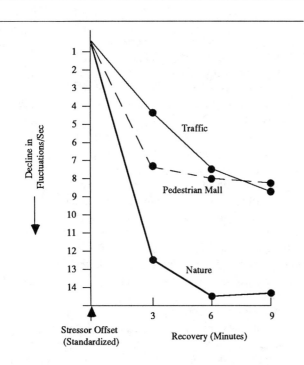

Figure 3. Skin conductance (SCR) during recovery from stress. (From Ulrich and Simons 1986)

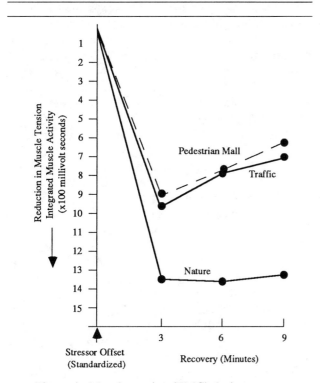

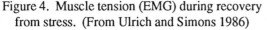

Figure 4. Muscle tension (EMG) during recovery from stress. (From Ulrich and Simons 1986)

section, when an individual is at rest, a response of cardiac deceleration with respect to external stimulation indicates perceptual intake or attention/interest (Coles 1984, Lacey and Lacey 1970). On the other hand, acceleration suggests perceptual rejection of an external stimulus. Accordingly, the results support the conclusion that perceptual intake may have been higher while individuals experienced the natural settings. These findings raise the possibility that intake/ attention-eliciting properties of nature may be an important mechanism in restoration during leisure experiences in natural environments. Authors in behavioral medicine and environment-behavior fields have advanced the notion that external distraction or attention with respect to a positive, nontaxing stimulus can effectively reduce stress or anxiety (e.g., Kaplan and Kaplan 1982, Stoyva and Anderson 1982).

Importantly, the physiological data above suggest the possibility that the natural settings elicited responses that included a parasympathetic nervous system component. Parasympathetic influences are associated with perceptual sensitivity and restoration of physical energy. Another noteworthy finding from this study was the rapidity of recuperation during natural exposures. After 4-6 minutes of exposure to the natural environments compared to the urban experiences, significantly greater recuperation was evident in all physiological measures (Figures 2-4). In view of the quickness of recovery influences, it seems plausible to speculate that even short duration leisure contacts with nature might be important to many urbanites in fostering restoration from mild stressors such as daily hassles or annoyances (Ulrich et al., in press). While the findings cannot be generalized directly to longer term leisure experiences in natural environments, including wilderness recreation, the results probably are relevant to advancing our understanding of mechanisms involved in the stress reduction that many wilderness users report is a very important benefit of their experiences—as discussed in the previous section.

Apart from physiological and psychological components, stressor effects often include reduced performance levels on tasks involving attention and cognitive processing (Glass and Singer 1972). Recently two studies investigated whether enhanced task performance is among the benefits of restorative leisure experiences in natural environments (Hartig et al. 1990). Findings from the first study suggested that a group who participated in a backpacking trip, compared to control groups, evidenced somewhat higher performance on a proofreading test. Also, the backpacking group had higher scores in terms of overall positive feelings. Results from the second study suggested that following a stressor, individuals who had taken a 40-minute walk in a natural setting had more positively toned feelings than subjects who had experienced either an urban walk or who relaxed while reading magazines or listening to music. However, there were no differences in recovery among the three groups as indicated by physiological data such as blood pressure and heart rate. In view of the rapidity of stress recovery that can occur during nature exposures (Ulrich and Simons 1986), it seems possible that potential differences in physiological recuperation may not have been detected because recordings were delayed until after the 40-minute recovery/leisure periods (Hartig et al. 1990).

Apart from these leisure-related investigations, a growing number of studies have reported substantial restoration benefits of nature exposures in health care and other stressful situations. Ulrich found that hospital patients recovering from surgery had more favorable postoperative courses if their windows overlooked trees rather than a brick building wall (Ulrich 1984). In the hospital study, therapeutic influences of the natural window views were evident in behavioral indicators, including shorter length of stay, lower intake of strong pain drugs, and more favorable evaluations by nurses. The hospital results are echoed in findings from research conducted in prisons suggesting that cell window views of nature are associated with lower frequencies of stress symptoms such as digestive illness and headaches, and with fewer sick calls by prisoners (Moore 1982, West 1986). Katcher and his colleagues used a combination of physiological and verbal measures to show that passive contemplation of a different configuration of natural content (an aquarium) reduced stress associated with dental surgery (Katcher et al. 1984).

STRESSFUL EFFECTS OF CHALLENGING OUTDOOR EXPERIENCES

Implicit in the above survey of findings was the perspective that stress tends to be a deleterious phenomenon, and that reduction of stress is beneficial. However, a different interpretation of stress usually underpins outdoor recreation programs which deliberately involve participants in challenging activities that are psychologically and physiologically stressful. The rationale for such programs often rests on the assumption that certain stressful or risky activities are appraised by many participants as positive or even exhilarating, and accordingly have beneficial consequences. Some programs are based on the premise that even quite negatively stressful activities are warranted if they also produce important long-term benefits such as enhanced self-esteem or identity.

A few studies have used verbal measures to assess anxiety or psychological duress elicited by challenging wilderness programs. For instance, Ewert (1988) used a mail questionnaire to measure situational fears of Outward Bound participants before their courses, immediately after, and one year after the courses ended. His findings suggested moderate levels of anticipatory anxiety for certain specific situational stressors in the physical environment (e.g., venomous snakes), and moderate intensity levels for several sociological or psychological fears (e.g., "letting myself down," "not fitting in" to the group). Data obtained immediately after the courses suggested that the Outward Bound experience significantly reduced levels of fear for several of the situations, although the findings also implied that fear remained at fairly moderate levels for many situations. Comparatively little additional lowering of fear appraisals for the situations occurred during the year following the courses.

It appears that no research has yet used psychophysiological methods to examine either possible long-term beneficial "after effects" or persistent stress influences of a stressfully challenging recreation experience. However, a few investigations have employed physiological measures to assess the extent to which specific challenging activities may be *immediately* taxing or stressful. In one study, heart rate was monitored continuously while subjects engaged in a sequence of high "ropes course" events (Little et al. 1986). After completion of three events that involved physical exertion, mean heart rate for the subjects had risen to 110 bpm. The fourth event—called a Zip Line—required comparatively little physical exertion; subjects stepped off a high platform and rode down a 315' cable in a seat harness attached to the line by a pulley. The first segment of the trip was freefall of 20 feet. During the Zip Line event, mean heart rate rose to 180 bpm. This finding implies that the psychological thrill or stress/anxiety of the Zip Line experience, not physical exertion, was largely responsible for the extreme cardiac reactivity reflected in the mean heart rate increase of 66 bpm. In the case of four subjects (total=14), maximum heart rate during the Zip Line reached at least 220 bpm. For older or unfit participants, any positive dimension of such an experience probably could only be psychological; the physiological effects of the event might be considered so stressful as to present a health risk.

Bunting and her colleagues used a combination of verbal and physiological measures to investigate stress associated with rock climbing and rappelling (Bunting et al. 1986). None of the individuals in the study had previous experience with these challenging, risky activities. Measures included self-ratings of anxiety, heart rate recordings, and stress hormones in urine (epinephrine and norepineph-rine). Data were obtained for each measure during a lengthy baseline period, during a three-hour anticipatory period, and after each activity. Findings from all measures converged in indicating that both physically fit and low-fit subjects experienced substantial anticipatory stress, with low-fit individuals experiencing the highest levels. For instance, the mean heart rate of the low-fit group just prior to rappelling was 127 bpm. Levels of stress hormones were higher for both fit and low-fit subjects during the anticipation phase than during baseline; epinephrine excretion during anticipation was especially high for the low-fit group, suggesting greater anticipatory stress. As expected, stress hormone levels were generally highest after the activities, reflecting the combined effects of physical exertion and psychological stress on neuroendocrine responses.

Although the amount of psychophysiological research on challenging recreation activities is limited, findings nonetheless indicate clearly that the short-term effects of such activities can include negative stress—e.g., anxiety, perhaps cardiovascular stress, and high levels of circulating stress hormones that might have deleterious influences. It appears that the "eustress" or beneficial stress hypothesis regarding challenging outdoor programs may not apply to some individuals from the standpoint of short-term or immediate influences. Certain challenging activities may place excessive or even hazardous physiological demands on some individuals, including those with low levels of physical fitness and those with *strong psychological reactivity* to the risk or thrill associated with the activities.

RESEARCH NEEDS, DIRECTIONS, AND CHALLENGES

Because only a limited amount of leisure research to date has used psychophysiological methods, there are conspicuous research needs in most areas relating to leisure consequences. A priority need is for research that identifies effects on physiological well-being that may be outside the conscious awareness of leisure participants (e.g., reduced blood pressure), and hence may not have been identified previously by studies using verbal methods. Another major requirement is for a program of psychophysiological studies to corroborate benefits already identified by verbally based approaches. Most findings in leisure research have been obtained from verbal methods such as questionnaires; where possible, it is important that these findings be validated by obtaining convergent results from psychophysiological or other procedures.

Achieving the great potential of psychophysiology for leisure research will require major efforts in undertaking both laboratory and field studies. Laboratory studies using physiological measures offer some very important advantages, such as precise, temporally continuous recordings of several indicators in different bodily systems. But the extent to which laboratory findings can be extended to real world situations often is limited by external and ecological validity considerations. One general strategy for advancing research on leisure benefits would be to rely heavily on laboratory studies for initial testing of hypotheses or for identifying relationships or main effects. Such laboratory findings could then be confirmed in field studies that usually would be more time consuming and costly than the laboratory predecessors, but might be stronger from the standpoint of external or ecological validity concerns. Although field studies have certain important strengths, they often present difficult control problems because the complexity of real situations typically introduces several variables or variations in conditions that can be excluded or held constant in laboratory research.

Whether conducted in laboratory or field settings, psychophysiological research generally requires technical expertise and other knowledge in areas unfamiliar to leisure researchers with social science backgrounds—e.g., electrical apparatus, physiology, biochemistry. This point implies that progress in applying psychophysiological methods to leisure issues will occur much faster if leisure scientists work together with psychophysiologists in interdisciplinary teams having the necessary range of skills.

For the purpose of identifying research needs, it is useful to distinguish two broad categories of leisure research on the basis of the temporal nature of the consequences in question. One category is concerned with short-term consequences—i.e., beneficial effects that can be detected during or immediately following a leisure experience (e.g., positive emotional responses, lower blood pressure). The second broad category investigates comparatively long-term consequences for well-being—i.e., effects that can be detected days or even weeks after a leisure or recreation episode. Regarding the former, physiological methods are exceptionally well-suited to the continuous monitoring of short-term effects or responses, especially when the leisure experience is passive or involves little physical activity. Research is also needed on the short-term or immediate psychophysiological consequences of *active* leisure experiences. However, this direction presents investigators with difficult challenges stemming from the fact that nearly all physiological responses are affected by physical activity or exercise. For instance, if recordings of blood pressure were obtained for an active wilderness hiker, the data could not be used for inferring, say, stress-reducing influences of natural scenery, unless the design controlled for the effects on blood pressure of the hiker's physical exertion, among other factors. Overcoming the confounding effects of exertion will require carefully conceived research designs that, for instance, hold physical exertion constant while relating possible variations in physiological indicators to systematic changes in other components of the leisure experience.

Apart from studies of short-term effects, there is a clear need for research that documents longer term psychophysiological consequences of leisure. From a long-term perspective, it becomes important to know, for example, whether stress reduction associated with a wilderness fishing trip might persist for a few days after the experience. The determination of possible long-term psychophysiological benefits of leisure episodes will eventually require longitudinal or follow-up studies that span several weeks or months. This research direction is especially important because if long-term benefits are documented (e.g., a persistent reduction in blood pressure associated with repeated leisure episodes), it may prove warranted to link the consequences to health-related benefits such as decreased risk for hypertension. One promising approach for investigating long-term benefits is psychoimmunology. In recent years medical studies have found that stress can have suppressive effects on the immune system, as evidenced, for instance, in lower levels of lymphocytes (e.g., Schleifer et al. 1983). In turn, such immunosuppressive influences can be associated with increased susceptibility to illness. Conceivably, future leisure research might reveal that an important benefit of frequent or prolonged restorative experiences is an increase in immune functioning and accordingly greater resistance to illness.

Another important issue relating to long-term consequences concerns the extent to which challenging, stressful outdoor recreation programs may have beneficial effects in the long run. As discussed in an earlier section, there is limited evidence from psychophysiological studies suggesting that certain challenging activities can have immediate or short-term effects that are quite negatively stressful for some participants. There is a conspicuous need for psychophysiological research that tests whether such influences are indeed transformed over time into benefits that justify the short-term stressful consequences.

Finally, the earlier discussion of benefits associated with natural environments implies a research consideration that applies to both short-term and long-term contexts. In studies concerned with positive physiological consequences tied to natural settings, research designs should be quasi-experimental, or have control groups or other environmental comparisons, to allow sound inferences regarding the role of nature. In the absence of such designs, findings regarding nature will be vulnerable on the grounds, for instance, that a comparable leisure activity in different surroundings (e.g., walking in a city) conceivably could produce similar consequences.

SUMMARY AND CONCLUSION

In addition to their importance for investigating benefits derived from physical exercise, physiological measures have great promise for identifying many other leisure consequences that may or may not be related to physical exertion, such as stress recovery. The main focus of this paper is on the use of psychophysiological methods for investigating the role of leisure activities and leisure environments, particularly natural environments, in helping people cope with stress. "Psychophysiological" refers to approaches that measure physiological responses as they relate to attention, cognition, emotions, and stress-related reactions.

Compared to verbal measures, physiological measures used in psychophysiology have certain significant advantages such as allowing temporally continuous recordings of influences of leisure experiences. Also, findings obtained from physiological procedures tend to have scientific credibility, often carry weight in environmental impact statements, and can be considered permissible data by courts. On the other hand, physiological methods tend to be time consuming and expensive, especially compared to verbal measures. Some physiological procedures are difficult and awkward to use in field studies, and are better suited to laboratory conditions. Importantly, physiological research approaches can identify certain effects on well-being that probably are outside the conscious awareness of leisure participants, and accordingly may not be identified or assessed with validity using verbal measures (e.g., influences on blood pressure). For decades, physiological measures have been of major importance in identifying detrimental human effects of toxic substances in the environment. Only recently has an effort been made in using this powerful category of methods to identify what may eventually prove to be several important benefits of leisure in natural environments.

From a physiological perspective, a stress response in contrast to relaxation is associated with increased physiological activity evident in many bodily responses—e.g., heart rate, blood pressure, skin conductance, muscle tension, blocking of alpha EEG activity, and higher levels of stress hormones such as epinephrine. Also, there is considerable evidence that different emotional reactions or states—which are important components of stress or well-being—are associated with different physiological reactions. Several theoretical perspectives on human-environment interactions converge in predicting that if individuals are stressed, leisure encounters with most natural settings will have stress-reducing influences, whereas exposures to many urban environments may hamper recuperation. Findings from scores of studies using verbal measures indicate that various stress mitigation benefits are consistently rated by outdoor recreationists as very important consequences of their leisure experiences. To date, only a small amount of research has used physiological methods to investigate stress reduction benefits of leisure encounters with natural environments. Although limited, the findings strongly suggest that recuperation from stress occurs much faster and more completely when individuals are exposed to natural rather than urban environments. Results suggest that responses to natural views include a parasympathetic system component, but this may not be the case for urban scenes. Likewise, findings from verbal methods indicate that more recuperation in the psychological component of stress can be produced by natural environments. Heart rate data raise the possibility that intake/attention-eliciting properties of nature may be one important mechanism in the rapid-onset restoration from stress that can occur during leisure experiences in natural settings.

Some outdoor recreation programs are based on the assumption that quite challenging or negatively stressful activities are justified because they may produce important long-term benefits such as enhanced self-esteem or identity. Findings from psychophysiological research on challenging activities indicate that the short-term or immediate effects of such activities can include negative stress—as indicated, for instance, by cardiovascular responses and high levels of circulating stress hormones that might have deleterious influences. This research suggests that the "eustress" or beneficial stress hypothesis regarding challenging programs may not apply to some participants from the standpoint of immediate consequences. Apart from the issue of short-term consequences, there is a need for research that investigates longer term psychophysiological influences of leisure, including challenging programs.

Achieving the great potential of psychophysiology for leisure research will require programs that include both laboratory and field studies. A priority need is for research that cross checks the results of verbally based methods with those obtained from physiological and behavioral measures. Over time, such triangulation will contribute to a deeper and better grounded understanding of stress reduction and other consequences of leisure.

ENDNOTES

[1] Ulf Dimberg and Roger S. Ulrich in paper on autonomic reactions to spatially restricted and open environments, in preparation.

LITERATURE CITED

Ajzen, I. 1985. From intentions to action: A theory of planned behavior. In: Kuhl J.; Bechman J., eds. Action-control: From cognition to behavior. Heidelberg: Springer: 11-39.

Baum, A.; Fleming, R.; Singer, J. 1985. Understanding environmental stress: Strategies for conceptual and methodological integration. In: Baum, A.; Singer, J. E., eds. Advances in environmental psychology, vol. 5: Methods in environmental psychology. Hillsdale, NJ: Lawrence Erlbaum: 185-205.

Baum, A.; Singer, J. E.; Baum, C. S. 1982. Stress and the environment. In: Evans, G. W., ed. Environmental stress. New York, NY: Cambridge University Press: 15-44.

Bunting, C. J.; Little, M. J.; Tolson, H.; Jessup, G. 1986. Physical fitness and eustress in the adventure activities of rock climbing and rappelling. Journal of Sports Medicine and Physical Fitness. 26: 11-20.

Cohen, S. 1978. Environmental load and the allocation of attention. In: Baum, A.; Singer, J. E.; Valins, S. eds. Advances in environmental psychology, vol. 1. Hillsdale, NJ: Lawrence Erlbaum.

Coles, M. G. H. 1984. Heart rate and attention: The intake-rejection hypothesis and beyond. In: Coles, M. G. H.; Jennings, J. R.; Stern, J. A., eds. Psychophysiological perspectives. New York, NY: Van Nostrand: 276-294.

Darwin, C. 1872. The expression of emotion in man and animals. London: Murray.

Davis, R. L. 1973. Selected motivational determinants of the recreational use of Belle Isle Park in Detroit. Ann Arbor: University of Michigan, School of Natural Resources. M.S. thesis.

Dimberg, U. 1986. Facial reactions to fear-relevant and fear-irrelevant stimuli. Biological Psychology. 23: 153-161.

Dimberg, U. 1987a. Facial reactions, autonomic activity and experienced emotion: A three component model of emotional conditioning. Biological Psychology. 24: 105-122.

Dimberg, U. 1987b. Facial reactions and autonomic activity to auditory stimuli with high and low intensity. Psychophysiology. 24: 586.

Dimberg, U. 1990. Facial electromyography and emotional reactions. Psychophysiology. 27:481-494.

Driver, B. L. 1975. Quantifications of outdoor recreationists' preference. In: Smissen B.; Meyers, J., eds. Research: Camping and environmental education, HPEP series No. 11. University Park, PA: Pennsylvania State University: 165-187.

Driver, B. L.; Cooksey, R. W. 1980. Preferred psychological outcomes of recreational fishing. In: Barnhart A.; Roelofs, T. D., eds. Catch-and-release fishing as a management tool: A national sport fishing symposium. Arcata, CA: Humboldt State University: 27-40.

Driver, B. L.; Green, P. 1977. Man's nature: Innate determinants of response to natural environments. In: Children, nature, and the urban environment. USDA Forest Service Report NE-30. Upper Darby, PA: Northeastern Forest Experiment Station: 63-70.

Driver, B. L.; Knopf, R. C. 1976. Temporary escape: One product of sport fisheries management. Fisheries. 1(2): 24-29.

Ekman, P.; Levenson, R. W.; Friesen, Wallace V. 1983. Autonomic nervous system activity distinguishes among emotions. Science. 221: 1208-1210.

Evans, G. W.; Cohen, S. 1987. Environmental stress. In: Stokols, D.; Altman, I., eds. Handbook of environmental psychology (2 vols.). New York, NY: John Wiley: 571-610.

Ewert, A. 1988. The identification and modification of situational fears associated with outdoor recreation. Journal of Leisure Research. 20: 106-117.

Glass, D. C.; Singer, J. E. 1972. Urban stress: Experiments on noise and social stressors. New York, NY: Academic Press.

Grings, W. W.; Dawson, M. E. 1978. Emotions and bodily responses: A psychophysiological approach. New York, NY: Academic Press.

Hartig, T.; Mang, M.; Evans, G. W. 1990. Perspectives on wilderness: Testing the theory of restorative environments. In: Easley, A. T.; Passineau, J.; Driver, B. L., eds. The use of wilderness for personal growth, therapy, and education. USDA Forest Service GTR RM-193. Fort Collins, CO: Rocky Mountain Forest and Range Experiment Station.

Heywood, L. A. 1978. Perceived recreation experience and the relief of tension. Journal of Leisure Research. 10: 86-97.

Kaplan, R.; Kaplan, S. 1989. The experience of nature. New York, NY: Cambridge University Press.

Kaplan, S.; Kaplan, R. 1982. Cognition and environment. New York, NY: Praeger.

Kaplan, S.; Talbot, J. F. 1983. Psychological benefits of a wilderness experience. In: Altman, I.; Wohlwill, J. F., eds. Human behavior and environment, vol. 6: Behavior and the natural environment. New York, NY: Plenum: 163-203.

Katcher, A. H.; Segal, H.; Beck, A. 1984. Comparison of contemplation and hypnosis for the reduction of anxiety and discomfort during dental surgery. American Journal of Clinical Hypnosis. 27: 14-21.

Knopf, R. C. 1983. Recreational needs and behavior in natural settings. In: Altman, I.; Wohlwill, J. F., eds. Human behavior and environment, vol. 6: Behavior and the natural environment. New York, NY: Plenum: 205-240.

Lacey, J. I. 1967. Somatic response patterning and stress: Some revisions of activation theory. In: Appley, M. H.; Trumbull, R., eds. Psychological stress: Issues in research. New York, NY: Appleton-Century-Crofts.

Lacey, J. I.; Lacey, B. C. 1970. Some autonomic-central nervous system interrelationships. In: Black, P., ed. Physiological correlates of emotion. New York, NY: Academic Press: 205-227.

Little, M. J.; Bunting, C. J.; Gibbons, E. S. 1986. Heart rate responses to high ropes course events. Texas HPERD Journal. October: 38-42.

Manfredo, M. J.; Driver, B. L.; Brown, P. J. 1983. A test of concepts inherent in experience-based management of outdoor recreation areas. Journal of Leisure Research. 15: 263-283.

Milgrams, S. 1970. The experience of living cities. Science. 167: 1461-1464, 1468.

Moore, E. O. 1982. A prison environment's effect on health care service demands. Journal of Environmental Systems. 11: 17-34.

Petty, R. E.; Cacioppo, J. T. 1983. The role of bodily responses in attitude measurement and change. In: Cacioppo J. T.; Petty R. E., eds. Social psychophysiology: A sourcebook. New York, NY: Guilford: 51-101.

Schleifer, S. J.; Keller, S. E.; Camanno, M., et al. 1983. Suppression of lymphocyte stimulation following bereavement. Journal of the American Medical Association. 250: 374-377.

Stainbrook, E. 1968. Human needs and the natural environment. In: Man and nature in the city. Proceedings of a symposium sponsored by the Bureau of Sport Fisheries and Wildlife. Washington, DC, October 21-22, 1968. Washington, DC: U.S. Department of the Interior: 1-9.

Stoyva, J.; Anderson, C. 1982. A coping-rest model of relaxation and stress management. In: Goldberger, L.; Breznitz, J., eds. Handbook of stress: Theoretical and clinical aspects. New York, NY: The Free Press: 745-763.

Tinsley, H. E. A.; Kass, R. A. 1979. The latent structure of the need satisfying properties of leisure activities. Journal of Leisure Research. 11: 278-291.

Tinsley, H. E. A.; Teaff, J. D.; Colbs, S. L.; Kaufman, N. 1985. A system of classifying leisure activities in terms of the psychological benefits of participation reported by older persons. Journal of Gerontology. 40: 172-178.

Tinsley, H. E. A.; Tinsley, D. J. 1988. An expanded context for the study of career decision making, development and maturity. In: Walsh, W.B.; Osipow, S.H., eds. Career decision making. Hillsdale, NJ: Lawrence Erlbaum Associates: 213-264.

Ulrich, R. S. 1979. Visual landscapes and psychological well-being. Landscape Research. 4: 17-23.

Ulrich, R. S. 1981. Natural versus urban scenes: Some psychophysiological effects. Environment and Behavior. 13: 523-556.

Ulrich, R. S. 1983. Aesthetic and affective response to natural environment. In: Altman, I.; Wohlwill, J. F., eds. Human behavior and environment, vol. 6: Behavior and the natural environment. New York, NY: Plenum: 85-125.

Ulrich, R. S. 1984. View through a window may influence recovery from surgery. Science. 224: 420-421.

Ulrich, R. S. 1988. Toward integrated valuation of amenity resources using nonverbal measures. In: Peterson, G. L.; Driver, B. L.; Gregory, R., eds. Amenity resource valuation: Integrating economics with other disciplines. State College, PA: Venture Publishing, Inc.: 87-100.

Ulrich, R. S.; Simons, R. F. 1986. Recovery from stress during exposure to everyday outdoor environments. In: Wineman, J.; Barnes, R.; Zimring, C., eds. Proceedings of the Seventeenth Annual Conference of the Environmental Design Research Association, April, 1986, Atlanta. Washington, DC: EDRA: 115-122.

Ulrich, R. S.; Simons, R. F.; Losito, B. D., et al. [In press]. Stress recovery during exposure to natural and urban environments. Journal of Environmental Psychology.

Weiss, L.; Baum, A. 1987. Physiological aspects of environment-behavior relationships. In: Zube, E. H.; Moore, G. T., eds. Advances in environment, behavior, and design, vol. 1. New York, NY: Plenum: 221-247.

West, M. J. 1986. Landscape views and stress response in the prison environment. Seattle: University of Washington, Department of Landscape Architecture. 125 p. M.L.A. thesis.

II.

STATE-OF-KNOWLEDGE CHAPTERS

B. Psychological Measures

Leisure and Self-Actualization

Mihaly Csikszentmihalyi
Department of Behavioral Sciences
University of Chicago
Chicago, Illinois

Douglas A. Kleiber
Department of Recreation and Leisure Studies
University of Georgia
Athens, Georgia

THE VARIED MEANINGS OF LEISURE

Despite its rapid development, the field of leisure studies still suffers from a certain amount of terminological confusion. Lack of clarity affects even its central concept, namely, leisure itself. For some the term is simply assumed to be a synonym for free time. Others use it to refer to specific, culturally defined recreational activities. Still others reserve the use of the term for a positive experiential state, generally attended by feelings of freedom and intrinsic motivation. And finally, it has been observed that for the ancient Greeks "true" leisure only obtained when individuals used their freedom to explore the limits of their potentialities and to expand the range of their mental, physical, and social skills, what today we might call *self-actualization.*

This paper addresses the prospect of resurrecting a concept of leisure in this last sense. But before exploring what leisure as self-actualization might mean nowadays, it will be useful to review briefly the other denotations by which leisure is more commonly understood, and to identify when and to what extent self-actualization is associated with them.

Leisure as Discretionary Time

In all human groups, there are certain things people must do to stay alive; they must extract calories from the environment, for example, and transform them for human consumption. These obligatory activities take more or less time, but they always leave a certain amount of it free to be used for purposes that are not dictated by the necessity of survival.

The amount of discretionary time available appears to have fluctuated widely through different historical periods. According to some anthropologists, men and women in hunting and gathering societies only needed to work for 3 to 4 hours a day, and spent the rest of the day in leisure (Lee 1975, Sahlins 1972). By contrast, from the mid-Eighteenth century to the beginnings of the Twentieth, workers in industrialized nations were often forced to work in factories from dawn to dusk, 6 days a week, with almost no time to use at their discretion (Thompson 1963).

The current situation in technologically advanced societies is somewhere in between the lackadaisical situation of the hunter-gatherers and the worst excesses of the Industrial Revolution. Most everywhere an 8-hour workday prevails, for a total of 40 hours per week—thus leaving about 72 hours a week free, after subtracting 8 hours a day for sleeping. This proportion between obligatory and discretionary time seems to be fairly standard among many forms of life; for instance, it is very similar to the time budget of the free ranging African baboon (Altmann and Altmann 1970, Altmann 1980).

But even this simple distinction between obligatory and discretionary time is difficult to establish with precision. In our studies of U.S. workers, for example, we found that of the 8 hours typically spent on the job, the average person only worked 6, and spent the remaining 2 chatting with co-workers, daydreaming, or otherwise engaged in freely chosen activities (Csikszentmihalyi and Graef 1980, Csikszentmihalyi and LeFevre 1989, Graef et al. 1983). Conversely, "free" time is never entirely free. In the first place, about 40 hours per week are devoted to general maintenance functions that are neither clearly obligatory, nor fully discretionary. The bulk of this time is taken up by driving to and from work, shopping, household chores, eating, dressing, and personal hygiene. These maintenance tasks take up a great deal of time, they are often resented by the person doing them, but their constraint is quite different from that of work.

That leaves 30 hours a week of more or less pure discretionary time. In our society, the single largest activity to fill up this time is television viewing—about 14 hours per week, on the average (see Kubey and Csikszentmihalyi 1990, Robinson 1981, Szalai 1972). But how "free" is this time, after all? Family responsibilities, religious obligations, and strong personal ambitions may drive the person to use any moment left over from work on projects that are dictated by external compulsions. Staffan Linder (1970), the Swedish economist, has proposed that in a competitive market economy people are driven to consume in leisure so as to match the value of what they would earn if they were working—thus slowly driving out "cheap" leisure activities like poetry or contemplation, and maximizing instead energy-intensive and otherwise costly forms of leisure.

Even these few examples should indicate that the concept of discretionary time does not provide an unambiguous definition of leisure. To summarize, in the first place, about one-third of the time spent at work is devoted to activities that if they were done elsewhere we would call leisure; conversely much "free" time is not discretionary. Secondly, it is often unclear whether a discretionary activity is freely chosen, or engaged in by some external or internalized compulsion. And finally, as we shall see later, much of the time free from obligations is experienced as a negative condition, as a state of depressing apathy worse than the experience of work. In such cases, it would be difficult to argue that leisure led to self-actualization.

Leisure as Activity

It was Kelly (1982: 20) who noted the paradox that although the definition of leisure in terms of activities is perhaps the least defensible theoretically, it is the one most often used by researchers and by various recreational agencies. There are at least two major problems with this practice. In the first place, it is difficult to know a priori what activities should be included in the leisure category. Is playing golf still leisure if one does it primarily to secure a business deal? Is work not leisure for the surgeon who enjoys operating more than anything else? When should we count gardening, working (or playing) with computers, running a ranch, or writing a book as leisure, and when should we count these as work?

The way out many researchers take is to count as leisure only those activities that the culture unequivocally places in that category. Such things as fishing, hunting, bowling, cycling, or playing chess and bridge are rarely done for productive purposes. The main reason people invest time and energy in them is for recreation. The problem with this expedient, however, is that it minimizes leisure as a phenomenon, vastly underestimating its frequency. This is because people do not engage in active recreation all that often. Although they may check several leisure pursuits on a questionnaire, thereby making it seem that their participation in such activities is an important part of their lives, sports, games, and other active leisure take up at most about 1% of a typical adult's life. When we add to this participation in clubs, cultural activities, movies and theatre, the frequency only goes up to about 2% (Csikszentmihalyi and Graef 1980).

This does not mean that recreational leisure activities are qualitatively unimportant. But it does suggest that at least quantitatively such activities are less important than they are usually thought to be. If only 2% of waking time is devoted to them, what happens to the other 28% of life that is discretionary? Part of the answer is obvious: passive leisure activities like TV and reading take up slightly more than a third of it; socializing—chatting with family, friends and neighbors—take up another third. But that still leaves quite a few hours each week for the kind of idiosyncratic leisure that does not show up on most surveys.

As it has been argued elsewhere (Csikszentmihalyi 1981), one might make the case that a single intense leisure experience is more significant in determining the course of a person's life than thousands of more mundane obligatory experiences. A special fishing trip might be remembered forever, and its story told to one's grandchildren. A bowling trophy may become the centerpiece of the den for years to come. The quilt sewn in one's free time might become an heirloom to future generations. Thus, the frequency with which one does an activity might not be its most important feature. But if this is true, then what counts is not the activity per se, but the quality of the experience it provides. And this consideration leads us naturally to the third main way in which leisure has been defined.

Leisure as Experience

In the last 15 years or so, there has been an increasing tendency to define leisure not in terms of the obligatory vs. discretionary dimension, or in terms of whether the activity is culturally defined as leisure, but more in terms of whether it provides a certain subjective state that could be reasonably identified with leisure. If a man does experience leisure, then he may be on the job immersed in work, and yet we would think of what he does as leisure. But if the same man was fishing on his vacation and felt constrained to do it, we would not say that he was in leisure.

The most popular candidates for what constitutes the leisure experience were proposed by the psychologist John Neulinger (1981). He suggested that when an activity is freely chosen, and when it is pursued for its own sake, the activity should be considered leisure. Freedom and intrinsic motivation are its hallmarks. This formulation has been widely adopted by other researchers (e.g., Iso-Ahola 1980, Tinsley and Tinsley 1986).

The experiential definition of leisure is, of course, closely related to the cultural definition. For instance, in studies of US workers it has been found that adults feel free only about 15% of the time they are working, and they are intrinsically motivated only about 5% of the time; whereas when doing sports or games they feel free about 90% of the time, and intrinsically motivated 40% of the time (Csikszentmihalyi and Graef 1980, Graef et al. 1983).

In fact, it is this close overlap that makes one somewhat suspicious of the current experiential definition. It seems possible that when people report whether they are free and intrinsically motivated, they base their judgment not on what they actually *feel*, but on the cultural label of the activity. If they are working they say they are not free, when they watch TV they say the opposite; not because this is what they are actually experiencing, but because work is supposed to be obligatory, and watching TV is clearly a free choice, and therefore it should be leisure.

A recent study (Csikszentmihalyi and LeFevre 1989) supports this interpretation. A group of adult urban workers tended to report more positive experiential states—such as potency, creativity, and concentration—when they were working than when they were involved in leisure activities. Nevertheless, when working they were much more likely to say that they did "wish to be doing something else" than

when in leisure, despite the fact that when working their experiential state was more positive. Similar results have been found with teenagers, who often feel more positive experiences in school than in leisure, yet they invariably feel unfree and unmotivated in school (Csikszentmihalyi and Larson 1984). Apparently the quality of immediate experience gets filtered through cultural expectations which then color our reports of what we experience.

How cultural expectations develop about whether work or leisure should be more enjoyable is well illustrated in a study of traditional Italian farming families. In the oldest generation, very positive experiential states, including freedom and intrinsic motivation, were reported 60% of the time in everyday work activities, and only 20% of the time in leisure. The middle generation reported 40% of their most positive experiences in work, 40% in leisure. The youngest generation was almost the mirror image of their grandparents: 20% reported freedom and intrinsic motivation in work, 75% in leisure (Delle Fave and Massimini 1988: 201).

Another possible drawback of the experiential definition is that many activities that are freely chosen and intrinsically rewarding have outcomes that are difficult to reconcile with the previously mentioned conceptions of leisure. For example, many juvenile delinquents report stealing and acts of vandalism as free and intrinsically motivated (Csikszentmihalyi and Larson 1978). Members of Japanese motorcycle gangs describe their shenanigans in similar terms (Sato 1988). Television viewing, which people report to be freely chosen and intrinsically motivated, generally produces depressed moods and physical apathy (Csikszentmihalyi and Kubey 1981, Kubey and Csikszentmihalyi 1990).

There are two ways to circumvent this problem. One is to admit that leisure is often tiresome, depressing, criminal, or at least "anomic" (Gunter and Gunter 1980, Kleiber 1985, Samdahl 1987). Or one can stipulate that we shall not call an activity "leisure" unless, in addition to all the other requirements, it also leads to a greater variety of positive, culturally acceptable experiences and perhaps even to self-actualization. This latter strategy may not correspond well with contemporary meanings of the term, but it leads us to reconsider leisure's ancient traditions.

Leisure as Self-Actualization

Throughout much of the history of the West, leisure was prized because it represented an opportunity for pursuing excellence and thereby achieving the highest priority of life. The Greeks idealized leisure as schole, a condition of life characterized by freedom from necessity which made it possible to explore one's potentialities and to develop one's character (de Grazia 1962, Hemingway 1988). It is from this term that the words "scholar," "scholastic," and "school" derive—all of them indicating ways to improve one's native abilities through disciplined practice. Thus, the value of leisure was not that it offered relaxation, pleasure, or recreation; on the contrary, it required effort in order to provide a sense of accomplishment and enhanced self-esteem.

In light of contemporary critical perspectives, it is easy to see this idealization of leisure as a way for the social elite of the classical world to establish its moral superiority, and hence to buttress its power, over the laboring classes that had neither the time nor the symbolic skills for pursuing refined leisure activities. According to many Marxist and deconstructionist critics, the notion of leisure as self-actualization is simply a clever propaganda move in the eternal class struggle. Those who can afford it will sing its praise in order to impress those who cannot.

A longer look at history, however, suggests that enduring social forms and cultural values tend to have an adaptive function. If the search for self-actualization only served the interests of a small minority, and harmed the rest of society, its value by now would have been tarnished. If leisure has been held in high account over the better part of 25 centuries, it must have an adaptive value for humankind, as has been cogently argued by Huizinga (1955) and Pieper (1952), among others.

To be self-actualizing, leisure need not be associated with high culture and elitism. As people wrest freedom from constraining and oppressive circumstances, at all levels of society, they are faced with the problem of using that freedom meaningfully. This is the challenge that Marx and many others saw for every human being. Yet, as we have shown, the activities in which people choose to invest their free time usually do little to expand their sense of well-being, or to cultivate a sense of self in the ways that Plato and Aristotle deemed appropriate for a free person.

TOWARD A
NEW UNDERSTANDING

Should an activity be called leisure only when freedom leads to self-actualization? Such an alternative might be tempting to those involved in leisure studies and leisure services who seek to establish the legitimacy (i.e., the benefits) of leisure. The deeper question, however, is how to transform free time, that ambivalent gift of abundance and security, into self-actualizing leisure. As a start, we might wish to define leisure in this sense as a *context of expressive freedom that is experienced as such.* It is easy for a person to recognize

freedom in terms of lack of obligations, constraints, and preoccupations. But whether that experience leads toward self-actualization is another question. To provide a better understanding of how this might occur, we need a closer look at the process of self-actualization.

To examine the relevance of this subject to the context of contemporary leisure, it is useful to review briefly what some recent thinkers have said about self-actualization. In the last quarter century, the most influential work on this subject was done by the psychologist Abraham Maslow. He defined self-actualization as "... the full use and exploration of talents, capacities, potentialities..." (Maslow 1970: 150); and he believed that every person, after having satisfied more urgent and basic needs, was motivated to self-actualize. He saw self-actualization as sparked by "peak experiences," or moments of one's "greatest maturity, individuation, fulfillment—in a word, [one's] healthiest moments" (Maslow 1968: 97).

It is our claim that leisure offers unique conditions for self-actualization that more constrained contexts do not, particularly as it allows an individual to broaden his or her experience while involved in culture-affirming practices (Kelly 1987). But even this outcome is not sufficient for self-actualization to occur. In describing the full use of talents and capabilities, Maslow emphasizes that self-actualization cannot be achieved through some smorgasbord of experience and sensations. Involvement in an activity must be deep, sustained, and disciplined to contribute to an emerging sense of self. This is especially important to note at a time when leisure practices are criticized for responding too readily to market demands and to the mass media, helping to perpetuate a superficial consumer mentality, instead of cultivating more complex and profound experience (Goodale and Godbey 1988, Linder 1970).

In contrast to leisure of this type, work and other institutionally restricted contexts may give more room for disciplined involvement even if they generally constrain the kind of exploration and experimentation that is also necessary for self-actualization. This has led to the common assumption that enjoyment and expressive behavior is incompatible with serious, focused, disciplined involvement; work, in other words, cannot be enjoyable, and leisure cannot be serious. But more sophisticated models of intrinsic motivation incorporate both exploration and focused involvement, and in so doing provide an example of how both work and leisure might promote self-actualization.

Self-Actualization and the Flow Experience

A line of research that bears on the issue of leisure and self-actualization is the one that has focused on the phenomenology of enjoyment or optimal experience. This research, originally inspired by Maslow's work, initially involved interviews with hundreds of people pursuing active forms of leisure such as rock-climbing, dancing, basketball, chess, and music composition, in an attempt to discover what features of these activities were perceived as rewarding, and what the psychic rewards of the activities were. In the course of these and of later studies it was found that whenever people enjoy what they are doing, they report very similar experiential states that distinguish the enjoyable moment from the rest of life. The same dimensions are reported in the context of enjoying chess, climbing mountains, playing with babies, reading a book, or writing a poem. These dimensions are the same for young and old, male and female, American or Japanese, rich or poor (Csikszentmihalyi 1975, Csikszentmihalyi and Csikszentmihalyi 1988). In other words, the phenomenology of enjoyment seems to be a panhuman constant. When all the characteristics are present, we call the state of consciousness a *flow experience,* because many of the respondents said that when what they were doing was especially enjoyable it felt like being carried away by a current, like being in a flow. Consequently the theoretical model that describes intrinsically rewarding experiences is known as the flow model.

The first subjective condition that separates a flow experience from everyday consciousness is the merging of action and awareness. The mind slips into the activity as if actor and action had become one. The duality of consciousness which is typical of ordinary life disappears; we no longer look at what we are doing from the outside, we become what we do. The climber feels part of the rock, the sky, and the wind; the chess player merges with the field of forces on the board; the dancer cannot be told from the dance; in reading fiction "while you read you are the patient pool or cataract of concepts which the author has constructed... The will is at rest amid that, moving like a gull asleep on the sea" (Gass 1972: 32).

This intense involvement is only possible when a person feels that the opportunities for action in the given activity (or challenges) are more or less in balance with his or her ability to respond to the opportunities (or skills). The opportunity for action may be something concrete and physical, like the peak of a mountain to be scaled; or it can be something abstract and symbolic, like a set of musical notes to be performed, a story to be read, a puzzle to be solved. Similarly, the skill may refer either to a physical ability, or to the mastery of manipulating symbols.

When the challenges are relatively greater than the skills, there is a sense of frustration that eventually results in worry and then anxiety; in the opposite case, when one's skills are greater than what is possible to do, one feels progressively more bored. But when a person feels that skills are fully engaged by challenges, he or she enters the state of flow, even if only temporarily—as the tennis player knows when a close volley is exchanged, or when the singer hears her voice following the ideal notes envisioned by the composer, or when the angler sees the fish rising to the fly.

A flow experience usually takes place when the activity provides a clear goal for the person to pursue. The goal may be something obvious like winning a game, reaching the top of the mountain, or completing a poem; or it may be an ad hoc goal that the person formulates on the spur of the moment, like mowing the lawn in a certain way, or ironing a shirt in a determined sequence of moves. A goal is necessary so that a person may get feedback to his or her actions, so that at any given moment they know whether the responses were appropriate to the challenges. Without a goal there cannot be meaningful feedback, and without knowing whether one is doing well or not it is very difficult to maintain involvement. It is important to realize, however, that the goal is not sought for itself; it is sought primarily because it makes the activity possible. A climber does not climb in order to reach the top; he reaches the top to define the climb. Similarly, poets do not write so they will have poems; they create poems so they can write.

When a person finds a goal which presents a certain range of opportunities for action that matches his or her skills, attention becomes so concentrated on the activity that all irrelevant concerns tend to be excluded from awareness. The past and the future fade away, elbowed out by the urgency of the present. The usual hobgoblins of the mind, the anxieties of everyday life—insecurity, guilt, jealousy, financial worries—disappear. The reason for this clarity is simple. Consciousness cannot process more than a limited range of information at the same time (Csikszentmihalyi 1978, Eysenck 1982, Hasher and Zacks 1979, Kahneman 1973). When all the attention is absorbed by the challenges of the activity, there is simply not enough left to notice anything else. Hence, the perfect attentional focus of the athlete, the religious mystic, the artist, the climber hanging over the precipice by his fingertips, or the reader completely taken by the characters and by the plot of a novel. There are few things as irritating as being distracted by outside stimuli when immersed in an enjoyable book, or when trying to play a musical instrument. While reading a novel, a few extraneous words one overhears can destroy the slowly constructed fictional world and bring us back to everyday reality, thereby destroying the enjoyment derived from having responded to the opportunities offered by the author with the skills of one's imagination.

One of the consequences of this complete concentration is that the person loses the sense of self-consciousness that always shadows our actions in everyday life. Attention is so completely absorbed in the task that there is not enough left over to contemplate the self. This adds to the liberating feeling flow provides; no longer restricted to the confines of one's self-image, it is possible to transcend the boundaries of one's being. The puny individuality of the climber merges with the majestic environment of sky and stone. The musician's self expands to embrace the harmony of the spheres. The reader's identity grows from roaming the faraway world created by the writer. Thus we reach a paradoxical conclusion: whereas the self disappears during a flow experience, it reappears afterwards stronger than it had been before, because climbing the mountain or playing the new song has expanded its limits. In concrete terms, this is what self-actualization implies.

Thus flow makes it possible for people to have new experiences without worrying about unpleasant consequences. This is true even when the person is involved in dangerous activities such as spelunking, sky diving, or rock-climbing. Because these activities are clearly demarcated, and appropriate rules are identified, the participant is able to anticipate risks and minimize the unexpected. When reading a novel about a war, a plague, or a cosmic journey, we can vicariously participate in these events without running risks. In this sense, leisure provides perhaps the most supportive environment for the growth of the self. At work and in contexts of social responsibility one is always exposed to the dangers of "real" life, and thus one tends to remain wary and self-conscious. One can best learn about the possibilities of the self when one feels free to make mistakes.

A matching of challenges and skills with clear goals and immediate feedback, a depth of concentration that prevents worry and the intrusion of unwanted thoughts into consciousness and results in a transcendence of the self—these are the universal characteristics associated with enjoyable activities. When these dimensions of experience are present, the activity becomes *autotelic,* or rewarding in itself, even though initially one may have been forced to do it, or did it for some extrinsic reason like the promise of a good grade, a useful diploma, or a paycheck. If during the activity one starts to experience flow, the activity becomes autotelic, or worth doing for its own sake.

What people enjoy the most in their lives is almost never something passive, like watching television or being entertained. When a seemingly passive activity such as reading is enjoyed, it is because it is turned into an active pursuit. The reader chooses the book, identifies with the characters, recreates visually the places and the events described, anticipates turns of the plot, and responds with empathy, yet critically, to the writer's craft (Neill 1988). In other words, he or she turns reading into a flow activity.

It is important in this context to stress the difference between enjoyment, which tends to require activity and ability; and pleasure, which is often passive and rarely leads to self-actualization. Flow depends on the use of skills, and on gradual increments of challenges and skills so that boredom or anxiety will not take over. Pleasure, on the other hand, is homeostatic: pleasurable experiences like resting when tired, drinking when thirsty, or having sex when aroused, do not require complex skills and can be repeated over and over and still be pleasurable. For this very reason, pleasure does not drive us to develop new potentialities, and thus does not lead to personal growth. Enjoyment, on the other hand, drifts into boredom unless a person keeps taking on new challenges and increases his or her abilities; therefore to maintain enjoyment one is forced to grow.

Of course, some activities are intended to provide enjoyment. This is true of games, sport, music, literature, the other arts, and religious ceremonies. The quality of life depends more on these opportunities to experience flow than on the size of the Gross National Product. But it would be a mistake to think that only playful activities can do this. Over the course of time we have separated work and leisure to the extent that now we think only unproductive leisure can be enjoyable, and productive work must necessarily be unpleasant. Nothing is further from the truth. Leisure begins to be thought of as the sole source of enjoyment only when a culture loses its capacity to make everyday life enjoyable. The ideal condition is one where work, family life, politics, friendship, and community interaction provide most of the optimal experiences that enrich life; leisure, if not integrated within those contexts, is needed only to experiment with new potentialities of being.

When reviewing conceptualizations of self-actualization from the Aristotelian concept of entelecheia to the concept of flow in our own days, a few constants seem to recur time after time. In the first place, there is the idea of *exploring alternatives*—trying out new ways of being. In the flow model, this is reflected by the experiential rewards of finding new challenges. There is the notion of *growth*, of stretching one's physical and mental potentialities until new skills are acquired. There is the idea of *affirming and building upon the best practices of one's culture.* In the flow model, this process is described as the dynamic need to constantly take on new challenges and develop new skills to avoid the conditions of anxiety and boredom. These three processes help us find out what the self could become, and they help us to act on that knowledge.

The problem is that in real life leisure seldom involves self-actualization as defined here. Of course, there are many leisure activities that offer the taste of new experiences, that help develop new skills, that reach down into healthy values. Unfortunately, however, what we most often do in our free time is redundant, passive, and to put it kindly, not up to the highest peaks of human accomplishment. Television viewing, the most frequent leisure activity for most people, and informal socializing, the next most frequent one, rarely provide opportunities of this sort. Does this mean that we should forget about using self-actualization as part of the definition of leisure, or does it mean that most of what we think of as leisure is not leisure at all, but only a worthless form of relaxation?

Some people might want to resolve this dilemma by pointing out that self-actualization is a value-laden concept and that social scientists should be value-free. Therefore it would be best to leave such notions out of the definition of leisure altogether. Unfortunately this solution will not work, because ignoring self-actualization is just as much a value choice as it is to feature it prominently. Those who insist that spending one's free time in a saloon, or glued to a TV set, or taking recreational drugs is no different than learning to sail or playing the flute, do so because they value individual choice more than anything else. They feel that nothing is more important than allowing people their freedom, even if its exercise leads to "wasting" time or to personal harm. We might agree with this position, but only because we value freedom more than the chance for self-actualization. In other words, the only way we can justify rejecting one set of values is by turning to another.

The only viable solution may be to recognize the justice of both claims. On the one hand, it is true that people, when given a choice, tend to fill their free time with activities that, like watching television, do not require effort and the extension of skills. On the other hand, if we value personal growth, we must also recognize that some activities are better suited to provide it than others. And in that case it makes sense to ask ourselves how we can support those forms of leisure that have a better chance of leading to self-actualization.

PROMOTING FLOW AND SELF-ACTUALIZATION IN LEISURE

The Family

It seems likely that the ability to use leisure time for personal growth is a meta-skill, a generalized disposition one learns in the first years of life. It is impossible to overestimate the impact of early experiences on a person's ability to use free time constructively. Some children grow up constantly bored, dissatisfied with what they have, unable to become involved with opportunities around them. Others grow up in a constant state of vigilance, always fearing that some unexpected threat will require defensive action. Neither line of development is likely to result in adults who will employ their leisure for self-actualization.

Recent studies suggest that parents can help children to become involved spontaneously with growth-producing activities by providing a context in which attention can be directed freely to opportunities for action, instead of being tied down in constant hassles. Parents who set clear rules and invest time in monitoring the behavior of their children, yet give them choices and challenges, make it possible for the children to save energy from the usual conflicts of family life, and to invest that saved energy into exploring new possibilities and into developing their skills (Rathunde 1988, in press).

In addition to helping develop a generalized control over attention, the family can help children to get involved in specific forms of leisure. It is quite common for people who master challenging leisure pursuits to have learned them from their parents. For instance a large proportion of the rock-climbers interviewed in *Beyond Boredom and Anxiety* had been introduced to climbing by their fathers, and those who were, enjoyed it more than those who had learned it later from others (Csikszentmihalyi 1975). The three teenage Polgar sisters, who share the top ranks among women chess players in the world, were taught to play by their parents when they were two years old.

There are other opportunities for families to use free time constructively. Common meals provide one of the few occasions in contemporary life when parents and children find themselves in the same place, in a relaxed atmosphere, and generally in a positive mood. Families that use the dinner table as a playing field in which ideas, opinions, jokes, and hopes are exchanged will be way ahead of those families in which mealtimes are wasted in withdrawal or in watching television. But even watching television, if done with some care, can turn into a growth-producing activity.

The more thoughts and emotions one brings to turn passive viewing into a participatory, critical, interactive involvement, the more children learn to use their mind and senses when they watch, instead of just blanking out in front of the tube.

In our studies, we find over and over again that the fondest memories people have of their past tend to involve family outings and vacations. Typical of such memories that serve as cornerstones for one's past would be an evening spent around a fireplace, drinking hot chocolate and singing old songs, after a vigorous day of cross-country skiing in the forest. When the entire family is together, doing the same thing—especially when it is something novel, and demanding—there develops an atmosphere of common purpose and good feeling that is usually absent from everyday life when children go to school in the morning, parents come home tired in the evening, and seldom is the whole family on the same wavelength. Vacations provide the opportunity to experience that "collective effervescence" that sociologist Emile Durkheim and anthropologist Victor Turner, among others, have claimed to be among the most powerful human experiences.

It should be quite clear that it is not easy for parents to create such a context for self-actualization. It takes quite a bit of extra effort to protect children from excessive attentional demands, yet provide them with the right amount of challenge; to introduce them to activities which match their skills; to plan the kind of outings and vacations that will serve as signposts to the future. In fact, these things won't happen unless parents are able and willing to invest their attention in such goals. And the time and attention needed for this purpose must be taken from more seductive recreations, like drinking that extra glass of liquor, reading one more section of the paper, or watching one more episode of that sitcom. Yet nothing will affect the future quality of children's lives as much as the energy invested in helping them learn how to use leisure constructively.

School and Leisure

It is somewhat ironic that the word "school" is rooted in the Greek word for leisure, schole. Contemporary education has very little of the freedom for experimentation, self-expression, and dialogue that the ancient Greeks found to be such an ideal context for learning. Formal public education has been continuously criticized for being anti-intellectual and for deadening the enthusiasm to learn. Various alternatives have been sought in the name of progressive education. Many attempts have been made to restore the enthusiasm for learning that young children bring to school; but as a compulsory system of social control and socialization, public education does not make intrinsic interest in learning a high priority. Certainly this is shortsighted when one considers that people will spend a large portion of their lives in free time, and that this time is likely to be wasted if people learn to hate learning in school.

On the other hand, there is evidence that at least some students in some classroom situations find learning as enjoyable as any leisure activity can be (Csikszentmihalyi 1982, Csikszentmihalyi and Larson 1984). When the school is active and involving, and thereby flow-producing, it is doing its job—maximizing children's investment of attention in skills that will be important to their future and to the community. When the school succeeds in promoting the pursuit of greater intellectual and practical challenges, it helps the process of self-actualization. Children tend to report that the teachers who made the greatest impression on them were those who themselves experienced flow in teaching (Csikszentmihalyi 1986, Plihal 1982). Enjoyment of learning is contagious—unfortunately, we have not learned how to use this simple knowledge in our formal educational system.

Beyond intensely involving learning activities, schools could also offer opportunities for reflection, intellectual play, and exploration. These forms of leisure enhance the germination of new ideas that might lead to creativity and hence belong in the context of a truly "liberal" education (Green 1968). "Breaks" within a rigorous curriculum, if appropriately integrated, could become a source of enrichment for both individuals and the school at large.

Although it is tempting to imagine what a really leisurely, or scholastic, educational system might be like, we must also deal with the rather dismal reality of what forms of leisure currently exist in schools. Nancy King (1987) has identified three kinds of play that take place in schools: illicit, sanctioned, and real. Illicit play includes drug use and delinquency, as well as whispering, teasing, and joking in class. Sanctioned play is the set of formally organized extra-curricular activities. Real play includes socializing in hallways and the cafeteria during recess, and it is the closest to leisure as conceived here. Schools might contribute more to the self-actualization of children by finding ways of creatively expanding the time allotted to casual interaction among classmates in a stimulating environment than by resorting to evermore complicated teaching technologies and cognitive theories.

As to extracurricular activities, their instrumental purposes and institutional constraints tend to undermine any leisure experience they might provide (Kleiber and Roberts 1987). Student councils, sport teams, and newspaper production are sponsored by the school administration, and students often see them as work, a source of status rewards and college entrance credentials rather than an outgrowth of intrinsic interest. Nevertheless, students can choose them, and to the extent that they are structured to allow for self-direction and progressive mastery, they can promote flow and self-actualization.

Teenagers generally report that involvement in sports, games, art, music performance, and hobbies are the most demanding and most enjoyable activities in their lives, whether done in school or out of school (Csikszentmihalyi and Larson 1984). We might think of them as "transitional activities," because they offer the experience of freedom and intrinsic motivation within structured and highly skilled systems of participation, systems that require discipline and engage the adolescent in a culturally integrative world of symbols and knowledge. Such activities thus create a psychological bridge between the light-hearted play world of childhood and the adult world where disciplined commitment is required. To the extent that extracurricular activities are both enjoyable and demanding, they provide possibilities for self-actualization within the context of schools (Kleiber et al. 1986).

Leisure with Peers

Being with friends, or at least with peers, is generally the most positive experience for both young people and old. We feel most happy, cheerful, alert, sociable, and free not when we are alone; not when we are with our spouse, parents, and children; certainly not when we are with our boss or co-workers; but when we are in the company of friends (Larson et al. 1986). But being with friends is not necessarily self-actualizing. The emphasis on positive affect does not afford much in the way of accurate feedback. While the very best of friends can be honest and critical of each other, most casual friendships do not provoke the kind of dissonance that is challenging and growth-producing.

Adolescents, especially, get few "stop" messages from friends, thus amplifying the tendency towards deviant behavior. When with friends, adolescents are most likely to report feeling happy and excited, but also least likely to feel in control (Csikszentmihalyi and Larson 1984). Highly intense, expressive, innovative behavior might be playlike and enjoyable, and it may serve the individuation aspects of identity formation; but if it is out of control and destructive to oneself and to others, it undermines any flow experience that may be produced and is personally and socially disintegrative. By creating disorder between the goals of the self and the goals of others, it can be self-actualizing only in a limited and distorted sense.

Whether we like it or not, however, peers are going to play an enormous role in the life experience of most people. Relatively few persons learn to enjoy solitude, which is a prerequisite for the more complex stages of self-actualization. People generally dread being alone to such an extent that they never try meditation, close reflection, or intense aesthetic experience; thus they never taste the fruits of that vita contemplativa that thrives in solitude and that our ancestors believed to be one of the highest states human beings could achieve (the other being the vita activa of political involvement) (see Arendt 1959 and Pieper 1952). Instead, most people will gravitate to each other's company, hoping to find in mutual stimulation the rewards of living.

Therefore, any program that tries to enhance the benefits of leisure must keep in mind the fact that companionship is in itself one of the most rewarding dimensions of experience. Freely chosen peers are best, but as Sherif and Sherif (1964) have shown in their famous "Robbers' Cave" group experiments, it is relatively easy to create bonds even among strangers in a play setting, just by introducing competition between randomly assembled groups. If the ultimate goal is to encourage self-actualization rather than just provide opportunities for leisure, the program will have to take into account the power of peer relations to cause harm as well as good.

Leisure and the Community

The communities in which we live cry out to be designed better to facilitate self-actualizing leisure. It is true that most neighborhoods attempt to provide opportunities for the active involvement of children and adults—swimming pools, clubs, athletic associations, libraries, youth centers. Although even in an inner-city community, middle-school age children report participating in an average of six different organized activities (Littell and Wynn[1]), the frequency of such activities is likely to be rather low when compared with unsupervised peer interactions (Csikszentmihalyi and Larson 1984). Young people prefer to spend time where they can be in each others' company away from adult interference—malls, streets, empty lots, and parks are more likely to be the settings for youth leisure, and the content of it is more likely to involve destructive or alienating activities.

In *Tools for Conviviality*, Ivan Illich (1973) suggests that post-industrial society must find ways to place access to resources in the hands of those people who can most effectively use them. From short-wave radios to television transmitters, from control over the police to control of the schools, communities, rather than giant bureaucracies or anonymous multinational corporations, should be empowered to decide the allocation of common resources. All of us should be involved in deciding what opportunities for action our communities should have—what parks, libraries, learning centers; how much nature and beauty should be preserved. These considerations lead us back again to the ancient Greeks, for whom politics and leisure were just as inseparable as learning and leisure were (see Hemingway 1988). What should I do with my free time? Why, obviously, invest it in an activity that will develop your potential. And what should I do with my developing potential? Obviously, you should use it for the common good—to improve life in the community.

Politics has lost much of its lustre since the heyday of Athens. Most of us are ready to leave the reins of the community in the hands of real estate speculators, the owners of large construction firms, and other parties whose interest in the common good is usually very limited and self-serving. It is said that of the more than three million inhabitants of the city of Los Angeles, no more than a hundred lawyers and newsmen are more than vaguely aware of the policies being implemented in their City Hall (Didion 1989: 99). As long as most citizens ignore politics, thinking of it as a necessary evil, it will always remain an unsavory practice controlled by selfish interests. But if we take the shaping of the future of our communities as the great challenge it is, we shall discover that the Greeks knew what they were saying when they talked about politics as the highest form of leisure. The most satisfying way to actualize the self is by helping others do the same.

ENDNOTES

[1] Joan Littell and J. Wynn in unpublished manuscript on the availability and use of resources for middle-school age children in two communities, Chapin Hall Center for Children in Chicago, 1989.

LITERATURE CITED

Altmann, J. 1980. Baboon mothers and infants. Cambridge, MA: Harvard University Press.

Altmann, S. A.; Altmann, J. 1970. Baboon ecology: African field research. Chicago, IL: University of Chicago Press.

Arendt, H. 1959. The human condition. Chicago, IL: The University of Chicago Press.

Csikszentmihalyi, M. 1975. Beyond boredom and anxiety: the experience of play in work and games. San Francisco, CA: Jossey-Bass. 231 p.

Csikszentmihalyi, M. 1978. Attention and the holistic approach to behavior. In: Pope, K. S.; Singer, J. L., eds. The stream of consciousness. New York, NY: Plenum: 335-58.

Csikszentmihalyi, M. 1981. Leisure and socialization. Social Forces. 60: 332-40.

Csikszentmihalyi, M. 1982. Learning, flow and happiness. In: Gross, R., ed. Invitation to life-long learning. New York, NY: Fowlett: 167-87.

Csikszentmihalyi, M. 1986. L'insegnamento e la trasmissione dei memi. In: Massimini, F.; Inghilleri, P., eds. L'esperienza quotidiana. Milano: Angeli: 197-214.

Csikszentmihalyi, M.; Csikszentmihalyi, I., eds. 1988. Optimal experience: psychological studies of flow in consciousness. New York, NY: Cambridge University Press. 416 p.

Csikszentmihalyi, M.; Graef, R. 1980. The experience of freedom in daily life. American Journal of Community Psychology. 8: 401-14.

Csikszentmihalyi, M.; Kubey, R. 1981. Television and the rest of life. Public Opinion Quarterly. 45: 317-28.

Csikszentmihalyi, M.; Larson, R. 1978. Intrinsic rewards in school crime. Crime and Delinquency. 24: 322-35.

Csikszentmihalyi, M.; Larson, R. 1984. Being adolescent: conflict and growth in the teenage years. New York, NY: Basic Books. 332 p.

Csikszentmihalyi, M.; LeFevre, J. 1989. Optimal experience in work and leisure. Journal of Personality and Social Psychology. 56:815-22.

de Grazia, S. 1962. Of time, work, and leisure. New York, NY: Twentieth Century Fund. 548 p.

Delle Fave, A.; Massimini, F. 1988. Modernization and the changing context of flow in work and leisure. In: Csikszentmihalyi, M.; Csikszentmihalyi, I., eds. Optimal experience: psychological studies of flow in consciousness. New York, NY: Cambridge University Press: 193-213.

Didion, J. 1989. Letter from Los Angeles. The New Yorker. April 24: 88-99.

Eysenck, M. W. 1982. Attention and arousal. Berlin: Springer Verlag.

Gass, W. H. 1972. Fiction and the figures of life. New York, NY: Vintage.

Goodale, T.; Godbey, G. 1988. The evolution of leisure. State College, PA: Venture Publishing, Inc. 291 p.

Graef, R.; Csikszentmihalyi, M.; McManama Giannino, S. 1983. Measuring intrinsic motivation in everyday life. Leisure Studies. 2:155-168.

Green, T. 1968. Work, leisure, and the American school. New York, NY: Random House. 175 p.

Gunter, B. G.; Gunter, N. 1980. Leisure styles: a conceptual framework for modern leisure. Sociological Quarterly. 21: 361-74.

Hasher, L.; Zacks, R. T. 1979. Automatic and effortful processes in memory. Journal of Experimental Psychology. General, 108: 356-88.

Hemingway, J. 1988. Leisure and civility: reflections on Greek ideal. Leisure Sciences. 10: 179-81.

Huizinga, J. 1955. Homo ludens. Boston, MA: Beacon Press. 220 p.

Illich, I. 1973. Tools of conviviality. New York, NY: Harper Press. 135 p.

Iso-Ahola, S. 1980. Social psychology of leisure and recreation. Dubuque, IA: W. C. Brown. 436 p.

Kahneman, D. 1973. Attention and effort. Englewood Cliffs, NJ: Prentice-Hall.

Kelly, J. R. 1982. Leisure. Englewood Cliffs, NJ: Prentice-Hall. 426 p.

Kelly, J. R. 1987. Freedom to be: toward a new sociology of leisure. New York, NY: MacMillan. 248 p.

King, N. 1987. Elementary school play. In: Block, J.; King, N., eds. School play. New York, NY: Garland: 143-56.

Kleiber, D. 1985. Motivational reorientation and the resource of leisure. In: Kleiber, D.; Maehr, M., eds. Motivation and adulthood. Greenwich, CT: JAI Press: 217-50.

Kleiber, D.; Larson, R.; Csikszentmihalyi, M. 1986. The expense of leisure in adolescence. Journal of Leisure Research. 18(3): 169-176.

Kleiber, D.; Roberts, G. 1987. High school play. In: Block, J.; King, N., eds. School play. New York, NY: Garland: 193-218.

Kubey, R.; Csikszentmihalyi, M. 1990. Leisure and the benefits of television. New Brunswick, NJ: L. Erlbaum.

Larson, R.; Mannell, R.; Zuzanek, J. 1986. Daily well-being of older adults with family and friends. Psychology and Aging. 1(2): 176-126.

Lee, R. B. 1975. What hunters do for a living. In: Lee, R. B.; de Vore, I., eds. Man the hunter. Chicago, IL: Aldine: 30-48.

Linder, S. 1970. The harried leisure class. Irvington, NY: Columbia University Press. 182 p.

Maslow, A. 1968. Towards a psychology of being. New York, NY: Van Nostrand Reinhold. 240 p.

Maslow, A. 1970. Motivation and personality. New York, NY: Harper & Row. 369 p.

Neill, V. 1988. Lost in a book: the psychology of reading for pleasure. New Haven, CT: Yale University Press.

Neulinger, J. 1981. The psychology of leisure. Springfield, IL: C. C. Thomas. 302 p.

Pieper, J. 1952. Leisure: the basis of culture. New York, NY: The New American Library. 127 p.

Plihal, J. 1982. Intrinsic rewards in teaching. Chicago, IL: The University of Chicago. Ph.D. Dissertation.

Rathunde, K. 1988. Optimal experience and the family context. In: Csikszentmihalyi, M.; Csikszentmihalyi, I., eds. Optimal experience: psychological studies of flow in consciousness. New York, NY: Cambridge University Press: 342-63.

Rathunde, K. [In press]. The context of optimal experience: an exploratory study of the family. New Ideas in Psychology.

Robinson, J. 1981. How Americans use time. New York, NY: Praeger.

Sahlins, M. 1972. Stone age economics. Chicago, IL: Aldine.

Samdahl, D. 1987. The self and social freedom. Champaign, IL: The University of Illinois. 202 p. Ph.D. Dissertation.

Sato, I. 1988. Bosozoku: flow in Japanese motorcycle gangs. In: Csikszentmihalyi, M.; Csikszentmihalyi, I., eds. Optimal experience: psychological studies of flow in consciousness. New York, NY: Cambridge University Press: 92-117.

Sherif, M.; Sherif, C. 1964. Reference groups. Chicago, IL: Regnery.

Szalai, A., ed. 1972. The use of time. The Hague: Mounton.

Thompson, E. P. 1963. The making of the English working class. New York, NY: Vintage.

Tinsley, H.; Tinsley, D. 1986. A theory of the attributes, benefits, and causes of the leisure experience. Leisure Sciences. 8(1): 1-45.

Self-Identity Benefits of Leisure Activities

Lois M. Haggard
Survey Research Center
University of Utah
Salt Lake City, Utah

Daniel R. Williams
Department of Forestry
Virginia Polytechnic Institute and State University
Blacksburg, Virginia

The authors would like to thank Irwin Altman and Daniel Dustin for their helpful comments on an earlier draft of this chapter.

INTRODUCTION

We have been rather eclectic in our approach to the topic of specifying and measuring the self-identity benefits of leisure activities. We have drawn from such predictable fields as psychology and recreation, and also from some less predictable fields such as philosophy and popular literature. We proceed by first describing the current status of scientific research and theory on the self and identity affirmation from a social psychological point of view. According to this view, recreation activities embody distinct and measurable identity images. Recreationists select activities partially on the basis of the identity images symbolized by the activity. Affirmation of these identity images may be considered one of the outcomes and potential benefits of participation in a leisure activity.

In the latter sections, we remove ourselves from our roles as strictly neutral scientific observers, and examine some of the value judgments implied by self-affirmation theory and by the recreation and leisure field. Although self-affirmation is almost unequivocally considered good, recent research in the field of psychology indicates that not all the identities people seek to affirm are healthy and adaptive. Thus, not all the identity affirmation that occurs during leisure activities is necessarily good or healthy for the individual. This challenges the needs-satisfaction models of leisure and recreation which lend unconditional support to the self-serving needs of the individual. In light of these findings, we search for definition of an optimal state of self-affirmation in leisure and recreation. In doing so, we examine the meaning of leisure benefits in a broad sense, drawing on leisure scientists and philosophers. We also examine sociological and psychological literature that helps to place leisure identity affirmation in the context of this broad definition. The literature offers a view of identity and individuality that seeks a standard of "goodness" that transcends strictly individual desires. This view allows us, in a final section, to propose prescriptions for the leisure sciences regarding nurturance of the optimal state of self-affirmation in leisure activities.

The Self-Affirming Potential of Recreation Situations

It seems natural for leisure scientists to study self-esteem and the self-concept because recreation and leisure situations seem so powerful in their effect on the self-concept. One of the major reasons to suspect that recreation situations will be strong in their ability to provide self-affirmation is freedom of choice. Freedom of choice is a primary defining criterion in people's perceptions of leisure, that is, behavior that an individual performs freely is likely to be defined by the individual as leisure behavior (Driver and Tocher 1970, Roadburg 1983). There are two aspects of freely performed behaviors that promote self-affirmation: their greater influence on self-perceptions, and their ability to be "customized" to meet precise needs of the individual.

Freely performed behaviors influence one's self-perceptions more so than constrained behaviors. Early tests of cognitive dissonance (Linder et al. 1967) and self-perception theories (Bem 1972) manipulated freedom of choice and found that situations in which the subject had high freedom of choice were more likely to produce attitude change. This was because subjects perceived freely performed behaviors as representative of their selves. In a study of self-concept change, freedom of choice and self-presentations (positive or negative) were manipulated (Rhodewalt and Augustsdottir 1986). The researchers found that behavior of the no-choice subjects reinforced existing self-images (positive or negative), but only those subjects who perceived freedom of choice incorporated *new* identity images into their self-concepts.

In terms of the "custom fit" offered by leisure situations, freely performed behaviors allow the individual to construct with more control and precision those situations that will affirm the images he or she desires. Knopf (1987), Driver and Tocher (1970), and others suggest that recreation is an attempt to "restructure the environment" periodically to meet needs that are not met by everyday experience. According to this view, "everyday" environments are more restrictive than recreation environments, and the motivation for recreating (re-creating) results from a discrepancy between a desired state (recreation) and an actual (everyday) state. Thus, another benefit of freedom of choice lies in freedom from restrictions that inhibit achievement of some desired state, one aspect of which is expression of desired identity images.

The Self

Implicit in the social psychological formulation of the self-concept is that the self is multidimensional. Much of the clinical psychology and recreation and leisure literature focuses on a single dimension of the self, that of self-esteem, or the evaluative (good-bad) dimension. Current trends in the field of psychology emphasize cognitive processes and information structures. From the cognitive perspective, the old preoccupation with a unidimensional self-esteem seems overly simplistic. Instead, the self is viewed as a complex phenomenon composed of a structure of cognitive self-

images (such as self-as-mother, -naturalist, or -honest person); self-esteem (the affective or evaluative dimension); and, in a broader context, all the motivational aspects of the self (active processes that seek out and create opportunities for self-definition).

The cognitive dimension.—The cognitive dimension of our self-concept, or self-schema, is a sum of all the self-relevant information we have accumulated and selected to remember over our lifetimes. This includes current cognitions about our house, children, leisure activities, ancestors, reputation, etc., as well as memories of our experiences in the past and projections of ourselves into the future. These individual self-relevant cognitions are also known as identity images. As Swann (1987:1044) suggests, "a self-conception is analogous to a composite of all the frames in a motion picture film, whereas a self-image is analogous to a single frame in that film."

The affective dimension.—The affective dimension is commonly referred to as self-esteem and consists of self-evaluations, or how we feel about ourselves in general and in specific situations. It is not clear how affect is formed, how it is stored in memory, or how evaluations of specific self-images impact our overall self-esteem. Some researchers have suggested that self-esteem is a weighted sum of all our self-cognitions (weighted by positive or negative evaluations of each self-cognition) in an expectancy-value framework (Fishbein and Ajzen 1975). Others emphasize the active and dynamic influence of self-esteem on the formation of our self-cognitions. For instance, Swann and Pelham[1] found that individuals with low self-esteem preferred situations which offered negative feedback, such as relationships in which they were perceived unfavorably. By selecting situations that provided negative feedback, their repertoire of self-cognitions contained an over-representation of negative self-cognitions.

The motivational dimension.—The Swann and Pelham study[1] implies the existence of a motivational component of the self. The rich history of research on the self suggests that, over the course of human development, we experience significant motivation to understand ourselves, as well as to be understood more clearly by those around us. The motivational dimension of the self is a dynamic entity that organizes and activates cognitions and behaviors that allow specific self-definitions to be affirmed or denied in our everyday existences, thereby affording greater self-awareness and expression. Csikszentmihalyi and Rochberg-Halton (1981) observed that the motivational aspects of the self allow us to "cultivate" identities, as opposed to having our social and physical environments impose a given identity upon us (cf., Schlenker 1984, 1986;

Swann 1983, 1987; Tedeschi 1983). The motivational aspect is significant because it removes human development from the characterization of reaction to one's environment, toward a more proactive transaction with one's social and physical environments.

The Self-Affirmation Process

The three components of the self work together in a process of self-affirmation. As a cognitive process, the self selectively attends to, encodes, and retrieves information that is relevant to other self-cognitions stored in memory. The affective component further directs our attention toward aspects of ourselves that we highly value. As a motivational process, the self selects and creates situations that serve identity functions such as consistency, definition, and esteem. The self-affirmation process has been elaborated by Schlenker (1984) who proposes that individuals continuously strive to validate cognitive self-images which Schlenker terms "desired identity images." According to Schlenker, we do not typically seek to validate all images equally. Rather, we focus primarily on those images that are positive and desirable (as in self-enhancement theories of Jones 1975, and Jones and Pittmann 1982), as well as believable. Identity images are maintained through a process in which individuals operate on their social realities in order to create validating situations. Schlenker proposes that the identity maintenance process consists of the following mechanisms:

> 1) displays of the signs and symbols of their identities (e.g., style of dress, house furnishings); 2) selective performance of jobs or tasks that permit identities to be built and maintained, including one's selection of an occupation and hobbies; 3) selective affiliation with others whose appraisals are supportive; 4) interpersonal behaviors designed to shape others' responses; and 5) cognitive activities such as selective attention, recall, and interpretation of self-relevant information (Schlenker 1984: 99).

The second mechanism, "selective performance of jobs or tasks . . . including . . . hobbies," addresses recreation behavior directly. The other identity maintenance mechanisms, although not as direct, bear a clear resemblance to behaviors typical of recreation situations.

In summary, the self is a complex entity, consisting of an infinite number of cognitions or self-images, an affect or esteem component, and a motivational, or dynamic process that actively searches for and creates opportunities for self-definition. Kihlstrom and Cantor (1983: 35) cite evidence that the self-schema is "chronically activated in memory"

and that self-relevant information is encoded without conscious intent and outside of conscious awareness. Thus, the breadth and depth of influence of the self on our lives may be more significant than any of us consciously recognize.

AN EXAMINATION OF RECREATION IDENTITIES

Despite a rapidly growing literature in psychology, we know little about how important leisure is to self-affirmation. Therefore, to establish the context for our subsequent discussion, we will review briefly some of our research on leisure and self-affirmation.

To explore the self-affirmation process in recreation and leisure situations, Haggard (1989) examined the cognitive identity images related to eight recreation activities. The purpose of the study was to explore the potential for recreation activities to serve as symbols for participants' identities. That is, if participants of recreation activities define and express their identities through leisure activities, one should be able to characterize recreation activities on the basis of the identity images they symbolize. Furthermore, if recreation participants are "improving" their self-concepts through recreation participation, it is likely to be in the domains for which the recreation activities serve as symbols. Haggard and Williams[2] asked students registered in eight different university activity classes (volleyball, weight training, racquetball, backpacking, kayaking, outdoor cooking, folk guitar, and chess) to define the characteristics of participants in their activity in order to demonstrate that the eight activities embodied quantifiable identity images that may play a role in the self-affirmation process—the process of defining ourselves as individuals.

Study Methods

Participants

The study described here employed 168 students enrolled in university recreation and leisure activity courses. Each activity was represented by approximately 20 participants. Because it was suspected that experience level may interact with the meaning of the activity for the participant, beginning, intermediate, and advanced participants were recruited in each activity group. In most of the activity courses, participants had at least some prior experience with the activity. In the beginning level courses, students may not have had experience performing the activity per se, but had presumably anticipated the course, who would be there, what fellow participants in that activity would be like, and whether they wanted to be a member of that group. Thus, even beginning level participants would likely have formed cognitions with respect to their selected activity, and the personality characteristics of its participants.

Use of activity participants only.—It was important that respondents in the study be participants in the recreation activity. In a pilot study, respondents were not screened with respect to their participation in the activity. The difference between that group's responses and the study group's responses was interesting. The two sets of responses were quite similar in terms of denotative meaning, but the terms used by participants to describe members of their group were more positive in connotation than terms used by nonparticipants. For instance, nonparticipants described weight lifters as "vain" and "conceited," whereas participants described members of their group as "concerned with physical appearance." The evidence that participants view themselves (or members of their group) in positive terms is consistent with Schlenker's (1984) notion that individuals will select themselves into situations that validate desirable identity images. This evidence does not, however, allow for inferences as to the direction of causality. Weight trainers may view "concern with physical appearance" as a positive trait before selecting weight training as an activity for themselves, or they may initially view weight trainers as vain, but change the valence of this trait as their experience in the activity continues over time.

Freedom of choice/self-determination.—An important aspect of the participants in the study is that they selected themselves into the class. A validity check in a similar study with identical activity courses indicated that participants perceived their behavior to be self-determined. Fewer than 1% of the respondents in that study disagreed with the statement, "I am taking this class because I really want to."

Selection of Activities

The study employed a factorial design in the selection of the eight recreation activity groups. The two factors selected represent a priori dimensions on which activities were believed to differ. The first factor consisted of required physical exertion (high, low). Activities were assigned by the experimenter into the high or low exertion category. For the second factor, activities within each physical exertion group were selected to represent a range of "primitiveness" of recreation activity environments. To select activities on the basis of primitiveness, a group of 34 independent raters (undergraduate social psychology students) rated each of 25 recreation activities on a scale from 1 (urban) to 5 (primitive)

on the basis of the primitiveness of the environment in which the activity would most likely be performed. This yielded a design with three low exertion activities: chess, guitar, and outdoor cooking (low, medium, and high primitiveness, respectively); and three high physical exertion activities, in order from urban to primitive: weight training, volleyball, and kayaking. Racquetball and backpacking were added to the list to increase the number of activities.

Selection of Attributes

Attributes were generated using an open-ended instrument adapted from an instrument used by McGuire and Padawer-Singer (1976) in their research on the "spontaneous self-concept." This methodology was a reaction to McGuire's perception that too often in research on the self-concept, respondents had been required to respond to a limited and sometimes arbitrary set of researcher-supplied attributes. The open-ended instrument consisted of the following instructions:

> Please take five minutes to write down on this sheet all of the things you can think of about people who play volleyball in their spare time. You may use a single word, a couple of words, or a whole sentence, whichever you prefer, to report each thing as you think of it.

The instructions were followed by a request to, "Tell me what volleyball players (weight lifters, kayakers, etc.) are like," and 15 blank lines. Each group of activity participants responded to this questionnaire with respect to their selected activity only. This procedure yielded a total of over 1,200 individual responses for all groups combined.

Results

Analysis

Three different data reduction techniques were applied to the data: a card-sort technique yielded salient categories of activity participant attributes, or identity images; quantitative prototypicality ratings yielded a measure of prototypicality of a wide range of attributes for each activity; and multidimensional scaling techniques yielded attributes, or identity images, that were uniquely associated with each of the activities scaled. Each of these techniques will be discussed in turn.

Salient Attributes

Attributes supplied by each activity participant were those attributes that were salient to that person at the time they completed the open-ended instrument. In order to get a sense of what classes or categories of attributes were salient to members of each group, attributes for each activity were sorted by independent raters using a card-sort technique (see Haggard 1989 for a detailed description of this technique). This purged the list of obvious redundancies and identified slightly broader classes of salient attributes. The card-sort technique resulted in 106 activity-relevant attribute categories, each containing anywhere from 2 to 30 individual attributes. For instance, for backpackers, a category that emerged was labeled "adventurous." This category included attributes such as "adventurous," "like to explore," "risk-takers," and "excitement people." Each category (such as adventurous) was considered representative of an identity image for members of that recreation activity group. The salient attributes for each activity group are displayed in Table 1.

Prototypical Attributes

Approximately two weeks after initial contact, members of the original respondent groups were asked to quantify the attributes in terms of their perceptions of how prototypical (Cantor and Mischel 1979) each attribute was of members of their activity group. The attribute list rated by the respondents included the 106 salient attribute categories identified by the card-sort technique, as well as nine general self-esteem attributes (e.g., competent, proud, etc.). Attributes were rated on a scale from 0% to 100% (i.e., "The adjective on the left applies to what percent of all backpackers?"). All 115 attributes appeared on each questionnaire, and participants of a given activity were asked to make prototypicality judgments regarding only the activity in which they were participating (i.e., kayakers were not asked to decide what a prototypical chess player was like). Attributes that received high scores for being prototypical of members of their group are considered representative of identity images for which there is consensus among participants of that activity. In other words, many or most of the participants of that activity may be bolstering these identity images through participation in the activity. These prototypical identity images are displayed in Table 2. Attributes displayed are the 10 highest rated attributes for each activity group.

Unique Attributes

Identity images resulting from the prototypicality ratings tended to be similar for similar recreation activities (e.g., kayakers, backpackers, and outdoor cooking enthusiasts all rated "like scenic beauty" as being very prototypical of members of their group. A question that could be asked at this point is: "How are the activities different?" To isolate the unique identity images associated with each of the recreation activities, multidimensional scaling (MDS) was performed on the 8 recreation activities, using as input the prototypicality ratings of the 115 attributes.

The MDS plot that resulted (see Figure 1) indicates which activities provide similar identity images (activities that are close together) and which provide unique identity images (activities that are farther apart on the plot). From examination of the primary axes and relative position of the activities in Figure 1, it appears that the horizontal axis of the plot (dimension 1) is defined by primitiveness (or indoor versus outdoor). In fact, the configuration of activities along the horizontal axis is correlated $r=.86$ (6) with the original ratings supplied by the 35 independent raters used for original categorization of the activities. The vertical axis (dimension 2) appears to be defined by physical exertion (or physical versus cognitive/creative). This configuration along horizontal and vertical axes is not entirely surprising, as it merely validates the two a priori dimensions on which the activities were initially selected.

Using a process that employed discriminant analysis, matrix algebra, and correlation (described in greater detail in Haggard 1989), the primary axes were rotated eight separate times, once for each recreation activity. After each rotation, Pearson correlation was used to isolate the original attributes that defined each axis, thereby disclosing the unique attributes afforded by each activity. The results of this exercise appear in Table 3. Attributes that are displayed are those that received the 10 highest correlations with that activity dimension.

Discussion

According to the self-affirmation perspective, recreation activities may serve identity functions because they symbolize distinct identity images. The study identified the identity images associated with eight different recreation activities. Although it was a select group of respondents (about 20 participants per activity, registered for university activities courses), the findings were replicated (Haggard and Williams[3]) for a subset of identity images and activities with a different sample from the same population. Some identity

Table 1. Ten most salient attributes for eight recreationist groups; attributes most often reported by participants in open-ended instruments.

Weight Trainers	Kayakers	Backpackers	Volleyball Players
Health conscious	Enjoy water sports	Loves fresh air	Competitive
Concerned with physical appearance	Adventurous	Likes scenic beauty	Active
Athletic	Fun-loving	Adventurous	Sports-minded
Positive	Outdoorsy	Fun-loving	Energetic
Determined	Conservationist	Outdoorsy	Team player
Healthy	Thrill seeker	Nature lover	Coordinated
Physically fit	Independent	Needs a break from society	Healthy
Self-respecting	Social	Fun	Athletic
Dedicated	Playful	Independent	Physically fit
Ego-motivated	Athletic	Relaxed	Casual

Folk Guitarists	Racquetball Players	Chess Players	Outdoor Cooking Enthusiasts
Enjoy music	Competitive	Strategic	Outdoorsy
Easy going	Strategic	Intelligent	Nature lover
Creative	Energetic	Analytical	Like to cook
Patient	Health conscious	Logical	Adventurous
At peace with themselves	Agile	Able to concentrate	Like food
Introspective	Mentally quick	Competitive	Back to nature
Expressive	Fun	Problem solver	Fun-loving
Mellow	Positive	Math-minded	Fun
Talented	Physically fit	Quiet	Naturalist
Relaxed	Coordinated	Cerebral	Conservationist

Table 2. Attributes with ten highest mean prototypicality ratings for eight recreationist groups; Study participants reported that most (a high percentage of) activity participants possess these attributes.

Weight Trainers	Kayakers	Backpackers	Volleyball Players
Health conscious	Enjoys water	Loves fresh air	Competitive
Enjoy music	Likes scenic beauty	Likes scenic beauty	Active
Concerned with physical appearance	Adventurous	Active	Sports-minded
Competitive	Loves fresh air	Adventurous	Energetic
Loves fresh air	Active	Able	Team player
Perfectionist	Health conscious	Fun-loving	Coordinated
Self-reliant	Fun-loving	Outdoorsy	Health conscious
Athletic	Nature lover	Interesting	Playful
Proud	Outdoorsy	Nature lover	Healthy
Positive	Fun	Needs a break from society	Ego-motivated

Folk Guitarists	Racquetball Players	Chess Players	Outdoor Cooking Enthusiasts
Enjoy music	Competitive	Strategic	Likes scenic beauty
Easy going	Active	Intelligent	Independent
Creative	Able to concentrate	Analytical	Outdoorsy
At peace with themselves	Strategic	Logical	Needs a break from society
Introspective	Energetic	Able to concentrate	Nature lover
Enjoy scenic beauty	Athletic	Competitive	Active
Casual	Healthy	Problem solver	Health conscious
Expressive	Good problem solver	Determined	Enjoy cooking
Mellow	Competent	Math-minded	Adventurous
Determined	Playful	Mentally quick	Loves fresh air

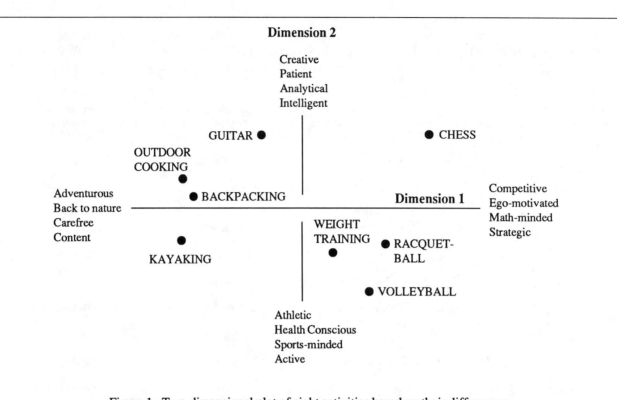

Figure 1. Two-dimensional plot of eight activities based on their differences
with respect to the prototype attributes they provide.

images may be relatively stable over time and across social and cultural groups, especially those identity images that inhere in the activity itself (such as "team-player" for volleyball and "logical" for chess). Other identity images will change as the focus shifts to other populations and as time and technology change the physical and/or social definitions of the activities. For instance, a prototypical bicycle rider of the 1950s may have been a freckle-faced teenager in tennis shoes on a bike equipped with wire baskets and handlebar streamers. The cyclist of today is an athlete with lycra shorts over bulging quadriceps on a bicycle with drop handlebars and a small cordura pack under the seat.

Three different types of attribution were offered by using three different methods to analyze the data. First, the top-of-the-head attributes, those initially supplied in the open-ended instrument, are the salient characteristics. Second, the attributes deemed characteristic of most activity participants are prototypical attributes, or those that are associated in a probabilistic way with the participants. These differ from the salient characteristics in that they are not necessarily the first characteristics that come to mind, instead they are the result of comparing and rating a large number of characteristics according to the likelihood that the

recreationist would possess them. Third, the attributes that resulted from correlation with the activity dimensions are attributes that are uniquely symbolized by that activity. In the case of some activities, such as backpacking and kayaking, the attributes are similar and often the same. This would indicate that the activities symbolize the same identity images, and may even be substitutable to some degree. Unique characteristics would be the focus in studies of the differences in identities symbolized by recreation activities. For instance, volleyball and racquetball would seem to be quite similar activities. Indeed, a comparison of the attributes associated with each recreationist group indicate that they do symbolize similar identities. However, according to our data, volleyball offers the athletic, health conscious, team player attributes as symbols; whereas racquetball offers the math-minded, able to concentrate, analytical and successful attributes. The two activities would seemingly attract two different types of individuals with different identity needs.

Of course, these data are preliminary. The study described above was not a critical experiment. Its purpose was demonstration of a concept: that recreation activities serve as symbols for identity images. It also described the content

Table 3. Attributes that most uniquely define each of eight recreationist groups.
These attributes correlated highly with each activity dimension on a multidimensional scaling of the activities.

Weight Trainers	Kayakers	Backpackers	Volleyball Players
Ego-motivated	Outdoorsy	Nature lover	Ego-motivated
Athletic	Fun-loving	Naturalist	Competitive
Competitive	Sociable	Outdoorsy	Concerned with physical appearance
Concerned with physical appearance	Loves fresh air	"Granola"	Sports-minded
Sports-minded	Naturalist	Likes scenic beauty	Proud
Team player	Nature lover	Fun-loving	Team player
Health conscious	Rugged	Adventurous	Athletic
Proud	Adventurous	Easy going	Strategic
Physically fit	Fun	Back to nature	Health conscious
Playful	Likes scenic beauty	Free	Energetic

Folk Guitarists	Racquetball Players	Chess Players	Outdoor Cooking Enthusiasts
Patient	Competitive	Analytical	Nature lover
Creative	Ego-motivated	Math-minded	Naturalist
Introspective	Strategic	Able to concentrate	Likes scenic beauty
Intelligent	Concerned with physical appearance	Quiet	"Granola"
Quiet	Proud	Strategic	Outdoorsy
Analytical	Math-minded	Cerebral	Back to nature
At peace with themselves	Able to concentrate	Logical	Easy going
Competent	Analytical	Competitive	Adventurous
Determined	Successful	Good problem solver	Fun-loving
Conservationist	Sports-minded	Mentally quick	Free

of the identity images, as opposed to continuing to refer to an abstract concept: volleyball symbolizes athleticism and health consciousness, chess symbolizes analytical and logical skills, etc. The study has served to fill a conceptual void between participation in recreation activities and some sort of "improvement" in the self-concept, the improved condition being reinforcement of certain facets of our identities and the definition of ourselves as individuals. The questions that remain include whether recreationists select themselves into activities on the basis of these attributes, whether the attri-butes or identity images are actually reinforced or acquired with continued participation and how quickly identity images change (cf., Williams et al. 1988), whether participants' perceptions of the activity change with continued participation, along with a number of other developmental and conceptual issues.

THE SELF-AFFIRMATION BENEFITS OF RECREATION AND LEISURE

To briefly summarize the information presented thus far, people strive to create identities for themselves. Leisure activities, primarily because they are unconstrained, may be particularly good vehicles for identity affirmation. People probably create given identities for themselves, partly by selecting themselves into given recreation activities which serve to bolster and/or furnish the identity images associated with that activity.

In terms of using affirmation as a model for describing benefits, an implicit value judgment is that self-affirmation is a goal of recreation behavior, and that achievement of this goal is unequivocally good. As Swann and Pelham[1] demonstrated, however, some individuals seek to affirm negative self-images.

Another issue that brings to light instances of seemingly "good" and "bad" self-affirmation is that of the two distinct motives for self-affirmation: believability and desirability. Schlenker (1984: 26) argues that the two are "coexisting components of all self-identifications." Although it is easy for most of us to see the advantages of holding desirable beliefs about oneself, not all individuals appear motivated by the desirability component. Swann (1983, 1987), as has already been mentioned, cites cases in which persons with negative self-views prefer self-consistent (negative) feedback to feedback that is esteem-enhancing. This view is quite provocative in that it suggests different levels of functioning with regard to the self- process. At the most functional level would be emotionally healthy individuals,

who seek to validate self-images that are both desirable and believable, as Schlenker (1984) suggests. At another level, less emotionally healthy individuals have fully functioning self-processes that are operating to validate dysfunctional self-images (e.g., "I couldn't succeed, even if I tried" or "I don't deserve anything better"). These individuals find the less desirable images more believable, and the believability component wins out. Our culture generally considers these individuals less healthy than those who achieve a balance between desirability and believability.

Other examples of phenomena in which self-affirmation takes on a decidedly negative cast may be found upon cursory examination of self-affirmation in recreation and leisure. Some recreationists display signs and symbols of a recreation activity that they do not actively participate in. There are the "lodge-sitters" at ski resorts who hang out in expensive ski clothing, but do not ski. There are "gearheads" who wear high-tech hiking boots around town, but do not hike. From the derogatory terms "lodge-sitter" and "gearhead" it is apparent that these individuals are not well thought of by at least some segments of society. As Schlenker (1986) suggests, there may be an implicit bias against behaviors motivated by public self-presentational behavior and status-seeking.

Another example of "bad" self-affirmation includes cases in which one individual harms another or the environment in his or her striving for self-identification. A case is cited by Sax (1980) in his description of an off-road motorcyclist who blares across a fragile desert ecosystem to affirm his sense of power and self-efficacy. Whether a person is excessively focused on public or private self-awareness; or he or she is seeking to validate unbelievable or undesirable self-images; or he or she is harming other people, the environment, or wildlife species; the above examples serve to demonstrate a single point: there seem to be gradations of goodness in the various manifestations of self-affirmation (cf., Dustin 1984).

The Implied Benefits of the Rec-Leisure Ethic

A brief review of some recent efforts to redirect the attention of the parks and recreation field to the merits of ethical and philosophical study of leisure may help to understand the question of the relative benefits of self-affirmation in leisure. While the benefits of play, recreation, and leisure have always been strongly rooted in moral philosophy, philosophical inquiry into the realm of leisure has seen renewed vigor of late (Dustin 1984, 1985; Hemingway 1986, 1988; Sylvester 1987). These same writers have noted a dearth of philosophical discussion of leisure functions, values, or benefits (particularly in the research journals), despite parks and recreation having origins in the progressive reforms of the early century (Duncan 1985). Still, with these reformist origins, the parks and recreation profession has never refrained from championing the virtues of leisure, recreation, and play. Popular arguments in support of the moral value of leisure have included Olmstead's statements about the value of nature and open space (Wellman 1987), the early efforts to "organize" playgrounds in cities as a way to promote more wholesome play for children (Duncan 1985), and the "wilderness cult" that saw wilderness recreation as a means to preserve the uniquely American character of individualism that was seen as instrumental to democratic government (Nash 1982).

In essence, the recreation movement has been built on a moral philosophy that sees leisure as "a therapeutic mode in society" (Hemingway 1987), and leisure service providers often see themselves as "serving others in their search for self-fulfillment" (Dustin 1984: 49). Consequently, much of the empirical literature is directed at documenting the therapeutic benefits of leisure—restoration for work, release of stress, creation of jobs, and a sense of freedom and identity. But to speak of leisure as a therapeutic mode in society makes leisure a derivative good, a good valued on the primacy of some other good (i.e., social harmony). According to Hemingway (1987: 7) "we in leisure studies...do our subject something of an injustice by continuing to discuss its importance in derivative terms. To do so places leisure, both logically and conceptually, in a derivative, subsidiary position."

While in Hemingway's view we fail to place sufficient intrinsic value on leisure, even the social value of leisure has been questioned by both students of leisure (Dustin 1984, Hemingway 1986, Sylvester 1987) and society (Lasch 1979, Linder 1970). At best, the value of leisure depends on the extent to which it serves the limited and negative function of "distracting us from our conditions rather than allowing us to engage ourselves with the world" (Hemingway 1986: 63). At its worst, mass leisure is seen as contributing to a sick society, one in which its members are alienated and isolated from others and themselves (Lasch 1979).

Many of these commentators have hinted that the difference between self-indulgence and self-fulfillment (potentially the difference between good and bad self-affirmation) has to do with the extent to which leisure does not drive one inward to avoid social conditions, but serves to draw attention to such conditions. For example, Hemingway (1988) suggests that even in addressing leisure as a spiritual condition, the leisure field has mistakenly focused on references to Aristotelian leisure as an inward (contemplative) process

rather than as the "development of civil character." According to Hemingway (1988: 82), Aristotelian leisure represented the central virtues of civility, "combining reflection and action with deeply rooted attachment to one's community." The specific function of leisure was the cultivation of civil character defined as the capacity for sharing existence. Such capacity requires that "autonomous individuals" be attentive toward people and open toward the truth so that people "are able to come together in pursuit of themselves and the world around them" (p. 183). The highest good in life, therefore, was an enduring quality of happiness that comes from a life spent in virtuous action. The shame of modern leisure, Hemingway laments, is that recreation, as immersion in amusement and as diversion from work and social ills, is misunderstood for leisure. "This leads us away from any true confrontation with ourselves, our lives, and our society" (p. 190).

While a growing number in the leisure field are beginning to question unbridled self-fulfillment (cf., Dustin 1984), stronger condemnations of leisure come from contemporary social critics who see our ego-centered striving for personal growth and self-expression as indications that we have taken the "Me Generation" search for self-fulfillment too far. One of the first to question the kind of individualism that is the companion to the leisure ethic was Philip Slater in his book *The Pursuit of Loneliness*. Slater (1970: 26) wrote:

> Individualism finds its roots in the attempt to deny the reality of human interdependence. One of the major goals of technology in America is to "free" us from the necessity of relating to, submitting to, depending upon, or controlling other people. Unfortunately, the more we have succeeded in doing this the more we have felt disconnected, bored, lonely, unprotected, unnecessary, and unsafe.

Christopher Lasch (1979) sees the trivialization of leisure more directly linked to the problem of individualism and the self-awareness movement. In his book *The Culture of Narcissism*, he describes "the culture of competitive individualism, which in its decadence has carried the logic of individualism to the extreme of war of all against all, the pursuit of happiness to the dead end of a narcissistic preoccupation with the self" (p. 21). Drawing on Huzinga's *Homo Ludens* he later indicts leisure and sport suggesting that "the masses now crave 'trivial recreation and crude sensationalism' and throw themselves into these pursuits with an intensity far beyond their intrinsic merit" (p. 186).

Yankelovich (1981), in a more optimistic treatment, sees the quest for self-fulfillment as reflecting a kind of "psychology of affluence." The "old rules" specifying social norms and roles and requiring self-sacrifice, have given way to a new license to explore the self. Clinging to the "presumption of ever-expanding affluence" Yankelovich notes "people unwittingly bring a set of flawed psychological premises to their search for self-fulfillment, in particular the premise that the self is a hierarchy of inner needs, and self-fulfillment an inner journey to discover these" (p. 8). What makes Yankelovich more hopeful is that he sees this search as a transition to a new "ethic of commitment" replacing the current self-indulgence ethic and its predecessor, the self-denial ethic, with the new ethic reflecting a more expressive as opposed to material definition of well-being.

At issue in all these criticisms is the extent to which modern society has lost the ability to provide meaning and direction to life and the role of leisure in restoring these qualities. Authors like Slater and Lasch make a strong case for the decline of what anthropologists call social solidarity (Redfield 1947) as they try to document the loss of true freedom in society, the growing alienation from work and social life, and the decline of meaning-giving institutions such as religion, family, and community. For these writers leisure remains to fill the void of meaning in modern society, but it may contribute as much to the problem as it resolves.

Leisure is supposed to provide a measure of control (and therefore improved self-esteem and perception of competence) in a society increasingly controlled by government, technology, and corporations. Leisure is supposed to provide a sense of involvement in an otherwise disorganized, secular, and individualistic world. However, if the search for identity through leisure results in an inward search for self-fulfillment, then the benefits of leisure may be to only distract us from the very conditions that give rise to the therapeutic need. Thus, leisure serves only the limited value of dulling our senses to the real conditions in society. Rather than being a therapeutic mode in society, leisure may be symptomatic, if not etiologic for the alienation and isolation in modern society.

For many, the extreme individualism that pervades our culture is seen as more directly responsible for these social ills than leisure (Bellah et al. 1985, Lasch 1979, Slater 1970). Leisure is implicated, however, because the freedom from constraining social roles and norms that leisure provides also promotes individualism. Nash (1982) makes the link when he suggests that the wilderness preservation movement was encouraged by the belief that democracy depended on individualism, the kind of individualism that the wilderness frontier inspired. Thus, wilderness recreation, the Boy Scout movement, and more recently "adventure programming" have their roots in the virtues of individualism and self-sufficiency.

A case could be made that the recreation profession is caught up in the "Me Generation" much like the rest of society. Dustin (1984) has prodded the leisure service professions to recognize that self-fulfillment is easily confused with self-indulgence, or as Yankelovich (1981) put it, that many self-fulfillment strategies are flawed. Dustin questions the "ethical propriety of the current professional practice" asking whether we are obliged to educate the public about such things. Sax (1980) raises similar questions with respect to the National Park Service policy of promoting intensive consumption or industrial tourism in place of "extensive experience." To what extent are the leisure service professions responsible for promoting these flawed strategies of self-fulfillment? Do we tacitly endorse them by simply reflecting the value orientations of society at large? What, for example, is the message of slogans along the lines of "Life. Be in it?"

As we have seen in the criticisms of Yankelovich, Lasch, and Slater, leisure is very often regarded as part of the problem, if not a symptom of it. The individualism that is often associated with the search for self-fulfillment through leisure may have undesirable consequences. Self-affirmation may get confused with self-indulgence. What concerns us here is that we want to avoid making the same grandiose claims about self-affirmation. We are still living in the "Me Generation." People are still inclined to see all the talk about self-fulfillment as a license to get theirs while the getting is good.

Beyond Self-Indulgence: The New Individualism

By questioning the benefits of a self-indulgent ethic in the leisure sciences, one must also question needs-satisfaction models of leisure. The problem, it seems, is that these models seldom step back from the self-serving needs of the individual to question the validity of the needs themselves. Authors such as Hemingway (1988), Dustin (1984), and Sylvester (1987) have begun to address some of the assumptions of needs-satisfaction models in the leisure profession. These authors observe that the values these models imply often seem to be in conflict with other values of society at large, and that perhaps the ethical dilemma emerges from an inattentiveness to the distinction between self-indulgence and self-fulfillment.

Relatively recent work on individualism may provide a key to distinguish self-indulgence from self-fulfillment. Self-affirmation can be interpreted as striving for individuation. It is the process of affirming what is "me" versus what is "not me." It gives us reassurance of who we are as individuals. As one looks at the attributes recreationists used to describe themselves in Tables 1 through 3, one notices that many of the attributes are quite individualistic in nature. Weight trainers describe themselves as "ego-motivated" and "self-reliant," and chess players describe themselves as "competitive." But not all attributes in recreationists' self-descriptions are individualistic. Some attributes are explicitly socially or community oriented (team player, sociable). Many other attributes exhibit an unmistakable communal character (playful, fun-loving, easy going, conservationist).

The current debate on individualism looks at both the individualistic and the communal side of our individual identities. It attempts to reconcile the discrepancy between the belief that individualism is a fundamental and beneficial quality of the American character and the apparent self-destructive and socially destructive effects of individualism and self-indulgence when they are taken to their extremes (Bellah et al. 1985, Lasch 1979, Sampson 1988, Spence 1985). Authors who point to the destructive power of individualism do not actually see individualism as "bad," but merely ambiguous (e.g., Spence 1985). At its best, individualism offers us internal locus of control, a competitive spirit, a reinforcement of freedom and achievement, and a clear differentiation between ourselves and others that endows us with natural rights as American citizens. At its worst, however, individualism leads us to participate in competitive achievement-striving behavior patterns that endanger our well-being and leads us to ignore communal aspects of our identities and shirk responsibility for our fellow humans, and in a broader sense, all aspects of our communities, including political involvement, and urban and natural environments.

Sampson (1988) offers us a new definition of individualism. Sampson's individualism promises freedom and achievement, but does not create the barriers between ourselves and others that lead to irresponsibility for fellow beings and the environment. He calls this form of individualism "ensembled individualism." Sampson's ensembled self is one who defines him or herself,

> . . . through relationship and connection . . . not . . . separate actors seeking somehow to mesh their behavior together, but rather from thoroughly interdependent actors whose very design for being includes working on behalf of larger interests (p.21).

One of the characteristics of the ensembled self is the tendency to define oneself "in relation to" groups, such as family, culture, and species. The ensembled self has a fluid self-other boundary that includes certain others in a given context. He or she also acknowledges that he or she will not always be in control and does not have to continuously strive

to control the environment. The antithesis of the ensembled self, the self-contained self, has a rigid self-other boundary that excludes all others (family, culture, and species, etc.). In addition, the self-contained individual strives to maintain a sense of control over the environment (in one case typified by the competitive and achievement-striving Type-A personality).

Sampson's ensembled self is not immersed in "Me Generation" self-indulgence. If the ensembled self acts morally, it is because she or he feels connected with others in the community, not separate from and in competition with others. Acting in ways that hurt other members of the community (neighborhood community, human community, community of living things, etc.) would result in a net loss to the community, and would thereby hurt the ensembled self because of its sense of connection to that community. The experience of the ensembled self is that of being a part of the community, and the community, in turn, defines the ensembled self.

Perhaps the most thorough recent work on the subject of commitment and sense of community comes from Robert Bellah et al. (1985) who referred to a sense of identity similar to Sampson's ensembled identity: "This alternative sense of identity in which the person is never wholly separate from others is clearest in the family. It is a context in which identity is formed in part through identifying with and incorporating aspects of other members" (p. 135). Bellah et al. make a convincing argument that commitment does not necessitate conformity. On the contrary, they see lack of commitment as strangely incompatible with conformism, explaining that "when one can no longer rely on tradition or authority, one inevitably looks to others for anxious confirmation of one's judgments" (p. 147-8). And they provide an insight into the dialectical relationship between the public and private selves:

> Perhaps the notion that private and public life are at odds is incorrect. Perhaps they are so deeply involved with each other that the impoverishment of one entails the impoverishment of the other . . . They are, instead, two halves of a whole, two poles of a paradox. They work together dialectically, helping to create and nurture one another (p.163).

Like the recreationists in our study who defined themselves using attributes such as "sociable" and "team players," it is possible to strive for individuality through commitment to one's community.

The view that individuality and community work together dialectically is important in grasping the meaning of the ensembled self. One could think of identity and community as different, mutually exclusive ends of a single continuum, but we believe this to be an inaccurate representation. Individualism exists in the context of the community, and likewise, community consists of freely behaving individuals. Altman and Gauvain (1981) suggest that identity/community as a dialectic is endowed with features of oppositional tension and a unified system. As opposing tensions, individuality and communality are in a dynamic relationship, "with one pole of the opposition dominating at one time, and the other dominating on other occasions, although neither completely or totally suppresses the other . . . [As elements of a unified system,] oppositional poles help define one another, and without such contrasts neither would have meaning" (Altman and Gauvain 1981: 285). It is in this sense of a dialectic that Bellah et al. (1985: 135) maintain that "community is not a collection of self-seeking individuals, . . . but a context within which personal identity is formed." According to Altman and Gauvain, another feature of a dialectic is that the relationships between opposites are dynamic, the relationship changing over time. "Sequential or cumulative changes involve the Hegelian idea of a thesis and antithesis being resolved in a synthesis that incorporates the opposites into a new phenomenon" (p. 286). In the case of identity/community, our self-definitions are constantly being reworked. Our identities change as we identify with different individuals, groups, activities, and communities. Communities change as their composition of individuals change and as the individuals seek new value structures to deal with changing roles, situations, and problems. What is the cultural synthesis that is emerging from the identity/community dialectic? What forces do these authors see shaping Western culture toward an optimal state of individuality/communality? Bellah et al. envision a social movement, a personal transformation among large numbers of people, a social ecology movement which links us to the conception of the common good. They recommend that the level of public discourse be raised so that the fundamental problems of self-contained individualism are addressed rather than obscured.

> Reducing the inordinate rewards of ambition and our inordinate fears of ending up as losers would offer a great change in the meaning of work in our society and all that would go with such a change. To make a real difference, such a shift in rewards would have to be a part of a reappropriation of the idea of vocation or calling, a return in a new way to the idea of work as a contribution to the good of all and not merely as a means to one's own advancement (Bellah et al. 1985: 287-8).

CONCLUSIONS

In specifying and measuring the self-identity benefits of leisure activities, we began by demonstrating that leisure activities symbolize identity images. These images may be seen as an outcome or product of participation in a leisure activity. Some authors (Swann 1983, 1987) suggest that individuals seek out situations (such as leisure activities) that serve to validate their preconceived notions of who they are. Other authors (Schlenker 1984) suggest that we select situations that move us toward desired views of ourselves. Although both views emerge from neutral positivistic approaches, they seem to imply that affirmation of our identities is desirable. Although there are a few exceptions (Swann and Pelham[1]), there is rarely a case made for the potential for gradations of goodness in identity affirmation.

The implicit values of the leisure professions, especially needs-satisfaction models in the professions, also tend to suggest that the appropriate focus is on the self-serving needs of the individual. According to at least some authors (e.g., Dustin 1984, Hemingway 1988), however, the problem with leisure identities today is the inward-focused, self-indulgent quality that is reinforced by such needs-satisfaction models. It is not that needs-satisfaction models are inappropriate altogether. It is that they are too narrow in their definition of needs, that is, focusing solely on the self-perceived desires of the individual and disregarding a basic facet of the human condition—that we do not always adequately perceive our own needs.

Converging on this dilemma are a number of social scientists who suggest that the solution may lie in a broadening of the definition of the self. These scientists suggest that we, as individuals, may better achieve self-fulfillment if we define ourselves as part of a community and in relation to aspects of that community. They suggest that it is through a sense of connection to the community, and commitment to our goals and callings that we may closer approximate self-fulfillment.

Yankelovich (1981) suggests that there already exists a social movement characterized by a hunger for deeper personal relationships and a growing conviction that a "me first, satisfy all my desires attitude leads to relationships that are superficial, transitory and ultimately unsatisfying" (p. 248). He supports a view that, at least to a point, social ills are self-correcting, because people feel good when they perceive that what they are doing is good for others as well as themselves.

McAvoy,[4] in response to increasing impacts on wildlife and the natural environment in general, has developed a five-point plan for the implementation of what he refers to as "an environmental ethic." He calls for the leisure profession to formulate a code of environmental ethics, including protection and preservation, respect for elements in nature, and the differentiation between activities on the basis of their moral goodness. His criteria for determining moral goodness is based on the benefits or detriments of an act to the "community of living things" (see also Dustin 1989). Another phase of McAvoy's solution is education about the implications of various recreation activities for the living community, and a sensitivity to and understanding of the natural environment and the responsibility of stewardship. He calls for science to assist in making a determination as to the amount of care needed for certain environments through understanding natural processes, and assessing environmental impacts and guidelines of practice. Some public relations work must also be done to procure a general acceptance of the ethic, as well as interventions and political advocacy. Finally, he suggests that we nurture our dreams of a better future, capture each individual's imagination, and inspire them to action.

As for a prescription for social scientists, we may more fully recognize their own roles as moral decisionmakers. Historically, the separation between science and ethics was not as strong. According to Bellah et al. (1985: 298), a nineteenth century college graduate was to be a "man of learning" who would have "an uplifting and unifying influence on society," and social scientists felt obliged to speak to the "major ethical questions of the society as a whole." E.F. Schumacher (1977) suggests there is currently an inappropriate overreliance on empiricism to address social problems. Not that empiricism itself is inappropriate, but that it is emphasized to the exclusion of philosophical and ethical issues. Bellah et al. (1985) concur and suggest that social science cannot be value free, especially when it addresses public philosophy. "To attempt to study the possibilities and limitations of society with utter neutrality, as though it existed on another planet, is to push the ethos of narrowly professional social science to the breaking point" (p. 286).

For the study of the self-identity benefits of leisure, there will always be uncertainty regarding good and bad self-affirmation, just as there will always be uncertainty about what is and is not leisure. This uncertainty comes from the nature of leisure itself. Sylvester reminds us that leisure is not a thing like a rock, but a concept borne in the mind. Because leisure is of human creation, researchers give it meaning rather than "discover" its nature. "Rather than initially examining *what is*, [researchers] are asserting what leisure *ought to be* for empirical purposes" (Sylvester 1987: 184).

As Sylvester (1987) argues, science and philosophy need to be more equal partners in the search for what is good. Social science cannot tell us what the benefits of leisure are

without first prescribing what leisure is. That prescription must be guided by sound philosophy, a process that has been neglected thus far in leisure science. Thus, researchers carry an important responsibility in how they give meaning to leisure, a responsibility that requires incorporating philosophy and ethics into leisure research. With such a prescription, social science can broaden our knowledge of our selves; knowledge which can bring wisdom to our ethical judgments. Only by integrating philosophy with social science will we be able to reduce the uncertainty that surrounds the meaning and value of leisure.

ENDNOTES

[1] William Swann and Brett Pelham in manuscript on embracing the bitter truths—positivity versus authenticity in social relationships, submitted for publication.

[2] Lois M. Haggard and Daniel R. Williams in paper on identity affirmation in resource recreation—a conceptual framework. University of Utah.

[3] Lois M. Haggard and Daniel R. Williams in paper on identity affirmation in resource recreation—an empirical investigation of desire for leisure identities. University of Utah.

[4] Leo McAvoy in paper on an environmental ethic for recreation and parks, presented at the Congress of the National Recreation and Park Association, Indianapolis, October 1988.

LITERATURE CITED

Altman, I.; Gauvain, M. 1981. A cross-cultural and dialectic analysis of homes. In: Liben, L.; Patterson, A.; Newcombe, N., eds. Spatial representation and behavior across the lifespan. New York, NY: Academic Press: 283-320.

Bellah, R. N.; Madsen, R.; Sullivan, W. M., et al. 1985. Habits of the heart: individualism and commitment in American life. Berkeley, CA: University of California Press. 298 p.

Bem, D. 1972. Self-perception theory. In: Berkowitz, L., ed. Advances in experimental social psychology. Vol. 6. New York, NY: Academic Press.

Cantor, N.; Mischel, W. 1979. Prototypes in person perception. In: Berkowitz, L., ed. Advances in experimental social psychology. Vol. 12. New York, NY: Academic Press.

Csikszentmihalyi, M.; Rochberg-Halton, E. 1981. The meaning of things: domestic symbols and the self. New York, NY: Cambridge University Press.

Driver, B. L.; Tocher, R. 1970. Toward a behavioral interpretation of recreation engagements with implications for planning. In: Driver, B. L., ed. Elements of outdoor recreation planning. Ann Arbor, MI: University Microfilms.

Duncan, M. 1985. Back to our radical roots. In: Goodale, T; Witt, P., eds. Recreation and leisure: issues in an era of change. State College, PA: Venture Publishing, Inc.: 407-415.

Dustin, D. L. 1984. Recreational limits in a world of ethics. Parks and Recreation. 19(3): 49-51,70.

Dustin, D. L. 1985. To feed or not feed the bears: the moral choices we make. Parks and Recreation. 20(10): 54-57,72.

Dustin, D. L. 1989. Recreation rightly understood. In: Goodale, T.; Witt, P., eds. Recreation and leisure: issues in an era of change, 3rd ed. State College, PA: Venture Publishing, Inc.

Fishbein, M.; Ajzen, I. 1975. Belief, attitude, intention, and behavior. Reading, MA: Addison-Wesley. 578 p.

Haggard, L. M. 1989. The "self" concept in recreation activity participation. Salt Lake City, UT: University of Utah. 81 p. Ph.D Dissertation.

Hemingway, J. L. 1986. The therapeutic in recreation: an alternative perspective. Therapeutic Recreation Journal. 20(2): 59-68.

Hemingway, J. L. 1987. Leisure studies in the university: an interdisciplinary approach. SPRE Annual on Education. 2(1): 29.

Hemingway, J. L. 1988. Leisure and civility: reflections on a Greek ideal. Leisure Sciences. 10(3): 179-191.

Jones, E. E. 1975. Ingratiation: a social psychological analysis. New York, NY: Irvington.

Jones, E. E.; Pittman, T. S. 1982. Toward a general theory on self-preservation: defined by attributions sought by actor.

In: Suls, J.; Greenwald, A. G., eds. Psychological perspectives on the self, Vol. 1. Hillsdale, NJ: Erlbaum: 231-262.

Kihlstrom, J.; Cantor, N. 1983. Mental representations of the self. In: Berkowitz, L., ed. Advances in experimental social psychology. Vol. 16. New York, NY: Academic Press: 1-47.

Knopf, R. 1987. Human behavior, cognition, and affect in the natural environment. In: Stokols, D.; Altman, I., eds. Handbook of environmental psychology. New York, NY: Wiley and Sons: 783-825.

Lasch, C. 1979. The culture of narcissism: American life in an age of diminishing expectations. New York, NY: W. W. Norton. 447 p.

Linder, D. E.; Cooper, J.; Jones, E. E. 1967. Decision freedom as a determinant of the role of incentive magnitude in attitude change. Journal of Personality and Social Psychology. 6: 245-254.

Linder, S. B. 1970. The harried leisure class. Irvington, NY: Columbia University Press. 182 p.

McGuire, W. J.; Padawer-Singer, A. 1976. Trait salience in the spontaneous self-concept. Journal of Personality and Social Psychology. 33: 743-754.

Nash, R. 1982. Wilderness and the American mind. 3rd ed. New Haven, CT: Yale University Press. 425 p.

Redfield, R. 1947. The folk society. American Journal of Sociology. 52(4): 293-308.

Roadburg, A. 1983. Freedom and enjoyment: disentangling perceived leisure. Journal of Leisure Research. 15: 15-26.

Rhodewalt, F.; Augustsdottir, S. 1986. The effects of self-presentation on the phenomenal self. Journal of Personality and Social Psychology. 50: 47-55.

Sampson, E. 1988. The debate on individualism: indigenous phychologies of the individual and their role in personal and societal functioning. American Psychologist. 43(1): 15-22.

Sax, J. L. 1980. Mountains without handrails: reflections on the national parks. Ann Arbor, MI: University of Michigan Press. 152 p.

Schlenker, B. R. 1984. Identities, identification, and relationships. In: Derlaga, V., ed. Communication, intimacy and close relationships. New York, NY: Academic Press: 71-104.

Schlenker, B. R. 1986. Self-identification: toward an integration of the private and public self. In: Baumeister, R. F., ed. Public self and private self. New York, NY: Springer-Verlag: 20-62.

Schumacher, E. F. 1977. A guide for the perplexed. New York, NY: Harper and Row. 147 p.

Slater, P. E. 1970. The pursuit of loneliness: American culture at the breaking point. Boston, MA: Beacon Press. 154 p.

Spence, J. 1985. Achievement American style: the rewards and costs of individualism. American Psychologist. 40(12): 1285-1295.

Swann, W. 1983. Self-verification: bringing social reality into harmony with the self. In: Suls, J.; Greenwald, A. G., eds. Psychological perspectives on the self. Vol. 2. Hillsdale, NJ: Erlbaum: 33-66.

Swann, W. 1987. Identity negotiation: where two roads meet. Journal of Personality and Social Psychology. 53: 1038-1051.

Sylvester, C. D. 1987. The ethics of play, leisure, and recreation in the twentieth century, 1900-1983. Leisure Sciences. 9(3): 173-188.

Tedeschi, J. T. 1983. In: Suls, J.; Greenwald, A., eds. Psychological perspectives on the self. Vol. 2. Hillsdale, NJ: Erlbaum.

Wellman, J. D. 1987. Wildland recreation policy. New York, NY: John Wiley. 284 p.

Williams, D. R.; Haggard, L. M.; Schreyer, R. 1988. The role of wilderness in human development. In: Wilderness Benchmark 1988: Proceedings of the National Wilderness Colloquium. USDA Forest Service, Southeastern Forest Experiment Station. Gen. Tech. Report SE-51.

Yankelovich, D. 1981. New rules: searching for self fulfillment in a world turned upside-down. New York, NY: Bantam Books. 280 p.

The Personal and Social Benefits of Sport and Physical Activity[1]

Leonard M. Wankel
Department of Recreation and Leisure Studies
University of Alberta
Edmonton, Alberta,
Canada

Bonnie G. Berger
Department of Physical Education
Brooklyn College of the City University of New York
Brooklyn, New York

The authors express their appreciation to Barry McPherson, Judy Sefton and Gary Smith for their valuable input and helpful comments on an earlier draft of this chapter.

Sport permeates all aspects of modern society. Its presence and influence are everywhere. Magnificent sport facilities dot the environment; runners, joggers, and walkers crowd park trails and suburban streets; sport headlines spill out of the sport sections onto the front pages of daily newspapers; annual sporting equipment sales total billions of dollars; assorted health and activity classes fill the program brochures of a variety of educational and recreational agencies; politicians eagerly seek out associations with sport figures and sport events thus affirming the political power of sport.

Despite its widespread recognition and considerable influence, sport has an elusive and often paradoxical quality which makes formal definition difficult. This is aptly illustrated by a quotation from America's leading popular sport magazine.

> Nobody has ever been able to say what sport is quite. But life would hardly be the same without it. Perhaps that's because sport means a number of opposite things. It means fact and it means fancy. It is as tangible as a golf club and as intangible as a dewy morning; exciting as a photo finish, serene as ebb tide. It is competition, composure, memory, anticipation. Sport is not all things to all people. But today it is something in more different ways to more people than it has ever been before. It is play for many and work for a few. It is what no one has to do and almost everyone wants to do. It represents, on the one hand challenges willingly accepted—and on the other, gambits willingly declined. Its colors are as bright as a cardinal's feathers; as soft as midnight on a mountain trail. It is as loud as a stadium at the climax of a World Series—and as quiet as snow. It is exercise and rest. It is man exuberant and man content... Sport is a wonderful world (Sports Illustrated 1981).

No single definition of sport has gained general acceptance. Rather, various definitions have been accepted by various authors to suit their particular purposes. Some definitions are very exclusive and specify a number of delimiting characteristics which exclude some activities frequently considered to be sport. Other more inclusive definitions specify few delimiting characteristics and include activities that are not generally considered to be sport (Kelly 1982). Despite this variability there is growing consensus that three elements are central to sport: competition—the striving to exceed the performance of others or one's own previous performance; physical prowess—the importance of physical skill developed through exertion and practice; and the presence of rules to provide structure and organization (Kelly 1982, Loy 1968, Snyder and Spreitzer 1989). Within public recreation agencies, a fourth defining element is commonly added, that being that sport is a component or subset of recreation. It is one type of leisure activity (cf., Alberta Recreation and Parks, Sport Development Policy 1983).

Within this chapter these four characteristics will be accepted as a general operational definition of sport. In applying this definition, however, the elements will be applied loosely with primary emphasis placed upon the physical activity and recreation dimensions. This will enable accommodation of the broadened perspective of sport reflected in the mass "sport for all" movement (Claeys 1985, McIntosh 1980), in which sport is defined as ... "free, spontaneous physical activity engaged in during leisure time to include sports proper and various other physical activities provided they demand some effort" (Council of Europe 1976: 2). It will, however, preclude extensive consideration of professional sport because it does not meet the recreation element of the definition.

In any serious attempt to evaluate the outcomes of sport involvement, one immediately encounters contrasting, and even contradictory claims. On one hand, critics have condemned modern sport for excessive violence, overemphasis on winning, and exploitation of individuals. On the other hand, sport proponents have extolled the contributions of sport to health, personal fulfillment, enjoyment, and community integration. These contrasting perspectives are read-ily apparent in the popular press as well as in more scholarly publications (cf., Martens 1978, Morgan and Goldston 1987, Smoll et al. 1988, Underwood 1980).

As numerous authors have observed (e.g., Csikszentmihalyi 1982, Martens 1976, Orlick 1975), it is futile to ask whether sport is good or bad. Sport, like anything, is not a priori good or bad but rather has the potential for producing both positive and negative outcomes. Hence, the salient question is ... "what conditions are necessary for sport to have beneficial outcomes?" To systematically assess the potentially positive outcomes of sport, and the conditions necessary for maximizing these outcomes, a theoretical model is essential. Csikszentmihalyi (1982) has proposed a model for this purpose.

The model (Figure 1) is based on the premise that four main types of consequences are of major importance when evaluating any sport activity. Two of these consequences are at the individual level: personal enjoyment and personal growth; while two are at the community level: social harmony/integration and social growth/change. In terms of this model, an ideal sport activity is one that contributes significantly to all four types of outcomes. Conversely, a sport is considered to be limited to the extent that it fails to contribute to the various desired outcomes. For example, a sport that is enjoyable but does not lead to personal growth, social

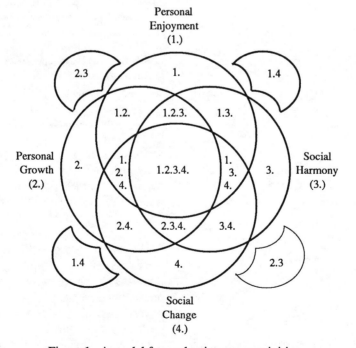

Figure 1. A model for evaluation sport activities.

Source: Csikszentmihalyi 1982:125.

harmony, or desirable social change (i.e., "1" in Fig. 1) is less desirable than one which is both enjoyable and leads to significant physical and psychological development (i.e., "1.2" in Fig. 1).

This four-component model will be used as the framework for our discussion of sport benefits. Specific benefits to be considered under each type of value are summarized in Table 1. Different dimensions within the overall sport experience (Table 2) are of varying importance to the realization of particular benefits.

PERSONAL ENJOYMENT

By delimiting our consideration of sport to recreational sport, we by definition are speaking of sport involvement which is freely chosen because of anticipated intrinsic rewards. Therefore, it is self-evident that such sport provides something akin to enjoyment for the participants. Otherwise, they would soon cease to participate. Indeed the argument that sport is fun, that large numbers enjoy it and thus participate, is a common justification for publicly sponsored sport programs. At the same time, this type of thinking has tended to prevent any systematic analysis of what fun is and what specifically leads to fun. In recent years, however, attempts have been made to go beyond such tacit acceptance to consider what factors influence the quality of the sport experience.

Studies indicate that fun or enjoyment is one of the most important reasons for participating in sport or physical activity. This is true for young people engaged in organized youth sport programs (Fry et al. 1981, Gill et al. 1983, Gould

et al. 1982, Sapp and Haubenstricker[2]) and for adults engaged in sport or physical activity (Canada Fitness Survey 1983; Miller Lite Report 1983; Palm 1978; Wankel 1985a, 1988). Limited evidence also indicates that enjoyment is related to future participation. Scanlan and Lewthwaite (1986), in a study of young competitive wrestlers, reported a correlation of .70 between enjoyment of the sport and intention to participate the next year.

With respect to outcome information, participants also generally indicate that they had fun while participating in sport. Wankel (1982) found that over 98% of boys (N=808) from the sports hockey, baseball, or soccer reported that they enjoyed playing their sport the past year. Similarly, over 96% of girls (N=896) participating in the sports softball, soccer, volleyball, basketball, and gymnastics reported that they liked playing their sport (Wankel 1983). Such results must be interpreted with caution however, for as in all recreation programs, a self-selection process occurs. The least satisfied individuals drop out. Hence, season-end reports on fun or enjoyment are somewhat biased.

Information collected during the season, however, also indicates generally high fun levels. Harris (1984: 381), in an ethnographic study of two youth baseball teams, concluded that "organized sport is fun for the players." In a season-long investigation of fun in the team sports soccer, hockey, and ringette, Wankel (1985b) reported average fun levels of 5.03 on a 7-point Likert scale.

Some progress has been made in delineating the nature of fun in sport and the factors facilitating it. Wankel and Sefton (1989) observed that, over a series of 10 games, level of reported fun (7-point Likert scale) was consistently related to positive affect as measured by semantic differential

Table 1. Types of benefits from sport.

I Personal Enjoyment	II Personal Growth	III Social Harmony	IV Social Change
Enjoyment/fun Flow	Physical health -cardiorespiratory -muscular strength -muscular endurance -flexibility -bone structure -weight management Psychological well-being -anxiety reduction -depression reduction	Socialization Intergroup relations Community integration	Educational attainment Social status Social mobility

Table 2.   Dimensions of sport.

I	II	III	IV	V	VI
Participant Dimension	Involvement Dimension	Activity Dimension	Social Dimension	Leadership Dimension	Motivational Dimension
Age	Participant	Training dimensions	Individual sport	Informal/spontaneous	Achievement/competitive
Sex	Spectator	-intensity	Dual sport	Formal/organized	Affiliation
Personality	Official	-duration	Team sport		Fitness/health
		-frequency			Relaxation
		Environmental demands			
		-open			
		-closed			

scales (mean r = .55). The authors concluded ... "clearly fun is a positive affective state associated with such feelings as happy, cheerful, and friendly as opposed to sad, irritable, and angry."

Several studies have identified factors important to fun or enjoyment. Wankel and Kreisel (1985a) utilized a Thurstonian paired-comparison procedure to scale the importance of 10 factors to youth enjoyment in the sports hockey, baseball, and soccer. Five items, which the authors interpreted as being intrinsic motivation factors—excitement of the sport, personal accomplishment, improving one's sport skills, testing one's skills against others, and just doing the skills—were most important to enjoyment. The social factors—being on a team and being with friends—were of secondary importance. Winning the game, getting rewards, and pleasing others—items which were classified as outcome-oriented or extrinsic motivation factors—were of least importance to enjoyment. This ordering of the factors was very consistent across the 7-8, 9-10, 11-12, and 13-14 age levels and the different sports soccer, baseball, and hockey. Similar results were obtained in a study of girls, ages 9 to 14 years, who participated in soccer, softball, basketball, volleyball, or gymnastics (Wankel 1983). Watson (1976, 1984) examined the sources of enjoyment of young Australian baseball participants. He found that intrinsic factors, those focusing on the excitement of game interaction and the achievement-oriented activities of skill acquisition and game competence, were more important than social factors and extrinsic (reward-oriented) factors.

Perception of one's ability or competence and self-reports of how well one performs have consistently been related to enjoyment. A study of the enjoyment of competitive wrestlers, ages 9 to 14 years (Scanlan and Lewthwaite 1986), indicated that perception of ability was positively related to enjoyment. Similarly, Brustad (1988) reported that a competence-like measure of intrinsic motivation was positively related to reported enjoyment in competitive youth basketball. "How well one played" consistently predicted fun in hockey/ringette across 10 games in the Wankel and Sefton (1989) study. In related research, demonstration of personal ability has been shown to be an important determinant of satisfaction in sport (Roberts and Duda 1984, Spink and Roberts 1980). While game outcome has been shown to affect fun or enjoyment, it has consistently been shown to be less important than personal success (Roberts and Duda 1984, Scanlan and Lewthwaite 1986, Spink and Roberts 1980, Wankel and Sefton 1989).

The importance of challenge to intrinsic motivation is emphasized in the "flow theory" of Csikszentmihalyi (1975; Csikszentmihalyi and Kleiber, this volume). Total immersion in an activity, the state of flow, most frequently results when one faces challenges appropriate to one's skills. Chalip et al. (1984) found that, regardless of the particular sport or level of organization, challenge was positively related to positive affect. Level of challenge experienced in a game was also a consistent predictor of reported fun in the Wankel and Sefton (1989) study.

Adults influence the enjoyment of youth sport participants. The enjoyment of wrestlers has been shown to be positively related to high adult satisfaction with performance, positive adult involvement and interactions, and low frequency of negative parental interactions (Scanlan and Lewthwaite 1986). In another study, parental pressure was negatively related to boys' and girls' enjoyment in basketball (Brustad 1988). With respect to leadership practices, athletes whose coaches gave high levels of positive reinforcement and support were found to like both the sport and their teammates more than did athletes from teams that were given less supportive and more punitive feedback (Smith and Smoll 1984). It is noteworthy that the athletes' perceptions of their coaches' behaviors were more important to their reactions than were the coaches actual objective behaviors.

Research on youth sport attrition has indicated that although many of those leaving a sport do so in order to participate in another activity, there are also a number who leave for more negative reasons (Gould 1987). Excessive pressure to win or to perform well is one frequently reported negative factor (Orlick 1974, Pooley,[3] Robertson 1982). Wankel and Kreisel[4] reported little overall consensus among youth sport participants on aspects reducing sport enjoyment. Some dislike factors, however, distinguished between athletes who intended to continue playing the sport the next year and those who did not. A factor analysis of 26 dislike items resulted in 6 factors. Five of these factors distinguished between those who intended to participate and those who did not. These factors pertained to lack of involvement, perceived lack of ability, too serious orientation with excessive emphasis on winning, dissatisfaction with one's coach and/or teammates, and aversive situations such as injury, razzing, or rule violations by opponents.

There is a paucity of research on adult enjoyment of organized sport. Snyder and Spreitzer (1979), however, included intrinsic interest as a key variable in their model of life-long sport involvement. Research supports the importance of enjoyment to continued involvement in physical activity (Heinzelmann and Bagley 1970, Wankel 1985a).

Measures of enjoyment have been restricted to self-report measures. Likert-type inventories (5- or 7-point scales) have been the preferred instruments (Brustad 1988, Scanlan and Lewthwaite 1986, Wankel and Sefton 1989). Although some researchers have employed simple one-item scales (Wankel and Sefton 1989), multi-item scales are recommended because of their greater reliability.

A Thurstone paired-comparison technique enables interval level scaling of different enjoyment factors (Wankel and Kreisel 1985a). Although this procedure produces a more precise measure than the Likert methodology, research indicates that the two techniques yield generally similar results for sport enjoyment (Wankel and Kreisel 1985b). Therefore, the additional time required for the Thurstone methodology may not be warranted. Semantic differential measures have been utilized successfully to assess mood states (Chalip et al. 1984, Csikszentmihalyi and Larson 1984, Kleiber et al. 1986, Wankel and Sefton 1989).

While many of the separate measures which have been employed to assess fun/enjoyment/satisfaction/positive affect can be criticized for questionable reliability and validity, the consistency of the accumulated results with these different measures is impressive. There is considerable convergence in the accumulated evidence regarding the importance of different factors affecting the youth sport experience. Perceived competence or ability, realistic task challenge, and a supportive environment are important to enjoyment.

There are a number of lines of promising research which warrant further study. The research of Csikszentmihalyi and associates in comparing adolescent experiences in sport to those in other life areas should be replicated and extended. It would be useful to investigate such comparisons for different age groups and for different individual variables. There is a particular need for more research on the experience of different adult populations in sport. Further research is needed on how different organizational structures, leadership practices, and other situational variables influence sport enjoyment. Research is also needed to identify how the various dimensions of activity (Table 2) affect enjoyment in various population groups. Finally, aside from research on aspects affecting fun, there is a need to investigate how separate enjoyment interludes relate to overall life satisfaction. How does fun affect overall happiness, mental health, and life satisfaction?

PERSONAL GROWTH

Personal growth includes a variety of individual factors. In this chapter, the effects of sport and physical activity involvement upon the individual will be considered in terms of two major aspects: physical health benefits and psychological benefits. Since both of these outcomes are examined in some detail in earlier chapters of this volume (cf., Froehlicher and Froehlicher; Paffenbarger, Hyde, and Dow; Hull), we will just summarize the major benefits and identify activity considerations for facilitating these benefits. Much of the research in this area pertains to systematic individual or group exercise programs. The motivation for involvement in these programs may be quite varied. In addition to the intrinsic, enjoyment-based orientation emphasized in the preceding section, the extrinsic motivation to gain various health benefits is of major importance.

Physical Health Benefits

Traditionally, health has been viewed as a dichotomous variable; an individual is either sick or healthy. This disease model of health (i.e., health is the absence of disease) is gradually being replaced, however, by a more complex model. According to this newer perspective, health is viewed as a continuum from extreme illness (near death) to optimal well-being. There is increasing evidence to indicate that involvement in physical activity is one important factor facilitating the development of positive health. As noted in Table 1, the type and extent of one's physical activity directly affects a wide spectrum of health indices: cardiorespiratory fitness, strength, endurance, flexibility, weight management, bone density, and even longevity (e.g., Froehlicher and Froehlicher, this volume; Paffenbarger et al. 1986; Sharkey 1984; Spirduso and Eckert 1989).

Cardiorespiratory Fitness

Cardiorespiratory fitness reflects the ability to take in, transport, and utilize oxygen. The heart, like any muscle, must be exercised to develop strength and efficiency. Beyond the effects on the heart itself, cardiorespiratory training increases the efficiency of the respiratory muscles, improves total lung capacity, increases pulmonary blood flow, reduces blood pressure and resting heart rate, and improves the high density lipid to low density lipid (HDL/LDL) ratio (Paffenbarger et al. 1986, Pollock et al. 1984, Sharkey 1984). See Froehlicher and Froehlicher in this volume for an indepth analysis of cardiovascular benefits.

The American College of Sports Medicine (1978) has suggested that, in order to maintain a desirable level of cardiorespiratory fitness, a person should exercise in his/her age-adjusted heart rate training zone for 15 to 60 minutes, 3 to 5 days a week. The necessary duration is dependent on the intensity of the activity. Optimal cardiovascular development requires exercising beyond an intensity threshold (a heart rate in the range of 130 beats per minute, Sharkey 1984); however, even low intensity exercise may result in decreased risk of coronary heart disease (Paffenbarger et al. 1986). Although age may influence the rate of change, evidence indicates that training at any age is associated with improved cardiorespiratory ability (Simons-Morton et al. 1987, Stamford 1988).

Muscular Strength

Muscular strength is the maximal force exerted in a single muscular contraction. While strength seems of little priority in everyday modern living, it takes on significance during emergency situations, vigorous sport, or under conditions of debilitating illness. Strength becomes of more general importance in an aging population because the age-related decline in strength can severely restrict activity. Hence, the maintenance of adequate strength is of increasing significance, given the current demographic trend toward an older population (McPherson 1986a, and this volume; Spirduso and Eckert 1989). Physical strength decreases with the age-related atrophy of skeletal musculature after 40 or 50 years of age (Buskirk and Segal 1989). At the present time, it is unclear whether decreased muscular activity causes the decline, whether the decline leads to less activity, or whether there is a combination of the two explanations (Spirduso 1986). Fortunately, the decline in physical strength can be modified substantially with exercise. Thus, exercise becomes increasingly important for the maintenance of muscular strength as a person ages. Much of the muscle frailty in the elderly can be prevented and/or decreased. With a well-designed strength training program, a sedentary adult can achieve a 50% increase in muscular strength within 6 months. This can be accelerated through more rigorous training (Sharkey 1984).

Muscular Endurance

Enhanced muscular endurance is also a direct result of sport and exercise programs. Muscular endurance, the ability to repeat a movement over and over, is more important than strength in executing everyday tasks. It is necessary for climbing stairs, carrying groceries, walking moderate to long distances, and for doing any number of routine or recreational activities. Endurance is very specific to each muscle group. Many people have considerable muscular endurance in their legs because of daily use patterns, but little in their arms. Muscular endurance is highly trainable and can be increased by as much as 100% in a relatively short period of time (Sharkey 1984). Greater muscular endurance leaves one less fatigued and with greater energy reserves to pursue a variety of leisure activities, thus contributing to the quality of life.

Flexibility

Flexibility, the range of motion through which a limb is able to move, is specific to each joint in the body (Sharkey 1984). Flexibility-increasing stretching exercises are important for all individuals, from elite athletes to people suffering from movement-limiting diseases such as arthritis. Since flexibility is lost through physical inactivity and is associated with the aging process, older members of the population need to participate in regular stretching exercises. Hatha yoga and rhythmic gymnastics are ideal flexibility-producing activities in which people of all ages can participate.

Bone Structure

Strong healthy bones are important to healthy, active living and are the direct result of active sport participation. Unfortunately, the skeletal structure has been taken for granted for too long. Only recently has attention been focused on the problems and causes of osteoporosis. Osteoporosis, the demineralization or decalcification of bone, most commonly affects the long bones of the body. Women are affected to a much greater extent than men. Lack of physical activity, along with low estrogen levels and calcium deficiency, has been identified as a contributor to osteoporosis (Smith et al. 1981, Stillman et al. 1986). In general, decalcification begins in women between the ages 30 to 35 years and in men between the ages 50 to 55 years. Once it begins, demineralization continues at a rate of approximately 1 to 3% per year in both women and men (Snow-Harter 1987). In women, however, the rate is amplified a further 6% after menopause due to the resulting hormonal changes (Smith and Gilligan 1986, Stillman et al. 1986).

Moderate programs of weight-bearing exercise seem to delay and possibly prevent demineralization for several decades. Jogging, running, and weight training are better than swimming or bicycling because they place greater stress on the long bones of the body. Since physically active individuals have stronger bones, the bone loss that eventually occurs is not as incapacitating. Calcium supplements and estrogen replacement therapy can help to *maintain* bone mass. In contrast, a joint approach of exercise and calcium supplements may help to *increase* bone density. As for all types of benefits, there is an optimal level of exercise. Too much exercise, as signaled by amenorrhea in women, can be deleterious to bone strength (Wells 1985).

Weight Management

Despite the increased awareness of basic nutritional concepts, individuals of all ages experience difficulty in maintaining a healthful and desirable body composition. Regular exercise combined with sensible eating habits is the most successful way to establish and maintain a healthful body composition.

Any type of exercise increases caloric expenditure and thus is conducive to weight loss. The amount of caloric expenditure is determined by the type, intensity, and duration of exercise. This may be illustrated by a simple example. A runner who runs a mile in 8 to 10 minutes consumes approximately 100 calories depending on body weight. A walker who walks for 30 minutes at a moderate 15-minute/mile pace consumes approximately 200 calories. Thus moderate exercise performed for a longer period of time can be more effective for weight loss than more intense exercise.

For weight loss, or more accurately loss of body fat, a combined program of exercise and caloric restriction is ideal. The exercise promotes loss of fat while preserving lean muscle and cellular fluids (Sharkey 1984). The loss of fat results in an improved appearance which is intrinsically rewarding. Exercise reduces fluid loss and decreases the daily weight fluctuations that plague many dieters. It also helps to maintain muscle tissue during weight loss and reduces the need for excessive caloric reduction and the resultant energy loss.

Combining exercise with caloric restriction has several additional advantages. A lowered caloric intake that is maintained longer than several weeks often results in a slower than usual metabolic rate and, thus, in a need for an even greater decrease in caloric intake. A vicious cycle then begins. The dieter reduces caloric intake, requires fewer calories than before, and then must eat even less to continue losing weight. Exercise prevents or reduces this "hibernation" effect (Webb 1986). Exercise also increases caloric output both during activity and for some time after exercise (Gaesser and Brooks 1984) and potentiates the thermic effect of food (Horton 1986). When exercising immediately before or after a meal, the increase in metabolic rate exceeds the sum of the increase in metabolic rates with exercise or eating alone—at least in lean individuals (Segal and Gutin 1983). In addition, moderate exercise does not seem to increase appetite (Dickson-Parnell and Zeichner 1985).

Summary

Physical activity relates to a number of physical health benefits. A variety of exercise and sporting activities provide opportunities for varying degrees and types of vigorous movement. The particular physical benefit obtained depends upon the specific activity and the state of the individual. Activities such as gymnastics, swimming, and calisthenics which involve a number of different types of movement of many large muscle groups make a greater overall physical health contribution than do more specialized sport activities. For optimal physiological training effects, quite precise activity specifications are available (American College of Sports Medicine 1986). However, when health benefits are distinguished from fitness benefits, it is apparent that even low intensity activity has considerable health benefits (Haskell et al. 1985, Paffenbarger and Hyde 1988). In this context, regular participation in a wide variety of physical activities contributes substantially to physical health.

Psychological Well-Being

Substantial research evidence supports the association of psychological well-being with regular involvement in physical activity (Berger and Hatfield, in press; Morgan and Goldston 1987; Sachs and Buffone 1984; Sacks and Sachs 1981). The exact nature of this relationship, however, is still unclear. Lack of agreement with respect to theoretical as well as operational definitions has resulted in disparate results and confused interpretations. Frequently, studies have not specified the type of activity sufficiently to enable precise classification of the dimensions of activity. Beyond those conceptual and definitional problems, a number of research design and methodological inadequacies have marred much of the research (Hughes 1984, Morgan and O'Connor 1988). Despite these limitations, progress has been made in clarifying the relationship of activity and well-being.

In the present discussion, emphasis will be placed upon identifying major considerations and key issues in facilitating psychological benefits of sport and physical activity. This consideration of psychological benefits will be restricted to two areas—anxiety and depression.

Anxiety and Tension Reduction

Anxiety, a general foreboding about some impending disaster that may be real, imaginary, or unknown, is a serious health hazard in North America. The 1-month prevalence rate for anxiety disorders in the U.S.A. is 7.3% of the general population (Landers 1989). Anxiety is generally differentiated into two types, state anxiety and trait anxiety (Spielberger 1987, Spielberger et al. 1970). State anxiety refers to a transitory condition associated with increased autonomic nervous system activity and subjective experiences of apprehension. It is associated with stress and the resulting threat and frustration. State anxiety varies across time according to the situation. Common symptoms include high levels of activation, tension, nervousness, worry, nausea, tiredness, and headaches. Trait anxiety, on the other hand, refers to an individual difference variable, a more permanent personality characteristic. It is the proneness to experience state anxiety in a variety of situations. Individuals high in trait anxiety tend to experience greater state anxiety in stressful situations than do individuals low in trait anxiety. Commonly used measures of anxiety in exercise research are the State-Trait Anxiety Inventory (Spielberger et al. 1970) for both trait and state anxiety and the Tension/Anxiety scale of the Profile of Mood States (McNair et al. 1971) for state anxiety.

Noncompetitive, aerobic, individual, rhythmic physical activity has repeatedly been associated with decreases in tension and state anxiety in normal populations. These populations, which are not unusually anxious to begin with, typically report feeling better after exercising (Bahrke and Morgan 1978; Berger 1984a, 1984b; Berger and Owen 1983, 1987; Boutcher and Landers 1988; Morgan 1987; Steptoe and Bolton 1988; Steptoe and Cox 1988; Wilson et al. 1981). Since the benefits in state anxiety are short-term rather than long-term, a regular physical activity program must be maintained for any sustained benefit.

Nevertheless, the benefits do seem to last longer than do those of other stress reduction techniques. Raglin and Morgan (1987) compared the influence of exercise and quiet rest on the state anxiety and blood pressure of normotensive men. Subjects were assessed before and immediately after 40 minutes of either quiet rest or involvement in a variety of physical activities. Follow-up state anxiety and blood pressure measures were also taken 20 minutes later, and at 1, 2, and 3 hours post-treatment. Results indicated that state anxiety was reduced immediately after the exercise, but not after the quiet rest. Exercisers also continued to report significant reductions in state anxiety as long as 3 hours later. For exercisers, the reductions in systolic blood pressure remained depressed for 3 hours; the diastolic reductions remained for 2 hours after exercise. On the other hand, blood pressure reductions returned to baseline 20 minutes after the quiet rest treatment.

Thayer (1987) also reported tension reduction benefits that lasted for several hours after exercise in a nonclinical population. He found that a 10-minute walk resulted in tension levels which were significantly below pre-test levels at 30, 60, and 120 minutes post-exercise. Significant decreases in tiredness and increases in energy also were reported 30 and 60 minutes after walking.

Highly stressed individuals and members of psychiatric populations have reported decreases in both state and trait anxiety after exercising (Brown 1987; Long 1983, 1985). In other words, highly anxious individuals tend to report both short- and long-term benefits from exercising. Illustrative of the nature of the long-term benefits, Long (1983) reported impressive results of exercise and stress-inoculation training for sedentary adults (24 to 65 years of age). Subjects were volunteers who responded to a newspaper announcement of a treatment program for adults who needed help in coping with stress. The participants' initial trait anxiety scores were similar to those reported for psychiatric patients. The exercisers reported significant reductions in state and trait anxiety after participating in a jogging program for 10 weeks. Furthermore, the exercisers reported continued benefits 3 months after completing the program (Long 1983). The participants still reported reduced anxiety and greater self-efficacy 15 months after completion of the jogging program (Long 1985). Long and Haney (1988a, 1988b) have reported similar long-term benefits for other high-stressed adults.

Exercise is frequently prescribed for the treatment of anxiety. Sixty percent of 1,750 physicians polled reported that they prescribed exercise for the management of anxiety (Ryan 1983). The types of exercise prescribed, in order of preference, were: walking, swimming, cycling, strength training, and running. Exercise has been shown to be as effective as other stress management techniques in reducing ongoing anxiety levels. More specifically, exercise has been reported to be as effective as the relaxation response (Berger et al. 1988), stress inoculation (Long 1983, 1985), and quiet rest (Bahrke and Morgan 1978, Raglin and Morgan 1987).

Typical of these studies, Berger and colleagues compared the psychological benefits of jogging, the relaxation response, a discussion group that included considerable group interaction and support, and a lecture-control situation (Berger et al. 1988). Three hundred and eighty-seven college students were randomly assigned to one of the four conditions for treatment over a 4-month period. Psychological stress was measured by the six subscales of the Profile of Mood States (POMS)(McNair et al. 1971): tension-anxiety, depression-dejection, anger-hostility, vigor-activity, fatigue-inertia, and confusion-bewilderment. As expected, jogging, the relaxation response, and the social support treatment groups were all more effective in reducing short-term psychological stress than was the lecture-control class. The finding that students in both the jogging and the relaxation

response treatment conditions reported significantly greater benefits than did those in the discussion group indicates that these treatment effects were in addition to any effects due to social interaction and camaraderie.

Information about considerations for selecting activities to have optimal anxiety reducing effects, as well as other desirable psychological consequences, will be discussed at the end of this section.

Depression Reduction

Depression, a heterogeneous group of depressive disorders, is characterized by generalized feelings of pessimism, despair, sadness, self-hate, and hopelessness (Klerman 1979). The ultimate behavioral expression of depression is suicide. Irritability, indecisiveness, fatigue, loss of appetite, and social withdrawal are less severe manifestations (Akiskal and McKinney 1975, Penfold 1981). Although anxiety and depressive disorder covary (Greist 1987), depression has replaced anxiety as the most common psychological complaint (Greist 1987, Klerman 1979). It is especially prevalent in women (Justice and McBee 1978, Penfold 1981).

Exercise has many advantages as a treatment modality for depression. It is effective, inexpensive, convenient, and has none of the somatic side effects of the tricyclic antidepressants. Approximately 80% of 1,750 physicians surveyed indicated that they prescribed exercise for the management of depression (Ryan 1983). Although somewhat less consistent, the research results of the relationship between exercise and depression parallel those previously reported for exercise and anxiety.

A number of researchers have reported involvement in activity to be associated with decreased depression in normal populations (Berger 1984a, 1987; Berger and Owen 1983, 1988; McCann and Holmes 1984; Sime 1987; Simons and Birkimer 1988). Other researchers, however, have reported no changes in depression for normal populations (Morgan 1983). It is likely that these disparate findings reflect some of the methodological differences and limitations noted earlier. With respect to the inadequacies of much of the research, Hughes (1984) reported that only 14% of 1,100 published articles in the area met his criteria established for scientific rigor.

The measure of depression that has been most successful when employed with nonclinical populations has been the depression subscale of the POMS. This measure reflects a state measure of mood rather than a stable personality characteristic. Although exercisers may not be especially depressed to begin with, as reflected by pre-exercise tension T-scores between 45 and 55 (50 is the mean), after exercise their scores are even lower (Berger and Owen 1983, 1988).

Long-term decreases in depression following exercise have been reported in a variety of depressed populations. Greist and colleagues (1979) reported that an exercise program of walking and jogging was as effective as two kinds of psychotherapy for depressed college students who sought treatment at a university counseling center. The students reported continued benefits as long as six months after treatment. Greist (1987) reported similar results in a second study comparing the effectiveness of jogging, Benson's relaxation response, and group psychotherapy in a group of depressed volunteers who were recruited through newspaper advertisements. Moderately depressed males (ages 26 to 53) who participated in aerobic exercise 4 times a week over 10 weeks reported significant decreases in depression as measured by the Beck Depression Inventory (Beck 1967) at 6 and 21 months following treatment (Sime 1987). Post-coronary patients with moderate depression have reported psychological benefits from exercise lasting as long as 4 years (Kavanagh et al. 1977). Hospitalized psychiatric populations also report decreases in depression after exercising (Bosscher,[5] Martinsen 1987, Martinsen et al. 1985).

Possible Underlying Mechanisms and Program Implications

Although exercise has been associated with both reduced anxiety levels and decreased depression, the underlying mechanisms mediating the relationships have not been determined. A variety of mediating mechanisms have been suggested. Some benefits might result from psychological processes such as distraction or time-out from daily stress, social interaction, feelings of accomplishment, and enhanced self-confidence and self-esteem (Bahrke and Morgan 1978; Long 1983, 1985). Physiological mechanisms, which may mediate psychological benefits, include elevated endorphin levels, increased body temperature, changes in respiratory patterns, increased blood flow and oxygenation to the central nervous system, and catecholamine changes (Sachs 1984, Sime 1987). For detailed reviews of these mechanisms see Berger and Hatfield (in press) and Morgan and O'Connor (1988). These suggested mechanisms have implications for designing activity programs for mental health benefits.

A psychological explanation for mental health benefits of exercise places emphasis on the attitude or state of mind of the individual during the activity. Enjoyment of the activity and escape or time-out from on-going life stress are important. As previously discussed, enjoyment or fun is an individual perception highly related to perceived competence and activity preference. Individual preferences may relate to activity type (e.g., jogging, cross-country skiing,

biking), activity intensity level, environmental conditions, competition, and individual versus group format (Berger and Owen 1988, Heinzelmann and Bagley 1970, Wankel 1985a).

Several researchers have reported positive psychological effects of activity programs even when the activity level was not sufficient to produce an aerobic training effect (Berger and Owen[6] 1988, Brown and Siegel 1988, Steptoe and Cox 1988, Thayer 1987). In one study, Hatha yoga participants who focused on a variety of stretching postures and on rhythmical, diaphragmatic breathing reported significant short-term reductions in tension, depression, anxiety, and confusion (Berger and Owen[6] 1988). Hatha yoga results in few, if any, aerobic training benefits. In another study, Brown and Siegel (1988) reported that exercise, regardless of its aerobic qualities, was an effective buffer against the negative health impact of stress. In addition, some evidence indicates that too intense exercise can negate the psychological benefits associated with activity (Berger and Owen[7] 1988, Morgan et al. 1988, Steptoe and Bolton 1988, Steptoe and Cox 1988). Evidence also indicates that, apart from the activity itself, aversive environments can undermine psychological benefits of activity. Berger and Owen (1986) reported no psychological benefits of activity when the physical environment was extremely hot. A number of authors have emphasized that a competitive orientation can be counterproductive (Hackfort and Spielberger 1989, Morgan et al. 1988). High pressure "win at all costs" organized competitions, whatever the activity, should be avoided if stress is to be reduced.

Some research attention has been addressed to the type of thought occurring during physical activity. Associative thinking refers to thought processes focusing on the individual and his/her engagement in the task at hand. Dissociative thinking, on the other hand, refers to thought processes focused on objects external to the participant's body and its engagement in the ongoing activity. Each type of thinking has advantages for certain situations. Dissociative thinking, taking one's thoughts away from oneself and his/her problems, may yield stress relief and facilitate persistence (Pennebaker and Lightner 1980). This may be particularly useful for beginning exercisers who still are uncomfortable with the physical sensations of exertion. Associative thinking pertaining to the task and one's involvement in it tends to be advantageous for better performance in elite-level distance running (Morgan and Pollock 1977).

Task demands also appear to influence the psychological benefits of physical activity. Closed skills, those performed with little reference to the environment (e.g., jogging, swimming), can afford greater opportunities for creative, reflective thinking (Berger and Mackenzie 1980, Glasser

1976, Sheehan 1988, Strauss 1986). Open skill activities such as tennis, baseball, and squash require greater external attentional demands. Engagement in such activities may (Cliff 1981) or may not (Weinberg et al. 1988) result in psychological benefits. Additional research is required to specify the particular activity and individual considerations essential to psychological explanations for improved physical activity benefits.

As with the psychological explanations, there is a lack of clarity concerning the physiological mechanisms which may mediate beneficial psychological effects of activity (Morgan and O'Connor 1988). For any physiologically based model it would appear that the basic dimensions of activity (intensity, duration, frequency, type) would be relevant considerations. Aerobic exercise (e.g., running, swimming) is the activity type which has most commonly been shown to produce psychological benefits (Berger et al. 1988; Berger and Owen 1983, 1987; Boutcher and Landers 1988; Long 1983, 1985; Long and Haney 1988a, 1988b; Raglin and Morgan 1987).

Adequate intensity is required to produce a physiological training effect; as previously indicated, however, too much intensity may undermine enjoyment and its positive psychological effect. Although further research is required to identify more precise guidelines for the optimal intensity level, Boutcher and Landers (1988) reported reduced anxiety levels to be associated with exercise (running) at 80% of maximal heart rate for 20 minutes in trained subjects. Well-conditioned individuals who had run at least 30 miles per week for the last 2 years reported significant decreases in anxiety (POMS). In contrast, nonrunners reported no decreases after the high intensity exercise. Too frequent, high intensity training is contraindicated for enhancing psychological well-being. Overtraining over a 10-day period resulted in increased anger, depression, and fatigue in a group of collegiate swimmers (Morgan et al. 1988). At the present time, it seems that moderate intensity exercise is most likely to be associated with favorable mood alteration.

With respect to exercise duration, some researchers have reported psychological benefits from as little as 8 to 30 minutes of exercise (Berger 1986; Berger et al. 1988; Berger and Owen 1983, 1988; Boutcher and Landers 1988; Steptoe and Bolton 1988; Steptoe and Cox 1988). Results of other research studies suggest that increasing the duration from 30 to 45 to 60 minutes may result in greater psychological benefits (Carmack and Martens 1979, Glasser 1976, Mandell 1979).

In summary, although some very tentative guidelines are available for establishing physical activity programs for psychological benefits, much more research is needed. Information concerning exercise intensity, duration, and

frequency would be of particular value. Certainly, much more controlled systematic research is needed before any clarity will be established as to underlying mechanisms mediating such effects (Morgan and O'Connor 1988). In the ensuing sections attention will be turned from the individual benefits of sport to the social benefits.

SOCIAL OUTCOMES OF SPORT[8]

Any consideration of socialization and social integration must be framed within the contrasting perspectives of social stability/harmony and social change. Successful adaptation within any social system requires assimilation of the requisite norms and values. At the same time, because systems are imperfect and inequities exist, change is desirable. The relationship between different social groups constitutes one important aspect of stability and change within a society. An ever present issue is to what extent these groups, be they based on religion, gender, age, ethnicity, socio-economic status, or a particular interest, are to be assimilated or allowed to maintain their separate identity and diversity. Although different countries have adopted different official approaches which vary in emphasis (e.g., the Canadian cultural mosaic versus the American melting pot), all positions reflect some balancing on the continuum between uniformity and diversity. Further, at any given time the emphasis may shift one way or the other on the continuum. Extreme positions are not generally considered desirable. With respect to intergroup relations, cooperation and sharing for mutual and shared benefit are deemed preferable to intergroup hostility and destructive behaviors. Such intergroup harmony, however, should not come at the expense of a disadvantaged group. Demands for social change increase when systematic inequities are considered unjustified. The following two sections will address the relation of sport to the contrasting perspectives of social harmony and social change.

SOCIAL INTEGRATION

Sport can serve as a vehicle for the transmission of knowledge, values, and norms. The specific values conveyed may be those of the dominant society or conversely those of a divergent subgroup. Hence, sport might contribute either to differentiation and stratification or to integration in the overall society. Socialization is a dynamic two-way process. Not only are minorities socialized into dominant structures, but they also change the exisitng structure. Thus, while minortiy groups (e.g., European hockey players) play the dominant form of activity in the society (North American hockey), they also introduce changes into that sport (e.g., greater emphasis on speed and finesse rather than strength and intimidation).

A number of authors (Allison and Luschen 1973, Axthelm 1970, Boersma 1979, Cleaver 1976, Guttman 1978) have described the adaptation of various sports to suit the values of specific cultures. Although the same sport may be played, it is played in different ways, with different emphases, adaptations and meanings to reflect the particular culture of the players.

From a social stratification perspective, evidence indicates that different sports appeal to different socioeconomic classes and reinforce differences. Participation rates in different sports reflect class differences (Greendorfer 1978, Loy 1972, Luschen 1969). Renson[9] indicates how the sports played by different classes serve as symbols of status and function, thus contributing to stratification in Belgian society.

Sport may also serve to transmit general values. According to Snyder and Spreitzer ... "a common justification for sport in schools is that participation in sport serves to transmit the values of the larger society. In other words, the youngster is ostensibly learning not only to play a specific sport but to 'play the game of life'" (1989: 44-45). Snyder (1972) studied the values conveyed through the dressing room slogans of high school coaches. In general, the slogans imbued values pertaining to the importance of commitment, self-discipline and hard work, loyalty and devotion to the team, and winning.

Edwards (1973) investigated the "American Sports Creed" as reflected in journal and newspaper writings on sport. He concluded that the central value orientation of American sport was "individual achievement through competition" (1973:334). He further identified seven central themes as constituting the "Creed": character, discipline, competition, physical fitness, mental fitness, religiosity, and nationalism.

Similar types of values were identified in a descriptive study of quotations from coaches printed in the media guides of collegiate and professional athletic organizations (Snyder and Spreitzer 1989). Similarly, Nixon (1979), in a study of 525 college students, found that four of Edwards' values were strongly supported. Ninety-five percent of the respondents agreed that sport develops self-discipline, 87% agreed that athletes enjoy better health, 85% agreed that sport builds character and citizenship, while 81% agreed that sport develops leadership qualities. Only 23% of the respondents thought that sport had value as preparation for life, and only 15% thought sport fostered belief in God and country. Fine

(1987) also noted that the values emphasized in the context of Little League Baseball were generally consistent with those identified by Edwards. He noted four basic value themes: the importance of effort; sportsmanship; the value of teamwork; and the manner of handling or accepting winning and losing.

Spreitzer and Snyder (1975), in a study of 500 respondents in a midwestern U.S.A. metropolitan area, found that most people thought that sport had positive value for society as well as for the individual. Nearly 90% of the respondents considered sport to be valuable in teaching self-discipline, 80% felt that sport promoted the development of fair play, and 70% thought that it fostered authority and good citizenship. Males and females expressed similar views about the values of sport.

Despite the apparent widespread belief in the socializing value of sports, substantive evidence to support these beliefs is lacking. A number of reviewers of the research literature have concluded that there is little evidence to indicate that sport involvement produces desirable personality or character development, moral development, or social values (Loy and Ingham 1973; McPherson 1986b, chapter 2; McPherson et al. 1989; Stevenson 1975, 1985).

Research on the relationship of athletic involvement and delinquency rates has generally indicated a negative association (Donnelly 1981, Hastad et al. 1984, Purdy and Richard 1983, Segrave 1983). The relationship has been found to be strongest for elementary and high school athletes of lower socioeconomic class. This statistical association, however, does not imply that sport causes a decrease in delinquency. A variety of factors other than the positive influence of sport may account for this relationship (Segrave 1983, Segrave and Hastad 1984). A lack of longitudinal studies precludes elimination of such alternate explanations as a selection of less delinquent individuals into sport or elimination of the delinquent-prone from sport prior to study by researchers. Further, it is questionable if this relationship holds for older age groups, especially in view of the considerable recent publicity given to rule violations, cheating, drug abuse, and violence by college and professional athletes.

Aggression has become more endemic in sport as greater emphasis has been placed on the importance of winning. Assaultive acts have become more common-place in many team sports, especially hockey, and have been related to a variety of instrumental and expressive functions (Bredemeier 1985; Colburn 1985, 1986; Goldstein 1983; Vaz 1977; Widmeyer 1984). Bredemeier and Shields (1987) report that sport involvement is associated with a lower level of moral reasoning. College basketball players were more egocentric in their moral reasoning than were nonathletes.

Youthful participants in contact sports at a summer camp were also more egocentric than were participants in other sports.

The reality of sport might not reflect people's wishes. Larson et al. (1975) found that parents' perceptions of current emphases within a youth hockey league differed from their expressed preferences. The parents felt that winning and learning to compete were emphasized more than desirable. They felt that more emphasis should be placed upon developing skills, learning sportsmanship, and having fun. An extensive study of parent attitudes toward the conduct of hockey programs in Ontario indicated considerable dissatisfaction (McPherson and Davidson 1980). Much of the criticism of nondesirable practices in youth sport or the questioning of coaching practices is not directed at the official or intended objectives or values, but rather at some of the nonofficial emphases. That is, many coaches and other adults emphasize, or are perceived to emphasize, values different from those espoused in official league constitutions. This discrepancy has been at least partially responsible for the development of a number of coaching leadership programs to improve the quality of leadership in youth sports (Wiggens 1987).

Limited research has been conducted on the effects of sport participation upon intra- and intergroup relations. Meyers (1962) organized 180 Regular Officers Training Corps students into 60 3-man teams and studied their reactions to involvement in a recreational rifle tournament over several weeks. The effects of competition and level of success on esteem for teammates were observed, perceived acceptance of self by teammates, and perceptions of where blame should be placed for poor team performance. Competitive teams improved more on self-esteem than did noncompetitive teams, and successful teams improved on self-esteem while unsuccessful teams deteriorated. Level of success influenced the effect of competition with successful competitive teams reporting more favorable relationships between teammates. Contrary to predictions, low success competitive teams had better adjustment scores than low success noncompetitive teams. The finding that team success is positively related to internal team dynamics is supported by research in the area of group/team cohesion. Martens and Peterson (1971) found that team cohesion on intramural basketball teams was positively related to both team success and satisfaction. The authors suggest a circular relationship between the variables with cohesion increasing success, success increasing satisfaction, and satisfaction increasing cohesion.

The early Robbers Cave Study of Sherif and associates (1961) remains the most definitive study available on the potential of sport involvement to alter intra- and interteam relations. By randomly assigning boys at a summer camp to competing teams and through a series of intergroup competitions and a competitive-based reward system, the investigators demonstrated the potential of intergroup competition to markedly affect friendship structures and interpersonal relations. Intragroup relations were strengthened while relations between members of competing teams became strained and even hostile. Subsequent introduction of external threats and superordinate goals (e.g., the need for all groups to cooperate to deal with a breakdown in the water system and a shortage of food) resulted in cooperation and improved interpersonal relations.

General research on group identification and in-group and out-group behaviour (Tajfel 1978) indicates that even involvement in very short-standing groups with minimal social interaction can have important influences on how individuals act toward each other. With more extended involvement and greater stakes involved, such as in many sport competitions, it is likely that these effects are increased dramatically.

Examples are readily apparent from sport where the composition of sport teams influence individual and group relations. One prominent example is when bitter rivals from competing NHL teams suddenly become teammates on a national team to compete in an international hockey series. At the community level, friendship groups can frequently be seen to shift as a result of boys/girls selecting or being selected for different sport teams.

No simple generalization can be drawn concerning the effects of sports on group harmony. On the basis of the existing research, it is likely that sharing experiences and working together under conditions of competitive stress will draw teammates closer. It is not unusual, however, to find strong rivalries and even hostilities between teammates. Although this is definitely the exception rather than the rule, a number of successful teams (e.g., New York Yankees and Oakland Athletics championship baseball teams and Oakland Raiders championship football team) gained notoriety for their interpersonal conflicts. With respect to intergroup relations, no simple effect of sport involvement is apparent. As Luschen (1970) notes, sport by nature requires both competition and cooperation from opposing players/teams. Which element is emphasized will dictate the predominant outcome in terms of intergroup relations. If striving to do one's best and testing of oneself against a worthy opponent is the orientation, it is likely that positive interpersonal relations will result. On the other hand, if the game outcome is emphasized, and winning is given primary emphasis rather than the process of competing, negative relations are likely to accrue. The social context and expectations provided emphasize these different outcomes. For example, the rugby tournament, where considerable emphasis is placed on socializing with opponents off the playing field, is in marked contrast to the norms of professional hockey or football where off-field fraternizing with the opposition, especially prior to a big game, is strongly discouraged, if not forbidden.

International sport competition has been associated with both positive and negative outcomes in terms of international relations. On the positive side, examples are available at the individual level of athletes from different countries forming friendships, even to the extent of marital unions. Sport also has occasionally served an important role in international diplomacy (e.g., "ping pong diplomacy," "good will games"). On the other hand, international sporting events have served as the immediate stimuli for triggering major international incidents.

Although sport proponents advocate the role of sport in modeling improved race relations, there is little evidence that permanent changes in attitude or prejudice occur due to participation on interracial teams (Chu and Griffey 1982, 1985; Rees and Miracle 1984). As in other areas, however, outcomes are probably variable depending upon the particular context. Particular outcomes reflect the specific emphasis, leadership, and social context. Such variable outcomes are evident in the literature on ethnicity and sport. Research on soccer teams at the community level has indicated that assimilation of ethnic groups into the mainstream society may occur when the team represents diverse ethnic groups (McKay 1975, Pooley 1976). But if a club is composed of a homogenous ethnic group, assimilation is less likely (Frogner 1985). Under these later conditions, integration into the ethnic community is more likely than assimilation into the mainstream society.

Sport may serve to strengthen community ties in modern urbanized society. Anderson and Stone (1981) refer to how sport events and the reporting of sports can foster "imaginary intimate" and "quasi-intimate" relationships to help satisfy the human need for belonging. Cialdini and associates (1976) reported the tendency for college students to wear more college colors, jackets, etc., the day following a win then after a loss. They interpret this as indicating a desire to identify with a winner and to "bask in the reflected glory" of the college team. On a larger scale, casual observation indicates the tendency for entire nations to celebrate or mourn with their country's successes and failures (e.g., reactions in Canada to results of Canada vs. U.S.S.R. World Cup Hockey, and Ben Johnson's winning and then losing a gold medal at the 1988 Olympic Games). Finally, Wilkerson and Dodder (1987) have identified a positive relationship between success of local high school athletic teams and level of social integration (collective conscience) in the community.

Although much has been written about the socialization effects of sport and the impact of sport on social integration, the research on which this literature is based has major limitations. The evidence is either of an anecdotal nature or is based on self-report measures. Many of these later measures have been of questionable reliability and validity. Further, most of the research has utilized correlational research designs which cannot demonstrate causality. Hence, although the accumulated evidence suggests a number of generalizations, these must remain tentative awaiting the results of well designed longitudinal research employing appropriate measurement tools (Coakley 1986).

In conclusion, in this section it has been observed that sport has the potential for fostering desirable values as well as social integration. For these positive outcomes to be realized, however, a number of conditions must be met. To this end, several researchers/authors have suggested guidelines for youth sport leadership practices (Gould 1982, Martens 1982, Smith and Smoll 1984). Essentially these recommendations focus on the importance of keeping winning in perspective and emphasizing a positive, enjoyable youth sport experience which facilitates the development of desirable skills and behavioral practices for all participants. Emphasis is placed on the importance of positive role models and the use of positive reinforcement to encourage the desired behaviors. A number of coaching development programs have been developed to foster such approaches (National Coaching Certification Program 1979, Wiggens 1987).

SOCIAL CHANGE

Social change frequently results when a group of individuals collectively acquire a shared perception of beliefs, values, goals, and actions concerning desired changes in the society. The desired changes may be relatively minor and incremental, reflecting a reformist perspective to change (e.g., fine tune the current system to provide more equitable opportunities); or more wide-sweeping, systemic changes reflecting a radical perspective that the whole system should be replaced or at least drastically overhauled. Paralleling the nature of the changes undertaken, the actions of the group to bring about the desired changes may vary considerably in level of planning and organization.

Changes within sport and general societal change have a two-way interactive relationship. General societal changes impact upon and change sport, while at the same time, changes within sport impact upon and facilitate change in the overall society. Typically, sport has been considered to be one of the most traditional, most conservative elements in society (Snyder and Spreitzer 1989). Nevertheless, it has not always been so and need not be so. Sport has the potential for markedly different outcomes. Perhaps the most vivid current example of how sport can serve as an agent for social change is the Dubin Enquiry currently under way in Canada. This enquiry into the problem of drugs in sport has focused media and public attention on a hidden or largely ignored social problem which permeates all aspects of society. As such, the enquiry has ramifications far beyond the world of track and field and sport.

Reference is frequently made to the potential of sport to serve as a vehicle for improving the life chances of disadvantaged individuals or groups. The rags to riches stories of selected athletes who have risen from humble beginnings in poverty to positions of prominence and affluence are presented as exemplary models of social mobility. Although such examples do exist, they undoubtedly constitute the exception rather than the rule. According to Lapchick (1987), the odds of an American high school basketball or football player becoming a professional player is approximately 10,000 to 1. Further, many of those who do sign professional contracts, have very short careers. The financial rewards are often fleeting. An athlete may just begin to enjoy the trappings of wealth and comfort when his/her professional career is cut short and there is no continuing source of income to sustain that lifestyle. Research on former players from a variety of sports (e.g., boxing, hockey, soccer) indicates that social and economic gains made as a result of sport during one's playing career are frequently lost after retirement (Houlston 1982; Lever 1969; Semyonov 1984, 1986; Smith and Diamond 1976; Weinberg and Arond 1952). It is increasingly recognized that sport involvement does not really provide a viable alternative to education and work as a means for achieving success and upward mobility.

An alternate hypothesis is that sport might facilitate social mobility in an indirect manner through facilitating educational attainment at the high school and college levels. There is some evidence to indicate that former high school and college athletes who graduate, earn more and have higher occupational prestige than do nonparticipants from the peer group (Howell et al. 1984, Picou et al. 1985, Sack and Thiel 1979). It is not clear, however, how this improved position comes about as a variety of explanations might account for the observed relationship (McPherson et al. 1989, Snyder and Spreitzer 1989).

Research comparing the academic achievement of athletes and nonathletes has yielded contradictory results. Some researchers report a positive relationship between sport participation and academic achievement (Buhrman 1971, Schafer and Armer 1968), others report negative relationships (Purdy et al. 1982) and others report no consistent results (Curtis and McTeer,[10] Hanks and Eckland 1976, Lapchick 1987, Shapiro 1984). These conflicting results indicate that a number of other factors must be taken into consideration in attempting to make any reasonable interpretation of the relationship between athletic involvement and academic achievement. Factors which have been shown to influence this relationship include level of competition, academic emphasis of institution, specific sport, gender, and socioeconomic status (Lapchick 1987, Sack 1987).

As was the case for socialization and social integration, it must be concluded that there is a lack of conclusive evidence to demonstrate the effectiveness of sport as an agent of social mobility or social change. Once more, however, it would appear that given the existence of the appropriate leadership and social context, positive outcomes in these areas might result.

CONCLUSION

Sport participation can result in a number of benefits. In terms of Csikszentmihalyi's four-component model, it has been shown that there are a number of potential benefits in each of the areas: personal enjoyment, personal growth, social harmony, and social change. In every case, however, the realization of these outcomes is contingent upon participation in an appropriate program. In the case of physical health benefits, this is essentially an activity program consisting of appropriate type, intensity, duration, and frequency of activity to produce the particular benefit desired. For personal enjoyment and psychological benefits to accrue, the particular activity considerations remain important, but in addition, the whole organizational and social context also becomes significant. Especially important to enjoyment are activity challenges appropriate to the individual's skill level and a positive, supportive social environment. With respect to social outcomes, sport has the potential to promote social harmony between groups or to foster greater rivalry and conflict. Similarly, although sport participants are often considered to hold very conservative, traditional values, sport has the potential to serve as an agent for social change. Which outcomes prevail depend upon the leadership and what values are emphasized in a particular sport context.

Given the extremely broad scope of potential outcomes, it is impossible to recommend appropriate research designs for investigating overall sport benefits. In researching any particular outcome, considerations must be given to clearly operationalizing the particular construct while manipulating, or systematically observing, variations in the dimensions of interest (Table 2) while controlling for extraneous influences. One generalization across different types of sport benefits is that there is a need for more longitudinal research. This is true with respect to physical health benefits, psychological benefits, and social outcomes.

ENDNOTES

[1] In this chapter, "sport" is defined broadly in the European "Sport for All" tradition. However, because of the common narrower definiton of the term, physical activity has been added to the title to clearly indicate the scope of the discussion.

[2] Molly Sapp and John Haubenstricker in paper on motivation for joining and reasons for not continuing in youth sport progams in Michigan, presented at the AAHPER National Convention, Kansas City, MO, 1978.

[3] John Pooley in paper on dropouts from sport (a case study of boys' age group soccer), presented at the American Alliance for Health, Physical Education, Recreation and Dance National Conference, Boston, MA, April 1981.

[4] Leonard M. Wankel and Philip S. Kreisel in paper on factors detracting from enjoyment and influencing withdrawal from youth sport programs, presented at the Fifth World Sport Psychology Congress, Copenhagen, Denmark, 1985.

[5] Rudolf Bosscher in unpublished manuscript on aerobic and nonaerobic physical exercise with depressed psychiatric patients (an experimental investigation).

[6] Bonnie G. Berger and David R. Owen in unpublished manuscript on the process of mood alteration with yoga and swimming (aerobic exercise not necessary).

[7] Bonnie G. Berger and David R. Owen in unpublished manuscript on preliminary analysis of a causal relationship between swimming and anxiety—fatigue may negate the psychological benefits.

[8] For a more comprehensive discussion of many of the topics in this section, see McPherson et al. 1989.

[9] R. Renson in paper on social status symbolism of sport stratification, presented at the International Congress of the Physical Activity Sciences, Quebec City, Canada, July 1976.

[10] James E. Curtis and William G. McTeer in paper on sport involvement and academic attainment in university (two studies from the Canadian case), presented at the Olympic Scientific Congress, Eugene, OR, July 1984.

LITERATURE CITED

Akiskal, H. S.; McKinney, W. T. 1975. Overview of recent research in depression: Integration of ten conceptual models into a comprehensive clinical frame. Archives of General Psychiatry. 32: 285-305.

Alberta Recreation and Parks. 1983. Sport development policy. Edmonton, AB: Government of Alberta.

Allison, M.; Luschen, G. 1973. A comparative analysis of Navaho Indian and anglo basketball sport systems. International Review of Sport Sociology. 14(3-4): 75-86.

American College of Sports Medicine. 1978. Position statement on the recommended quantity and quality of exercise for developing and maintaining fitness in healthy adults. Medicine and Science in Sports. 10: vii-x.

American College of Sports Medicine. 1986. Guidelines for graded exercise testing and exercise prescription, 3rd ed. Philadelphia, PA: Lea & Febiger.

Anderson, D. F.; Stone, G. P. 1981. Sport: A search for community. In: Greendorfer, S. L.; Yiannakis, A., eds. Sociology of sport: Diverse perspectives. West Point, NY: Leisure Press: 164-172.

Axthelm, P. 1970. The city game. New York, NY: Harper and Row.

Bahrke, M. S.; Morgan, W. P. 1978. Anxiety reduction following exercise and meditation. Cognitive Therapy and Research. 2: 323-333.

Beck, A. T. 1967. Depression: Clinical, experimental, and theoretical aspects. New York, NY: Harper and Row.

Berger, B. G. 1984a. Running away from anxiety and depression: A female as well as a male race. In: Sachs, M. L.; Buffone, G. W., eds. Running as therapy: An integrated approach. Lincoln, NE: University of Nebraska Press: 138-171.

Berger, B. G. 1984b. Running toward psychological well-being: Special considerations for the female client. In: Sachs, M. L.; Buffone, G. W., eds. Running as therapy: An integrated approach. Lincoln, NE: University of Nebraska Press: 172-197.

Berger, B. G. 1986. Use of jogging and swimming as stress reduction techniques. In: Humphrey, J. H., ed. Current selected research in human stress (vol. 1). New York, NY: AMS Press: 169-190.

Berger, B. G. 1987. Stress levels in swimmers. In: Morgan, W. P.; Goldston, S. E., eds. Exercise and mental health. Washington, DC: Hemisphere Publishing Corp.: 139-143.

Berger, B. G.; Friedmann, E.; Eaton, M. 1988. Comparison of jogging, the relaxation response, and group interaction for stress reduction. Journal of Sport and Exercise Psychology. 10: 431-447.

Berger, B. G.; Hatfield, B. D. [In press]. Exercise and stress reduction. New York, NY: AMS Press.

Berger, B. G.; Mackenzie, M. M. 1980. A case study of a woman jogger: A psychodynamic analysis. Journal of Sport Behavior. 3: 3-16.

Berger, B. G.; Owen, D. R. 1983. Mood alteration with swimming—swimmers really do "feel better." Psychosomatic Medicine. 45: 425-433.

Berger, B. G.; Owen, D. R. 1986. Mood alteration with swimming: A re-evaluation. In: Vander Velden, L.; Humphrey, J. H., eds. Current selected research in the psychology and sociology of sport (vol. 1). New York, NY: AMS Press: 97-114.

Berger, B. G.; Owen, D. R. 1987. Anxiety reduction with swimming: Relationships between exercise and state, trait, and somatic anxiety. International Journal of Sport Psychology. 18: 286-302.

Berger, B. G.; Owen, D. R. 1988. Stress reduction and mood enhancement in four exercise modes: Swimming, body conditioning, hatha yoga, and fencing. Research Quarterly for Exercise and Sport. 59: 148-159.

Boersma, J. 1979. Baseball: Oriental style. Soldiers. 34: 28-31.

Boutcher, S. H.; Landers, D. M. 1988. The effects of vigorous exercise on anxiety, heart rate, and alpha activity of runners and nonrunners. Psychophysiology. 25: 696-702.

Bredemeier, B. J. 1985. Moral reasoning and the perceived legitimacy of intentionally injurious sport acts. Journal of Sport Psychology. 7: 110-124.

Bredemeier, B. J.; Shields, D. L. 1987. Moral growth through physical activity: A structural/developmental approach. In: Gould, D.; Weiss, M. R., eds. Advances in pediatric sport sciences (vol. 2). Champaign, IL: Human Kinetics: 143-165.

Brown, J. D.; Siegel, J. M. 1988. Exercise as a buffer of life stress: A prospective study of adolescent health. Health Psychology. 7: 341-353.

Brown, R. S. 1987. Exercise as an adjunct to the treatment of mental disorders. In: Morgan, W. P.; Goldston, S. E., eds. Exercise and mental health. Washington, DC: Hemisphere: 131-137.

Brustad, R. J. 1988. Affective outcomes in competitive youth sport: The influence of intrapersonal and socialization factors. Journal of Sport and Exercise Psychology. 10(3): 307-321.

Buhrman, H. G. 1971. Scholarship and athletics in junior high school. International Review of Sport Sociology. 7: 119-131.

Buskirk, E. R.; Segal, S. S. 1989. The aging motor system: Skeletal muscle weakness. In: Spirduso, W. W.; Eckert, H. M., eds. Physical activity and aging. Champaign, IL: Human Kinetics: 19-36.

Canada Fitness Survey. 1983. Fitness and lifestyle in Canada. Ottawa, Ontario: Fitness and Amateur Sport, Government of Canada.

Carmack, M. A.; Martens, R. 1979. Measuring commitment to running: A survey of runners' attitudes and mental states. Journal of Sport Psychology. 1: 25-42.

Chalip, L.; Csikszentmihalyi, M.; Kleiber, D.; Larson, R. 1984. Variations of experience in formal and informal sport. Research Quarterly for Exercise and Sport. 55: 109-116.

Chu, D.; Griffey, D. 1982. Sport and racial integration: The relationship of personal contact, attitudes and behavior. In: Dunleavy, A. D.; Miracle, A.; Rees, C. R., eds. Studies in the sociology of sport. Fort Worth, TX: Texas Christian University Press: 271-282.

Chu, D.; Griffey, D. 1985. The contact theory of racial integration: The case of sport. Sociology of Sport Journal. 2(4): 323-333.

Cialdini, R.; Borden, R.; Thorne, A., et al. 1976. Basking in reflected glory: Three (football) studies. Journal of Personality and Social Psychology. 34: 366-375.

Claeys, U. 1985. Evolution of the concept of sport and the participation/nonparticipation phenomenon. Sociology of Sport Journal. 2(3): 233-239.

Cleaver, C. G. 1976. Japanese and Americans: Cultural parallels and paradoxes. Minneapolis, MN: University of Minnesota Press.

Cliff, M. B. 1981. The psychological and physical effects and implications of therapeutic tennis instruction. Dissertation Abstracts International. 41: 4272B.

Coakley, J. J. 1986. Socialization and youth sports. In: Rees, C. R.; Miracle, A. W., eds. Sport and social theory. Champaign, IL: Human Kinetics: 135-143.

Colburn, K. 1985. Honor, ritual and violence in ice hockey. Canadian Journal of Sociology. 10(2): 153-170.

Colburn, K. 1986. Deviance and legitimacy in ice hockey: A microstructural theory of deviance. The Sociological Quarterly. 27: 63-74.

Council of Europe. 1976. European sport for all charter. Resolution (76)41. Strasbourg, France.

Csikszentmihalyi, M. 1975. Beyond boredom and anxiety: The experience of play in work and games. San Francisco, CA: Jossey-Bass.

Csikszentmihalyi, M. 1982. The value of sports. In: Partington, J. T.; Orlick, T.; Salmela, J. H., eds. Sport in perspective. Ottawa: Coaching Association of Canada: 122-127.

Csikszentmihalyi, M.; Larson, R. 1984. Being adolescent: Conflict and growth in the teenage years. New York, NY: Basic Books.

Dickson-Parnell, B. E.; Zeichner, A. 1985. Effects of a short-term exercise program on caloric consumption. Health Psychology. 4: 437-448.

Donnelly, P. 1981. Athletics and juvenile deliquents: A comparative analysis based on a review of literature. International Review for the Sociology of Sport. 16: 415-431.

Edwards, H. 1973. Sociology of sport. Homewood, IL: Dorsey Press.

Fine, G. A. 1987. With the boys. Chicago, IL: The University of Chicago Press.

Frogner, E. 1985. On ethnic sport among Turkish migrants in the Federal Republic of Germany. International Review for the Sociology of Sport. 20(1/2): 75-85.

Fry, D. A. P.; McClements, J. D.; Sefton, J. M. 1981. A report on participation in the Saskatoon Hockey Association. Saskatoon, Canada: SASK Sport.

Gaesser, G. A.; Brooks, G. A. 1984. Metabolic bases of excess post-exercise oxygen consumption: A review. Medicine and Science in Sports and Exercise. 16: 29-43.

Gill, D.; Gross, J. B.; Huddleston, S. 1983. Participation motivation in youth sports. International Journal of Sport Psychology. 14: 1-14.

Glasser, W. 1976. Positive addiction. New York, NY: Harper and Row. 159 p.

Goldstein, J. H. 1983. Sports violence. New York, NY: Springer-Verlag.

Gould, D. 1982. Fostering psychological development in young athletes: A reaction. In: Orlick, T.; Partington, J. T.; Salmela, J. H., eds. Mental training for coaches and athletes. Ottawa: Coaching Association of Canada: 52-56.

Gould, D. 1987. Understanding attrition in children's sport. In: Gould, D.; Weiss, M. R., eds. Advances in pediatric sport sciences (vol. 2). Champaign, IL: Human Kinetics: 61-86.

Gould, D.; Feltz, D.; Weiss, M. R.; Petlichkoff, L. 1982. Participation motives in competitive youth swimmers. In: Orlick, T.; Partington, J. T.; Salmela, J. H., eds. Mental training for coaches and athletes. Ottawa: Coaching Association of Canada: 57-59.

Greendorfer, S. L. 1978. Social class influence on female sport involvement. Sex Roles. 4: 619-625.

Greist, J. H. 1987. Exercise intervention with depressed outpatients. In: Morgan, W. P.; Goldston, S. E., eds. Exercise and mental health. Washington, DC: Hemisphere Publishing Corp.: 117-121.

Greist, J. H.; Klein, M. H.; Eischens, R. R., et al. 1979. Running as treatment for depression. Comprehensive Psychiatry. 20: 41-54.

Guttman, A. 1978. From ritual to record: The nature of modern sports. Irvington, NY: Columbia University Press.

Hackfort, D.; Spielberger, C. D., eds. 1989. Anxiety in sports: An international perspective. New York, NY: Hemisphere Publishing Corp. 275 p.

Hanks, M. P.; Eckland, B. K. 1976. Athletics and social participation in the educational attainment process. Sociology of Education. 49: 271-294.

Harris, J. C. 1984. Interpreting youth baseball: Players' understandings of fun and excitement, danger and boredom. Research Quarterly for Exercise and Sport. 55: 379-382.

Haskell, W. L.; Montoye, H. J.; Orenstein, D. 1985. Physical activity and exercise to achieve health-related physical fitness components. Public Health Reports. 100(2): 202-212.

Hastad, D. N.; Segrave, J. O.; Pangrazi, R.; Petersen, G. 1984. Youth sport participation and deviant behavior. Sociology of Sport Journal. 1(4): 366-373.

Heinzelman, F.; Bagley, R. W. 1970. Response to physical activity programs and their effects on health behavior. Public Health Reports. 85(10): 905-911.

Horton, E. S. 1986. Metabolic aspects of exercise and weight reduction. Medicine and Science in Sports and Exercise. 18: 10.

Houlston, D. R. 1982. The occupational mobility of professional athletes. International Review of Sport Sociology. 17(2): 15-26.

Howell, F. M.; Miracle, A. W.; Rees, C. R. 1984. Do high school athletics pay?: The effects of varsity participation on socioeconomic attainment. Sociology of Sport Journal. 1(1): 15-25.

Hughes, J. R. 1984. Psychological effects of habitual aerobic exercise: A critical review. Preventive Medicine. 13: 66-78

Justice, B.; McBee, G. W. 1978. Sex differences in psychological distress and social functioning. Psychological Reports. 43: 659-662.

Kavanagh, T.; Shephard, R. J.; Tuck, J. A.; Qureshi, S. 1977. Depression following myocardial infarction: The effects of distance running. In: Milvey, P., ed. Annals of the New York Academy of Sciences, 301. New York, NY: New York Academy of Sciences: 1029-1038.

Kelly, J. R. 1982. Leisure. Englewood Cliffs, NJ: Prentice-Hall.

Kleiber, D.; Larson, R.; Csikszentmihalyi, M. 1986. The experience of leisure in adolescence. Journal of Leisure Research. 18(3): 169-176.

Klerman, G. L. 1979. The age of melancholy. Psychology Today. 12(4): 36-42, 88.

Landers, S. 1989. In the U.S., mental disorders affect 15 percent of adults: NIMH analyzes monthly prevalence rates. APA Monitor. 20(1): 16.

Lapchick, R. E. 1987. The high school athlete as the future college student-athlete. Journal of Sport and Social Issues. 11(1,2): 104-121.

Larson, D.; Spreitzer, E.; Snyder, E. E. 1975. Youth hockey programs: A sociological perspective. Sports Sociology Bulletin. 4: 55-63.

Lever, J. 1969. Soccer: Opium of the Brazilian people. Transaction. (December): 2, 36-43.

Long, B. C. 1983. Aerobic conditioning and stress reduction: Participation or conditioning? Human Movement Science. 2: 171-186.

Long, B. C. 1985. Stress-management interventions: A 15-month follow-up of aerobic conditioning and stress inoculation training. Cognitive Therapy and Research. 9: 471-478.

Long, B. C.; Haney, C. J. 1988a. Coping strategies for working women: Aerobic exercise and relaxation intervention. Behavior Therapy. 19: 75-83.

Long, B. C.; Haney, C. J. 1988b. Long-term follow-up of stressed working women: A comparison of aerobic exercise and progressive relaxation. Journal of Sport and Exercise Psychology. 10: 461-470.

Loy, J. W., Jr. 1968. The nature of sport—a definitional effort. Quest. 10 (May): 1-15.

Loy, J. W., Jr. 1972. The interdependence of sport and culture. International Review of Sport Sociology. 2: 127-141.

Loy, J. W., Jr.; Ingham, A. 1973. Play, games and sport in the psychosociological development of children and youth. In: Rarick, G. L., ed. Physical activity: Human growth and development. New York, NY: Academic Press.

Luschen, G. 1969. Social stratification and social mobility among young sportsmen. In: Loy, J. W.; Kenyon, G. S., eds. Sport, culture and society. New York, NY: MacMillan: 258-276.

Luschen, G. 1970. Cooperation, association, and contest. Conflict Resolution. 14: 21-34.

Mandell, A. 1979. The second second wind. Psychiatric Annals. 9: 57-69.

Martens, R. 1976. Kid sports: A den of iniquity or land of promise? In: Proceedings of the National College Physical Education Association for Men. University of Illinois at Chicago Circle.

Martens, R. 1978. Joy and sadness in children's sport. Champaign, IL: Human Kinetics.

Martens, R. 1982. Coaching to enhance self-worth. In: Orlick, T.; Partington, J. T.; Salmela, J. H., eds. Mental training for coaches and athletes. Ottawa: Coaching Association of Canada: 48-52.

Martens, R.; Peterson, J. A. 1971. Group cohesiveness as a determinant of success and member satisfaction in team performance. International Review of Sport Sociology. 6: 49-61.

Martinsen, E. W. 1987. Exercise and medication in the psychiatric patient. In: Morgan, W. P.; Goldston, S. E., eds. Exercise and mental health. Washington, DC: Hemisphere Publishing Corp.: 85-95.

Martinsen, E. W., Medhus, A.; Sandvik, L. 1985. Effects of aerobic exercise on depression: A controlled study. British Medical Journal. 291: 109.

McCann, I. L.; Holmes, D. S. 1984. Influence of aerobic exercise on depression. Journal of Personality and Social Psychology. 46: 1142-1147.

McIntosh, P. 1980. 'Sport for all' programmes throughout the world (Report prepared for UNESCO, Contract No. 207604). New York, NY: UNESCO.

McKay, J. 1975. Sport and ethnicity: Acculturation, structural assimilation, and voluntary association involvement among Italian immigrants in Metropolitan Toronto. Waterloo: University of Waterloo: M.Sc. thesis.

McNair, D. M.; Lorr, M.; Droppleman, L. F. 1971. Profile of mood states manual. San Diego: Educational and Industrial Testing Service. 27 p.

McPherson, B. D. 1986a. Sport, health, well-being, and aging: Some conceptual and methodological issues and questions for sport scientists. In: McPherson, B. D., ed. Sport and aging. Champaign, IL: Human Kinetics: 3-23.

McPherson, B. D. 1986b. Socialization theory and research: Toward a "new wave" of scholarly inquiry in a sport context. In: Rees, R.; Miracle, A. eds. Sport and social theory. Champaign, IL: Human Kinetics: 111-134.

McPherson, B. D.; Curtis, J.; Loy, J. 1989. The social significance of sport. Champaign, IL: Human Kinetics.

McPherson, B. D.; Davidson, L. 1980. Minor hockey in Ontario: Toward a positive learning environment for children in the 1980's. Toronto: Ontario Government Bookstore.

Meyers, A. 1962. Team competition, success and the adjustment of group members. Journal of Abnormal and Social Psychology. 65(5): 325-332.

Miller Lite report on American attitudes toward sports. 1983. Milwaukee, WI: Miller Brewing Company.

Morgan, W. P. 1983. Physical activity and mental health. In: Eckert, H. M.; Montoye, H. J., eds. Exercise and health: The academy papers, No. 17. Champaign, IL: Human Kinetics Publishers: 132-145.

Morgan, W. P. 1987. Reduction of state anxiety following acute physical activity. In: Morgan, W. P.; Goldston, S. E., eds. Exercise and mental health. Washington, DC: Hemisphere: 105-109.

Morgan, W. P.; Costill, D. L.; Flynn, M. G., et al. 1988. Mood disturbance following increased training in swimmers. Medicine and Science in Sports and Exercise. 20: 408-414.

Morgan, W. P.; Goldston, S. E., eds. 1987. Exercise and mental health. Washington, DC: Hemisphere. 196 p.

Morgan, W. P.; O'Connor, P. J. 1988. Exercise and mental health. In: Dishman, R. K., ed. Exercise adherence: Its impact on public health. Champaign, IL: Human Kinetics: 91-121.

Morgan, W. P.; Pollock, M. L. 1977. Psychologic characterization of the elite distance runner. In: Milvy, P. V., ed. Annals of the New York Academy of Sciences. New York, NY: New York Academy of Sciences: 381-403.

National Coaching Certification Program. 1979. Ottawa: Coaching Association of Canada.

Nixon, H. L. 1979. Acceptance of the 'dominant American sports creed' among college students. Review of Sport and Leisure. 4: 141-159.

Orlick, T. 1974. The athletic dropout: A high price for inefficiency. CAHPER Journal. November-December: 21-27.

Orlick, T. 1975. The sports environment: A capacity to enhance—a capacity to destroy. In: Rushall, B. S., ed. The status of psychomotor learning and sport psychology research. Dartmouth, NH: Sport Science Associates: 2.1-2.18.

Paffenbarger, R. S.; Hyde, R. T. 1988. Exercise adherence, coronary heart disease and longevity. In: Dishman, R. K., ed. Exercise adherence: Its impact on public health. Champaign, IL: Human Kinetics: 41-74.

Paffenbarger, R. S.; Hyde, R. T.; Wing, A. L.; Hsieh, C. 1986. Physical activity, all-cause mortality, and longevity of college alumni. New England Journal of Medicine. 314: 605-613.

Palm, J. 1978. Mass media and the promotion of sports for all. In: Landry, F.; Orban, W., eds. Physical activity and human well being. Miami, FL: Symposium Specialists: 273-279.

Penfold, S. P. 1981. General papers: Women and depression. Canadian Journal of Psychiatry. 26: 24-31.

Pennebaker, J. W.; Lightner, J. M. 1980. Competition of internal and external information in an exercise setting. Journal of Personality and Social Psychology. 39: 165-174.

Picou, J. S.; McCarter V.; Howell, F. M. 1985. Do high school athletics pay? Some further evidence. Sociology of Sport Journal. 2(1): 72-76.

Pollock, M. L.; Wilmore, J. H.; Fox, S. M. 1984. Cardiorespiratory function. In: Pollock, M. L.; Wilmore, J. H.; Fox, S. M., eds. Exercise in health and disease. Philadelphia, PA: W. B. Saunders: 53-96.

Pooley, J. 1976. Ethnic soccer clubs in Milwaukee: A study in assimilation. In: Hart, M., ed. Sport in the socio-cultural process. 2nd Edition. Dubuque, IA: W. C. Brown: 475-492.

Purdy, D. A.; Eitzen, S. D.; Hufnagel, R. 1982. Are athletes also students? The educational attainment of college athletes. Social Problems. 29(4): 439-448.

Purdy, D. A.; Richard, S. 1983. Sport and juvenile delinquency: An examination and assessment of four major theories. Journal of Sport Behavior. 6(4): 179-193.

Raglin, J. S.; Morgan, W. P. 1987. Influence of exercise and quiet rest on state anxiety and blood pressure. Medicine and Science in Sports and Exercise. 19: 456-463.

Rees, C. R.; Miracle, A. W. 1984. Participation in sport and the reduction of racial prejudices: Contact theory, superordinate goals, hypothesis or wishful thinking. In: Theberge, N.; Donnelly, P., eds. Sport and the sociological imagination. Fort Worth, TX: Texas Christian University Press: 140-152.

Roberts, G. C.; Duda, J. 1984. Motivation in sport: The mediating role of perceived ability. Journal of Sport Psychology. 6: 312-324.

Robertson, I. 1982. Sport in the lives of Australian children. In: Orlick, T.; Partington, J.; Salmela, J., eds. Mental training for coaches and athletes. Ottawa: Coaching Association of Canada: 61-63.

Ryan, A. J. 1983. Exercise is medicine. The Physician and Sports Medicine. 11: 10.

Sack, A.; Thiel, R. 1979. College football and social mobility: A case study of Notre Dame football players. Sociology of Education. 52: 60-66.

Sack, A. L. 1987. College sport and the student-athlete. Journal of Sport and Social Issues. 11(1,2): 31-48.

Sacks, M. H.; Sachs, M. L., eds. 1981. Psychology of running. Champaign, IL: Human Kinetics. 279 p.

Sachs, M. L. 1984. The runner's high. In: Sachs, M. L.; Buffone, G. W., eds. Running as therapy: An integrated approach. Lincoln, NE: University of Nebraska Press: 273-287.

Sachs, M. L.; Buffone, G. W., eds. 1984. Running as therapy: An integrated approach. Lincoln, NE: University of Nebraska Press. 229 p.

Scanlan, T.; Lewthwaite, R. 1986. Social psychological aspects of competition for male youth sports participants: IV. Predictors of enjoyment. Journal of Sport Psychology. 8: 25-35.

Schafer, W. E.; Armer, M. 1968. Athletes are not inferior students. Trans-Action. 5: 21-26, 61-62.

Segal, K. R.; Gutin, B. 1983. Thermic effects of food and exercise in lean and obese women. Metabolism. 32: 581-589.

Segrave, J. 1983. Sport and juvenile delinquency. In: Terjung, R., ed. Exercise and sport science review. Vol. 11. Philadelphia, PA: Franklin Institute Press: 181-209.

Segrave, J.; Hastad, D. 1984. Interscholastic athletic participation and delinquent behavior: An empirical assessment of relevant variables. Sociology of Sport Journal. 1(2): 117-137.

Semyonov, M. 1984. Sport and beyond: Ethnic inequalities in attainment. Sociology of Sport Journal. 1(4): 358-365.

Semyonov, M. 1986. Occupational mobility through sport: The case of Israeli soccer. International Review for the Sociology of Sport. 21(1): 23-31.

Shapiro, B. J. 1984. Intercollegiate athletic participation and academic achievement: A case study of Michigan State University student-athletes, 1950-1980. Sociology of Sport Journal. 9(1): 46-51.

Sharkey, B. J. 1984. Psychology of fitness (2nd ed.). Champaign, IL: Human Kinetics. 365 p.

Sheehan, G. 1988. Running "comfortable." The Physician and Sportsmedicine. 16(7): 41.

Sherif, M.; Harvey, O. J.; White, B. J., et al. 1961. Intergroup conflict and cooperation: The Robbers Cave Experiment. Norman, OK: The University Book Exchange, The University of Oklahoma. 212 p.

Sime, W. E. 1987. Exercise in the prevention and treatment of depression. In: Morgan, W. P.; Goldston, S. E., eds. Exercise and mental health. Washington, DC: Hemisphere Publishing Corp.: 145-152.

Simons, C. W.; Birkimer, J. C. 1988. An exploration of factors predicting the effects of aerobic conditioning on mood state, Journal of Psychosomatic Research. 32: 63-75.

Simons-Morton, B. G.; O'Hara, N. M.; Simons-Morton, D. G.; Parcel, G. S. 1987. Research Quarterly for Exercise and Sport. 4: 295-302.

Smith, E. L.; Gilligan, C. 1986. Exercise, sport, and physical activity for the elderly: Principles and problems of programming. In: McPherson, B. D., ed. Sport and aging. Champaign, IL: Human Kinetics: 91-105.

Smith, E. L.; Sempos, C. T.; Purvis, R. W. 1981. Bone mass and strength decline with age. In: Smith, E. L.; Serfass, R. C., eds. Exercise and aging: The scientific basis. Hillside, NJ: Enslow: 850-865.

Smith, M. D.; Diamond, F. 1976. Career mobility in professional hockey. In: Gruneau, R. S.; Albinson, J. G., eds. Canadian sport: Sociological perspectives. Don Mills, Ontario: Addison-Wesley: 275-293.

Smith, R.; Smoll, F. 1984. Leadership research in youth sports. In: Silva, J. M.; Weinberg, R. S., eds. Psychological foundations of sport. Champaign, IL: Human Kinetics: 371-386.

Smoll, F.; Magill, R.; Ash, M., eds. 1988. Children in sport. Champaign, IL: Human Kinetics.

Snow-Harter, C. 1987. Biochemical changes in postmenopausal women following a muscle fitness program. The Physician and Sports Medicine. 15: 90-96.

Snyder, E. E. 1972. Athletic dressing room slogans as folklore: A means of socialization. International Review of Sport Sociology. 7: 89-102.

Snyder, E. E.; Spreitzer, E. 1979. Lifelong involvement in sport as a leisure pursuit: Aspects of role construction. Quest. 31(1): 57-70.

Snyder, E. E.; Spreitzer, E. 1989. Social aspects of sport. Third edition. Englewood Cliffs, NJ: Prentice Hall.

Spielberger, C. D. 1987. Stress, emotions and health. In: Morgan, W. P.; Goldston, S. E., eds. Exercise and mental health. Washington, DC: Hemisphere: 11-16.

Spielberger, C. D.; Gorsuch, R. L.; Lushene, R. E. 1970. STAI manual. Palo Alto, CA: Consulting Psychologists Press.

Spink, K.; Roberts, G. C. 1980. Ambiguity of outcome and causal attributions. Journal of Sport Psychology. 2: 237-244.

Spirduso, W. W. 1986. Physical activity and the prevention of premature aging. In: Seefelt, V., ed. Physical activity and well-being. Reston, VA: American Alliance for Health, Physical Education, Recreation and Dance: 142-160.

Spirduso, W. W.; Eckert, H. M., eds. 1989. Physical activity and aging: American Academy of Physical Education Papers No. 22. Champaign, IL: Human Kinetics. 201 p.

Sports Illustrated. 1981. 19(2): 108.

Spreitzer, E.; Snyder, E. E. 1975. The psychosocial functions of sport as perceived by the general population. International Review of Sport Sociology. 10(3-4): 87-95.

Stamford, B. A. 1988. Exercise and the elderly. In: Pandolf, K. B., ed. Exercise and sport sciences reviews. New York, NY: Macmillan: 341-379.

Steptoe, A.; Bolton, J. 1988. The short-term influence of high and low intensity physical exercise on mood. Psychology and Health. 2: 91-106.

Steptoe, A.; Cox, S. 1988. Acute effects of aerobic exercise on mood. Health Psychology. 7: 329-340.

Stevenson, C. 1975. Socialization effects of participation in sport: A critical review of the literature. Research Quarterly. 46: 287-301.

Stevenson, C. 1985. Socialization research. In: Chu, D.; Segrave, J. O.; Becker, B. J., eds. Sport and higher education. Champaign, IL: Human Kinetics.

Stillman, R. J.; Lohman, T. G.; Slaughter, M. H.; Massey, B. H. 1986. Physical activity and bone mineral content in women aged 30 to 85 years. Medicine and Science in Sports and Exercise. 18: 576-580.

Strauss, R. H. 1986. Take a walk. The Physician and Sports Medicine. 14(10): 23.

Tajfel, H. 1978. The achievement of group differentiation. In: Tajfel, H., ed. Differentiation between social groups: Studies in the social psychology of intergroup relations. New York, NY: Academic Press: 77-98.

Thayer, R. E. 1987. Energy, tiredness, and tension effects of a sugar snack versus moderate exercise. Journal of Personality and Social Psychology. 52: 119-125.

Underwood, J. 1980. The writing is on the wall. Sports Illustrated. 19(May): 36-72.

Vaz, E. W. 1977. Institutionalized rule violations in professional hockey: Perspectives and control systems. CAHPER Journal. 48(3): 6-14.

Wankel, L. M. 1982. Factors affecting sport participation. Ottawa: Fitness and Amateur Sport, (Project No. 265-003-02). 115 p.

Wankel, L. M. 1983. Factors influencing girls' enjoyment of sport. Ottawa: Fitness and Amateur Sport, (Project No. 217). 64 p.

Wankel, L. M. 1985a. Personal and situational factors affecting exercise involvement: The importance of enjoyment. Research Quarterly for Exercise and Sport. 56(3): 275-282.

Wankel, L. M. 1985b. Personal and situational factors affecting youth sport enjoyment and involvement. Ottawa: Fitness and Amateur Sport, (Project No. 400-0060). 72 p.

Wankel, L. M. 1988. Exercise adherence and leisure activity: Patterns of involvement and interventions to facilitate regular activity. In: Dishman, R. K., ed. Exercise adherence: Its impact upon public health. Champaign, IL: 369-396.

Wankel, L. M.; Kreisel, P. S. 1985a. Factors underlying enjoyment of youth sports: Sport and age group comparisons. Journal of Sport Psychology. 7: 51-64.

Wankel, L. M.; Kreisel, P. S. 1985b. Methodological considerations in youth sport motivation research: A comparison of open-ended and paired comparison approaches. Journal of Sport Psychology. 7: 65-74.

Wankel, L. M.; Sefton, J. M. 1989. A season-long investigation of fun in youth sports. Journal of Sport and Exercise Psychology. 11:355-366.

Watson, G. G. 1976. Reward systems in children's games: The attraction of game interaction in Little League Baseball. Review of Sport and Leisure. 1: 93-121.

Watson, G. G. 1984. Competition and intrinsic motivation in children's sport and games: A conceptual analysis. International Journal of Sport Psychology. 15: 205-218.

Webb, P. 1986. Direct calorimetry and the energetics of exercise and weight loss. Medicine and Science in Sports and Exercise. 18: 3-5.

Weinberg, R.; Jackson, A.; Kolodny, K. 1988. The relationship of massage and exercise to mood enhancement. The Sport Psychologist. 2: 202-211.

Weinberg, S. K.; Arond, H. 1952. The occupational culture of the boxer. American Journal of Sociology. 57: 460-469.

Wells, C. L. 1985. Women, sport, and performance: A physiological perspective. Champaign, IL: Human Kinetics Publishers. 333 p.

Widmeyer, N. 1984. Aggression—performance relationships in sport. In: Silva, J.; Weinberg, R., eds. Psychological foundations of sport. Champaign, IL: 274-286.

Wiggens, D. K. 1987. A history of organized play and highly competitive sport for American children. In: Gould, D.; Weiss, M. R., eds. Advances in pediatric sport sciences. Champaign, IL: Human Kinetics: 1-25.

Wilkerson, M.; Dodder, R. A. 1987. Collective conscience and sport in modern society: An empirical test of a model. Journal of Leisure Research. 19(1): 35-40.

Wilson, V. E., Berger, B. G.; Bird, E. I. 1981. Effects of running and of an exercise class on anxiety. Perceptual and Motor Skills. 53: 472-474.

Programmed, Nonclinical Skill Development Benefits of Leisure Activities

A. T. Easley
School of Natural Resources
Sir Sandford Fleming College
Lindsay, Ontario

The past four decades have witnessed a tremendous increase in the use of the wilderness, or outdoors generally, as a "classroom" for a variety of educational purposes. The more widely known recent phenomenon is referred to as "outdoor education" or "environmental education," where typically the curriculum elements from school are taught in an outdoor setting.

Another significant educational use of the outdoors has been through the development of "adventure/challenge" or "wilderness education" programs. The foundations of many of these programs are based on the educational philosophy of Kurt Hahn, the founder of the "Outward Bound" movement. Because Outward Bound schools exist in over 17 countries of the world and have a history of over 40 years, they have been the subject of many studies and research efforts.

Outward Bound and its derivative programs have a variety of educational goals. Outward Bound has "personal growth through challenge" as its consistent goal. As its name implies, the National Outdoor Leadership School (NOLS), has as a goal the development of leadership in the individual participants. Other programs have objectives ranging from survival to environmental or self-awareness.

The success of these structured outdoor programs and the beneficial consequences to the students are dependent on many things such as curriculum elements, teaching environment, equipment, and of course, high quality leadership and favorable safety records.

The objective of this chapter is to present a review of the theories, research, and literature which may be useful in developing a framework for further research on the nature and benefits to the participants, and to the environment itself, of these structured outdoor experiences. This chapter first examines the literature related to experiential education as used in structured outdoor programs. Next, different types of structured programs and their objectives are described. Then the documented and speculated beneficial consequences are discussed.

EXPERIENTIAL EDUCATION IN STRUCTURED OUTDOOR PROGRAMS

Education is essential to ensure that citizens are environmentally literate and sensitive to the concept of wilderness or resource stewardship and to the necessity for conservation and preservation of natural resources. To instill these values, it is necessary to face the challenge of changing individuals so that their actions reflect evolved awareness.

Educational methods used to instill resource-oriented values and beneficial behavior, while interacting with those resources, reflect the proposition put forth by Ranney (1984):

> Consciousness or awareness that survives comes about through education, actual restructuring and rethinking. "I hear, I forget; I see, I remember; I do, I understand" seems to be the most effective rule when creating change.

Thus, experiential education is seen to be the method of choice when trying to create change.

Experiential learning has been defined as learning which occurs when changes in judgments, feelings, knowledge, or skills result from living through an event or events (Chickering 1963 cited in Kraft, n.d.). Put more simply, experiential education comes through experience.

The concept of experiential education is not new. "With a view to action, experience seems in no respect inferior to art, and men of experience succeed even better than those who have a theory without experience" (Aristotle cited in Kraft, n.d.). However, in our culture which is increasingly information-rich but experience-poor, we traditionally educate through assimilating information. We are taught via symbolic mediums, through distilled experiences of others, and by direct memory-to-memory transfer (Kraft, n.d.).

The overwhelming dominance of education that emphasizes vicarious experience is an injustice. Gibbons (1986 cited in Kraft, n.d.) states that to prepare students for transformation, transition, and societal change, the classroom is too narrow an environment; the learner must deal more directly with personal and social issues (including resource stewardship) through concrete experience. Kraft (n.d.) states that every major national study of the problems of youth, adolescents, high schools, and universities in the 1970s made recommendations concerning the need for experiential modes of learning for most, if not all youths, in the last quarter of the 20th Century.

The outdoors or wilderness[1] is an ideal medium for applying the tools of experiential education, which explains its use by virtually all of the structured outdoor programs such as NOLS and Outward Bound. Experiential learning appears to be etched more permanently and deeply on the brain of the learner as all learning can be associated with concrete actions and events, not just abstract symbols or general principles (Kraft, n.d.). Such education could help the American public restructure its environmental consciousness and result in the acquisition of skills, such as minimum impact techniques or behaviors that are more sensitive to resource stewardship. Such learning is essential because traditional education is primarily seen as a promotion of the status quo and a passing on of a stagnant cultural heritage, where the vicarious symbolic modes of the traditional educational practices are conducive to producing a passive citizenry (Kraft, n.d.). Thus, experiential education could be an essential tool for ensuring an active, articulate, informed citizenry that can speak out in defense of our natural resources.

Coleman (1974 cited in Kraft, n.d.) analyzed the differences between experiential and classroom learning. He found that information assimilation (classroom learning) depends largely on artificial motivation. Grades are the external motivators that must be applied to motivate the learner. It seems obvious that nonformal (nonschool) groups need to utilize different methods of learning as grades are not motivators. Even in school situations, the threat of grades is a negative reinforcer and fails to motivate some students. In contrast, motivation is intrinsic in experiential learning. Learning how to cook over an open fire, learning appropriate backpacking techniques, and learning how to stay warm in inclement weather, each result in the specific useful (i.e., valued) skill that motivates such learning.

Coleman (1974 cited in Kraft, n.d.) also found that information assimilation is highly dependent on the symbolic medium of language. Thus, persons who have learned the symbolic medium poorly, those who are still too young to have learned it well, and those culturally disadvantaged in linguistic and verbal skills, are groups which have difficulty with traditional modes of learning. If, for example, the target group to be educated about the value of appropriate behavior in wilderness environments is the American public, then it is possible that a significant proportion of the public would fall into Coleman's category of individuals who have difficulty with information assimilation modes of learning. As will be pointed out later, many structured outdoor programs have had great success in imparting significant life skills as well as outdoor skills to their specific populations using the experiential techniques common in outdoor programs.

The psychological rationales for advocating experiential education are varied. Recent research on Piaget's stages of development provides the strongest case for use of experiential learning modes such as those used in outdoor programs. In his original research, Piaget (1954 cited in Sakofs 1983) identified various stages of cognitive development in children. He found that children moved from concrete, operational thought to formal or abstract thought around age 11. At this point, according to Piaget, children are capable of cognitively dealing with abstract concepts. It seemed reasonable, therefore, for schools to develop lessons that were based on abstract thinking through use of books rather than structuring more costly, time consuming experiential lessons (Sakofs 1983). Seemingly, book learning was justified because children were supposed to be capable of learning solely by abstract manipulations of the mind after age 11.

However, Maynard (1975 cited in Sakofs 1983) found that large percentages of junior and senior high school students are not capable of formal/abstract thoughts, and many adults never reach Piaget's formal operational state. Thus, research indicates that traditional education emphasizes methods of knowledge acquisition that require people to use cognitive skills they do not possess (Sakofs 1983).

Humanistic psychologists also made their case for experiential education to help students achieve their highest potential. Abraham Maslow (1968 cited in Kraft, n.d.) stated that the experiences in which we uncover our intrinsic selves are apt to be unique moments in which a person discovers his/her true identity, not the traditional learning situations in schools. Carl Rogers (1969 cited in Kraft, n.d.) emphasized experiential philosophies in the role of the teacher as a facilitator, the involvement of the student in the selection of what is to be learned, and that the motivation of the learner is due to his or her own intrinsic reasons. Erikson (1963 cited in Kraft, n.d.) bemoaned the imbalance between passive stimulation and active outlet in education. He advocated experiential learning as more likely to aid progress in nurturing important life values such as trust, autonomy, positive identity, intimacy, and integrity.

It is apparent that experiential education does not occur without the intent and know-how to make it happen. Nowhere is experiential learning more developed than in the many structured wilderness experience/education programs in existence today. Programs like NOLS, Outward Bound, as well as countless children's camps, and agency-supported programs like Boy Scouts and youth conservation work programs, utilize this education-through-experience to impart a variety of beneficial skills to their participants. To understand the scope of learning transmitted by these programs, the wide range of these structured programs will be described.

STRUCTURED OUTDOOR PROGRAMS: SOME EXAMPLES

Structured outdoor recreational experiences are provided by a wide range of programs—nonprofit and commercial, run by professionals or by volunteers, and formal or informal in structure. This section will describe the major programs or types of programs to help capture their wide-ranging objectives and goals.

Outward Bound

Outward Bound uses challenging activities in a wilderness setting to teach students more about themselves. Kurt Hahn founded the school in 1941 based on the conviction that high adventure in the outdoors, guided by caring and competent instructors, teaches essential lessons of self-respect, tenacity, respect for others, and reverence for life (Canadian Outward Bound Wilderness School 1985).

Outward Bound teaches the skills necessary to survive in the wilderness while providing opportunities to confront and experience nature in a highly personal way and to learn from that experience. Introspection and contemplation are placed side by side with vigorous physical activity. Programs are also geared to the idea that humans are social animals and, as much as each individual needs to know about himself, he must also learn about living with others (Maynard 1969).

Outward Bound training aims at self-confrontation and self-discovery by involving students in a continuing sequence of physical stress situations that increase in difficulty and complexity, but are structured in such a way as to ensure a maximum probability of success. Mental stress is usually the result of the accompanying fear produced by the situations which involve real physical danger and the implicit pressure to carry on activities which most participants believe are beyond their capacity to complete successfully. By accepting these challenges it is believed that the participants are led to a reevaluation of the potential of themselves and others. It is believed that a person who experiences self-discovery in one environment can transfer the underlying lesson of his experience to other environments (Smith 1971).

The Outward Bound educational method is based primarily on experiential self-teaching. Instructors demonstrate, but quickly stand aside to encourage students to learn first hand. This learning-by-doing philosophy is the foundation of Outward Bound's experiential program.

The benefits attributed to Outward Bound are numerous. The focus of the experience, however, is not primarily based on development of hard skills. Appreciation and awareness of the natural environment happens naturally on an Outward Bound course. Being in close contact with wilderness can serve to inspire a sense of the environment and one's responsibility for it, but wilderness preservation and resource conservation philosophies are not generally expounded as part of the normal curriculum. There is a focus in Outward Bound courses, however, on minimum impact use of the natural environments in which courses take place.

The primary purpose or focus of Outward Bound courses is more individual/personal, as are the benefits of Outward Bound courses. The opportunity to expand capabilities, push back limits, challenge fears, and learn how to function effectively under stress and uncertainty are a few of the life skill benefits that are attributed to an Outward Bound experience. Besides individual growth, intensive teamwork necessitates learning to cooperate and to contribute in a group—an important benefit in today's society. Specific wilderness skills (camp craft, navigation, emergency first aid, rock climbing, kayaking, nutrition, etc.) are concrete benefits gained by the participants in an Outward Bound course.

In keeping with the emphasis of Outward Bound courses on an individual's change and development, numerous studies have attempted to measure the benefits attributed to the Outward Bound experience. Independent studies by Smith (1971) and Wetmore (1972) measured different personality traits before and after an Outward Bound experience. Smith found that some personality factors of young men seemed to have changed significantly, but afterwards there were no real changes in school attendance behavior. Wetmore found that there were distinctly positive changes in self-concept experienced by adolescent boys due to the Outward Bound experience. However, he found that this benefit decreased after the participants returned to their home environment.

The therapeutic potential of the Outward Bound process in treating juvenile delinquents was examined by Wright (1983). He found significant increases in self-esteem, self-empowerment (self-efficacy and locus of control), internality, and cardiovascular fitness, but no significant gain in problem-solving skills. Kelly and Baer (1971) found that recidivism rates were half of the base rate 9 months after an Outward Bound experience. However, 5 years after the Outward Bound experience, recidivism was not significantly lower for past participants than for juveniles who had not experienced the Outward Bound course.

The cautious conclusion of a review of all the studies (Wright 1983) was that participation in an Outward Bound program may increase the delinquent's self-esteem and internality, while reducing the likelihood of further contact with the juvenile justice system during the first year after the program. The fact that problem-solving skills were not improved is significant as an ability to successfully resolve intra- and inter-personal problems is necessary when the delinquent returns to the community.

Many have advocated that Outward Bound is a unique educational enterprise which uses experience as its major learning medium (Bacon 1983, Putnam 1984, Richards 1977). The direct experience provided by Outward Bound is aimed at helping participants to discover their strengths and capabilities, to build their confidence, and to cause them to re-examine their values.

The National Outdoor Leadership School (NOLS)

The National Outdoor Leadership School (NOLS) is a nonprofit, tax exempt educational organization incorporated as a private licensed school. It was established in 1965 to teach skills and knowledge necessary to be comfortable in the wilderness, in order to protect the user and the environment. NOLS combines the tradition of a programmed outdoor recreation experience with specific educational objectives: leadership development, outdoor skills, minimum impact conservation techniques, and expedition dynamics (Williams and Nickerson[2]).

The courses which NOLS offers provide relatively inexperienced individuals with an opportunity to explore remote wilderness areas they would otherwise never get to see, and to go there safely and with minimal environmental impact. Along the way they learn the value of outdoor leadership and about their own resources to deal with the challenges of wilderness travel and living.

NOLS takes the approach that the education of users in the skills and ethics of wilderness travel is the key to continued "use" of wildlands without creating adverse environmental impact. It is the school's belief that there is no point in putting aside wildlands for public use and protection unless the public is educated enough to know how to use wilderness without destroying it (NOLS 1986).

Education of the public about resource stewardship, about wilderness values, and about how to enjoy wilderness without stressing people or the environment, is exemplified in the kind of experiential education that NOLS offers (Hendee 1985). The NOLS program teaches safety, judgment, leadership, expedition behavior, outdoor living and travel skills, minimum impact camping, environmental ethics, natural sciences, and ecology.

The NOLS' experiential educational basis is evident. In the 1986 Annual Report the NOLS educational techniques are described as follows:

> NOLS achieves its goals, not by the traditional lecture style with occasional lab sessions and field trips—but by direct exploration and practice of skills in the outdoor classroom. The NOLS program encourages students to figure out what questions need to be asked and to use their judgment to find solutions which work best in each particular situation. NOLS gives students an education far beyond the scope and depth of that provided by the traditional classroom (NOLS 1986).

NOLS also encourages environmental awareness and understanding through the wilderness setting of their courses, as well as through a specific curriculum that covers geology, flora and fauna identification, and ecosystem relationships. The importance of resource conservation is also a specific subject throughout a typical course.

Course objectives are developed to allow each participant to:

- accept responsibility for the safety of themselves and the expedition;
- observe and experiment with the effectiveness and appropriateness of various leadership styles;
- test their own leadership style and skills through opportunities to be "leader-of-the-day";
- learn outdoor living skills such as cooking and baking, nutrition and rationing, fishing, climate control, physiology, and equipment care and selection; and
- learn travel techniques required in an expedition.

A wide range of benefits to participants in a NOLS course have been reported. Recent studies indicate that in addition to wilderness skills (Easley et al. 1986) there are substantial personal growth benefits even though they are perceived as a byproduct of a NOLS experience and are not the major emphasis of the NOLS curriculum (Driver et al. 1990, Easley 1985, Shin 1988). The nature and magnitude of reported skill benefits are discussed in a subsequent section of this chapter.

Wilderness Vision Quest

Wilderness Vision Quest is an experiential program founded by Michael H. Brown in 1976. The program is a camping and backpacking experience founded on an intimate encounter with nature. It is designed to help people grow in their appreciation of the natural world and, through the use of tools and techniques of self-discovery, is reported (Brown 1984) to lead to "the awakening of deep inner-life resources which lie dormant in all of us" (functions such as intuition, imagination, inspiration, and insight).

The structured program led by Brown emphasizes the spiritual dimensions of our contact with the natural world and calls for a deliberate focus on, and conscious effort to work towards, the constructive discovery, exploration, healing, enrichment, and growth of the human spirit (Brown 1984). Brown further suggests that organizations like Outward Bound and NOLS lead people into wild country simply

to wait for or hope that special and memorable experiences will occur. Wilderness Vision Quest participants are taught a wide variety of methods and techniques for deepening their appreciation of the natural world and for facilitating the process of self-discovery. Brown has developed an eleven step process that "gently and carefully guides the inner journey" (Brown 1984).

The program is designed to consciously and deliberately move people toward inner-life dimensions through the careful use of specific methods and techniques for expanding and heightening awareness. Through a combination of physical activity, light diet, exposure to the cycles and rhythms of nature, and carefully selected individual and group processes, the experiences of both the wilderness and inner lives are supposedly intensified (Brown 1984).

Benefits of the Wilderness Vision Quest program all accrue to the individual's development. Resource management issues and camping skills are not a part of the program. However, the use of wilderness or outdoor settings serves some function as a means of instilling general wilderness appreciation and values. By combining the inspiring wilderness qualities of naturalness and solitude with group and personal experience, Wilderness Vision Quest promotes connectedness to the natural world as well as self-awareness.

The major focus and intended benefits of Wilderness Vision Quest are to help participants release stress and tension, clarify values, and get in touch with the meaning and purpose of their lives. The participants challenge their own limits in one way or another, which are claimed to result in deeper self-knowledge and development of latent human potential.

Brown (1984) describes the benefits of a Wilderness Vision Quest as the chance to leave behind patterns and beliefs that keep us feeling separate and alone. He believes that, through observing and participating fully in nature, the participants discover the units of life and the importance of their part in it. Empowered by this perspective, the participants are seen as returning to daily life changed in a positive way—open, responsive, alive, and more able to align their actions in the world with their deepest values.

Universities

Universities use the outdoors for a variety of structured leisure and educational activities. First, and closely related to scientific use, is the use of structured, programmed activities for field trips; for subjects and study areas for theses, dissertations, and other reports; and for instructional examples. According to Hendee and Roggenbuck[3] the major emphases of these programmed wilderness-related courses in universities (that included field trips) were to increase understanding of: wilderness appreciation and use, wilderness and resource protection and management, and resource legislation and allocation. The benefits of these types of educational uses are directly related to both cognitive and affective development of individuals and supposedly lead to the obvious concomitant beneficial consequences.

A second educational use by universities is more akin to recreational use. It is the use of the outdoors as a setting for teaching woodsmanship and survival skills (Hendee et al. 1978). This includes formal courses with field trips, as well as university outing clubs and outdoor centers. The benefits of these activities are largely recreational, but some positive resource management attitudes and use ethics are likely due to the experiential nature of the program of activities.

A third component of programmed skill development activities by universities is the existence of cooperative programs. Work study and internship programs have been developed between individual resource management agencies and universities related to wildland and resource management (DuLac et al., in press). The resulting benefits of such educational activities accrue solely to the individuals involved, but clearly relate to the skill development benefits of structured programs even though achieved through resource management agencies rather than educational or adventure programs.

Other Groups

There are literally thousands of programs run by agencies and institutions (such as Boy Scouts, Girl Scouts, YMCA, YWCA, churches, elderhostels, conservation groups, and in Canada, the very effective Junior Forest Wardens program) that offer programs of skill development. These programs typically use outdoor areas and experiential educational techniques to impart both skills and knowledge. The Boy Scouts, for example, have always held outdoor living skills and ethics related to resource conservation as the pinnacle of achievement. The nature of these programs usually has an educational component. It is not possible, however, to identify what this component is in all cases, or whether specific, enduring skills are imparted to individual participants. In the absence of quantitative evidence, it is speculated that general resource appreciation and ethics, or at least sensitivity, are the result of many of these programs.

Similarly, it is not possible to determine if experiential education occurs in these programs. The nature of the activities may be experiential, but it is not known if actual experiential education is planned and implemented. The educational and skill development benefits of these programs are speculated by the author to be a direct function of the ability and insight of the leaders, surely the focus for another paper.

Summer Outdoor Youth Programs

Organized summer camps (through agencies, groups, and institutions) also are seen as programmed, skill development, and generally leisure-time programs which generate beneficial consequences to individuals. Most summer camps have educational objectives that are ecological and/or outdoor skill-related, although there is no way of knowing if these are true experiential education processes or just leisure activities with a recreational value.

Summer camps have been attended by many of America's youth and thus are an important force in shaping resource attitudes and behaviors. Most of the benefits research has been directed at personal growth rather than measuring evolving environmental consciousness or skill development. A literature review (Johnson and Driver[4]) of studies evaluating the benefits of youth camping was undertaken to develop a list of possible benefits that accrue to summer camp participants. The benefits that were reported in the review were numerous, falling into four categories: improvement in work attitudes, habits and skills; increased ability to get along with others; increased self-confidence; and improvement in basic orientation to life. The review was compiled as a basis for evaluating the long-term benefits of the Youth Conservation Corps (YCC). From 1972 to about 1982 YCC was an environmental education/work program where enrollees (age 15-18) live in a camp environment and participate in 30 hours of conservation work on public lands and 10 hours of environmental education per week. Since about 1982, it has been largely a conservation work program with reduced attention to environmental education. Longitudinal/panel studies of YCC participants in the late 1970s document a wide variety of benefits in all four categories identified by the Johnson and Driver[4] review and considerable differential benefits by different type of enrollee (Johnson and Driver 1982, Ross and Driver 1986, 1988).

SKILLS AND PERSONAL BENEFITS GAINED FROM STRUCTURED OUTDOOR EXPERIENCES

Self-Confidence

Extensive reviews of research evaluating changes in self-concept as a result of outdoor adventure programs indicate many methodological problems in study designs and mixed findings in program outcomes (Burton 1981, Ewert 1982, Shore 1977). There seems to be evidence, however, that the "stress/challenge" approach of Outward Bound can produce significant and enduring changes in a variety of components of self-concept. Support for an increase in self-confidence from outdoor programs can be found in Nye's (1976) work on Outward Bound, Kaplan's (1974) work using subjects from an "outdoor challenge" program, and the early work of Clifford and Clifford (1967) also on Outward Bound. Additional results on a variety of personal benefits related to programmed or structured outdoor experiences can be found in the works of Heaps and Thorstenson (1974), Berstein (1972), Winkie (1976), and Adams (1969).

Ewert (1982) prepared a comprehensive review and analysis of over 50 studies on self-concept and other psychological outcomes related to wilderness/adventure education. Shore (1977) had previously done a similar comprehensive review and critical evaluation of studies related specifically to Outward Bound. A dissertation by Burton (1981) is also particularly important because of its analysis of studies related to Outward Bound.

In the field of wilderness/adventure education, much of the research on self-concept has been done at various Outward Bound schools. The body of literature is vast. Thomas (1985) relates that more than 30 doctoral dissertations have been completed which relate to Outward Bound in the United States alone, with additional research having been done at schools in Britain and West Germany. Burton (1981), as cited by Thomas (1985: 13), found that:

> Of the 161 studies examined, 50 had used self-concept or a component of self-concept as the outcome variable. Of the 38 selected studies (those Burton determined had the most valid research design), self-concept was used in 17 (45%). Further, of all the variables chosen for the Outward Bound-type research, self-concept showed the most consistent positive change.

Because several comprehensive reviews already exist (Burton 1981, Ewert 1982, Shore 1977), only a few selected studies are reviewed here.

Beker (1960) designed a study to evaluate emotional and social growth of 13 school classes of sixth graders participating in 5-day school camping programs as a part of their regular school curriculum. Four nonparticipating classes provided control subjects. A 47-item check list was developed as a means of studying self-concept. Most of the items were original, although some were chosen from other studies. Significant and marked positive changes in self-concept were shown by the campers. The control group did not reflect these changes. The results suggest that school camping can have a marked positive impact on children's self-concepts.

Jones and Swan (1972) evaluated an outdoor education program for sixth grade children. They sent questionnaires to the parents within 10 days of their children returning from camp. Many of the parents felt the program benefited their children in many ways, including improving their attitudes toward school and self-confidence. They also reported that many parents felt participating in an outdoor education program improved their children's peer relationships.

Swan (1977) addressed the importance of wilderness experience in the development of human consciousness and emphasized that the purpose of environmental education is to develop educational programs aimed at the expansion and synthesis of the human potential. He insisted that being placed in the wilderness environment brings joy and can bring what Maslow called "peak experience." From his point of view, natural areas are reservoirs of life-nourishing energy which must be preserved to perpetuate a healthy people.

In a study of wilderness use as a functional reinforcement, Rossman and Ulehla (1977) interviewed and administered the reward value questionnaire, expectation questionnaire, and a final questionnaire to 47 male and 47 female undergraduate students who had participated in a wilderness experience. They found that a majority of the subjects felt that the emotional or spiritual experience, challenge and adventure, aesthetic enjoyment of natural settings, and escape from urban stress were important aspects of the wilderness experience.

A similar study was carried out by Brown and Haas (1980) with users of the Rawah Wilderness as subjects. They found that the outcome domains of wilderness experience were related to Nature, Escape Pressures, Achievement, Autonomy, Reflection on Personal Values, Sharing/Recollection, Risk Taking, and Meeting/Observing other people. They concluded that such information would aid in the development of more specific, quantifiable, and evaluative management objectives. This information could also provide a basis for developing recreation inventories, selecting management tools and techniques, and developing visitor information packages. The information might also aid in the differential economic valuation of wilderness recreation activity and experience opportunities.

To determine whether the effect of long-term camping experience upon personality affects work orientation and interpersonal orientation, Bridgewater (1981) administered Jackson's Personality Research Form (PRF) (Jackson 1974) and Rotter's Internal-External Locus of Control Scale (I-E) (Rotter 1963) to 37 students in the National Outdoor Leadership School Wilderness Course. Using the pre-test and post-test of those instruments, the study revealed that there were significant differences in 8 out of 21 items on the I-E Scale at the .05 level. On the PRF, male subjects moved significantly away from impulsivity. There was more deliberation before these subjects spoke or expressed their feelings or wishes.

Kaplan (1984) evaluated a wilderness program in Michigan's Upper Peninsula by assessing the following data sources: 1) questionnaires completed by the 49 participants in the last 2 years of the program; 2) familiarity and preference ratings of photographs; 3) reactions to the solo experience; and 4) ratings of moods and feelings both before and at the conclusion of the program. She found that the program resulted in many psychological benefits to the participants.

Ewert (1986) divided the benefits of participation in outdoor adventure recreation into psychological categories (e.g., self-concept, confidence, self-efficacy, sensation-seeking, actualization, well-being, personal testing); sociological categories (e.g., compassion, group cooperation, respect for others, communication, behavior feedback, friendship, belonging); educational categories (e.g., outdoor education, nature awareness, conservation education, problem-solving, value-clarification, outdoor techniques, improved academics); and physical categories (e.g., fitness skills, strength, coordination, catharsis, exercise, balance). Through a review of literature, he identified the critical need for an increase in the attention shown to adventure activities by the professional researcher.

Ewert (1982) discusses the work of Dickinson[5] at the National Outdoor Leadership School (NOLS). Using a relatively small sample of 42 students from 3 selected courses, he administered the Tennessee Self-Concept Scale (TSCS) as a pre-test on the first day of the course and as a post-test on the last day of the course. A third administration of the instrument was given to participants 5 months after completion of the course. The study apparently had no matching control group. Dickinson's analysis revealed that the population experienced a positive change in self-concept as measured by the TSCS as a result of the NOLS course and that the changes apparently persisted for the 5-month follow up period. All 10 scales of the TSCS (self-criticism, total positive self, identity, self-satisfaction, behavior, physical self, moral-ethical self, personal self, family self, and social self) showed significant positive changes at the .05 level of significance.

Dickinson's study is one of the few research efforts that deals with a nonstress challenge program (i.e., NOLS) and with a "normal," although self-selecting population. It was, however, an undergraduate project and may not have been subjected to professional peer review.

A study by Kimball (1979) also used the TSCS on a population of students enrolled in a variety of so-called "wilderness experience" courses. Like Dickinson's study, it used a pre- and post-administration of the TSCS without a control group. While Dickinson's subjects were enrolled in 5-week standard wilderness courses at NOLS, Kimball's work was based on 14-day experiences by subjects who participated in perceived "high-stress" activities, such as rock climbing, river rafting, and a solo experience. Using t-tests of pre/post differences in TSCS scores, Kimball found positive changes in all 10 TSCS scales. Again, the difficulties of making definite conclusions and generalizations without a control group were manifest. Kimball's findings did, however, support several previous studies (Berstein 1972, Clifford and Clifford 1967, Heaps and Thorstenson 1974, Nye 1976).

Easley (1985) conducted a study on the influence of instructor personality on self-concept changes in students in a 5-week NOLS course. The research used a pre-treatment/post-treatment administration of the TSCS to 355 students in the treatment group, where the treatment was a NOLS course. A control of 50 students consisted of students scheduled to take a NOLS course. Significant gains in self-concept were found, using ANCOVA analysis procedures, on 7 of the 10 TSCS scales. The only scales not showing significant change were satisfaction, personal self, and self-criticism.

A recent study by Thomas (1985) attempted to determine the influence of course length on the self-concept change of a relatively young (average age 15.14) group of 134 participants at the Minnesota (now Voyageur) Outward Bound School. His study design included both experimental and control groups in courses of two different lengths. For the 14-day course, there were 38 subjects in the experimental group and 14 subjects in the control group. For the longer course of 21 days, there were 70 in the experimental group and 12 in the control group. The study employed a pre/post/follow-up design using the TSCS. He mailed pre-test and post-test instruments and found no statistically significant differences in pre-test and post-test changes between the 14-day, 21-day, or control groups, although the slight differences found favored the experimental groups. Thomas used the ANCOVA procedure to adjust for the pre-test scores in the three groups. However, there is no mention that the homogeneity-of-slopes had been tested by including the interaction effects of the pre-test and experimental or control group. Such unequal sample group sizes and potential heterogeneity of variances would have indicated this procedure prior to the normal ANCOVA adjustment of post-test scores. Thomas did find significant changes (p<.01) when comparing pre-test and follow-up self-concept scores for the younger students (age <15.14 years). Older students experienced no such follow-up test changes.

Self-actualization is commonly mentioned when the psychological benefits of wilderness are discussed (Driver 1987, Driver and Brown 1986, Ewert 1986, Roggenbuck,[6] Young and Crandall 1986). Roggenbuck[6] suggested self-actualization as the ultimate health benefit of a wilderness experience.

To determine whether or not an Outward Bound experience would assist in the self-actualization process, Vander Wilt and Klocke (1971) administered the Personal Orientation Inventory to 20 participants in a 3-week Minnesota Outward Bound course. Specific activities of the students during the course included rock climbing, canoeing, rappelling, a 3-day solo experience, etc., and numerous in-depth discussions of these experiences. Using a pre-test and post-test design, Vander Wilt and Klocke concluded that significant positive changes occurred in the female participants at p<0.10 on the Time Ration, Support Ration, Self-Acceptance, Nature of Man, and Capacity for Intimate Contact scales. When they compared pre-test and post-test scores of the male members of the sample, they found no significant differences at p<0.10. Significant differences occurred in the positive direction at the 0.10 level on 7 of the 12 scales when the entire group was compared.

Davis (1972) suggested that positive effects of fear, as experienced in rock climbing, can play a role in increasing self-actualization and self-awareness. He sent questionnaires to 408 graduates of an Outward Bound School. The questionnaires consisted of a two-part rating scale designed to indicate the intensity of fear experienced at specific moments during the participant's first vertical rock climb and subsequent rappel. The subjects were also asked for short verbal descriptions reflecting upon their feelings of fear and enthusiasm prior to, during, and after the activities. On the basis of the replies, he concluded that overcoming fear results in new levels of self-awareness and self-actualization. He pointed out that fear must be overcome and transformed into enthusiasm before self-actualization could be expected.

Scott (1974) presented a persuasive suggestion of a connection between self-actualization and wilderness use. He expected that wilderness experiences are more likely to foster self-actualization and the occurrence of peak experiences than outdoor activities in less primitive environments. Although his connection was not based on empirical studies, he postulated self-actualization and wilderness use by analyzing the writings and lives of men such as George Catlin, John Muir, Henry Thoreau, and Aldo Leopold who had "peak experiences" while in the wilderness. He speculated that these men were self-actualizing individuals who used wilderness experiences to further their growth.

A direct test of the effects of the wilderness experience on self-actualization was carried out by Lambert et al. (1978). They examined changes in self-actualization values as a function of participation in college classes that included a wilderness experience. Two program groups and two control groups were utilized in this study. All subjects in each group were administered the Personal Orientation Inventory (POI) at the beginning and end of their respective classes. No significant differences pre- and post-course were found with the POI.

Leiweke (1976) carried out a study to determine whether self-actualization was significantly increased as a result of a 24-day Outward Bound experience. His study took place in 1974 at the Texas Outward Bound School. Using a pre-test and post-test of the POI, observation, and student journals, he concluded that there was a significant change in self-actualization by the participants.

Papantones (1977) designed a study to examine whether the use of Transactional Analysis was an effective method of increasing self-actualization in a resident camp setting. The study was quasi-experimental in design with a population that had already been chosen and assigned to specific camp sessions. He used a control group consisting of 84 campers and an experimental group consisting of 163 adolescent males. The control group took part in group sessions with their leaders while the experimental group took part in a Transactional Analysis Group Program in a 5-day resident camp program at Andrews Air Force Base. Using a pre-test and post-test of the POI, he found that both groups demonstrated significant changes in self-actualization (t=14.08, p<0.05 for control group; t=21.00, p<0.05 for experimental group). A follow-up survey revealed that they had gained much valuable knowledge from their experience.

Vogel (1979) set out to investigate whether an Outward Bound type of program conducted by Project Urban Suburban Environments (USE) in New Jersey, resulted in changes in the participants. The study involved 39 individuals enrolled in a 16-day Project USE course as an experimental group, and 20 individuals who would take the course later that year as a control group. Through the pre-test and post-test of the POI, individual journals, and instructors' evaluation, the study revealed that the experimental group post-test scores were significantly higher than those of the control group on several scales of Inner-Support. The analyses also revealed that the experimental group had positive correlation between their self-actualization scores measured by the POI and self-perception of personal change scores measured by course description. Vogel concluded that this form of training can lead to higher levels of self-actualization for participants and increased awareness of self-perception of personal change.

Two of the most recent studies on wilderness use and self-actualization were carried out by Young and Crandall (1984, 1986). The first study was designed to test three hypotheses: that wilderness users are more self-actualized than nonusers; that among present nonusers, those who intend to use wilderness will be more self-actualized than those who never intend to; and that among the wilderness users, frequent users are more self-actualized than less frequent users.

Young and Crandall (1984) used two samples to test the level of self-actualization, one from the general public and the other from a group of wilderness users of the Boundary Waters Canoe Area Wilderness (BWCAW) in the Superior National Forest. Because of the time required and previous insensitivity of the POI, they used a short form of the POI which had high reliability (r=0.75, p<0.001) and correlation (d=0.64, p<0.001 level) with the longer form. This study indicated there were significant differences between wilderness users' scores and nonusers' scores. They also found that there was a trend for potential users to be slightly more self-actualized than potential nonusers. However, frequent wilderness users were found to be no more self-actualized than occasional wilderness users.

To examine the possibility of individual changes in self-actualization with continued wilderness visits over a period of time, Young and Crandall (1986) conducted a 5-year longitudinal study. They collected the data in 1979 in the BWCAW for the first administration of the POI. After examining the frequency of wilderness use, they sent POI questionnaires to the panel members annually. Through this study, they found that panel members' self-actualization scores were significantly higher in 1984 than 1979 (p<0.001), and that active users had significantly higher scores than inactive users.

Shin (1988) reported on research designed to determine to what extent participation in a 5-week NOLS course increased the self-actualization of participants and whether participants' personal variables were correlated with any change. A pre-test and post-test control group design was employed to administer Jones and Crandall's Short Index of Self-actualization to 163 students in the treatment group. A control group of 138 students consisted of students scheduled to take a NOLS course. Significant increases in positive

self-actualization were found. Participants' sex, age, previous wilderness experience, place of residence, and education showed no significant effect on self-actualization changes. The major conclusions from the research were that changes in self-actualization did occur as a result of a 5-week wilderness experience and that these changes occurred regardless of participants' backgrounds.

From the studies cited here, and from the detailed reviews of the many studies by Ewert (1982), Shore (1977), and Burton (1981), it seems that wilderness education/adventure courses have indeed resulted in changes to participants. As Ewert (1982: 17) points out:

> While there has been a wide variance in the design and conclusion-generating ability of these works, there can be little doubt that many of these types of programs have done something to the participant. That something has often been a positive enhancement of the self-concept.

Outdoor Skills

The development of specific outdoor skills is a ubiquitous and important part of most outdoor programs. However, few research studies have addressed changes in the actual outdoor skill level of participants. Kaplan (1974) published one of the few studies that purported to measure, on the basis of pre-test and post-test self-reports, changes in outdoor skills as a result of a wilderness skills program. She found that 7 out of 10 specific activity-based skills, (finding food, rock climbing, ecology, map reading, using compass, knowledge of woods, and setting up camp) changed as a result of a program. No change was reported in first aid skill, outdoor cooking, or fire building. Johnson and Driver (1982) found a wider variety of outdoor skill acquisition from participation in the Youth Conservation Corps. The importance of outdoor skill development in many programs and the findings from Kaplan and Johnson and Driver result in the hypothesis that students receive significant gains in outdoor skill as a result of their participation in these programmed experiences.

Robertson reported on two interesting studies related to reported vs. actual camping behaviors (often skill-based) and the source of information related to those behaviors. Her studies result in two major conclusions related to skill development. One study (Robertson 1986) reported that visitors were accurate in reporting their perceived camping behaviors when compared to actual observed behavior. Her second work (Robertson[7]) revealed some interesting but surprising results. Over one-third (37%) of the visitors in her study of reported vs. actual camping behavior reported that their primary source of wilderness visitor information had been formal classes, including wilderness courses, outdoor organizations, and employment training. The same percentage of visitors perceived formal classes (viz, programmed recreational experiences) as the most effective source of wilderness information. In addition, past related literature (Bradley 1978, Clark et al. 1972, Fazio 1979, Oliver et al. 1985) supports personal contact and formal training as the most effective wilderness education approaches particularly related to minimum impact skills. However, based on Robertson's studies, a significant relationship was not found between the source of information and appropriateness of wilderness behavior. In other words, formal teaching as a common source of wilderness information is perceived as effective by visitors, managers, and researchers, but was not found to be related to appropriate back-country behavior.

A recent exploratory study on perceived benefits of a NOLS course by Driver et al. (1990), used a "one-shot" longitudinal sample of past students (1974, 1975, 1981, 1982, 1983). It showed a relatively high mean (7.8 out of 9) desirability of the respondents for the benefit of "Outdoor Skills," a high mean (3.7 out of 5) perceived change in those skills as a result of the NOLS course, and the influence of a NOLS course being rated highest (4.1 out of 5) of the 19 clustered benefits studied. The exploratory nature of the research prevents generalization but clearly indicates that participants not only valued the significant increase in their outdoor skills but that the NOLS curriculum and programmed experiential courses were the causal agent.

There is still much to be learned or validated about the internalization of wilderness skills that seem to result from many of the programmed skill-developing courses. The usual lack of longitudinal follow-up of past participants precludes any firm conclusions about the long-term impact of the skill development aspects of these programs.

Leadership Skills

Leadership development is a principal focus at NOLS and in other programs and, therefore, it is hypothesized that students should perceive and receive gains in this important outcome. Very little research has been done on the question of leadership skill development as a result of an outdoor program. No objective measures of changes in leadership skill are typically done, but a subjective assessment done as part of the post-course evaluation by instructors indicates that positive changes are perceived to take place in many students. Baker (1975), however, found no changes in leadership behavior as a result of an outdoor skills course at NOLS using a standard instrument, the Leadership Opinion Questionnaire.

A recent study of NOLS (McDannold 1985) using the Hersey and Blanchard (1982) Situation Leadership Model reported that students' leadership effectiveness scores increased from a pre-course mean score of +9.30 to a post-course mean score of +11.10. This change was significant at the .05 level. The leadership style, however, as rated by the instrument, was not significantly changed by the course experience.

There seems to be a dearth of research related to leadership development in outdoor programs. It is speculated by this author that leadership still remains as a "fuzzy" concept which has not been well specified and operationalized. The plethora of "executive development" and/or "leadership" courses suggest a potentially fruitful (and perhaps somewhat urgent) area of research.

FUTURE EFFORTS AT CHARACTERIZING BENEFICIAL CONSEQUENCES: A PRELIMINARY PROGNOSTICATION

There appears to be a definite need to develop a taxonomy of wilderness/adventure education programs. Programs currently exist which use natural areas as classrooms that range in objectives from the therapeutic/personal growth orientation of Outward Bound and its derivative programs, through the type of skills/leadership programs represented by NOLS. The principal focus of many of these programs is not adequately understood, nor is their value to the students or the wilderness. The number and diversity of objectives of the programs are increasing. Hale (1978), for example, described over 200 such programs which offer outdoor adventure and skill development as a component of their curriculum. In addition, Hendee and Roggenbuck[3] determined that there were 542 wilderness-related courses taught within colleges and universities in the U.S. They determined that about 30% of the course instructors listed the first objective of the course as "wilderness appreciation, use, enjoyment, and skills." An additional 40% listed this objective as the second major purpose of the course. The courses represented student enrollment of over 8,000 students per year. Further definition of the specific beneficial consequences related to appreciation, use, and enjoyment seems to be needed.

Once an adequate taxonomy of objectives and course types has been developed, it may be possible to explore a second major issue related to wilderness education, that is, how these courses relate to, encourage, or solidify the personal values gained by the students; and how these values and skills transfer to everyday life. Little work has been done on how these courses influence student perceptions of the wilderness values of nature appreciation, freedom, solitude, simplicity, and spiritual and aesthetic insight (Hendee et al. 1978). The fundamental questions yet to be answered deal with the values of these educational wilderness experiences and the types of educational approaches that will maximize these values in the hearts and minds of the students. Different methodological approaches may be necessary to address these issues. Research efforts which utilize qualitative research methods rather than objective or self-report instruments may be the necessary first step to provide the answers to the many questions that remain.

There has not been sufficient empirical evidence gained by previous research to confidently conclude the nature and extent of student skill development or leadership abilities as a result of wilderness/adventure courses. MacNeil (1975), Lyman (1975), and Iida (1975) have suggested the need for better experimental designs with sufficient sample sizes and control groups, as well as careful attention to "artifacts" such as maturation, history, and testing reactance. While progress has been made, methodological problems still remain.

For example, Easley (1985) and Shin (1988) both reported decline in post-test scores on the TSCS of the control group (post-tested just prior to the start of the course) in research on NOLS. The implication of a decline in post-test scores is worthy of some discussion. One might speculate on several reasons for the phenomena, including behavior of young subjects experiencing freedom after having been pre-tested in their home environment.

Koepke offers a more plausible and less speculative reason based on her study at the Colorado Outward Bound School. She found that the students "experience(d) a high anxiety level just prior to the course" (Koepke 1973: 5). She also reported an inverse relation between a student's self-perception and the level of anxiety experienced. Rhodes (1973: 164) pointed out that "anticipatory anxiety on the part of the participants prior to the beginning of the training experience...can easily bias the results of pre-training measures." Kimball (1979: 156) related the problems of administering a psychometric survey to students while "on a course" and recommended that "testing should occur in a quiet classroom-like atmosphere." The testing procedures used by both Easley (1985) and Shin (1988) were designed to reduce this reported pre-course anxiety, but it is possible that the drop in TSCS scales reported for control students was, in fact, a result of the perceived challenges ahead or of the testing instrument itself. This potential anxiety effect has great significance for pre-test and post-test administration of psychometric instruments and should be subjected to further research.

Many other predictors of student outcomes should be examined. For example, much of the research reviewed has not addressed the role of the wilderness environment, or degree of solitude experienced on programmed courses. Other factors that should be examined as possible predictors of student outcomes would include specific program curriculum elements and perhaps even some measure of the strength of interpersonal relationships developed by the students while on a course.

Further research efforts should focus on the two outcomes of outdoor skills and leadership skill. Initial efforts might be devoted to determining the criterion measures of these outcomes, their operationalization, and the degree of change produced in students using the techniques extant in structured programs. Extension of this work could involve limited experimental manipulation of a package of different teaching strategies for use on some courses to determine their differential effectiveness. This would be particularly germane to student gains in leadership skill, both as perceived by the student and as measured by objective instruments.

Much of the reported research addressed only one specific student outcome, the objective measure of self-concept. It would be an interesting research project, perhaps using survey research methods rather than experimental methods, to determine what specific effects these programs have in the longer run on various aspects of students' lives after their experience. Such research would probably be based on subjective self-perception by former students, but other more quantifiable research objectives could be developed related to employment patterns in outdoor programs, selection of college major, repeat attendance at structured programs, and involvement in environmental organizations. Comparisons with an equivalent control group of students who have not experienced such structured programs might lead to some interesting revelations on the longer term effects of such a program. The exploratory work by Driver et al. (1990) is a step in the right direction and the methodology offers much promise.

Further examination and definition of the influence of various well-defined components of program curricula should be undertaken. Some research has already demonstrated a potentially strong influence of the curriculum on a variety of student outcomes (Scherl 1989). More precise definition of which components influence which outcomes would be of assistance in developing new course proposals and revising existing course teaching strategies to achieve specific outcomes.

The final prognostication is that there seems to be sufficient empirical evidence on self-concept to warrant a higher priority to research on other outcome measures, such as outdoor skills and leadership skill development.

ENDNOTES

[1] Wilderness in the context of this paper does not refer to the "W" Wilderness of the National Wilderness Preservation System but to any area with wild or wilderness-like conditions.

[2] D. R. Williams and N. Nickerson in paper on measuring satisfaction of NOLS students, 1985.

[3] J. C. Hendee and J. W. Roggenbuck in paper on wilderness-related education as a factor increasing demand for wilderness, presented at the 1984 International Forest Congress in Quebec City.

[4] L. A. Johnson and B. L. Driver in unpublished literature review of studies of the benefits of youth camping and outdoor survival programs, 1982.

[5] R. Dickinson in report on a study to determine self-concept change through a program of wilderness skill development, University of Northern Colorado, 1979.

[6] J. W. Roggenbuck in paper on health benefits of wilderness use, prepared for Dr. Hendee, Assistant Director of the USDA Forest Service, Southeastern Forest Experiment Station, Asheville, NC, 1984.

[7] R. D. Robertson in paper on conceptualizing recreation behavior—an examination of Fishbein-Ajzen model as a framework for wilderness education.

LITERATURE CITED

Adams, W. D. 1969. Survival training: its effect on the self-concept and selected personality factors of emotionally disturbed adolescents. Logan, UT: Utah State University. 388 p. Ph.D. dissertation.

Baker, E. D. 1975. Change in leadership behavior attitudes affected by participation in basic courses at the National Outdoor Leadership School. University Park, PA: Penn State University. M.S. thesis.

Bacon, S. 1983. The conscious use of metaphor in Outward Bound. Denver, CO: Colorado Outward Bound School.

Beker, J. 1960. The influence of school camping on the self-concepts and social relationships of sixth grade children. Journal of Educational Psychology. 51(6): 352-356.

Berstein, A. 1972. Wilderness as a therapeutic behavior setting. Therapeutic Recreation Journal. Fourth Quarter: 160-161, 185.

Bradley, J. 1978. A human approach to reducing wildland impacts. Proceedings of the Wildland Recreation Impacts Conference. USDA Forest Service, USDI National Park Service. R-6-001-1979.

Bridgewater, H. G. 1981. The effect of a ninety-four day wilderness camping program upon personality. Oklahoma City, OK: Oklahoma State University. 121 p. Ph.D. dissertation..

Brown, M. 1984. Wilderness vision quest. In: Martin, V.; Inglis, M., eds. Wisconsin: Wilderness the way ahead: 213-218.

Brown, P. J.; Haas, G. E. 1980. Wilderness recreation experiences: the Rawah case. Journal of Leisure Research. 12(3): 229-241.

Burton, L. M. 1981. A critical analysis and review of the research on Outward Bound and related programs. Dissertation Abstracts International. 42: 158-B.

Canadian Outward Bound Wilderness School. 1985. The Canadian Outward Bound Wilderness School. Can. Outward Bound Pamph., 16 pp.

Clark, R. N.; Burgess, R. L.; Hendee, S. C. 1972. The development of anti-litter behavior in a forest campground. Journal of Applied Behavior Analysis. 5(1): 1-5.

Clifford, E.; Clifford, M. 1967. Self-concepts before and after survival training. British Journal of Social and Clinical Psychology. 6: 241-248.

Davis, R. W. 1972. The fear experience in rock climbing and its influence on self-actualization. In: Shore, A., ed. Outward Bound: a reference volume. Greenwich, CT: Outward Bound, Inc: 83-85

Driver, B. L. 1987. Benefits of river and trail recreation: the limited state of knowledge and why it is limited. In: Seguire, S., ed. Proceedings, First International Congress on Trail and River Recreation, Vancouver, May 31-June 4, 1986: 44-58.

Driver, B. L.; Brown, P. 1986. Probable personal benefits of outdoor recreation. In: A literature review: President's Commission on Americans Outdoors, Washington, DC: 63-70 values section.

Driver, B. L.; Peterson, G. L.; Easley, A. T. 1990. Benefits perceived by past participants in the NOLS Wind River Wilderness Course. In: Easley, A. T.; Passineau, J.; Driver, B. L., eds. The use of wilderness for personal growth, therapy and education. GTR RM-193. Fort Collins, CO: USDA Forest Service, Rocky Mountain Forest and Range Experiment Station.

DuLac, D.; Blackwell, J.; Lennon, T., et al. [In press]. Partnerships for recreation on the national forests. In: Proceedings, National Recreation Strategy Symposium—America's great outdoors. 1987 November 15; Lake Geneva, WI.

Easley, A. T. 1985. The personality traits of wilderness leadership instructors at NOLS: the relationship to perceived instructor effectiveness and the development of self-concept in students. Blacksburg, VA: Virginia Polytechnic Institute and State University. 182 p. Ph.D. dissertation.

Easley, A. T.; Roggenbuck, J. W.; Ratz, J. 1986. Wilderness education at NOLS: student outcomes and correlates of perceived instructor effectiveness. In: Lucas, R. C., ed. Proceedings, National Wilderness Research Conference: current research. Fort Collins, CO: 377-384.

Ewert, A. 1982. Outdoor adventure and self-concept: a research analysis. Eugene, OR: University of Oregon, Dept. of Recreation and Park Management.

Ewert, A. 1986. Values, benefits and consequences in outdoor adventure recreation. In: A literature review: President's Commission on Americans Outdoors, Washington, DC: 71-80.

Fazio, J. R. 1979. Communicating with the wilderness user. University of Idaho College of Forestry, Wildlife and Range Science Bull. no. 28.

Hale, A., ed. 1978. Directory-programs in outdoor adventure activities. Mankato, MN: Outdoor Experiences.

Heaps, R. A.; Thorstenson, C. T. 1974. Self-concept changes immediately and one year after survival training. Therapeutic Recreation Journal. Second quarter: 60-63.

Hendee, J. C. 1985. Wilderness...the next twenty years. National Outdoor Leadership School, distinguished lecturer series. 1(1): 14.

Hendee, J. C.; Stankey, G. H.; Lucas, R. C. 1978. Wilderness management. US Forest Service, Misc. Pub. No. 1365.

Hersey, P.; Blanchard, K. 1982. Management of organizational behavior: utilizing human resources (4th ed.). Englewood Cliffs, NJ: Prentice-Hall Inc.

Iida, M. 1975. Adventure-oriented programs: a review of research. In: van der Smissen, B., ed. Research camping and environmental education. State College, PA: Penn State HPER Series No. 11: 219-241.

Jackson, D. W. 1974. Personality research form. In: Bridgewater, H. G. 1981. The effect of a ninety-day wilderness camping program upon personality. Oklahoma City, OK: Oklahoma State University. Ph.D. disertation: p. 56.

Johnson, L. A.; Driver, B.L. 1982. An approach to measuring the perceived benefits to volunteers in natural resource agencies. In: Proceedings, Volunteers in the backcountry. Pinkham Notch, New Hampshire, May 21-22, 1982. Durham, NH: University of New Hampshire: 80-88.

Jones, O. E.; Swan, M. D. 1972. Parents' perceptions of resident outdoor education, Rockford Outdoor School and Taft Campus, Illinois, a comparison, Spring 1971. Taft Campus Occasional Paper No. 4. Oregon, IL: Northern Illinois University, Taft Campus, Department of Outdoor Teacher Education.

Kaplan, R. 1974. Some psychological benefits of an outdoor challenge program. Environment and Behavior. 6 (1): 101-116.

Kaplan, R. 1984. Wilderness perception and psychological benefits: an analysis of a continuing program. Leisure Science. 6(3): 271-290.

Kelly, F.; Baer, D. 1971. Physical challenge as a treatment for delinquency. Crime and Delinquency. 13: 437-445.

Kimball, R. 1979. Wilderness experience program: final evaluation report. Doc. 179 327. Washington, DC: US Educational Resources Information Center.

Koepke, S. M. 1973. The effects of Outward Bound participation upon anxiety and self-concept. (ERIC Document Reproduction Service No. ED 099 162).

Kraft, R. J. [n.d.]. Towards a theory of experiential learning. In: Kraft, R. J.; Sakofs, M., eds. The theory of experiential education. Boulder, CO: Association for Experiential Education. 1985: 7-38.

Lambert, M. J.; Segger, J. F.; Stanley, J. S., et al. 1978. Reported self-concept and self-actualizing value changes as a function of academic classes with wilderness experience. Perceptual and Motor Skills. 46: 1035-1040.

Leiweke, J. T. 1976. The influence of the twenty-day Outward Bound experience on self-actualization. St. Louis, MO: St. Louis University. 148 p. Ph.D. dissertation.

Lyman, R. D. 1975. Therapeutic camping as a treatment modality for the emotionally disturbed. In: van der Smissen, B., ed. Research camping and enviromental education, Penn State HPER Series No. 11: 243-351.

Maynard, L. 1969. Outward Bound: nature as teacher. Saturday Review. May, 17: 76-77.

McDannold, D. S. 1985. A study of leadership of the National Outdoor Leadership School. Thesis, honors degree, University of Waterloo, Canada.

MacNeil, B. B. 1975. The background of therapeutic camping. Journal of Social Issues. 13(1): 3-14.

National Outdoor Leadership School. 1986. NOLS 1986 Annual Report. 16 p.

Nye, R. P. 1976. The influence of an Outward Bound program on the self-concept of participants. Dissertation Abstracts International. 37(01): 142-A.

Oliver, S; Roggenbuck, J. W.; Watson, A. E. 1985. Education to reduce impacts in forest campgrounds. Journal of Forestry. April.

Papantones, M. 1977. A transactional analysis group program designed to increase the self-actualization of adolescent males in a resident camping setting as measured by the POI. Washington, DC: George Washington University. 103 p. Ph.D. dissertation.

Putman, R. 1984. The rationale for Outward Bound. Eskdale, Holmroot Cumbria: Eskdale Outward Bound School.

Ranney, S. 1984. Working to conserve wild America: the wilderness movement in the US. In: Martin, V.; Inglis, M., eds. Wisconsin: Wilderness the way ahead: 78-87.

Richards, G. E. 1977. Some educational implications and contributions of outward bound. Tharwa, A.C.T.: Australian Outward Bound School.

Rhodes, J. S. 1973. The problem of individual change in Outward Bound: an application of change and transfer theory. Dissertation Abstracts International. 33: 4922A.

Robertson, R. D. 1986. Actual versus self-reported wilderness visitor behavior. In: Lucas, R. C., ed. Proceedings - National Wilderness Research Conference: current research. Ogden, UT: U.S. Department of Agriculture, Intermountain Research Station, General Technical Report INT-212: 326-332.

Ross, D. M.; Driver, B. L. 1986. Importance of appraising responses of subgroups in evaluations: Youth Conservation Corps. Journal of Enviornmental Education. 17(3): 16-23.

Ross, D. M.; Driver, B. L. 1988. Benefits of residential and nonresidential Youth Conservation Corps camps. Journal of Outdoor Education. 22: 14-20.

Rossman, B. B.; Ulehla, Z. J. 1977. Psychological reward values associated with wilderness use: a functional-reinforcement approach. Environment and Behavior. 9(1): 41-66.

Rotter, J. B. 1963. Internal-external locus of control reinforcement. Psychological Monographs. 80(1): 1-28.

Sakofs, M. 1983. Piaget—a psychological rationale for experiential education. In: Kraft, R. J.; Sakofs, M., eds. The theory of experiential education. Boulder, CO: Association for Experiential Education. 1985: 159-160.

Scherl, L. M. 1989. The wilderness experience: psychological and motivational considerations of a structured experience in a wilderness setting. James Cook University of North Queensland. Ph.D. Dissertation.

Scott, N. 1974. Toward a psychology of wilderness experience. Natural Resource Journal. 14: 231-237.

Shin, W. S. 1988. The influence of a wilderness course on the self-actualization of the students. University of New Brunswick, Canada. M.S. thesis.

Shore, A. 1977. Outward Bound: a reference volume. Greenwich, CT: Outward Bound, Inc.

Smith, M. 1971. An investigation of the effects of an Outward Bound experience on selected personality factors and behaviors of high school juniors. Univ. of Oregon. 170 p. Ph.D. dissertation.

Swan, J. A. 1977. The psychological significance of the wilderness experience. The Journal of Environmental Education. 8: 4-7.

Thomas, S. E. 1985. The effect of course length on self-concept changes in participants of the Minnesota Outward Bound Junior Program. Buffalo, NY: State University of New York. Ph.D. dissertation.

Vander Wilt, R. B.; Klocke, R. A. 1971. Self-actualization of females in an experimental orientation program. Journal of Women Deans and Counsellors. 34: 125-129.

Vogel, R. M. 1979. The effects of Project USE training (adventure training). Philadelphia, PA: Temple University. 143 p. Ph.D. dissertation.

Wetmore, R. C. 1972. The influence of Outward Bound school experience on the self-concept of adolescent boys. Boston, MA: Boston University. 150 p. M.S. thesis.

Winkie. P. A. 1976. The effects of an Outward Bound school experience on levels of moral judgment and self-concept. Dissertation Abstracts International. 37(12): 7657-A.

Wright, A. N. 1983. Therapeutic potential of the Outward Bound process: an evaluation of a treatment program for juvenile delinquents. Therapeutic Recreation Journal: 2nd Quarter: 33-42.

Young, R. A.; Crandall, R. 1984. Wilderness use and self-actualization. Journal of Leisure Research. 16(2): 149-160.

Young, R. A.; Crandall, R. 1986. Self-actualization and wilderness use: a panel study. In: Lucas, R. C., ed. Proceedings, National Wilderness Research Conference: current research. Fort Collins, CO. July 23-26, 1985: 385-388.

Recreation for the Mentally Ill

Lynn Levitt
Behavioral Sciences Department
School of Humanities
New York Institute of Technology
Central Islip, New York

Although the value of recreation for the mentally ill has been recognized for many years, it wasn't until after WWII that psychiatrists and others began to recognize the therapeutic value of recreation (O'Morrow 1980). Recreation is viewed as therapeutic for patients/clients because it is supposed to provide an outlet for hostility and other emotions; reduce social isolation, boredom, and loneliness; provide diversional activities; increase socialization; encourage independence, growth, and development; increase self-esteem and self-confidence; develop new skills and interests; improve health and physical fitness; and encourage individual and group decisionmaking (Davis 1952; Frye and Peters 1972; Haun 1961,1965; Menninger 1948; Nesbitt 1977; O'Morrow 1980; The Hospital Recreation Section of the American Recreation Society 1953; West 1979).

Since several of these benefits address many of the symptoms of mental and emotional disturbance (e.g., poor interpersonal relationships, depression, withdrawal, lack of self-esteem), recreation appears to have the potential to lessen or alleviate these symptoms and hence improve the physical, emotional, and mental health of the patient (Frye and Peters 1972, Li 1981, Menninger 1948). However, do the results of empirical research support this contention?

In examining the effects of recreation participation on the mentally ill, one realizes that the mentally ill participate in both structured and unstructured recreation activities. While unstructured recreation activities may be therapeutic for mentally ill patients/clients (Frye 1969), if recreational activities aren't structured, many mentally ill individuals tend to be listless, inactive, or spend a lot of time doing nothing in their free time (Conroy et al. 1981, Frye and Peters 1972, Harrington and Cross 1962, Jenkins et al. 1977, McClannahan 1973, Quilitch and Dare de Longchamps 1974). Therefore, the results of research reviewed in this chapter are based almost exclusively on structured recreation programs designed to bring about changes in the behavior and attitudes of the mentally ill and hence the label "therapeutic."[1]

THE NATURE OF RECREATION PROGRAMS

There is great diversity in the nature of recreation programs for mentally and emotionally disturbed individuals in terms of duration, the patients/clients, the staff, the patient/staff ratio, the setting, and the recreation activities themselves. Based on the recreation activities offered, recreation programs for the mentally ill can be divided into the following three categories: 1) mixed recreation activities/programs consisting of some combination of activities such as arts and crafts, walking, games, music, and sports (Altarez 1938, Bernstein 1985, Eler 1987, Jenkins et al. 1977, Kelly et al. 1983, Schwab et al. 1985); 2) physical exercise programs (primarily jogging or running) (Allen 1980, Conroy et al. 1982, Greist et al. 1979a, Kern et al. 1984, Watters and Watters 1980); and 3) therapeutic camping programs[2] (Banaka and Young 1985, Barker and Weisman 1966, Remar and Lowry 1974, Stich and Senior 1984). Since there is considerably more research on therapeutic camping programs than either mixed recreation activities or physical exercise programs, the nature of therapeutic camping programs will be reviewed separately.

Mixed Recreation Activities and Physical Exercise Programs

Most of these recreation programs last a few weeks, but some can be as short as a day (Voight 1988). Most of the research has been conducted with children (Altaraz 1938; Black et al. 1975; Eason et al. 1982; Kern et al. 1982, 1984; Santarcangelo et al. 1987; Schleien et al. 1987; Watters and Watters 1980) and adolescents (Reid et al. 1988, Stermac and Josefowitz 1985, Voight 1988, Witman 1987). However, other programs include only adults (Beal et al. 1977; Gordon et al. 1966; Greist et al. 1979a, 1979b; Harrington and Cross 1962; Wong et al. 1987), limit their sample to elderly patients (D'Urso and Logue 1988, Kelly et al. 1983, Schwab et al. 1985), or include mixed-age groups (Lewinsohn and Graf 1973, Wassman and Iso-Ahola 1985).

Usually small samples of less than 10 patients/clients (Black et al. 1975; Eler 1987; Kern et al. 1982, 1984; McClung 1984; Reid et al. 1988; Reynolds and Arthur 1982; Santarcangelo et al. 1987; Stermac and Josefowitz 1985; Watters and Watters 1980; Wong et al. 1987), or from 10-20 patients/clients (Allen 1980; Conroy et al. 1981, 1982; Wassman and Iso-Ahola 1985; Witman 1987) participate in these programs. Some programs are larger with 20-50 participants or more (Beal et al. 1977, Jenkins et al. 1977, Kelly et al. 1983, Lewinsohn and Graf 1973, Voight 1988).

Most recreation programs are usually mixed-sex groups (Bernstein 1985, Eason et al. 1982, Kern et al. 1982, Lewinsohn and Graf 1973, Voight 1988, Wassman and Iso-Ahola 1985) or all males (Allen 1980, Black et al. 1975, Reid et al. 1988, Watters and Watters 1980, Wong et al. 1987). Studies of elderly samples usually have more females than males (Jenkins et al. 1977), although the reverse can be true (Kelly et al. 1983).

Some recreation programs include individuals with various disorders such as schizophrenia, depression, anxiety disorders, drug abuse, behavioral disorders, autism, demen-

tia, and manic depression (Allen 1980, Bernstein 1985, Conroy et al. 1982, Harrington and Cross 1962, Kelly et al. 1983, Lewinsohn and Graf 1973, Miller 1987, Reid et al. 1988, Stermac and Josefowitz 1985, Voight 1988, Witman 1987). However, other programs are limited to individuals with the same diagnosis such as autism (Black et al. 1975; Kern et al. 1982, 1984; Santarcangelo et al. 1987; Schleien et al. 1987; Watters and Watters 1980), schizophrenia (Beal et al. 1977, Eler 1987, McClung 1984, Wong et al. 1987), or depression (Greist et al. 1979a, Wassman and Iso-Ahola 1985). The recreation programs consist of either hospitalized inpatients (Conroy et al. 1982, Eler 1987, Kelly et al. 1983, Santarcangelo et al. 1987, Voight 1988, Witman 1987), outpatients (D'Urso and Logue 1988, Harrington and Cross 1962), or both (Lewinsohn and Graf 1973).

The criteria for selection in physical exercise programs is often based, in part, on approval by medical or other personnel and/or passing a physical examination (Conroy et al. 1981; Greist et al. 1979a, 1979b; Kern et al. 1982, 1984; Reid et al. 1988; Solomon and Bumpus 1978; Voight 1988). In one program patients were eliminated if they were on antidepressant drugs (Greist et al. 1979b). Sometimes the patients/clients are volunteers (Bernstein 1985, Conroy et al. 1981, Lewinsohn and Graf 1973).

Therapeutic Camping Programs

Although some camping programs are day camps (Bergan 1958, Lee 1983, Orbach 1966), most are short-term camping programs with overnight stays ranging from a few days to a few weeks (Baer et al. 1975, Banaka and Young 1985, Herr 1975, Kaplan and Reneau 1965, Lowry 1974, Rerek 1973, Shearer 1975, Smith 1959, Weisman et al. 1966). Usually mountainous, forested regions such as national parks and forests, state parks, or forest preserves are used (Ackerman et al. 1959, Hobbs and Radka 1976, McDonald 1974, Neffinger et al. 1984, Polenz and Rubitz 1977, Reitman and Pokorny 1974, Shearer 1975, Tuttle et al. 1975), although some programs take place in rugged, backcountry wilderness areas (Coffey and Ferree 1974, Collingwood 1972, Kistler et al. 1977). Typically, camping sites with developed facilities such as cabins, a dining hall, or recreational building are chosen (Ackerman et al. 1959, Acuff 1961, Barker and Weisman 1966, Henke and Kuhlen 1943, Herr 1977, McFarland et al. 1967, Middleman and Seever 1963, Morse 1947, Ramsey 1969, Reitman and Porkorny 1974, Rerek 1973, Rickard et al. 1971, Smith 1959, Weisman et al. 1966, Winter and Winter 1968). Usually small groups of less than 10 to midsize groups of up to 50 participants are taken camping (George and Gibson 1959, Hobbs and Shelton 1972, Kistler et al. 1977, Langsner and Anderson 1987,

McCreary-Juhasz and Jensen 1968, Neffinger et al. 1984, Orbach 1966, Polenz and Rubitz 1977, Rickard et al. 1971, Stimpson and Pederson 1970, Tuttle et al. 1975, Weisman et al. 1966). Camper/staff ratios range from approximately 1/1 (Jerstad and Stelzer 1973, McDonald 1974) to 3/1 or 5/1 (Neffinger et al. 1984, Peterson and Acuff 1955, Stoudenmire and Comola 1973).

Programs for emotionally disturbed children and adolescents are usually restricted to either all males or all females (mostly all-male) with a wide variety of disorders (e.g., phobias, hostility, withdrawal, adjustment problems, delinquency). On the other hand, programs for chronic mentally ill adults from state mental hospitals or institutions are invariably mixed-sex groups of different ages although a few programs limit their populations to geriatric patients/clients (Lee 1983, Rerek 1973). Some come from community mental health programs or private hospitals (George and Gibson 1959, Orbach 1966). Camping programs for mentally ill adults usually include schizophrenics or schizophrenics in combination with other diagnostic categories (Acuff 1961, Banaka and Young 1985, Bergan 1958, George and Gibson 1959, McFarland et al. 1967, Peterson and Acuff 1955, Shearer 1975, Whittekin 1967). Participants are usually volunteers selected for such programs by the staffs (e.g., Lowry 1974, Orbach 1966, Ramsey 1969, Stich and Senior 1984). Certain children and adolescents are eliminated depending on the nature of the program (Kelly and Baer 1969, Lee 1983, McNeil 1957, Ramsey 1969, Remar and Lowry 1974, Stich and Senior 1984, Weisman et al. 1966). The staffs of therapeutic camping programs consist of a combination of professionals and nonprofessionals. While the importance of staff selection has been noted (Smith 1959), the criteria for selection of the staff are usually not stated.

EXPERIMENTAL DESIGN AND METHODOLOGY

The majority of researchers investigating the effects of therapeutic camping, plus a few researchers investigating effects of other type recreation programs on the mentally ill, have used either Campbell and Stanley's one-shot case study (Campbell and Davis 1940, Caplan 1967, George and Gibson 1959, Jerstad and Stelzer 1973, Kaplan and Reneau 1965, Kistler et al. 1977, Remar and Lowry 1974) or the one group pre-test/post-test design (Jensen et al. 1968, McClung 1984, McCreary-Juhasz and Jensen 1968, Orbach 1966, Stimpson and Pederson 1970, Stoudenmire and Comola 1973, Stermac and Josefowitz 1985, Tuttle et al. 1975).

Some researchers added control or comparison groups (Banaka and Young 1985; Beal et al. 1977; Conroy et al. 1982; Eler 1987; Greist et al. 1979a, 1979b; Kelly and Baer 1968, 1971; Kelly et al. 1983; Ritter and Mock 1980; Shniderman 1974; Stich 1983; Voight 1988; Watters and Watters 1980; Witman 1987; Wright 1983). When the sample size was small, several investigators relied on quasi-experimental designs such as the single-subject design (Eason et al. 1982; Kern et al. 1982, 1984; Reid et al. 1988; Santarcangelo et al. 1987; Wong et al. 1987). A few studies were correlational rather than experimental (Lewinsohn and Graf 1973, Wassman and Iso-Ahola 1985). The data were often observational or anecdotal in nature (e.g., Altaraz 1938, Bernstein 1985, Byers 1978, Caplan 1967, D'Urso and Logue 1988, Eells 1947, George and Gibson 1959, Goodrich 1947, Jerstad and Stelzer 1973, Landes and Winter 1966, Lowry 1974, McDonald 1974, Middleman and Seever 1963, Miller 1987, Morse 1947, Neffinger et al. 1984, Peterson and Acuff 1955, Smith 1959, Solomon and Bumpus 1978, Stich and Senior 1984). Some researchers have used instruments such as personality tests, attitude and rating scales, questionnaires, daily journals, file data, psychological tests, or self-reports (Baer et al. 1975; Banaka and Young 1985; Collingwood 1972; Conroy et al. 1982; Greist et al. 1979a; Katz and Kolb[3]; Kelly et al. 1983; Kelly and Baer 1968, 1969; McClung 1984; Mondell et al. 1981; Polenz and Rubitz 1977; Ritter and Mock 1980; Stermac and Josefowitz 1985; Stich 1983; Stimpson and Pederson 1970; Tuttle et al. 1975; Voight 1988; Witman 1987; Wright 1983).

In analyzing the data from therapeutic camping programs, only a few researchers used statistical tests of significance (Baer et al. 1975, Banaka and Young 1985, Henke and Kuhlen 1943, Herr 1975, Hughes 1979, Kelly and Baer 1968, Mondell et al. 1981, Orbach 1966, Polenz and Rubitz 1977, Ritter and Mock 1980, Ryan and Johnson 1972, Shniderman 1974, Stimpson and Pederson 1970, Tuttle et al. 1975, Wright, 1983). However, statistical tests of significance were used more frequently in studies examining the effects of participation in other type recreation programs (Conroy et al. 1981, 1982; Lewinsohn and Graf 1973; Stermac and Josefowitz 1985; Voight 1988; Watters and Watters 1980; Witman 1987). Still other investigators relied on percentages or frequency data (Allen 1980, Eason et al. 1982, Reid et al. 1988, Santarcangelo et al. 1987, Wong et al. 1987).

Only a handful of researchers have conducted any follow-up studies (Baer et al. 1975; Banaka and Young 1985; Barker and Weisman 1966; Eason et al. 1982; Greist et al. 1979a, 1979b; Jensen et al. 1968; Kistler et al. 1977; Ramsey 1969; Rickard and Dinoff 1967; Ritter and Mock 1980).

THERAPEUTIC BENEFITS OF RECREATION

The results of the majority of studies indicate that recreation participation is therapeutic for mentally ill patients participating in mixed recreation activities, physical exercise, or therapeutic camping programs. There are a few studies, however, that indicate no effects or negative effects from recreation participation. The therapeutic benefits are discussed for each of the three types of recreation programs.

Mixed Recreation Activities Programs

The therapeutic benefits of participating in mixed recreation activities programs (e.g., arts and crafts, sports, games, music, exercise, ballet, walking) for mentally and emotionally disturbed individuals include the following:

- Patients taken off prescription drugs (Schwab et al. 1985).
- Decrease in inappropriate or disruptive behaviors and/or increase in appropriate behaviors (Altarez 1938, Bernstein 1985, Campbell and Davis 1940, Eason et al. 1982, Kelly et al. 1983, Santarcangelo et al. 1987, Schlein et al. 1987, Schwab et al. 1985, Stermac and Josefowitz 1985, Wong et al. 1987).
- Increased quantity and quality of social interactions (Beal et al. 1977, Bernstein 1985, Campbell and Davis 1940, Eler 1987, Schwab et al. 1985).
- Repressed emotions released (Altarez 1938).
- Improved functioning level (Altarez 1938).
- Increased range of interests (Campbell and Davis 1940).
- Transfer of improved patients to other wards (Campbell and Davis 1940).
- Improved client-staff interactions (Bernstein 1985, Schwab et al. 1985).
- Enhanced self-concept (Bernstein 1985).
- Increased cooperation and trust (Witman 1987).
- Increased fun for the patients (Miller 1987, Stermac and Josefowitz 1985, Witman 1987).

In addition, a significant negative correlation between recreation participation and depression has been reported (Wassman and Iso-Ahola 1985). Depressed subjects were also found to engage in fewer activities and/or repeat them less frequently (Lewinsohn and Graf 1973).

Although the results of most studies indicate beneficial effects from participating in mixed recreation activities, some studies indicate no effects on the behaviors of certain patients (Black et al. 1975, Schwab et al. 1985). Kelly et al. (1983) found no statistically significant changes in the functioning of elderly patients with long-term medical and psychiatric disabilities as a result of participating in a recreation program. Witman (1987) found no improvement in the cooperation and trust of adolescent patients following a social recreation program (but found improvement following an adventure program).

Physical Exercise Programs

The therapeutic benefits of physical exercise programs (mostly jogging or running) for mentally and emotionally disturbed individuals include the following:

- Decrease in inappropriate behaviors and an increase in appropriate behaviors (Allen 1980; Kern et al. 1982, 1984; Reid et al. 1988; Watters and Watters 1980).
- Increased interest in and improved attitudes toward school (Allen 1980, Kern et al. 1982).
- Depressive symptoms alleviated (Conroy et al. 1981, 1982; Greist et al. 1979a, 1979b; Solomon and Bumpus 1978).
- Reduced anger, restlessness, tension, stress, anxiety, and frustration (Conroy et al. 1981, 1982; Solomon and Bumpus 1978).
- Increased self-esteem, self-concept, and sense of competence and mastery (Conroy et al. 1981, McClung 1984).
- Improved physical health and fitness (Conroy et al. 1982).
- Decreased sleep disturbances (Conroy et al. 1981, 1982).
- Enhanced social interactions (Conroy et al. 1981).
- Increased joy (Conroy et al. 1981).

Results of research indicate, however, that participation in physical exercise programs can have no effects or even negative effects. Conroy et al. (1982) found physical exercise did not ameliorate many disturbing feelings or elicit a wide range of positive affects such as cooperation. Kern et al. (1984) found no decrease in stereotypic behaviors of three autistic children following 15 minutes of a mild exercise (ballplaying). Reid et al. (1988) reported no consistent increase in intelligible appropriate speech to prosocial, compliant behavior following physical exercise. Voight (1988) found a ropes course to have a significant negative effect on stress and a slightly negative effect on the mood of adolescents in terms of anxiety, depression, fatigue, regression, and guilt when compared to nonparticipating controls.

Therapeutic Camping Programs

The benefits of therapeutic camping for mentally and emotionally disturbed individuals include the following:

- Improved physical health, fitness, and increased appetites (Caplan 1967, Collingwood 1972, Reitman and Pokorny 1974, Wright 1983).
- Enhanced self-concept, self-esteem, and self-confidence (Coffey and Ferree 1974, Collingwood 1972, Hobbs and Shelton 1972, Hughes and Dudley 1973, Kelly and Baer 1969, Kimsey and Frost 1971, McCreary-Juhasz and Jensen 1968, McDonald 1974, Muller 1971, Shank 1975, Stimpson and Pederson 1970, Weisman et al. 1966, Winter and Winter 1968, Wright 1983).
- Increased initiative (Weisman et al. 1966).
- Increased patient enthusiasm and fun (Kistler et al. 1977, Neffinger et al. 1984, Reitman and Pokorny 1974, Whittekin 1967).
- Improved school attitudes and behaviors (Behar and Stephens 1978, Coffey and Ferree 1974, Rawson 1973, Rickard and Dinoff 1967, Shniderman 1974).
- Discharge from hospitals, shorter hospital stays, and reduced recidivism rates (Acuff 1961; Arthur et al. 1976; Baer et al. 1975; Barker and Weisman 1966; Jerstad and Stelzer 1973; Kelly and Baer 1968, 1971; Lowry 1974; Peterson and Acuff 1955; Rerek 1973; Weisman et al. 1966; Willman and Chun 1973).
- Changes in group problem solving (Rickard et al. 1971, 1975).
- Fewer emotional problems and pathological symptoms (Behar and Stephens 1978, Henke and Kuhlen 1943, Ritter and Mock 1980, Rosen 1959, Shearer 1975, Stoudenmire and Comola 1973, Whittekin 1967, Winter and Winter 1966).
- Development of new interests and improved skills (Banaka and Young 1985, McCreary-Juhasz and Jensen 1968, Reitman and Pokorny 1974).
- Establishment of friendships (Barker and Weisman 1966, Lee 1983, Remar and Lowry 1974).

- Increased quality and quantity of social interactions (Banaka and Young 1985, Herr 1977, Hobbes and Radka 1976, Hughes 1979, Kaplan and Reneau 1965, Kelly and Baer 1968, Lowry 1974, McCreary-Juhasz and Jensen 1968, Rawson 1973, Reitman and Pokorny 1974, Shearer 1975, Smith 1959, Tuttle et al. 1975).
- Improved patient-staff relationships (George and Gibson 1959, Herr 1975, Kaplan and Reneau 1965, McFarland et al. 1967, Ramsey 1969, Reitman and Pokorny 1974, Rerek 1973, Smith 1959).

Some studies indicate, however, that therapeutic camping can have negative effects including passive aggressive behavior, hostility, regressive behavior, increased anxiety and guilt, depression or suicide, or no effects on certain behaviors (Byers 1978, Henke and Kuhlen 1943, Langsner and Anderson 1987, McDonald 1974, Muller 1971, Orbach 1966, Polenz and Rubitz 1977, Ritter and Mock 1980, Ryan and Johnson 1972, Shniderman 1974). Redl (1974) even cautions against the psychopathologic risks of camp life.

ISSUES AND RECOMMENDATIONS

Experimental Design and Methodology

While there are a relatively large number of studies on the effects of therapeutic camping programs as compared to other type recreation programs for mentally and emotionally disturbed individuals, some of the criticisms directed at research on therapeutic camping programs (Gibson 1979; Levitt 1982, 1988) can also be levied at these other type recreation programs (Kennedy 1987).

Although most research findings appear to support the contention that participation in recreation activities is therapeutic for mentally ill and emotionally disturbed individuals, the validity of these findings needs to be questioned because of weaknesses in experimental design and methodology. Since many of the recreation programs were evaluated without the use of control or comparison groups, and subjects were not randomly assigned to treatment conditions, the internal and external validity of these designs is weak.

The use of control or comparison groups can help eliminate (or suggest) other causal explanations and/or enhance the credibility of recreation as a viable treatment in alleviating symptoms of mental illness. For example, Watters and Watters (1980) reported a decrease in self-stimulatory behaviors of autistic children after jogging, but not after watching television or doing regular academic work. They were, therefore, able to attribute the decrease in negative behaviors to physical exercise rather than to a change or break in the subjects' usual academic routine. On the other hand, Morgan (1979) reported a reduction in anxiety following physical exercise as well as biofeedback and a quiet rest period. He therefore suggested that diversion (getting away from it all) and not physical exercise per se is the crucial ingredient in reducing anxiety. Greist et al. (1979a, 1979b) found a 10-week running program to be as effective a treatment in alleviating depressive symptoms in moderately depressed patients as either time-limited or time- unlimited psychotherapy.

The internal validity of these designs is also weak because the treatment, i.e., the recreation intervention, may be confounded with other factors such as spontaneous remission, the Hawthorne effect, environmental change, increased perceived control, other therapies used in conjunction with the recreation activities, or drug treatment (Allen 1980, Apter 1977, Clark and Kempler 1973, Conroy et al. 1981, Hobbs and Radka 1975, Hughes 1979, Iso-Ahola 1980, Kern et al. 1984, Morgan 1979, Santarcangelo et al. 1987, Schwab et al. 1985, Stermac and Josefowitz 1985, Watters and Watters 1980, Witman 1987).

There are also problems with the samples selected. Most studies use small, often biased samples thereby limiting the generalizability of the results to other populations. Even if the sample size is relatively large for studying the effects of a recreation program, there may be too few patients in each diagnostic category to compare statistically (Harrington and Cross 1962). Other sources of possible sample bias include high attrition rate (Kelly et al. 1983), the use of one sex only (Allen 1980), the subjects' memory and their ability or willingness to cooperate (Harrington and Cross 1962), and the chronicity of the patients' physical and mental disabilities (Kelly et al. 1983). Since sex differences in response to therapeutic camping have been found with emotionally disturbed children (Ryan and Johnson 1972), these issues become more salient.

There are also difficulties in assessing changes in the behavior of patients/clients as a result of recreation participation (Kelly et al. 1983, McGuire 1985). Since most of the observations involving therapeutic camping programs were based on participant observation by the staff involved, and only a few researchers reported interrater reliability (Banaka and Young 1985, Orbach 1966), biases could have resulted. However, in most of the research involving other type recreation programs, some form of interrater reliability was reported (Beal et al. 1977, Eason et al. 1982, Kern et al. 1984, Reid et al. 1988, Santarcangelo et al. 1987, Stermac and

Josefowitz 1985, Watters and Watters 1980). Although some investigators used reliable and valid instruments (Kelly et al. 1983, Voight 1988), the instruments used in therapeutic camping studies generally lacked reliability and validity. This appears to support Touchstone's (1975) contention that researchers in psychiatric hospitals tend to rely on nonstandardized, in-house evaluation tools rather than standardized instruments, and the lack of reliable and valid instruments is one of the difficulties in doing research in these settings.

The importance of developing specialized recreation and leisure instruments has been emphasized (Annand 1977, Iso-Ahola 1988, Neal 1970), and there have been successful efforts to develop reliable and valid leisure assessment instruments (Ellis and Niles 1985, Ellis and Witt 1986, Howe 1984). In addition, Saslow (1978) recommends a multidimensional approach in which a variety of objective and subjective tools are used from a variety of perspectives to assess changes in campers' feelings, behaviors, and skills. Saslow's suggestion of assessing behavior change from a variety of perspectives is important because in at least one program, the staff did not perceive the negative feelings of the campers (Polenz and Rubitz 1977).

Another important factor that may affect the outcome is the time when subjects are tested. Morgan (1979) found that anxiety increased immediately after vigorous running but decreased 10-30 minutes later. Kelly et al. (1983) stated that the time delay between their community program and observations of patients on hospital units at the completion of the entire program may have affected their results.

In addition, since statistical tests were rarely used in analyzing the data from therapeutic camping studies, we do not know if the results of these studies are statistically significant. The use of statistical tests of significance would enhance the scientific credibility of the findings. If conditions do not permit the use of statistical tests of significance (e.g., very small sample), then frequency data or percentage changes should be used. In fact, Hunter (1983) recommends that therapeutic recreation researchers consider reporting amount of change by frequency to record individual improvements rather than use statistical tests which measure group change.

Most importantly, though, without short-term and long-term follow-up studies, we do not know if the therapeutic benefits of recreation participation for mentally and emotionally disturbed individuals are permanent or generalize to other settings and/or populations. Although the findings of some follow-up studies indicate that the beneficial effects of recreation participation can last from several months to 2 years and do generalize to other settings (Eason et al. 1982; Greist et al. 1979a, 1979b; Kern et al. 1982; Ritter and Mock 1980), the results of other studies indicate that the beneficial effects return to baseline or may even become worse once the recreation program ends (Allen 1980, Banaka and Young 1985, Reid et al. 1988). In addition, a 9-month follow-up study by Gordon et al. (1966) indicated ex-patients who were interested in sports in the hospital seldom participated in the community (although this was not true for more passive activities).

Finally, there are certain ethical issues to consider when conducting research involving recreational programs for mentally and emotionally disturbed individuals. Ethical issues become salient when one uses single-subject designs in which a necessary treatment is given and then withdrawn, or in true experimental designs when the control group does not receive a potentially beneficial treatment (Dattilo 1986, Weiner 1979). Also, if patients benefit from participating in a particular recreation program for a few weeks, they may feel "let down" when the program ends (Conroy et al. 1982, Reynolds and Arthur 1982), or their behavior may became worse (Reid et al. 1988). Other ethical concerns in doing follow-up studies on psychiatric patients have been discussed (Showstack et al. 1978). Some of these ethical concerns, though, can be partly overcome either by administering the recreation program to the control group after completion of the experiment, or with single-subject designs, continuing the recreation program after completion of the study.

Thus, if future research is to become more acceptable to the scientific community and is to provide a stronger data base from which to argue for financial support of such programs, there must be improvements in experimental design and methodology (e.g., use of control groups, reliable and valid measures, follow-up studies, statistical tests of significance) with due consideration given to the ethics involved. If possible, the use of true experimental designs with control groups and randomization of subjects (Campbell and Stanley 1963) should be used. However, if conditions are not feasible (e.g., too few subjects, randomization is not possible, or there are no control groups available) (Mannell 1983, Weiner 1979), then the use of quasi-experimental designs should be considered. In particular, the single-subject design has been recommended (Dattilo 1986, Mannell 1983, Weiner 1979) and used by several investigators. In this design a subject serves as his/her own control and certain threats to internal validity can be controlled, but the external validity is weak because results cannot be generalized to larger populations (Weiner 1979). Ellis and Witt (1983) recommend the use of more advanced experimental designs such as randomized block, split-plot, or hierarchial designs because these designs are useful in explaining other variables that may directly influence the outcomes of experiments (e.g., type of recreation activity, nursing home, or recreation therapist). Thus, with improved systematic

research we can begin to ensure accountability and improve the quality of the therapeutic recreation services (Beddall and Kennedy 1985, Compton 1984, Iso-Ahola 1988, Mannell 1983).

Finally, more recreation practitioners need to become involved in research. Although the majority of practitioners recognize the importance of, and hold favorable attitudes toward, evaluation of their clients, few actually do research partly because of barriers that exist in conducting such research (Beddall and Kennedy 1985, Bullock et al. 1984, Touchstone 1975, Witt 1988). In a psychiatric setting, for example, some of these problems include lack of reliable evaluation instruments, lack of professional time to do evaluation, and lack of adequately trained personnel to do the research (Touchstone 1975). Certain of these problems can be overcome by conducting interdisciplinary research with university faculty and other professionals who have the necessary research skills. Other suggestions to deal with these problems have been recommended (Compton 1984, Witt 1988).

Therapeutic Aspects of Recreation

To date we still do not know what is therapeutic about participating in a recreation activity. It may be either participating in the recreation activity itself or some other underlying mechanism(s) that is(are) responsible for the beneficial effects.

It has been suggested that the therapeutic benefits of participating in physical exercise programs could be due to factors other than physical exercise. The therapeutic benefits of running or jogging may be attributed to developing a sense of mastery and control, learning patience, symptom relief, biochemical/physiological changes, distraction or diversion, or consciousness alteration rather than the running/jogging per se (Greist et al. 1979b; Kern et al. 1982, 1984; Morgan 1979; Solomon and Bumpus 1978). Reid et al. (1988) suggest that a change from nonphysical to physical, or a cathartic experience could have accounted for some of the effects of their physical exercise program. However, fatigue has been ruled out as an explanation for the therapeutic effects following physical exercise (Kern et al. 1982, 1984; Reid et al. 1988).

Likewise, we still do not understand what is therapeutic about camping in a wilderness or wilderness-like setting. The flora and fauna of wilderness, the uniqueness of wilderness, the low level of stimulation of wilderness, the aesthetic or spiritual value of wilderness, the isolation of wilderness from the stresses of the city, or the ability of wilderness to evoke coping behaviors have been cited as the possible factors that produce the therapeutic gains (Acuff 1961, Apter 1977, Bernstein 1972, Neffinger et al. 1984, Thomas[4]). Moreover, it is not known if the beneficial effects of therapeutic camping programs are dependent on the natural environment, or if these same benefits could be achieved in other settings.

The possibility also exists that some other confounding factor (e.g., increased perceived control, the Hawthorne effect, environmental change) rather than the recreation activity itself is the therapeutic agent. Iso-Ahola (1980) states that it is not the recreation activity itself but the extent to which these recreational activities induce a sense of personal responsibility and control over one's behavior, environment, and entire life that is important. Since prior investigators have indicated the importance of increased perceived control and responsibility (Bernstein 1985, Coviensky and Buckley 1986, Iso-Ahola and Mobily 1982, Langer and Rodin 1976, Wassman and Iso-Ahola 1985), this may indeed be an important factor to be considered in developing a recreation program. An increase in patients' control and responsibility has already been achieved in various recreation programs by having the patients/clients decide to participate in the program, choose their own activities, plan menus and events, and prepare the food (Ackerman et al. 1959, McFarland et al. 1967, Peterson and Acuff 1955, Smith 1959, Whittekin 1967).

Hopefully, if researchers include certain control and/or comparison groups in their studies in the future, we may begin to understand just what is(are) the therapeutic agent(s) in recreation participation.

Program Planning

While there are beneficial effects for mentally ill patients participating in recreation programs, it is still not clear what characteristics of these programs produce the therapeutic effects. We need to know what factors of recreation programs produce therapeutic benefits for whom, under what conditions, and why (Compton 1984, Connolly 1984, Mannell 1983). Without such information we do not know what aspects of the program to change or improve (Rickards 1985). However, based on past recreation programs we are just beginning to understand how some of these factors affect the participants.

To begin with, it has been shown that the nature of the activity (i.e., the type, duration, and intensity of the recreation activity) may have differential effects on patients' behaviors. Kern et al. (1984) reported that 15 minutes of vigorous exercise (jogging) reduced stereotypic behaviors in autistic children, but 15 minutes of mild exercise (ballplaying) did not. Vigorous jogging also led to a decrease in

state anxiety for "normals" and highly anxious individuals (Morgan 1979) while a moderate amount of jogging relieved depression (Conroy et al. 1982), and meditative, long-distance running produced still other effects (Solomon and Bumpus 1978). Conroy et al. (1982) found that psychotic patients became less symtomatic in the longer 6-week program of lesser jogging than in a one-week pilot program of more vigorous jogging. It is therefore important to further investigate the impact of various styles of running (Greist et al. 1979b) and longer, more intensive exercise periods of jogging (Watters and Watters 1980). To date, though, there seems to be some agreement that running or jogging for mentally ill individuals should be noncompetitive and not exceed the patient's adaptive capacity (Conroy et al. 1981, Greist et al. 1979a, Solomon and Bumpus 1978). Also, it may be advantageous if the therapist runs with his/her patients/clients (Kostrubala 1976).

The duration of the recreation activity may also affect the outcome (Gupta et al. 1974). Although Allen (1980) did not find much difference between a 5- or 10-minute jog, she cites studies showing a 10-minute jog is necessary for a physical conditioning effect. With therapeutic camping programs, a 1- or 2-day program may be too short to expect desired behavior changes necessary for normal functioning (Shea 1977, Turner 1976), and little is known about the effects of repetitive camping experiences. Thus, much more information on the duration of recreation intervention, the number of sessions, and the length of each session necessary to produce the therapeutic effects is needed.

Moreover, participation in a particular recreation activity may produce changes in certain behaviors but not in others. Kern et al. (1982) stated that jogging may be a more effective treatment for only some types of self-stimulatory behaviors. Watters and Watters (1980) found that physical excercise led to a decrease in self-stimulatory behaviors but not in the levels of correct question answering for autistic children.

Since researchers have already reported differences in recreation participation based on an individual's diagnosis, age, race, and mood (Campbell and Davis 1940, Miller 1987), these factors must be taken into account before planning recreation activities. In fact, Hoffman (1981) recommends a prescriptive approach to activity selection in which individual information, program information, support systems, and the client's main goal are necessary prerequisites to selecting recreation activities that will help the client reach his/her goal.

Since patients with different diagnoses respond differently to the same recreation activity, there appears to be a need to match the recreation activity and benefits more specifically to the different diagnostic categories (Campbell and Davis 1940, Davis 1950). Miller (1987) reported that the most active players of computer games were "others" (e.g., mixed diagnostic features, drug abusers), delusionals, and secondary depressives, while the least active players were schizophrenics and unipolars. Further, a physical exercise program may have proved too stimulating for some schizophrenics (Conroy et al. 1982) and a ropes course too invasive and demanding for emotionally disturbed adolescents (Voight 1988).

Campbell and Davis (1940) suggest more simple activities for organic cases and more complex activities for functional cases. Physical exercise such as running/jogging is not recommended and may even be detrimental or dangerous for patients with more severe diagnoses such as the schizoid, psychotic, withdrawn, or borderline individual (Solomon and Bumpus 1978), or severely depressed individuals (Greist et al. 1979a, 1979b.). Wassman and Iso-Ahola (1985) claim that structured activities may prove more motivating for depressed patients than unstructured activities, and Stoudenmire (1977) states that camp activities for emotionally disturbed children should incorporate educational and emotional objectives.

Different type therapeutic camping programs may also be needed for adolescents, chronic mentally ill adults, and less disturbed adults (Remar and Lowry 1974). Certain camping therapies have proven more successful with certain types of boys than others (Rickard et al. 1971; Winter and Winter 1968, 1966). Kelly and Baer (1971) have reported that certain types of Outward Bound programs proved more successful in reducing recidivism than others. They found that juvenile delinquents responded more positively to Outward Bound programs that were action-oriented, physically challenging programs with periods of high excitement and real danger followed by relatively quiet periods. Thus, juvenile delinquents may be particularly well-suited for programs that emphasize camping in rugged, backcountry, wilderness areas. However, certain qualities of Outward Bound may make it an inappropriate treatment for urban juvenile delinquents or for students with psychological fears and difficulties (Katz and Kolb[3]). The ultimate goals of therapeutic camping programs may have to be modified for long-term clients versus acute short-term or day care clients (Arthur et al. 1976). Criteria for selection and elimination of participants in recreation programs is also needed. Usually the criteria for patients participating in therapeutic camping programs are based on diagnosis, but other criteria such as psychosocial dysfunction or length of hospitalization have been suggested as being important (Ramsey 1969, Stich and Senior 1984). For physical exercise programs, patients generally have to pass a medical or physical exam (Conroy et al.

1982, Greist et al. 1979b, Solomon and Bumpus 1978). D'Urso and Logue (1988) recommend that patients be given a choice to participate.

The importance of selecting good staff and group leaders in enhancing the effects of the treatment have been emphasized (McClung 1984, Witman 1987). Witman (1987) suggests the inclusion of professionals in addition to the activity staff. In selecting the staff for the more rugged camping programs such as Outward Bound, selection is geared to those with the functionally relevant skills needed to implement the program (Collingwood 1972). With therapeutic camping programs, a 1/1 camper/staff ratio for adolescents and 3/1 or higher ratio for chronic mentally ill adults has been suggested (Remar and Lowry 1974).

Since negative effects of therapeutic camping on patients and staff have been observed, research is also needed on the nature of workshops and/or meetings for the participants and staff both before and after the camping experience. In particular, more information on the negative effects of camping programs on the staff is needed.

To begin to understand what factors of the recreation program contribute to the therapeutic effects, Connolly (1984) suggests a tool called the Program Plan Description form that describes the nature of the recreation program (e.g., content, characteristics, and structure of the program). If researchers begin to use this form, perhaps some comparisons among recreation programs can begin to be made.

Further, since there are low rates of participation in recreation activities by mentally ill persons, we also need to identify techniques that will motivate patients/clients to participate and maintain their interest in recreation activities while in the hospital and later in the community (Bullock et al. 1984, Compton 1984). One technique found to be effective in increasing appropriate play behavior in autistic children is suppression of self-stimulatory behaviors (Koegel et al. 1974). Quilitch and Dare de Longchamps (1974) found an increase in recreation participation for 10 days after a ticket contingency ("buying" bingo cards after participating in 20 minutes of supervised volleyball and billiards) was removed. The use of reinforcers and refreshments, or providing simple recreation materials and prompting patients to use the materials increased recreation attendance and participation of nursing home residents (Gillepsie et al. 1984; Jenkins et al. 1977; McClannahan 1973; McClannahan and Risley 1975a, 1975b). Others suggest that an increase in recreation attendance and participation by the elderly may be achieved by varying the leaders and co-participants of recreation activities (McGuire 1985) or selecting activities that are mentally stimulating or based on the motivations for leisure expressed by the elderly (MacAvoy[5] 1977). In another study peer modeling and cognitive self-guidance had immediate (but not long-lasting) effects on the social play of emotionally disturbed children (Reynolds and Arthur 1982).

Other investigators have found that modifications of the physical environment can increase recreation participation and/or modify other behaviors. Black et al. (1975) reported that a stark environment (i.e., empty room) led to more negative behaviors in autistic children while a theraplay environment (i.e., confined space designed to facilitate a movement flow) led to more positive behaviors. McPherson (1977) cited studies that indicate that hyperactive behavior in children can be reduced through initial contact with novel stimuli and certain types of music or moving stimuli. Finally, since chronic clients often have a lot of free time but do not know how to make use of the resources in a community (Coviensky and Buckley 1986), more research on the effects of leisure counseling programs on the recreation participation of ex-patients living in the community needs to be conducted.

SUMMARY AND CONCLUSIONS

Results of studies indicate that participating in different type recreation activities is therapeutic for mentally and emotionally disturbed individuals. Recreation participation appears to alleviate many symptoms of mental illness such as depression, anxiety, withdrawal, low self-esteem, disruptive behaviors, and poor interpersonal relationships. However, since much of this past research was methodologically flawed, more improved, systematic empirical research needs to conducted. Further research on the effects of leisure counseling programs on recreation participation for patients and ex-patients is also needed.

In an era of accountability and cutting programs, a cost-effectiveness analysis of each program needs to be conducted and disseminated to other professionals. Although Haun (1965) warned against comparing recreation programs to other treatments for the mentally ill, the cost-effectiveness of a recreation program would appear to be a prerequisite if it is to be integrated as a permanent part of an individual's rehabilitative program. Already the low cost of operating one physical exercise (running) program (Greist et al. 1979a, 1979b) and two therapeutic camping programs (Banaka and Young 1985, Stich 1983) as compared to traditional psychotherapies has been demonstrated.

In conclusion, it is hoped that with improved empirical research concerning some of the issues addressed in this paper, individuals can argue more forcefully for the inclusion of such programs in the treatment of mentally and emotionally disturbed individuals.

ENDNOTES

[1] This would concur with the 1969 definition of therapeutic recreation by the National Therapeutic Recreation Society as "a process which utilizes recreation services for the purposive intervention in some physical, emotional, and/or social behavior to bring about a desired change in the behavior and to promote the growth and development of the individual" (West 1979). However, there has been an ongoing debate about the nature and purpose of recreation versus therapeutic recreation (Ball 1970, Dixon 1978, Frye 1969, Frye and Peters 1972, Haun 1965, Mobily 1985).

[2] Since most camping programs for emotionally disturbed children and chronic mentally ill adults do not take place in backcountry wilderness, the term "therapeutic camping" will be used throughout this paper. However, other terms such as wilderness therapy, camp challenges (Banaka and Young 1985, Neffinger et al. 1984), experiential therapeutic camping (Stich 1983, Stich and Senior 1984), sociotherapeutic camping (Ramsey 1969), camping therapy (Remar and Lowry 1974), and psychiatric camping therapy (Lowry 1974) have also been used.

[3] R. Katz and D. Kolb in unpublished report on Outward Bound and education for personal growth, Office of Juvenile Delinquency, HEW Grant No. 66013.

[4] John Thomas, in a paper presented to the 1979 First Annual Convention of the Wilderness Psychology Group, University of Montana, Missoula, MT.

[5] Leo MacAvoy in unpublished research report for the Minnesota Department of Natural Resources, St. Paul, MN, 1976.

LITERATURE CITED

Ackerman, O. R.; Mitsos, S. B.; Seymour, M. A. 1959. Patients go camping in Indiana. Mental Hospital. 10: 16-17.

Acuff, S. H. 1961. Camping: Transition between hospital and home for the adult mentally ill. Journal of Health, Physical Education and Recreation. 32: 24-25, 62.

Allen, J. I. 1980. Jogging can modify disruptive behaviors. Teaching Exceptional Children. 12: 66-70.

Altarez, I. M. 1938. Recreation as a factor in handling maladjusted individuals. Mental Hygiene. 22: 276-285.

Annand, V. 1977. A review of evaluation in therapeutic recreation. Therapeutic Recreation Journal. 11(2): 42- 47.

Apter, S. J. 1977. Therapeutic camping: An alternative strategy for troubled children. Journal of Clinical Child Psychology. Winter: 73-75.

Arthur, T. E.; McK. Phillips, G.; Thomas, S. B. 1976. Camping by objectives. Therapeutic Recreation Journal. 10(4): 132-138.

Baer, D. J.; Jacobs, P. J.; Carr, F. E. 1975. Instructors' ratings of delinquents after Outward Bound survival training and their subsequent recidivism. Psychological Reports. 36: 547-553.

Ball, E. L. 1970. The meaning of therapeutic recreation. Therapeutic Recreation Journal. 4(1): 17-18.

Banaka, W. H.; Young, D. W. 1985. Community coping skills enhanced by an adventure camp for adult chronic psychiatric patients. Hospital and Community Psychiatry. 36(7): 746-748.

Barker, B.; Weisman, M. 1966. Residential camping: Imaginative program helps chronic mental patients. Journal of Rehabilitation. 32: 26-27.

Beal, D.; Duckro, P.; Elias, J.; Hecht, E. 1977. Graded group procedures for long-term regressed schizophrenics. The Journal of Nervous and Mental Disease. 164(2): 102-106.

Beddall, T.; Kennedy, D. W. 1985. Attitudes of therapeutic recreators toward evaluation and client assessment. Therapeutic Recreation Journal. 19(1): 62-70.

Behar, L.; Stephens, D. 1978. Wilderness camping: An evaluation of a residential treatment program for emotionally disturbed children. American Journal of Orthopsychiatry. 48(4): 644-653.

Bergan, J. F. 1958. Day camp in Connecticut. Mental Hospital. 9: 12-13.

Bernstein, A. 1972. Wilderness as a therapeutic behavior setting. Therapeutic Recreation Journal. 6(4): 160-161, 185.

Bernstein, B. 1985. Becoming involved: Spolin theater games in classes for the educationally handicapped. Theory Into Practice. 24(3): 219-223.

Black, M.; Freeman, B. J.; Montgomery, J. 1975. Systematic observation of play behavior in autistic children. Journal of Autism and Childhood Schizophrenia. 5(4): 363-371.

Bullock, C. C.; McGuire, F. M.; Barch, E. M. 1984. Perceived research needs of therapeutic recreators. Therapeutic Recreation Journal. 18(3): 17-24.

Byers, S. E. 1978. Counselor skill-training in a year round therapeutic wilderness camp: Effect on camper and counselor behaviors during problem solving sessions. Dissertation Abstracts International. 39(3-B): 1469.

Campbell, D. D.; Davis, J. E. 1940. Report of research and experimentation in exercise and recreation therapy. American Journal of Psychiatry. 96(2): 915-933.

Campbell, D. T.; Stanley, J. C. 1963. Experimental and quasi-experimental designs for research. Chicago, IL: Rand McNally College Publishing Co.

Caplan, R. B. 1967. Tent treatment for the insane—An early form of milieu therapy. Hospital and Community Psychiatry. 18: 145-146.

Clark, J.; Kempler, H. L. 1973. Therapeutic family camping: A rationale. Family Coordinator. 22: 437- 442.

Coffey, J. V.; Ferree, J. 1974. Buddies, backpack and blisters. The School Counselor. 21: 230-232.

Collingwood, T. R. 1972. Survival camping with problem youth. Rehabilitation Record. 13: 22-25.

Compton, D. M. 1984. Research priorities in recreation for special populations. Therapeutic Recreation Journal. 18(1): 9-17.

Connolly, P. 1984. Analyzing program cause as well as effect: A method for program analysis. Therapeutic Recreation Journal. 18(1): 31-39.

Conroy, R. W.; Smith, K.; Alexander, E., et al. 1981. Total fitness as a psychiatric hospital program. Bulletin of the Menninger Clinic. 45: 65-71.

Conroy, R. W.; Smith, K.; Felthous, A. R. 1982. The value of exercise on a psychiatric unit. Hospital and Community Psychiatry. 33: 641-645.

Coviensky, M.; Buckley, V. C. 1986. Day activities programming: Serving the severely chronic client. Occupational Therapy in Mental Health. 6(2): 21-30.

Dattilo, J. 1986. Single-subject research in therapeutic recreation: Applications to individuals with disabilities. Therapeutic Recreation Journal. 20(1): 76-87.

Davis, J. E. 1950. Modern dynamics of rehabilitation for the psychotic patient. Mental Hygiene. 343: 423-437.

Davis, J. E. 1952. Clinical applications of recreational therapy. Springfield, IL: Charles C. Thomas.

Dixon, J. 1978. Expanding individual control in leisure participation while enlarging the concept of normalcy. Therapeutic Recreation Journal. 12(3): 20-24.

D'Urso, M.; Logue, G. 1988. Competitive adapted sports for impaired older adults. Therapeutic Recreation Journal. 22(4): 56-64.

Eason, L. J.; White, M. J.; Newsom, C. 1982. Generalized reduction of self-stimulatory behavior: An effect of teaching appropriate play to autistic children. Analysis and Intervention in Developmental Disabilities. 2: 157-169.

Eells, E. P. 1947. From the Sunset Camp Service League: Camp as a therapeutic community. The Nervous Child. 6: 225-231.

Eler, B. J. 1987. Social interaction in a drama-dance group of hospitalized schizophrenics. Dissertation Abstracts International. 47(08): 2803A-2804A.

Ellis, G. D.; Niles, S. 1985. Development, reliability, and preliminary validation of a brief leisure rating scale. Therapeutic Recreation Journal. 19(1): 50-61.

Ellis, G. D.; Witt, P. A. 1983. Improving research designs in therapeutic recreation. Therapeutic Recreation Journal. 17(4): 27-35.

Ellis, G. D.; Witt, P. A. 1986. The leisure diagnostic battery: Past, present, and future. Therapeutic Recreation Journal. 20(4): 31-47.

Frye, V. 1969. A philosophical statement on therapeutic recreation services. Therapeutic Recreation Journal. 3(4): 11-14.

Frye, V.; Peters, M. 1972. Therapeutic recreation: Its theory, philosophy, and practice. Harrisburg, PA: Stackpole Books.

George, G. R.; Gibson, R. W. 1959. Patient-staff relationships change with environment. Mental Hospital. 10: 18-19.

Gibson, P. M. 1979. Therapeutic aspects of wilderness programs: A comprehensive literature review. Therapeutic Recreation Journal. 13(2): 21-33.

Gillepsie, K.; McLellan, R. W.; McGuire, F. M. 1984. The effect of refreshments on attendance at recreation activities for nursing home residents. Therapeutic Recreation Journal. 19(3): 25-29.

Goodrich, L. 1947. How much decentralized camping can do for the child. The Nervous Child. 6: 202-210.

Gordon, H. L.; Rosenberg, D.; Morris, W. E. 1966. Leisure activities of schizophrenic patients after return to the community. Mental Hygiene. 50: 452-459.

Greist, J. H.; Eischens, R. R.; Klein, M.; Faris, J. W. 1979a. Antidepressant running. Psychiatric Annals. 9(3): 23-33.

Greist, J. H.; Klein, M., H.; Eischens, R. R., et al. 1979b. Running as a treatment for depression. Comprehensive Psychiatry. 20(1): 41-54.

Gupta, V. P.; Sharma, T. R.; Jaspal, S. S. 1974. Physical activity and efficiency of mental work. Perceptual and Motor Skills. 38: 205-206.

Harrington, J. A.; Cross, K. W. 1962. A preliminary investigation of leisure in psychiatric patients. Mental Hygiene. 46: 580-597.

Haun, P. 1961. Contributions of hospital recreation to the care and treatment of patients. The Welfare Reporter; progress in the public field. 12: 3-13.

Haun, P. 1965. Medicine, psychiatry and recreation. In: Haun, P., ed. Recreation: A medical viewpoint. New York: Teachers College Press of Columbia University: 49-98.

Henke, M. W.; Kuhlen, R. G. 1943. Changes in social adjustment in a summer camp: A preliminary report. The Journal of Psychology. 15: 223-231.

Herr, D. E. 1975. Camp counseling with emotionally disturbed adolescents. Exceptional Children. 41(5): 331-332.

Herr, D. E. 1977. Institutionalized adolescents' perceptions of a summer camp program. Adolescence. 12(47): 421-431.

Hobbs, T. R.; Radka, J. E. 1975. A short-term therapeutic camping program for emotionally disturbed adolescent boys. Adolescence. 10: 447-455.

Hobbs, T. R.; Radka, J. E. 1976. Modification of verbal productivity in shy adolescents during a short-term camping program. Psychological Reports. 39: 735-739.

Hobbs, T. R.; Shelton, G. C. 1972. Therapeutic camping for emotionally disturbed adolescents. Hospital and Community Psychiatry. 23: 298-301.

Hoffman, M. B. 1981. Recreation therapy: A prescriptive approach. Therapeutic Recreation Journal. 15(3): 16-21.

The Hospital Recreation Section of the American Recreation Society. 1953. Basic concepts of hospital recreation: A study of prevailing concepts of recreation for the ill and disabled. Washington, DC: American Recreation Society.

Howe, C. 1984. Leisure assessment instrumentation in therapeutic recreation. Therapeutic Recreation Journal. 18(2): 14-24.

Hughes, H. M. 1979. Behavior change in children at a therapeutic summer camp as a function of feedback and individual versus group contingencies. Journal of Abnormal Child Psychology. 7(2): 211-219.

Hughes, A. H.; Dudley, H. K. 1973. An old idea for a new problem: Camping as a treatment for the emotionally disturbed in our state hospitals. Adolescence. 8: 43-50.

Hunter, I. R. 1983. Methodological issues in therapeutic recreation research. Therapeutic Recreation Journal. 17(2): 23-32.

Iso-Ahola, S. E. 1980. Perceived control and responsibility as mediators of the effects of therapeutic recreation on the institutionalized aged. Therapeutic Recreation Journal. 14(1): 36-43.

Iso-Ahola, S. E. 1988. Research in therapeutic recreation. Therapeutic Recreation Journal. 22(1): 7-13.

Iso-Ahola, S. E.; Mobily, K. E. 1982. Depression and recreation involvement. Therapeutic Recreation Journal. 16(3): 48-53.

Jenkins, J.; Felce, D.; Lunt, B.; Powell, L. 1977. Increasing engagement in activity of residents in old people's homes by providing recreational materials. Behavior Research and Therapy. 15: 429-434.

Jensen, S. E.; McCreary-Juhasz, A.; Brown, J. S.; Hepinstall, E. M. 1968. Brief communications and clinical notes: Disturbed children in a camp milieu. Canadian Psychiatric Association Journal. 13: 371-373.

Jerstad, L.; Stelzer, J. 1973. Adventure experiences as treatment for residential mental patients. Therapeutic Recreation Journal. 7(3): 8-11.

Kaplan, H. K.; Reneau, R. F. 1965. Young patients enjoy therapeutic camping. Mental Hospitals. 16: 235-237.

Kelly, F. J.; Baer, D. J. 1968. Outward Bound schools as an alternative to institutionalization for adolescent delinquent boys. Boston, MA: Fandel Press, Inc.

Kelly, F. J.; Baer, D. J. 1969. Jesness Inventory and self-concept measures for delinquents before and after participation in Outward Bound. Psychological Reports. 25: 719-724.

Kelly, F. J.; Baer, D. J. 1971. Physical challenge as a treatment for delinquency. Crime and Delinquency. 17: 437-445.

Kelly, G. R.; McNally, E.; Chamblis, L. 1983. Therapeutic recreation for long-term care patients. Therapeutic Recreation Journal. 17(1): 33-41.

Kennedy, D. W. 1987. Leisure and mental illness: A literature review. Therapeutic Recreation Journal. 21(1): 45-50.

Kern, L.; Koegel, R. L.; Dunlap, G. 1984. The influence of vigorous versus mild exercise on autistic stereotyped behaviors. Journal of Autism and Developmental Disorders. 14(1): 57-67.

Kern, L.; Koegel, R. L.; Dyer, K. D., et al. 1982. The effects of physical exercise on self-stimulation and appropriate responding in autistic children. Journal of Autism and Developmental Disorders. 12(4): 399-419.

Kimsey, L. R.; Frost, M. 1971. Long term camping for emotionally disturbed boys. Diseases of the Nervous System. 32: 35-40.

Kistler, K. S.; Bryant, P. M.; Tucker, G. J. 1977. Outward Bound—Providing a therapeutic experience for troubled adolescents. Hospital and Community Psychiatry. 28(11): 807, 812.

Koegel, R. L.; Firestone, P. B.; Kramme, K. W.; Dunlap, G. 1974. Increasing spontaneous play by suppressing self-stimulation in autistic children. Journal of Applied Behavior Analysis. 7: 521-528.

Kostrubala, T. 1976. The joy of running. Philadelphia, PA: J. B. Lippincott.

Langer, E.; Rodin, J. 1976. The effects of choice and enhanced personal responsibility for the aged: A field experiment in an institutional setting. Journal of Personality and Social Psychology. 34: 191-198.

Landes, J.; Winter, W. 1966. A new strategy for treating disintegrating families. Family Process. 5: 1-20.

Langsner, S. J.; Anderson, S. C. 1987. Outdoor challenge education and self-esteem and locus of control with children with behavior disorders. Adapted Physical Activity Quarterly. 4: 237-246.

Lee, J. A. 1983. The group: A chance at human connection for the mentally impaired older person. Social Work with Groups. 5(2): 43-55.

Levitt, L. 1982. How effective is wilderness therapy: A critical review. Proceedings of the Third Annual Conference of the Wilderness Psychology Group; July 8-10, 1982; West Virginia University, Morgantown, West Virginia.

Levitt, L. 1988. Therapeutic value of wilderness. In: Wilderness Benchmark 1988: Proceedings of the National Wilderness Colloquium. January 13-14, 1988; Tampa, Florida: 156-168.

Lewinsohn, P. M.; Graf, M. 1973. Pleasant activities and depression. Journal of Consulting and Clinical Psychology. 41(2): 261-268.

Li, R. K. K. 1981. Activity therapy and leisure counseling for the schizophrenic population. Therapeutic Recreation Journal. 15(4): 44-49.

Lowry, T. P. 1974. Camping as a short term private psychiatric hospital. In: Lowry, T. P., ed. Camping therapy: Its uses in psychiatry and rehabilitation. Springfield, IL: Charles C. Thomas: 59-62.

MacAvoy, L. H. 1977. Leisure components of the geriatric day care center program. Therapeutic Recreation Journal. 11(2): 55-58.

Mannell, R. C. 1983. Research methodology in therapeutic recreation. Therapeutic Recreation Journal. 17(4): 9-16.

McClannahan, L. E. 1973. Recreation programs for nursing home residents: The importance of patient characteristics and environmental arrangements. Therapeutic Recreation Journal. 7(2): 26-31.

McClannahan, L. E.; Risley, T. R. 1975a. Activities and materials for severely disabled geriatric patients. Nursing Homes. 24: 10-13.

McClannahan, L. E.; Risley, T. R. 1975b. Design of living environments for nursing-home residents: Increasing participation in recreation activities. Journal of Applied Behavior Analysis. 8(3): 261-265.

McClung, S. B. 1984. A rock-climbing program as therapy for the chronically mentally ill. Dissertation Abstracts International. 45(04): 1292B.

McCreary-Juhasz, A.; Jensen, S. E. 1968. Benefits of a school camp experience to emotionally disturbed children in regular classrooms. Exceptional Children. 34: 353-354.

McDonald, M. C. 1974. Adventure camping at Oregon State Hospital. In: Lowry, T. P., ed. Camping therapy: Its uses in psychiatry and rehabilitation. Springfield, IL: Charles C. Thomas: 16-31.

McFarland, F. W.; Martin, R. C.; Williams, T. A. 1967. Staff attitudes and patient behavior change on camping trip. Hospital and Community Psychiatry. 18: 296-298.

McGuire, F. A. 1985. Recreation leader and co-participant preferences of the institutionalized aged. Therapeutic Recreational Journal. 19(2): 47-54.

McNeil, E. B. 1957. The background of therapeutic camping. Journal of Social Issues. 13: 3-14.

McPherson, I. T. 1977. A review of literature: Control of hyperactive children in recreational activities. Therapeutic Recreation Journal. 11(2): 59-65.

Menninger, W. C. 1948. Recreation and mental health. Recreation. Nov.: 340-346.

Middleman, R.; Seever, F. 1963. Short-term camping for boys with behavior problems. Social Work. 8: 88-95.

Miller, R. E. 1987. Method to study anhedonia in hospitalized psychiatric patients. Journal of Abnormal Psychology. 96(1): 41-45.

Mobily, K. 1985. A philisophical analysis of therapeutic recreation: What does it mean to say "We can be therapeutic?" Part II. Therapeutic Recreation Journal. 19(2): 7-14.

Mondell, S.; Tyler, F. B.; Freeman, R. W. 1981. Evaluating a psychotherapeutic day camp with psychosocial competence and goal attainment measures. Journal of Clinical Child Psychology. 10(3): 180-184.

Morgan, W. P. 1979. Anxiety reduction following acute physical activity. Psychiatric Annals. 9(3): 36-45.

Morse, W. C. 1947. From the University of Michigan Fresh Air Camp: Some problems of therapeutic camping. The Nervous Child. 6: 211-224.

Muller, D. J. 1971. Post-camping depression: A lethal possibility. American Journal of Psychiatry. 128(1): 141-143.

Neal, L. L. 1970. Trends in therapeutic recreation research. In: Berryman, D. L.; Arje, F. B., eds. Therapeutic recreation annual, Vol. VII. Washington, DC: National Therapeutic Recreation Society of National Recreation and Parks Association: 20-24.

Neffinger, G. G.; Schiff, J. W.; Abrams, S. 1984. The wilderness challenge: An adjunctive treatment. In: Pepper, B.; Ryglewicz, H., eds. Advances in treating the young chronic patient. New directions for mental health services, no. 21. San Francisco: Jossey-Bass: 99-102.

Nesbitt, J. S. 1977. The benefit of leisure service and participation to people who are handicapped. In: Fain, G. S.; Hitzhusen, G. L., eds. Therapeutic recreation state of the art. Arlington, VA: National Recreation and Park Association: 9-15.

O'Morrow, G., S. 1980. Therapeutic recreation: A helping profession. Reston, VA: Reston Publishing Company, Inc.

Orbach, C. E. 1966. Camping experiences for psychiatric patients from a day care hospital. Journal of Psychiatric Nursing. 4: 571-585.

Peterson, B. F.; Acuff, S. H. 1955. An experiment in living. Mental Hospital. 6: 8-9.

Polenz, D.; Rubitz, F. 1977. Staff perceptions of the effect of therapeutic camping upon psychiatric patients' affect. Therapeutic Recreational Journal. 11(2): 70-73.

Quilitch, H. R.; Dare de Longchamps, G. 1974. Increasing recreational participation of institutional neuro-psychiatric residents. Therapeutic Recreation Journal. 8(2): 56-59.

Ramsey, G. V. 1969. Sociotherapeutic camping for the mentally ill. In: Bindman, A. J.; Siegel, A. D., eds. Perspectives in community mental health. Chicago, IL: Aldine: 324-334.

Rawson, H. E. 1973. Residential short-term camping for children with behavior problems: A behavior-modification approach. Child Welfare. 52(8): 511-520.

Redl, F. 1974. Psychopathologic risks of camp life. In: Lowry, T. P., ed. Camping therapy: Its uses in psychiatry and rehabilitation. Springfiled, IL: Charles C. Thomas: 76-88.

Reid, P. D.; Factor, D. C.; Freeman, N. L.; Sherman, J. 1988. The effects of physical exercise on three autistic and developmentally disordered adolescents. Therapeutic Recreation Journal. 22(2): 47-56.

Reitman, E. E.; Pokorny, A. D. 1974. Camping at a psychiatric day center. In: Lowry, T. P., ed. Camping therapy: Its uses in psychiatry and rehabilitation. Springfield, IL: Charles C. Thomas: 63-67.

Remar, M. E.; Lowry, T. P. 1974. Camping therapy in the Commonwealth of Massachusetts. In: Lowry, T. P., ed. Camping therapy: Its uses in psychiatry and rehabilitation. Springfield, IL: Charles C. Thomas: 13-15.

Rerek, M. D. 1973. Senior citizen camping: An innovative program in community psychiatry. Journal of the Bronx State Hospital. 1(2): 85-87.

Reynolds, R. P.; Arthur, M. H. 1982. Effects of peer modeling and cognitive self guidance on the social play of emotionally disturbed children. Therapeutic Recreation Journal. 16(1): 33-40.

Rickard, H. C.; Dinoff, M. 1967. Behavior change in a therapeutic summer camp: A follow-up study. Journal of Genetic Psychology. 110: 181-183.

Rickard, H. C.; Serum, C. S.; Forehand, R. 1975. Problem-solving attitudes of children in a recreation camp and in a therapeutic camp. Child Care Quarterly. 4(2): 101-107.

Rickard, H. C.; Serum, C. S.; Wilson, W. 1971. Developing problem solving attitudes in emotionally disturbed children. Adolescence. 6: 451-456.

Rickards, W. H. 1985. Perspectives on therapeutic recreation research: Opening the black box. Therapeutic Recreation Journal. 19(2): 15-23.

Ritter, D. R.; Mock, T. J. 1980. Carryover effects of a summer therapeutic daycamp program on children's classroom behavior: A one-year follow-up. Journal of School Psychology. 18(4): 333-337.

Rosen, H. 1959. Camping for the emotionally disturbed. Children. 6(3): 86-91.

Ryan, J. L.; Johnson, D. T. 1972. Therapeutic camping: A comparative study. Therapeutic Recreation Journal. 6(4): 178-180.

Santarcangelo, S.; Dyer, K.; Luce, S. C. 1987. Generalized reduction of disruptive behavior in unsupervised settings through specific toy training. The Journal of the Association for Persons with Severe Handicaps. 12(1): 38-44.

Saslow, L. D. 1978. A multidimensional approach to camper assessment. Therapeutic Recreation Journal. 12(4): 30-35.

Schleien, S. J.; Krotee, M. L.; Mustonen, T., et al. 1987. The effect of integrating children with autism into a physical activity and recreation setting. Therapeutic Recreation Journal. 21(4): 52-62.

Schwab, M.; Rader, J.; Doan, J. 1985. Relieving the anxiety and fear in dementia. Journal of Gerontological Nursing. 11(5): 8-15.

Shank, J. 1975. Therapeutic recreation through contrived stress. Therapeutic Recreation Journal. 9(1): 21-25.

Shea, T. M. 1977. Camping for special children. St. Louis: The C. V. Mosby Co.

Shearer, R. M. 1975. Camping as a therapeutic experience for depressed and schizophrenic patients. Hospital and Community Psychiatry. 26: 494, 497.

Shniderman, C. M. 1974. Impact of therapeutic camping. Social Work. 19: 354-357.

Showstack, J. A.; Hargreaves, W.; Glick, I. D.; O'Brien, R. S. 1978. Psychiatric follow-up studies. The Journal of Nervous and Mental Diseases. 166(1): 34-43.

Smith, B. K. 1959. Patients go camping in Texas. Mental Hospital. 10: 17-18.

Solomon, E. G.; Bumpus, A. K. 1978. The running mediation response: An adjunct to psychotherapy. American Journal of Psychotherapy. 32(4): 583-592.

Stermac, L.; Josefowitz, N. 1985. A board game for teaching social skills to institutionalized adolescents. Journal of Child Care. 2(3): 31-38.

Stich, T. F. 1983. Experiential therapy. Journal of Experiential Education. 5(3): 23-30.

Stich, T. F.; Senior, N. 1984. Adventure therapy: An innovative treatment for psychiatric patients. In: Pepper, B.; Ryglewicz, H., eds. Advances in treating the young adult chronic patient. New directions for mental health services, no. 21. San Francisco, CA: Jossey-Bass: 103-108.

Stimpson, D. V.; Pederson, D. M. 1970. Effects of a survival training experience upon evaluation of self and others for underachieving high school students. Perceptual and Motor Skills. 31: 337-338.

Stoudenmire, J. 1977. Including educational and perceptual training in a therapeutic camp for emotionally disturbed children. Therapeutic Recreation Journal. 11(1): 12-15.

Stoudenmire, J.; Comola, J. 1973. Evaluating Camp Climb-Up: A two week therapeutic camp. Exceptional Children. 39: 573-574.

Touchstone, W. A. 1975. The status of client evaluation within psychiatric settings. Therapeutic Recreation Journal. 9(4): 166-172.

Tuttle, L. P.; Terry, D.; Shinedling, M. M. 1975. Note on increase of social interaction of mental patients during a camp trip. Psychological Reports. 36: 77-78.

Turner, A. L. 1976. The therapeutic value of nature. Journal of Operational Psychiatry. 7: 64-74.

Voight, A. 1988. The use of ropes courses as a treatment modality for emotionally disturbed adolescents. Therapeutic Recreation Journal. 22(2): 57-64.

Wassman, K. B.; Iso-Ahola, S. E. 1985. The relationship between recreation participation and depression in psychiatric patients. Therapeutic Recreation Journal. 19(3): 63-70.

Watters, R. G.; Watters, W. E. 1980. Decreasing self-stimulatory behavior with physical exercise in a group of autistic boys. Journal of Autism and Developmental Disorders. 10(4): 379-387.

Weiner, A. 1979. A quasi-experimental approach to evaluating recreation programs: Time-series analysis. Therapeutic Recreation Journal. 13(1): 32-38.

Weisman, M. N.; Mann, L.; Barker, B. W. 1966. Camping: An approach to releasing human potential in chronic mental patients. American Journal of Psychiatry. 123(2): 166-172.

West, R. E. 1979. Therapeutic recreation services as a component of optimal health care in a general hospital setting. Therapeutic Recreation Journal. 13(3): 7-11.

Whittekin, R. G. 1967. Imaginative themes enliven day camp. Hospital and Community Psychiatry. 8: 237-238.

Willman, H. C.; Chun, R. Y. F. 1973. Homeward Bound: An alternative to the institutionalization of adjudicated juvenile offenders. Federal Probation. 37: 52-58.

Winter, W. D.; Winter, L. M. 1966. Therapeutic camping: An experience in group living. Corrective Psychiatry. 12: 449-459.

Winter, W. D.; Winter, L. M. 1968. Clinical experiences with therapeutic camping. Adolescence. 3: 203-216.

Witman, J. P. 1987. The efficacy of adventure programming in the development of cooperation and trust with adolescents in treatment. Therapeutic Recreation Journal. 21(3): 22-29.

Witt, P. A. 1988. Therapeutic recreation research: Past, present, and future. Therapeutic Recreation Journal. 22(1): 14-23.

Wong, S. E.; Terranova, M. D.; Bowen, L., et al. 1987. Providing independent recreational activities to reduce stereotypic vocalizations in chronic schizophrenics. Journal of Applied Behavior Analysis. 20: 77-81.

Wright, A. N. 1983. Therapeutic potential of the Outward Bound process: An evaluation of a treatment program for juvenile delinquents. Therapeutic Recreation Journal. 17(2): 33-42.

Spiritual Benefits of Leisure Participation and Leisure Settings

Barbara L. McDonald
Strategic Assessment Branch
National Oceanic and Atmospheric Administration
Forestry Sciences Lab
Athens, Georgia

Richard Schreyer
Department of Forest Resources
College of Natural Resources
Utah State University
Logan, Utah

THE NATURE OF SPIRITUALITY

Spiritual experiences are among the most fundamental of human experiences and may occur in a variety of situations and settings. A setting that is often neglected as a major source of spiritual experience is the leisure setting. The enjoyment connotations of leisure may at times make it appear inappropriate for the more serious or reverential aspects of spirituality. However, spiritual experiences within leisure may, in fact, be widespread.

While spiritual experiences within leisure may be significant, very little is actually known about the spiritual characteristic of leisure, and even less attention has been devoted to it from a management/planning perspective (McDonald 1989). When the topic does arise, it is often not treated seriously, or it is treated as inappropriate for discussion.

McDonald et al. (1988) suggest two major reasons for lack of attention to this topic. First, the Constitution mandates separation of church and state. Spirituality connotes relationships to doctrinaire religions, and thus has often been viewed as inappropriate for government involvement. Much leisure research is government funded, further contributing to the lack of research attention to spiritual values. Second, because of the dearth of research in this area within leisure, there is little understanding of what the term functionally means, leading to ambiguity in operational applications.

Definition of Spirituality

For many, spirituality implies a relationship to some notion of a Divine Being. Spiritual experience, however, is not necessarily synonymous with religious experience. A more general definition might suggest an individual's attempt to understand his/her "place" in the universe. This often implies a relationship to a specific deity, although this is not necessary. Spirit refers to the nontangible elements of existence upon which life may be presumed to be based. This relates to the nonphysical, nonrational, nonempirical elements of human consciousness. A dictionary definition of spirit is "animating, fundamental, or vital principle held to give life to physical organisms," also "immaterial intelligent or sentient part of a person." These definitions exemplify the dualistic nature of spiritual connotations—the more universal nature of the spiritual domain and the human response to that universal concept.

McDonald et al. (1988) suggest that a key element in spirituality is the relationship between "self" and "other." They suggest that the self may be construed generically, such as one's culture or species. Likewise, "other" may imply a notion of God, but could also represent interrelationships with any entity or entities that represent "not-self." "It is the interaction of self and other within the wilderness context that defines (solely on a personal level) the true meaning of wilderness spirituality" (p. 194).

William James (1936) concluded, after years of studying the reported religious experiences of many individuals, that the spiritual domain exists in the shape of a personal god or gods, or is conceived as a "stream of ideal tendency" within the eternal world. James further noted that two broad characteristics of the religious life are that the observed world is only a part of a greater spiritual universe from which it acquires its larger significance, and that a harmonious relationship with the spiritual universe is the ultimate end.

Mircea Eliade, an historian of religion, describes the distinction between the "sacred" and the "profane." Profane implies that which we experience as a direct part of our tangible existence, our daily experiences. Sacred, on the other hand, represents our experience with consciousness that is different than the profane. "Man becomes aware of the sacred because it manifests itself, shows itself, as something wholly different from the profane" (Eliade 1957: 11). The sacred, therefore, is the manifestation of experience that is distinctly different from our everyday existence and consciousness.

The manifestation of the sacred can happen in any situation (e.g., during leisure), and a range of settings, symbols, or objects may serve to catalyze the experience. To persons traditionally exposed to more rational interpretations of reality, an understanding of the concept of the sacred is less accessible. Many public resources that provide settings for leisure pursuits are planned and managed by professionals trained in rational/empirical approaches to dealing with such places. To consider a rock as sacred may threaten the managerial precepts and guidelines that are the foundation of their professional modus operandi, yet this is precisely what Eliade suggests the sacred can mean.

In this paper, the terms religious, sacred, and spiritual are used interchangeably. While we recognize that these terms denote different meanings, the various sources we used sometimes referred to the religious, sometimes to the sacred or the spiritual. The scarcity of available references to the spiritual domain as it may relate to leisure created the need to use a wider range of terms and meanings. Given the subjectivity of the topic, there cannot be ultimate technical definition of spirituality.

The Significance of Spirituality

While interpretations of the meaning of spirituality differ, there is no question that it represents a significant element of life that has practical implications for individual and cultural development. Such forces seem to be deep-rooted in human consciousness. Attempts to understand and explain the unknown and likely unknowable questions regarding the supernatural and mystical exist as far back in history as human symbols. Burial sites, stone formations, petroglyphs, myths, and stories indicate that prehistoric human activities often centered on spiritual rituals and beliefs. These activities suggest that early societies attempted to understand and influence natural and supernatural forces to help them in this life and potential after life. Physical relics and surviving stories are evidence of a spiritual lifestyle that included rituals, celebrations, and other similar activities.

Regardless of diverse personal and cultural interpretations, the spiritual domain seems to possess universal elements. When discussed in this paper, spiritual domain is meant to include the recognized and often unrecognized relationships between things, but from the self-other perspective. Spirituality seems to be a uniquely human concept. Throughout human history, various cultures have passed along spiritual beliefs through surprisingly similar art and literature (Campbell 1986). The world-wide similarities between religious myths and beliefs may be partly explained by communication through storytelling, art and dance, and ultimately through the written word and electronic media. These religious stories were also likely passed along in ritual, drama, and celebration, implying a relationship between leisure and the spiritual domain of life. In fact, time is usually set aside for spiritual ritual and celebration, much as time is set aside for leisure.

Today, spiritual values, beliefs, and practices remain important to the individual and to society. Even as we have become more of a global society, each culture's particular spiritual values and beliefs continue to play a valuable role in (social and political) identification, community and cultural organization, and individual development. Luckmann (1967) described an evolution in religion toward a more personal interpretation, warning not to mistake this "invisible religion" for a reduction in religious values. The emergence of science and technology has not lessened the importance of our philosophical, ethical, and spiritual lives. It has, however, relegated the discussion of spiritual values more to nonscientific outlets. The balance of scholarly research toward technology is not indicative of the sustained interest in philosophical and spiritual topics (Walker 1989).

Spirituality and Leisure

The essence of all religious thought is the "belief that life has purpose" (Gaer 1963). But there is little widespread agreement about the nature of that purpose. The struggle to know, and the undeniable power of the unknown, give birth to spiritual values, practices, and beliefs. An individual's work hours (to earn the means of survival) provide, in one sense, a purpose for life. But humans search for purpose beyond mere subsistence. The search is, inevitably, a search for meaning beyond the physical aspects of staying alive. Why do we live? Why must we die? Humans live for more than sustenance, so they struggle to understand existence beyond the time that is necessary to provide these basic needs, that is, during leisure (Mills 1985).

Leisure provides an opportunity for individual expression that is well suited to such personal inquiry. The nature of leisure itself tends to promote philosophical perspectives of life. According to Godbey (1989):

> The nature of leisure is subjective and dialectic. Recreation and leisure behavior is ultimately infinite, nonrational, and full of meaning which is, or can be, spiritual.

The Dynamics of Spirituality

It is difficult to characterize the nature of spiritual experience in leisure. Given the subjective nature of the topic, people may have spiritual experiences and not interpret them as such, or find it difficult to verbalize what they have felt. There is also the question of to what extent such experiences may catalyze or alter behavior (Schreyer and Driver 1989), i.e., do they make a difference in people's lives?

Various ways have been used to organize this concept. For instance, McDonald et al. (1988) identified four "levels" of wilderness spiritual experience: 1) sacred places and things, 2) cultural heritage, 3) organized group experience, and 4) individual experiences.

Stokols,[1] in a paper attempting to define views of people-environment relationships, contrasted the "spiritual" view with the "instrumental" view. The spiritual approach emphasizes use of the environment as an end in itself, with emphasis on symbolic and affective features, where quality of environment is measured in terms of the richness of psychological and sociocultural meanings, as well as considerations of comfort and health. In contrast, instrumental views tend to see environments as tools for advancing human interests, where emphasis is on the material features of the environment, and quality is defined primarily in terms of comfort and health criteria.

Stokols[1] also suggested that spiritual environmental views include an integration of public and private domains, that environments are viewed as "dynamic and organic extensions of individuals and groups," with environmental research being pointed toward enhancing the awareness, participation and cohesion of environmental users. For both McDonald et al. and Stokols, environmental spiritual views relate the physical environment to a human interpretation of that environment. The two concepts are woven tightly.

The framework used to characterize spiritual experience for the rest of this paper will emphasize the distinction of *content* and *process*. The two are inextricably intertwined—there can be no process without content, and no content without process. However, an understanding of the nature of the dynamics of spirituality and of the benefits derived requires an understanding of the difference. People who are uncomfortable with the notion of spirituality manifested in leisure are often prone to be side-tracked by the content, as opposed to focusing on the nature of the process.

Content represents the specific object of spirituality. This may involve a particular religious belief system; some symbolic entity, such as a particular nation and its ideology; or a particular environment that is considered sacred. The content is a function of a person's development, social systems, personal philosophy, and/or culture.

The process component focuses on the psychological thought processes that occur leading up to an experience of spirituality. The processes that go on in the mind may be universal—what a person experiences may be similar whether the content is a specific religious ritual or participation in a leisure activity. Of course, as with any complex psychological phenomenon, it is likely that there is considerable variation in the nature of the experience people describe as spiritual. However, by attempting to better understand the nature of these processes, the functional significance of spirituality to the individual and to culture may be characterized.

Various processes appear as precursors to spiritual experience, such as participation in ritual, use of symbols, communion (with nature, God, etc.), music and dance, and contemplation (d'Aquili 1985). These processes may be similar regardless of the values or beliefs brought to the activity. Within these processes, religions and belief systems facilitate spirituality. The resulting feelings of spirituality may be similar, regardless of the belief system or content involved.

Leisure is also a process. Research has attempted to characterize what the essential elements of the process of leisure are, such as the experience of freedom, intrinsic motivation, and the loss of self-awareness (Neulinger 1983, Samdahl and Kleiber[2]). The purpose here is not to debate the meaning of leisure, but to suggest that there is a need to better understand how the process of leisure may enhance spiritual experience and benefit. If leisure experiences differ significantly qualitatively from other elements of life, they may in fact be a particularly useful ground for the development of spiritual activity, especially if more constrained life situations do not allow people the opportunity to escape the instrumental or the profane.

The remainder of the paper will address these dimensions in more detail. We will examine the different processes that have been used to characterize spiritual experience. Then we will look at the specific domains of content, particularly as they relate to leisure and leisure settings. The processes used to catalyze such experiences will be examined, and the benefits which may accrue from such experiences will be discussed. Finally, we will examine research needs and management implications.

THE PROCESS OF SPIRITUALITY

The experience of spirituality is one that spreads across a wide array of human activity. There appear to be strong similarities between spiritual experiences described by persons in widely varying situations, ranging from formal religious ceremonies to leisure settings. This suggests that the processes of thought in these cases may possess similar elements, and that it is primarily the object of the spiritual expression that differs. This section will first address how the spiritual experience has been described and how it is similar to various states of consciousness related to leisure pursuits and settings. Finally, we will look at technical attempts to characterize such experiences.

The Religious Experience

The religious experience has been characterized as a profound state of consciousness, in which the individual transcends the bounds of normal existence and experiences perceptions of phenomena that are uninterpretable in objective circumstances. The experience, as Maslow describes it, is often communicated as intensely personal, private, and illuminating (Maslow 1970).

Explanations for such experiences are couched in the particular sociocultural context in which they occur. However, the ways people express what they have felt, across the full range of doctrines or cultural views, have strong similarities. Maslow emphasized the universal nature of this experience across religions, cultures, political ideologies, professions, and individuals, which he referred to as the "core religious experience." "This private religious experience is shared by all the great religions including the aesthetic ones like Buddhism, Taoism, Humanism, or Confucianism" (Maslow 1970: 28).

Two points are central to this discussion. First, the human mind tends to experience that which it senses through a psychophysiological process that is shared in common. There is no doubt that there are variations in that "wiring" that will lead to radically different thought processes (Vonnegut 1975). To the extent that such aberrations create dramatic visions, the line between religious vision and mental illness may be hard to draw (Scheff 1966). However, the nature of religious experience expressed by most people is likely the function of similar means of sensing the world and of interpreting that world internally.

The second point is that people will interpret that perceptual experience in terms of their own personal meanings. These meanings are a function of one's culture, developmental history, and adopted formal beliefs. The process of religious experience is likely a shared perceptual process, but the interpretation varies according to the meanings that a given individual will apply to them.

States of Consciousness

These processes are presumed to be independent of context. In other words, a spiritual experience in any situation may be interpreted as having common characteristics. The key element is the state of consciousness that people attain during such experiences. This altered state of consciousness may occur during leisure as well. Although some research has been conducted on leisure and organized religions, very little research has been conducted on leisure and individual spiritual experiences (Ng[3]).

The state of consciousness is a subjective notion, as we can only know what the individual can articulate (Laing 1967). However, there have been attempts to characterize the commonalities among those expressions. Spiritual experiences are generally considered extreme states of consciousness, and as such are examined as special, ephemeral occurrences. According to Maslow (1970), these spiritual experiences were essentially equivalent to what he has labeled "peak" experiences.

A peak experience may be considered a period of time in which one experiences "self-actualization," which Maslow (1968) characterizes as a sense of personal fulfillment at the maximum level of human performance. It involves situations where the individual becomes egoless, where space and time become relatively insignificant, and the person's identity becomes merged with action and attainment of a greater sense of the whole. In other words, such experiences represent extreme states of human consciousness, and people who have such experiences tend to describe them in similar ways.

A similar construct that has also been frequently applied to leisure settings is Csikszentmihalyi's (1975) conception of the "flow" experience. Csikszentmihalyi has studied persons in various forms of human endeavor and found that descriptions people give of the subjective aspects of their experience, when highly involved, tend to be similar. This notion of flow may be applied to a variety of contexts, but it is likely applicable to what may be characterized as a spiritual experience as well.

The flow experience is represented by a merging of action and awareness. The person does not consciously think about the action that is being taken, even though the person is aware of those actions. There is a focusing of attention on a narrow set of stimuli. The person filters out extraneous information and concentrates only on that sensory information immediately relevant to what is being addressed. Csikszentmihalyi refers to Maslow in this regard in describing it as a "narrowing of consciousness" or a "giving up the past and the future" (Maslow 1971, cited in Csikszentmihalyi 1975). Flow experiences involve a loss of sense of self. There is not so much a sense of self-consciousness as there is an awareness of the immediate circumstance of what is occurring. And yet there is a heightened awareness of internal processes. As Csikszentmihalyi notes, "This heightened awareness obviously occurs in Yoga and many religious rituals" (p. 43).

This theme is recognized in such books as *The Inner Game of Tennis* (Gallwey 1974), in which the author espouses the "art of relaxed concentration" as a means for attaining self-awareness. This sense of focus is oriented toward personal challenge and fulfillment. Murphy and White (1978) describe many spiritual aspects that are experienced by persons participating in sports. They characterize through participant narratives various "mystical sensations" in sports, such as a sense of acute well-being, peace, calm and stillness, detachment, freedom, floating, ecstasy, control, instinctive action and surrender, mystery and awe, feelings of immortality, unity, altered perceptions of space and time, out-of-body experiences, and awareness of the "Other."

Through research conducted in cooperation with *Runner's World* magazine, Glasser (1976) concluded that running can produce the type of mental state to which meditators aspire. Glasser theorized that running activates an ancient neural need to run for survival. In addition, Glasser theorized that during running, the individual is less

self-critical than during any other activity that can be done alone. These two conditions, self-acceptance and the primitive need to run, can create a transcendental state in the brain.

Neuroscientists are just beginning to study the transcendental state. One theory is that activities such as marathon running and meditation inhibit the neurotransmitter serotonin (Mandell, cited in Clifford 1987). This in turn causes the brain's temporal lobes and limbic system to boost electrical discharges. Old stimuli and memories are then processed as if they are "new and full of meaning." Other scientists agree in general that an increase in electrical charges within the brain is responsible for the transcendental state (Persinger, cited in Clifford 1987; d'Aquili 1985).

A theory advanced by d'Aquili (1985) to explain the persistence of ritual in human societies is that prolonged, repetitive, rhythmic stimuli causes the simultaneous firing of the sympathetic and parasympathetic nervous systems, creating a euphoric feeling of unity within the individual. This feeling of unity can take on any culturally defined meaning, such as communitas tribus (tribal unity), communitas hominus (unity of mankind), or communitas universalis (unity of all things). The specific content of these experiences is determined by individual, social, and cultural values, but the process leading to the feeling is similar.

Past experiences, ritual, and extended intense experience seem to play a role in the creation of the transcendental state, lending support to the importance of the social-psychological realm in the spiritual experience. Within or outside of leisure, another characteristic of activity leading to a feeling of communitas, may be instances where the mind must encourage the body to persevere. Examples in leisure include marathon running and rock climbing. Examples perhaps "outside" of leisure may be meditation, or working out a challenging math problem. Of course, it may be argued that leisure may usually be characterized by feelings of communitas, regardless of when or why the activity is engaged in.

One of the critical elements in translating these processes into what may be interpreted as a spiritual experience is receptivity. Receptivity has been identified as a basic characteristic of leisure (Hendee and Brown 1988, Pieper 1963). Receptivity is an open-minded attitude that is not merely passive (although it may incorporate some characteristics of passivity). A desirable and perhaps necessary characteristic of spiritual experience is receptivity to what various dimensions, such as time, space, emotions, or physical conditions, are offering the individual.

The Wilderness Experience

Perhaps one of the most generally cited notions of the combination of extreme states of consciousness and spiritual endeavor related to leisure is the wilderness experience. Obviously, there is no such thing as "the" wilderness experience, as it is a function of what people are seeking, what they perceive, and it is colored by our meanings, symbols, and needs (Knopf 1983, Stankey and Schreyer 1987).

The wilderness experience has cognitive and affective components that interact and may potentially produce a transcendent experience (Stankey and Schreyer 1987). Ulrich (1983) suggests that a person's initial affective state will influence the ways in which the environment is perceived. In other words, if a person is looking for or expecting a spiritual or transcendent experience, then what is encountered may be more likely to catalyze that happening. This may serve to attain higher states of consciousness or self-awareness (Scott 1974, Young and Crandall 1984).

In fact, Scott (1974) suggested that the major writers on wilderness, such as Muir, Catlin, Thoreau, and Leopold, used language describing wilderness experiences that were very close to notions of transcendent or peak experiences. He suggested they used such environments as vehicles for self-actualization.

Scott (1974: 233) used a framework of altered states of consciousness to analyze the nature of the experience being described by such writers. He noted:

> . . . the reverie of Catlin is a meditative state mediated by the parasympathetic component of the autonomic nervous system and the treetop adventure of Muir would be an ecstatic state resulting from stimulation of the sympathetic division of this system.

In summary, spiritual experiences are seen to be individual and intense. They are interpreted through the values and the context of the individual. The subjective elements of such experiences tend to be described in terms that parallel certain states of consciousness that have been ascribed to, but certainly not limited to, leisure experiences and settings. The process of the leisure experience is very compatible with the notion that persons may derive spiritual experiences under such circumstances.

THE CONTENT OF SPIRITUAL EXPERIENCES

The previous section attempted to identify the common threads of spiritual experience as a psychological process. What is most commonly thought of in terms of spirituality, however, is the specific content. We will examine the application of content to leisure spirituality under two topics: spirituality as applied to a specific religious doctrine or philosophy, and spirituality as applied to a place or setting. The two are not mutually exclusive, but do involve different sources of emphasis.

Religious Beliefs

It is not necessary to go into detail concerning the array of beliefs represented by the world's religions. The permutations of belief are exceedingly diverse. However, there are also commonalities. James (1936) concluded that all religions agree that some notion of spirit or an unseen universe exists, and that this existence can act upon the known universe. Furthermore, James asserts that the religions agree that an entity is really affected for the better when its life is placed into the "hands" of this existence (Klein 1984). When one surrenders oneself (or is receptive) to the universal spirit and its ability to act upon or within the known world, then one believes his/her life has been improved. James (1936) observes that the concept of the divine cannot be a single concept, but is a group of concepts, different for different individuals, depending on their past and present needs.

These values are expressed through different belief systems, which are acted out in a variety of ways. There are different ways in which various religious belief systems direct the expression of spirituality in terms of the places, the objects, the symbols, and the situations in which spiritual experience is to occur. This will affect the ways in which a person may seek to use leisure for spiritual encounter.

Judeo-Christian religions have traditionally emphasized a dualism between the mortal and the Deity. This of course varies in degree, and the element of communion is a common theme. However, there is a stronger sense of separation between the sacred and the profane than with other belief systems. For instance, among Native American cultures, spirituality was often an integral aspect of daily interactions with the functions of life (Brown 1982). The basic idea is that their religion was equivalent to their lifestyle (McDonald 1987). This conception is shared in many other belief systems and philosophies, such as Taoism, which emphasizes the interrelatedness of all experiences (McDonald et al. 1988).

Such interrelatedness within experiences would enhance the likelihood that spirituality would be a part of the leisure experience. For instance, Navajos will incorporate religious rituals as an integral aspect of deer hunting (Johnson[4]). While the dualistic nature of Judeo-Christian religions makes the connection between spirituality and leisure less fundamental, there are many ways in which the leisure setting is seen as a means of creating spiritual awareness, such as within religious youth camps.

If religion is an integral part of one's life, regardless of the belief system, then leisure time will likely involve elements of spirituality. Religions may use leisure settings for specific spiritual events or teachings. In some cases, the line between leisure pursuit and formal religious activity becomes blurred. To the extent that formal religious beliefs are a part of the individual's life, they will affect the manifestation of spirituality in leisure.

Spirituality and Place

Sacred Space

Throughout history, cultures have attributed special meanings to certain settings. Beyond the trees, rocks, etc., the place takes on special meaning. In many cases, these places have a religious or spiritual connotation. Thus, there is a tendency for people to develop attachments with settings that go beyond their physical function. This represents a sense of "place" (Tuan 1976).

This sense of place may be very specific, such as a sacred rock, or it may be very broad, such as a philosophy in which one is connected to the earth and all living things. "If spirit is the life-giving principle and many nonhuman forms have life, then it is possible that they also have spirit, or are spiritual. Many individuals in past and current societies have been spiritually inspired by the natural world" (McDonald 1989: 20). McDonald goes on to cite Watkins (1987): "We humans are related in life to all the life around us... The species that produced the typewriter reaches adulthood through the same process by which the spider grows, shares in the same mysterious spark and dance of creation. Biologist E. O. Wilson has dubbed this relatedness biophilia—the brotherhood of life."

This view of the spiritual importance of place has permeated virtually all cultures and religions. In Christianity the wilderness appears to have particular symbolic significance for spiritual experience. The notion of Christ going into the wilderness for spiritual inspiration and Moses receiving the Ten Commandments in the wilderness characterize a Judeo-Christian view of wilderness (Bratton 1986).

Early Christian theology saw earth as the creation of God. Therefore, the nature of God could be seen in the workings of natural systems (Norton 1987).

Buddha supposedly spent six years in the forest to find enlightenment. As previously mentioned, Taoism emphasizes the functional interconnectedness between humans and the community of life. And of course, many allusions to Native American spirituality in connection with the earth have been observed.

This connectedness with a place has been described by Tuan (1975) as "geopiety," a sense of reverence for the earth. Graber (1976) discusses the notion of "sacred space," or places that hold special significance to individuals, groups, or cultures. As quoted in McDonald et al. (1988: 196), Graber observes: "Some parts of space are wholly different from others. When the sacred reveals itself in space, man gains a fixed point of orientation in the chaotic relativity of the profane world. Sacred space is the site of power, and makes itself known by the effects of power repeating themselves there, or by the effects of power being repeated in ritual by man."

Such places may be specific human constructions, such as the Sistine Chapel. They may also be natural places. Just as the inspiration of a human place of worship may catalyze spiritual experiences, so may a natural setting if it is seen as being invested with such qualities.

Placing spiritual value on natural settings occurs in a range of cultures. The preservation of national parks and monuments is often viewed in a reverential framework. These areas are often referred to as our "national shrines" that serve as places of inspiration. While the objects of place reverence may be more specific than large environments, the key is that they possess some symbolic meaning for the perceiver. As McDonald et al. (1988: 197) note:

> Native Americans ascribed special significance to totems, often animals such as the bear. Americans today may feel inspired by the sight of eagles, the Grand Canyon, or even less spectacular but still meaningful naturally occurring life forms or systems. A focus by some groups on crystals is a recent example of the subcultural significance of specific natural objects.

These feelings can frequently be found in literature and in the expressions of communion with nature and its powerful qualities. Loren Eisley (1946: 195-196) said: "By the time I get to the wood I am carrying all manner of seeds hooked in my coat or piercing my socks or sticking by ingenious devices to my shoestrings. We, the seeds and I, ... sit down to rest, while I consider the best way to search for the secret of life." In Eisley's case, the environment is an essential ingredient in the search for life's meaning.

While any environment that may be used for leisure purposes may have the capacity to bring forth such feelings, some environments are culturally invested with meanings that make them particularly prone to support spiritual experiences. Perhaps the one that is most representative of that in American culture is wilderness.

Wilderness Experiences

Driver et al. (1987: 302) acknowledge the significant spiritual component underlying wilderness philosophy:

> Wilderness appreciation...began with the revolutionary idea that the least modified environments were the purest expressions of God's power and glory . . . Wilderness acquires importance as a setting for answering the deepest questions of human existence, for celebrating the creative power behind life and things, and for understanding the unity of them all.

Rationales for the preservation of wilderness are often couched in themes that emphasize "nature appreciation, education, freedom, solitude, simplicity, as well as spiritual, aesthetic, and mystical dimensions" (Hendee et al. 1968). Thus, the wilderness experience is frequently equated with the spiritual. While the process of the wilderness experience was described above, it is also important to emphasize that there is strong content reflected in the writings of wilderness advocates. This becomes a part of the emotional context that people will bring to the wilderness setting.

This content has been strongly articulated by the writers most revered by wilderness enthusiasts. As noted by Stankey and Schreyer (1987), John Muir considered wild nature the conductor of divinity and believed that wilderness should exist as a source of psychic and spiritual energy (Nash 1982). Arthur Carhart (1920) felt that "the individual with any soul cannot live long in the presence of towering mountains or sweeping plains without getting a little of the high moral standards of nature infused into his being." Joseph Wood Krutch (1958) observed that "wilderness and the idea of wilderness is one of the permanent homes of the human spirit." Roggenbuck et al. (1973) discussed the long term spiritual impact of wilderness through the words of Sigurd Olson:

> They think they go into the back country . . . to test themselves or to face a challenge, but what they really go for is to experience the spiritual values of wilderness . . .

Graber (1976) described the community of wilderness purists as a "sacred community," emphasizing the role of place as content in the development of shared spiritual values.

The spiritual connotation in the meaning of wilderness is hard to escape. The extent to which people share those particular values is of course extremely variable. However, to the extent that people do accept those values, they will see wilderness settings as appropriate places for spiritual experience.

> The only riches you can enjoy in the wilderness are the riches of the spirit, and through history people have gone to the wilderness to discover the spiritual riches within themselves. Wilderness is a place where we cannot escape the fundamental truth that what matters is not what we have, but what we are (Wootten 1985: 3).

FACTORS INFLUENCING SPIRITUAL EXPERIENCE

The process of spiritual experience may occur during leisure, and leisure settings may be seen as places appropriate for spiritual expression. In this section, we will examine some of the forces which may serve to precipitate spiritual experiences during leisure. A particular behavior such as contemplation or prayer, or the environment such as wilderness or a cathedral, may become catalysts for feelings one might characterize as spiritual. Individuals may consciously or unconsciously pursue leisure in these environments or through these behaviors in order to attain such experiences. We examine this through the contexts of sociocultural forces and environmental influences.

Sociocultural Forces

Cultures or subcultures share similar views of religion and the meaning of life. It becomes very important to share these, to reaffirm the rightness of those values (Berger and Luckmann 1966). Thus, cultures develop ways of expressing shared values and attainment of spiritual experience. In many cases, these experiences may appear to be "choreographed" in terms of their formality and procedure.

The Ways to Spiritual Experience

One example is the notion of a celebration, which is essentially a social communion. Pieper (1963: 56-57) emphasized the importance of celebration in the development of culture and spiritual beliefs. "To hold a celebration means to affirm the basic meaningfulness of the universe and a sense of oneness with it, of inclusion within it." He pointed out that early feasts and festivals without gods were un-known. Sunday in our culture carries with it both mixed meanings of religious significance and leisure. Many formal holidays have as their roots the worship of the divine (or have evolved from pagan ceremony).

A variety of vehicles are used in this context. They include symbolism and ritual, acts of communion, music and dance, and contemplation (d'Aquili 1985). Dewey (1958) notes that the word "symbol" is not only used to identify expressions of quantities and values in scientific fields such as mathematics, but is also used to identify deeply personal and social values, such as the flag or the crucifix.

The relevance of symbols and ritual to leisure need not be dwelled upon. The presence of symbols and ritual are abundant in leisure. Celebrations are generally considered synonymous with leisure. Music and dance, acts of contem-plation and communion are all fundamental elements of leisure experiences. And of course, the use of imagery in leisure, particularly in the context of the phenomenon we describe as play, is perhaps one of the basic definitions of the concept. Thus, the elements which serve to catalyze spiri-tual experiences in general are prevalent in leisure situ-ations, suggesting that people who seek to make spiritual uses of leisure will have many resources to support them.

There are voices who argue for perspective in relation-ship to these vehicles, in the sense that the vehicles may be seen as ends in themselves, as opposed to means to an end. According to Maslow (1970), many individuals "concre-tize" the symbols, words, or ceremonies, and elevate the concrete form to the sacred objects and activities, forgetting the origin of the sacred revelation. This may happen, according to Maslow, to individuals who are ignorant, naive, or who lack education. To them, the symbols may become more important than the object or experience.

Groups and Spirituality

The cultural bonding represented by shared spirituality can occur at all levels of social organization. It can occur at the broad cultural level, but it may also occur at the community or the group level. In fact, it has been suggested that shared spirituality may serve as an important means of strengthen-ing a sense of community among people. In the context of wilderness advocates, Graber (1976) observes: "The strik-ing uniformity of wilderness purists' beliefs, their member-ship in conservation organizations, their sense of identity, and their degree of emotional commitment suggest the emergence of something like a sacred community."

At the interpersonal level, shared spirituality may be strongly influenced by group dynamics. Other persons in the group may make it known that spiritual expression is a part of the agenda for the given leisure pursuit. This may give permission for others to make such expressions as well. It may also provide a certain amount of social pressure on persons in the group to have the expected type of experience. Such agendas may be a formal part of the situation, such as with organized groups like the Boy Scouts or with youth camps.

Social groups will develop norms of appropriate behav-ior for a given social situation. Such norms are as applicable in leisure situations as they are in other life situations. They may reinforce or deter an individual from spirituality during leisure. If the norm is to not be introspective or spiritual during a certain event, this will encourage participants not to engage in such experiences. Beyond behavioral norms, there may be norms that attend to the emotional domain as well, that is, how we are supposed to feel in a given situation. Hochschild (1979) refers to these as "feeling rules," and suggests that many emotions experienced in certain situ-ations may be as much a function of social definitions of appropriate emotion as they are innately expressed feelings.

The persons who have the most influence in determin-ing the norms and feeling rules are those who are most revered and respected. These are the people who are pre-sumed to know what the "right" thing to do or feel is. In the context of leisure, this is often expressed through the writ-ings of persons who are experts, the most skilled, or who have the most experience. They may often also evoke the significance of the spiritual components of the pursuit. Thus, the wilderness writers discussed above may create a strong atmosphere for the adoption of expectations for spiritual experience among wilderness enthusiasts.

At the most specific level, an individual's personality will have much to say about susceptibility or even willing-ness to engage in spiritual encounter. Just as some people have personalities that make it impossible for them to be hypnotized, there are others who do not easily experience the sensation of the spiritual. Maslow (1970) observed that some individuals, due to their particular nature, may always attempt to be rational, materialistic, or mechanistic. These types of individuals tend to become nonpeakers. Their view of life causes them to regard peak or transcendent experi-ences negatively, as reflecting a loss of control, as insanity, or as irrational and emotional. They therefore tend to avoid or supress such experiences.

On the other hand, there are persons who may be particularly sensitive, intuitive, and prone to spiritual expe-rience. At the extreme expression of this type of personality, we may refer to the individual as a mystic or a seer.

Environmental Influences

Much has been written about the spiritual and sacred quality of the natural environment in early societies and for contemporary cultures (Flamm 1988, Graber 1976, McDonald 1987). Cathedrals and churches are examples of indoor environments which evoke contemplative or spiritual feelings. On the other hand, prayer, meditation, or other contemplation may occur anywhere, even on a crowded bus.

In a broad sense, all leisure and spiritual experiences take place in settings that are culturally defined. The setting is the sum of physical, cultural, and emotional elements, but the relative importance of these elements may vary. In some cases, the physical environment may be necessary to invoke the spiritual condition; in others, the physical environment may be of little importance.

There is likely a continuum of the degree of importance the environment will play in affording spiritual experience. This is dependent on how the environment is perceived as an element in the spiritual experience. What aspects of natural settings can evoke such feelings? This is obviously related to what the individual is looking for. However, many notions of spirituality appear to derive from feelings of the grandeur and overpowering elements of nature. The sense of forces larger than what the human mind can comprehend may serve as a catalyst in this regard. It is interesting to note that many formal places of worship, such as cathedrals, appear to mimic nature in the sense of large open places that seem to reach to the sky. At a more microcosmic level, natural stimuli may provide a contrast to the harsh manmade world a person has to confront. These natural environments may provide an opportunity for individuals to engage in contemplative activities and facilitate conceptions of the spiritual.

The new science of chaos and fractal geometry bring to light interesting new theories of unity and the attractiveness of nature. The principles of fractal geometry and the concept of scale may stimulate appreciation for the structure and form of nature. The concept of the self-similarity of nature and the related concept of scale may provide the fixed point of orientation that Graber referred to. "In terms of aesthetic values, the new mathematics of fractal geometry brought hard science in tune with the particularly modern feeling for untamed, uncivilized, undomesticated nature" (Gleick 1987: 117).

Environments may serve as the repository of personal cultural heritage, which may have significant spiritual implications. This may be the reverence for places that have historical meaning, such as the Gettysburg battlefield, that ties into feelings for broader cultural values. It may also be much more deeply rooted in religious meaning, as in Native American identification with the places of their ancestors. Environments are repositories for our history, they capture the record of our existence. To the extent that our history has spiritual elements, the significance of places for cultural meaning and the maintenance of cultural continuity will be an important factor in the ways people experience such places. In the sense of serving as a catalyst, the intensity of the link of the individual to such meanings will enhance the likelihood that these places may be used for spiritual experience. Many leisure settings are places of significant historical and cultural experience, and a significant motivation for persons seeking to visit such places is to make this type of connection. While much of the interest in cultural resources is historical or empirical, there is also a recognition that such places have significant symbolic and personal meanings for members of various cultures.

THE BENEFITS OF SPIRITUAL EXPERIENCE

The benefits which may accrue from spiritual use of leisure and leisure settings are at best speculative, as there is virtually no research that addresses such an issue. Of course, the capacity to engage in spiritual expression in and of itself may be considered a benefit, and has been identified in lists of the various benefits of leisure (Schreyer and Driver 1989). Therefore, a major benefit of leisure may be to provide an opportunity to experience a sense of spirituality. This is of course subjective, but the perceived sense of spiritual experience may affect the individual in ways that involve the capacity for introspection, humility, and feelings of belonging. The role of leisure is that it may allow an opportunity to engage in this experience when the mind is not otherwise preoccupied or the individual is "busy." The belief that one's life has been improved by some new association or understanding of the spiritual universe may lead to other feelings characteristic of the spiritual experience, such as peace, comfort, zest, endurance, and re-creation. These feelings, in turn, can impart meaning to the more ordinary aspects and objects of one's life.

"The Way that can be described is not the eternal Way" (Watts 1975). According to Watts and the Taoistic philosophy, it is impossible to operationalize or scientifically measure spirituality. It may, as well, be unnecessary and counterproductive. The consequences of spiritual benefit are real to the individual, and it is their manifestation that lends credibility and reality to the concept of spiritual benefit. For example, research by Rossman and Ulehla (1977) on University of Colorado students indicated that one of the major perceived benefits from wilderness was having the chance for spiritually uplifting experiences. Regardless of the particular interpretations of spiritually uplifting experiences, the benefit was expressed as having the chance for such experiences.

A significant benefit from spiritual experience may be the potential for personal development. The confrontation with domains beyond one's personal life space may serve as a means for greater understanding. As McDonald et al. (1988: 194) describe it:

> This may occur suddenly (and be called a spiritual experience) or may develop over a period of time (and be called spiritual growth). The sudden awareness experience may be similar to the mystical experience, embracing such characteristics as ineffability, a feeling of knowledge, a short-lived experience, and a feeling of abeyance (James 1936). Spiritual growth, on the other hand, occurs over a period of time, but may include sudden experiences of insight and understanding ... This awareness impacts individuals to the degree that their view of their life-world is changed, reflecting the new awareness we labeled "spiritual growth." Spiritual growth, by definition, requires a change (in awareness), which is rarely planned or calculated.

In an effort to put structure on this process, McDonald[5] suggested a "Com-model," or model describing leisure participation that leads to a sense of community and broader appreciation for existence. This model describes a move from a sense of awareness to conscious choice to engage in constructive leisure activities. This leads to embracing the challenge of the activity, which enhances self-awareness. To the extent that this self-awareness leads to new insights and development, the individual will have a more positive attitude, which will encourage an increasing sense of commitment. Ultimately, this commitment will lead to a greater sense of connectedness with other persons/entities and a greater sense of community toward which the individual purpose is directed.

A related possible benefit is a greater sense of appreciation for the environment and the community of life. Many leisure experiences occur in natural settings. If they serve as the means to rewarding spiritual encounters that are related to heightened senses of awareness, then there may be a deeper sense of understanding of the value of such environments.

As spiritual experience implies a freedom from the normal constraints of life, it may allow for a greater degree of personal expression. This may allow the individual to explore new possibilities and opportunities for personal fulfillment and creativity. While we have noted the strong social forces which may influence such experiences, they can also be very personal and allow the individual to escape the constraints of social expectation.

A spiritual experience can also expand into social consciousness and increase the sense of connectedness or community for the individual. This connectedness may be with a group, a community, a nation, or the earth and its community of life and can be described as "being with" unity (community). In other words, there is a sense of harmony with some collective other. The beneficial aspects of this have to do with a sense of belonging, a sensitivity to the whole, and a sense of purpose and direction.

Another possible benefit is a sense of wellness and mental health. Access to spiritual experience may be a significant part of an individual's sense of control over life in response to the more pragmatic demands of life. Ragheb[6] identified spiritual wellness as one of six wellness measures correlated with leisure satisfaction. Spiritual wellness was measured using a self-report Likert scale item asking about spiritual wellness as a general construct. Spiritual wellness correlated significantly with all measures of leisure satisfaction, and was correlated most strongly with aesthetic/environmental leisure satisfaction at 0.35.

Finally, spiritual experience may be a source of creativity. Because such experience allows for an escape from the bounds of the tangible world and encourages new or different perception, it may afford the individual the opportunity for creative thought. Creativity involves new ways of understanding and describing that which we attempt to understand and interpret. The freer our perception and thought are, the more likely we are to develop those new ways. Thus, spirituality may have the potential to open new doors of perception and to provide a philosophical structure to communicate the creative process. Much of the world's creative works in science, drama, literature, music, and art were inspired by questions and meditations about the human spirit. These creations are often the result of leisure-related pursuits, either as nonwork endeavors, such as creating religious art as an act of worship; or as the object of leisure enjoyment, such as in drama or art exhibitions.

FUTURE DIRECTIONS

Managing for Spiritual Opportunities

The recognition of the nature and significance of spirituality in leisure implies that it can and should be consciously planned and managed for. Interestingly, there have been formal legal and policy declarations in the U.S. Government that provide for such management. McDonald et al. (1988) note that the USDA Forest Service Manual states: "The qualities of wilderness and wild areas . . . provide a refuge from civilization, give spiritual comfort, and preserve the flora and fauna for inspiration." They also cite Vest (1987) as noting that much of the language of the Wilderness Act implies spiritual values. "Religion . . . is at the core of wilderness solitude." They also cite the Code of Federal Regulations as saying "National Forest Wilderness resources shall be managed to promote, perpetuate, and, where necessary restore . . . specific values of solitude, mental challenge, scientific study, inspiration, and primitive recreation" (United States 36 CFR 1986).

There are a variety of ways in which the process of providing opportunities for spiritual expression may be approached. There must be a capacity to inventory leisure settings as to their spiritual potential. This may include recognition of cultural sites of historic significance or sacred spaces, places used systematically by groups for spiritual experience, and attributes of settings that may promote such experiences. Similarly, there needs to be an identification of those environmental elements that may hinder or make such experiences less likely to occur.

There is a need to assess the demand for such experiences, both existing and latent. Particularly, this assessment needs to be carried out across various subcultural groups within society in terms of their spiritual needs. Opportunities for such experiences must then systematically be incorporated into the planning process.

Actual provision of opportunities may include programming activities that promote spiritual experience such as yoga, as well as creative activities such as music or dance. It may also involve the conscious design of settings to promote opportunities for spiritual experience, both in terms of landscape design and facility design. Stokols[1] suggests the use of symbols and other physical elements that may serve as catalysts to spiritual experience. He even suggests the development of "global icons" which he considers "pictorial and graphic symbols of human fellowship that can be displayed within public and private settings to remind us of our common global interests and responsibilities. Ultimately, we must find ways to promote a better balance between the instrumental objectives of high technology and the spiritual dimensions of environmental design."

An important offshoot is to recognize that many people may not be consciously seeking a spiritual experience, but may in fact encounter it unintentionally (McDonald 1989). To the extent that planning, management, and design can provide for such opportunities, they may produce additional benefits beyond what the person has consciously sought.

Finally, there needs to be a sensitivity to the preservation of opportunities for such experiences. Increases in recreational demand, even for spirituality itself, may increase the potential impacts on the very places which may provide those opportunities. Further, the development and growth of society makes ever greater demands on resources. This development may infringe on the amount of space through which spiritual experience may be available. Of particular concern in this regard is maintaining the integrity of sacred spaces—places considered to have particular spiritual meaning by various subcultures.

Research Needs

Since little research has been carried out on spirituality in leisure per se, there is a wide potential for pursuing various research questions. The following are some potential research questions:

- What is the frequency of use of leisure for spiritual purposes? What is the relative importance of these uses to various individuals? What is the frequency of spiritual experience among persons who did not actively seek such experiences, and what were the circumstances?
- What types of persons seek such experiences?
- What types of activities or behaviors do people engage in who seek such experiences?
- What do people experience when they experience spirituality during leisure?
- What are the major catalysts of such experiences?
- What settings and/or aspects of settings facilitate such experiences?
- What is the range of such types of experiences, and how do they relate to people, activities, catalysts, and settings? Are there characteristics across the range of spiritual experience that are universal, and are there others that are idiosyncratic?
- How and to what extent are spiritual experiences related to personal growth and development?
- How do different subcultures within our society experience spirituality, where, and in what activities?
- To what extent do public providers of leisure services facilitate the desire for spiritual experiences? Are the opportunities provided equitable to various subcultures in this regard?

- What is the nature of "sacred space," and how is it defined by different cultures, subcultures, and groups?
- How does environmental design or active managerial intervention affect spirituality? (Stokols notes that designed settings are often separated by function, but that spirituality emphasizes integration and unity, presenting a potential conflict.)

This list is not intended to be exhaustive, so much as it suggests needed directions. Many other questions will obviously arise as research proceeds.

These research questions suggest a number of study approaches, incorporating the fields of recreation, psychology, sociology, philosophy, religion, anthropology, geography, and landscape architecture, among possible others.

Some research questions call for a new interpretation and notion of sacred space, celebration, and spiritual experience among cultures or investigating the use of landscaping in the orient to achieve feelings of solitude and reverence. Self-report measures may be applied to understanding the spiritual experience of current users of recreation opportunity. Existing or new psychological and sociological scales may be appropriate for user questionnaires and would provide for measures of reliability. Open-ended questions or personal interview techniques may be required to allow for the variety of responses anticipated and to clarify ideas, concepts, and beliefs about spiritual experience that would undoubtedly be a necessary part of this type of exploratory research. Tightly controlled studies using planning and management alternatives could be employed along with psychological measures and other self-reporting techniques. Longitudinal research would provide valuable information pertinent to human development questions and could be used within many of the suggested research methods and disciplines appropriate to spiritual studies.

Since little research has been conducted in this area, the need to explore a variety of research methodologies is obvious. Undoubtedly, different types of research approaches are needed to answer different questions. Consistent and acceptable operational definitions must be developed. To understand the phenomenon of spiritual experience within the recreation experience, scholars and researchers from many disciplines must be encouraged to apply their own techniques, and from this mosaic a better understanding of and appreciation for the importance of spiritual experience within the domain of recreation should emerge.

CONCLUSION

The presence of spirituality is pervasive in human society. It appears to be expressed during leisure in a wide variety of ways. Its significance has often been overlooked because it is less tangible than more concrete and understandable aspects of life. Nevertheless, it is one of the universal human experiences, and access to spiritual experience appears to provide the opportunity for considerable benefit, including feelings of peace, belonging, inspiration, and unity. If these benefits are then manifested through the individual's behavior, and if this behavior in turn improves the condition of the individual, community, environment, or planet, then the spiritual benefits of leisure may have far-reaching consequences.

ENDNOTES

[1] Daniel Stokols, in presentation on instrumental and spiritual views of people-environment relations: current tensions and future challenges, keynote address at the 10th Annual Conference of the International Association of People and their Surroundings; Technical University, Delft, The Netherlands, July 5-8, 1988.

[2] Diane M. Samdahl and Douglas A. Kleiber, in paper on self-awareness and the leisure experience, presented at the NRPA Leisure Researh Symposium; New Orleans, LA, October 18-19, 1987.

[3] David Ng, in paper on interrelationship between religion and leisure: perspectives and analysis, presented at the NRPA Leisure Research Symposium; Orlando, FL, 1984.

[4] J. Johnson, in paper on the experience of deer hunting, prepared for Utah State University class in Principles of Wildland Management; Logan, UT, 1988.

[5] Barbara L. McDonald, in paper on recreation as a spiritual experience: awareness, community, and meditative aspects, presented at the NRPA National Congress; New Orleans, LA, October 18-19, 1987.

[6] Mounir Ragheb, in paper on leisure and wellness, presented at the Southeastern Recreation Research Conference; Asheville, NC, February 1989.

LITERATURE CITED

Berger, P. L.; Luckmann, T. 1966. The social construction of reality. Garden City, NY: Anchor Books.

Bratton, S. P. 1986. Battling Satan in the wilderness: antagonism, spirituality, and wild nature in the four gospels. In: Lucas, R. C., comp. Proceedings, National wilderness research conference: current research; 1985 July 23-26; Fort Collins, CO. Gen. Tech. Rep. INT-220. Ogden, UT: USDA Forest Service, Intermountain Research Station: 406-411.

Brown, J. E. 1982. The spiritual legacy of the American Indian. New York, NY: The Crossroad Publishing Co.

Campbell, J. 1986. The inner reaches of outer space: metaphor as myth and as religion. New York, NY: Harper and Row, Inc.

Carhart, A. 1920. Recreation in the forest. American Forestry. 26(317): 268-272.

Clifford, T. 1987. Anatomy of ecstasy. American Health. 6(1): 53.

Csikszentmihalyi, M. 1975. Beyond boredom and anxiety. San Francisco, CA: Jossey-Bass.

d'Aquili, E. 1985. Human ceremonial ritual and modulation of aggression. Zygon. 20(1).

Dewey, J. 1958. Art as experience. New York, NY: Capricorn Books.

Driver, B. L.; Nash, R.; Haas, G. 1987. Wilderness benefits: a state-of-knowledge review. In: Lucas, R. C., comp. Proceedings, National wilderness research conference: issues, state-of-knowledge, future directions; 1985 July 23-26; Fort Collins, CO. Gen. Tech. Rep. INT-220. Ogden, UT: USDA Forest Service, Intermountain Research Station: 294-319.

Eisley, L. 1946. The immense journey. New York, NY: Random House.

Eliade, M. 1957. The sacred and the profane—the nature of religion. New York, NY: Harcourt, Brace & World.

Flamm, B. R. 1988. The future wilderness system. In: Freilich, H. R., comp. Wilderness benchmark 1988: Proceedings of the National Wilderness Colloquium. Gen. Tech. Rep. SE-51. Asheville, NC: USDA Forest Service, Southeastern Forest Experiment Station: 54-65.

Gaer, J. 1963. What the great religions believe. New York, NY: Dodd, Mead, and Co.

Gallwey, W. T. 1974. The inner game of tennis. New York, NY: Random House.

Glasser, W. 1976. Positive addition. New York, NY: Harper and Row.

Gleick, J. 1987. Chaos: making a new science. New York, NY: Penguin Books.

Godbey, G. 1989. Implications of recreation and leisure research for professionals. In: Jackson, E. L.; Burton, T. L., eds. Understanding leisure and recreation: mapping the past, charting the future. State College, PA: Venture Publishing, Inc.

Graber, L. 1976. Wilderness as sacred space. Washington, DC: Association of American Geographers Monograph Series.

Hendee, J.; Brown, M. 1988. How wilderness experience programs facilitate personal growth: an explanatory model. Renewable Resources Journal. 6(2): 9-16.

Hendee, J. C.; Catton, W. R.; Marlow, L. D.; Brockman, C. F. 1968. Wilderness users in the Pacific Northwest: their characteristics, values and management preferences. Research Paper PNW-61. Portland, OR: USDA Forest Service, Pacific Northwest Forest and Range Experiment Station.

Hochschild, A. R. 1979. Emotion work, feeling rules, and social structure. American Journal of Sociology: 551-574.

James, W. 1936. The varieties of religious experience. New York, NY: The Modern Library.

Klein, B. 1984. Movements of magic: the spirit of T'ai-Chi-Ch'uan. N. Hollywood, CA: Newcastle Publishing Co.

Knopf, R. C. 1983. Recreational needs and behavior in natural settings. In: Altman, I.; Wohlwill, J., eds. Behavior and the natural environment. New York, NY: Plenum: 205-240.

Krutch, J. W. 1958. Grand Canyon: today and all its yesterdays. New York, NY: William Morrow and Co. 256 p.

Laing, R. D. 1967. The politics of experience. New York, NY: Ballantine Books.

Luckmann, T. 1967. The invisible religion. New York, NY: MacMillan Co.

Maslow, A. 1968. Toward a psychology of being. 2nd ed. Princeton, NJ: Van Nostrand.

Maslow, A. 1970. Religions, values and peak experiences. New York, NY: Viking.

Maslow, A. 1971. The farther reaches of human nature. New York, NY: Viking.

McDonald, B. L. 1989. The outdoors as a setting for spiritual growth. Women in Natural Resources. 10(2): 19-23.

McDonald, B. L.; Guldin, R.; Wetherhill, R. C. 1988. The spirit in the wilderness: the use and opportunity of wilderness experience for spiritual growth. In: Freilich, H. R., comp. Wilderness benchmark 1988: Proceedings of the National Wilderness Colloquium. Gen. Tech. Rep. SE-51. Asheville, NC: USDA Forest Service, Southeastern Forest Experiment Station: 193-207.

McDonald, K. 1987. Sacred land in environmental planning. The Environmental Professional. National Association of Environmental Professionals. 9(1): 27-32.

Mills, A. S. 1985. Participation motivations for outdoor recreation: a test of Maslow's theory. Journal of Leisure Research. 17(3).

Murphy, M.; White, R. A. 1978. The psychic side of sports. Reading, MA: Addison Wesley.

Nash, R. 1982. Wilderness and the American mind. 3rd ed. New Haven, CT: Yale Univ. Press.

Neulinger, J. 1983. Value implications of denotations of leisure. In: Values and leisure and trends in leisure services. State College, PA: Venture Publishing, Inc.: 19-29.

Norton, B. G. 1987. The spiral of life: how it all works. Wilderness. Spring.

Pieper, J. 1963. Leisure: the basis of culture. New York, NY: Random House.

Roggenbuck, J. W.; Kienast, C. R; Middaugh, G. B. 1973. Quality recreation in wilderness. In: Brown, P. J.; Schomaker, J. H., eds. Recreation carrying capacity in wilderness—a series of topical papers. Logan, UT: Institute of Outdoor Recreation and Tourism, Utah State Univ: 1-12.

Rossman, B. B.; Ulehla, Z. J. 1977. Psychological reward values associated with wilderness use: a functional-reinforcement approach. Environment and Behavior. 9(1): 41-65.

Scheff, T. J. 1966. Being mentally ill. Chicago, IL: Aldine Publishing Co.

Schreyer, R.; Driver, B. L. 1989. The benefits of leisure. In: Jackson, E. L.; Burton, T. L., eds. Understanding leisure and recreation: mapping the past, charting the future. State College, PA: Venture Publishing, Inc.: 385-419.

Scott, N. R. 1974. Toward a psychology of wilderness experience. Natural Resources Journal. 14(2): 231-237.

Stankey, G. H.; Schreyer, R. 1987. Attitudes toward wilderness and factors affecting visitor behavior: a state-of-knowledge review. In: Lucas, R. C., comp. Proceedings, National wilderness research conference: issues, state-of-knowledge, future directions; 1985 July 23-26; Fort Collins, CO. Gen. Tech. Rep. INT 220. Ogden, UT: USDA Forest Service, Intermountain Research Station: 246-293.

Tuan, Y. 1976. Space and place. Minneapolis, MN: University of Minnesota Press.

Tuan, Y. 1975. Geopiety: a theme in man's attachment to nature and to place. In: Lowenthal, D.; Bowden, M. J., eds. Geographies of the mind. New York, NY: Oxford Univ. Press: 11-37.

Ulrich, R. S. 1983. Aesthetic and affective response to natural environments. In: Altman, I.; Wohlwill, J. F., eds. Behavior and the natural environment. New York, NY: Plenum: 85-125.

United States Code of Federal Regulations. 36 CFR Ch. 11 (July 1, 1986 Edition) Part 293—Wilderness Primitive Areas.

Vest, J. 1987. The philosophical significance of wilderness solitude. Environmental Ethics. 9: 304-327.

Vonnegut, M. 1975. The eden express. New York, NY: Bantam.

Walker, D. 1989. Philosophy professors leave Britain for American campuses. The Chronicle of Higher Education. March 8, 1989.

Watts, A. W. 1975. Tao: the watercourse way. New York, NY: Pantheon Books, Random House.

Wootten, H. 1985. Wilderness, values, and the search within ourselves. Habitat. 13(4): 2-3.

Young, R. A.; Crandall, R. 1984. Wilderness use and self-actualization. Journal of Leisure Research. 16(2): 149-160.

The Learning Benefits of Leisure

Joseph W. Roggenbuck
Department of Forestry
Virginia Polytechnic Institute and State University
Blacksburg, Virginia

Ross J. Loomis
Department of Psychology
Colorado State University
Fort Collins, Colorado

Jerome V. Dagostino
Department of Psychology
Colorado State University
Fort Collins, Colorado

INTRODUCTION

In this paper, we will focus on those purported leisure learning outcomes which society at large defines as desirable. We believe these socially accepted learning benefits to be:

- learning of specific recreational activities and skills in specific environments,
- learning about the natural and cultural environment,
- developing more positive attitudes about the environment and resource management and becoming more effective environmental decision-makers,
- learning different behaviors toward the environment,
- developing pride in the community and nation and becoming a more involved citizen, and
- learning about the self (Buhyoff and Brown[1]).

DEFINITIONS OF LEARNING

Psychologists and educators have generated mountains of work trying to answer the question, "What is learning?", and a complete discussion of this issue lies well beyond the scope of this effort. Indeed, Gagne and Dick (1983) estimated that it would take one researcher 5 years just to review the theory and applications of the subfield of learning called instructional psychology. Instructional psychology represents only one of many conceptual approaches that might be used to understand leisure learning. Given the futility of attempting to review all that is known about how learning happens, we have instead chosen to limit our inquiry to three tasks: 1) a description of two general approaches to learning—stimulus-response and cognitive; 2) development of an integrative model of leisure learning; and 3) a description of seven learning outcomes or experiences that result from leisure engagements.

Stimulus-Response versus Cognitive Learning

For the purpose of understanding leisure learning, it is useful to draw on a basic distinction from academic learning research that divides kinds of learning experiences into *stimulus-response* versus *cognitive*. Traditionally, psychologists have emphasized learning as an observable change in *behavior,* and conventional wisdom focused on two kinds of learning: classical conditioning or associative learning of facts and information patterned after the original work of Pavlov, and the behavioral change learning associated with the operant conditioning work of Skinner. Leisure theorists and recreation administrators—at least in outdoor settings—haven't given much attention to conditioned learning, probably because of its connotations of manipulation of recreational experiences with an accompanying loss of freedom. Yet administrators do use incentives, appeals, information, and feedback to modify littering and energy consumption behavior in recreational settings—often with considerable effectiveness—and this represents a kind of stimulus-response learning (Hines et al. 1986-87). Some mood or emotional learning, including feelings associated with attitudes, can also occur through a conditioning process. Learning of muscle responses and other kinds of skills can also be explained, in part, by classical stimulus-response psychology.

As early as the 1940s there were dissenting voices to the notions that learning was conditional changes in behavior. Tolman (1949) suggested that there were at least *six* kinds of learning, and his analysis put much more emphasis on the individual's perceptions and understanding of the world (rather than changes in behavior) than was the accepted wisdom of the time. Today, Tolman's ideas about learning are much more in vogue in the cognitive revolution in the study of learning (e.g., see Gardner 1985). This revolution has emphasized learning as changes in *mental* activities such as memory (Klatzky 1980) and other cognitive processes such as attention, seeing, talking, and solving problems (Bourne et al. 1979, Moates and Schumaker 1980). Furthermore, researchers such as Neisser (1982) have determined how memory works in natural contexts.

Cognitive learning can include the acquisition of such leisure-related *facts* as temperature of water at Yellowstone's thermal pools; such *concepts* as the interrelationships of water, heat, and rock strata of the Yellowstone geysers; *visual learning* and *memory* of the beauty of geysers; *meta-*

cognitions of the relationships between Yellowstone's Old Faithful and Norris geyser basins—both spatially and functionally; *schemata learning* which categorizes the geysers as part of Yellowstone's water system along with its lakes, rivers, and streams; and finally the cognitive aspects of both *mood* and affective or *attitudinal* learning.

An Integrative Model of Leisure Learning

Academic learning research and theory, instructional psychology, life-time learning (Cross 1981, Knowles 1984), experiential learning (Kolb 1984, Walter and Marks 1981), environmental or contextual learning (Falk and Balling 1982; Falk and Balling, in press), and visitor evaluation research all assist the understanding of leisure learning, and thereby, the benefits derived from it. Rather than propose a specific model or theory of leisure learning and benefit analysis, we have opted for an integrative approach. Admittedly, this strategy emphasizes a "bottom-up" approach to the problem whereby empirical research in specific leisure settings could be guided by an array of different theories of learning. The learning theory chosen would be determined by the specific learning outcome or experience under study, the context of the research setting, and the leisure population of interest. In time, perhaps a more grand theory or "top-down" approach to understanding leisure learning will evolve. Given, however, the wide array of experiences and behaviors as well as potential settings involved, it would seem unlikely that one approach or theory of learning would be adequate. Furthermore, topics like adult and experiential learning, the importance of understanding context or environmental variables, and visitor studies in leisure settings all provide insight into leisure learning by emphasizing the unique nature of nontraditional learning opportunities.

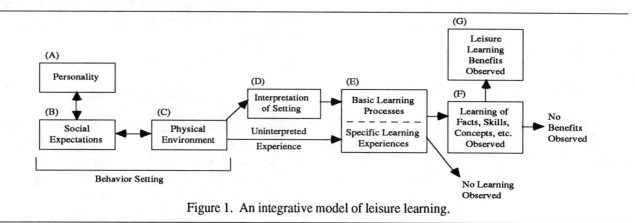

Figure 1. An integrative model of leisure learning.

Figure 1 displays a general model intended to guide understanding of leisure learning and benefits. It was derived from a general model of environmental adaptation (Fisher et al. 1984) and provides for integrating the different fields of inquiry about learning just discussed. Important to the model is the identification of different learning experiences that reflect not only a variety of learning opportunities, but also would lead to different leisure benefits.

Beginning at the left of the flow chart model in Figure 1 are three boxes representing personality (A), social expectations about leisure settings and experiences (B), and the physical environment (C). Leisure learning has to take into account the motivation and personality styles of the learning much in the way the adult learning movement has indicated. Consistent with behavior-setting research, an individual's reaction to his environment is a function of both the physical setting and the social expectations brought to that setting. Leisure learning may be direct and experiential in nature, as indicated by a direct line to the learning experiences in box E, or interpreted, as in the case of many visitor exhibits and environmental learning programs (D). Included in this box are variables of effective exhibit design and applications of instructional psychology to leisure time educational programs. Basic learning processes, whether stimulus-response or cognitive in nature, and a variety of learning experiences (or kinds of learning) are represented in box E and may or may not lead to factual learning, which may or may not be observed (F). Furthermore, there is no certainty that if learning does take place that the outcomes can be considered benefits. Box G in Figure 1 represents observed or measured benefits related to leisure learning.

When potential learners engage in a leisure time experience (e.g., hiking, sports, museum visiting), they bring along particular personality styles of learning and motivation as well as expectations about the experience and setting. They are confronted with a specific environment, interpreted or not, that promotes one or more learning experiences, such as motor learning or conditioning, to meet the demands of that setting. Specific learning experiences can be identified that are appropriate for a given setting. These experiences may be part of a formal leisure program curriculum, or they may be observed as part of the information outcomes of participation. Once the different kinds of learning experiences are identified, it is then possible to complete a benefits analysis on the learning observed.

Learning Outcomes

Learning and educational psychology have identified a variety of learning outcomes or kinds of learning. Seven of these outcomes seem to be the possible result of leisure engagements: behavior change and skill learning, direct visual memory, information (factual) learning, concept learning, schemata learning, metacognition learning, and attitude and value learning. Learning of *new behaviors or skills* during leisure and/or modifying old ones comes closest to being the kind of learning studied by traditional stimulus-response theorists. Recreation managers, programmers, and counselors have used educational intervention in an effort to teach new skills, influence where people go during their leisure time, and reduce the harmful impacts of their behavior on the environment or on other recreationists.

One of the products of the cognitive learning revolution mentioned earlier is a strong interest in understanding *visual memory*. We now know, for example, that our ability to recognize things we have seen before, even briefly, is very good (Shepard 1967). Remembering a painting seen in an art gallery or how sunsets looked during a wilderness outing are examples of visual memory. Recognizing from a picture an historic building seen during a vacation stop is an example of recognition memory. Such memory learning seems critically important to enjoyable leisure experiences. Before the recreationist can perceive, function in, and enjoy environments, he or she must be able to recognize various elements and scenes of the environment (Kaplan 1984). Also, the leisure enjoyment benefits of the recall phase of the recreational experience is not possible without visual memory, and visual memory requires cognition and learning. For pleasant memories to occur, the individual must have processed information, coded it in memory, and have the ability to bring it back to the "mind's eye" (Hammitt 1987).

Information or *factual learning* is probably the most common learning outcome of leisure engagements. Exhibits at visitor centers, ranger presentations around campfires, and park brochures all purport to teach facts. Examples of factual information provided include the names of the Union and Confederate generals at Gettysburg, the diet of the Anasazi Indians, and the frequency of eruption of the geysers at Yellowstone.

When cognitive psychologists studied learning, they quickly became interested in how individuals organize or make sense out of facts. One way this is done is to organize specific stimuli or information into categories or phenomena that show common attributes. These more general or higher order working units are *concepts*. Rosch (1973) has identified *natural* categories that people learn early in life to use to organize common features of the world around them. For example, trees have common attributes that distinguish them from animals. It is likely that a visitor to a museum full of different kinds of objects or a hiker on a nature trail is using natural concept learning in his or her exploration of the setting. At the same time, the museum or the nature trail likely contains information that "doesn't fit" existing mental categories, and is therefore puzzling. Park interpreters can assist learning by helping visitors incorporate factual information into existing, expanded, or more differentiated conceptual structures.

Related to concept learning is the discovery that large bundles of knowledge are stored in memory in the form of integrated units called *schemata*. Schemata form a framework for understanding and remembering new information. A schema takes in information from the environment, directs the search for information, and in turn can be changed by new information (Moates and Schumacher 1980). Schemata are therefore useful in understanding perception and the learning of prose materials. For example, schemata theory would explain why a history buff knowledgeable about the Civil War but visiting a famous battlefield for the first time, would experience very different kinds and amounts of learning than the first time visitor who is not a Civil War enthusiast. The history buff would already know the names of the key generals, the overall strategy of both commanding generals, and the importance of the lay of the land. These schemata would already exist in his or her memory. The casual, first-time visitor would have little of this information, and what information he or she had would have little organization. These two individuals would respond to historical interpretation and the setting itself in very different ways.

Researchers in education have become aware of the importance of the self-perceptions learners have on *how* they learn and *how* they orient themselves to the learning environment. For example, Hood (1984) has shown that some people avoid art museums because they perceive themselves as not knowing how to deal with art museums and feeling uncomfortable in that setting. In contrast, art museum patrons who visit often feel at home in an art museum. These percepts, or *metacognitions,* combine orientation to a place with impressions of one's level of mastery. If one has appropriate orientation to a setting or content, one will both feel more comfortable and learn more. This seems especially important in leisure settings, many of which are novel. Orientation metacognitions that involve cognitive mapping of the environment are also critical to learning (Porteous 1977).

Leisure activities involve many opportunities for learning both *attitudes* and broader, more pervasive *values.* A personal history of many camping and wilderness experiences is likely to contain learned attitudes about nature, conservation, and the "right" behaviors that go with being a good camper. Attitude learning has been studied as a problem in classical association (Byrne and Clore 1970) or as a form of cognitive learning acquired, for example, through

observing others (Bandura 1977). It involves changes in beliefs (knowledge), feelings, and behavior toward a specific object or event. Value learning is closer to schemata learning mentioned earlier when several points of information, including attitudes, are incorporated into a coherent mental structure (Smith 1969). Thus, a parent who regularly takes a child on Saturdays to a science center is not only reflecting specific values about the importance of science, but also a value system about parenting and appropriate leisure time activities.

EVIDENCE OF LEISURE LEARNING

We are taking two approaches to document the learning benefits of leisure. The first is to explore the meanings of leisure engagements to participants. We will be reporting whether recreationists in their subjective descriptions of their experiences cite learning as a component or value of their leisure. We will also be comparing the relative importance of learning to other reported outcomes of leisure. Our second approach is to review and report actual increases in various categories of learning due to leisure engagements. Thus, we will have subjective reports of the extent to which learning is a desired and perceived benefit of leisure, and empirical measures of gains in mood, memory, knowledge, attitudes, values, and behavior due to leisure.

Learning as a Motive for Leisure

Several leisure theorists have asked recreationists for their reasons for engaging in leisure time activities in general or for participating in their favorite activities. Beard and Ragheb (1980) developed a Leisure Satisfaction Scale designed to measure the extent to which individuals perceive that certain personal needs are met or are satisfied through leisure activities. The scale assessed six types of leisure outcomes: psychological, educational, social, relaxational, physiological, and aesthetic. Students rated relaxational outcomes as most important and physiological benefits as least important. Educational benefits, i.e., intellectual stimulation and learning about selves and surroundings, tied for fourth position in importance with aesthetic benefits. The mean score of the educational factor was 2.5 on a 5-point scale, indicating that the desire for education was between "seldom" and "sometimes" true.

Hawes (1978) did a nationwide household survey to determine the kinds of satisfaction derived by women and men from their three favorite recreational activities. From a list of 32 possible types of satisfaction, both men and women rated "peace of mind" as the most important satisfaction. Women rated "a chance to learn new things" and "it gives me a chance to develop a skill" as second and eighth most important. Men rated these two benefits as eighth and sixth most important, respectively. Other learning-related outcomes ranked in the top half were "I like it because I have a feeling of mastery of the activity" for men and women, and "It gives me a chance to be alone with my thoughts" for women.

Pierce (1980a) surveyed urban residents to determine the extent to which they received the following types of satisfaction from their free time activity: intimacy, relaxation, achievement, power, time filling, and intellection. The intellection factor included such items as "It was intellectually stimulating," "It enlivened my mind," "I learned something new," and "I learned more about myself." Both men and women in the sample rated relaxation as most important. The women, however, rated intellection as their second most important type of satisfaction; for men intellection ranked fourth.

The findings from these three surveys suggest that while learning is not the most important desired outcome from generalized leisure time activities, it is often among the more sought after benefits. Indeed, for women, it was the second most satisfying outcome, following only the pervasively important "relaxation" motive.

We now turn to desired benefits from engagement in specific recreational activities. The learning motive fell in the most important quartile of all motivating forces for reading for pleasure (Hawes 1978; Pierce 1980a, 1980b; Tinsley and Kass 1979); attending plays, concerts, and lectures (Tinsley et al. 1977, Tinsley and Kass 1979); and making crafts (Hawes 1978). For almost all studies reviewed, the desire to learn new things while socializing/partying (Hawes 1978), driving for pleasure (Hawes 1978), visiting wilderness (Driver et al. 1987, Lucas 1964, Rossman and Ulehla 1977, Wellman et al. 1982), and visiting nature centers (Blahna and Roggenbuck 1979) were among the top 25% of all reasons listed. Learning most frequently fell in the second most important quartile among reasons for participation in ORV use (Driver and Knopf 1976, Driver et al. 1987, Schreyer et al. 1981), canoeing and rafting (Driver et al. 1987, Graefe et al. 1981, Knopf et al. 1983, Schreyer and Roggenbuck 1978), reservoir use (Driver et al. 1987), and hunting (Decker et al. 1980, Driver and Knopf 1976, More 1973, Potter et al. 1973). The importance of gaining new knowledge through camping varied a great deal from study to study, ranging from the third quartile to the first quartile in rank among motives listed (Hawes 1978, Hollender 1977, Pierce 1980a). Learning importance for fishing (Adams 1979, Driver and Bassett 1975, Driver and Knopf 1976, Hawes 1978) and national park visitation

(Wellman et al. 1982) tended to fall in the third quartile in importance, but the one study on national park visitors is almost certainly unrepresentative, because its subjects were beach users of Cape Hatteras—a recreation area.

For many physical activities like scuba diving (Tinsley and Kass 1978, 1979), bicycling and jogging (Tinsley et al. 1977; Tinsley and Kass 1978, 1979), and many sports activities like golf and tennis (Driver and Knopf 1976), bowling (Hawes 1978), and swimming (Driver and Knopf 1976, Hawes 1978), learning was very low in importance compared to other motivating forces. Picnicking also scored low on the learning motive (Hawes 1978), and this was also the case for passive leisure activities like watching television (Pierce 1980a, Tinsley and Kass 1978), attending sports events (Hawes 1978, Tinsley and Kass 1978), and listening to music (Hawes 1978; Pierce 1980a, 1980b). Finally, some studies showed that learning was a more important motive for women than for men for leisure activities in general (Hawes 1978, Pierce 1980a), for creative crafts and handicrafts (Hawes 1978), for gardening/landscaping (Hawes 1978), and for camping (Hawes 1978, Pierce 1980a).

Measures of Leisure Learning Outcomes

Behavior Change and Skill Learning

Research on the learning of new behaviors during leisure has focused on the effectiveness of planned interventions by recreation managers, interpreters, and counselors to teach new skills, influence people to visit new places, and to teach low impact behaviors. Sometimes observation has been used to measure the incidence of new behaviors, but more often self-reports by recreationists about their behavior have been employed.

Skill learning.—Leisure pursuits have been shown to increase skill levels, especially when the recreationist has "hands-on" involvement with the task, performs the task in the relevant setting, and/or completes a programmed learning task. For example, Sneider, Eason, and Friedman (1979) found that exhibits contained in the Star Games exhibition of the University of California, Berkeley museum increased students' ability to operate telescopes, explain proper stargazing, and perform well on an astronomy quiz. That treatment groups had significantly higher scores over a control group that visited the museum but not the Star Games exhibition was explained by the hands-on activities required by the exhibits. Likewise, O'Connor (1983) found that active participation in an Old Sturbridge Village living history program taught high school students 19th century labor skills such as food preparation and tool making.

Organizations like the Boy Scouts, the Girl Scouts, the National Outdoor Leadership School, and Outward Bound Schools are also deeply involved with teaching new skills in leisure settings. In addition, many high schools and colleges provide field trips to natural environments—sometimes for academic credit—for the purpose of teaching outdoor skills. For example, Kaplan (1974) measured the outdoor skills of adolescent participants in a 2-week outdoor challenge program in the backcountry of Michigan's Upper Peninsula. Before and after measures indicated that the students' skills in finding food, rock climbing, knowledge of ecology, map reading, using compasses, knowledge of the roads, and setting up camp improved significantly during the course. Of these, rock climbing and compass use skills increased the most. Only for first aid, fire building, and outdoor cooking was there no significant gain; and for fire building and outdoor cooking, abilities were high going into the program.

Influencing site and route choice.—A body of forest recreation research has examined the nature, extent, and causes of change in recreation site selection due to management intervention. In one of the earliest studies, Lime and Lucas (1977) sent a brochure to recreationists visiting high-use zones in the Boundary Waters Canoe Area Wilderness, informing them about patterns of use and attractions in the area. A follow-up survey after the subsequent summer season demonstrated that one-third of their contacts had used a new entry point to the BWCAW, most had selected a more lightly used canoe route, and three-fourths said the brochure influenced their choice of a travel route and time of trip.

Roggenbuck and Berrier (1982) evaluated the use of an informational brochure and ranger contacts to encourage behavior shifts of campers away from a heavily used meadow in Shining Rock Wilderness of North Carolina. The informational messages, delivered either by trailhead brochures or by the brochure plus a ranger contact at the problem meadow, described problems of impacts and congestion at the meadow and identified the location and characteristics of five alternative, more lightly used campsites within a mile of the spot. Under the control condition, 62% of all wilderness user groups camped in the problem meadow; the percentage dropped to 44% with the brochure alone, and to 33% under the brochure and personal contact condition.

Krumpe and Brown (1982) also had success in changing behavior of recreationists in a wildland setting. They developed a brochure which used a decision tree format to describe 28 lightly used trails in the backcountry of Yellowstone National Park. They cited evidence that people process information in a sequential flow when they attempt to reach a decision, and thus felt that the decision tree format would facilitate behavior change. They gave the brochure to backpackers when they received their backcountry use permits at ranger stations in the park. Under the control condition (no information), only 14% of all groups took one of the 28 lightly used trails; this number increased significantly to 37% with the brochure's use. Inexperienced hikers were more likely to choose one of the recommended trails.

Huffman and Williams (1987) followed the Krumpe and Brown study by developing a user-friendly microcomputer program that permitted backcountry hikers in Rocky Mountain National Park to gain information on trail attributes in the sequence of their relative importance to individual decisionmaking. Twenty-nine different trails were included in the decision aid, and hikers received the information at a park visitor center when they applied for their backcountry use permits. Under the control condition (no information), about 17% selected one of the 29 trails. When a brochure describing these trails was distributed to hikers, 38% of the groups selected one of the trails. When hiker groups accessed the same information on the microcomputer, 60% of all groups selected one of the 29 trails. These findings suggest that computerized information organized in a fashion most meaningful for the user accomplishes substantial behavior change.

Learning low impact behaviors.—Visits to parks and nature education programs have long been thought to promote a responsible land ethic. For example, the Smokey The Bear fire prevention program communicated in our national forests is credited with cutting the number of forest fires by half (USDA Forest Service 1976). In the last couple of decades, researchers have begun to document the alleged reductions in impact behaviors due to nature programs and park visits. For example, Fazio (1974) found that backpackers who had seen one of several interpretive displays or programs explaining the reasons for regulations regarding behavior in Rocky Mountain National Park had a significantly higher propensity to observe the rules than those who had not been exposed to the interpretive contact.

Roggenbuck and Passineau (1986) conducted a study at Indiana Dunes National Lakeshore to assess the effectiveness of interpreter-guided field trips in changing the behavior of grade school visitors. The children's behavioral intentions to not litter, to recycle materials, and to act in various ways to protect natural and cultural resources increased significantly from pre-trip to post-trip. Post-test scores of the control group that didn't visit the park did not increase over their pre-test measures, and the children's scores after the field trip were significantly higher than comparable post-test scores of the control group.

Actual littering behavior was also observed among field trip participants. When anti-littering messages were given to the children at the start of the field visit, they picked up 66% of the litter that had been planted along their trail. When the message was coupled with role modeling of finding and picking up a piece of litter by the park naturalist, 90% of all planted litter was retrieved by the children. Approximately three-fourths of the way through the field visit, the children were given a souvenir button in a small envelope. Without the knowledge of the children, observations were made of the extent to which the button envelope was discarded on the ground. Even though more than 350 children received the souvenir button envelope, not one was ever found on the forest floor.

Oliver et al. (1985) used informational prompts in a developed campground to reduce littering and tree damage behavior. Under the control condition, 82% of all camper parties left at least one piece of litter at their campsite at their departure; the number of pieces per campsite averaged 3.9. Tree damage was also high, with 38% of all groups damaging at least one tree and an average of 1.1 incidents of damage per group. Three interventions were used to change the impact behavior: a brochure described the extent, consequences, and costs of the impacts and their management; the same brochure plus a ranger contact at the campsite reinforcing the message; and the brochure, personal contact at the campsite, *and* a request for camper assistance in reporting impact behaviors to the park ranger. All treatments reduced impact behaviors. The brochure plus contact was significantly better than the brochure alone, reducing groups with littered campsites from 67% to 41% and groups causing tree damage from 20% to 4%. Interestingly, the request for assistance in rule enforcement did not have any additional positive behavior change effects among study participants. Under this condition, 46% of all groups left litter in their campsite; 10% damaged trees.

Finally, Vander Stoep and Gramman (1988) conducted a research program at Shiloh National Military Park to determine whether pro-social behavior prompts, information, and incentives would reduce the impacting behavior of youth groups on historical cannon, statues, and monuments. Three treatments were tested: an awareness of consequences message (AC); the AC message plus a resource protection message (RP); and the AC message, the RP message, and an incentive for being a guardian of the resource. All three interventions resulted in significant improvements in behavior. Contrary to study hypotheses, the succeeding and more complex treatments did not have an additional effect on reducing damaging behavior over the simple awareness of consequences message.

Direct Visual Memory

Memory learning is important for subsequent use and enjoyment of "pictures from the past." Our fascination with photographs, and now portable VCRs, may be an indication of the importance we attach to recognition memory (Barnard et al. 1980). These authors analyzed recall and recognition memory for objects in a history museum under different conditions of number of objects seen. Limiting the number of objects viewed aided memory, and subjects could recognize more objects than they could recall.

Much of the assessment of "visual memory" learning in outdoor leisure settings has been done by Kaplan (1984) and by Hammitt (1978, 1980, 1981, 1982, 1987). Their work recognizes that before one can perceive, function in, and enjoy environments, one must be able to recognize various elements and scenes of the environment. In addition, Hammitt (1987), in particular, acknowledges the leisure enjoyment benefits of the recall phase of the recreational experience.

Kaplan (1984) assessed gains in familiarity with scenes of a natural area that was the location of a 9-day outdoor challenge program. She showed program participants 24 photos of the study area and 3 similar control photos at 3 different points in time: just prior to going into the woods, as soon as a 2-day solo during the program ended, and after the 9-day program. Familiarity ratings were greater for all area photos and for none of the control photos after the experience. More experienced outdoorsmen rated familiarity with the scenes higher before the program than did inexperienced individuals, but there was no difference between the two groups after the event. Thus, on-site experiences of short duration seem to overwhelm the visual learning of past experience.

Hammitt reports visual learning benefits of recreational visits to the Cranberry Glades Botanical Area of West Virginia and the Great Smoky Mountains National Park. At the West Virginia area, he showed 400 visitors photos of scenes taken from the boardwalk through the bog (Hammitt 1978, 1980, 1982). In addition, some photos from a similar bog environment in Michigan were included. The study subjects' familiarity with the on-site photos increased because of the walk, but scenes taken from the Michigan bog were not recognized (Hammitt 1978, 1982). Increases in post-trip familiarity were not greater for those visitors who saw area photos before their hike on the boardwalk than those who had not. Thus, the on-site experience seems to be most important in visual memory. Also, the single visit of first-time users was enough to increase their familiarity to levels expressed by the more experienced visitors.

Hammitt (1987) explored the relationship between placing interpretive signs with a short text along a trail to a waterfall in the Great Smoky Mountains National Park and familiarity with scenes at those spots. His hypothesis was that the greater informational content of the signs would draw park visitors into the scene, and more information about the scene would be coded in memory. Results partially confirmed the hypothesis. Four of the eight signs posted showed a statistically significant increase in familiarity; two others had increases that were not significant.

Information (Factual) Learning

By far the greatest amount of work done on the learning benefits of leisure experiences and settings has addressed factual learning. Some of the research on this topic likely also taps higher orders of learning, like concept learning, schemata learning, and metacognition learning. However, because most leisure researchers have not based their inquiries on theories of learning psychology, they do not conceptualize their work in terms of levels of learning. Therefore, they do not report findings in terms of higher and lower orders of learning, and it is difficult for us to make the appropriate distinctions among their reports of learning. Also, since the amount of research on informational learning in leisure situations is substantial, we have divided our summary into leisure learning at parks and natural areas, museums or visitor centers, outdoor/environmental/wilderness courses, and school-based field trips to outdoor settings.

Parks and natural areas.—Feldman (1978) attempted to increase knowledge about the environment among recreating motorists at a park in New York state through an interpretive message on a tape cassette and in a brochure. He distributed the interpretive media to recreationists as they began their tour of the park, and measured short-term retention of information after the tour. Using 10 multiple choice items, he found that both the cassette tape and brochure increased learning over the control (i.e., no information condition). Indeed, the brochure was better than control on nine items; the cassette tape was better than the control on all 10 items. The brochure and the cassette tape differed on only 2 of the 10 knowledge questions, with the brochure effecting higher learning scores.

Fazio (1979) completed one of the first analyses of learning of appropriate low-impact camping techniques in wilderness through interventions by various educational media. Working in Rocky Mountain National Park, he provided informational messages in a brochure, a trailhead sign, a visitor-activated slide/sound exhibit, a half-hour color television program, and a newspaper feature article.

Since few backpackers in the park saw the newspaper article and the television program, those treatments were dropped. He compared before and after treatment scores on a combined knowledge-wilderness sensitivity index with a possible range of 0 to 100. The slide exhibit alone, the slide exhibit plus the brochure, and the slide exhibit plus the trailhead sign were the only treatments that resulted in significant knowledge increases, and these increases exceeded 13 points. The trailhead sign and the brochure were not by themselves very effective.

McAvoy and Hamborg (1984) developed a 10-item true-false test to assess the knowledge levels of Boundary Waters Canoe Area Wilderness users about rules and regulations for low impact use of the area. Sample subjects attained an overall mean score of 8.2 correct out of the 10 items. No statistical difference was found by primary source of information about the rules and regulations, but permit brochures and visits to the Forest Service visitor center tended to result in higher scores. Long-term visitors to the area (having five or more visits) did score significantly higher than more recent visitors, suggesting that learning did occur over time.

Nielsen and Buchanan (1986) compared the learning benefits that resulted from interpretive programs on fire ecology and fire management among visitors to Grand Teton National Park. The field experiment indicated that both the automated audiovisual slide program about wildfire and a naturalist's talk about fire while a recent burn was in view increased knowledge of fire ecology significantly over the control situation. However, the two treatments did not differ. Knowledge scores on a 10-point scale increased from 5.4 for control to 7.4 for the interpreter-guided tour; scores for the automated audiovisual program increased by 2.1.

Sieg, Roggenbuck, and Bobinski (1988) provided a workshop on the natural and cultural history of the New River Gorge National River to whitewater rafting guides in an effort to improve their interpretations and increase subsequent knowledge levels among their guests. A subjective measure of amount of interpretation provided by guides increased significantly from before to after the training workshop (increasing from a mean response of 5.2 to 6.0 on a 7-point scale). Increased knowledge levels were also significant. During the control condition (before the workshop), passengers ending their river trip averaged 5.4 items correct out of 13 on the river history and ecology test. After the workshop, post-trip scores increased to 8.8. Knowledge gain from the river trip was 1.8 during the control condition; during the treatment condition (after the workshop) knowledge gain averaged 5.2. These scores reflect ample knowledge gains for river guests due to National Park Service-sponsored training of private concessionnaires in a park.

Outdoor/wilderness/environmental education.—
Dowell and McCool (1986) tested the effectiveness of three methods of teaching Boy Scouts a "leave no trace" ethic: a slide show alone, a booklet alone, and a booklet and slide show. A knowledge test of wilderness ecology and leave no trace practices was administered to a control group, to groups immediately after they received the educational program, and one month after the program. Knowledge of wilderness ecosystem scores were 11.0 for the control group; this increased to 12.1 for the combined educational treatments, and to 12.6 one month after the treatment. Both the post-test and the retention scores were significantly greater than the control group's. The three different media treatments did not differ from each other. Even more significant gains in knowledge of appropriate wilderness use practices were achieved due to the educational programs; scores rose from a mean of 3.8 under control to 6.4 for treatment post-test and 5.8 for retention. For the knowledge of skills, the slide program appeared better than the booklet condition.

The Boundary Waters Canoe Area Wilderness has an outreach program to teach volunteer leaders in communities in the region about wilderness concepts, values, and low-impact practices. Training workshops typically last from 1 to 4 hours. Jones and McAvoy (1988) evaluated knowledge gains by program participants both immediately after and about 3 months later. Knowledge levels were high going into the workshop, averaging 9.9 on a 12-point scale. Nevertheless, knowledge gains were significant, reaching 11.6 immediately following the workshop and 11.1 after the 3-month period.

Finally, Gamble (1988) compared the effectiveness of outdoor education experiences and computer-assisted instruction in learning of environmental concepts. In the two study treatments, one group of fifth grade students received 4 hours of instruction over a 4-day period in an outdoor education camp; the other group received the same content indoors in computer-aided instruction in 4 hours over a 4-day period. Both groups scored similarly on pre-tests of factual knowledge about the environment. After-treatment tests indicated that students in the outdoor education program had significant gains in comprehension and application of the material, but those in the computer-assisted instruction did not.

Museums and visitor centers.—Museums have invested considerable effort in documenting what visitors learn from exhibits and how to enhance learning. Variables of research interest have been meaningfulness, whole verus distributed task learning, amount of practice, and use of prose (Moates and Schumacher 1980). Past work has demonstrated that exhibits often don't provide their full learning potential (Fortner 1986, Shettel 1973). Such findings have led to innovations in exhibit design and pedagogy, and this in turn has led to increased factual as well as conceptual learning (Griggs 1981, Griggs and Manning 1983, Screven 1986). Science center research by Eason and Linn (1976) and Borun (1977) has also demonstrated factual learning, when effective exhibit techniques are used. Stronck (1983) compared cognitive and affective learning from museum visits by fifth, sixth, and seventh graders who received either a structured tour by docents or a less structured tour led by the classroom teacher. Greater cognitive learning occurred in the structured program, but more positive attitudes about the museum's content resulted from the more informal tour.

Evaluations of the learning benefits of visitor centers are surprisingly few. One interesting study examined information recall, subjective self-assessments of learning, and enjoyment at 17 visitor centers in parks in England. Prince (1982) noted that displays with texts, models, and artifacts had the highest information scores, as did displays relating parts of organisms and systems making up the whole. Overall enjoyment of the visitors was very high, but the link between visitors' information recall and enjoyment was minimal.

Using learning theory, Moscardo and Pearce (1986) theorized that any learning requires that people access mental schemata, process information, and adapt existing schemata to permit incorporation of the new information. This is a very active process, requiring mindfulness on the part of the participant. Mindfulness, therefore, becomes an indicator of learning and is evidenced by attention given to the task or the activity. Mindfulness had a substantial positive correlation (.40) with visitor enjoyment, and visitor enjoyment was strongly correlated (.65) with visitors' subjective evaluations of their own knowledge gain. For certain kinds of visitor centers—namely those with historic themes, highly specific and appealing conservation themes, and with variety in kinds of high quality interpretive techniques used—mindfulness, subjective knowledge, information recall, and enjoyment were all positively correlated.

Field trips to outdoor settings.—A popular use of outdoor leisure settings for learning is the field trip originating from school classrooms. Questions are increasingly asked whether learning actually occurs on such trips, or if the field trip is simply a pleasurable "skip day" from the monotonous classroom. Some of the best and most theoretically grounded leisure learning research has addressed these questions.

Roggenbuck and Passineau (1986) evaluated the learning effectiveness of a field visit by fourth, fifth, and sixth grade children to an historical area of Indiana Dunes National Lakeshore. Two different types of guided walks were provided: a lecture walk where the park interpreter told the story of Indians, fur traders, and early pioneer farmers with little student involvement; and an activity walk where the story was the same but students also engaged in activities that demonstrated story content. A control group of comparable school children did not visit the park. Pre-test and post-test measures of knowledge were gained within a few days before and a week after the field visit.

The school children's knowledge of how Indians, fur traders, and early pioneers made a living, adapted to their environment, and influenced each other, along with knowledge of national park values and appropriate visitor behavior, increased dramatically—improving by about 10 percentage points on correct responses. Knowledge gains on the pioneer farmers' independence and interdependence, their use of renewable resources, and their cultivation and use of diverse resources were also significant, but absolute increases in correct answers were only about five percentage points from pre-trip to post-trip. The children's scores did not improve on a matching test which required the integration of ideas about all three earlier cultures. This suggests that the field trip was not as successful in teaching higher level concepts as it was on the lower level, factual information. Finally, the activity learning treatment was not more effective than the lecture mode. Indeed, on some items, the lecture style demonstrated greater gains. It appeared that the activities, many of which were designed to be fun, distracted children from task and fact learning.

Some of the most innovative and provocative research in the entire area of the learning benefits of visits to leisure settings has been carried out by Falk, Balling, and their associates (Balling et al.,[2] Balling and Falk,[3] Falk 1983, Falk and Balling 1980, Falk et al. 1978, Martin et al. 1981). Their work has had the general goal of understanding the amount and kind of learning resulting from field trips to outdoor settings, zoos, or museums; but more specifically has assessed the effect of student and environmental variables on types and content of learning. Over time their research has identified and clarified the important role of familiarity, novelty, and cognitive development level on task and setting learning in outdoor environments.

Falk et al. (1978) evaluated the learning benefits of elementary school field trips to a wooded setting in a nonurbanized area near Washington, DC. Their research premise was that children unfamiliar with the outdoor environment lack the necessary cognitive schemata to learn assigned task concepts, and would instead explore the environment to attain comfortable orientation and cognitive structure. The authors, therefore, hypothesized one of two scenarios. Children unfamiliar with the outdoor environment would learn little about specific field trip tasks on their first field trip visit to the outdoor center, but if not con-

strained from exploration, would increase in knowledge about the setting. If constrained from exploratory behavior by task-oriented objectives, they would learn neither tasks nor the setting. In contrast, children familiar with the field environment would focus on the trip's learning tasks, and would indeed have significant gains in task knowledge. Results showed that the familiar group scored higher in knowledge of the outdoor setting going into the experiment, but both groups increased similarly in gaining knowledge during their field visit. On the other hand, the unfamiliar group did not increase in knowledge of the field trip's instructional task (i.e., learning about vegetation density), but the familiar group's concept learning increased significantly.

Falk and Balling (1980) continued this thread of research by examining the relationship between novelty, complexity, and relevance of the field trip setting to the learning of specific lesson facts and concepts versus more generalized nontask learning. Again, they found that novelty was the most useful predictor, and that there are optimum levels of environmental novelty for task learning, and that familiarity relates to novelty. At very low levels of setting novelty, children were bored and little lesson learning occurred. At very high levels of novelty, children seemed uncomfortable, engaged in increased social interaction with friends, increased horseplay, and increased exploratory behavior. Little task learning occurred. In contrast, lesson learning was highest at mid-range of novelty of the outdoor setting, and concepts learned on a 1-day field trip were remembered well 1 month after the activity. The authors hypothesized that the learning curve for nontask or exploratory behaviors was likely a mirror image of the task-related learning curve, i.e., nontask-related learning was highest under conditions of low and high novelty.

Martin et al. (1981) attempted to gain greater experimental precision and understanding of the effect of environmental novelty on kinds and availability of learning by using a within-subject design. A total of 63 grade school children participated in an ecology learning program, and each student made a field visit to a familiar environment (the schoolyard) and a novel environment (a mid-Atlantic forest and old field environment). The experiment was then repeated, with each subject again going to both the novel and the familiar field environments. In all cases, the teacher and program content were the same, and there were pre-test and post-test measures of performance of the lesson's ecological activity. Results indicated that novice students' performance on the ecological activity increased significantly due to a field visit to the schoolyard, but that the same novice students' task performances did not increase due to the field trip to the novel environment. In contrast, the repeaters in the experiment showed significant increases in lesson concept learning due to the schoolyard visit and also the natural (novel) area field trip. A separate test of exploratory or setting learning (nonlesson task learning) in the natural areas showed that novices' scores increased, but that repeaters to the same natural environment did not increase in setting knowledge. A ceiling effect in setting knowledge appeared to have occurred, and children on the second visit seemed to have focused on the field trip's learning tasks.

Falk and Balling (1982) extended their previous research by examining the relationships among cognitive developmental level, novelty, familiarity, and task-directed learning on field trips to outdoor environments. The field trip study objective was for elementary school children to learn more about trees. The control or familiar field visit was to a wooded area behind the subjects' school, and the treatment or novel situation was a day visit to a nature center. Developmental level was taken into account by including a third-grade class and a fifth-grade class in the experiment. As expected, there was a significant interaction between subjects' cognitive development level and novelty of environment on extent of learning about trees. The third graders learned most from the visit to the wooded area in their schoolyard; the fifth graders learned most from the field trip to a wooded area at the more distant nature center. Researchers cited observational measures of behavior of the two groups in the two environments to support their belief that third graders found the schoolyard wooded area to have optimal novelty, while the nature center was too novel. In contrast, for the fifth graders the schoolyard was so familiar that it was boring, but the nature center had optimal novelty.

Balling, Falk and Aronson[2] continued to advance their research on field trip learning by using research findings on the importance of levels of novelty to develop pre-trip orientation materials for fourth grade children on a single visit to a zoological park. The lesson task of the field trip was to learn about mammals that swim. The researchers developed three kinds of pre-trip materials: cognitive (conceptual and factual information about aquatic mammals), observational (suggestions on how and what to observe when watching animals), and orientation (descriptions of the zoo and the field trip experience, including location of snack bar and gift shop). There were also two control conditions: no pre-trip material, and no pre-trip material and no field trip.

All groups who went on the field trip learned more about aquatic mammals than did the group that did not, and retention of information after 90 days was still significantly higher than control. Of the three pre-trip informational treatments, the group that received the orientation materials showed the greatest learning gains. The authors conclude that such orientation information permits students to formulate a cognitive map of the zoo, negate the necessity for considerable exploratory behavior, and permit students to focus on the learning task at hand.

Concept Learning

Much of the informational or factual learning documented in the previous section likely included concept learning. However, leisure researchers have tended not to break down and report types of learning beyond the knowledge, attitude, and behavior categories. Few studies found in the leisure literature clearly distinguish between factual learning and the formulation of new concepts by the organization of phenomena that share common attributes.

As discussed earlier, Roggenbuck and Passineau (1986) evaluated whether a field trip to Indiana Dunes National Lakeshore resulted in increased learning for the grade school participants. The students did make significant gains in factual learning. However, when these students were asked to integrate their knowledge into a more generalized *concept* on the activities and characteristics of the three cultural groups studied, post-trip scores were no higher than pre-trip scores, and field trip participants did not score any higher than a control group that didn't visit the park.

Kern and Carpenter (1986) found that a field lab in contrast to a classroom lab increased learning at higher cognitive levels. College students in an earth science course did not differ in their learning of factual information across the two lab conditions. However, individuals in the field condition demonstrated substantially greater abilities to apply, analyze, and synthesize information gained. They were able to better understand processes and how attributes of the environment fit together to form higher level, functioning units.

Lucas and McManus (1986) found that the ability of museum visitors to sort illustrations of living creatures into categories based on features such as color or anatomy was determined largely by the amount of feedback provided by the exhibit setting. DeWaard et al. (1974) also noted that for the feedback to help concept learning, it must contain pertinent and directive information.

In conclusion, little of substance can be said about increases in concept learning during leisure experiences. This is in large part due to the failure of leisure researchers to conceptualize and measure cognitive learning at this level of differentiation. For those few studies that have specifically addressed this higher level of learning, results are mixed.

Schemata Learning

Cognitive differentiation theory proposes that as one's knowledge about a subject increases, one's mental schemata—or bundles of knowledge stored in memory that act as a framework for understanding and remembering new information—tends to be reorganized and to become more differentiated. Level of schemata development thus influences and is influenced by learning. Little work has been done by leisure researchers on mental schemata development.

Lee and Uzzell (1980) found that visitors' schemata about farms was more differentiated after they went to an interpretive program on farming and rural life than before. Nicol (1969) provided learning stations based on clusters of related concepts such as functions of shearing and grinding molars, unusual teeth, and the teeth of the walrus at the Boston Children's Museum. Results of pre- and post-test comparisons suggested that children were learning concepts about teeth and possibly a schema for how teeth work in general. Wright (1980) suggests that children who learn formal classroom information about the human body system and then visit a health exhibit may acquire a more integrated or assimilated set of knowledge than children exposed to the classroom information alone. That is, the exhibit may develop schemata for the integration of body function knowledge. Furthermore, schemata theory helps to explain why stories, whether presented in written form in a museum label or told around a campfire, can be such effective learning devices (Rumelhart 1975, 1977).

Metacognition Learning

Leisure researchers have interest in metacognition learning because it explains how people perceive their environment, how comfortable they feel in it, and how they find their way in it. Orientation becomes critically important and influences what people learn. Koran et al. (1983a, 1983b, 1984) have repeatedly emphasized the need for museum research to provide some kind of guidance information with the content information of an exhibit, as well as providing opportunities for visitors to be active rather than passive. Screven (1974, 1975) has also focused attention on the need for instructional or guidance panels and devices in exhibits to orient the visitor and increase learning.

Another kind of metacognition learning is the development of cognitive maps about the environment. Such cognitive maps are mental structures which contain information about how the environment is organized (Knopf 1981). These internalized models portray the significant elements of the external environment and the relations among them. They permit the individual to make sense out of the environment, to structure what would otherwise be fragmented and perplexing. The lack of such mental or cognitive maps frustrates learning and enjoyable use of the environment.

Knopf (1981) tested the purported link between cognitive map development and learning at Gettysburg National Military Park. Visitors there have a choice of several kinds of interpretive media. Two of the interpretive facilities, i.e., the Electric Map and the Cyclorama, are primarily orientational in nature, and remaining interpretive media such as the auto tour and the visitor center are primarily factual in nature. Knopf predicted that first-time park visitors would learn more from attending orientational programs, especially when those orientational programs were attended early during the Gettysburg visit. Results confirmed study hypotheses. Visitors who attended in sequence the electric map, cyclorama, and auto tour, or the sequence of electric map, auto tour, and cyclorama learned the most. Groups who learned the least attended one of the nonorientational programs first, programs such as the auto tour or the visitor center. These findings link cognitive map theory, schemata development, familiarity, and novelty as key constructs in predicting and understanding leisure learning.

Attitude and Value Learning

Leisure researchers who have studied learning have tended to emphasize factual knowledge, attitude change, and behavior change. They have also searched for relationships among these three learning outcomes, i.e., they have tended to subscribe to conceptual systems that suggest an increase in knowledge tends to increase positive attitudes which tend to increase positive behavior. Some research in museums indicates that attitude change is apt to be a part of other learning going on at the time (Borun 1977, Boggs 1977).

Park visits.—Nielsen and Buchanan (1986) developed and tested an automated slide program and a naturalist-guided boat tour of a forest fire area to increase knowledge of fire ecology and support for natural fire management (i.e., the "let-burn" policy) among visitors to Grand Teton National Park. Both interpretive treatments were effective in increasing positive attitude scores and neither program was better than the other.

Olson et al. (1984) studied the effects of a brochure, a series of on-site signs, and personal services including off-site presentations and on-site guided hikes, on changes in levels of knowledge and attitudes about wildflower picking, burn vegetation, grazing, cut timber, camping, confining visitors, restricting uses, picnicking, set asides of land, trapping, and alcohol use at a state nature preserve. Pre-visit and post-visit measures showed significant changes in knowledge and attitudes, with a significant and positive relationship between increases in knowledge and positive attitude changes. The brochures had the largest attitude gain, followed by personal services and signs on-site.

Cable et al. (1987) evaluated the gain in positive attitudes about forestry and forest management resulting from a visit to the interpretive facilities at Petawawa National Forestry Institute in Ontario in 1982 and 1983. Visitors demonstrated significantly more favorable attitudes on five of seven forestry topics in 1982 and on one of four topics in 1983 as a result of their visit. The most positive gain was for prescribed burning, with a 17.7% increase in support. However, overall support for the forestry practices and agencies only reached 55% and 48% on the post-visit tests in 1982 and 1983, respectively.

Environmental education.—Roggenbuck and Passineau (1986) found that a field trip visit to an historical site at Indiana Dunes National Lakeshore significantly increased school children's attitudes toward protection of park resources, the conservation of park resources, and visiting parks and historic sites. Student gains were not significant on the desire to learn more about parks. Perhaps the field visit answered the questions students had, and they felt a satiation effect at the end of the 2-hour hike through the historical site.

Shepard and Speelman (1985-86) studied changes in adolescents' attitudes toward conservation principles and toward plants and animals with poor reputations after a 3- to 5-day stay at Ohio 4-H camps. Students who selected an outdoor education program that included sensory awareness and basic ecological concepts were compared to those who didn't select this environmental program. Overall, there was no difference in post-trip attitudes between the two groups. However, rural children tended to improve significantly, leading the authors to suggest that the urban children be acclimatized into the environment before moving on to the more conceptual material. First-time campers tended to improve more than experienced campers on attitudes toward conservation principles. Perhaps a ceiling effect had been reached for the experienced camp visitor.

Jones and McAvoy (1988) tested whether a USDA Forest Service wilderness education workshop on wilderness values and appropriate behavior was effective in fostering positive attitudes about wilderness use and management. Workshop participants' attitudes and behavioral beliefs about wilderness were assessed immediately prior to, immediately after, and 12 to 15 weeks after the course. Favorable attitudes increased significantly from pre-test to post-test, and retained their high level over the extended period. Also, absolute attitude values were high. On a possible range of -9 to +9, mean attitude scores were -4.9 on

the pre-test, and they increased to 7.4 and 7.0 on immediate post-test and retention. Behavioral belief scores could range from -90 to +90; participants scored 57.5 on the pre-test, 82.2 on immediate post-test, and 73.8 on retention measure.

Finally, Reames and Rajecki (1988) implemented a zoo outreach program for preschool children. They took live animals and other educational materials about animals to the children's day care centers and assessed whether such close contact with the animals fostered positive attitudes. Attitudes were measured before and after the visit. For the seven animals shown to the children, attitude scores increased on four. Only for the rabbit, parrot, and alligator did scores not increase. On the five animals covered in the presentation but for which no live specimen was available, children's positive attitudes increased on only one.

Summary

The above rather lengthy review of the learning outcomes of leisure suggests the following general conclusions:

- Leisure researchers have tended not to approach the study of learning benefits from theories of learning psychology. As a result, research has failed to adequately address the hierarchical nature of learning, and has produced few cumulative findings.
- Leisure research has focused on factual information gain, attitude change, or behavior change. Among these, there is ample evidence that people do make significant gains in behavior or skill and informational knowledge during leisure participation. Evidence of attitude change is less compelling.
- Visual and recognition memory learning and mood change occur during leisure experiences, but surprisingly little empirical research has focused on these kinds of learning.
- Little research has focused on the conceptual, schemata, and metacognition levels of learning in leisure settings. This is a surprising and constraining knowledge gap, for this type of learning is especially important for orienting oneself and comprehending novel leisure settings.
- Almost all leisure learning research has focused on learning that is aided by educational or interpretive interventions. There is a need for assessment and evaluation of learning by recreationists who experience leisure environments without guides, programs, and educational materials.

- Research on leisure learning benefits has given many inconsistent and sometimes contradictory results. This seems due in part to inadequate theoretical foundations, but more often seems the result of inadequate research methods. More careful operationalization of research variables and more frequent use of experimental designs are needed.

- Many individual differences and contextual variables affect degree and nature of learning in leisure settings, including level of cognitive development and familiarity and novelty of the environmental setting.

ENVIRONMENTAL SENSITIVITY AND CITIZENSHIP: AN EXAMPLE OF A LEISURE LEARNING BENEFIT

Our review of leisure learning outcomes suggests that individuals engaged in leisure activities or participating in activities in leisure settings often increase in level of skill, grow in knowledge of facts and concepts, store images and associated mood states in memory, develop more complex and efficient frameworks and categories for organizing knowledge, and experience changes in attitudes or values. These learning outcomes likely result in benefits to the individual and to society, but acquired skills or knowledge can have dehabilitating effects. For example, American youth often learn to use drugs during their leisure time. Such drugs often result in changes of mood states—even feelings of euphoria—but their long-term effects would not be considered beneficial.

Is there empirical evidence that leisure learning benefits individuals and society? As a case study, let us turn to environmental sensitivity and citizenship. Early in our discussion, we noted claims that leisure learning can foster both increased understanding and empathy for the environment *and* motivation to take actions to protect it (Buhyoff and Brown[1]). Recently, Hungerford[4] noted the key elements or absolutes necessary for individuals to become active and responsible environmental citizens. These included sound problem identification skills, a degree of *environmental sensitivity*, sound issue investigation and evaluation skills, knowledge of and perceived skill in the use of citizenship action strategies, and an internal locus of control (an individual's feeling of empowerment that he or she can influence the course of events).

Environmental sensitivity is a set of affective characteristics which result in an individual viewing the environment from an empathetic perspective. Sia et al. (1985-86), Hines et al. (1986-87), Sivek (1987), and Marcinkowski (1988) have all found environmental sensitivity to be a major predictor of environmentally literate individuals and environmentally responsible behavior. For example, Sia et al. (1985-86) found that only perceived skill in using environmental action strategies exceeded level of environmental sensitivity as the key predictors in explaining environmental behavior of Sierra Club members. For a sample of Elderhostel members, level of environmental sensitivity was the most important predictor. Sivek's research among members of Trout Unlimited, Ducks Unlimited, and the Wisconsin Trappers Association confirmed Sia's findings, as did Marcinkowski's work with additional Sierra Club and Audubon Society members. Additional research suggests that while irresponsible environmental behavior can be changed without developing environmental sensitivity, *long-term* environmentally responsible citizenship appears to require it (Hungerford[4]).

Environmental educators have searched for the precursors to or causes of environmental sensitivity, in an effort to better learn how to develop this affect among their students. Again, active citizen conservationists and educators were queried to determine what most prompted their involvement and success in environmental issues. The most consistent and important explanatory variable was long-term experience with relatively pristine environments, beginning at an early age (Marcinkowski 1988, Peterson 1982, Sia et al. 1985-86, Tanner 1980). These outdoor experiences typically included hunting, fishing, family vacations/outings, and camping begun early in life and continued to the present. The outdoor environments need not be wilderness, but often seemed to produce feelings of awe and wonder. Secondly, the environmental activists tended to state that they experienced the outdoors alone or with only one or two others; and any companions, usually family members or teachers, were influential role models.

These findings confirm the importance of informal leisure engagements in developing environmental sensitivity, and indirectly in fostering environmental activism. Indeed, environmental educators have expressed doubt that the emotional bonding with the environment required for sensitivity can be taught in the classroom (Hungerford[4]). Marcinkowski, Volk, and Hungerford (1989), in their address to the UNESCO conference on environmental education, called environmental sensitivity a *pre-goal* or *foundation goal* for environmental education curricula—a prerequisite to classroom environmental education. They note that outdoor education/recreation is the best available method for fostering environmental sensitivity, and the best available resources are natural environments, outdoor education centers, recreation areas, school camping programs, national parks, youth programs, and nature and environmental centers.

ENDNOTES

[1] Gregory J. Buhyoff and Perry J. Brown in paper on social and individual learning benefits from recreational enjoyments presented at 6th National Environmental Design Research Association Conference, Lawrence, Kansas; April 21, 1975.

[2] John D. Balling, John H. Falk, and Ruth Aronson in paper on pre-trip orientation—an exploration of effects on learning from a single-visit field trip to a zoological park, in preparation.

[3] John D. Balling and John H. Falk in paper on classroom vs. field trip science experiences, presented at the 1983 Annual Meeting of the National Association for Research in Science Teaching, Dallas, Texas; April 5-8, 1983.

[4] Harold R. Hungerford in research report on citizenship behavior in environmental education. Science Education Program, Department of Curriculum and Instruction, Southern Illinois University.

LITERATURE CITED

Adams, S. W. 1979. Segmentation of a recreational fishing market: a canonical analysis of fishing attributes and party composition. Journal of Leisure Research. 11(2): 82-91.

Bandura, A. 1977. Social learning theory. Englewood Cliffs, NJ: Prentice Hall. 247 p.

Barnard, W.; Loomis, R. J.; Cross, H. A. 1980. Assessment of visual recall and recognition learning in a museum environment. Bulletin of the Psychonomic Society. 16(4): 311-313.

Beard, J. G.; Ragheb, M. G. 1980. Measuring leisure satisfaction. Journal of Leisure Research. 12(1): 20-33.

Blahna, D. J.; Roggenbuck, J. W. 1979. Planning interpretation which is "in tune" with visitor expectations. Journal of Interpretation. 4(2): 16-19.

Boggs, D. L. 1977. Visitor learning at the Ohio Historical Center. Curator. 20(3): 205-214.

Borun, M. 1977. Measuring the immeasurable: a pilot study of museum effectiveness. Washington, DC: Association of Science-Technology Centers. 14 p.

Bourne, L. E., Jr.; Dominowski, R. L.; Loftus, E. F. 1979. Cognitive processes. Englewood Cliffs, NJ: Prentice-Hall. 408 p.

Byrne, D.; Clore, G. L. 1970. A reinforcement model of evaluative responses. Personality: An International Journal. 1: 103-128.

Cable, T. T.; Knudson, D. M.; Udd, E.; Stewart, D. J. 1987. Attitude changes as a result of exposure to interpretive messages. Journal of Park and Recreation Administration. 5(1): 47-59.

Cross, K. P. 1981. Adults as learners. San Francisco, CA: Jossey Bass. 300 p.

Decker, D. J.; Brown, T. L.; Gutierrez, R. J. 1980. Further insights into multiple satisfactions approach for hunter management. Wildlife Society Bulletin. 8(4): 323-331.

DeWaard, R. J.; Jagmin, N.; Maiso, S.; McNamara, P. A. 1974. Effects of using programmed cards on learning in a museum environment. The Journal of Educational Research. 67(10): 457-460.

Dowell, D. L.; McCool, S. F. 1986. Evaluation of a wilderness information dissemination program. In: Lucas, R. C., comp. Proceedings: National Wilderness Research Conference: Current Research. USDA Forest Service Gen. Tech. Rep. INT-212: 494-500.

Driver, B. L.; Bassett, J. R. 1975. Defining conflicts among river users: a case study of Michigan's Au Sable River. Naturalist. 26(2): 19-23.

Driver, B. L.; Knopf, R. C. 1976. Temporary escape: one product of sport fisheries management. Fisheries. 1(2): 21-29.

Driver, B. L.; Nash, R.; Haas, G. 1987. Wilderness benefits: a state-of-knowledge review. In: Lucas, R. C., compiler. Proceedings, National Wilderness Research Conference: Issues, State-of-Knowledge, Future Directions. USDA Forest Service Gen. Tech. Rep. INT-220: 294-319.

Eason, L.; Linn, M. C. 1976. Evaluation of the effectiveness of participatory exhibits. Curator. 19(1): 45-62.

Falk, J. H. 1983. Field trips: a look at environmental effects on learning. Journal of Biological Education. 17(2): 137-142.

Falk, J. H.; Balling, J. D. 1980. The school field trip: where you go makes a difference. Science and Children. 17(6): 6-9.

Falk, J. H.; Balling, J. D. 1982. The field trip milieu: learning and behavior as a function of contextual events. Journal of Educational Research. 76: 22-28.

Falk, J. H.; Balling, J. D. [In press]. The relationship of context to learning: field trip versus classroom science experiences. ILVS Review: A Journal of Visitor Studies.

Falk, J. H.; Martin, W. W.; Balling, J. D. 1978. The novel field-trip phenomenon: adjustment to novel settings interferes with task learning. Journal of Research in Science Teaching. 15(2): 127-134.

Fazio, J. R. 1974. A mandatory permit system and interpretation for backcountry user control in Rocky Mountain National Park: an evaluation study. Fort Collins, CO: Colorado State University. 246 p. Ph.D. dissertation.

Fazio, J. R. 1979. Communicating with the wilderness user. University of Idaho College of Forestry, Wildlife, and Range Experiment Stn. Bull. No. 28. Moscow, ID. 65 p.

Feldman, R. L. 1978. Effectiveness of audio-visual media for interpretation to recreating motorists. Journal of Interpretation. 3(1): 14-19.

Fisher, J. D.; Bell, P. A.; Baum, A. 1984. Environmental psychology. New York, NY: Holt, Rinehart and Winston. 472 p.

Fortner, R. W. 1986. A multi-phased evaluation of the impact of a non-school science exhibition. Rockville, MD: National Oceanic and Atmospheric Administration. 13 p.

Gagne, R. M.; Dick, W. 1983. Instructional psychology. In: Rosenzweig, M. R.; Porter, L. W., eds. Annual review of psychology. 34: 261-295. Palo Alto, CA: Annual Reviews, Inc.

Gamble, S. C. 1988. Outdoor education and computer-assisted instruction in teaching critical thinking regarding environmental concepts. In: Legg, M., ed. National Association of Interpretation 1988 Research Monograph: 65-70.

Gardner, H. 1985. The mind's new science. New York, NY: Basic Books. 423 p.

Graefe, A. R.; Ditton, R. B.; Roggenbuck, J. W.; Schreyer, R. 1981. Notes on the stability of the factor structure of leisure meanings. Leisure Sciences. 4(1): 51-65.

Griggs, S. A. 1981. Formative evaluation of exhibits at the British Museum. Curator. 24(3): 189-201.

Griggs, S. A.; Manning, J. 1983. The predictive validity of formative evaluation of exhibits. Museum Studies Journal. 1(2): 31-41.

Hammitt, W. E. 1978. A visual preference approach to measuring interpretive effectiveness. Journal of Interpretation. 3(2): 33-37.

Hammitt, W. E. 1980. Designing mystery into trail-landscape experiences. Journal of Interpretation. 5(1): 16-19.

Hammitt, W. E. 1981. The familiarity-preference component of on-site recreational experiences. Leisure Sciences. 4(2): 171-193.

Hammitt, W. E. 1982. Attention, familiarity, and effective interpretation. Journal of Interpretation. 7(2): 1-9.

Hammitt, W. E. 1987. Visual recognition capacity during outdoor recreation experiences. Environment and Behavior. 19(6): 651-671.

Hawes, D. K. 1978. Satisfactions derived from leisure-time pursuits: an exploratory nationwide survey. Journal of Leisure Research. 10(4): 247-264.

Hines, J. M.; Hungerford, H. R.; Tomera, A. N. 1986-87. Analysis and synthesis of research on responsible environmental behavior: a meta-analysis. The Journal of Environmental Education. 18(2): 1-8.

Hollender, J. W. 1977. Motivational dimensions of the camping experience. Journal of Leisure Research. 9(2): 133-141.

Hood, M. G. 1983. Staying away—Why people choose not to visit museums. Museum News. 61(4): 50-57.

Huffman, M. G.; Williams, D. R. 1987. The use of micro-computers for park trail information dissemination. Journal of Park and Recreation Administration. 5: 34-46.

Jones, P. E.; McAvoy, L. H. 1988. An evaluation of a wilderness user education program: a cognitive and behavioral analysis. In: Legg, M., ed. National Association of Interpretation 1988 Research Monograph: 13-20.

Kaplan, R. 1974. Some psychological benefits of an outdoor challenge program. Environment and Behavior. 6(1): 101-116.

Kaplan, R. 1984. Wilderness perception and psychological benefits: an analysis of a continuing program. Leisure Sciences. 6(3): 271-290.

Kern, E. L.; Carpenter, J. R. 1986. Effect of field activities on student learning. Journal of Geological Education. 34: 180-183.

Klatzky, R. L. 1980. Human memory: structures and processes. San Francisco, CA: W. H. Freeman. 358 p.

Knopf, R. C. 1981. Cognitive map formation is a tool for facilitating information transfer in interpretive programming. Journal of Leisure Research. 13(3): 232-242.

Knopf, R. C.; Peterson, G. L.; Leatherbery, E. C. 1983. Motives for recreational river floating: relative consistency across settings. Leisure Sciences. 5(3): 231-255.

Knowles, M. S. 1984. The adult learner: a neglected species. Houston, TX: Gulf. 292 p.

Kolb, D. A. 1984. Experiential learning: experiences as the source of learning and development. Englewood Cliffs, NJ: Prentice-Hall, Inc. 256 p.

Koran, J. J., Jr.; Lehman, J. R.; Shafer, L. D.; Koran, M. 1983a. The relative effects of pre- and post-attention directing devices on learning from a "walk through" museum exhibit. Journal of Research in Science Teaching. 20(4): 341-346.

Koran, J. J., Jr.; Longino, S. J.; Shafer, L. D. 1983b. A framework for conceptualizing research in natural history museums and science centers. Journal of Research in Science Teaching. 20(4): 324-340.

Koran, J. J., Jr.; Morrison, L.; Lehman, J. L., et al. 1984. Attention and curiosity in museums. Journal of Research in Science Teaching. 21(4): 345-355.

Krumpe, E. E.; Brown, P. J. 1982. Redistributing backcountry use through information related to recreation experiences. Journal of Forestry. 80: 360-362, 364.

Lee, T. R.; Uzzell, D. L. 1980. The educational effectiveness of the farm open day. Perth: Countryside Commission for Scotland. 48 p.

Lime, D. W.; Lucas, R. C. 1977. Good information improves the wilderness experience. Naturalist. 28(4): 18-21.

Lucas, R. C. 1964. Wilderness perception and use: the example of the Boundary Waters Canoe Area. Natural Resources Journal. 3(3): 394-411.

Lucas, A. M.; McManus, P. 1986. Investigating learning from informal sources: listening to conversations and observing play in science museums. European Journal of Science Education. 8(4): 341-352.

Marcinkowski, T. J. 1988. An analysis of correlates and predictors of responsible environmental behavior. Carbondale, IL: Southern Illinois University. 749 p. Ph.D. dissertation.

Marcinkowski, T. J.; Volk, T. L.; Hungerford, H. R. 1989. An environmental education approach to the training of middle level teachers: a teacher education programme specialization. Paris, France: UNESCO. 177 p.

Martin, W. W.; Falk, J. H.; Balling, J. D. 1981. Environmental effects on learning: the outdoor field trip. Science Education. 65(3): 311-316.

McAvoy, L. H.; Hamborg, R. 1984. Wilderness visitor knowledge of regulations: a comparison of visitor contact methods. Journal of Interpretation. 9(1): 1-10.

Moates, D. R.; Schumacher, G. M. 1980. An introduction to cognitive psychology. Belmont, CA: Wadsworth. 365 p.

More, T. A. 1973. Attitudes of Massachusetts hunters. In: Hendee, J. C.; Schoenfeld, C., eds. Human dimensions in wildlife programs. Washington, DC: Wildlife Management Institute: 72-76.

Moscardo, G.; Pearce, P. L. 1986. Visitor centers and environmental interpretation: an exploration of the relationship among visitor enjoyment, understanding, and mindfulness. Journal of Environmental Psychology. 6(2): 89-108.

Neisser, U. 1982. Memory observed: remembering in natural contexts. San Francisco, CA: W. H. Freeman. 433 p.

Nicol, E. H. 1969. The development of museum exhibits (report no. 5-0245). Boston, MA: The Children's Museum. 114 p.

Nielsen, C.; Buchanan, T. 1986. A comparison of the effectiveness of two interpretive programs regarding fire ecology and fire management. Journal of Interpretation. 11(1): 1-10.

O'Connor, D. E. 1983. Learning about the American economy through living museums. Social Education. 47(1): 40-43.

Oliver, S. S.; Roggenbuck, J. W.; Watson, A. E. 1985. Education to reduce impacts in forest campgrounds. Journal of Forestry. 83(4): 234-236.

Olson, E. C.; Bowman, M. L.; Roth, R. E. 1984. Interpretation and nonformal education in natural resources management. Journal of Environmental Education. 15: 6-10.

Peterson, N. J. 1982. Developmental variables affecting environmental sensitivity in professional environmental educators. Carbondale, IL: Southern Illinois University. 109 p. Masters thesis.

Pierce, R. C. 1980a. Dimensions of leisure I: satisfaction. Journal of Leisure Research. 12(1): 5-19.

Pierce, R. C. 1980b. Dimensions of leisure III: characteristics. Journal of Leisure Research. 12(3): 273-284.

Porteous, J. D. 1977. Environment and behavior. Menlo Park, CA: Addison-Wesley. 446 p.

Potter, D. R.; Hendee, J. C.; Clark, R. N. 1973. Hunting satisfaction: game, guns, or nature. In: Hendee, J. C.; Schoenfeld, C., eds. Human dimensions in wildlife programs. Washington, DC: Wildlife Management Institute: 62-71.

Prince, D. R. 1982. Countryside interpretation: a cognitive evaluation. Museums Journal. 82(3): 165-170.

Reames, J.; Rajecki, D. W. 1988. Changing preschoolers' attitudes toward animals: a zoo program and an evaluation. In: Legg, M., ed. National Association of Interpretation 1988 Research Monograph: 27-38.

Roggenbuck, J. W.; Berrier, D. L. 1982. A comparison of the effectiveness of two communication strategies in dispersing wilderness campers. Journal of Leisure Research. 14(1): 77-89.

Roggenbuck, J. W.; Passineau, J. 1986. Use of the field experiment to assess the effectiveness of interpretation. In: McDonald, B.; Cordell, K., eds. Proceedings, Southeastern Recreation Research Conference. Recreation Technical Assistance Office, Institute of Community and Area Development. Athens, GA: University of Georgia: 65-86.

Rosch, E. H. 1973. Natural categories. Cognitive Psychology. 4: 328-350.

Rossman, B. B.; Ulehla, Z. J. 1977. Psychological reward values associated with wilderness use—a functional-reinforcement approach. Environment and Behavior. 9(1): 41-66.

Rumelhart, D. E. 1975. Notes on a schema for stories. In: Bobrow, D. G.; Collins, A. M., eds. Representation and understanding: studies in cognitive science. New York, NY: Academic Press. 427 p.

Rumelhart, D. E. 1977. Introduction to human information processing. New York, NY: Wiley. 306 p.

Schreyer, R.; Jacob, G. R.; White, R. G. 1981. Environmental meaning as a determinant of spatial behavior in recreation. In: Frazier, J.; Epstein, B., eds. Proceedings of Applied Geography Conference. Binghamton, NY: SUNY Dept of Geography: Vol. 4, 294-300.

Schreyer, R.; Roggenbuck, J. W. 1978. The influence of experience expectation on crowding perceptions and social-psychological carrying capacities. Leisure Sciences. 1(4): 373-394.

Screven, C. G. 1974. Learning and exhibits: instructional design. Museum News. 52(5): 67-75.

Screven, C. G. 1975. The effectiveness of guidance devices on visitor learning. Curator. 18(3): 218-243.

Screven, C. G. 1986. Exhibitions and information centers: some principles and approaches. Curator. 29(2): 109-137.

Shepard, R. N. 1967. Recognition memory for words, sentences, and pictures. Journal of Verbal Learning and Verbal Behavior. 6: 156-163.

Shepard, C. L.; Speelman, L. R. 1985-86. Affecting environmental attitudes through outdoor education. Journal of Environmental Education. 17(2): 20-23.

Shettel, H. H. 1973. Exhibits: Art form or educational medium? Museum News. 52(1): 32-41.

Sia, A.; Hungerford, H.; Tomera, A. 1985-86. Selected predictions of responsible environmental behavior: an analysis. The Journal of Environmental Education. 17(2): 31-40.

Sieg, G. E.; Roggenbuck, J. W.; Bobinski, C. T. 1988. The effectiveness of commercial river guides as interpreters. In: Proceedings 1987 Southeastern Recreation Research Conference. Feb.18-20, Asheville, NC. Athens, GA: Dept. of Recreation and Leisure Studies, Univ. of Georgia: 12-20.

Sivek, D. J. 1987. An analysis of selected predictors of environmental behavior of three conservation organizations. Carbondale, IL: Southern Illinois University. 166 p. Ph.D. Dissertation.

Smith, M. B. 1969. Social psychology and human values. Chicago, IL: Aldine. 438 p.

Sneider, C.; Eason, L.; Friedman, A. 1979. Summative evaluation of a participatory science exhibit. Science Education. 63(1): 25-36.

Stronck, D. R. 1983. The comparative effects of different museum tours on childrens' attitude and learning. Journal of Research in Science Teaching. 20(4): 283-290.

Tanner, R. T. 1980. Significant life experiences. A new research area in environmental education. The Journal of Environmental Education. 11(4): 20-24.

Tinsley, H. E. A.; Barrett, T. C.; Kass, R. A. 1977. Leisure activities and need satisfaction. Journal of Leisure Research. 9(2): 110-120.

Tinsley, H. E. A.; Kass, R. A. 1978. Leisure activities and need satisfaction: a replication and extension. Journal of Leisure Research. 10(3): 191-202.

Tinsley, H. E. A.; Kass, R. A. 1979. The latent structure of the need satisfying properties of leisure activities. Journal of Leisure Research. 11(4): 278-291.

Tolman, E. C. 1949. There is more than one kind of learning. Psychological Review. 46: 144-155.

USDA Forest Service. 1976. Forest interpreter's primer on fire management. U.S. Government Printing Office. Washington, DC. 70 p.

Vander Stoep, G. A.; Gramman, J. H. 1988. Use of interpretation as an indirect visitor management tool: an alternative to regulation and enforcement. In: Legg, M., ed. National Association of Interpretation 1988 Research Monograph: 47-55.

Walter, G. A.; Marks, S. E. 1981. Experiential learning and change theory, design and practice. New York, NY: Wiley & Sons.

Wellman, J. D.; Dawson, M. S.; Roggenbuck, J. W. 1982. Park managers' predictions of the motivations of visitors to two National Park Service areas. Journal of Leisure Research. 14(1): 1-15.

Wright, E. L. 1980. Analysis of the effect of a museum experience on the biology achievement of sixth-graders. Journal of Research in Science Teaching. 17(2): 99-104.

Developmental Benefits of Play for Children

Lynn A. Barnett
Department of Leisure Studies
University of Illinois
Champaign, Illinois

INTRODUCTION

The topic of play has for many years occupied the writings of philosophers, educators, and others concerned with the development of the child. Indeed, a number of the most prominent theories of play were formulated in the 19th century. In the early 20th century, descriptive accounts of play were quite common in the literature (e.g., Griffiths 1935, Lehman and Witty 1927, Markey 1935). For the most part, however, any comprehensive, empirical, or systematic treatment of play had not been conducted during these years. Fortunately, this situation has changed markedly in the past decade (cf., Rubin et al. 1983). In the last 5 years alone, more than 40 research-based books have been published in the area of children's play, and more than 500 journal articles, book chapters, and conference presentations have appeared.

With this surge of scholarly interest, then, it should not be an unwieldy task to answer the question, "What are the developmental benefits of play to the child?" In the following pages, we shall objectively and critically investigate the demonstrated benefits of play for the development of the young child. We will explore and question the evidence which purports to demonstrate a relationship between the child's play and his/her cognitive, social, emotional, and physical development. And we shall critically reflect on the pronouncement made at the First National Conference on the Vital Role of Play in Learning, Development, and Survival (Washington, DC, May 2-3, 1979) that:

> Play is vital to the healthy development of all of the so-called higher animals. Play is a biological imperative. Play for your life: the stakes are survival.

PLAY AND CULTURATION

Groos (1898, 1901) early postulated that play was the very "stuff of childhood," and that a period of immaturity (childhood) was necessary in order that organisms might play. Moreover, he postulated that the length of the play period varies directly with the organism's position on the phylogenetic scale: the more complex the organism the longer its period of immaturity (and hence the longer its period of play). These longer periods of immaturity in more complex species were regarded as necessary to allow for the practice of those instinctively based skills which were critical for survival during adulthood. Groos considered play to emanate from a general instinctual impulse and to be completely adaptive and necessary for the survival of the species: play exists so that the young of the species can practice instinctively based behaviors before they are needed in perfected form in adulthood. For some animals, instinctive behaviors arrived fully developed so that, as a result, there was no need for a period of play to exist for them. However, for the other more complex organisms, the life-sustaining instincts emerged in an undeveloped form during childhood. Play thus allowed the exercise, elaboration, and perfection of these behaviors before they became necessary for survival in adulthood.

Like Groos, Bruner (1974) also posited an evolutionary and functional explanation for children's play. He combined evidence from comparative research (cf., Bekoff 1972; Fagen 1981; Hinde 1971; Lorenz 1970, 1971; Muller-Schwarze 1978; Smith 1978) with his own expertise in cognitive development in children. In considering the crucial functions of play, Bruner (1974, 1983) stressed that: (a) play results in a reduction in the seriousness of the consequences of errors; (b) it is characterized by a very loose connection between means and ends, allowing frequent opportunities to try combinations of skills that would hardly be tried under functional pressures of survival; (c) in play there is an underlying scenario in which children create a rich and idealized imitation of real life; (d) children use play to transform the external world according to their own perceptions and wishes; and (e) play can function as a problem-solving situation which then serves as a source of pleasure when solutions are successfully discovered. Thus, in congruence with comparative and cross-cultural literature (see Schwartzman 1978 for a review), Bruner depicts childhood as an outcome of evolutionary adaptations that, to a certain degree, are similar in man and great apes. Selection has favored pressure-free periods of time in childhood (play) during which the subroutines of adult skilled action can be acquired through observational learning and imitation. These activities are incorporated in playful combinations and varied ad libitum without much risk.

Conversely, some ethologists question the benefits brought about by the evolution of play, arguing that only a relatively small amount of play can be observed (MacKinnon 1971, Schaller 1963), and in addition, that increased exploratory and playful behaviors can increase the danger of predation and mortality (Berger 1972, Teleki 1973). However, the majority of researchers (cf., Bekoff 1972, Loizos 1967, Poirier 1972, Suomi and Harlow 1971, Wilson and Kleiman 1974) have viewed play as an important factor in evolutionary adaptation. The fact that play characterizes only higher vertebrates—there is, for example, no evidence of play in reptiles—raises the question of whether and how play may be interrelated to the evolution of a larger brain.

Play is a significant process of adaptation. The potential risk of an increased exposure to the danger of predation or other dangers during play appears in quite another light in relation to human evolution. If play has contributed to the evolution of culture, then the price of increased mortality due to predation and other dangers has been outweighed many times by the benefits inherent in the development of culture. Among other dangers, predation has been virtually eliminated, to the point of making extremely rare zoo specimens out of dangerous, predatory animals.

Several other authors have also considered the general evolutionary aspects of play, for example, the role of play in human culture (Erikson 1977, Huizinga 1955). Huizinga examined artists' contributions to civilizing culture and he suggested that human beings should be classified as *Homo ludens* rather than *Homo sapiens*. A culturally based explanation for play was early introduced by Friedrich von Schiller, an eighteenth century poet who also wrote a treatise on play. Schiller's interest in play emanated from his concern with aesthetic education. In his letters entitled "On the Aesthetic Education of Man," Schiller (1875) argued that the purpose of play was to establish a sense of aesthetic appreciation in humankind. Play was considered to be the medium through which the player could transform and transcend reality, thereby gaining an appreciation of culture and of the world.

PLAY AND COGNITIVE DEVELOPMENT

One of the critical benefits of a child's play has long been thought to be its contribution to the child's thinking ability. Children have been shown to acquire knowledge most easily through play across a variety of contexts. The characteristic exploration and manipulation often found in play enables the child to learn more about the specific characteristics of objects and others, and also about how they can relate interactively to the outer world. This idea of playfulness being related to learning dates back several centuries (Comenius 1657) and has been consistently applied to contemporary educational systems (e.g., Rousseau, Pestalozzi, Froebel, Montessori).

Empirical work on the cognitive correlates and consequences of playful experience has been the topic of much recent attention. Play has been linked theoretically and empirically to two modes of cognitive thought: convergent and divergent problem-solving ability (Vandenberg 1980). Convergent problems are those that have a single, correct solution, whereas divergent tasks have multiple solutions.

Many authors have argued that the child's thought processes, both convergent and divergent, are very much influenced by playful activities and interactions. Other investigators have attempted to demonstrate that cognitive abilities can be enhanced using play materials and play scenarios, thus being viewed as support for their contention that play contributes to children's cognitive development. The specific ways in which play contributes to these abilities, however, remains unclear at this time.

Play and Convergent Thinking Ability

Problem-Solving Ability

As far back as Groos (1898, 1901) it has been hypothesized that one of the important functions of play is that it relates directly to problem-solving ability, providing the individual with the specific skills to solve a variety of problems posed in life's circumstances. Play is regarded as an orientation which affords the individual the ability to apply much of his/her playful experience with objects and procedures to real-life problems which didn't appear in the original play situation. It is speculated that by exploring and manipulating objects in play, individuals learn the properties of those objects as well as their potential for application to various other problem situations.

Research with animals.—Much of the evidence to support this position comes from studies of tool-use in animals, showing their relation to previous object play experience (Bruner 1972, Candland et al. 1978, van Lawick-Goodall 1970; but see McGrew 1977). Van Lawick-Goodall (1968) conducted extensive observations of chimpanzees using tools. Her naturalistic research showed that chimps will examine and play with objects with their only reward being the pleasure of manipulating the objects. These observations, with accompanying detailed chronicles of playful activity preceding skilled tool use, have been confirmed with other monkeys as well (Kawai 1965). There is also supporting literature that shows that the deprivation of object play opportunities leads to severely limited tool use and/or problem-solving ability in animals (Barnett 1976; Bernstein 1962; Birch 1945a, 1945b; Jackson 1942; Menzel et al. 1970; Schiller 1875).

Tool-using abilities have been noted in species other than primates. Wasps, birds, fish, ants, and sea otters have all been observed to use objects as tools (Wilson 1975). A wealth of observational research also indicates that species below birds on the phylogenetic scale do not play (cf., Fagen 1981 for a review). Thus, there are species who are capable

of using tools but who do not play. These examples could be used to argue that play is therefore not a necessary prerequisite for tool use; however, this conclusion may be premature. As Wilson (1975) noted, the tool-using behaviors of these species are very stereotyped and elementary, and do not bear strong resemblance to the skilled tool-use of higher order animals.

One of the most fundamental characteristics of play is recognized to be the typical experimentation with new behaviors, where the player dismantles old behaviors and recombines them in new and entertaining ways (Bruner 1972, Fagen 1988, Loizos 1967). It has been reliably observed that as we move down the phylogenetic scale, the flexibility that a species demonstrates to be able to dismantle and recombine its behaviors decreases. At the low end of the phylogenetic scale, Lorenz (1956) labeled these behaviors as "vacuum" activities, where behaviors are exhibited out of their normal context. This appearance of activities out of context produces new responses to situations, thereby generating novel uses and adaptations of the animal's previously stereotyped behaviors. Lorenz regarded these vacuum activities as the phylogenetic precursors to play, and said they could provide the flexibility that is required to developing simple tool-using skills in species that are lower on the phylogenetic scale and are not capable of playing. Thus, it has been hypothesized that the phylogenetic precursors of play are responsible for the development of the primitive use of objects as tools in the way that play contributes to the development of tool-use in species higher on the phylogenetic scale.

Thorndike (1901) and Hobhouse (1901) early intimated that play experiences are potentially important for insightful problem-solving ability. Early observational studies by Bingham (1929), Kluver (1937), Kohler (1925), and Yerkes (1927) demonstrated that chimpanzees showed remarkable problem-solving abilities that could not be solely explained by trial and error efforts. Birch (1945a, 1945b) and Jackson (1942) systematically sought to investigate this, and concluded that play provided the chimps with the opportunity to develop a generalized scheme with objects, which was then used more specifically when it was required later to solve a task. Schiller (1952, 1957) attempted to replicate and extend Birch's findings. He found support for the problem-solving function of play, and concluded that "the lack of opportunity to play...definitely retarded their development in manipulation" (Schiller 1957: 266).

Schiller's interpretation of the consequences of play led to an implicit model of problem-solving. His results support the argument that playful experience with objects is important for the development of insightful tool-using abilities; however, he deviated from Birch and Jackson concerning the ways in which play operates to aid subsequent tool-use. Schiller argued that play develops specific behaviors that are used in a problem-solving task, while Birch and Jackson held that play develops a generalized schema of action that is mobilized in the specific way that is called for to solve the task.

One difficulty with the early empirical efforts of Birch, Schiller, and Jackson was that there was no attempt to control for the animals' other nonplay experiences with the sticks. It thus remains unclear at this juncture whether it was the chimps' actual play experience with the stick, or merely exposure to the stick which was the crucial factor for successful solution of the task.

All of this research—the observations of van Lawick-Goodall (1970) and others and the experiments of Birch, Schiller, and Jackson—taken together suggests that play is a critical factor in both the generation of new, adaptive behaviors, as well as in the cultural distribution of skills that are already established (Vandenberg[1]). Van Lawick-Goodall's data illustrates that young animals learn skills from adults through observational learning, and that they use play to perfect these skills and abilities. The findings of Birch, Jackson, and Schiller show that play is important in the production of novel behaviors which could subsequently be applied to new problem situations. While these conclusions are plausible interpretations, they should be considered tentative, since the authors failed to make the important distinction between play and exploration (cf., Hutt 1979, Weisler and McCall 1976), and since precise definitions of what constituted play were for the most part absent. In fact, it has been argued that these experiments were not really concerned with play at all, but that the investigators merely used the term "play" to describe the situation where there were no apparent environmental demands placed on the animal.

Research with children.—Much of this animal research was subsequently extended to investigations with infants and young children (Alpert 1928; Barnett 1976; Brainard 1930; Ling 1946; Matheson 1931; Menzel et al. 1970; Moriya 1937a, 1937b; Pepler 1979; Pepler and Ross 1981; Richardson 1932, 1934; Smith and Dutton 1979; Sylva 1974, 1977; Sylva et al. 1976; Vandenberg 1978a). Sylva and her colleagues attempted to extend the findings of Birch and Schiller to preschool children between 3 and 5 years of age. The task was similar, and the children were given the opportunity, in varying conditions, to play with the objects that would later be used to solve the task. Appropriate experimental controls were instituted to discount the "mere exposure" hypothesis, and detailed coding of behaviors both before and during the problem-solving task were conducted. In general, Sylva and her colleagues found that

the children who were allowed to play with the materials that would later be used in a task subsequently performed better on that task than the children who had no opportunity for play experiences.

While encouraging, several important methodological problems prevent an unbridled acceptance of the conclusions from this research. Barnett (1976) and Vandenberg[2] attempted to resolve some of these concerns, as well as to expand their investigations of the play experience and the problem-solving behaviors that are required for successful completion. Using the same basic research paradigm, and with children of similar age, Barnett was able to show that many of Sylva et al.'s conclusions were premature, and that the physical manipulation so characteristic of play is more beneficial to problem-solving than visual learning or passive participation. In addition, Vandenberg found that the relationship between play and problem-solving was mediated by many individual and situational variables, such as age and task characteristics, and that the play experience best facilitates the problem-solving ability of those children whose ability was most commensurate with the demands of the task situation.

The studies by Barnett, Vandenberg, and later research by Smith and Dutton (1979) suggest that the process by which play contributes to problem-solving is a complex one. More recently, some of the experimental methodology used in these studies has been criticized, particularly because of the likelihood of experimenter bias and lack of adequate control groups (Cheyne 1982; Simon and Smith 1983, 1985; Smith and Simon 1984). Specifically, when Simon and Smith (1983) and Smith et al. (1985) controlled for potential biases that may have been due to scoring and treatment procedures, they were unable to replicate the superiority of the play condition found by Smith and Dutton (1979). Simon and Smith (1985) were also unable to replicate the superiority of the play group in the earlier Smith and Dutton study when they controlled for exposure to the experimental situation by using independent observers and scorers in addition to an alternate control group. Finally, Smith et al. were unable to replicate their earlier work, and they found that unconscious experimenter bias probably contributed to the group differences that were found.

In summary, the research cited above generally supports the contention that play may have a significant impact on problem-solving ability, although the way in which it makes this contribution is still unclear. Efforts to identify specific behaviors in play which would be responsible for later successful problem-solving have not proven fruitful. It appears from the above research that there is no direct correspondence between playful experience and subsequent task performance. Play is not necessary for producing the correct solution to a task, since many children performed well on the experimental tasks without any prior related play experience. Rather, what the literature does suggest is that it is more likely that play provides the individual with a flexible approach to his/her environment, and contributes to the development of a generalized mode of cognitive approach which the individual utilizes in the problem situation.

Play and Conservation

Several researchers have attempted to produce empirical support to show that play facilitates children's ability to conserve. Conservation, a term stemming from Piaget, refers to the child's comprehension that certain properties of objects and relationships will remain invariant in spite of perceptual transformations. Piaget's (1932) observation that preschool children are not able to solve problems involving conservation has been supported by a wealth of research on most continents. He suggested that one reason that children have difficulty with conservation is that they are not able to grasp the principle of reversibility, that is, that if a liquid is poured back from a tall narrow glass into its original shorter, wider glass, the level of the liquid will be the same as it was before the liquid was poured into the taller, narrow glass.

Fink (1976) attempted to demonstrate the relationship between a child's play and his/her ability to conserve by using sociodramatic play with kindergarten children. His play training group, in contrast to two control groups, did show significant increases in a social role-taking task, but no differences were found for either conservation of number or conservation of quantity. Golomb and Cornelius (1977) believed that making children aware of the change from fantasy to reality would help promote their acquisition of conservation of quantity. They used a different type of play training than Fink used, which involved first engaging the child in symbolic play, and then maneuvering the child into verbally explaining the make-believe transformations that had occurred in the play. Their findings were in support of the hypothesis: prior to the training none of the preschool children showed conservation ability, but on the post-test, 10 out of the 15 subjects in the experimental play training group gave conservation responses compared with only 1 subject in the control group. A later partial replication by Guthrie and Hudson (1979) casts doubt on the generalizability of Golomb and Cornelius' findings. In fact, Guthrie and Hudson concluded that the conservation tests alone may have contributed more to the children's attainment of conservation than the play training.

Several theorists, most notably Piaget and Vygotsky, have contradictory thoughts about the role of play in the development of logical thinking ability. Fink's (1976) and

Guthrie and Hudson's (1979) finding that play training did not facilitate young children's acquisition of conservation of number and quantity provide support for Piaget's view that play does not result in the acquisition of new cognitive structures due to its primarily assimilatory nature. It actually would have been surprising had the efforts to replicate the Golomb and Cornelius (1977) study been successful. Conservation appears to develop very slowly through childhood, and with relatively little transfer from one type of conservation to another. Thus, many children are able to conserve liquid quantity and yet not understand conservation of weight or volume. It would have proven interesting to find that only three sessions on role reversibility could have transferred to the ability to conserve liquid quantity.

Play and Divergent Thinking Ability

There are two common lines of thought about the way in which play contributes to the development of divergent thinking ability. The first mode regards play as contributing to developmental thinking ability by virtue of its characteristic experimental and flexible nature. Once the child has discovered the properties of an object, or mastered a skill, he/she begins to actively experiment with the object in new and creative ways. This experimentation in play adds variability (Sutton-Smith[3] 1967) and flexibility (Bruner 1973) to the child's repertoire of responses. As noted earlier, the separation of exploration and play (Hutt 1979, Weisler and McCall 1976) makes this distinction between the child gaining familiarity with the properties of an object, and then subsequently experimenting with that object in unique combinatorial ways. This experimentation in play, termed diversive exploration by Hutt (1970) has been described as a more advanced activity, following the specific investigation of the object, or specific exploration (Hutt 1970, 1982). Hutt observed that diversive exploration is typically characterized by a more relaxed and varied approach to play objects, involving trial and error and the chance combinations of responses, and it is a form of variation-seeking with an object and a child's own behaviors (Sutton-Smith[3]). Bruner (1973) described this experimental quality in play as a combinatorial flexibility in which the child's skills form subroutines which are then experimented with and later incorporated into more complex activities. The benefit of this experimental nature in play is that it provides the child with a broad repertoire of skills and responses, and with a flexible approach which is used to effectively solve a divergent thinking task or problem.

A second way of viewing the relationship between play and divergent thinking ability is by focusing on the symbolic, pretense nature that characterizes much of young children's play. It has been posited by several theorists that play serves to facilitate the child's transition from concrete to abstract thought processes (Piaget 1951, Smilansky 1968, Vygotsky 1967). In play, children often assign the meaning of an object to a symbol, a process termed representation. According to Piaget (1951), the meanings of symbols are, in part, evoked through assimilation, which is the dominant element in play. Hence, it is argued, the symbolic representations that are so often produced in play form part of the process through which the child develops the ability to think abstractly. Vygotsky (1967) clarified the way that this transformation from the child's ability to move from concrete thinking to abstract thinking occurs. He explained that in play, a thought is typically separated from an object, for example, a stick becomes a horse. The mechanism that causes the transition in play is that the stick "becomes a pivot for severing the meaning of horse from a real horse" (Vygotsky 1967: 546). Play allows young children the only context in which thoughts can be freed from the constraints imposed by the real world.

Several researchers have reliably noted the existence of a developmental sequence in play that goes from the concrete to the abstract (cf., Watson and Fischer 1977). Fein (1975) observed that initially the child relies on an object which is prototypical; however, as the child's thinking matures, s/he is able to use a less similar object to symbolize another object in play. Fenson and Ramsay (1980) viewed this progression as a process of decentration whereby the child gradually becomes less dependent on actions focused on him/her self. The ability to think of objects in more abstract and less self-centered terms, which is practiced in play, facilitates divergent problem-solving ability because it requires the child to make a variety of free associations in his/her mind.

In summary, symbolic play involves the child using one object to signify another and can therefore be viewed as an elementary form of representational thought. In play, the child's thoughts can be separated from the concrete and moved into the abstract, and this may be done at an earlier age when the child might be otherwise incapable of abstract thought. Play affords the opportunity to practice and vary this newly acquired ability to think abstractly. This is a significant process for creativity since it allows the child to focus beyond the obvious, to make novel associations, and to engage in imaginative activity during play and subsequent divergent problem-solving. It still remains to be shown whether these processes in play do indeed correlate with increases in creativity.

Play and Creativity

Intuitively, it seems eminently plausible that play and creativity are strongly related—they both seem to be of the same fabric. Both activities share a healthy disregard for the usual and familiar, and both involve the creation of something novel from something commonplace. This apparently close relationship between play and creativity has been the topic of many empirical efforts.

Torrance (1961) and Wallach and Kogan (1965) observed that playfulness was one of the personality traits that seemed to differentiate between more creative and less creative children. Lieberman (1965) similarly posited a correspondence between playfulness and divergent thinking ability in her studies of kindergarten children. From this research she found strong correlations between five playfulness traits and three measures of divergent thinking ability: ideational fluency (the ability to generate a large number of responses that conform to a certain criterion), spontaneous flexibility (the ability and disposition to vary responses), and originality (the ability to generate unique responses). Durrett and Huffman (1968) were able to replicate Lieberman's findings with Mexican-American kindergarten children.

Singer and Rummo (1973) also examined the relationship between divergent thinking ability (ideational fluency), creativity, and playfulness. Their research reported that highly creative boys were more communicative, curious, humorous, playful, and expressive; but for girls, none of the play measures were related to creativity alone, but they interacted with measures of intelligence. These findings were further explicated by Hutt and Bhavnani (1976) who found that more girls could be classified as "nonexploratory" in their play, while boys tended to be more "inventive explorers." In their study, inventive play correlated positively with measures of divergent thinking ability, but primarily for boys. Johnson (1976) found high correlations between several measures of divergent thinking and the frequency with which low socioeconomic preschoolers engaged in sociodramatic play, an advanced form of pretend play in which two or more children adopt roles and attempt to recreate real-life situations. He found that only social fantasy play, and not nonsocial fantasy play, was related to performance on the divergent thinking tasks. He suggested that the factor common to both divergent thinking and social fantasy play might be ideational fluency. In a later replication and extension, Barnett and Kleiber (1982) found that the relationship between play and divergent thinking reported by the previous authors was confounded with intelligence. In addition, they also confirmed earlier findings that gender differences mediated the findings, such that a positive relationship between play and divergent thinking could be observed for girls, but a negative or absent relationship was present for boys.

Singer and Rummo's (1973) study and Barnett and Kleiber's (1982) study both raise the possibility that playfulness and creativity are both related but through a third variable—intelligence (see also Williams and Fleming 1969). A reanalysis of Lieberman's (1965) data with mental age held constant, showed that the correlations between playfulness and creativity were considerably reduced. Due to the correlational nature of this research, it is not clear whether playfulness determines creativity or whether creativity determines playfulness. The weakness of these studies is that it is not possible to determine whether play experiences cause developmental change or whether the association between play and creativity is simply the result of a similar cognitive style. It is not surprising, therefore, that most of the more recent studies about this presumed relationship have employed experimental rather than correlational research strategies.

In one of the first of the experimental studies, Sutton-Smith (1968) argued that play contributes to creativity by increasing the child's repertoire of novel associations with objects. Dansky and Silverman (1973) improved upon some of the methodological weaknesses of Sutton-Smith's study by dividing preschool children into three groups: a play group which was allowed to play with a set of common household objects, an imitation group which mimicked the experimenter's actions with the same objects, and a control group which had no contact at all with the objects. Results of a creativity test involving the same objects that were used in the treatment conditions showed that the children in the play group generated more unusual responses than the children in the other two groups. In addition, they observed that the children who were in the play condition were able to make more use of environmental cues as they searched for responses to the task. Dansky and Silverman hypothesized that the children who had played may have come into the testing situation with a more playful attitude, which then allowed them to approach the divergent task with more flexibility, curiosity, spontaneity, and interest.

In a follow-up study (Dansky and Silverman 1975), they concluded that play creates a generalizable set for the production of novel responses to objects, an ability which they referred to as associative fluency. They stated that the results of their two investigations "lend strong support to the notion that play creates a set, or attitude, to generate associations to a variety of objects whether or not these objects are encountered during play activity." It appears that the symbolic transformations that occur in make-believe play are the

key link between play and this type of creative thinking (Li 1978). In these transformations, children typically distort reality to fit their whims and wishes, resulting in the generation of novel associations and combinations of ideas. This thesis is in agreement with Piaget's (1951: 162) statement: "play constitutes the extreme pole of assimilation of reality to the ego, while at the same time it has something of the creative imagination which will be the motor of all future thought and even of reason."

Dansky (1980b) explored the possibility that the lack of situational constraints inherent in free play settings is responsible for the gains in cognitive ability reported above, and not the free play behavior itself. He found that the mere opportunity to engage in free play does not automatically lead to increases in creative thinking ability. According to Dansky, there must be make-believe in free play in order to see gains in creative thinking. He also found that many preschool children did not regularly exhibit make-believe in their play—an observation also found in the play of children in the United States (Christman 1979, Feitelson and Ross 1973, Rosen 1974), England (Smith and Dodsworth 1978, Tizard et al. 1976), Canada (Rubin et al. 1976), and Israel (Feitelson 1959, Smilansky 1968).

Dansky (1980a) further examined the role of make-believe or fantasy in play and the way in which it might contribute to the child's creativity. He found that the beneficial effects of free play on creativity were limited to those children who typically engaged in make-believe play in the classroom. Based on this and earlier findings, he hypothesized that some of the cognitive processes that are involved in make-believe or fantasy play, such as free association and symbolic thinking, are strikingly similar to those involved in divergent thinking ability. Pepler examined the effect of play experiences on the child's divergent thinking ability (Pepler 1979, Pepler and Ross 1981). She found that children who had divergent play experiences performed better on a divergent thinking task than children in any of the other groups. Results in the second study indicated that children who had certain types of divergent play experiences were more imaginative on divergent thinking tasks, suggesting that it is not play *per se*, but play with unstructured play materials, that contributes to creativity.

Critique and Summary

In summary, there is some support for suggesting that play is related to the child's creative ability. Taken together, the studies presented above indicate that through play experiences, children perform better on divergent thinking tasks than children with imitation, intellectual, convergent, or neutral experiences. This research also suggests several processes by which play may contribute to creativity. First, there may be a generalized transfer of a playful attitude or a flexible response set from the play to the problem-solving situations. Hence, children with play experiences have been shown to be more flexible, curious, spontaneous, and interested in the task (Dansky and Silverman 1973, 1975). Second, the characteristic investigation and experimentation in play may generate a more specific transfer of novel responses to the task situation. Dansky and Silverman (1973) found that children with play experiences made more use of previous play activities to generate responses on a divergent thinking task than nonplaying children. Third, it is possible that the symbolic activity in play may well facilitate the child's creative performance. Although they did not systematically measure symbolic activity, the data suggests that the children who benefitted most from their play experiences were those whose play contained many elements of make-believe and fantasy. Several authors have suggested that the cognitive skill of being able to shift one's attention from the concrete to the abstract during play may be similar to the skill that is required to generate a variety of novel responses on a divergent thinking task (Johnson 1976, Singer and Rummo 1973).

Several individual and situational factors may well interact with the processes that govern the relationship between play and creativity. For example, there is some research that indicates that children with a predisposition for make-believe play (Dansky 1980a) or for inventive exploration (Hutt and Bhavnani 1976) tend to be more creative. Other research suggests that characteristics of the play experience (Matthews 1977, 1978), such as the structure of the play materials (Dreyer and Rigler 1969, Goldman and Chaille,[4] Pepler 1979, Pepler and Ross 1981, Pulaski 1973), nature of the task (Kogan and Morgan 1969), social interaction (Griffing,[5] Johnson 1976), or adult intervention (Bishop and Chace 1971, Darvill 1982, Johnson and Ershler 1982) affect subsequent divergent thinking ability.

Several significant conceptual problems with this literature have been identified. First, most of the researchers have not explored the possibility that differences in individual personality traits or behavioral styles among the children may have contributed to performance on many of the problem-solving tasks. Lieberman (1965) and Singer and Rummo (1973) have found significant relationships between the child's playfulness traits (cognitive spontaneity, social spontaneity, physical spontaneity, manifest joy, sense of humor) and creative thinking ability. Other investigators have found that the child's predisposition to engage in exploratory or make-believe play, as well as his/her cognitive style (Kogan 1983), also contributes to the effects of play on the child's problem-solving ability (Dansky 1980b, Feitelson and Ross 1973, Hutt and Bhavnani 1976).

Second, there are several gaps in understanding the relationship between play and problem-solving ability (Vandenberg[6]) which may be due to the failure to distinguish play behavior from exploration (Wohlwill 1987). This omission is crucial because play has consistently been distinguished empirically from exploration on the basis of behavioral and physiological responses to novel stimuli, and it has also been distinguished theoretically with regard to motivation and learning (Barnett 1974; Barnett and Wade 1979; Barnett et al.;[7] Hughes and Hutt 1979; Hutt 1966, 1967, 1970, 1976, 1979; Hutt and Bhavnani 1976; Nunnally and Lemond 1973). A child confronted by a novel, uncertain, complex, or discrepant object or situation engages in a process of specific exploration, investigating the physical properties of the object in an apparent attempt to answer the question, "What can this object do?" (Hutt 1976). This specific exploration seems to be similar to curiosity, which has been equated with divergent thinking ability in young children (Arasteh 1968). Play (also referred to in Hutt's model as diverse exploration), alternately, occurs only in a known environment and only when a child has already acquired all the information about the object s/he wanted. Thus, any object-related learning that takes place during diverse exploration or play is considered incidental. The question addressed by the child becomes, "What can I do with this object?" (Hutt 1966, 1976). Diverse exploration appears to be similar in appearance to various behaviors described by others as dramatic, symbolic, fantasy, thematic, or sociodramatic play in which the child uses an object for a variety of purposes and/or as a substitute for a missing object.

It may well be that diverse exploration is dependent upon or related to specific exploration. The ability to transform or substitute one object or role for another appears to be based on their shared physical properties or characteristics (Fein 1975). It appears likely that specific exploration provides the child with the knowledge about an object's physical properties and characteristics that is necessary before s/he can use the object in a variety of ways, many of which may be fairly conventional or common. The behaviors observed in diverse exploration and symbolic play are similar to the divergent thinking process in which the child generates uncommon or unusual responses. Other parallels noted in the literature are the idea that both symbolic play and creativity are thought to involve the nonevaluative association of a wide variety of schemas and that both require the capability to focus on more than a single aspect of an object or situation at a time. Play has been long thought to contribute to creative thinking by providing the child with a wide behavioral repertoire from which to make associations (Sutton-Smith 1968).

An additional limitation concerns the manner in which play has been operationally defined in many of these studies. Play is commonly defined as behavior that is intrinsically motivated, pleasurable, flexible, and nonliteral in nature (cf., Rubin et al. 1983). Many of the play conditions described in the preceding studies exhibit few if any of these characteristics. Also, most of the play training procedures were highly structured and involved an adult modeling or prompting the child to instigate a play activity or interaction. Just how intrinsically motivated this interaction is is open to questionable interpretation. In addition, some of the studies cited above have looked at social play and how it might be related to divergent thinking ability, while others have looked at solitary play. It might be important to more systematically examine these two forms of play so that the common or distinct processes that mediate the play-creativity relationship can be delineated. Until these problems with independent variables (i.e., separating play from other behaviors and operationalizing play in a manner consistent with its definitional characteristics) are solved, it is not possible to demonstrate that it is play *per se* that is responsible for any increases in cognitive processing or performance.

Recent reviews of this play research also critically include the authors' frequent failure to control for possible experimenter effects (Cheyne 1982, Smith and Simon 1984), a failure to determine whether gains from play experience are "real" and not transitory (Pepler 1982, Vandenberg[6]), and a frequent failure to demonstrate that play did indeed occur in the play-experience conditions (Christie and Johnson 1983, Smith and Whitney 1987, Vandenberg[6]). Of these criticisms, Smith and Whitney (1987) concluded that the possible contaminating experimenter effect was the most critical. In the four experimental studies that showed positive relationships between play and creativity (Dansky 1980a; Dansky and Silverman 1973, 1975; Li 1978), all of the experimental conditions and tests were administered by the same experimenter, who also presumably was aware of the research hypotheses of the study. Several attempts to replicate these earlier positive findings failed when precautions against experimenter effects were instituted (Simon and Smith 1985, Smith and Simon 1984). Additional research found that, when the possibility of experimenter effects and testing bias were eliminated, no significant relationship between play and creativity was found (Pepler and Ross 1981, Smith and Whitney 1987).

In conclusion, then, it is difficult to substantiate a causal relationship between children's play behavior and cognitive ability.

Play and Language

The idea that play and language are interrelated is not surprising since both serve several joint functions in the young child's life: first, both involve a communicative function of sharing objects with others (Dunn and Wooding 1977, Werner and Kaplan 1963); and second, children use both play and language to experiment and thereby learn about symbolic transformations and various self-other relationships (Bruner 1977, Bruner and Sherwood 1976).

A correspondence between symbolic play and language has been proposed on theoretical grounds by McCune-Nicolich (1981), Piaget (1951), and Werner and Kaplan (1963). As was the case with other aspects of cognitive development, language and play have been found to be mutually reinforcing (Reynolds 1972). Whereas play clearly precedes the advent of language, play is in one sense itself a form of language because it incorporates symbolic representation. Piaget viewed thought and language as separate though related systems having a common origin in the symbolic processes expressed through play and imitation. Hence, the ability to represent objects, actions, and feelings in symbolic play is paralleled by a corresponding ability to represent those phenomena in language (Nicolich 1977). In both the comprehension and the production of language, the child is required to master the phonological, syntactic, and semantic rules that must be followed if s/he is to convey his/her intended meaning (Athey 1974). Play has been regarded as instrumental in developing both the comprehension and production aspects of language.

Piaget (1926) explained that children progressed from a limited self-centered, egocentric use of language to a broader based other-centered use of language. From this perspective, language is dependent on thought, and children's thought is dependent on experience and social interaction (cf., Duncan 1972). Play is regarded as one of the most prevalent events in early childhood that provides both experience and social interaction. Piaget identified the representational function provided by play and suggested that play is facilitative of children's aural language comprehension. That is, children who are allowed to play what they hear will have a better understanding of what they hear and, therefore, will recall more of what they have heard. Playing out a story forces a child to do several things: first, the child becomes actively involved in the experience—they are no longer just hearing words, they are recreating events. Second, in order to physically recreate the events, the child must create a mental representation of the events. Third, the child must engage in social interaction to coordinate his/her play, and this social interaction acts further to help the child create a mental representation of the event.

A number of developmental consistencies between play and language have been observed in young children. Just as children move from the use of single words to combinations of words in language, they move from the performance of single scheme to multiple scheme sequences in play (McCune-Nicolich and Bruskin 1982). Also, temporal correspondences have been shown between the ages at which children attain developmental stages in play and in language (McCune-Nicolich and Bruskin 1982, Shore et al. 1984). Observations such as these seem to suggest a strong relationship between symbolic play and language ability.

A number of studies have found support for this relationship, demonstrating positive correlations between symbolic play and language during the early stages of language acquisition in both normal and language-impaired children (Bates et al. 1975, Lowe and Costello 1976). Fein (1975) reported multivariate findings demonstrating that it is symbolic play that is closely related to language production and comprehension, while other types of play are not. Largo and Howard (1979) obtained positive correlations between pretend play and receptive language, while Rosenblatt (1977) found that children who learned language early also engaged in more representational play than other children.

Observational studies by Garvey (1974, 1979) have shown that children also gain valuable language practice from sociodramatic play. This advanced form of symbolic play requires that children use two types of verbal exchanges: pretend communications which are appropriate for their chosen roles, and metacommunications which are used to structure and perpetuate the play episode. This latter type of exchange is used to assign roles, to specify the make-believe identities of objects, to play story plots, and to secure the cooperation of other players. Garvey found that children constantly switch between pretend communications and metacommunications while engaging in sociodramatic play episodes. In addition, studies of autistic children (Sigman and Ungerer 1981) and retarded children (Jeffree and McConkey 1976, Kahn 1975) have found a positive relationship between symbolic play and language, and Steckol and Leonard (1981) reported improvement in communicative competence following training in symbolic play.

When language-impaired children are compared to normal children who are matched on age (e.g., Brown et al.,[8] Fein,[9] Lovell et al. 1968), results have generally supported a close relationship between play and language. However, when normal children have been matched on language ability with language-impaired children, a direct relationship between play and language has not been consistently supported. Terrell et al. (1984) found that language-impaired children show a higher level of play than normal

children. Roth and Clark (1987) also found differences between the symbolic play and language skills of normal and language-impaired children, but in the opposite direction: the play of their language-impaired subjects was less sophisticated than the play shown by their language-matched normal peers.

These discrepant findings may be due to age and language level differences between the subjects in the two studies. Roth and Clark's (1987) subjects were older and had more advanced language skills than in the Terrell et al. (1984) study. The relationship between play and language may change relative to increasing age and/or linguistic maturity (Roth and Clark 1987). Another possible explanation for these variant findings is that the measure of symbolic play selected in these two studies was not accurate. Studies of normal children's symbolic play have often focused on the children's object transformations in play (Elder and Pederson 1978, Fein 1975, Jackowitz and Watson 1980), while these two studies focused on children's appropriate use of toys, or representational play (Veneziano 1981). Because the cognitive skills required for these two different types of play may be different, it may not be appropriate to view them as equivalent in empirical research.

Smilansky (1968) showed that training in sociodramatic play could be used to increase the language performance of low socioeconomic children in Israel. Her study was partially replicated in the United States by Lovinger (1974), who found that sociodramatic play training resulted in increases in the number of words the children used in free play and also in the children's verbal expressiveness scores. It is difficult to reliably interpret the findings of these studies, however, since neither study involved a control group that would show whether similar differences might have been obtained with another type of training procedure which also encouraged a lot of verbal interaction. A similar criticism can be found with Collier's (1979) investigation of Cazden's (1979) hypothesis that language play leads to increased metalinguistic awareness. While the findings pointed to the beneficial effect of a play experience group, the lack of a "no treatment" control group makes it impossible to conclude that the gains were brought about solely by the language games in the play condition.

Several investigators have demonstrated that this sociodramatic play training is facilitative of young children's comprehension of stories (Pellegrini and Galda 1982, Saltz and Johnson 1974, Saltz et al. 1977). While taking care to eliminate many of the methodological concerns raised with the preceding studies, this research found positive results. The studies provided evidence to support the contention that play facilitates children's story comprehension; however, none of this research provides any indication as to what aspects of the play situation were important to increased comprehension.

Conflicting findings were obtained by Yawkey and Silvern[10] who also looked at the relationship between play and reading comprehension. Their results indicated that children who played recalled more of the story they had read than the other groups of children, but that there was no difference in comprehension between the play and control groups. In a follow-up study, Silvern (1980) compared a similar play condition with a picture condition and two control conditions, and results again indicated no significant differences in comprehension between the play and other research groups. The apparent discrepancy between the Saltz studies and the Pellegrini and Galda study with the Silvern investigation might be reconciled if the many differences between them are noted. The former studies used stories that were familiar to the children and found positive results for play experiences, while the Silvern study found no positive results for play. Also, in all of the studies the experimenter was directly involved in the children's play; however, in Silvern's studies the children were playing individually, whereas in the other studies the children were playing in groups. Also, Silvern did not provide any training experiences where such experiences were provided in the other studies.

Five experimental conditions were used by Silvern in follow-up research to attempt to resolve some of these inconsistencies (Silvern et al.[11]). In the first study, the researchers found that the children needed certain types of experiences in play in order for play to be facilitative. In the second study, the findings indicated that the children in the play condition performed significantly better on recall of a story they had read than children in various discussion conditions. Finally, using many of the same procedures but testing for alternate explanatory hypotheses, these researchers found that the play experiences that are facilitative are most operative when the conditions are unfamiliar and the presence of adults is more facilitative than directive (Silvern et al.[11]).

The conclusion from this literature regarding the relationship between play and language development is that social interaction appears to be necessary for the normal course of language growth, but play is probably not.

PLAY AND SOCIAL DEVELOPMENT

Research with Animals

Many primate ethologists have posited that the key elements of the animal's social life, the development of social bonds, grooming, components of sexual behavior, and aggression, are, to some degree, learned and rehearsed during social play (Mason 1967, Poirier and Smith 1974). Laboratory studies have documented the need for social play interaction in order for full and normal social development to occur in many animals. These studies have generally found that much of what is considered "normal" development does not occur unless an animal has had the opportunity for peer play group interaction.

Play and Social Adjustment

The importance of the peer group has been documented by Harlow's (1969) studies on the relative importance of the mother and the peer group to the social development of young rhesus monkeys. Harlow's (1969) deprivation studies provide evidence that peer play interaction is more important for the development of normal social behaviors than maternal interaction. Even brief daily play sessions between infants raised with surrogate mothers fully compensated for their lack of real mothering. At similar chronological ages, these infants developed a repertoire of infant-infant play relations and, later on, adult sexual behaviors, as varied as that of infants raised with mothers in the playpen. Surrogate-raised infants who were allowed 20 minutes of play per day with their peer group were considerably better adjusted adults than infants raised with their mothers alone.

As Bekoff (1972) noted, play with peers is important enough that peer play interaction can override the effects of maternal separation making it a less traumatic experience, as demonstrated above by Harlow (1969) with rhesus monkeys and by Tisza et al. (1970) with hospitalized children. Harlow et al. (1971), studying the social recovery of isolated monkeys, stated that the most critical and valid measures of social recovery were those of social contact and play. Mason's work (1961, 1963) clearly showed that animals with restricted social play experiences (those raised in isolation) show strikingly abnormal sexual, grooming, and aggressive patterns. Laboratory studies suggest that the full development of an animal's biological potential requires the stimulation and social forces normally encountered in the peer play group as well as in the larger social group (Harlow 1963, 1966; Mason 1963, 1965).

One of the most conclusive research efforts on the value of an enriched play environment was undertaken over a period of 12 years, from 1960 to 1972, by a team of biologists and psychologists led by Rosenzweig (Rosenzweig 1966, 1971; Rosenzweig and Bennett 1976, 1977a, 1977b; Rosenzweig et al. 1978; Rosenzweig et al. 1968). Very early in their experiments it was found that rats that spent 4 to 10 weeks in an enriched environment with frequent changes in playthings differed markedly from the rats in the impoverished environments without playthings. For example, the rats with enriched play had greater weight of the cerebral cortex, stronger nerve endings and transmitters, and greater enzyme activity. When the experiments were replicated 16 times with the same strain of rats, the same pattern of differences was repeatedly found. Only when the play environment was changed and new challenges were offered the rats were there any decisive anatomical and chemical changes in the brain. Several follow-up studies showed that the changes in the brain that were observed were not due to amount of handling, stress, or maturational differences. The researchers thus concluded that play experiences were of critical benefit, finding that two hours a day of enriched play experience over a 30-day period were sufficient to produce changes in the brain weight of the experimental rodents.

Play and Social Integration

Social play is one of the modes by which animals appear to maintain familiarity with other group members. Play has been said to help establish and maintain social affinities among group members. It is noteworthy that play is rare among adults where social relations are already well established. Play may be considered one of the means of exchange whereby social animals maintain their familiarity with one another as individuals (Etkin 1967). In play, young social animals learn their place in the group and develop appropriate in-group feelings and behaviors. Play has been said to maintain peer relations in social mammals.

Play facilitates the individual's integration into its troop and eventual reproductive success. During play, animals learn patterns of social cooperation, without exceeding certain limits of aggression. Diamond (1970) noted that cooperation of this kind brings its own rewards. Aggressive, noncooperative animals may be socially rejected, and perhaps physically excluded from the group. Play behavior relates to learning in early infancy and to the behavioral dialogue between mother and offspring, as well as between peers.

Harlow (1966) stated that the successful initiation of social or interactive play is crucial to the development of an age-mate affectional system. If youngsters lack the oppor-tunity to play, they are faced with the options either of being maladjusted or of being excluded from the social group (Carpenter 1965). The integration of an individual into a peer play group allows juveniles the opportunity to establish relationships that will later help maintain group unity. The play group is perhaps the major context for learning social skills, and as such it is regarded as an important factor in social integration (Hall 1968, Jay 1963).

Play and Social Communication

Play behavior has been said to serve to fully acquaint an animal with its species-specific, and perhaps group-specific, "communication matrix" (cf., Bekoff 1977, Darwin 1898, Poole 1978, W. J. Smith 1977, Symons 1978b, West 1974). Isolation studies have clearly documented that socially deprived animals have problems with response integration and communication (Baldwin and Baldwin 1974; Chepko 1971; Harlow and Harlow 1965; Muller-Schwarze 1968, 1971). Although socially deprived animals have been shown to exhibit several components of normal social behavior, these components are not combined into an integrated pattern and effectively applied in social interactions. The effectiveness of an animal's social interaction depends upon its experiences with others in both sending and receiving communicative messages. Messages within the communication matrix can only be effective if individuals know and understand their meaning. Animals raised in isolation without the benefit of social experiences (such as are provided in play) are both poor senders and poor receivers of information, and thus have overall inept communicative ability. These animals are incapable of response integration in an appropriate context.

An aspect vital to learning the rules of appropriate play behavior is the development of communicative ability. Bateson (1955, 1956) noted that play can only occur when primates are capable of some degree of metacommunication to carry the message, "this is play." Altmann (1965) emphasized that it is the development of a system of metacommunication, communication about communication, that allows the animal to fully participate in adult behaviors. One of the most important social functions of play, then, is the learning of proper social communication (but see Baldwin and Baldwin 1974, Bekoff 1974, Symons 1974). During play, infants learn that there are restraints upon the recombination of communicative acts. They learn that certain sequences (communication chains) are far more useful to them as individuals than are others. The sequences in which communication units are strung together is learned, and the mode of recombination for each animal depends upon previous social experiences. Perhaps within the play group animals learn to predict one another's behaviors. The value of such predictability is quite obvious if one considers the fate of an animal continually emitting inappropriate responses.

The relative success or failure of any social animal relates to its ability to associate properly with its role, to communicate using the appropriate signals at the appropriate time. Each animal assumes various roles during the daily cycle; each role entails a set of communicative actions. Animals must learn, by the juvenile stage, to alternate between what may be termed "primary" and "secondary" responses. They must be able to switch from one role to another, called code switching, without interference. The appropriate use of these responses can be learned and practiced, with minimal risk, during play behavior.

Play and the Adult Dominance Hierarchy

It has been argued that the basis of the adult dominance hierarchy in many species of animal may well be formed in the play group; play behavior helps the young find their place in the existent social order (Carpenter 1934). In the course of play, young animals may compete for food or sleeping position, as well as for other things. Through trial and error in play, and through the constant repetition of certain behaviors that are characteristic of play, it has been suggested that an infant learns the limits of its capabilities.

Early dominance patterns appear in rough-and-tumble play. Wrestling bouts characteristic of play give a growing primate practice in behavior that, at least in part, influences its social position. Although dominance among the young is mostly a function of relative size, during play juveniles gain social experience and become familiar with both dominant and subordinate positions (Dolhinow and Bishop 1970). The play group provides a context in which mistakes and experimentation can go without punishment or threat of danger from others. Adjustments appear during play (e.g., animals learn each other's aggressive and defensive capabilities) enabling a young primate to function properly as an adult of the species and to occupy a place within the group's social organization. The play group is the center for experimental social learning because its members, mostly peers, are young and are unable to inflict much damage.

The argument that play functions to establish a dominance order is generally well recognized in the primate literature (Carpenter 1934; Dolhinow 1971; Fagen 1976; Gottier 1972; Hall 1965; Harlow 1969; Harlow and Harlow 1965; Jolly 1972; Poirier 1969, 1970, 1972; Poirier and Smith 1974; Rosenblum 1961; Suomi and Harlow 1971). However, there are some others who disagree with this position (cf., Smith 1982). Aldis (1975: 173) directly challenged the dominance-play hypothesis, arguing that although the establishment of rank order relationships may

be an effect of play, play does not appear to be designed to achieve this goal: ". . . the influence of play on rank order relationships is probably only adventitious: it is difficult to believe that the survival value of play depends primarily on its effect on rank order relationships."

While high rank contributes to reproductive success, an evolutionary perspective entails the view that frequent, vigorous, sustained, competitive playfighting during youth is adaptive. Perhaps in some cases the sacrifice of playfighting experience is more than offset by the advantages to be gained from constantly asserting dominance. Symons (1978a) found that playfights between males were less likely to become antagonistic than were playfights involving a female, perhaps because playfighting experience is more important to male than to female reproductive success and selection has favored immature males who inhibit aggression and dominance assertion during play. Bekoff (1972) reported little evidence in the literature that animals use play or solicit play in order to deceive each other. While deception may occur at a level too subtle to have been detected by observers, an animal that practiced the crude deception of soliciting play in order to approach or threaten a subordinate would quickly run out of play partners. Fear is the enemy of play and the basis of dominance (Fagen 1981).

The dominance hypothesis of play states that playfighting functions as a kind of bluff or threat. But if play had this function, animals could be expected to react to play initiation or solicitation as they do to a threat, with submission, or much more rarely, with escalation. Every feature in which playfighting contrasts with fighting—the inhibition in play, the high frequency of play, the attractiveness of play, its regular occurrence between unevenly matched animals, the initiation of play by subordinate animals and by obviously outclassed animals, the ability of the dominant animals and animals of superior ability to solicit play successfully, the failure of playfights to terminate when it becomes clear which animal is superior—indicates that playfighting is not designed to establish rank order and, more to the point, that the establishment of rank order is unlikely to be an incidental effect or byproduct of playfighting. The adaptive significance of a playfight is more in the playfighting itself than in the outcome; the adaptive significance of a status contest is more in the outcome than in the means by which the outcome is achieved.

In addition, it can be argued that playfights could not establish rank and remain playful. An activity that is designed appropriately to establish rank order by physical contest—in terms of precision, economy, and efficiency is fighting. In short, the opposite of the dominance hypothesis is more correct: frequent, vigorous, sustained, competitive playfighting can exist only when the players are not thereby contesting status.

Research with Children

From the Piagetian perspective, the child is intrinsically motivated to engage in social interactions (Piaget 1970). Several researchers have investigated the idea that important social gains are made through the child's playful experiences (Garvey 1977, Greif 1977, Hartup 1978). Examples of such social skills that show gains through play interactions are cooperation, helping, sharing, and success at solving social problems through acceptable means. Some of the social-cognitive areas which have undergone investigation with play include the development of perspective-taking skills (Chandler 1973, Damon 1978, Mead 1932, Smilansky 1968), moral judgement, social attributional skills, and conceptions of friendship (Shantz 1975).

There are two competing hypotheses about the relationship between play and social development. The first hypothesis is that fantasy play is related to and causes (at least to some extent) the development of social and social-cognitive skills. Smilansky (1968) argued that children exhibit a high level of social and social-cognitive skills when they share a fantasy theme with one another and maintain this type of play for an extended period of time. According to Smilansky and others (cf., Bruner 1974, Mead 1932, Singer 1973, P. K. Smith 1977), the act of engaging in social fantasy play serves to exercise and consolidate the child's emerging social skills of empathy, role-taking, self-control, sharing, and cooperation. The child's pretend play can be regarded as essentially a social activity that stimulates the acquisition and appreciation of different social roles, social constructs, and their defining qualities. Fantasy play often serves to consolidate the child's social skills, which can then be appropriately transferred to a nonplay situation. Pretend play is thus important to the child's social development since it provides the structure within which the child can experiment with new skills, providing support and feedback on growing social competencies.

The second hypothesis is that sociodramatic play is merely a reflection of the child's egocentric thought and the primacy of assimilation over accommodation. Therefore, it is reasonable to find a positive relationship between the child's egocentric perspective-taking and his/her incidence of fantasy play. Piaget (1932) considered peer interaction and not play to be causally related to the development of social cognition. The child's symbolic play, according to Piaget (1951) exemplifies the inadequacy of his/her early thought processes and the subordination of reality to fit his/her own whims and desires. Thus, play was viewed as "pure assimilation," a clear example of the child's egocentric perspective of the world. In this way of thinking, the role of imaginative play in social development was seen merely as a method of exercising newly developed cognitive skills, having minimal relation to social progress.

Initial support for these hypotheses emanates from observational studies of the play activities of young children. These studies report significant correlations with indices of peer popularity and the incidence of both dramatic play (Marshall 1961, Rubin and Maioni 1975) and rough-and-tumble play (Coie and Kupersmidt 1983, Dodge and Frame 1982, Neill 1976, Pellegrini 1988). For example, Rubin and Maioni (1975) found a significant positive relationship between the frequency of dramatic play of preschool children and their scores on classification and role-taking tests. Notably, they also found a negative relationship between the frequency of functional, practice play and these same tests. In another study, Rubin (1976) obtained a significant positive correlation between the observed incidence of associate play in preschool children and their scores on a role-taking task, as well as a negative correlation between unoccupied and parallel play and role-taking skill. The authors thus concluded that active peer interaction was positively correlated with social-cognitive development, while passive peer interaction was negatively correlated with this type of development.

Cragg[12] found a significant positive relationship between kindergarteners' group play styles and both role-taking and sharing behaviors. In a subsequent study, Rubin (1980) observed that children in naturalistic settings who initiate and with whom other children initiate active interactions are less verbally egocentric than their less social preschool peers. Johnson (1976) reviewed the literature that showed that lower socioeconomic preschoolers consistently show less sociodramatic and symbolic play than their middle class agemates (e.g., Sigel and McBane 1967, Smilansky 1968), and linked these findings to the observation that lower class preschoolers also tend to be less able to classify (Sigel and McBane 1967), assume roles (Bearison and Cassel 1975), and exhibit divergent thinking skills than their middle class agemates. While these studies do indicate a possible link between some social-cognitive abilities and play, their correlational nature does not allow us to infer a causal relationship. These results may just as easily indicate that role-taking skills are a prerequisite to dramatic or social play interactions.

Connolly conducted research which illustrates a relationship between social pretend play and social competence (Connolly 1980, Connolly and Doyle 1984). In a study of preschool and early school-age children, ratings of the frequency and quality of social play were compared with several measures of social competence. The findings indicated that fantasy play measures could be significant predictors of social competence outcome measures: children who engaged in greater amounts of social fantasy play or more complex play were more socially skilled. While these findings may be encouraging, given the correlational nature of this study, the question of causality still remains unanswered.

Stronger support for the presumed play-social development relationship can be found in studies which report experimental attempts to train social skills through dramatic play. The majority of these studies follow a similar experimental paradigm: children are provided with a series of adult-led sessions in fantasy play, and their post-test scores on various measures of social or social-cognitive development are then compared to those of children who received no such play training.

One of the first such attempts to train social and/or social-cognitive skills through play was conducted by Smilansky (1968). Working with disadvantaged children, she found that sociodramatic play training lead to greater verbal communication skills, more positive affective behavior, and less aggression. These latter abilities have been regarded by some (e.g., Mussen and Eisenberg-Berg 1977) to be partly dependent on the development of social cognition: that is, the better able the child is to role-take, the less likely s/he will be to engage in egocentric speech and aggressive behaviors and the more likely she/he will be to display altruistic acts (e.g., Rubin and Schneider 1973). Unfortunately, much of the early Smilansky data are not quantitative in nature, and the significance of her findings are suspect.

Saltz and Johnson (1974), working with preschool disadvantaged children, examined the effects of similar thematic play training experiences. Their findings, replicated in a follow-up study with a similar sample (Saltz et al. 1977), showed that children who received the thematic-fantasy play training were better on role-taking and empathy tests than children who received no such training. Unfortunately, the measures were taken only as post-test scores, and it is unclear whether role-taking skills were equivalent among the children at the start of the training procedure. An additional problem was that the particular test that was used (Borke 1973) only taps a very primary level of social-cognitive development, and has been argued by some as measuring egocentric projection rather than empathy (Rubin 1980, Shantz 1975). Moreover, other reports have questioned the ecological, convergent, and discriminant validity of this measure (Rubin 1978, Rubin and Maioni 1975).

Several other research efforts (Burns and Brainerd 1979, Fink 1976, Iannotti 1978, Rosen 1974, Smith and Syddall 1978, Spivack and Shure 1974) have provided promising but as yet inconclusive support for the thesis that sociodramatic play causes social-cognitive growth. One major problem with many of these training studies is that the outcome measures of role-taking or empathy are either inappropriate, invalid, or ill-conceived (Krasnor and Rubin,[13] Rubin and Pepler 1980). In many cases, directed play experiences are confounded with adult tuition, so that it is not clear whether it is the fantasy play or the adult tuition which accounted for any of the advances or associations with social or social-cognitive development that were observed.

All in all, then, there appears to be limited support for the premise that spontaneously and voluntarily generated fantasy play leads to social and social-cognitive development. When small groups of children are led in dramatic play by adult tutors, significant effects can be detected. However, these data do not allow us to answer the question of whether it is the play experience which is the significant force in developmental gains. While there are few studies that suggest a direct causal link between fantasy play and social skill development, it would be premature to conclude that such a causal relationship does not exist. It is plausible that pretense behaviors reflect newly acquired social-cognitive ability which may be strengthened and consolidated through play. As such, then, play could be considered to be adaptive.

PLAY AND EMOTIONAL DEVELOPMENT

Sigmund Freud (1955) argued that play allowed the mastery of anxiety-producing events. Individuals were thought to master the traumatic events of childhood through compulsive repetition of the behavioral and contextual components of these events. If children were not allowed to master these traumatizing events through their play, they were considered to be at risk for adult psychopathology. Thus, to Freud, the mastery of behaviors or events in childhood via repetition and practice in play was thought to serve a crucial role in adulthood.

Neo-Freudian theorists view play as serving a cathartic (rather than mastery) role in normal development. For the neo-Freudians, play is thought to provide an avenue for the weakening of childhood tensions, anxieties, and aggressive impulses. Dramatic play around conflictful and anxiety-ridden themes helps the child, not only in the resolution of the conflict, but also in freeing energy for "more impersonal cognitive tasks" (Axline 1969, Erikson 1963, Freud 1970, Gould 1972, Johnson 1969, Murphy 1956, Peller 1971,

Sarnoff 1976, Singer 1973). This cathartic view of play has led to modern-day forms of play therapy, one purpose of which is to allow the expression and release of anxiety-inducing impulses (cf., Axline 1969, Schaefer 1976, Schaefer and O'Connor 1983, Wehman 1977).

To date, there is some direct evidence which confirms the view of play as anxiety-reducing. Symmonds (1946) was among the first to attempt an empirical test of this hypothesis, finding a positive correlation between anxiety and fantasy in young children. In his discussion, he suggested that fantasy play served as an appropriate outlet for a child's expression of anxiety.

Several other individuals have focused on hospitalized children as a population for examining the emotional benefits that play can effect. Much of this research, however, confounds other environmental conditions with the effects of participation in play and activity programs (Bolig 1980, Goslin 1978, Hodapp 1982). For example, investigation by Prugh et al. (1953) of improved ward management versus traditional ward management included the availability of an activities program as one of several characteristics in the improved ward management condition. Although children experiencing improved ward management were less upset than those subjected to the traditional style, there is no way of gauging the influence of play or the activities program. Bopp (1967) also investigated the effects of two conditions: a play/activities program and a no preparation/restricted visiting condition. She found no significant post-hospitalization differences, but like Prugh et al.'s (1953) study, there were several confounding variables with the play experience. Johnson (1969) compared children in isolation who received individualized play sessions with children who did not, and found no significant differences, as judged from their parents' perspective. Bolig (1980), however, found that the more time children spent in a supervised play/activities program, the more internal (locus of control) they became. He interpreted this finding as support for the idea that play, activities, and/or the relationships established through play, can contribute to an increased perception of control over stressful events. Bolig went on to suggest that children who became more internal may be able to cope more effectively with subsequent events by being more active, inquiring, and demanding of the environment than previously. Case studies (cf., Byers 1972, Erikson 1958, Noble 1967) have shown play sessions to be effective in reducing anxiety associated with specific hospital procedures; and field studies suggest even more generalized reduction of anxiety through participation in play and activities (Hall 1977, Stacey et al. 1970).

Gilmore (1966) was among the first to experimentally examine the effects of play experiences in alleviating anxiety with a hospitalized population. In the first of three studies he compared observations of 18 hospitalized children (presumed to be anxious) to 18 elementary school children of the same chronological age. He observed all children on three occasions with three sets of toys, all of which were novel and related to the hospital setting. Results indicated that the hospitalized children preferred the hospital-relevant toys more than did the control children, both in amount of toy contact and in stated verbal preference. To eliminate any biases due to a modeling effect, he conducted a second study to experimentally manipulate the anxiety factor. Gilmore hypothesized that the children would play initially with the toys relevant to the source of their anxiety (auditory or visual), and that this toy preference would extinguish across a second testing session since the source of the anxiety was removed. The findings were contradictory: while the auditory fear group played longer with the auditory toys when they anticipated a loud sound than when it was removed, the visual fear group showed little difference in choice of play materials across the sessions. In addition, the control group played more with the visual toys during the first session and longer with the auditory toys during the second session. A third study was introduced to sort through some of these difficulties. Again, the findings in the third study were contradictory, with all groups showing a preference for the visual over the auditory toys. Methodological problems prevent any clear interpretation of this data as supportive or not for an emotional role for play in the child's development.

In two studies, Barnett (Barnett 1984, Barnett and Storm 1981) attempted to experimentally test the anxiety-reducing motivation for play with preschool children. The findings indicated that the anxious children returned to baseline levels of anxiety following the play session, and their play was very much focused on the toys that were featured in the film. The videotaped play sessions allowed detailed observations and comparisons of the way in which the anxious children were able to "work through" their distress. A follow-up study was conducted to test the paradigm in a more natural field setting, and to expand the investigation to further explore the ways in which children use play to work through their conflict (Barnett 1984). The separation anxiety that children naturally experience on the first day of school was used to represent levels of the anxiety factor. Physiological and behavioral measures were used to divide preschool subjects into two groups: those that showed high distress on both measures (high anxiety group), and those that showed low distress on both measures (low anxiety group). Half of the subjects in each group were then allowed to play freely in a large play room, while the other half were not allowed a play experience (they passively listened to a story). Subjects within each of these conditions were again divided to incorporate a social versus nonsocial manipulation to see if the presence of peers had an inhibiting (Freud 1955) or beneficial (Eriksson 1972, Levin and Wardwell 1962) effect on anxiety resolution. The major result of the study was that support was again found for the importance of a play period which the children used to neutralize the anxiety they were feeling. An additional finding of interest was the way in which this was done: the children predominantly used fantasy play to reenact the departure of their mothers, often changing the outcome or reversing roles to achieve a more pleasant and/or controlled result. The presence of peers seemed to interfere with the anxiety resolution, since the child was not fully able to create his personally desired scenario. These two studies, taken together, can be viewed as providing tentative support for the notion that play can be important for the young child in successfully dealing with unpleasantness in his environment. Clearly, further efforts need to extend this preliminary research to different settings, and to children across different age and cultural backgrounds.

PLAY AND PHYSICAL DEVELOPMENT

Play as Energy Expenditure

In the late nineteenth century, Spencer (1873) put forth the proposition that play existed for physiological purposes. His ideas were drawn from his interest in what he believed to be a universal tendency for animals and humans to be active. Spencer further hypothesized that the actions engaged in by an organism varies according to its status in the phylogenetic hierarchy. Thus, with increased status, proportionally less time was spent "absorbed in providing for immediate needs." Given that less nervous energy was expended to maintain life among "higher" than "lower" animals, the former group had more energy to discharge on nonlife-supporting endeavors. These latter activities, carried on without regard for ulterior benefit and spurred on by the replenished or revitalized nerves, he labeled "play."

A number of early 20th century psychologists have offered theoretical, but not empirical, support for this surplus energy explanation for play. Tolman (1932), for example, suggested that once the primary needs for food, sex, contact, and rest were met, the organism would find itself in a physiologically homeostatic condition. However, if quiescence lasted for too long a period of time, the organism would find itself in a condition of having too much unspent energy. Tolman wrote that the secondary need for play, when pressed into action, could alleviate the negative condition of having surplus energy.

Over the years, proponents of the surplus energy theory have been criticized by theorists and researchers alike (cf., Barnett 1978, Ellis 1973, Levy 1977, Rubin et al. 1983). At the most basic level, there does not appear to be any empirical support for the existence of a hydraulic-energy system functioning within the human species (Beach 1945); and yet, Berlyne's (1960) theory of arousal motivation rests squarely on the assumption that neural needs and their satisfaction are responsible for play and exploratory activities.

Play and Physical Ability

Young animals tend to play more than do adult animals (Baldwin and Baldwin 1974; Dolhinow and Bishop 1970; Hinde 1971; Loizos 1966, 1967; Muller-Schwarze 1971; West 1974). This age-dependent scheduling of play may be explained as a consequence of natural selection, assuming that play results in immediate costs (e.g., diversion of time and energy from other activities) and eventual benefits (due to increased physical capacity caused by the training effects of play).

Several authors have argued that play experience is likely to improve physical ability by enhancing strength, endurance, and skill (cf., Brownlee 1954, Dobzhansky 1962, Fagen 1976, Smith 1982, Symons 1978a). Strength and endurance of particular muscle groups, maximum work rate, and endurance in whole-body work, such as running and swimming, have all been shown to adapt to a program of regular exercise. Muscle mass (Astrand and Rodahl 1970), heart size (Poupa et al. 1970), capillary density (Bloor and Leon 1970, Tomanek 1970), and vital capacity (Ekblom 1969) can also adapt to exercise. Indeed, growth rate (Ekblom 1969) and possibly even length of life (Arshavsky 1972) can respond adaptively and positively to a program of regular physical exercise, provided that the exercise program begins sufficiently early in development, before growth ceases in adulthood.

Regular performance of physical work by an animal tends to increase that animal's capacity to perform that work. Such "enrichment" of the animal's environment through regular work and exercise results in enduring adaptive physiological changes in mammals of several species, and particularly in young mammals.

Brain structure, like the structure of muscle, bone, and other somatic components, may respond adaptively to experience. Brain components exhibit measurable anatomical, cytological, and biochemical training responses. These responses appear to be specific to certain types of experience. In fact, play and exploration are the only behaviors known to mediate this response (Ferchmin and Eterovic 1977, Ferchmin et al. 1975, Ferchmin et al. 1980, Greenough 1978).

Experiments on environmentally induced growth of cerebral cortex indicate with increasing precision that the specific experience responsible for these changes is participation in playful social interaction, playful object manipulation, or performance of playful body movements. These experiments have ruled out many plausible alternatives to play experience, including observation by the subject of other rats housed in enriched environments that produce cortical growth (Ferchmin et al. 1975), nonplayful training of motor skills (Ferchman and Eterovic 1977), mere group living (Rosenzweig et al. 1968), or learning by operant conditioning (Rosenzweig et al. 1968). Recent reviews of these sophisticated experiments on play can be found in Bennett (1976), Rosenzweig and Bennett (1977a, 1977b), and Greenough (1978).

Brownlee (1954) and Geist (1971) argued that an animal that would not be expected to regularly exercise certain muscle groups (e.g., those needed for predation, escape, fighting, or reproduction) in a functional context until adulthood might well suffer from the physiological consequences of its inactivity, whereas an animal that regularly exercised such muscle groups in a nonfunctional context ("play") would train itself physically, in preparation for adulthood. Brownlee cited additional muscle groups that are regularly used by young animals in functional contexts, but that are not used in play. As argued above, current understanding of the physiology of exercise in mammals further supports Brownlee's hypothesis, suggesting that regular vigorous exercise must take place before adulthood to ensure adequate training. Once growth ceases, exercise is less effective and is therefore more costly in terms of time and energy. In adulthood, exercise will often occur in a functional context. Moreover, training of some physiological functions in adulthood appears to be impossible. For these reasons alone, it is argued, young animals play.

But why playful rather than serious forms of activity? From a strictly physiological point of view, vigorous exercise in a nonplay context does not differ from vigorous exercise in play. Functional forms of fighting, escape, and predation could be extremely costly in terms of time, energy, and survivorship, since they would tend to expose the young animal to very real dangers. In addition, the partner in such serious interactions should be selected to fight back, attack, or escape in ways that were not only functional, but that also produced the smallest possible physical training response in the animal initiating the interaction. In play, on the other hand, the choice of schedule and intensity is left to the individual, and natural selection should act on the behavioral composition, frequency, duration, and intensity of play bouts in order to produce optimal, age-specific, species-specific, and sex-specific exercise programs (Brownlee

1954). That is, play should train muscles or muscle groups that would otherwise only be used in such vigorous adult activities as prey-catching, fighting, predator avoidance, and mating (Ewer 1968, Wilson 1971). Differential recruitment of muscle fibers and muscle groups (Basmajian 1972, 1974; Taylor 1978) is significant in this context because certain components of muscle are generally accompanied by considerable stress or danger to the organism. Muscle components normally used only in emergencies could be recruited in play for training purposes. If recruited out of their "normal" sequence, they might impart an unusual, playful quality to the animal's movement.

Often many of these behaviors seem designed for sensorimotor stimulation as well as for physical exercise. Aldis (1975) noted that play movements can effectively stimulate the vestibular apparatus, an inner ear sensory organ involved in maintaining the body's balance in space. In play, animals balance (Delacour 1933), slide (Aldis 1975, Emory 1975, Geist 1971, Nance 1975, Schaller 1963, Stevenson 1976), and fall, apparently on purpose (Aldis 1975, Bourliere et al. 1970, Donald 1948, Emory 1975, Nolte 1955, Sugiyama 1965, Symons 1978a). Motives as such can invite play (Aldis 1975). In addition to sliding, passive transport in play may include riding waves (Peterson and Bartholomew 1967), jets of water, or waterfalls (Knappen 1930, Roberts 1934, Stoner 1947). Young wild primates and small children may even drop objects, apparently for the sole purpose of watching them fall (Baldwin and Baldwin 1977, Horr 1977, Kummer 1968).

Vestibular stimulation in play is often seen with young children. Aldis (1975) presented an excellent review of this aspect of human play, from the earliest games of parents with their infants to amusement park rides. Clark et al. (1977) showed that exposure to vestibular stimulation accelerates motor development in infants, an effect apparently recognized by Plato (1926: 5), who recommended that babies be rocked and carried. This regime is advisable, according to Plato, because when bodies receive most food, and when growth occurs most rapidly, without plenty of suitable exercise countless evils are produced in the body. (For an experimental demonstration of this, see Hedhammar et al. 1974.) Therefore, according to Plato, young animals need the most exercise and exercise the most.

Our concept of play as physical training has not improved significantly in the two millenia since Plato. Questions about ultimate causation and evolutionary significance of play-induced modifications in development remain to be formulated, directly tested, and ultimately answered.

SUGGESTIONS FOR FUTURE RESEARCH

If we wanted to conduct the ultimate test to demonstrate the benefits of play for the child, it would be very easy to conceive and design. Unfortunately, it could not be conducted.

A causal relationship, in a true experimental paradigm, between play and development would require that a randomly selected and wide-ranging group of children differing in characteristics such as age, social class, ethnicity, family background, configuration, and environment, etc., be deprived of play. Systematically, some of the children would be play-restricted from birth, some from 2 months of age, some from 4 months of age, some from 6 months of age, etc., and concomitant measures of cognitive, social, physical, and emotional development taken. Each child would have to be experimentally matched to several counterparts of the same intelligence, language ability, mental age, chronological age, family constellation, birth order, social ability, personality configuration, and many others. In addition, for half of these play-restricted children, play would be introduced at varying ages and to varying degrees. By following this paradigm, and employing scrupulously clean measures and procedures all along the way, I am convinced that we would then be able to write the definitive monograph detailing the developmental benefits of play for children.

The absurdity of this research plan is obvious, but it illustrates the frustrations in attempting to conclusively demonstrate a causal relationship between play and development. That is why much of the experimental research that is cited above has been criticized for multiple reasons, and the observational research leaves our causal question unanswered. While there are some strong suggestions of a critical significance for play in development from the animal literature, the generalizability of findings on rhesus monkeys to human toddlers is not as clear-cut as we need to be able to extrapolate.

Given this quandry, we can either give up all hope and turn to needlepoint, or we can attempt to do the best we can (scientifically and methodologically) and perhaps, through consensus, we might be able to arrive at a commonly-held conjecture. I'd like to offer two suggested research directions which I feel would add substantively to our speculations about why children (and others) play as we move closer to the issue of causality.

Longitudinal Research

While we obviously need to drop our "play deprivation" manipulation proposed above, the use of longitudinal field-based research would serve a valuable function. A research program needs to be conducted which concurrently assesses play as well as convergent and divergent cognitive ability, social development, emotional development, and physical ability. Since much of the literature in each area has been criticized on methodological grounds, particular care would need to be devoted to valid and comprehensive measures of each developmental aspect. In addition, play would have to be defined as completely as possible, both with quantitative and qualitative measures of internal predispositions to be playful, and behaviorally through activity and preference data. As noted above, as wide-ranging a sample of children and context should be used as possible, incorporating the literature on cross-cultural, social class, and ethnic diversity in both play and developmental stages.

This research would allow us to move toward directionality in generating a predictive model of play and child development. Parallel research questions could be investigated that would move us closer to looking at the functional significance of play. For example, "As the child increases in cognitive ability, does he also increase in cognitive play?" And, "As the child increases in cognitive play, does he also increase in cognitive ability?" Play could be modeled to predict performance, and inversely, performance could be modeled to predict play.

The long-term relationship between play and divergent thinking ability, for example, within a specific population of children, would also be chronicled through this longitudinal research plan. At present, there are only a few recent studies which have attempted research of this type, and the longest duration for assessing a child's developmental change was two years (Clark et al.,[14] Johnson and Ershler,[15] Smith et al. 1981). In addition, all of these studies narrowly defined the population, and various developmental assessments that were used have been criticized for validity and procedural issues. A more comprehensive and rigorous research program needs desperately to be conducted.

Exceptional Children

If play experiences naturally benefit the cognitive and/or social and/or emotional and/or physical development of the child (and we just do not know how to empirically demonstrate it), then it should follow that children who are developmentally atypical should not play in the same way that more "normal" children do. Thus, another convergent approach to examining developmental benefits of play is to compare "special" children (that is, those significantly below and significantly above an average level) to children who are within the normative range. In methodological terms, measures of development can be used as the independent variable(s), and play indices can serve as the dependent variables.

There has been some previous research with children who are delayed in intellectual, social, emotional, and physical development (for reviews, see Barnett and Kane 1985, Quinn and Rubin 1984), although inconsistent findings, definitional problems, methodological inadequacies, and statistical flaws abound throughout much of this work. In contrast, there is relatively little literature which looks at the play of children who are developmentally advanced. Clearly, then, a great deal of research study is needed with children who are not functioning at an "age-appropriate level" of development. And, in addition to the theoretical importance of research in revealing much about the developmental benefits of play, a great deal of practical significance as well could be achieved. The diagnosis, assessment, and treatment of exceptional children could be ultimately enhanced. However, without the appropriate research as a foundation, errors in judgement about the use of play in these ways could easily be made.

ENDNOTES

[1]Brian Vandenberg in paper on play—dormant issues and new perspectives, presented at Center for Early Education and Development, Round Table Conference, University of Minnesota, Minneapolis, MN, 1979.

[2]Brian Vandenberg in paper on the role of play in the development of insightful tool-using abilities, presented at the American Psychological Association, Toronto, Canada, 1978.

[3]Brian Sutton-Smith in paper on current research and theory on play, games and sports; presented to the first National Conference on Mental Health Aspects of Sports, Exercise and Recreation, American Medical Association, Atlantic City, NJ, 1975.

[4]J. Goldman and C. Chaille in paper on object use in the preschool—an undeveloped resource, presented at the Biennial Meeting of the Society for Research in Child Development, 1981.

[5]P. Griffing in paper on a follow-up study of sociodramatic play among black school age children representing two social class groups, presented at the Biennial Meeting of the Society for Research in Child Development, 1981.

[6]Brian Vandenberg in paper on play—a casual agent in problem solving?, presented at the meeting of the American Psychological Association, Montreal, Quebec, 1980.

[7]Lynn A. Barnett, Michael J. Ellis, and Robert J. Korb in internal report on arousal modulation as a function of visual complexity, University of Illinois Children's Research Center, Champaign, IL, 1974.

[8]J. Brown, A. Redmond, K. Bass, J. Liebergott, and S. Swope in paper on symbolic play in normal and language-impaired children, presented at the Annual Convention of the American Speech and Hearing Association, Washington, DC, 1975.

[9]Greta Fein in paper on imagination and play—some relationships in early development, presented at the meeting of the American Psychological Association, Toronto, Ontario, 1978.

[10]Thomas D. Yawkey and Steven B. Silvern in paper on an investigation of imaginative play and language growth in five, six and seven-year-old children, presented at the Annual Meeting of the American Educational Research Association, San Francisco, CA, 1979.

[11]Steven B. Silvern, Peter A. Williamson, Janet B. Taylor, Elaine Surbeck, and Michael F. Kelley in paper on young children's story recall as a product of play, story familiarity and adult intervention, presented at the Annual Meeting of the American Educational Research Association, New York, 1982.

[12]S. Cragg in unpublished manuscript on the effects of empathy, role-taking and play on altruism, University of Waterloo, 1977.

[13]Linda Krasnor and Kenneth H. Rubin in paper on preschoolers' verbal and behavioral solutions to social problems, presented at the Annual Meeting of the Canadian Psychological Association, Ottawa, Ontario, 1978.

[14]P. Clark, P. Griffing, and L. Johnson in paper on symbolic play and creativity—contemporary and longitudinal relationships, presented at the Annual Meeting of the American Educational Research Association, New Orleans, LA, 1988.

[15]James E. Johnson and Joan Ershler in paper on developmental changes in imaginative play and cognitive ability of preschoolers, presented to the American Psychological Association, Montreal, Quebec, 1980.

LITERATURE CITED

Aldis, O. 1975. Play fighting. New York, NY: Academic Press. 319 p.

Alpert, A. 1928. The solving of problem situations by preschool children. Teachers College Contractual Education. Number 323. 69 p.

Altmann, S. A. 1965. Sociobiology of rhesus monkeys. II. Stochastics of social communication. Journal of Theoretical Biology. 8: 490-522.

Arasteh, J. D. 1968. Creativity and related processes in the young child: a review of the literature. Journal of Genetic Psychology. 112: 77-106.

Arshavsky, I. A. 1972. Musculoskeletal activity and rate of entropy in mammals. Advances in Psychobiology. 1: 1-52.

Astrand, P. O.; Rodahl, K. 1970. Textbook of work physiology. New York, NY: McGraw-Hill. 669 p.

Athey, I. 1974. Syntax, semantics, and reading. In: Guthrie, J. T., ed. Cognition, curriculum, and comprehension. Newark: International Reading Association.

Axline, V. 1969. Play therapy. New York, NY: Ballantyne. 374 p.

Baldwin, J. D.; Baldwin, J. I. 1974. Exploration and social play in squirrel monkeys. American Zoologist. 14: 303-315.

Baldwin, J. D.; Baldwin, J. I. 1977. The role of learning phenomena in the ontogeny of exploration and play. In: Chevalier-Skolnikoff, B.; Poirier, F. E., eds. Primate biosocial development. New York, NY: Garland: 343-406.

Barnett, L. A. 1974. An information processing model of children's play. Urbana, IL: University of Illinois. 122 p. M.S. thesis.

Barnett, L. A. 1976. The contrast between play and other forms of learning in preschool children's problem-solving ability. Urbana, IL: University of Illinois. 219 p. Ph.D. dissertation.

Barnett, L. A. 1978. Theorizing about play: critique and direction. Leisure Sciences. 1(2): 113-129.

Barnett, L. A. 1984. Young children's resolution of distress through play. Journal of Child Psychology and Psychiatry. 25(3): 477-483.

Barnett, L. A.; Kane, M. J. 1985. Individual constraints on children's play. In: Wade, M. G., ed. Constraints on leisure. Springfield: Charles C. Thomas: 43-82.

Barnett, L. A.; Kleiber, D. A. 1982. Concomitants of playfulness in early childhood: cognitive abilities and gender. Journal of Genetic Psychology. 141: 115-127.

Barnett, L. A.; Storm, B. 1981. Play, pleasure and pain: the reduction of anxiety through play. Leisure Sciences. 4(2): 161-175.

Barnett, L. A.; Wade, M. G. 1979. Children's play and the processing of information: an integrative study. Leisure Sciences. 2(1): 13-38.

Basmajian, J. V. 1972. Electromyography comes of age. Science. 176: 603-609.

Basmajian, J. V. 1974. Muscles alive: their functions revealed by electromyography. 3rd ed. Baltimore, MD: Williams & Williams.

Bates, E.; Camaioni, L.; Volterra, V. 1975. The acquisition of performatives prior to speech. Merrill-Palmer Quarterly. 21: 205-226.

Bateson, G. 1955. A theory of play and fantasy. Psychiatric Research Reports. 2: 39-51.

Bateson, G. 1956. The message "This is play." In: Schaffner, B., ed. Group processes. New York, NY: Macy Foundation: 145-246.

Beach, F. A. 1945. Current concepts of play in animals. American Naturalist. 79: 523-541.

Bearison, D. J.; Cassel, T. Z. 1975. Cognitive decentration and social codes: communicative effectiveness in young children from differing family contexts. Developmental Psychology. 11: 29-36.

Bekoff, M. 1972. The development of social interaction, play, and metacommunication in mammals: an ethological perspective. Quarterly Review of Biology. 47: 412-434.

Bekoff, M. 1974. Social play in mammals. American Zoologist. 14: 265-436.

Bekoff, M. 1977. Mammalian dispersal and the ontogeny of individual behavioral phenotypes. American Naturalist. 111: 715-732.

Bennett, E. L. 1976. Cerebral effects of differential experience and training. In: Rosenzweig, M. R.; Bennett, E. L., eds. Neural mechanisms of learning and memory. Cambridge, MA: MIT Press: 279-287.

Berger, M. E. 1972. Population structure of olive baboons in the Laikipia district of Kenya. East African Wildlife Journal. 10: 159-164.

Berlyne, D. E. 1960. Conflict, arousal, and curiosity. New York, NY: McGraw-Hill. 350 p.

Bernstein, I. S. 1962. Response to nesting materials of wild born and captive born chimpanzees. Animal Behavior. 10: 1-6.

Bingham, H. C. 1929. Parental play of chimpanzees. Journal of Mammalogy. 8: 77-89.

Birch, H. G. 1945a. The relation of previous experience to insightful problem-solving. Journal of Comparative Psychology. 38: 367-383.

Birch, H. G. 1945b. The role of motivational factors in insightful problem-solving. Journal of Comparative Psychology. 38: 295-317.

Bishop, D. W.; Chace, C. A. 1971. Parental conceptual systems, home play environment and potential creativity in children. Journal of Experimental Child Psychology. 12: 318-338.

Bloor, C. M.; Leon, A. S. 1970. Interaction of age and exercise on the heart and its blood supply. Laboratory Investigations. 22: 160-165.

Bolig, R. 1980. The relationship of personality factors to responses to hospitalization in young children admitted for medical procedures. Columbus, OH: The Ohio State University. 130 p. Ph.D. dissertation.

Bopp, J. 1967. A hospital play program, unrestricted visiting and rooming-in: their effects upon children's post-hospital behavior. East Lansing, MI: Michigan State University. 146 p. Ph.D. dissertation.

Borke, H. 1973. Interpersonal perception of young children: egocentrism or empathy? Developmental Psychology. 9: 102-108.

Bourliere, F.; Hunkeler, C.; Bertrand, M. 1970. Ecology and behavior of Lowe's guenon in the Ivory Coast. In: Napier, J. R.; Napier, P. H., eds. Old world monkeys: evolution, systematics, and behavior. New York, NY: Academic Press: 297-350.

Brainard, P. P. 1930. The mentality of the child compared with that of the apes. Journal of Genetic Psychology. 37: 268-293.

Brownlee, A. 1954. Play in domestic cattle: an analysis of its nature. British Veterinary Journal. 110: 48-68.

Bruner, J. S. 1972. Nature and uses of immaturity. American Psychologist. 27: 687-708.

Bruner, J. S. 1973. Organization of early skilled action. Child Development. 44: 1-11.

Bruner, J. S. 1974. Child's play. New Scientist. 62: 126-128.

Bruner, J. S. 1977. Early social interaction and language acquisition. In: Schaffer, H. R., ed. Studies in mother-infant interaction. London: Academic Press.

Bruner, J. S. 1983. The legacy of Nicholas Hobbs: research on education and human development in the public interest. Peabody Journal of Education. 60(3): 60-69.

Bruner, J. S.; Sherwood, V. 1976. Peekaboo and the learning of rule structures. In: Bruner; J. S.; Jolly, A.; Sylva, K., eds. Play: its role in development and evolution. New York, NY: Basic Books: 277-285.

Burns, S. M.; Brainerd, C. J. 1979. Effects of constructive and dramatic play on perspective taking in very young children. Developmental Psychology. 15: 512-521.

Byers, M. L. 1972. Play interviews with a five-year-old boy. Maternal-Child Nursing Journal. 1(2): 133-141.

Candland, D. K.; French, J. A.; Johnson, C. N. 1978. Object-play: test of a categorized model by the genesis of object-play in *Macaca fuscata*. In: Smith, E. O., ed. Social play in primates. New York, NY: Academic Press: 259-296.

Carpenter, C. R. 1934. A field study of the behavior and social relations of red howling monkeys. Comparative Psychology Monographs. 10: 1-168.

Carpenter, C. R. 1965. The howlers of Barro Colorado Island. In: DeVore, I., ed. Primate behavior. New York, NY: Holt, Rinehart, & Winston: 250-291.

Cazden, C. 1979. Peekaboo as an instructional model: discourse development at home and school. Papers and Reports on Child Language Development. 17: 1-29.

Chandler, M. J. 1973. Egocentrism and antisocial behavior: the assessment and training of social perspective taking skills. Developmental Psychology. 8: 326-332.

Chepko, B. D. 1971. A preliminary study of the effects of play deprivation on young goats. Zeitschrift Fuer Tierpsychologie. 28: 517-526.

Cheyne, J. A. 1982. Object play and problem-solving: methodological problems and conceptual promise. In: Pepler, D. J.; Rubin, K. H., eds. The play of children: current theory and research. White Plains, NY: S. Karger: 79-96.

Christie, J. F.; Johnson, E. P. 1983. The role of play in social-intellectual development. Review of Educational Research. 53: 93-115.

Christman, M. L. 1979. A look at sociodramatic play among Mexican-American children. Childhood Education. 56: 106-110.

Clark, D. L.; Kreutzberg, J. R.; Chee, F. K. W. 1977. Vestibular stimulation influence on motor development in infants. Science. 196: 1228-1229.

Coie, J.; Kupersmidt, J. 1983. A behavioral analysis of emerging social status in boys' groups. Child Development. 54: 1400-1416.

Collier, R. G. 1979. Developing language through play. Elementary School Journal. 80: 89-92.

Comenius, J. A. 1657. Opera didactica omnia. Amsterdam. (reprinted in 1968, Orbis pictus. New York, NY: Bardeen.)

Connolly, J. A. 1980. The relationship between social pretend play and social competence in preschoolers: correlational and experimental studies. Concordia University. 253 p. Ph.D. dissertation.

Connolly, J. A.; Doyle, A. 1984. Relation of fantasy play to social competence in preschoolers. Developmental Psychology. 20: 797-806.

Damon, W. 1978. The social world of the child. San Francisco, CA: Jossey-Bass. 361 p.

Dansky, J. L. 1980a. Make-believe: a mediator of the relationship between play and associative fluency. Child Development. 51: 576-579.

Dansky, J. L. 1980b. Cognitive consequences of sociodramatic play and exploration training for economically disadvantaged preschoolers. Journal of Child Psychology and Psychiatry. 20: 47-58.

Dansky, J. L.; Silverman, I. W. 1973. Effects of play on associative fluency in preschool-aged children. Developmental Psychology. 9: 38-43.

Dansky, J. L.; Silverman, I. W. 1975. Play: a general facilitator of associative fluency. Developmental Psychology. 11: 104.

Darvill, D. 1982. Effect of play with relevant and non-relevant materials on problem solving. Waterloo, Ontario: University of Waterloo. 151 p. Master's thesis.

Darwin, C. R. 1898. The expression of emotions in man and animals. New York, NY: Appleton.

Delacour, J. 1933. On the Indochinese gibbons. Journal of Mammalogy. 14: 71-73.

Diamond, J. M. 1970. Assembly of species communities. In: Cody, M. L.; Diamond, J. M., eds. Ecology and evolution of communities. Cambridge, MA: Belknap Press of Harvard University Press: 342-444.

Dobzhansky, T. 1962. Mankind evolving. New Haven: Yale University Press. 381 p.

Dodge, K.; Frame, C. 1982. Social cognitive biases and deficits in aggressive boys. Child Development. 53: 620-635.

Dolhinow, P. J. 1971. At play in the fields. Natural History. 80: 66-71.

Dolhinow, P. J.; Bishop, N. 1970. The development of motor skills and social relationships among primates through play. Minnesota Symposium on Child Psychology. 4: 141-198.

Donald, C. H. 1948. Jackals. Journal of Bombay Natural History Society. 47: 721-726.

Dreyer, A.; Rigler, D. 1969. Cognitive performance in Montessori and nursery school children. Journal of Educational Research. 62: 411-416.

Duncan, S. 1972. Some signals and rules for taking speaking turns in conversations. Journal of Personality and Social Psychology. 23: 283-292.

Dunn, J.; Wooding, C. 1977. Play in the home and its implications for learning. In: Tizard, B.; Harvey, D., eds. Biology of play. Philadelphia, PA: Heinemann, London & Lippincott: 45-58.

Durrett, E.; Huffman, W. 1968. Playfulness and divergent thinking among Mexican-American children. Journal of Home Economics. 60: 355-358.

Ekblom, B. 1969. Effect of physical training in adolescent boys. Journal of Applied Physiology. 27: 350-355.

Elder, J. L.; Pederson, D. R. 1978. Preschool children's use of objects in symbolic play. Child Development. 49: 500-504.

Ellis, M. J. 1973. Why people play. Englewood Cliffs, NJ: Prentice-Hall. 173 p.

Emory, G. R. 1975. The patterns of interaction between the young males and group members in captive groups of *Mandrillus sphinx* and *Theropithecus gelada*. Primates. 16: 317-334.

Erikson, E. H. 1958. Play interviews for four-year-old hospitalized children. Monographs of the Society for Research in Child Development. 23(4).

Erikson, E. H. 1963. Childhood and society. New York, NY: W. W. Norton. 445 p.

Erikson, E. H. 1977. Toys and reasons: stages in the ritualization of experience. New York, NY: W. W. Norton. 182 p.

Eriksson, B. 1972. Physical training, oxygen supply and muscle metabolism in 11-13 year old boys. Acta Physiologica Scandinavia. Supplement 384.

Etkin, W. 1967. Social behavior from fish to man. Chicago, IL: University of Chicago Press. 205 p.

Ewer, R. F. 1968. Ethology of mammals. New York, NY: Plenum. 418 p.

Fagen, R. 1976. Exercise, play, and physical training in animals. In: Bateson, P. P. G.; Klopfer, P. H., eds. Perspectives in ethology. vol. 2. New York, NY: Plenum: 189-219.

Fagen, R. 1981. Animal play behavior. New York, NY: Oxford University Press. 684 p.

Fagen, R. 1988. Animal play and phylogenetic diversity of creative minds. Journal of Social and Biological Structures. 11(1): 79-82.

Fein, G. 1975. A transformational analysis of pretending. Developmental Psychology. 11: 291-296.

Feitelson, D. 1959. Some aspects of the social life of Kurdish Jews. Jewish Journal of Sociology. 1: 201-216.

Feitelson, D.; Ross, G. S. 1973. The neglected factor—play. Human Development. 16: 202-223.

Fenson, L.; Ramsay, D. 1980. Decentration and integration of the child's play in the second year. Child Development. 51: 171-178.

Ferchmin, P. A.; Eterovic, V. A. 1977. Brain plasticity and environmental complexity: role of motor skills. Physiological Behavior. 18: 455-461.

Ferchmin, P. A.; Bennett, E. L.; Rosenzweig, M. R. 1975. Direct contact with enriched environment is required to alter cerebral weights in rats. Journal of Comparative and Physiological Psychology. 88: 360-367.

Ferchmin, P. A., Eterovic, V. A.; Levin, L. E. 1980. Genetic learning deficiency does not hinder environment-dependent brain growth. Physiological Biology. 24: 45-50.

Fink, R. S. 1976. Role of imaginative play in cognitive development. Psychological Reports. 39: 895-906.

Freud, A. 1970. The symptomatology of childhood. In: Eissler, R. S.; Freud, A.; Hartmann, H., et al., eds. Psychoanalytic study of the child. Vol. 25. New York, NY: International Universities Press.

Freud, S. 1955. Beyond the pleasure principle. In: Strachey, J., ed. The standard edition of the complete psychological works of Sigmund Freud. Vol. XVIII. London: Hogarth: 7-64.

Garvey, C. 1974. Some properties of social play. Merrill-Palmer Quarterly. 20: 163-180.

Garvey, C. 1977. Play. Cambridge, MA: Harvard University Press. 133 p.

Garvey, C. 1979. Communicational controls in social play. In: Sutton-Smith, B., ed. Play and learning. New York, NY: Gardner Press: 109-126.

Geist, V. 1971. Mountain sheep: a study in behavior and evolution. Chicago, IL: University of Chicago Press. 383 p.

Gilmore, J. B. 1966. Play: a special behavior. In: Haber, R. N., ed. Current research in motivation. New York, NY: Holt, Rinehart & Winston: 343-354.

Golomb, C.; Cornelius, C. B. 1977. Symbolic play and its cognitive significance. Developmental Psychology. 13: 246-252.

Goslin, E. 1978. Hospitalization is a life crisis for the preschool child: a critical review. Journal of Community Health. 3: 321-346.

Gottier, R. F. 1972. Factors affecting agonistic behavior in several subhuman species. Genetic Psychology Monographs. 86: 177-218.

Gould, R. 1972. Child studies through fantasy. New York, NY: Quadrangle. 292 p.

Greenough, W. T. 1978. Development and memory: the synaptic connection. In: Teyler, T., ed. Brain and learning. Stamford, CT: Greylock Publishers: 127-145.

Greif, E. B. 1977. Peer interaction in preschool children. In: Webb, G., ed. Social development in childhood. Baltimore, MD: Johns Hopkins University Press.

Griffiths, R. 1935. The study of imagination in early childhood and its function in mental development. London: Routledge. 367 p.

Groos, K. 1898. The play of animals. New York, NY: D. Appleton & Co. 341 p.

Groos, K. 1901. The play of man. New York, NY: D. Appleton & Co. 412 p.

Guthrie, K.; Hudson, L. M. 1979. Training conservation through symbolic play: a second look. Child Development. 50: 1269-1271.

Hall, D. J. 1977. Social relations and innovation: changing the state of play in hospitals. Boston, MA: Routledge & Kegan Paul. 222 p.

Hall, K. R. L. 1965. Behavior and ecology of the wild patas monkey in Uganda. Journal of Zoology. 148: 15-87.

Hall, K. R. L. 1968. Behavior and ecology of the wild patas monkey in Uganda. In: Jay, P., ed. Primates: studies in adaptation and variability. New York, NY: Holt, Rinehart & Winston: 32-120.

Harlow, H. F. 1963. Basic social capacity of primates. In: Southwick, C. H., ed. Primate social behavior. Princeton, NJ: D. Van Nostrand Co.: 153-160.

Harlow, H. F. 1966. Learning to love. American Scientist. 54: 244-272.

Harlow, H. F. 1969. Age-mate or peer affectional systems. In: Lehrman, D. S.; Hinde, R. A.; Shaw, E., eds. Advances in the study of behavior. Vol. 2. New York, NY: Academic Press: 334-384.

Harlow, H. F.; Harlow, M. K. 1965. The affectional systems. Behavior of Nonhuman Primates. 2: 287-334.

Harlow, H. F.; Harlow, M. K.; Suomi, S. 1971. From thought to therapy: lessons from a primate laboratory. American Scientist. 59: 538-549.

Hartup, W. 1978. Peer relations and the growth of social competence. In: Kent, M. W.; Rolf, J. E., eds. The primary prevention of psychopathology. Vol. 3. Hanover: University Press of New England.

Hedhammer, A.; Wu, F.-M.; Krook, L., et al. 1974. Overnutrition and skeletal disease: an experimental study in growing Great Dane dogs. Cornell Veterinarians. 64, Supplement 5.

Hinde, R. A. 1971. Development of social behavior. Behavior of Nonhuman Primates. 3: 1-68.

Hobhouse, L. T. 1901. Mind in evolution. London: MacMillan. 415 p.

Hodapp, R. M. 1982. Effects of hospitalization on young children: implications of two theories. Children's Health Care. 10: 83-86.

Horr, D. A. 1977. Orang-utan maturation: growing up in a female world. In: Chevalier-Skolnikoff, S.; Poirier, F. E., eds. Primate biosocial development. New York, NY: Garland: 289-321.

Hughes, M.; Hutt, C. 1979. Heart-rate correlates of childhood activities: play, exploration, problem-solving and daydreaming. Biological Psychology. 8: 253-263.

Huizinga, J. 1955. Homo ludens. New York, NY: Beacon. 229 p.

Hutt, C. 1966. Exploration and play in children. Symposium of the Royal Zoological Society of London. 18: 23-44.

Hutt, C. 1967. Temporal effects on response decrement and stimulus satiation in exploration. British Journal of Psychology. 58: 365-373.

Hutt, C. 1970. Specific and diversive exploration. Advances in Child Development and Behavior. 5: 119-180.

Hutt, C. 1976. Exploration and play in children. In: Bruner, J. S.; Jolly, A.; Sylva, K., eds. Play: its role in development and evolution. New York, NY: Basic Books: 202-215.

Hutt, C. 1979. Exploration and play. In: Sutton-Smith, B., ed. Play and learning. New York, NY: Gardner Press: 175-194.

Hutt, C. 1982. Towards a taxonomy and conceptual model of play. In: Hutt, C.; Rogers, J.; Hutt, S. J., eds. Developmental processes in early childhood. London: Routledge & Kegan Paul.

Hutt, C.; Bhavnani, R. 1976. Predictions from play. Nature. 237: 171-172.

Iannotti, R. J. 1978. Effects of role-taking experiences on role taking, empathy, altruism, and aggression. Developmental Psychology. 14: 119-124.

Jackowitz, E.; Watson, M. 1980. Development of object transformations in early pretend play. Developmental Psychology. 16: 543-549.

Jackson, T. A. 1942. Use of the stick as a tool by young chimpanzees. Journal of Comparative Psychology. 34: 223-235.

Jay, P. 1963. Mother-infant relations in langurs. In: Rheingold, H. L., ed. Maternal behavior in mammals. New York, NY: Wiley: 282-304.

Jeffree, D.; McConkey, R. 1976. Observation scheme for recording children's imaginative doll play. Journal of Child Psychology and Psychiatry. 17: 189-197.

Johnson, J. E. 1976. The relations of divergent thinking and intelligence test scores with social and nonsocial make-believe play of preschool children. Child Development. 47: 1200-1203.

Johnson, J. E.; Ershler, J. 1982. Curricular effects on the play of preschoolers. In: Pepler, D. J.; Rubin, K. H., eds. The play of children: current theory and research. Basel, Switzerland: S. Karger: 130-143.

Johnson, J. M. 1969. The effects of a play program on hospitalized children. Columbus, OH: The Ohio State University. 97 p. Master's thesis.

Jolly, A. 1972. Troop continuity and troop spacing in *Propithecus verreauxi* and *Lemur catta* at Berenty. Folia Primatologica. 17: 335-362.

Kahn, J. V. 1975. Relationship of Piaget's sensorimotor period to language acquisition of profoundly retarded children. American Journal of Mental Deficiency. 6: 640-643.

Kawai, M. 1965. Newly acquired pre-cultural behavior of the natural troop of Japanese monkeys on Koshima Island. Primates. 6: 1-30.

Kluver, H. 1937. Re-examination of implement-using behavior in a Cebus monkey after an interval of three years. Acta Psychologie. 2: 347-397.

Knappen, P. 1930. Play instinct in gulls. Auk. 47: 551-552.

Kogan, N. 1983. Stylistic variation in childhood and adolescence: creativity, metaphor, and cognitive style. In: Flavell, J.; Markman, E., eds. Handbook of child psychology. Vol. 3. New York, NY: Wiley: 630-706.

Kogan, N.; Morgan, F. T. 1969. Task and motivational influences on the assessment of creative and intellective ability in children. Genetic Psychology Monographs. 80: 91-127.

Kohler, W. 1925. The mentality of apes. New York, NY: Harcourt Brace. 342 p.

Kummer, H. 1968. Two variations in the social organization of baboons. In: Jay, P. C., ed. Primates: studies in adaptation and variability. New York, NY: Holt, Rinehart & Winston: 293-312.

Largo, R. H.; Howard, J. A. 1979. Developmental progression in play behavior of children between nine and thirty months. II. Spontaneous play and language development. Developmental Medical Child Neurology. 21: 492-503.

Lehman, H. C.; Witty, P. Z. 1927. The psychology of play activities. New York, NY: Barnes. 242 p.

Levin, H.; Wardwell, E. 1962. The research uses of doll play. Psychological Bulletin. 59: 27-56.

Levy, J. 1977. Play behavior. New York, NY: Wiley. 232 p.

Li, A. K. F. 1978. Effects of play on novel responses of preschool children. Alberta Journal of Educational Research. 24: 31-36.

Lieberman, J. N. 1965. Playfulness and divergent thinking: an investigation of their relationship at the kindergarten level. Journal of Genetic Psychology. 107: 219-224.

Ling, B. C. 1946. The solving of problem-situations by the preschool child. Journal of Genetic Psychology. 68: 3-28.

Loizos, C. 1966. Play in mammals. Symposium of the Royal Zoological Society of London. 18: 1-9.

Loizos, C. 1967. Play behaviour in higher primates: a review. In: Morris, D., ed. Primate ethology. Chicago, IL: Aldine: 176-218.

Lorenz, K. Z. 1956. Plays and vacuum activities. In: Autuori, M., et al., eds. L'instinct dans le comportement des animaux et de l'homme. Paris: Masson et Cie.: 633-645.

Lorenz, K. Z. 1970. Studies in animal and human behavior. Vol. 1. Cambridge, MA: Harvard University Press.

Lorenz, K. Z. 1971. Studies in animal and human behavior. Vol. 2. Cambridge, MA: Harvard University Press.

Lovell, K.; Hoyle, H. W.; Siddall, M. Q. 1968. A study of some aspects of the play and language of young children with delayed speech. Journal of Child Psychology and Psychiatry. 9: 41-50.

Lovinger, S. L. 1974. Sociodramatic play and language development in preschool disadvantaged children. Psychology in the Schools. 11: 313-320.

Lowe, M.; Costello, A. 1976. Manual for the symbolic play test; experimental edition. London: NFER. 245 p.

MacKinnon, J. 1971. The orangutan in Sabah today. Oryx. 11: 141-191.

Markey, F. 1935. Imaginative behavior of young children. Child Development Monographs. 18. 139 p.

Marshall, H. 1961. Relations between home experiences and children's use of language in play interactions with peers. Psychological Monographs. 75: 2-77.

Mason, W. A. 1961. The effects of social restriction on the behavior of rhesus monkeys. I. Free social behavior. Journal of Comparative Physiological Psychology. 54: 287-290.

Mason, W. A. 1963. The effects of environmental restriction on the social development of rhesus monkeys. In: Southwick, C. H., ed. Primate social behavior. Princeton, NJ: D. Van Nostrand: 161-173.

Mason, W. A. 1965. The social development of monkeys and apes. In: DeVore, I., ed. Primate behavior. New York, NY: Holt, Rinehart & Winston: 514-543.

Mason, W. A. 1967. Motivational aspects of social responsiveness in young chimpanzees. In: Stevenson, H. W., ed. Early behavior: comparative and developmental approaches. New York, NY: Wiley: 103-126.

Matheson, E. 1931. A study of problem solving behavior in preschool children. Child Development. 2: 242-262.

Matthews, W. S. 1977. Modes of transformation in the initiation of fantasy play. Developmental Psychology. 13: 212-216.

Matthews, W. S. 1978. Sex and familiarity effects upon the proportion of time young children spend in spontaneous fantasy play. Journal of Genetic Psychology. 133: 9-12.

McCune-Nicolich, L. 1981. Toward symbolic functioning: structure of early pretend games and potential parallels with language. Child Development. 52: 785-797.

McCune-Nicolich, L.; Bruskin, C. 1982. Combinatorial competency in symbolic play and language. In: Pepler, D. J.; Rubin, K. H., eds. The play of children: Current theory and research: White Plains, NY: S. Karger: 30-45.

McGrew, W. C. 1977. Socialization and object manipulation of wild chimpanzees. In: Chevalier-Skolnikoff, S.; Poirier, F. E., eds. Primate biosocial development: biological, social and ecological determinants. New York, NY: Garland: 261-288.

Mead, M. 1932. An investigation of the thought of primitive children with special reference to animism. Journal of the Royal Anthropological Institute. 62: 173-190.

Menzel, E. W. Jr.; Davenport, R. K. Jr.; Rogers, C. M. 1970. The development of tool using in wild-born and restriction-reared chimpanzees. Folia Primatologica. 12: 273-283.

Moriya, M. 1937a. An observation of problem-solving behavior in preschool children. I. Application of the principle of the lever. Japanese Journal of Experimental Psychology. 4: 63-81.

Moriya, M. 1937b. An observation of problem-solving behavior in preschool children. II. Aplication of the principle of the lever (continued). Japanese Journal of Experimental Psychology. 4: 147-160.

Muller-Schwarze, D. 1968. Play deprivation in deer. Behaviour. 31: 144-162.

Muller-Schwarze, D. 1971. Ludic behavior in young mammals. In: Sterman, M. B.; McGinty, D. J.; Adinolfi, A. M., eds. Brain development and behavior. New York, NY: Academic Press: 229-249.

Muller-Schwarze, D. 1978. Evolution of play behavior. Stroudsburg, PA: Dowden, Hutchinson & Ross. 396 p.

Murphy, L. B. 1956. Personality in young children. Vol. 1. New York, NY: Basic Books.

Mussen, P.; Eisenberg-Berg, N. 1977. Roots of caring, sharing and helping. San Francisco, CA: Freeman. 212 p.

Nance, J. 1975. The gentle Tasaday: a Stone Age people in the Philippine rain forest. New York, NY: Harcourt Brace Jovanovich. 465 p.

Neill, S. 1976. Aggressive and non-aggressive fighting in twelve- to thirteen-year-old pre-adolescent boys. Journal of Child Psychology and Psychiatry. 17: 213-220.

Nicolich, L. M. 1977. Beyond sensorimotor intelligence: assessment of symbolic maturity through analysis of pretend play. Merrill-Palmer Quarterly. 23: 89-101.

Noble, E. 1967. Play and the sick child. London: Farber & Farber. 165 p.

Nolte, A. 1955. Field observations on the daily routine and social behaviour of common Indian monkeys, with special reference to the bonnet monkey. Journal of Bombay Natural Historical Society. 53: 177-184.

Nunnally, J. C.; Lemond, L. C. 1973. Exploratory behavior and human development. In: Reese, H., ed. Advances in child development and behavior. Vol. 8. New York, NY: Academic Press.

Pellegrini, A. D. 1988. Elementary-school children's rough-and-tumble play and social competence. Developmental Psychology. 24(6): 802-806.

Pellegrini, A. D.; Galda, L. 1982. The effects of thematic fantasy play on the development of children's story comprehension. American Educational Research Journal. 19: 443-452.

Peller, L. E. 1971. Models of children's play. In: Herron, R. E.; Sutton-Smith, B., eds. Child's play. New York, NY: Wiley: 110-125.

Pepler, D. J. 1979. The effects of play on convergent and divergent problem solving. Waterloo, Ontario: University of Waterloo. 243 p. Ph.D. dissertation.

Pepler, D. J. 1982. Play and divergent thinking. In: Pepler, D. J.; Rubin, K. H., eds. The play of children: current theory and research. White Plains, New York: S. Karger: 64-78.

Pepler, D. J.; Ross, H. S. 1981. The effects of play on convergent and divergent problem solving. Child Development. 52: 1202-1210.

Peterson, R. S.; Bartholomew, G. A. 1967. The natural history and behavior of the California sea lion. American Society of Mammalogists, Special Publication No. 1. 79 p.

Piaget, J. 1926. The language and thought of the child. New York, NY: Harcourt Brace. 246 p.

Piaget, J. 1932. The moral judgment of the child. New York: Free Press. 410 p.

Piaget, J. 1951. Play, dreams and imitation in childhood. New York, NY: W. W. Norton. 296 p.

Piaget, J. 1970. Piaget's theory. In: Mussen, P. H., ed. Carmichael's manual of child psychology. Vol. 1. New York, NY: Wiley.

Plato. 1926. Laws. Bury, R. G. tr. two vols. (Loeb Classical Library, 9.) Cambridge, MA: Harvard University Press.

Poirier, F. E. 1969. Behavioral flexibility and intertroop variation among Nilgiri langurs of South India. Folia Primatologica. 11: 119-133.

Poirier, F. E. 1970. The communication matrix of the Nilgiri langur of South India. Folia Primatologica. 13: 92-136.

Poirier, F. E. 1972. Primate socialization. New York, NY: Random House. 260 p.

Poirier, F. E.; Smith, E. O. 1974. Socializing functions of primate play. American Zoologist. 14: 275-287.

Poole, T. B. 1978. An analysis of social play in polecats with comments on the form and evolutionary history of the open mouth play face. Animal Behavior. 26: 36-49.

Poupa, O.; Raksuan, K.; Ostadal, B. 1970. The effect of physical activity upon the heart of vertebrates. Medicine in Sport Science. 4: 202-233.

Prugh, D.; Staub, E.; Sands, H., et al. 1953. A study of the emotional reactions of children and families to hospitalization and illness. American Journal of Orthopsychiatry. 23: 70-106.

Pulaski, M. A. 1973. Toys and imaginative play. In: Singer, J. L., ed. The child's world of make-believe. New York, NY: Academic Press: 74-103.

Quinn, J. M.; Rubin, K. H. 1984. The play of handicapped children. In: Yawkey, T. D.; Pellegrini, A. D., eds. Child's play: developmental and applied. Hillsdale, NJ: Lawrence Erlbaum Associates: 63-80.

Reynolds, P. C. 1972. Play and the evolution of language. New Haven, CT: Yale University. 170 p. Ph.D. dissertation.

Richardson, H. M. 1932. The growth of adaptive behavior in infants: an experimental study of seven age levels. Genetic Psychology Monographs. 12: 195-359.

Richardson, H. M. 1934. The adaptive behavior of infants in the utilization of the lever as a tool: a developmental and experimental study. Journal of Genetic Psychology. 44: 352-377.

Roberts, B. 1934. Notes on the birds of central and southeast Iceland, with special reference to food habits. Ibis. 4: 239-264.

Rosen, C. E. 1974. The effects of sociodramatic play on problem solving behavior among culturally disadvantaged preschool children. Child Development. 45: 920-927.

Rosenblatt, J. S. 1977. Developmental trends in infant play. In: Tizard, B.; Harvey, O., eds. Biology of play. Philadelphia, PA: Heinemann, London & Lippincott: 33-44.

Rosenblum, L. A. 1961. The development of social behavior in the rhesus monkey. Madison, WI: University of Wisconsin. 134 p. Ph.D. dissertation.

Rosenzweig, M. L. 1966. Environmental complexity, cerebral change, and behavior. American Psychologist. 21: 321-332.

Rosenzweig, M. L. 1971. Role of experience in development of neurophysiological regulatory mechanisms and in organization of the brain. In: Walcher, D. N.; Peters, D. L., eds. The development of self-regulatory mechanisms. New York, NY: Academic Press: 15-33.

Rosenzweig, M. L.; Bennett, E. L. 1976. Enriched environments: facts, factors, and fantasies. In: Petrinovich, L.; McGaugh, J. L., eds. Knowing, thinking and believing. New York, NY: Plenum Press: 179-213.

Rosenzweig, M. L.; Bennett, E. L. 1977a. Effects of environmental enrichment or impoverishment on learning and on brain values in rodents. In: Oliverio, A., ed. Genetics, environment and intelligence. New York, NY: Elsevier North-Holland: 163-196.

Rosenzweig, M. L.; Bennett, E. L. 1977b. Experiential influences on brain anatomy and brain chemistry in rodents. In: Gottlieb, G., ed. Studies on the development of behavior and the nervous system. Vol. 4, Early influences. New York, NY: Academic Press: 289-327.

Rosenzweig, M. L.; Bennett, E. L.; Hebert, M.; Morimoto, H. 1978. Social grouping cannot account for cerebral effects of enriched environments. Brain Research. 153: 563-376.

Rosenzweig, M. L.; Love, W.; Bennett, E. L. 1968. Effects of a few hours a day of enriched experience on brain chemistry and brain weights. Physiological Behavior. 3: 819-825.

Roth, F. P.; Clark, D. M. 1987. Symbolic play and social participation abilities of language-impaired and normally developing children. Journal of Speech and Hearing Disorders. 52: 17-29.

Rubin, K. H. 1976. The relationships of social play preference to role taking skills in preschool children. Psychological Reports. 39: 823-826.

Rubin, K. H. 1978. Role-taking in childhood: some methodological considerations. Child Development. 49: 428-433.

Rubin, K. H. 1980. Fantasy play: its role in the development of social skills and social cognition. New Directions in Child Development. 9: 69-84.

Rubin, K. H.; Maioni, T. L. 1975. Play preferences and its relationship to egocentrism, popularity, and classification skills in preschoolers. Merrill-Palmer Quarterly. 21: 171-178.

Rubin, K. H.; Pepler, D. J. 1980. The relationship of child's play to social-cognitive growth and development. In: Foot, H.; Chapman, T.; Smith, J., eds. Friendship and social relationships. London: Wiley: 209-233.

Rubin, K. H.; Schneider, F. W. 1973. The relationship between moral judgment, egocentrism, and altruistic behavior. Child Development. 44: 661-665.

Rubin, K. H.; Fein, G.; Vandenberg, B. 1983. Play. In: Hetherington, E. M., ed. Handbook of child psychology. Vol. IV - Socialization, personality, and social development. New York, NY: Wiley: 694-774.

Rubin, K. H.; Maioni, T. L.; Hornung, M. 1976. Free play behaviors in middle- and lower-class preschoolers: Parten and Piaget revisited. Child Development. 47: 414-419.

Saltz, E.; Johnson, J. 1974. Training for thematic-fantasy play in culturally disadvantaged children: preliminary results. Journal of Educational Psychology. 66: 623-630.

Saltz, E.; Dixon, D.; Johnson, J. 1977. Training disadvantaged preschoolers on various fantasy activities: effects on cognitive functioning and impulse control. Child Development. 48: 367-380.

Sarnoff, C. 1976. Latency. New York, NY: Aronson. 402 p.

Schaefer, C. E. 1976. Therapeutic use of child's play. New York, NY: Aronson. 684 p.

Schaefer, C. E.; O'Connor, K. J. 1983. Handbook of play therapy. New York, NY: Wiley. 489 p.

Schaller, G. B. 1963. The mountain gorilla: ecology and behavior. Chicago, IL: University of Chicago Press. 431 p.

Schiller, F. 1875. Essays, aesthetical and philosophical. London: Bell and Sons. 297 p.

Schiller, P. H. 1952. Innate constituents of complex responses in primates. Psychological Review. 59: 177-191.

Schiller, P. H. 1957. Innate motor action as a basis of learning: manipulative patterns in the chimpanzee. In: Schiller, C. M., ed. Instinctive behaviour. New York: International Universities Press: 264-287.

Schwartzman, H. B. 1978. Transformations: the anthropology of children's play. New York, NY: Plenum Press. 380 p.

Shantz, C. U. 1975. The development of social cognition. In: Hetherington, E. M., ed. Review of child development research. Vol. 5. Chicago, IL: University of Chicago Press.

Shore, C.; O'Connell, B.; Bates, E. 1984. First sentences in language and symbolic play. Developmental Psychology. 20: 872-880.

Sigel, I. E.; McBane, B. 1967. Cognitive competence and level of symbolization among five-year-old children. In: Helmuth, J., ed. Disadvantaged child. Vol. I. New York, NY: Brunner-Mazel.

Sigman, M.; Ungerer, J. 1981. Sensorimotor skills and language comprehension in autistic children. Journal of Abnormal Child Psychology. 9: 149-165.

Silvern, S. B. 1980. Play, pictures, and repetition: Mediators in aural prose learning. Educational Communication and Technology. 28: 134-139.

Silvern, S. B.; Williamson, P. A.; Waters, B. 1982. Play as a mediator in comprehension: an alternative to play training. Educational Research Quarterly. 7(3): 16-21.

Simon, T.; Smith, P. K. 1983. The study of play and problem-solving in preschool children: have experimenter effects been responsible for previous results? British Journal of Developmental Psychology. 1: 289-297.

Simon T.; Smith, P. K. 1985. Play and problem-solving: a paradigm questioned. Merrill-Palmer Quarterly. 31: 265-277.

Singer, J. L. 1973. The child's world of make-believe: experimental studies of imaginative play. New York, NY: Academic Press. 294 p.

Singer, J. L.; Rummo, J. 1973. Ideational creativity and behavioral style in kindergarten aged children. Developmental Psychology. 8: 154-161.

Smilansky, S. 1968. The effects of sociodramatic play on disadvantaged preschool children. New York, NY: John Wiley. 164 p.

Smith, E. O. 1978. A historical view of the study of play: statement of the problem. In: Smith, E. O., ed. Social play in primates. New York, NY: Academic Press: 1-32.

Smith, P. K. 1977. Social and fantasy play in young children. In: Tizard, B.; Harvey, D., eds. Biology of play. Philadelphia, PA: Heinemann, London & Lippincott: 123-145.

Smith, P. K. 1982. Does play matter? Functional and evolutionary aspects of animal and human play. Behavioural and Brain Sciences. 5: 139-184.

Smith, P. K.; Dodsworth, C. 1978. Social class differences in the fantasy play of preschool children. Journal of Genetic Psychology. 133: 183-190.

Smith, P. K.; Dutton, S. 1979. Play and training in direct and innovative problem-solving. Child Development. 50: 830-836.

Smith, P. K.; Simon, T. 1984. Object play, problem-solving and creativity in children. In: Smith, P. K., ed. Play in animals and humans. Oxford: Blackwell. 334 p.

Smith, P. K.; Syddall, S. 1978. Play and non-play tutoring in preschool children: Is it play or tutoring which matters? British Journal of Educational Psychology. 48: 315-325.

Smith, P. K.; Whitney, S. 1987. Play and associative fluency: Experimenter findings may be responsible for previous positive findings. Developmental Psychology. 23(1): 49-53.

Smith, P. K.; Dalgliesh, M.; Herzmark, G. 1981. A comparison of the effects of fantasy play tutoring and skills tutoring in nursery classes. International Journal of Behavioural Development. 4: 421-441.

Smith, P. K.; Simon, T.; Emberton, R. 1985. Play, problem solving and experimenter effects: a replication of Simon & Smith (1983). British Journal of Developmental Psychology. 3: 105-107.

Smith, W. J. 1977. The behavior of communicating. Cambridge, MA: Harvard University Press. 545 p.

Spencer, H. 1873. Principles of psychology. New York, NY: D. Appleton.

Spivack, G.; Shure, M. B. 1974. Social adjustment of young children. San Francisco, CA: Jossey-Bass. 212 p.

Stacey, M.; Dearden, R.; Pill, R.; Robinson, D. 1970. Hospitals, children, and their families. Boston, MA: Routledge & Kegan Paul. 188 p.

Steckol, K.; Leonard, L. 1981. Sensorimotor development and the use of prelinguistic performatives. Journal of Speech and Hearing Research. 24(2): 262-268.

Stevenson, M. F. 1976. Behavioural observations on groups of Callithricidae with an emphasis on playful behaviour. Jersey Wildlife Preservation Trust 13th Annual Report. 47-52.

Stoner, E. A. 1947. Anna hummingbirds at play. Condor. 49: 36.

Sugiyama, Y. 1965. Behavioral development and social structure in two troops of hanuman langurs. Primates. 6: 213-247.

Suomi, S. J.; Harlow, H. F. 1971. Monkeys at play. Natural History. 80: 72-75.

Sutton-Smith, B. 1967. The role of play in cognitive development. Young Children. 22: 361-370.

Sutton-Smith, B. 1968. The folkgames of American children. In: Coffin, T., ed. Our living traditions: an introduction to American folklore. New York, NY: Basic Books.

Sylva, K. 1974. The relationship between play and problem solving in children 3-5 years old. Cambridge, MA: Harvard University. 144 p. Ph.D. dissertation.

Sylva, K. 1977. Play and learning. In: Tizard, B.; Harvey, D., eds. Biology of play. Philadelphia, PA: Heinemann, London & Lippincott: 59-73.

Sylva, K.; Bruner, J. S.; Genova, P. 1976. The role of play in the problem-solving of children 3-5 years old. In: Bruner, J. S.; Jolly, A.; Sylva, K., eds. Play: its role in development and evolution. New York, NY: Basic Books: 244-260.

Symmonds, P. 1946. The dynamics of human adjustment. New York, NY: D. Appleton-Century. 666 p.

Symons, D. 1974. Aggressive play and communication in rhesus monkeys. American Zoologist. 14: 317-322.

Symons, D. 1978a. Play and aggression: a study of rhesus monkeys. Irvington, NY: Columbia University Press. 246 p.

Symons, D. 1978b. The question of function: dominance and play. In: Smith, E. O., ed. Social play in primates. New York, NY: Academic Press: 193-230.

Taylor, C. R. 1978. Why change gaits? Recruitment of muscles and muscle fibers as a function of speed and gait. American Zoologist. 18: 153-161.

Teleki, G. 1973. The predatory behavior of wild chimpanzees. Lewisberg, PA: Bucknell University Press. 232 p.

Terrell, B. Y.; Schwartz, R. G.; Prelock, P.; Messick, C. K. 1984. Symbolic play in normal and language impaired children. Journal of Speech and Hearing Research. 27: 424-429.

Thorndike, E. L. 1901. The mental life of monkeys. Psychological Review Monographs. 3: 57.

Tisza, V.; Hurwitz, I.; Angoff, K. 1970. The use of a play program by hospitalized children. Journal of the American Academy of Child Psychiatry. 9: 515-531.

Tizard, B., Philps, J.; Plewis, I. 1976. Play in preschool centers. II. Effects on play of the child's social class and of the educational orientation of the center. Journal of Child Psychology and Psychiatry. 17: 265-274.

Tolman, E. C. 1932. Purposive behavior in animals and man. New York, NY: Century Co. 463 p.

Tomanek, R. J. 1970. Effects of age and exercise on the extent of the myocardial capillary bed. Anatomical Record. 167: 55-62.

Torrance, E. P. 1961. Priming creative thinking in the primary grades. Elementary School Journal. 62: 139-145.

van Lawick-Goodall, J. 1968. A preliminary report on expressive movements and communication in the Gombe Stream chimpanzees. In: Jay, P. C., ed. Primates: studies in adaptation and variability. New York, NY: Holt, Rinehart & Winston: 313-374.

van Lawick-Goodall, J.. 1970. Tool-using in primates and other vertebrates. Advances in the Study of Behavior. 3: 195-249.

Vandenberg, B. 1978a. Play and development from an ethological perspective. American Psychologist. 33: 724-738.

Veneziano, E. 1981. Early language and nonverbal representation: A reassessment. Journal of Child Language. 8: 541-563.

Vygotsky, L. S. 1967. Play and its role in the mental development of the child. Soviet Psychology. 5: 5-18.

Wallach, M. A.; Kogan, N. 1965. Modes of thinking in young children. New York, NY: Holt, Rinehart & Winston. 357 p.

Watson, M. W.; Fischer, K. W. 1977. A developmental sequence of agent use in late infancy. Child Development. 48: 828-836.

Wehman, P. 1977. Helping the mentally retarded acquire play skills. Springfield, IL: Charles C. Thomas. 231 p.

Weisler, A.; McCall, R. B. 1976. Exploration and play: resume and redirection. American Psychologist. 31: 492-508.

Werner, H.; Kaplan, B. 1963. Symbol formation. New York, NY: Wiley. 530 p.

West, M. 1974. Social play in the domestic cat. American Zoologist. 14: 415-426.

Williams, T. M.; Fleming, J. W. 1969. Methodological study of the relationship between associative fluency and intelligence. Developmental Psychology. 1: 155-162.

Wilson, E. O. 1971. The insect societies. Cambridge, MA: The Belknap Press of Harvard University Press. 548 p.

Wilson, E. O. 1975. Sociobiology. Cambridge, MA: The Belknap Press of Harvard University Press. 697 p.

Wilson, S.; Kleiman, D. 1974. Eliciting play: a comparative study. American Zoologist. 14: 341-370.

Wohlwill, J. F. 1987. Introduction. In: Gorlitz, D.; Wohlwill, J. F., eds. Curiosity, imagination, and play: on the development of spontaneous cognitive and motivational processes. Hillsdale, NJ: Lawrence Erlbaum: 2-21.

Yerkes R. M. 1927. The mind of a gorilla. Genetic Psychology Monographs. 2(1 and 2): 1-193.

Mood as a Product of Leisure: Causes and Consequences

R. Bruce Hull, IV
Center for Urban Affairs
College of Architecture
Texas A & M University
College Station, Texas

INTRODUCTION

If any agreement concerning the nature of leisure exists, it is the common belief that leisure is a positive experience accompanied by satisfying and pleasurable moods, emotions, or feelings (Mannell 1980: 77).

The purpose of this paper is to demonstrate that mood is both a prevalent and a relevant product of leisure activities, worthy of management and study. The causes and consequences of mood are neither irrational nor intangible, despite some misconceptions to the contrary. Rather, mood is a predictable, measurable, and theoretically grounded product of leisure activities. Mood, in fact, may be one of the more relevant products of leisure management efforts.

The discussion which follows is not exhaustive, but rather attempts to frame the work on leisure-induced mood which is just now beginning in earnest. When possible, the findings and theories presented here are interpreted in the context of leisure and outdoor recreation, but many examples and interpretations are of a more general nature. Throughout the paper "R" is used to denote recreationist. The term "mood" is used to denote a specific set of subjective feelings which occur as a consequence of everyday leisure experiences (i.e., excitement, relaxation, awe, happiness). A detailed definition of mood is developed later in the chapter.

MOOD AS A PRODUCT OF LEISURE

Mood theory helps better understand the intrinsically rewarding feelings which characterize the experiential quality of leisure. Through use of mood theory and by explicitly researching specific moods rather than the more general phenomena of "feeling good" or "having fun," we may begin to better understand leisure. An analogy to the health fields helps illustrate the merit of being reductionist and focusing on specific moods which characterize a leisure experience. There are numerous aspects of human health: cardiovascular, immunal, skeletal, muscular, mental, and so on. To study one global concept such as "health" would constrain efforts to understand, predict, and manage these phenomena since the different aspects of health, although interrelated, respond differently to treatments and operate within different systems requiring different theories and experimental procedures.

Another advantage of explicitly studying leisure-induced mood is that mood has relevant and long lasting consequences on such things as the immune system, cognitive skills, and helping behavior. Thus, leisure and its consequent moods should be viewed as socially relevant and deserving of public attention. There is much more to leisure than having a good time. Ignoring the intricacies of leisure-induced mood limits our ability to focus research questions and foregoes an opportunity to demonstrate social relevance.

That recreationists experience moods becomes obvious when reading personal accounts of environmental experiences (e.g., Abbey 1961, Lopez 1986). These writers are inspirational in their introspective accounts of the mood they experience while at leisure. This intuitive, introspective evidence is supported by a limited but growing number of empirical and theoretical findings. For example, Shaffer and Mietz (1969) found that mood and aesthetic experiences were the primary reasons Rs gave for visiting natural areas (similar findings are reported by Hawes 1979 and Klausner 1967). Hammitt (1980) and More and Payne (1978) empirically demonstrated that moods varied as a result of participation in leisure activities. Stone (1987) traced the moods associated with different daily events of 79 persons for over 84 days and found that leisure events were significantly associated with positive and desirable moods; more so than most any other type of daily event. Bishop and Jeanrenaud (1976) found variations in end-of-day mood to be associated with leisure activities respondents participated in during the day. Mannell, Zuzanek, and Larson (1988) reported that leisure activities tend to evoke positive mood states. Ulrich (1983) extended aspects of emotion theory to explain preferences for natural landscapes. Hull and Harvey (in press) suggested that mood experienced in suburban parks covaries with types and amounts of park vegetation and is an important predictor of user preference.

Knopf suggests that the research community has not adequately addressed the leisure/mood relationship. He suggests that mood responses to leisure situations seem to be one of the implicitly agreed upon, commonly acknowledged, but least understood aspects of leisure research. "It would seem improbable that, with the prevailing interest in emotional response to natural environments in all forms of literature, practically no research has been conducted on the topic. But that is certainly the case" (Knopf 1987: 807).

From a more theoretical perspective Gunter (1987) identified eight properties of leisure, five of which seem related to moods (pleasure, enjoyment, fantasy, adventure, spontaneity). Similarly, Mercer (1976) suggested that the quest for excitement (a mood) is a major motivation for leisure pursuits. Elias and Dunning (1969) noted that opportunities to experience and express moods are severely limited in modern society and contend that moods evoked via leisure pursuits are critical to maintaining health and quality

of life. And Csikszentmihalyi (1975) theorizes that "flow" is a character of some leisure experiences: it is suggested here that one quality of "flow" might be a positive mood state. More specific inquiry may reveal specific types of moods which comprise and/or are associated with flow and other aspects of leisure.

These theoretical and empirical studies suggest that mood plays an important role in leisure experiences. However, it is unclear precisely what this role is and the extent of its impacts. Nonetheless, there can be little doubt that it is a salient product of most leisure experiences. Thus, it seems an important area for study. The following sections define mood in some detail in order to facilitate a more rigorous discussion of the topic as it pertains to leisure.

DEFINITION OF MOOD

Mood has been the focus of inquiry, speculation, and debate perhaps for as long as man has pondered his existence. Notable past contributors include Aristotle, Darwin, Dewey, Freud, William James, Kant, and Wundt. The works of these scholars, and the more recent scholars cited in this chapter, have not produced consensus. Most agree that mood consists of behavioral, physiological, and cognitive processes but there is considerable debate about the specific role of and interaction among these processes. The *behavioral* component of mood includes communication (i.e., facial expression), action (i.e., fight or flight), motoric responses, and attention. Several theorists (e.g., Izard 1971, 1977; Leeper 1970; Tomkins 1981) also suggest that mood is a motivator of behavior. The *physiological* component of mood includes changes in the arousal/activation level of the organism. It is not clear, however, whether each mood is associated with a unique physiological state (see Ekman et al. 1983, Mandler 1984, Schachter and Singer 1962). The *cognitive* component of mood includes self-awareness of one's mood state. It also includes, and here the debate starts to thicken, cognitive appraisals of situations which may precede and influence experienced mood.

This section attempts to develop a working understanding of mood. It attempts this by defining mood with respect to its causes, consequences, and associated feeling states. The causes and consequences of mood are addressed in the subsequent two sections. This section of the chapter focuses on the subjective feeling state.

How do we distinguish between the "cold" cognitive processes in consciousness which we do not feel (i.e., the mental act of adding two plus two) and the "hot" cognitive processes called mood which we do feel (i.e., feeling surprised, angry, or relaxed)? This is the dilemma faced when defining mood. One approach to solving this dilemma has been to search for behavioral, motoric, and physiological states which occur concurrently with subjective feelings of mood and to use these as indicators to denote the onset of mood. But even if these efforts were successful, we are still faced with the dilemma of describing the subjective state, the experience of mood.

Identifying the specific set of experiential states which are moods is complicated by three issues: 1) the fact that common, everyday language contains many mood-relevant words but that this everyday language is not acceptable for scientific use because it is necessarily redundant, over inclusive, and ambiguous (Fehr and Russell 1984, Mandler 1984); 2) the unlikelihood that the fundamental moods, which some argue are innate and shared by all humans, have simple English equivalent words which don't appear in other languages (see Wierzbicka 1986); and 3) cultural biases of researchers which cause them to emphasize socially relevant phenomena, i.e., it has been suggested that "western psychologists" only emphasize moods which have pragmatic consequences to socially relevant concerns such as difficult thought, coping with a challenge, capacity for love and work, and successful communication of complex ideas (Kagan 1984).

One major task in defining mood is to identify and define the specific qualities of mood which are familiar and which we each experience. There is agreement among persons that they experience love, excitement, fear, surprise, stress, and relaxation. But many other words descriptive of feelings also come to mind: there are literally thousands of such words in the English language. Are they all distinct moods? Is there some overarching or organizing hierarchy of moods? There have been numerous attempts to identify and theoretically justify the qualitatively different types of moods and the organizing principles behind them. These approaches are generally of two types: discrete moods organized around and derived from combinations of fundamental, prototypical moods; or gradient moods represented by and derived from different levels of basic dimensions of mood.

Notable proponents of discreet moods are Tomkins, Izard, and Plutchik. These theorists suggest there exist a limited number of fundamental moods that have innate, "hardwired," cognitive and physiological responses, and stimulus triggers. These fundamental moods then combine to form the infinite variety of subtle mood states with which we are familiar and have developed a lay vocabulary to describe. The fundamental moods generally number five to ten. Tomkins (1981) identifies fear, anger, enjoyment, disgust, interest, surprise, contempt, shame, and distress. Izard (1977) identifies fear, anger, joy, disgust, interest,

surprise, contempt, shame, sadness, and guilt. Plutchik (in Mandler 1984) identifies fear, anger, joy, disgust, anticipation, surprise, sadness, and acceptance. These theories are strengthened by one another in that they converge on six fundamental moods. However, they differ from one another in the process and mechanisms proposed to generate even these six moods. Two of the concerns mentioned above are potential problems for these theories: the definitions rely upon lay terms to describe the fundamental moods, and the assumption is made that English language terms capture moods presumed present in persons who speak languages which have no direct or simple translation for these terms.

In contrast to theories purporting several discreet, fundamental moods are theories and definitions of mood which purport several bipolar, orthogonal dimensions of mood. Shaver et al. (1987) suggest that these dimensions may be emergent properties which explain the covariation of fundamental, discrete moods; but it is not yet clear whether this is so. Mehrabian, Russell, Osgood, and others suggest, in contrast to proponents of fundamental moods, that several basic dimensions are the building blocks of all moods.

The theory adopted in this chapter as a means to describe, predict, and explain mood is based on dimensions. It will be referred to as PAD, which stands for Pleasure, Arousal, Dominance—the three major dimensions of mood. The theory has roots in the arousal work of Berlyne (1960); the evaluation, activity, and potency dimensions of Osgood and associates (e.g., Osgood et al. 1957, Osgood 1969); the theories of Mandler (1984) and Lang (1984); and the work by Mehrabian and Russell and associates (e.g., Mehrabian and Russell 1974, Russell and Pratt 1980, Russell and Snodgrass 1987, Russell and Steiger 1982, Ward and Russell 1981). This theory seems relevant for leisure concerns.

Mood is described using a three dimensional space with pleasure, arousal, and dominance as the dimensions (Fig. 1). The three dimensions are bipolar: very aroused to very sleepy, very pleasant to very unpleasant, very dominant to very submissive. Moods are described according to where they fall in the three dimensional space. For example, an arousing and pleasant environment is exciting, a pleasant and unarousing environment is relaxing, an unpleasant and unarousing environment is boring, and an unpleasant and arousing environment is hectic. An arousing, unpleasant, and submissive environment may result in anger, whereas if the environment were dominant, the result would be fear. These dimensions may not be independent; however for practical, descriptive purposes they are often thought of as such.

Arousal is the primary dimension in terms of theoretical importance. Berlyne (1960: 48) defines arousal as "one of the variables that would have to be assigned a value if the

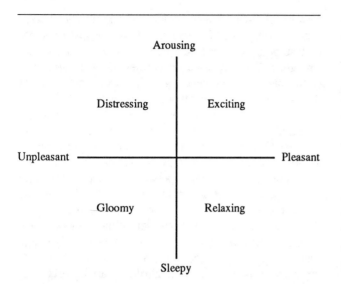

Figure 1. Two-dimensional model of mood. (This depicts two of the three proposed dimensions of PAD mood theory. The third dimension, dominance-submissive, runs orthogonally to these, out through the origin towards and away from the reader. This figure is adapted from Russell and Snodgrass 1987.)

psychological condition of a human being or higher animal at any particular time were to be adequately described. It is a measure of how wide awake the organism is, of how ready it is to react. The lower pole of the continuum is represented by sleep or coma, while the upper pole would be reached in states of frantic excitement." Dominance refers to the feeling of control and/or ability to manipulate a situation. It distinguishes, for example, between fear and anger. Pleasure is characterized by feelings of satisfaction, comfort, enjoyment, and beauty. It results, for example, from the successful attainment of a goal. Note that each dimension is bipolar, ranging from high to low.

Regardless of which specific subjective feelings qualify as moods, it is still necessary to distinguish among different levels of intensity of the subjective experience. It seems that situations when one merely is aware of their mood are qualitatively different from when one is totally consumed by a mood, and these situations, in turn, are different from situations when one is appraising a place as potentially evocative of a mood. For the purposes of effective communication among researchers, it is critical that these different qualities of feeling states be recognized and labeled. Simon (1982) and Russell and Snodgrass (1987) have developed more specific definitions and what follows borrows heavily from their work. *Mood* is defined as the subtle, subjective state of a person at any given moment. Persons are always in some mood. Mood influences and directs, but does not

disrupt cognition and behavior. Stone (1987) tracked people over many days and found evidence suggesting that people were always in some mood state and that these mood states have physiological correlates. Persons may or may not be consciously aware of their mood or its effects, but when asked to be introspective and provided with a verbal report instrument they are able to reliably assess their own mood. Thus, mood is defined as the subjective state which can be assessed through introspective appraisal and verbal report. An *emotional episode* includes conscious awareness of mood, the attribution of the mood to a specific cause, and a conscious plan of action corresponding to the mood or its cause. It is different from mood in that during an emotional episode the person is consciously aware of his current mood and has identified (perhaps inaccurately) a cause of the mood. Moreover, the person's plan for the immediate future (be it a behavior or a thought process) is directed at the cause of the mood with the intent of maintaining, enhancing, or changing the current mood. An example of an emotional episode is the prototypical emotional state such as fear where the person's behavior is motivated by the object causing the fear (e.g., fight or flight). Some intense leisure activities may produce emotional episodes—much more so than other aspects of day to day life. When one hunts, rafts, or climbs rocks, one is aware that it is the leisure experience which is the cause of one's mood. In addition, because it is a leisure activity where one has the freedom to chose one's plan, it is likely that the person's plan corresponds to the mood and its cause; thus satisfying all the criteria of the definition of an emotional episode.

The *emotional affordance* of an object, person, or situation refers to the cognitive appraisal persons make of the mood-inducing qualities of an object, person, or situation. It may not refer to the current mood state of the person making the appraisal. For example, a wilderness experience may be assessed as potentially relaxing, a white-water raft trip as potentially exciting, and camping with your mother-in-law may be viewed as potentially stressful. All these appraisals can be made while one is sitting at home, watching TV, feeling relaxed. Emotional affordance is an assessment of how one thinks one would be affected by an experience. It is an assessment of the anticipated impact of the object, place, or situation on the person rather than an assessment of the person's current mood resulting from an interaction with the object, place, or situation. The person's goals and past experiences may make her evaluation of emotional affordance unique.

Emotional disposition refers to the general tendency to be in one mood rather than another. A person may be generally happy or relaxed or nervous. This is a person's particular trait or temperament and it will influence one's current mood state.

LEISURE-RELATED "CAUSES" OF MOOD

The primary purpose of this section is to illustrate the enormous range of situational factors which influence mood states. Most of these factors covary with leisure experiences, many can be influenced by recreation management. Another purpose of this section is to further an understanding of mood by describing some of its causes. The impacts of environment on mood are well documented and only a select sample of the entire literature is reviewed here. Some of this information is presented in a recent review article by Russell and Snodgrass (1987).

Pre-Arrival Mood

The mood associated with the immediate past has a significant impact on current mood. A person's mood colors one's evaluations of situations—for example, when in a positive mood the cup looks half full. Thus, if one enters an environment in a good mood, one is likely to evaluate things positively and be more likely to maintain that good mood. This has implications for recreation. The on-site experience is likely to be colored by mood generated while planning the experience and traveling to the site. Planning involves numerous expectations and images about the recreation experience, and these by themselves have been found sufficient to alter mood in laboratory settings. Travel may be stressful or pleasant depending on comfort, the amount of control one has over the process, the social companionship, and the length of the trip. These factors can combine to produce strong positive or negative moods prior to arrival at a recreation site and thus influence the mood associated with the on-site recreation experience.

Imperceptible Stimuli

There are an infinite number of imperceptible stimuli which may impact mood. Just because a stimulus is outside the range of a sense organ does not prevent it from impacting humans. The most obvious examples include chemicals one breathes or ingests. Carbon monoxide, lead, and other chemicals cause feelings of fatigue, aggression, anxiety, and so on (Anderson 1982, Schulte 1963). Positively or negatively charged air ions are suggested to influence mood, although the evidence is conflicting (Hawkins 1981). Imperceptible sounds are also suggested to influence mood (Evans and Tempest 1972).

The potential impact of imperceptible stimuli seems significant in natural environments. Humans evolved in a natural environment and thus may be sensitive to that environment in ways which we are not consciously aware or perceptually sensitive. The types and amounts of sounds, smells, ions, and electromagnetic radiation in a natural setting are likely to be significantly different than what is found in a highrise building. Perhaps these imperceptible stimuli significantly impact mood in a fashion which cannot be duplicated by artificial environments or in overly developed recreation sites. Unfortunately, there is a dearth of research on this topic so no conclusion is available.

Perceptible Stimuli

Light, sound, smell, vibration, taste, temperature—all influence pleasure, arousal, and dominance. Mehrabian and Russell (1974) and Russell and Snodgrass (1987) summarize much of the available literature. The conclusion reached from this extensive literature is that mood can be manipulated through alterations of physical characteristics. For example, arousal may be increased by increasing light intensity or sound intensity, and pleasure may be manipulated by colors.

Collative Properties

Berlyne (1960) theorized and tested for generalizable properties of physical stimuli which determine the intensity of a person's exploratory effort focused on the stimuli. Wohlwill (1976) subsequently adopted and extended these properties to evaluate natural landscapes. These properties include: complexity, novelty, incongruity, surprisingness, and ambiguity. They reflect aspects of the stimulus field which engender an exploratory response in the observer. Part of the rationale behind the collative properties is the unrealistic expectation that any organism can respond specifically to each of the infinite number of possible variations in sensory stimuli. There must be some means by which the various sensory stimuli are aggregated over time, space, and sense organ. The organism, then, responds to this aggregation. The collative properties represent, in a manner which attempts to be generalizable to all stimuli, the amount of information present in the stimulus field. The more information there is, the more the effort required to decode it; hence, the higher the arousal of the organism. In the context of the mood theory presented above, the collative properties are related to the mood evoked by the stimuli because they influence the organism's level of arousal. Kaplan and Kaplan (1982) describe a similar information processing-based theory with slightly different terms: mystery, legibility, coherence, etc.

Berlyne identified these properties through experimentation using abstract, meaningless stimuli. Although they have been applied with some success in the past, they unfortunately don't work well as predictors of persons' moods, preferences, or beauty assessments in real environments. They simply don't account well for the mood-inducing qualities of environments which convey meaning (Fenton 1985, Whitfield 1983).

Meaning

Most physical settings contain (symbolize, convey, evoke) meaning about appropriate behaviors in the place and about the people who regularly use the place (Csikszentmihalyi and Rochberg-Halton 1981, Norman 1988, Rapoport 1982, Stokols 1981). Characteristics of outdoor recreation areas convey meaning about most every aspect of a recreation experience: parking lots are for cars, trails are for walking, ball fields for organized sport, scat symbolizes wildlife, fire rings represent camping, tents claim territory, graffiti and litter suggest a lack of supervision or lack of concern.

Meaning in the environment is used by Rs to evaluate obstacles which stand in the way of successfully completing a recreation experience and serves to identify the resources which are available to the R to help complete the recreation experience. For example, the meanings associated with (and moods evoked by) a clear, cool, small stream depends on whether one is thirsty, fishing, lost, or trying to canoe. If the environmental feature facilitates the plan (i.e., a small stream may be appropriate for having a cool drink), a different level of arousal and pleasure may result than if the feature hindered the objective (i.e., the small stream would be frustrating if one's heart were set on white-water rafting).

Another impact on mood of environmental meaning results from learned or innate mood reactions which occur in response to particular stimuli. The mood reaction occurs despite the R's activity. The meaning associated with an object can be sufficient to evoke either general arousal or a specific mood response. Mandler (1984) used a gun as an example of an object which, because of something learned, has acquired the ability to evoke arousal and fear in persons. Some objects and settings may evoke similar mood responses in all members of a group (culture). Nature (Knopf 1987, Ulrich 1983, Wohlwill 1983) and water (Hertzog 1985, Ulrich 1983) have been suggested as features which evoke pleasure and relaxation responses in most persons. However, these theories must account for the fact that nature has not always been associated with positive values (Nash 1973). Blood and snakes and fast moving objects are examples of environmental stimuli which may evoke innate, preprogrammed mood responses. Another example is the human face which evokes an expression of happiness in most infants (Izard 1977).

People

Arousing and salient features of any environment are the other persons present. People are unpredictable and powerful. They compete for resources and space (i.e., they can get in "line" before you, take the last chair, or eliminate solitude), they can threaten well-being (i.e., crime), and they can easily disrupt efforts to concentrate or relax (i.e., by striking up a conversation). People must be observed, analyzed, and their behavior predicted so that any threat to one's objectives may be mitigated. This requires increased attention and level of activation on the part of the observer (i.e., arousal). The presence of other persons also places enormous restrictions on one's own appropriate behavior since it is available for observation. The literatures on crowding, territory, and personal space are full of examples of the salience of people on the mood, satisfaction, and behavior of recreationists (e.g., Baum and Paulus 1987).

Recreation Activity

Four factors are likely to influence the mood associated with recreation activities.

Alertness.—Recreation activities range between the two extremes of risky behavior (i.e., rock climbing) and mentally vegetative, solitary behavior (i.e., sunbathing) in the level of activation required of the R. The solitary rock climber requires high levels of activation: physical skills must be accurate for precise bodily movements, sense organs (especially balance) must be alert, and cognitive processes must be sharp to evaluate route, positions, and holds—in short, success demands high levels of alertness. In contrast, a solitary sunbather is left with minimal demands on motor, sense, or cognitive systems—success depends only on the weather.

Other people.—Activities which involve other persons involve higher levels of arousal for all the reasons mentioned above in the discussion on people.

Activity environment fit.—Mood will be influenced by how well the environment facilitates the recreation activity. Some activities are less demanding in terms of specific environmental needs (i.e., picnicking, hiking) than are others (i.e., golf, hunting). If the activity is blocked by environmental obstacles, the resulting mood may be negative and intense.

Environment.—Finally, it is often the case that the environment associated with an activity is a source of pleasure and arousal despite other factors. Rock climbing is usually associated with views and rugged topography which enhance both pleasure (beauty) and arousal. Rafting and boating are usually associated with either placid, relaxing lakes or roaring, exciting rivers. Most activities, however, can be successfully undertaken in a variety of environmental conditions and thus the impact of environment on mood may not be exclusively associated with the activity. Nonetheless, whatever the environment is, it is likely to have a significant impact on mood state.

Memories

Changes in mood caused by recollection of a leisure experience have been shown to exist (Hammitt 1980), yet there is little research on this topic. Csikszentmihalyi and Rochberg-Halton (1981) examined the significance of household objects in persons' lives. They found that many objects which served as symbols of the past evoked strong mood reactions, in several cases the thought of losing these objects brought subjects to tears. Strong antidotal evidence exists to suggest that recalling and telling others about recreation experiences is a common event—the story about the fish that got away is a classic example. What purpose does this serve? Perhaps recollections evoke strong, positive moods—a desired and sought after state.

POTENTIAL CONSEQUENCES OF MOOD

The primary purpose of the following discussion is to summarize empirical research which illustrates the theoretical and socially relevant impacts of mood. An additional purpose is to further an understanding and definition of mood by detailing some of its consequences. The impacts of mood are divided into two categories: those that occur on-site, while engaged in a recreation experience; and those that occur off-site, after the person has encountered subsequent environments. It is important to note that many of the impacts of mood discussed below can occur without conscious awareness of mood or of the impacts. Also note the breadth of type and the magnitude of these impacts as well as their potential relevance to leisure research, management, and public policy. Many of the studies reviewed do not differentiate among emotion, affect, and mood, although it appears that they are addressing, at least in part, the concept of mood as it is defined here.

On-Site Impacts of Mood

Attention

Mood state influences what is attended to in the environment and therefore can have a profound impact on subsequent cognition and behavior (Frijda 1986, Izard 1984, Mandler 1984). Izard (1984) reviews studies where subjects were simultaneously exposed, for a very short duration, to a happy face in one eye and a sad face in the other. Persons in happy moods reported seeing the happy face more often than the sad. Broadbent and Gregory (1967) found that the mood content of words influenced whether or not the words were perceived. Thus, it seems the person's mood state and the mood-evoking potential of the stimuli influence a person's attention to that stimuli.

Cognition

Numerous significant cognitive processes are influenced by mood: they include memory, perception of control, attribution, and one's evaluations of situations. Gilligan and Bower (1984: 568) conclude that "an emotion can have a surprisingly strong influence on how someone thinks and acts in his social world . . . Emotion . . . seems to be inextricably related to how we perceive and think, influencing them at every turn." The effect of mood on *memory* is perhaps the best documented. Recall is more likely to be correct and efficient when the person doing the recalling is in a mood similar to the mood when the material was learned. Similarly, material/stimuli are remembered better if they evoke a mood similar to the current mood of the learner. It is not suggested that mood influences the absolute performance of memory (although this may be true). Rather, it is suggested that the availability of memories and the readiness with which they come to mind are influenced by mood. This, in turn, may have a significant influence on subsequent cognitive planning.

Mood can influence how one perceives one's self relative to the world (Moore et al. 1984). Positive moods tend to promote feelings of control, including internal locus of control. Mood also affects attribution. A person in a negative mood is more likely to be critical and accept blame even when blame is not appropriate. Conversely, a person in a positive mood is more likely to be persistent at tasks and have positive expectations of future performances. There is also evidence that mood influences transient qualities of personality and self-concept. Happy persons tend to describe themselves as productive, as having high self-esteem, and as possessing high levels of skill, competency, and proficiency. Similarly, mood tends to influence how persons perceive one another. "Happy people tend to be friendly, charitable, and merciful in their judgments of others; angry people tend to be the opposite" (Gilligan and Bower 1984: 567). Mood also influences decisions made about objects and situations. Marketing research has found that the mood evoked by advertisements and by the products themselves influences product acceptance (e.g., Batra and Ray 1986, Kardes 1986). Isen et al. (1987) suggest one possible mechanism for the impact of mood on cognition is that it influences the way cognitive material is organized. This consequently determines the way information is perceived, recognized, and associated with other information.

Behavior

Mood impacts behavior in part through its impact on cognition. Thus it is difficult to categorize some impacts as either cognitive or behavioral. In either case, the impacts on behavior are extensive and those discussed here include task performance, altruistic behavior, communication, and motivation. Performance of any task requires an appropriate level of arousal. The "Yerkes-Dodson" law suggests that the relation between arousal and performance is best represented by an inverse U. If arousal is too low, the person is not alert enough to function; if arousal is too high, then symptoms of nervousness and stress degrade performance. The optimal level of arousal is influenced by task complexity, familiarity, and skill level. This proposed relationship has been a basis for much theory, yet empirical support for it is not strong (Frijda 1986). Nonetheless, evidence of the interaction between the various aspects of mood and the quality of task performance is extensive. Moore et al. (1984) note that sadness tends to increase learning time. Isen et al. (1987: 1128) conclude that "... creativity ... can be facilitated by a transient pleasant affective state. Moreover, the affective state sufficient to do this can be induced subtlety, by small everyday events." Perceived dominance and control also influence performance (Mehrabian and Russell 1974). The greater the perceived control, the better the performance tends to be. Positive mood is also associated with willingness to delay gratification and suffer immediate costs for the promise of larger, long-term rewards and, hence, influences the types of tasks one pursues (Moore et al. 1984).

Prosocial behavior, such as altruistic and helping behaviors, tend to increase when persons are in positive moods. Berkowitz (1987: 722) suggests this is because "persons feeling happy…might interpret calls for assistance in a relatively favorable manner or might view positively those asking for help. In thinking positively about the world around them, they look at ambiguous people and behaviors in this generally positive light . . . They may even regard themselves more favorably than they otherwise are inclined to do, and this positive self-conception could facilitate socially positive behavior." Sherrod et al. (1977: 369) found strong impacts of mood on helping behavior and concluded: "If 10 minutes of attention to . . . [positive mood inducing stimuli] . . . can exert such effects on social behavior as those obtained in the present research, one wonders about the consequences of actual physical environments on mood and behavior. It appears that, other things being equal, the quality of the physical environment may strongly influence the way in which people respond to each other."

Positive, mildly arousing mood is associated with social interaction (Mehrabian and Russell 1974). On the other side of the coin, mood has been associated with antisocial behavior, such as cheating (Dinstbier 1984). Thus, the mood evoked by an environment is likely to influence the type and the intensity of human interaction which occurs there.

Mood has been presented by several theorists as a mechanism for motivating, organizing, and sustaining human behavior (Arnold 1970; Izard 1971, 1977; Leeper 1970; see also Frijda 1986 for a review). Some moods are seen as products of evolution in that they encourage response patterns which enhance chances of survival. "Each emotion that emerged over the course of human evolution added a different quality of motivation and new behavioral alternatives that increased adaptive prowess. For example, interest, a very important positive mood, motivates cognitive and motor search and exploratory behaviors, and anger mobilizes energy for physical action, as well as confidence in one's powers . . . Both interest and anger, like each of the emotions, are significant determinants of selective attention and hence of the contents of perception and cognition" (Izard 1984: 18). Leeper (1970) argues strongly against those who present emotion as a disorganizing response which disrupts behaviors (which is associated with the belief that mood is irrational). Leeper argues that disruption only occurs in extreme situations such as when all of the person's attempts have failed and nothing seems to work so the person becomes so frustrated that only disruptive, angry behavior results. He suggests that moods are subtle yet prevalent aspects of everyday life and work to *organize and direct* behavior. A point of concern about moods as viable motives for 21st century man is raised by Geist (1979:423): "In artificial environments, such as we occupy, severe intellectual control over our actions is essential, since our emotional responses need not be valid guides to the utility of our actions."

Physiology

Mood change, and mood in general, have physiological correlates. This aspect of mood is discussed in detail elsewhere (Frijda 1986; Ulrich, Dimberg and Driver, this volume). Suffice it to say that the impacts include the following: autonomic responses (i.e., heart rate, blood pressure, respiration, electrodermal activity, sweating, gastrointestinal and urinary activity, pupillary response, and trembling); hormonal changes (i.e., epinephrine, norepinephrine, ACHT, corticosteroids); and electrocortical responses (i.e., muscle tension).

Off-site Impacts of Mood

The cognitive, behavioral and physiological impacts of mood described above were presented from the perspective of the immediate impacts of current mood. The breadth and significance of these impacts are impressive in themselves, but the impact of mood is likely to be much more extensive. Persons "carry" moods from one situation into other situations. Thus, moods generated in one setting are likely to impact cognition and behavior in subsequent settings.

Planning

A person's past mood has the potential to color evaluations of new situations, the identification of future goals, and the development of future plans. Hence mood may influence future behaviors, moods, and cognitions. When persons enter an environment they evaluate it (Brunswik 1956, Ittelson et al. 1974), and as discussed above, these evaluations may be colored by current mood. These mood-colored evaluations will have the impact of perpetuating the current mood—when one starts off happy, one is more likely to evaluate situations positively and consequently may maintain the positive mood. Likewise, a person's current mood may influence goal and plan selection because mood impacts aspects of cognition such as memory recall. In the process of identifying a goal and constructing a plan which leads to its accomplishment, one must access and evaluate information from memory; and, since appraisal and memory recall are colored by mood state, the plan of future actions, and consequently the future behaviors, may be influenced by the current mood state. Thus, it seems likely that there is a long-term impact of mood induced by leisure.

Health

Mood impacts health in a variety of subtle yet significant ways which include the immune system, stress recovery, and strong self-concept. Stone et al. (1987: 988) demonstrated that daily fluctuations in self-reported mood correlated with changes in the "secretory immune system . . . [which is]. . . often described as the body's first line of defense against invading organisms." Their results suggest that subjects' immune systems were strongest during times of positive moods such as those that would be associated with leisure activities. Other researchers have demonstrated that mood state (especially depression) correlated highly with health indicators such as changes in the immune system and actual occurrences of cancer (Maddi et al. 1987, Shekelle et al. 1981).

Graef et al. (1983) found that persons experiencing intrinsically motivating experiences (i.e., experiences which produce positive mood) are more likely to have stronger self-concept. Literature reviewed by Moore et al. (1984) supports this conclusion. They report findings of positive mood being correlated with higher ratings of self-esteem. Thus, leisure activities may promote health by promoting positive moods and intrinsically motivating experiences which subsequently promote a strong sense of self-worth and ultimately a stronger sense of coherence (Antonovsky 1987).

MEASUREMENT OF MOOD

Mood states are subtle, often undetected by the person experiencing them. Normally we are not aware of our mood or how it impacts us. Kagan (1984) makes an analogy of this phenomenon to a disease or illness. In the early stages of an illness, one is generally unaware of the problem; if the illness progresses, one becomes aware of physical changes which are symptoms of the illness (e.g., pain, fever) but still remains unaware of the specific cause (i.e., virus, cancer, heart). Even a trained medical doctor has difficulty identifying and measuring the symptoms, let alone the specific cause of the symptoms. Moods are equally difficult to assess. There are three types of mood measures: assessment of nonverbal, motoric behavior (posture and facial expressions); assessment of physiological measures which covary with mood; and verbal reports of subjective feelings. There is no agreed upon assessment method because mood manifests itself differently under different conditions and because there is no agreed upon definition of mood. It is agreed that multiple measures are generally desirable.

Izard (1971) assessed mood through use of observable facial expressions. Fridlund and Izard (1983), Dimberg (1987), and others have extended this procedure by assessing facial electromyographic response patterns (imperceptible changes in facial muscles). These assessments seem to be reliable and sensitive indicators of the pleasure/displeasure mood response. However, Matsumoto (1987) notes methodological problems may exist in some studies (his critique pertains mainly to tests of the facial feedback hypothesis). Advances in physiological assessment technology enable more refined assessment of physiological indicators which tend to reflect the arousal component of mood (see Ekman et al. 1983; Frijda 1986; and Ulrich, Dimberg and Driver, in this volume).

There are many verbal report instruments. Instruments attempting to assess pleasure, arousal, and dominance have been developed by Russell, Mehrabian, and their colleagues (e.g., Mehrabian and Russell 1974, Russell and Mehrabian 1977, Russell and Pratt 1980, Russell et al. 1981). Many other instruments exist which focus on other aspects of mood (e.g., McNair et al. 1978, Nowlis 1965, Thayer 1967). Some of these self-report measures have been found to covary with physiological measures (e.g., Stone et. al. 1987, Thayer 1967).

Kagan (1984) notes that measurements meant to represent the three response systems (cognitive subjective assessment, physiological, and behavioral—including facial) represent different aspects of mood and should not be expected to converge in all cases. Lazarus et al. (1970) even suggest that assessments of the different systems should be expected to contradict each other given the complexity of the relationships between psychological coping strategies, cultural, and social constraints on expression, and innate biological programs. However, Dimberg (1987) has found some convergence.

Most mood measurement procedures are disruptive. Thus, the assessment of mood itself may alter the subject's mood state. Physiological measures require electrodes, wires, and laboratory instruments, as do assessments of facial electromyographic response patterns. Subjective, verbal reports require the person to stop what they would normally be doing and reflect on their mood state, something they would not normally do. The simple act of introspection and self-assessment may modify the mood. Moreover, many of these procedures are laboratory based and/or require subjects to depart somewhat from their normal behavioral patterns. Thus, the validity of mood assessments made while subjects have artificial purposes (i.e., instructed to "imagine you are climbing a mountain") or no purpose at all except to watch slides is questionable. Such is the case in many laboratory experiments where subjects are seated in

unfamiliar rooms and exposed to surrogate leisure experiences (e.g., pictures, stories, sounds) or surrogate situations (e.g., games, confederates). Obviously, there are numerous measurement issues which need to be resolved.

SUGGESTIONS FOR RESEARCH

Four broad areas of research need developing:

- Theoretical and empirical studies are needed to explore the role of mood in leisure activities. At this early stage in the development of the field, descriptive empirical studies are worthwhile. For example, little is known about the moods experienced during different recreation experiences or about the temporal characteristic of one's mood over a site visit and its relationship to short- and long-term user satisfaction and overall health and well-being.
- Development of nondisruptive, noninvasive mood measurement techniques is needed. Current methods are disruptive and many are laboratory bound. Because a person's plan for leisure activities plays such a significant role in determining mood state, it is important that ecologically valid research be conducted. That is, subjects should have actual leisure experiences (valid purposes) and not forced to be cognizant of experimental constraints.
- It is important that the socially relevant impacts of leisure-induced mood be documented so that leisure becomes recognized as socially relevant and worthy of investment and further research rather than being just a nice thing to do if enough resources are not already committed to other concerns.
- To improve management of recreation sites and leisure activities, research is needed to assess the impact on mood of manageable characteristics of the social and physical environment.

CONCLUSION

The purpose of this paper was to demonstrate that mood is a significant, prevalent, and relevant product of leisure activities. To accomplish this, an effort was made to develop a working understanding of mood by reviewing theories and findings. It was suggested that in order to understand mood it is necessary to understand its causes, its consequences, and the subjective feeling it produces. All three aspects of mood were discussed in this paper. Mood is a complex topic needing considerable additional scholarly inquiry before it is understood well enough for effective recreation management. It is important that this activity be focused on theories and empirical findings rather than semantics. This paper attempted to help frame this future inquiry.

Mood is an integral part of many leisure theories and is a likely product of leisure experiences. Mood can be significantly influenced by characteristics of the physical and social setting. Many of these characteristics are under the control of recreation managers. The significance of mood was demonstrated by noting the impacts of mood on cognition, behavior, and physiology. These impacts include learning, task performance, helping behavior, socialization, self-concept, and health. Perhaps the most significant, yet least understood impact of mood is its influence on the planning of future events and, as such, its influence on the behaviors and cognitions of persons long after they leave the leisure setting. It is important to note that the impacts of mood are socially relevant. And, it may not be unreasonable to suggest that mood is one of the more socially relevant products of leisure activities. In fact, the benefits resulting from mood induced by leisure experiences may be one of the major justifications to society for the expenditure of its resources on the provision, management, and study of leisure. There is much more to leisure than the intrinsic benefits of "enjoyment" and "having a good time." Studies of mood may help understand this and other aspects of leisure.

Despite the apparent significance of mood, little relevant research exists in the leisure and recreation fields. Four broad areas of research need developing: theoretical and empirical studies of the role of mood in leisure activities, improvements of noninvasive measurement technology, documentation of the socially relevant impacts of leisure-induced mood, and assessment and understanding of the impact on mood of manageable characteristics of the social and physical environment.

LITERATURE CITED

Abbey, E. 1961. Desert solitaire. New York, NY: Random House.

Anderson, A. C. 1982. Environmental factors in aggressive behavior. Journal of Clinical Psychiatry. 43:280-283.

Antonovsky, A. 1987. Unraveling the mystery of health: how people manage stress and stay well. San Francisco, CA: Jossey-Bass.

Arnold, M. B. 1970. Perennial problems in the field of emotion. In: Arnold, M. B., ed. Feelings and emotions. New York, NY: Academic Press.

Batra, R.; Ray, M. 1986. Affective responses to mediating acceptance of advertising. Journal of Consumer Research. 13: 234-249.

Baum, A.; Paulus, P. 1987. Crowding. In: Altman, I; Stokols, D., eds. Handbook of environmental psychology. New York, NY: John Wiley and Sons: 522-570.

Berkowitz, L. 1987. Mood, self-awareness, and willingness to help. Journal of Personality and Social Psychology. 52: 721-729.

Berlyne, D. 1960. Conflict, arousal, and curiosity. New York, NY: McGraw-Hill.

Bishop, D.; Jeanrenaud, C. 1976. End-of-day moods on work and leisure days in relation to extraversion, neuroticism, and amount of change in daily activities. Canadian Journal of Behavioral Science. 8: 388-400.

Broadbent, D. E.; Gregory, N. 1967. Perception of emotionally toned words. Nature. 215: 518-584.

Brunswik, E. 1956. Perception and the representative design of psychological experiments. Berkeley, CA: University of California.

Csikszentmihalyi, M. 1975. Beyond boredom and anxiety. San Francisco, CA: Jossey-Bass.

Csikszentmihalyi, M.; Rochberg-Halton, E. 1981. The meaning of things: domestic symbols and the self. Cambridge: Cambridge University Press.

Dimberg, U. 1987. Facial reactions, autonomic activity and experienced emotion: a three component model of emotional conditioning. Biological Psychology. 24: 105-122.

Dinstbier, R. A. 1984. The role of emotion in moral socialization. In: Izard, C. E.; Kagan, J.; Zajonc, R., eds. Emotion, cognition, and behavior. Cambridge: Cambridge University Press: 17-37.

Ekman, P.; Levenson, R. W.; Friesen, W. V. 1983. Autonomic nervous system activity distinguishing among emotions. Science. 221: 1208-1210.

Elias, N.; Dunning, E. 1969. The quest for excitement in leisure. Society and Leisure (Bulletin for sociology of leisure, education and culture; European Centre for Leisure and Education). 2: 50-85.

Evans, M. J.; Tempest, W. 1972. Some effects of infrasonic noise in transportation. Journal of Sound and Vibration. 22: 19-24.

Fehr, B.; Russell, J. A. 1984. Concept of emotion viewed from a prototype perspective. Journal of Experimental Psychology: General. 113: 464-486.

Fenton, D. M. 1985. Dimensions of meaning in the perception of natural settings and their relationships to aesthetic response. Australian Journal of Psychology. 37: 325-339.

Fridlund, A. J.; Izard, C. E. 1983. Electromyographic studies of facial expressions of emotions and patterns of emotions. In: Cacioppo, J. T.; Petty, R. E., eds. Social psychophysiology: a source book. New York, NY: The Guilford Press.

Frijda, N. H. 1986. The emotions. Cambridge: Cambridge University Press.

Geist, V. 1979. Life strategies, human evolution, environmental design: towards a biological theory of health. New York, NY: Springer-Verlag.

Gilligan, S. G.; Bower, B. H. 1984. Cognitive consequences of emotional arousal. In: Izard, C. E.; Kagan, J.; Zajonc, R., eds. Emotion, cognition, and behavior. Cambridge: Cambridge University Press: 547-588.

Graef, R.; Csikszentmihalyi, M.; Gianinno, S. M. 1983. Measuring intrinsic motivation in everyday life. Leisure Studies. 2: 155-168.

Gunter, B. G. 1987. The leisure experience: selected properties. Journal of Leisure Research. 19: 115-130.

Hammit, W. 1980. Outdoor recreation: is it a multi-phase experience. Journal of Leisure Research. 12: 107-105.

Hawes, D. K. 1979. Satisfactions derived from leisure-time pursuits: an exploratory nationwide survey. Journal of Leisure Research. 10: 247-264.

Hawkins, L. H. 1981. The influence of air ions, temperature, and humidity on subjective well-being and comfort. Journal of Environmental Psychology. 1: 279-292.

Hertzog, T. R. 1985. Analysis of preference for waterscapes. Journal of Environmental Psychology. 5: 225-241.

Hull, R. B.; Harvey, A. [In press]. Explaining the emotion experienced in suburban parks. Environment and Behavior.

Isen, A. M.; Daubman, K. A.; Nowicki, G. P. 1987. Positive affect facilitates creative problem solving. Journal of Personality and Social Psychology. 52: 1122-1131.

Ittelson, W. H; Proshansky, H. M.; Rivlin, L. G.; Winkel, G. H. 1974. An introduction to environmental psychology. New York, NY: Holt, Rinehart and Winston.

Izard, C. E. 1971. The face of emotion. New York, NY: Appleton-Century-Crofts.

Izard, C. E. 1977. Human emotions. New York, NY: Plenum.

Izard, C. E. 1984. Emotion-cognition relationships and human development. In: Izard, C. E.; Kagan, J.; Zajonc, R., eds. Emotion, cognition, and behavior. Cambridge: Cambridge University Press.

Kagan, J. 1984. The idea of emotion in human development. In: Izard, C. E.; Kagan, J.; Zajonc, R., eds. Emotion, cognition, and behavior. Cambridge: Cambridge University Press. 38-72.

Kaplan, S.; Kaplan R. 1982. Cognition and environment: functioning in an uncertain world. New York, NY: Praeger.

Kardes, F. R. 1986. Effects of initial product judgments on subsequent memory-based judgments. Journal of Consumer Research. 13: 1-11.

Klausner, S. Z. 1967. Sport parachuting. In: Slovenko, R.; Knight, J. A., eds. Motivations in play, games, and sports. New York, NY: Charles C. Thomas.

Knopf, R. 1987. Human behavior, cognition, and affect in the natural environment. In: Stokols, D.; Altman, I., eds. Handbook of environmental psychology. New York, NY: John Wiley and Sons: 783-826.

Lang, P. J. 1984. Cognition in emotion: concept and action. In: Izard, C.; Kagan, J.; Zajonc, R., eds. Emotion, cognition and behavior. Cambridge: Cambridge University Press: 192-226.

Lazarus, R. S.; Averill, J. R.; Opton, E.M. 1970. Towards a cognitive theory of emotion. In: Arnold, M., ed. Feelings and emotions: The Loyola Symposium. New York, NY: Academic Press: 207-232.

Leeper, R. W. 1970. The motivational and perceptual properties of emotions as indicating their fundamental character and role. In: Arnold, M., ed. Feelings and emotions: The Loyola Symposium. New York, NY: Academic Press: 151-168.

Lopez, B. 1986. Arctic dreams: imagination and desire in a northern landscape. New York, NY: Charles Scribner's Sons.

Maddi, S. R.; Bartone, P. T.; Puccetti, M. C. 1987. Stressful events are indeed a factor in physical illness: reply to Schroeder and Costa (1984). Journal of Personality and Social Psychology. 52: 833-843.

Mandler, G. 1984. Mind and body: psychology of emotion and stress. New York, NY: W.W. Norton.

Mannell, R. C. 1980. Social psychological techniques and strategies for studying leisure experience. In: Iso-Ahola, S., ed. Social psychological perspectives on recreation and leisure. Springfield, IL: Charles C. Thomas.

Mannell, R. C.; Zuzanek, J.; Larson, R. 1988. Leisure states and "flow" experiences: testing perceived freedom and intrinsic motivation hypotheses. Journal of Leisure Research. 20: 289-304.

Matsumoto. D. 1987. The role of facial response in the experience of emotion: more methodological problems and a meta-analysis. Journal of Personality and Social Psychology. 52: 769-774.

McNair, D. M.; Lorr, M.; Droppleman, L. F. 1978. Profile of mood states. San Diego: Educational and Industrial Testing Service.

Mehrabian, A.; Russell, J.A. 1974. An approach to environmental psychology. Cambridge, MA: MIT Press.

Mercer, C. 1976. Why do people take holidays? New Society. 26(August): 56-57.

Moore, B.; Underwood, B.; Rosenhan, D. L. 1984. Emotion, self, and others. In: Izard, C. E.; Kagan, J.; Zajonc, R., eds. Emotion, cognition, and behavior. Cambridge: Cambridge University Press: 464-483.

More, T. A.; Payne, B. R. 1978. Affective response to natural areas near cities. Journal of Leisure Research. 10: 7-12.

Nash, R. 1973. Wilderness and the American mind. New Haven, CT: Yale University Press.

Norman, D. 1988. The psychology of everyday things. New York, NY: Basic Books.

Nowlis, V. 1965. Research with the mood adjective check list. In: Tompkins, S. S.; Izard, C. E., eds. Affect, cognition, and personality. New York, NY: Springer.

Osgood, C. E. 1969. On the whys and wherefores of E, P, and A. Journal of Personality and Social Psychology. 12: 194-199.

Osgood, C. E.; Suci, G. J.; Tannenbaum, P. H. 1957. The measurement of meaning. Urbana, IL: University of Illinois Press.

Rapoport, A. 1982. The meaning of the built environment. Beverly Hills, CA: Sage.

Russell, J. A.; Mehrabian, A. 1977. Evidence for a three-factor theory of emotions. Journal of Research in Personality. 11: 273-294.

Russell, J. A.; Pratt, G. 1980. A description of the affective quality attributed to environments. Journal of Personality and Social Psychology. 38(2): 311-322.

Russell, J. A.; Snodgrass, J. 1987. Emotion and the environment. In: Altman, I.; Stokols, D., eds. Handbook of environmental psychology. New York, NY: John Wiley and Sons: 245-280.

Russell, J. A.; Steiger, J. H. 1982. The structure in persons: implicit taxonomy of emotions. Journal of Research in Personality. 16: 447-469.

Russell, J. A., Ward, L. M.; Pratt, G. 1981. Affective quality attributed to environments: a factor analytic study. Environment and Behavior. 13: 259-288.

Schachter, S.; Singer, J. E. 1962. Cognitive, social, and physiological determinants of emotional state. Psychological Review. 69: 379-399.

Schulte, J. H. 1963. Effect of mild carbon monoxide intoxication. Archives of Environmental Health. 7: 524-530.

Shaffer, R. ; Mietz, J. 1969. Aesthetic and emotional experiences rate high with northeast wilderness hikers. Environment and Behavior. 1: 187-197.

Shaver, P.; Schwartz, J.; Kirson, D.; O'Connor, C. 1987. Emotion knowledge: further exploration of a prototype approach. Journal of Personality and Social Psychology. 52: 1061-1086.

Shekelle, R. B.; Raynor, W. J.; Ostfeld, A. M., et al. 1981. Psychological depression and 17-year risk of death from cancer. Psychosomatic Medicine. 43: 117-125.

Sherrod, D.; Armstrong, D.; Hewitt, J., et al. 1977. Environmental attention, affect, and altruism. Journal of Applied Social Psychology. 7: 359-371.

Simon, H. 1982. Affect and cognition: comments. In: Clark, M. S.; Fiske, S. T., eds. Affect and cognition. Hillsdale, NJ: Lawrence Erlbaum Assoc.: 333-342.

Stokols, D. 1981. Group x place transactions: some neglected issues in psychological research on settings. In: Magnusson, D., ed. Towards a psychology of situations: an interactional perspective. Hillsdale, NJ: Lawrence Erlbaum Assoc.: 393-415.

Stone, A. A. 1987. Event content in a daily survey is differentially associated with concurrent mood. Journal of Personality and Social Psychology. 52: 56-58.

Stone, A. A.; Cox, D. S.; Valdimarsdottir, H., et al. 1987. Evidence that secretory IgA antibody is associated with daily mood. Journal of Personality and Social Psychology. 52: 988-993.

Thayer, R. E. 1967. Measurement of activation through self-report. Psychological Reports. 20: 663-678.

Tomkins, S. S. 1981. The quest for primary motives: biography and autobiography of an idea. Journal of Personality and Social Psychology. 41: 306-329.

Ulrich, R. S. 1983. Aesthetic and affective responses to natural environments. In: Altman, I.; Wolhwill, J., eds. Human behavior and environment: Vol. 6. Behavior and the natural environment. New York, NY: Plenum.

Ward, L. M.; Russell, J. A. 1981. The psychological representation of molar physical environments. Journal of Experimental Psychology: General. 110: 121-144.

Whitfield, T. W. 1983. Predicting preference for familiar, everyday objects: an experimental confrontation between two theories of asethetic behaviour. Journal of Environmental Psychology. 3(3): 221-237.

Wierzbicka, A. 1986. Human emotions: universal or culture specific. American Anthropology. 88(3): 584-594.

Wohlwill, J. F. 1976. Environmental aesthetics: the environment as a source of affect. In: Altman, I.; Wohlwill, J. F., eds. Human behavior and environment, Vol. 1. New York, NY: Plenum: 37-86.

Wohlwill, J. F. 1983. The concept of nature: a psychologist's view. In: Altman, I.; Wohlwill, J. F., eds. Human behavior and environment: Vol. 6. Behavior and the natural environment. New York, NY: Plenum: 5-37.

The Paragraphs about Leisure and Recreation Experience Preference Scales: Results from Two Inventories Designed to Assess the Breadth of the Perceived Psychological Benefits of Leisure

B. L. Driver
Rocky Mountain Forest and Range Experiment Station
USDA Forest Service
Fort Collins, Colorado

Howard E. A. Tinsley
Department of Psychology
Southern Illinois University
Carbondale, Illinois

Michael J. Manfredo
Department of Recreation Resources and Landscape
Architecture
College of Forestry and Natural Resources
Colorado State University
Fort Collins, Colorado

This and the previous nine chapters describe what are labeled psychological measures of the benefits of leisure in this volume. Several of the previous state-of-knowledge papers considered many types of benefits within a specific class (e.g., clinical, adventure recreation, learning), but generally they reported on studies in which different psychometric instruments were used to measure one or a few types of benefit. Most of those instruments were not originally developed within leisure contexts. In contrast, this chapter summarizes information about the psychological benefits of leisure gained from two inventories, each of which tap up to 44 "benefit themes." They are the Paragraphs About Leisure (PAL) developed by Tinsley and his associates, and the Recreation Experience Preference (REP) scales developed by Driver and his colleagues. These inventories were developed specifically to assess the relative importance of subjectively appraised leisure benefits and/or psychological outcomes that imply benefits.

This chapter contrasts the conceptual and applied orientations of the two teams of scientists who developed the PAL and REP instruments, provides sample results from their application, and develops the concept of psychological benefit. The purposes are to document the wide variety of psychological benefits available from leisure opportunities and to help clarify the concept of psychological benefit. The need for additional research on those psychological benefits which were not addressed in the foregoing chapters is stressed and specific directions to future research are suggested. An underlying theme is that the benefits of leisure occur in a *chain of causality,* with many of the highly specified benefits (e.g., companionship, competence testing) tapped by the PAL and REP scales serving as *intermediate outcomes* requisite to the gratification of particular psychological needs before more holistically defined human needs (e.g., personal growth, improved mental health, self-esteem, social bonding) can be met and their associated benefits realized.

THE TWO INVENTORIES

Although development of the inventories discussed here were truly team efforts, it is impossible to acknowledge all of the scientists who have contributed significantly. Of Tinsley's associates, Tom Barrett, Rick Kass, Sharon Bowman, and Diane Tinsley deserve special acknowledgement. Driver's associates include Perry Brown, Richard Knopf, Michael Manfredo, Glenn Haas, and Ray Cooksey. Our references to Tinsley and Driver generally include the notation "et al." to acknowledge the contributions of these associates.

Both the PAL and REP scales are founded on the notion that leisure opportunities are important in helping people meet basic psychological needs, especially those that are not fulfilled in nonleisure times and spaces. Since work was begun on each inventory, the orientations have changed somewhat. Tinsley et al. have retained the need gratification conceptual scaffolding and emphasize a "counseling" orientation, the objective of which is to assist recreationists in maximizing their leisure gratification. Driver et al. have moved more toward a psychologically based model which focuses on recreation demand for managerial purposes.

Paragraphs About Leisure

Conceptual Foundation

The genesis of Tinsley et al.'s interest in the psychological need-fulfilling benefits of leisure opportunities was outlined in one of their earliest reports. Tinsley, Barrett and Kass (1977) noted that since the turn of the century psychologists have been aware of the importance of individuals' jobs as a determinant of their mental health and life satisfaction. In contrast, Tinsley et al. (1977) pointed out that little systematic theory or research has been directed toward the effects of leisure activity on mental health, work adjustment, and life satisfaction. Although personality theorists long ago postulated that behavior is a function of needs, scholars began to conceptualize leisure choice as a function of the needs of the individual only in the late 1960s.

Ideally, individuals should be able to structure their leisure so as to maximize life satisfaction, raise self-esteem, and facilitate increased self-actualization. To do so, however, requires knowledge of the need-gratifying characteristics of the various leisure activities.

Early attempts to identify the type of needs most influential in leisure choice generally involved only a limited number of need dimensions. Hence, they failed to generate the breadth of information required regarding the extent to which leisure activities differ in their need-satisfying characteristics. This reasoning led Tinsley et al. (1977) to the conclusion that a systematic exploration of the full range of needs which might potentially be satisfied by participation in leisure activities was needed. Tinsley et al.'s goal, then, was to develop a reliable and valid psychometric inventory that assessed the full range of human needs gratified by leisure experience.

Before the PAL inventory is discussed, it is theoretically instructive to briefly describe Tinsley and Tinsley's (1986, 1988) view of the relation between need gratification and the concept of the psychological benefits of leisure. According to Tinsley and Tinsley (1986, 1988), leisure experiences result in the satisfaction of some of the psychological needs of the participant (see Fig. 1). This need gratification helps to maintain and enhance the physical health, mental health, and life satisfaction of the individual which, in turn, stimulate personal psychological growth. Tinsley and Tinsley (1986) believe that the dependence of physical health, mental health, life satisfaction, and personal growth on gratification of the individual's psychological needs is best represented by a stepwise model in which changes in need gratification must exceed a threshold before effects occur (see Figs. 2 and 3). Some minimal level of need gratification is a necessary but not sufficient condition for maintaining life satisfaction at or above the maintenance threshold (TM). Whenever a person's level of need gratification falls below the maintenance threshold, the probability increases that he or she will experience leisure deficit (i.e., chronic inadequacy of leisure experience). Failure to rectify

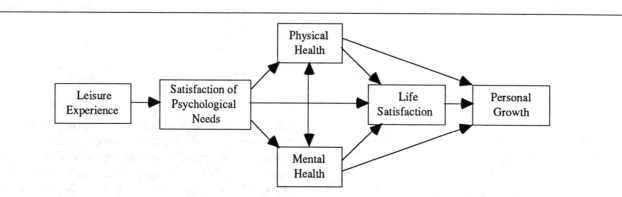

Figure 1. Relationships between leisure, psychological need fulfillment, and psychological benefit.

Source: Tinsley and Tinsley 1986.

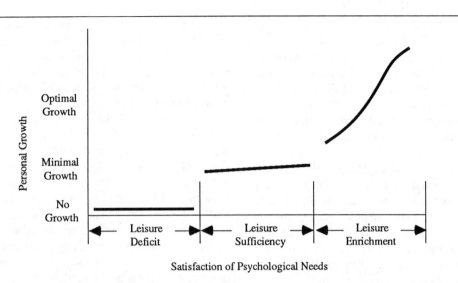

Figure 2. The relationship of psychological need satisfaction to personal growth.

Source: Tinsley and Tinsley 1986

this situation is postulated as resulting in a lack of personal growth (Fig. 2) and deterioration of the person's physical and mental health (Fig. 3). Tinsley and Tinsley (1986, 1988) postulate further that leisure sufficiency results from experiencing leisure frequently enough that the level of need gratification exceeds the maintenance threshold (TM) but not the growth threshold (TG). Persons who judge their life satisfaction to be high typically are motivated to avoid making personal changes. Consequently, persons experiencing leisure sufficiency may give minimal attention to

personal growth, but the primary result is maintenance of the status quo. Physical and mental health will remain largely unchanged under such circumstances (Fig. 3).

This model of the psychological benefits of leisure explicitly posits that the needs being gratified are *intervening variables,* with the results of this need gratification—physical and mental health, life satisfaction, and personal growth—clearly representing improved conditions, the definition of benefit adopted for this volume (see chapter by Driver, Brown, and Peterson).

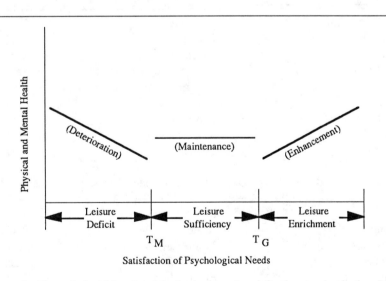

Figure 3. The relationship of psychological need satisfaction to physical and mental health.

Source: Tinsley and Tinsley 1986

Development of the PAL

Using this theoretical orientation as a guiding paradigm, Tinsley et al. began a program of research to map the domain of psychological needs which can be fulfilled or partially fulfilled through leisure and to develop reliable and valid psychometric instruments for quantifying the relative importance of each. This research resulted in the identification of 44 psychological needs that may be gratified by participation in leisure activities. An extensive review of the personality trait and testing literature was conducted in identifying those constructs (Tinsley et al. 1977). Early work indicated that several of these needs were generically related to many leisure activities (Tinsley and Kass 1978). The team identified 27 of the 44 need-gratifying dimensions which varied the most across leisure activities. These two groups are shown in Table 1. To reduce the complexity of the research task for participants, one version of the PAL was developed to measure these 27 dimensions. An alternative version contains scales for measuring all 44 of the need-satisfying constructs. In subsequent work, Tinsley and Kass (1979) factor analyzed the 27-scale form of the PAL and reported 8 more general "psychological benefits of leisure" which are described in Exhibit 1.

Each scale of the PAL consists of a single paragraph which describes the gratification of a particular psychological need. Respondents are instructed to indicate the extent to which each paragraph is an accurate statement about the leisure activity they are describing. Ratings are done on a 5-point Likert scale with response alternatives ranging from 1=Not True to 5=Definitely True (Tinsley and Kass 1978). The PAL thus quantifies the perceived degree to which a designated leisure activity provides opportunities to meet the targeted needs. It is important to understand that the PAL does not quantify how important it is to the respondent to have these needs met, nor does it measure respondents' reasons for choosing the activity. Instead, it measures the extent to which respondents report each need is gratified while participating in the activity being described.

The gain or improved condition (i.e., benefit) is sometimes more inferred than directly measured. For example, the benefit called Solitude (see Exhibit 1, no. 8) does not explicitly specify an improved condition. Recall, however, that the Tinsley and Tinsley (1986, 1988) paradigm views need gratification as an *intervening variable* which mediates the relation between leisure experiences and benefits such as physical health, mental health, and life satisfaction. Another important qualification is that the notion of need gratification presupposes a need which requires gratification. In the

Table 1. Psychological needs identified by Tinsley, Barrett, and Kass (1977).

Leisure Activity Specific: 27 needs which can be satisfied to a significantly greater degree through participation in some leisure activities than by participation in other leisure activities.

Ability Utilization	Creativity	Security
Achievement	Dominance	Self-Esteem
Activity	Exhibition	Sentience
Advancement	Getting Along with Others	Sex
Affiliation	Independence	Social Service
Aggression	Nurturance	Social Status
Authority	Play	Supervision
Catharsis	Responsibility	Understanding
Compensation	Reward	Variety

Leisure Activity General: 17 needs which are satisfied to approximately the same degree by all leisure activities.

Abasement	Infavoidance	Relaxation
Autonomy	Justice	Self-Control
Counteraction	Moral Values	Succorance
Defendence	Order	Task Generalization
Deference	Recognition	Tolerance
Harmavoidance	Rejection	

Exhibit 1. Psychological benefits of leisure: Description and reliability (in parenthesis) of factors derived from analysis of 27 leisure-specific need satisfier scales.

1. Self-expression[1] (.92)
    A complex benefit reflecting, in order of prominence:
    a. satisfaction of the individual's need to express oneself successfully through creative use of one's talents
    b. to undertake novel activities, often of benefit to others
    c. to enjoy recognition and power for these efforts

2. Companionship (.93)
    Satisfies the person's need to engage in playful but supportive relationships with others in which feelings are valued, self-expression is accepted, and one's feelings about self are enhanced.

3. Power (.97)
    Satisfies the individual's needs to be in control of the social situation and enjoy the center of attention, often at the expense of others.

4. Compensation (.80)
    Satisfies the person's needs to experience something new, fresh, or unusual; to satisfy needs not satisfied by their job or daily routine.

5. Security (.80)
    Satisfies the individual's need to be able to make a safe and secure, long-term commitment free of bothersome change, in which they will be rewarded for their efforts and receive a measure of recognition.

6. Service (.87)
    Satisfies the person's need to be of assistance to others.

7. Intellectual Aestheticism (.94)
    Satisfies the need of the individual for intellectual stimulation and aesthetic experiences.
        Note: This factor appears to be bipolar with low scores reflecting satisfaction of the individual's need for physical activity.

8. Solitude[2] (.93)
    Satisfies the person's need to do things alone without feeling threatened.

---

[1]Originally named self-actualization
[2]Originally named autonomy

Source: Tinsley 1984. (Reprinted by permission)

absence of an appropriate need, a condition may be neutral or even negative in its effect. For example, it seems likely that under some circumstances, experiencing solitude can be nonbeneficial. We will return to this issue in our final section.

Reliability and Validity of the PAL

Tinsley and Johnson (1984) have reported split-group reliabilities for the sample of 34 leisure activities listed in Table 2. (The "T" scores in that table will be explained shortly). The reliabilities were obtained by dividing the total sample of respondents who described a given leisure activity into two samples using an odd/even split. Then the mean score assigned the activity on each of the 44 scales was calculated independently for the two split groups, the two sets of scale scores were correlated, and the correlation was adjusted using the Spearman-Brown prophecy formula. The split-group reliabilities were .94 or higher for all leisure activities except attending popular musical performances (.86) and photography (.91). The reliabilities ranged upward to .98, with a median of .96. This provides convincing evidence of the stability of the results obtained by the PAL across independent samples.

The evidence for the validity of the PAL still must be regarded as preliminary. Nevertheless, more validity information is available for the PAL than for most of the other instruments developed to measure leisure constructs (see Tinsley and Tinsley 1988). Tinsley and Kass (1980a) reported a multitrait-multimethod analysis of the PAL and Leisure Activity Questionnaire (LAQ) based on a sample of 10 leisure activities. The LAQ is a 334 item instrument designed to measure the same 44 dimensions as the PAL. Convergent validity coefficients for the activities ranged from .68 to .88, with a median of .81. Both analysis of variance and factor analysis procedures revealed substantial evidence of discriminant validity for the PAL. The ANOVA F ratios for the variance components for both convergent and discriminant validity were significant, but the variance component due to method bias was not significant. The relative magnitude of the variance components suggested that the convergent and discriminant validity were of practical as well as statistical significance.

Convergent and discriminant validity were also evident in the results of the factor analysis. Convergent validity was indicated in the factor loadings of identical activities on their respective target factors. These ranged from .92 to .97. Discriminant validity was supported by the degree to which the factor loadings of other activities were lower than the factor loading of the activities which were hypothesized to define the factor. Significant differences in the predicted direction were observed in 178 of 180 comparisons.

Tinsley and Kass (1980b) reported a discriminant analysis in which the PAL was administered to one of two cross-validation groups. The developmental sample and the other cross-validation sample had completed the LAQ. The cross-validation hit rates for the PAL (i.e., 54% and 55%) were higher than those for the LAQ (i.e., 50% and 51%). The cross-validation hit rates of both instruments exceeded the expected chance rate by a ratio of 4.2 to 1.

Tinsley and Bowman (1986) compared the ratings of stamp collecting obtained from experienced stamp collectors and naive respondents. Significant differences were found on 16 of the 44 PAL scales. Omega squared values of .10 or greater were observed for the following scales: ability utilization (.23), creativity (.19), affiliation (.16), tolerance (.14), cooperation (.11), reward (.10), and abasement (.10). Omega squared values of this magnitude reveal differences in the perceptions of the two groups which are of practical as well as statistical significance. The results of Tinsley and Bowman (1986) provide further evidence of the discriminant validity of the PAL.

Results of Research with PAL

The PAL has been used in many studies to determine the psychological need-gratifying properties of a wide variety of leisure activities. Table 2 summarizes the results for an illustrative sample of 34 leisure activities. The Factor T-scores given in Table 2 reflect the relative importance of each of the eight psychological benefit factors described in Exhibit 1. T scores in the range from 45-55 are considered average. T scores in the range from 56-60 are above average and those above 60 are high. T scores in the below average and low ranges are those from 40-44 and below 40, respectively.

Table 3 depicts the psychological benefits of 18 leisure activities reported by elderly persons (Tinsley and Teaff 1983). Further analysis of this data revealed six leisure activity clusters (Tinsley et al. 1985) and three significant canonical variates (Tinsley et al. 1987; see Table 4). Canonical variate 1 indicates that women over 65 years of age of lower socioeconomic status and morale report Companionship to be the principal psychological need gratified by their leisure experiences. Research suggests that the elderly are especially vulnerable to loneliness, but the number of friends a person has is less related to loneliness than to the lack of relationships of mutual sharing. The loading of Nurturance, Social Service, and Cooperation on canonical variate 1 are consistent with this observation.

Canonical variate 2 indicates that women in the 55-65 age range were more likely than men or women over 65 to report Recognition to be the principal need gratified by their

Table 2. T scores of leisure activities on psychological benefit factors.

Activity	Self-Expression	Companionship	Power	Compensation	Security	Service	Intellectual Aestheticism	Solitude
				Psychological Benefit				
Attending popular musical performances	44	61	65	55	44	43	55	35
Baking and cooking	54	49	54	46	48	64	58	43
Bicycling	60	53	58	61	49	39	36	52
Bowling	49	48	45	45	50	49	36	44
Camping	58	56	43	63	49	53	49	50
Canoeing	58	55	39	64	61	52	39	53
Ceramics	54	43	41	48	54	47	55	60
Collecting autographs	52	45	38	60	72	45	56	60
Collecting stamps	48	35	36	49	61	43	53	64
Drinking and socializing	38	69	73	40	36	46	57	29
Going to movies	30	45	54	55	35	42	64	52
Hiking	60	59	36	65	53	61	47	56
Jogging	54	46	42	51	61	43	37	60
Lake fishing	51	54	60	65	45	51	53	59
Painting with oils, acrylics, or water colors	58	47	40	55	56	53	56	55
Photography	56	49	51	52	51	52	59	55
Picnicking	51	65	54	62	38	61	51	39
Playing cards	39	44	55	19	32	33	48	41
Playing chess	52	39	53	41	55	42	65	47
Playing golf	53	51	58	48	58	49	50	52
Playing guitar	54	58	60	46	57	58	57	50
Playing tennis	57	51	56	52	56	44	36	44
Playing volleyball	57	61	52	52	48	52	34	30
Raising house plants	51	50	48	46	56	66	62	60
Reading fiction	34	40	46	58	46	46	68	62
Roller skating	54	56	58	49	40	46	34	46
Shooting pool	46	48	65	36	41	44	48	48
Swimming	58	55	54	43	58	54	38	54
Vegetable gardening	65	50	39	53	61	76	47	54
Visiting friends/relations	47	70	63	46	59	72	59	29
Watching basketball	49	47	60	42	46	44	33	36
Watching television	19	30	45	52	31	36	51	58
Woodworking	59	47	45	51	59	58	48	57
Working crossword puzzles	32	23	28	31	33	35	61	63

Source: Tinsley and Tinsley 1988, page 243.

Table 3.   General level of 8 psychological benefits in 18 leisure activities known to be important to elderly people. [1]

Activity	Psychological Benefit							
	Self-Expression	Companionship	Power	Compensation	Security	Service	Intellectual Aestheticism	Solitude
Playing cards	A	A	A	L	L	L	A	L
Playing bingo	A	H	A	A	A	A	L	A
Watching sports (not on TV)	A	L	L	A	L	L	L	A
Bowling	A	H	A	A	A	A	L	A
Picnicking	L	A	A	H	L	A	A	L
Raising house plants	A	L	L	A	H	A	L	H
Collecting photographs	A	L	L	L	A	L	A	H
Collecting antiques	A	A	A	A	H	L	H	H
Knitting and crocheting	H	A	A	L	H	A	A	H
Woodworking	H	L	L	H	H	L	L	H
Ceramics	H	H	A	H	H	H	H	H
Dancing	H	H	H	H	H	A	L	L
Watching TV	L	L	L	L	L	L	L	A
Reading	A	L	A	H	H	A	H	H
Volunteer service activities	H	A	H	A	A	H	H	L
Volunteer professional activities	H	H	H	A	A	H	H	L
Attending meetings of social groups	A	H	H	A	L	H	H	L
Attending meetings of religious organizations	A	A	H	A	H	H	A	L

[1] L = below average to low, A = average, and H = above average to high.

Source: Tinsley and Teaff 1983.

Table 4. Correlation of psychological benefits and personal characteristics with canonical variates.

Psychological Benefits	Canonical Variates[1]		
	I	II	III
Affiliation	60	05	25
Cooperation	52	04	08
Nurturance	56	-12	18
Security	36	10	18
Supervision	50	34	21
Advancement	18	36	08
Reward	22	37	24
Self-esteem	13	40	09
Sentience	05	34	15
Creativity	14	30	46
Ability utilization	-05	22	43
Authority	04	-12	66
Dominance	10	-20	44
Responsibility	18	-09	38
Social service	34	04	54
Social status	19	-13	53
Achievement	18	13	29
Activity	11	18	22
Aggression	-05	-08	-09
Catharsis	28	-06	-13
Compensation	25	-28	12
Exhibition	-26	-16	00
Independence	07	-02	09
Play	16	24	08
Sex	-02	07	04
Understanding	20	28	29
Variety	11	19	11
Personal characteristics:			
Gender	48	85	21
Age	80	-38	43
Socioeconomic status	-65	02	72
Morale	-30	07	26
Physical health	26	-15	11
Canonical correlation	47[2]	26[2]	23[2]
Eigenvalue	22	07	05

[1] Decimal points have been omitted.

[2] $p \leq 0.001$.

Source: Tinsley, Colbs, Teaff, and Kaufman 1987.

leisure experiences. Tinsley and Faunce (1980) have shown that the decision of a woman to work as a homemaker instead of working outside the home is typically influenced more by her practical situation (e.g., family situation) than by her abilities and interests. Those who work outside the home report Recognition and Enhanced Self-Esteem to be important benefits, while Recognition is typically absent for homemakers (Tinsley and Tinsley 1989). Canonical variate 2 suggests that the leisure experiences of older women offer an alternate method of satisfying their need for Recognition and Self-Esteem.

Canonical variate 3 illustrates that persons over 65 years of age from higher socioeconomic backgrounds were most likely to report gratification of their needs for Power through their leisure experiences. This pattern stands in contrast to the conclusion of some (e.g., Gordon et al. 1976, Lawton et al. 1982) that increasing age is associated with an increasing orientation toward home-based, passive activities. Instead, for at least a significant subgroup of elderly persons, their economic security seems to free them to participate in activities in which they can rise to positions of power and influence.

The results of Tables 1-4 indicate some types of psychological benefits not discussed in the previous chapters and significant valuations placed on them. Together these results provide an overview of the research program of Tinsley and his associates and of the types of insights provided by their research approach.

Recreation Experience Preference Scales

Conceptual Foundation

Unlike Tinsley, Driver's training was not in psychology but in natural resource planning and policy analysis, with a heavy dose of economics. His interest in the needs-fulfilling function of amenity resources arose from his frustration at the lack of methods and instruments suitable for testing his belief that leisure was beneficial, especially leisure occurring in natural environments. Because of his early interest in environmental stress (Carson and Driver 1967), Driver was especially interested in the role of leisure and natural environments in stress mediation (see chapter by Ulrich, Dimberg and Driver).

Given the primitive nature of research on leisure in the mid-1960s it was neither feasible nor possible to investigate the benefits of leisure directly. Driver opted to evaluate these benefits indirectly by looking at the motivational bases of leisure choice. His goal was to develop a data base which would allow strong inferences to be made about how particular leisure activities and settings benefited different types of recreationists. This orientation led Driver to begin work in 1968 with graduate students at The University of Michigan on the development of psychometric instruments to identify and assess the relative importance of benefit-implying reasons why recreationists select particular activities and environments.

The early conceptual foundation, derived from consumer economics and the concept of expected utility, was based on the notion that specific vectors/dimensions of utility could be identified and their relative importance quantified. This belief ran counter to the then conventional wisdom in economics that perceived utility as a holistic abstraction that could not be quantified. Subsequently, Driver et al. modified that expected utility orientation to incorporate tenets of the expectancy valence model of psychology. This expanded model (unlike expected utility) explicitly endorses the notion that specific multiple dimensions of value (i.e., salient benefits and attributes) could both be identified and quantified for a particular choice object (Driver 1976).

Like the PAL, development of the REP scales was backed by the "unmet needs" hypothesis that leisure was beneficial in helping people gratify needs (defined largely by personality testing instruments) not satisfied by their nonleisure behavior. (See Driver and Knopf 1977 on the relationships between personality traits and recreation behavior.) The traits-based unmet needs tack proved difficult to relate to recreation area management, however, so a different approach was followed guided by the works of Lawler (1973) in industrial psychology and Fishbein and Ajzen (1975) in attitude theory and measurement (Haas et al. 1981, Manfredo et al. 1983).

Lawler's concepts are within the tradition of human motivation theories which suggest observable behavior can be explained by examining the determinants of motivation. Similar to the Tinsley et al. efforts, the Lawler approach is backed by the unmet needs hypothesis. Lawler (1973) suggested that human performances lead to a variety of outcomes, some of which are ends in themselves and some of which might be intermediate in achieving other outcomes. Furthermore, he suggested that the attractiveness of an outcome is determined by the extent to which it satisfies a human need, with needs defined as those outcomes which people seek as ends. Given the orientations of Driver et al., the outcomes of most interest were those that could be affected by management actions and those that connoted a benefit (e.g., improved physical health from the desire for Exercise/Physical Fitness, which is one of the REP scales).

Fishbein and Ajzen's theory of Reasoned Action become better known in the mid to late 1970s (Fishbein and Ajzen 1975, Ajzen and Fishbein 1980), and it was later refined by Ajzen (1985) into the theory of Planned Behavior.

As with Lawler's model, Fishbein and Ajzen's theory is based in expectancy-valence formulations of human decisionmaking. Specifically, under that model, choice of recreation would be a function of (1) the salient beliefs regarding the outcomes of making a specific recreation choice, (2) the strength of beliefs about these outcomes, (3) an evaluation of the desirability of these outcomes, and (4) beliefs about what others feel the person should choose and the motivation to comply with others. Since the focus of the Fishbein-Ajzen theory is upon behavioral prediction, and since it explicitly deals with beliefs about specific consequences of a particular leisure behavior, it has helped guide conceptualization of leisure benefits as advantageous outcomes or consequences.

Figure 4 (Brown 1984) shows the general conceptual model that guided the Driver et al. research. Note the box labeled Consumer Output which is defined as "recreation experience[s]" that serve as *intervening variables* in the production of benefits for individuals and society—shown in the last two boxes to the right. Thus, the concept of intervening variable is explicit in Figure 4, as is the strong applied orientation of the Driver et al. research.

The applied focus centered on two issues. First, Driver et al. were concerned with how amenity resource managers (who generally have little training in the social and behavioral sciences) could better understand and respond to the needs and demands of recreationists. Second, they wanted to identify ways in which the importance of these demands could be quantified more objectively. They believed this was necessary for the amenities to compete more fairly with data on "cash flows" generated to public agency treasuries from alternative-to-amenity uses of publicly administered resources. Thus, although the focus was on benefits to recreationists, Driver et al.'s research was directly concerned with the benefits and costs of basic recreation resource allocation decisions. A primary objective of that research was to enhance amenity resource managers' ability to specify management objectives and prescriptions that would provide recreation experience opportunities identified by the research on recreationists' motivations. This orientation later led to the practice of experience-based management of recreation settings, as reflected in Manfredo et al. (1983) and to use of the Recreation Opportunity Spectrum system (see Driver et al. 1987).

Recent efforts by Driver et al. have focused more explicitly on the last two "benefits as outputs" boxes of Figure 4 than did previous studies—as reflected by this volume.

Development of the REP Scales

As with Tinsley et al., the first task of Driver and his colleagues was to identify human needs that could be gratified by leisure behavior. Early pursuit of the unmet needs hypothesis led to the identification of many "reasons for recreating" from the personality trait literature (e.g., achievement, independence, and control). However, because the trait-defined needs generally did not have direct managerial relevance, most of the needs were derived from the leisure literature, from numerous focus group sessions conducted with recreationists, or serendipitously from the statistical clusterings of early item pools in which previously unanticipated need-implying constructs emerged as clusters. Subsequently, the items were refined and new ones added in many empirical replications in survey research that employed both personal interview schedules and mail questionnaires.

The relative importance of each item in the original version of the REP inventory was assessed using a response format that evaluated each scale item as to its "importance" as a reason for deciding to recreate in a particular activity at a certain place. The response alternatives ranged from Not At All Important to Extremely Important. At this time respondents completed the questionnaire when interviewed on site. Later, a different response format was introduced that asked respondents to indicate the contribution of each scale item to total expected satisfaction. Response alternatives ranged from Detracts Very Strongly through Neither Detracts Nor Adds to Adds Very Strongly. Most of the research using this response format employed questionnaires mailed to respondents 2-4 months after sample frames were developed from brief on-site interviews. The instructional set asked the subjects to assume they were to take an identical trip next year and then rate each item as to its expected affect on expected overall satisfaction from that future narrowly defined type of leisure engagement.

Most of the work in developing the REP scales was done by examining only the valence component of the respondents' leisure-related experience preferences, using either the "Importance" or "Adds To-Detracts From" response formats. Following the Fishbein and Ajzen model, recent applications of the scales have assessed not only the valence but the perceived likelihood of each experience occurring. The general title of the resultant scales has changed over time from "Unmet Needs," "Preferred Psychological Outcomes," and "Perceived Immediate Benefits" to the current name, "Recreation Experience Preference" (REP) scales, which has been in use since about 1982.

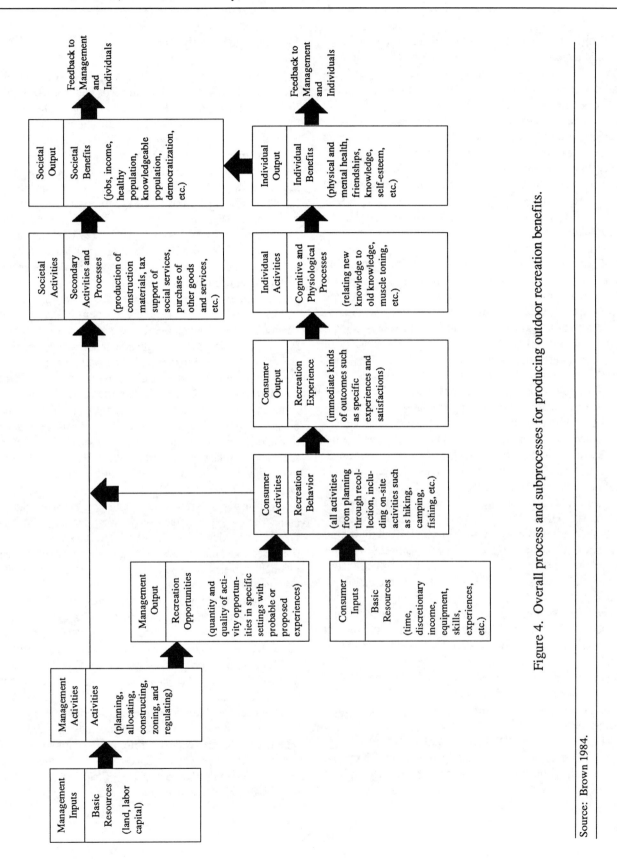

Figure 4. Overall process and subprocesses for producing outdoor recreation benefits.

Source: Brown 1984.

Currently, 43 REP scales exist to measure the extent to which specific experiences are desired and expected from leisure activities. The names of those scales are shown in Exhibit 2 along with the 19 more general recreation experience preference "domains" into which the 43 scales are grouped empirically. Most of the domains are relatively orthogonal. Some overlap is apparent in the scales and domains measured by the REP and PAL, but there are also substantial differences which reflect the different orientations and purposes of the two instruments.

Reliability and Validity of the REP Scales

From 1968 to about 1976, efforts concentrated solely on developing and refining the scales. From about 1976 to 1984, efforts were directed toward improving, confirming statistical properties, and applying the scales. At least 50 empirical studies have been conducted by Driver et al. to test the reliability and validity of the scales. Some studies included all 43 REP scales and others a subset of them. Space here does not permit an in-depth discussion of all studies for each of the 43 REP scales, but an overview will be provided of the tests of several types of reliability and validity.

Much of the scale development work focused on obtaining good statistical properties, such as maintaining an average Pearson correlation between items within a scale of at least .4, realizing a Cronbach alpha of .6 or higher, and maintaining independence (low correlation) between scales not in the same domain and between domains. These objectives have been met. The Cronbach alphas of most of the full-item scales exceed .75 (Driver[1]). Tinsley et al. (1982) computed the Cronbach alphas for 32 scales comprised of their best two ("core") items (i.e., not the full-item scales) for two large data sets. They found alphas ranging from a low of .46 to a high of .86, averaging .68 in one study and .72 in the other. Tinsley et al. (1982) also examined the split-group reliabilities of the 32 REP scales, again separately for 2 large data sets and for 6 separate recreation activities. Those split-group correlations ranged from .54 to .97 for one data set, with few of them lower than .65, and from .74 to .99 in the other study, with very few below .80.

Regarding stability over time (i.e., test-retest reliability), Graefe et al. (1981) indicated good stability over time for average scale and domain scores computed across subjects at different points in time. However, Manfredo (1984) and Williams (1988) determined that, when subjects are administered the REP instrument at different points in time (i.e., before, during, months after participation), there is no effect due to time, but there is a subject-by-time interaction. One reason for this finding may be recall bias, i.e., people are inaccurate in attempting to remember their feelings when

making a decision. Another explanation may be that, regardless of the instructional set which asks people to recall their reasons for participating, people's responses are influenced by their current state (i.e., needs that currently exist), expected state (what they would experience on the next visit), or realized state (i.e., what they actually experienced). In fact, there has been no study which provides the necessary test for effects due to time. Such a study should use a repeat measures design to compare administrations of REP scales that occur at the *same point* in time with respect to participation. For example, two time-lapsed measures could be taken of the same subjects before they engaged in the same recreation opportunity. This is an area that needs further research.

Several tests of different types of validity have been made, with some of them yet unreported. The nature of the scales, especially the large number of them, required that particular attention be given to the content validity of each scale. Opportunities for close scrutiny of such validity were afforded by the literally scores of empirical studies and clusterings of items that were done to refine items, achieve reasonable statistical independence between the scales and domains, and meet the statistical criteria of an average Pearson correlation of .4 between items within a scale and a Cronbach alpha of .6 or higher. Specifically, spuriously correlated items that did not fit logically with a construct being tapped by each scale were dropped. For example, tests of content validity (i.e., separate clustering and judgments about logical fits of items in clusters) were made for up to 15 different cuts of a particular data set, with these segmentations defined by type of activity, age, sex, etc. So long as at least two core items were used per scale from the inventory, the content validity of the scales have been upheld by many scientists using the scales (cf., Graefe et al. 1981). Naturally, problems have existed when one-item scales were used by some researchers.

Considerable developmental effort was also devoted to refinement of the item pool to achieve reasonable statistical independence between domains and between scales not in the same domain. That goal has been a difficult one to obtain; since each of the 43 scales usually tap positive aspects of the same type of behavior (leisure activity), the chance for intercorrelation is high. Nevertheless, very good statistical independence has been achieved between scales (not belonging to the same domain) and between domains (see footnote 1). By definition, scales within a domain show higher independence but do show structural differences when a hierarchial clustering algorithm is used.

Tinsley et al. (1982) concluded that the 35 scales and 18 domains they tested showed "acceptable...concurrent validity" based on discriminant analyses of two large data sets.

Exhibit 2. Recreation experience preference (REP) scales making up the recreation
experience preference domains.[1]

1. Enjoy nature
   A. Scenery
   B. General nature experience

2. Physical fitness

3. Reduce tension
   A. Tension release
   B. Slow down mentally
   C. Escape role overloads
   D. Escape daily routines

4. Escape physical stressors
   A. Tranquility/solitude
   B. Privacy
   C. Escape crowds
   D. Escape noise

5. Outdoor learning
   A. General learning
   B. Exploration
   C. Learn geography of area
   D. Learn about nature

6. Share similar values
   A. Be with friends
   B. Be with people having
      similar values

7. Independence
   A. Independence
   B. Autonomy
   C. Being in control

8. Family relations
   A. Family kinship
   B. Escape family

9. Introspection
   A. Spiritual
   B. Personal values

10. Be with considerate people
    (social security)

11. Achievement/stimulation
    A. Reinforcing self-confidence
    B. Social recognition
    C. Skill development
    D. Competence testing
    E. Seeking excitement
    F. Endurance
    G. Telling others

12. Physical rest

13. Teach/lead others
    A. Teaching/sharing skills
    B. Leading others

14. Risk taking

15. Risk reduction
    A. Risk moderation
    B. Risk prevention

16. Meet new people
    A. Meet new people
    B. Observe other people

17. Creativity

18. Nostalgia

19. Agreeable temperatures

[1]Individual REP scales are designated by the indented capital letters if there is more than one scale per domain and
by the name given the domain when there is only one scale per domain.

Rosenthal et al. (1982) tested for the construct validity of eight of the scales using multitrait-multimethod analyses and concluded that "the construct validity of seven of eight scales studied was verified."

Few studies have attempted to test the predictive validity of the scales, and we believe that those that have reflect design problems. A common problem has been attempts to predict a dependent variable (e.g., choice of a certain type of setting) from a particular REP scale when a priori logic would suggest little relationship should be expected between that REP scale and the dependent variables. However, in many applications of the scales, there is strong evidence of criterion validity; technical mountain climbers score highest on risk taking, photographers score high on creativity, low income inner city users of a nearby urban park rank stress-reducing experiences as most important, and so on.

Crandall et al.[2] did a validity study to test relationships between scores on four scales related to preferences for social interaction and scores on Eysenck's Personality Inventory (Eysenck and Eysenck 1963) which provided indexes of the respondents' tendencies toward introversion or extroversion. Modest correlations (generally .20 to .59) were found across the five activities and four scales studied. Lastly, Michaels and Driver,[3] in a yet unpublished study, found little evidence of social desirability bias in any of the scales using the Marlowe-Crowne Social Desirability Scale (Crowne and Marlowe 1964) and another test they developed.

In summary, it can safely be said that the REP scales seem to have reasonable validity and reliability. Further research is needed to make more definitive statements.

Results of Research with the REP Scales

The REP scales have been used widely by many scientists in several countries. Example results from some of those REP studies are given in Tables 5-7 and Figure 5. (Because the names given the scales have changed over time, some of the scales in Tables 5-7 will have labels different from those assigned them in Exhibit 2.)

Table 5 (Driver and Cooksey 1980) shows results from a study containing 24 REP scales which were administered to randomly selected recreationists using parks along the Huron River near Ann Arbor, Michigan. Note both the differences and similarities in REP scale scores within and between the activities. Figure 5 is based on responses of the fishermen in the Table 5 sample and shows that REPs differed significantly across the different market segments defined for that group. Specifically, those Huron River anglers were segmented into "Object Types" (called O-Types)

based on revelation of their eight most highly valued REPs. This clustering of people by these eight experience preferences yielded six O-Types (or experience-types). The mean scores of each O-Type on the eight experience preferences are plotted in Figure 5. Notice that Type 3 scored high and Type 4 scored low on all the eight REP scales, reflecting differing motivations. This technique of segmenting allows study of the social, demographic, and economic characteristics of each O-Type, thereby revealing how different types of users benefit in different ways.

Table 6 summarizes the overall mean scores on 16 REP domains (i.e., groups of REP scales—see Exhibit 2) of users of 15 different areas ranging from designated wilderness areas to highly used outdoor areas (Driver et al. 1987). As presented in Table 6, the results are not activity-specific (the mean scores cover all activities within each area), but focused almost entirely on back-pack camping and hiking. Rank orders of the mean scores are shown for each area. Note patterns of commonality across areas in those REPs ranked the highest. The standard deviations are not shown to avoid clutter, but the coefficients of variation were 20-50% of the means, reflecting in part the aggregation across activities. A more detailed discussion of the results appearing in Tables 5 and 6 appears in the sources cited.

Table 7 summarizes previously unreported data from studies done by B. L. Driver, Perry Brown, Ross Arnold, and Glenn Haas. The response format and coding were the same as for the Table 6 data. The generally sizable standard deviations shown in Tables 5 and 7 are typical and reflect the diversity of motivations, as indicated by the object types in Figure 5.

Though several are in progress, only one study has been reported (Manfredo et al. 1989) that attempted to measure benefits that are perceived to flow from recreation experiences as measured using the REP scales. Drawing on concepts from Bem (1970), the Manfredo et al. (1989) study was based on the following propositions: (1) human behaviors are directed by beliefs; (2) there is a vertical and horizontal organization of beliefs; (3) values are desired end-states or conditions that are defined as evaluative beliefs which serve as the foundation for many higher order beliefs; and (4) the benefits arising from recreation participation can be examined by assessing the extent to which it allows people to achieve or reinforce important values. The Manfredo et al. study developed an instrument composed largely of REP scale items and asked subjects to indicate how centrally important the selected REP outcome (e.g., family cohesion) was in their life and the extent to which hunting allowed them to achieve the desired end-states indicated by the REP scale used.

Table 5. Mean scores on preferred psychological outcome scales by participants in six activities in the Michigan Huron River study.

Psychological Outcome	Camping RO[1]	Camping x̄[2]	Camping (sd)[3]	Picnicking RO	Picnicking x̄	Picnicking (sd)	Swimming RO	Swimming x̄	Swimming (sd)	Boating RO	Boating x̄	Boating (sd)	Sailing RO	Sailing x̄	Sailing (sd)	Fishing RO	Fishing x̄	Fishing (sd)	Max. Diff. in x̄s[4]
1. Escape daily routine	1	4.7	(1.1)	1	4.3	(1.3)	2	4.4	(1.3)	2	4.2	(1.2)	1	4.1	(1.2)	2	4.2	(1.4)	
2. Physical rest	3	4.4	(1.4)	1	4.3	(1.4)	1	4.5	(1.2)	5	3.5	(1.5)	4	3.6	(1.5)	1	4.3	(1.4)	1.0
3. Enjoy nature	4	4.3	(1.2)	1	4.3	(1.3)	4	4.1	(1.3)	1	4.3	(1.2)	3	3.7	(1.3)	3	4.1	(1.4)	
4. Escape physical pressures	2	4.6	(1.4)	1	4.3	(1.6)	3	4.3	(1.4)	3	4.0	(1.5)	4	3.6	(1.4)	2	4.2	(1.5)	1.0
5. Tranquility - privacy	5	3.8	(1.3)	2	4.0	(1.3)	5	3.7	(1.3)	5	3.5	(1.3)	6	3.3	(1.3)	4	3.8	(1.3)	0.7
6. Be with other people	6	3.7	(1.3)	3	3.9	(1.3)	6	3.5	(1.2)	4	3.8	(1.2)	2	3.8	(1.2)	6	3.4	(1.3)	
7. Slow down mentally	5	3.8	(1.5)	5	3.4	(1.4)	6	3.5	(1.3)	7	3.1	(1.4)	7	3.2	(1.3)	5	3.5	(1.4)	0.7
8. Exercise - physical fitness	8	3.3	(1.5)	6	3.1	(1.5)	7	3.4	(1.4)	4	3.8	(1.4)	5	3.5	(1.5)	8	3.1	(1.7)	0.7
9. Escape role overloads[5]																			
10. Family togetherness	7	3.5	(1.3)	4	3.5	(1.5)	8	3.0	(1.4)	8	2.9	(1.5)	9	2.8	(1.4)	9	2.9	(1.5)	0.7
11. Learning - discovery	9	3.2	(1.2)	7	2.9	(1.3)	11	2.7	(1.3)	6	3.2	(1.2)	9	2.8	(1.2)	7	3.2	(1.3)	
12. Security	8	3.3	(1.5)	7	2.9	(1.5)	9	2.9	(1.6)	9	2.6	(1.4)	9	2.8	(1.4)	9	2.9	(1.6)	0.7
13. Nostalgia	10	3.1	(1.6)	8	2.8	(1.6)	10	2.8	(1.6)	10	2.5	(1.5)	11	2.5	(1.5)	7	3.2	(1.6)	0.7
14. Independence - autonomy	13	2.2	(1.0)	9	2.1	(1.1)	13	2.2	(1.0)	11	2.2	(1.0)	10	2.6	(1.1)	13	2.4	(1.1)	
15. Agreeable temperatures																9	2.9	(1.8)	
16. Teaching - sharing skills	13	2.2	(1.3)	11	1.9	(1.9)	14	1.9	(1.1)	11	2.2	(1.3)	10	2.6	(1.4)	11	2.6	(1.6)	0.7
17. Meet/observe other people	11	3.0	(1.3)	8	2.3	(1.3)	10	2.8	(1.4)	12	2.1	(1.1)	9	2.8	(1.3)	11	2.6	(1.4)	0.9
18. Introspection	12	2.4	(1.2)	8	2.3	(1.3)	12	2.3	(1.5)	11	2.2	(1.2)	12	2.1	(1.1)	11	2.6	(1.5)	
19. Achievement	13	2.2	(1.3)	13	1.7	(1.1)	15	1.7	(1.0)	10	2.5	(1.3)	8	3.1	(1.4)	10	2.7	(1.6)	1.4
20. Seek stimulation	15	2.0	(1.1)	12	1.3	(1.0)	14	1.9	(1.1)	13	1.9	(0.9)	11	2.5	(1.2)	14	2.2	(1.1)	0.7
21. Creativity	14	2.1	(1.3)	10	2.0	(1.2)	14	1.9	(1.2)	13	1.9	(1.1)	13	2.0	(1.2)	15	2.0	(1.3)	
22. Spiritual																12	2.5	(1.8)	
23. Social recognition	16	1.5	(0.9)	14	1.4	(0.9)	17	1.3	(0.8)	14	1.5	(0.9)	14	1.9	(1.1)	16	1.8	(1.3)	
24. Risk taking	17	1.4	(0.7)	14	1.4	(0.9)	16	1.4	(0.8)	14	1.5	(1.0)	14	1.9	(1.2)	17	1.5	(0.9)	
Sample Size	201			312			304			324			157			335			

[1] RO designates rank order of mean scores, with tied scores given the same rank.

[2] Rating was done on a 6-point Likert-type response format on which 1 designated "not important" and 6 designated "extremely important."

[3] sd = standard deviation.

[4] This column shows the maximum difference in mean scores across activities when means differed by at least 0.7.

[5] A blank cell indicates that the row outcome scale was not included in the questionnaire for the column activity.

Source: Driver and Cooksey 1980.

Results of this study indicate that hunting is perceived to contribute to important conditions in life, but not uniformly across all values examined. The condition ranked highest by the study group was Family Togetherness (mean of 4.4, where 5.0 represented a Most Important Condition in Life) toward which hunting (on the average) contributed a moderately high amount. Hunting also contributed high amounts to Relationships with Nature, Positive Self-Image, and Independence, all of which were strongly important (4.0) Conditions in Life. The intervening variable nature of the "valued" REPs is apparent.

The chapter in this volume by Ulrich, Dimberg, and Driver examines the restorative role of leisure environments and reports results of additional applications of the REP scales.

CONCLUSIONS AND FUTURE RESEARCH DIRECTIONS

The results from use of the PAL and REP scales support the following conclusions. First, it is clear that a wide variety of perceived psychological benefits can be inferred from these studies. Second, it is possible to identify subgroups of users engaging in the same activity at the same site which differ in the extent to which they value these benefits. Third, despite the differences in motivations between users, strong patterns of commonality exist in these psychologically measured dimensions of leisure choice which suggest there is predictability about these benefits. Fourth, it is clear that the benefits of leisure exist in a chain of causality, as depicted in Figures 1 and 4. The realization of one benefit represents both an outcome early in the chain and an input for the realization of

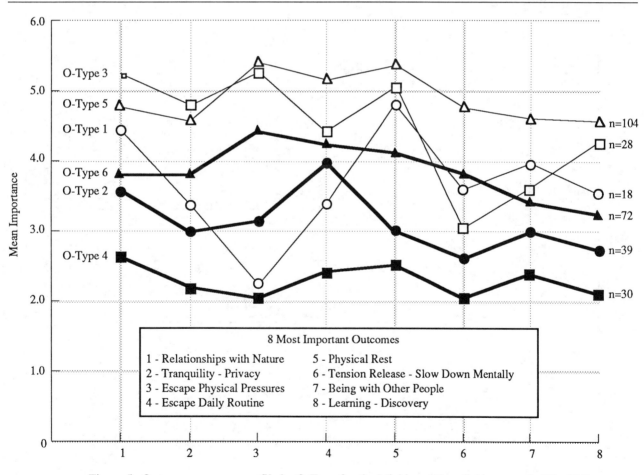

Figure 5. Outcome response profile by O-Type for the Michigan River fishing sample (N = 335).

Source: Driver and Cooksey 1980.

Table 6. Mean scores and their ranks (in parentheses) of responses to 16 recreation experience preference domains by users of eight designated wilderness, four undesignated wilderness, and three contrasting nonwilderness areas, with states in which located.[1]

Experience preference domains	Designated Wilderness							
	Weminuche (CO) (N = 313)	Maroon Bells (CO) (N = 268)	Flattops (CO) (N = 135)	Eagles Nest (CO) (N = 271)	Rawah (CO) (N = 212)	Linville Gorge (NC) (N = 249)	Shining Rock (NC) (N = 297)	Joyce Kilmer (NC) (N = 80)
1. Enjoy nature	1.5 (1)	1.5 (1)	1.5 (1)	1.5 (1)	1.7 (1)	1.5 (1)	1.6 (1)	1.4 (1)
2. Physical fitness	2.4 (4)	2.0 (2)	2.5 (5)	2.3 (2)	2.3 (3)	2.1 (2)	2.2 (2)	1.8 (2)
3. Reduce tensions	2.1 (2)	2.3 (4)	2.1 (2)	2.4 (3)	2.2 (2)	2.3 (3)	2.3 (3)	2.1 (3)
4. Escape noise/crowds	2.2 (3)	2.2 (3)	2.2 (3)	2.4 (3)	2.2 (2)	2.3 (3)	2.3 (3)	2.2 (4)
5. Outdoor learning	2.1 (2)	2.4 (5)	2.4 (4)	2.5 (4)	2.2 (2)	2.3 (3)	2.4 (4)	2.2 (4)
6. Sharing similar values	2.8 (5)	2.9 (6)	3.2 (8)	2.8 (4)	2.8 (4)	2.7 (4)	2.9 (5)	2.7 (6)
7. Independence	3.1 (7)	2.9 (6)	2.8 (7)	3.3 (7)	3.0 (6)	3.0 (7)	3.0 (6)	3.0 (8)
8. Family kinship	3.0 (6)	3.0 (7)	2.6 (6)	3.2 (6)	2.9 (5)	3.4 (9)	3.1 (7)	3.0 (8)
9. Introspection/spiritual	3.5 (8)	3.1 (8)	3.3 (9)	3.7 (8)	3.5 (7)	2.8 (5)	2.9 (5)	2.6 (5)
10. Considerate people	3.6 (9)	3.4 (9)	3.2 (8)	3.8 (9)	3.7 (8)	3.0 (7)	3.3 (8)	2.8 (7)
11. Achievement/stimulation	3.9 (11)	3.1 (8)	3.4 (10)	4.0 (11)	3.9 (10)	2.9 (6)	3.1 (7)	3.0 (8)
12. Physical rest	3.8 (10)	4.3 (10)	2.5 (5)	3.9 (10)	3.9 (10)	3.2 (8)	3.3 (8)	3.4 (9)
13. Teach/lead others	3.7 (10)	4.3 (10)	3.5 (11)	3.9 (10)	3.8 (9)	3.6 (10)	3.7 (9)	3.9 (10)
14. Risk taking	4.7 (12)	4.8 (12)	4.8 (13)	4.6 (12)	4.8 (10)	4.1 (11)	4.5 (10)	4.6 (12)
15. Risk reduction	4.8 (13)	4.7 (11)	4.7 (12)	4.7 (13)	4.8 (11)	4.7 (13)	4.7 (11)	4.7 (13)
16. Meet new people	5.6 (14)	5.3 (13)	5.5 (14)	5.5 (14)	5.8 (12)	4.6 (12)	4.5 (10)	4.5 (11)

Experience preference domains	Undesignated Wilderness				Nonwilderness Areas		
	Indian Peaks (CO) (N = 101)	Vermont (VT) (N = 415)	Commanche (CO) (N = 424)	Shoshone (WY) (N = 165)	Little Sahara (UT) (N = 421)	Arkansas River (CO) (N = 442)	Lake Shelbyville (IL) (N = 1,567)
1. Enjoy nature	1.8 (1)	2.5 (2)	1.7 (1)	1.9 (1)	2.4 (4)	1.7 (1)	3.1 (2)
2. Physical fitness	2.8 (4)	2.7 (4)	2.4 (2)	2.2 (3)	2.2 (3)	2.3 (4)	3.1 (2)
3. Reduce tensions	1.9 (2)	1.9 (1)	2.4 (2)	2.0 (2)	2.7 (5)	2.2 (3)	3.3 (4)
4. Escape noise/crowds	2.8 (4)	2.8 (5)	2.5 (3)	2.0 (2)	3.1 (9)	2.1 (2)	3.3 (4)
5. Outdoor learning	2.4 (3)	2.5 (3)	2.5 (3)	2.2 (3)	2.9 (8)	2.3 (4)	3.8 (6)
6. Sharing similar values	3.3 (6)	3.0 (7)	3.5 (7)	3.1 (7)	1.2 (1)	2.3 (4)	3.1 (2)
7. Independence	3.2 (5)	2.9 (5)	3.2 (4)	3.1 (7)	2.7 (6)	2.7 (5)	3.7 (5)
8. Family kinship	3.4 (7)	3.6 (9)	3.6 (8)	2.5 (4)	2.1 (2)	2.1 (2)	3.2 (3)
9. Introspection/spiritual	3.3 (6)	3.2 (8)	3.4 (6)	2.6 (5)	3.5 (12)	3.5 (8)	4.1 (8)
10. Considerate people	3.1 (4)	-	3.3 (5)	3.0 (6)	-	-	4.8 (10)
11. Achievement/stimulation	3.6 (8)	3.3 (9)	3.8 (9)	3.1 (8)	2.8 (7)	3.1 (6)	4.2 (9)
12. Physical rest	3.1 (4)	5.0 (11)	3.4 (6)	3.3 (9)	3.2 (10)	3.1 (2)	3.0 (1)
13. Teach/lead others	4.2 (9)	-	4.1 (10)	3.9 (10)	3.6 (13)	3.1 (6)	5.2 (11)
14. Risk taking	4.6 (10)	3.2 (8)	5.1 (13)	2.2 (3)	2.2 (3)	2.2 (3)	5.3 (12)
15. Risk reduction	4.7 (11)	-	4.5 (11)	4.9 (11)	3.3 (11)	3.4 (7)	-
16. Meet new people	5.1 (12)	4.5 (10)	4.9 (12)	4.9 (11)	3.5 (12)	4.0 (9)	4.0 (7)

1 Ratings were made on the following 9-point response format (with numerical codes used to compute means): Adds (to satisfaction): most strongly (1), strongly (2), moderately (3), a little (6), neither adds nor detracts (5); detracts: a little (6), moderately (7), strongly (8), most strongly (9). Coefficients of variation were 20-50% of the means.

Source: Driver et al. 1987.

Table 7. Responses of recreationists using the Arkansas River in Colorado to
Recreation Experience Preference scales.

Scale	Camping			Fishing			Hiking			Sightseeing		
	$\bar{x}$	SD	N	$\bar{x}$	SD	N	$\bar{x}$	SD	N	$\bar{x}$	SD	N
Reinforcing self-image	6.35	2.94	101	6.16	2.89	115	7.71	1.52	24	5.63	3.15	132
Skill development	6.44	2.67	103	7.07	2.02	116	7.75	1.29	24	5.42	3.00	130
Excitement	4.51	2.82	102	4.84	2.78	115	6.22	2.37	23	4.79	2.73	129
Telling others	6.50	2.02	104	6.10	2.11	116	6.46	2.13	24	7.09	1.79	131
Independence	6.26	2.65	102	6.48	2.48	116	6.96	2.49	25	6.07	2.48	130
Control-power	6.87	2.16	102	6.52	2.47	111	6.38	2.22	24	6.50	2.35	125
Risk taking	3.92	2.61	103	4.35	2.69	114	6.00	2.17	24	3.91	2.73	130
Equipment	7.12	2.00	104	7.30	1.77	118	6.58	2.43	24	5.70	2.78	132
Family togetherness	8.02	1.97	104	7.03	2.45	118	6.63	2.57	24	7.77	2.23	134
Being with friends	7.92	1.39	102	6.91	2.26	117	7.72	1.02	25	7.77	1.55	125
Being with similar people	7.49	1.98	104	7.23	2.10	117	7.63	1.21	24	7.38	2.04	136
Meeting new people	6.58	2.05	103	5.51	2.57	116	6.04	2.49	25	6.09	2.25	133
Observing other people	5.66	2.01	103	4.95	2.37	117	5.12	1.90	25	5.43	2.15	131
General learning	7.49	1.43	103	7.45	1.76	116	7.92	1.15	25	7.59	1.55	128
Exploration	8.12	0.85	101	7.48	1.19	114	8.42	0.69	24	8.09	0.92	128
Geography of area	7.33	2.07	103	6.72	2.41	116	8.28	0.84	25	6.86	2.54	133
Learn about nature	7.49	1.54	103	7.20	1.80	118	8.20	0.82	25	7.37	2.14	134
Scenery	8.46	0.71	101	7.87	1.53	118	8.52	0.65	25	8.60	0.66	135

Table 7. (continued)

Scale	Camping			Fishing			Hiking			Sightseeing		
	$\bar{x}$	SD	N	$\bar{x}$	SD	N	$\bar{x}$	SD	N	$\bar{x}$	SD	N
General nature experience	8.22	1.02	104	8.11	1.45	116	8.56	0.77	25	8.17	1.41	131
Spiritual	6.25	2.63	103	6.20	2.58	117	6.71	2.51	24	5.93	2.96	133
Introspection	5.97	2.70	101	5.49	2.79	116	6.28	2.67	25	5.53	2.95	132
Creativity	6.64	2.69	102	4.10	3.20	115	6.12	3.32	25	6.10	2.98	134
Exercise-physical fitness	7.57	1.14	103	7.84	1.20	114	8.29	0.91	24	7.29	1.27	124
Physical rest	8.21	1.07	102	8.11	1.38	118	7.16	1.97	25	7.78	1.79	135
Tension release	7.17	2.24	103	6.99	2.43	117	6.96	2.56	24	6.71	2.52	136
Slow down mentally	7.77	1.42	104	7.28	2.38	115	7.72	1.77	25	7.57	1.94	130
Escape role overloads	7.43	2.07	104	7.10	2.30	118	7.28	2.22	25	7.04	2.45	134
Escape daily routine	8.37	1.39	102	8.10	1.30	116	8.63	0.58	24	8.21	1.23	135
Tranquility	8.26	1.24	104	8.12	1.49	116	8.44	0.82	25	8.27	1.20	131
Escape crowds	7.84	0.92	101	7.86	1.02	115	8.13	0.98	24	7.75	0.98	127
Escape physical stressors	7.34	2.30	104	7.03	2.44	118	7.96	1.93	25	6.95	2.71	131
Social security	7.51	1.92	104	6.32	2.67	115	7.35	2.33	23	6.55	2.58	133
Escaping family	3.42	2.93	103	4.95	3.08	117	4.38	3.41	24	4.06	3.10	135
Teaching-sharing skills	6.40	2.40	104	6.50	2.08	113	6.79	2.00	24	5.95	2.73	133
Risk avoidance	6.09	2.76	100	5.80	2.76	115	5.26	2.73	23	6.28	2.79	134

a subsequent benefit later in the chain. For example, assume that a worker on a boring job realizes from leisure a *Compensation* benefit (Exhibit 1, No. 4; gratification of the need to experience something new) and that this benefit leads to better *mental health* of the bored worker. This can cause several beneficial consequences. For example, it might result in *improved work performance* which can lead to *a higher salary,* which, in turn, is perceived by our worker as creating *greater economic stability,* a condition shown by Campbell (1981) to be an important contributor to the end-state benefit of *life satisfaction.*

Tinsley, Driver, and their colleagues have characterized their inventories as measuring "perceived psychological benefits" of leisure (Brown 1981; Driver and Brown 1986; Driver and Knopf 1975, 1977; Tinsley 1984; Tinsley and Tinsley 1986). Both groups of scholars recognize that this label can be questioned, and both are aware of the shortcomings of current approaches.

Until recently, Driver et al. have relied mostly on an "inferential" definition of benefit, reasoning that if a particular REP scale were perceived as important it reflected a benefit. Current efforts are directed at defining the benefits more explicitly. Tinsley and Tinsley's (1986, 1988) model postulates that psychological need gratification is necessary for mental and physical health, personal growth, and life satisfaction. But the literature on human needs is fraught with disagreements about how many human needs exist and their importance. Also, the PAL measures perceived degree to which a need can be met by a designated leisure activity, not how important the satisfaction of that need is to the respondent. Thus, even though one is engaging in an activity that scores high on providing opportunities to meet particular needs, this does not mean that those benefits are in fact being derived. Tinsley and his associates are in the very early stages of constructing a scale to measure the psychological needs of the individual in an effort to address this weakness.

We believe that the PAL and REP scales do identify and measure intermediate benefits in the chain of benefits associated with leisure behavior. Our position has been that the notions of need gratification and pursuit of desired psychological outcomes or desired experiences through leisure activity, can perhaps best be understood as intervening variables. Like all intervening variables, need and preference gratification cannot be directly observed. The antecedents (i.e., leisure behavior) and consequences (i.e., life satisfaction, physical health) are more directly observable, and the credence given to the intervening variable is contingent upon its utility in explaining the relationships observed between the antecedents and consequences. For example, the REP scale called Tranquility/Solitude (4A in Exhibit 2)

does not necessarily imply that solitude is always beneficial. Instead, one must specify from a theoretical perspective those conditions under which it is and is not a benefit. As another example, Service (Exhibit 1, No. 6) is a PAL-derived psychological benefit that "satisfies the person's need to be of assistance to others." This implies that something good will happen under some not well-defined circumstances if this need is met. To relate the gratification of this need to better mental health or life satisfaction, the mechanism(s) by which the intervening variable of Service contributes to those beneficial outcomes must be specified in more detail.

The chain of causality in benefit formation raises two problems. The first and probably least significant is that of terminology. Clearly, different terms are needed for referring to the psychological needs (and benefits) close to the beginning of the chain, behaviorally observable conditions in the middle of the chain such as physical and mental health, and more abstract end-state benefits such as life satisfaction, self-actualization, and personal growth. The use of a single term (i.e., psychological benefit) to refer to such disparate outcomes is confusing and inadequate. Future research should strive for clearer terminology.

A second problem raised by this model concerns the point(s) in the causal chain at which the benefits of leisure can be measured most meaningfully. Obviously, for predictive purposes the greatest precision will be achieved between proximal constructs because of the rapidly increasing number of intervening variables that enter as one proceeds through the chain. Increased research attention needs to be devoted to documenting the dynamics by which leisure experiences are converted to the various postulated psychological benefits. It is only through such research that we can document the benefits of leisure and give it firmer footing in a Protestant Ethic society.

Other improvements are needed in research on the psychological benefits of leisure. Greater care must be taken to define more clearly than in the past why variables are posited to be a benefit. The definition of a benefit as an improved condition, a gain, or an advantageous change (see the introductory chapter to this volume) should help in this endeavor. The future research task is to specify the psychological benefits of leisure more definitively. Once identified, research is needed to measure the magnitude of these benefits and to investigate causal relationships between characteristics of the recreationists, specific types of benefit at different places in the chain of benefits, and the dependency of these benefits on particular leisure activities and setting attributes. Care must also be taken in future research to clearly explicate the theoretical relationships between those benefits which occur early in the chain of causality (i.e., those abstract intervening variables) and those more objectively measured beneficial changes which occur subsequently. Our confidence in the status of these intervening variables as mediators of the later psychological benefits will be increased by the use of psychometric instruments such as the PAL, the REP scales, and other instruments in cross-validating the results obtained with one instrument at a particular place in the chain.

As more research is done on the benefits of leisure, it is clear that more study will be needed of the psychological benefits, which we have defined as intervening variables in the chain of benefit causality that go from antecedent condition through motivation and participation to the realization of end-state benefits. Much will be left out, and our understanding will be severely impaired, if we look only at the end-state benefits—many of which cannot be defined without the proposed comprehensive approach that includes analysis of all links in the chain of benefits.

ENDNOTES

[1] B.L. Driver in unpublished paper on item pool for scales designed to quantify the psychological outcomes desired and expected from recreation participation, 1977.

[2] R. Crandal, E. Pavia-Krueger, and W.M. Gilker in paper on relationship between personality inventories and specific leisure satisfaction, presented at Southwest Sociological Association, Houston, Texas, April 3, 1980.

[3] Michaels and Driver paper is available from Driver.

LITERATURE CITED

Ajzen, I. 1985. From intentions to action: A theory of planned behavior. In: Kuhl, J.; Bechman, J., eds. Action-control: From cognition to behavior. Heidelberg: Springer: 11-39.

Ajzen, I.; Fishbein, M. 1980. Understanding attitudes and predicting social behavior. New York, NY: Prentice Hall, Inc.

Bem, D. J. 1970. Beliefs, attitudes, and human affairs. Belmont, CA: Brooks/Cole. 114.

Brown, P. J. 1981. Psychological benefits of outdoor recreation. In: Kelly, J. R., ed. Social benefits of outdoor recreation. Urbana-Champaign, IL: University of Illinois, Dept. of Leisure Studies: 13-17.

Brown, P. J. 1984. Benefits of outdoor recreation and some ideas for valuing recreation opportunities. In: Peterson, G. L.; Randall, A., eds. Valuation of wildland resource benefits. Boulder, CO: Westview Press: 209-220.

Campbell, A. 1981. The sense of well-being in America: Recent patterns and trends. New York, NY: McGraw Hill. 263 p.

Carson, D. H.; Driver, B. L. 1967. Environmental stress. American Behavioral Scientists. 8-11.

Crowne, D.; Marlowe, D. 1964. The approval motive. New York, NY: John Wiley and Sons.

Driver, B. L. 1976. Quantifications of outdoor recreationists' preferences. In: Van der Smissen, B.; Meyers, J., eds. Research: Camping and environmental education. HPEP Series No. 11. University Park, PA: Pennsylvania State University: 165-187.

Driver, B. L.; Brown, P. J. 1986. Probable personal benefits of outdoor recreation. In: A Literature Review. President's Commission on Americans Outdoors. Washington, DC: Government Printing Office: 63-67 of Values Section.

Driver, B. L.; Brown, P. J.; Gregoire, T.; Stankey, G. H. 1987. The ROS planning system: Evolution and basic concepts. Leisure Sciences. 9: 203-214.

Driver, B. L.; Cooksey, R. W. 1980. Preferred psychological outcomes of recreational fishing. In: Barnhart, R. A.; Roelofs, T. D., eds. Catch-and-release fishing as a management tool: A national sport fishing symposium. Arcata, CA: Humboldt State University: 27-40.

Driver, B. L.; Knopf, R. C. 1975. Temporary escape: One product of sport fisheries management. Fisheries. 1: 24-29.

Driver, B. L.; Knopf, R. C. 1977. Personality, outdoor recreation, and expected consequences. Environment and Behavior. 9: 169-193.

Driver, B. L.; Nash, R.; Haas, G. E. 1987. Wilderness benefits: A state-of-knowledge review. In: Lucas, R. C., comp. Proceedings, National Wilderness Research Conference: Issues, state of knowledge, future directions. General Technical Report INT-220. Ogden, UT: USDA Forest

Service, Intermountain Forest and Range Experiment Station: 294-319.

Eysenck, H. J.; Eysenck, S. B. G. 1963. Eysenck personality inventory. San Diego, CA: Educational and Industrial Testing Service.

Fishbein, M.; Ajzen, I. 1975. Belief, attitude, intention, and behavior. Reading, MA: Addison-Wesley Publishing Co. 578 p.

Gordon, C.; Gaitz, C.; Scott, J. 1976. Leisure and lives: Personal expressivity across the life span. In: Binstock, R.; Shanas, E., eds. Handbook of aging and the social sciences. New York: Von Nostrand Reinhold.

Graefe, A. R.; Ditton, R. B.; Roggenbuck, J. W.; Schreyer, R. 1981. Notes on the stability of the factor structure of leisure meanings. Leisure Sciences. 4(1): 51-65.

Haas, G. E.; Driver, B. L.; Brown, P. J. 1981. Measuring wilderness recreation experiences. In: Cannon, L., ed. Proceedings of The Wilderness Psychology Group Annual Conference. University of New Hampshire, Dept. of Psychology.

Lawler, E. E. 1973. Motivations in work organizations. Monterey, CA: Brooks/Cole. 224.

Lawton, M. P.; Moss, M.; Fulcomer, M. 1982. Determinants of the activities of older people. Philadelphia, PA: Philadelphia Geriatric Center.

Manfredo, M. J. 1984. Comparability of onsite and offsite measures of recreation needs. Journal of Leisure Research. 16(3): 245-249.

Manfredo, M.; Driver, B. L.; Brown, P. J. 1983. A test of concepts inherent in experienced-based setting management for outdoor recreation areas. Journal of Leisure Research. 15: 263-283.

Manfredo, M. J.; Sneegas, J. J.; Driver, B. L.; Bright, A. 1989. Hunters with disabilities: a survey of wildlife agencies and a case study of Illinois deer hunters. Wildlife Society Bulletin. 17: 213-229.

Rosenthal, D. H.; Driver, B. L.; Waldman, D. 1982. Construct validity of instruments measuring recreationists' preferences. Leisure Sciences. 5(2): 89-108.

Tinsley, D. J.; Faunce, P. S. 1980. Enabling, facilitating and precipitating factors associated with women's career orientation. Journal of Vocational Behavior. 17: 183-194.

Tinsley, H. E. A. 1984. The psychological benefits of leisure counseling. Society and Leisure. 7: 125-140.

Tinsley, H. E. A.; Barrett, T. C.; Kass, R. A. 1977. Leisure activities and need satisfaction. Journal of Leisure Research. 9: 110-120.

Tinsley, H. E. A.; Bowman, S. L. 1986. Discriminant validity of the Paragraphs About Leisure for expert and naive respondents. Educational and Psychological Measurement. 46: 461-465.

Tinsley, H. E. A.; Colbs, S. L.; Teaff, J. D.; Kaufman, N. 1987. The relationship of age, gender, health and economic status to the psychological benefits older persons report from participation in leisure activities. Leisure Sciences. 9: 53-65.

Tinsley, H. E. A.; Driver, B. L.; Ray, S. B.; Manfredo, M. J. 1986. Stability of recreation experience preference (REP) ratings for samples and individuals across three measurement periods. Journal of Education and Psychological Measurement. 46(4): 1105-1111.

Tinsley, H. E. A.; Driver, B. L.; Kass, R. A. 1982. Reliability and concurrent validity of the recreation experience preference scales. Journal of Educational and Psychological Measurement. 41(3): 897-907.

Tinsley, H. E. A.; Johnson, T. L. 1984. A preliminary taxonomy of leisure activities. Journal of Leisure Research. 16: 234-244.

Tinsley, H. E. A.; Kass, R. A. 1978. Leisure activities and need satisfaction: A replication and extension. Journal of Leisure Research. 10: 191-202.

Tinsley, H. E. A.; Kass, R. A. 1979. The latent structure of the need-satisfying properties of leisure activities. Journal of Leisure Research. 11: 278-291.

Tinsley, H. E. A.; Kass, R. A. 1980a. The construct validity of the Leisure Activities Questionnaire and of the Paragraphs About Leisure. Educational and Psychological Measurement. 40: 219-226.

Tinsley, H. E. A.; Kass, R. A. 1980b. Discriminant validity of the Leisure Activities Questionnaire and the Paragraphs About Leisure. Educational and Psychological Measurement. 40: 227-233.

Tinsley, H. E. A.; Teaff, J. D. 1983. The psychological benefits of leisure activities for the elderly: A manual and final report of an investigation. Carbondale, IL: Southern Illinois University, Department of Psychology.

Tinsley, H. E. A.; Teaff, J. D.; Colbs, S. L.; Kaufman, N. 1985. A system of classifying leisure activities in terms of the psychological benefits of participation reported by older persons. Journal of Gerontology. 49: 172-178.

Tinsley, H. E. A.; Tinsley, D. J. 1986. A theory of the attributes, benefits and causes of leisure experience. Leisure Sciences. 8: 1-45.

Tinsley, H. E. A.; Tinsley, D. J. 1988. An expanded context for the study of career decisionmaking, development and maturity. In: Walsh, W. B.; Osipow, S. H., eds. Career decisionmaking. Hillsdale, NJ: Lawrence Erlbaum Associates: 213-264.

Tinsley, H. E. A.; Tinsley, D. J. 1989. Reinforcers of the occupation of homemaker: An analysis of the need-gratifying properties of the homemaker occupation across the stages of the homemaker life cycle. Journal of Counseling Psychology. 36: 189-195.

Williams, D. R.; Ellis, G. D.; Nickerson, N. P.; Shafer, C. S. 1988. Contributions of time, format, and subject to variation in recreation experience preference measurement. Journal of Leisure Research. 20(1): 57-68.

II.

STATE-OF-KNOWLEDGE CHAPTERS

C. Sociological Measures

Benefits of Leisure for Family Bonding

Dennis K. Orthner
Human Services Research Laboratory
University of North Carolina at Chapel Hill
Chapel Hill, North Carolina

Jay A. Mancini
Department of Family and Child Development
College of Human Resources
Virginia Polytechnic Institute and State University
Blacksburg, Virginia

The potential value leisure experiences can play in family bonding is a comparatively new insight. Prior to the twentieth century, the primary source of family bonds was shared work and other family roles. Families were held together by strong external constraints and their complementary roles, particularly between husbands and wives (Levinger 1965). This was a preindustrial and early industrial time in which men and women had quite different patterns of socialization and in which their complementary roles were vital to individual and family success. With industrialization, however, family and gender became more interchangeable and family bonding shifted from "role taking" to "role making" as the major source of family integration (Aldous 1978). Thus, individual families became more dependent for their success on the ability of husbands and wives to reconcile their divergent needs and interests, rather than their abilities to submerge their individual needs and interests in favor of larger family goals.

This significant transformation in the Western family has been chronicled by a number of sociologists and historians. Most notably, Ernest W. Burgess (1923) recognized the early seeds of this transformation in the 1920s, and later labeled this a change in the family from an "institutional phase" to the contemporary "companionship" phase (Burgess and Locke 1945). It is noteworthy that Burgess identified the role of companionship in leisure as a primary ingredient of this change. In doing so, he acknowledged the central role that leisure and recreation experiences play in family experiences and the strength of family bonds.

The value that shared leisure experiences can have for families has been widely acknowledged. One study found that men and women ranked companionship highest on a list of nine goals of marriage (Levinger 1964). In another study, a national sample ranked such things as liking the same kind of activities as more important to marital success than having children or financial security (Roper Organization 1974).

By the 1980s, desires for companionship have reached almost universal proportions. When asked about their primary leisure objectives, a national sample of adults listed "spending time with your family" and "companionship" as their two most common objectives (United Media 1982). This extremely strong tie between leisure and family values led the authors of a report on American culture to conclude that the emerging "therapeutic" ideology of the family has now become the predominant perspective in Western society (Bellah et al. 1985). This ideology views love and marriage primarily in terms of psychological gratification, focusing new importance on shared time and interaction for family solidarity.

This increased value placed upon shared leisure experiences is supported by evidence of shared family time. For example, the Lynd's reported that shared family experiences were relatively rare in "Middletown" during the 1920s (Lynd and Lynd 1929). However, the follow-up study in the 1970s found that Middletown couples and families were now spending much more time together (Caplow et al. 1982). Kelly (1983) found in his national study that family activities had become a common "core" to individual leisure patterns and that this core of family activities remained important throughout the life course for both men and women. A recent national survey of time use found that home-based activities are by far the most common leisure activities among American adults (Decision Research 1987). When time diary data are analyzed, family activities become the most frequently engaged in by family members (Juster and Stafford 1985).

The number of studies examining the relationship between leisure and family variables is growing. But both the quality and quantity of the research remains somewhat limited. This paper attempts to stimulate further research by identifying the state of our knowledge on leisure benefits for family bonding. It also suggests several theoretical frameworks out of which this research might progress. One of the often heard cries from the literature is the absence of carefully developed theoretical frameworks linking leisure and family behavior. By articulating several alternative frameworks and proposing some research designs that might be developed, it is hoped that our understanding of this important relationship will be fostered.

LEISURE BENEFITS FOR FAMILIES

Although the above data suggest that shared leisure experiences have become increasingly important to families, they do not by themselves indicate how these leisure experiences impact on family bonds and solidarity. Even though couples and families may value interactions and interact more frequently during leisure time, this is not sufficient to justify an implied linkage between leisure experiences and family solidarity. There are many potential factors that influence the strength of a family relationship, including leisure experiences. It is the interactions between leisure experiences and other family dimensions that serve as a foundation for the theoretical frameworks reviewed later in this paper.

In order to organize the literature on family benefits, it is important to identify the family outcomes that represent these benefits. The literature on family outcomes is very extensive (cf., Sussman and Steinmetz 1987), although the research on interactions between leisure and family experi-

ences is limited. For purposes of this paper, family benefits are summarized into three dimensions: family satisfaction, family interaction, and family stability. In studies of family strength and relational qualities, these three dimensions appear to be the most commonly reviewed and they serve as primary indicators of the quality of family life.

Leisure and Family Satisfaction

Most of the research that has focused on family leisure behavior has examined its consequences for family satisfaction, and most often, martial satisfaction. Reviews of this literature by Orthner and Mancini (1980) and Holman and Epperson (1984) are acknowledged so this review will briefly summarize and update research findings in this area.

First of all, and most important, there is a consistent finding in the research literature that husbands and wives who share leisure time together in joint activities tend to be much more satisfied with their marriages than those who do not. This finding is consistent whether the data come from time diary-type information (Orthner 1975) or perceptions of sharing activities (Holman 1981, Holman and Jacquart 1988, Miller 1976). So pervasive is this relationship that there does not appear to be any recent study that fails to find an association between joint activities and marital satisfaction.

This finding has also been demonstrated in cross-cultural investigations. Palisi (1984) replicated Orthner's research in a cross-national study of marriages in Australia, England, and the United States. In all three samples, there was a strong, positive, and significant relationship between joint participation in leisure activities and marital well-being and happiness. Earlier studies in Australia had also confirmed this relationship (Bell 1975, Fallding 1961). In one of the few studies that has been done outside of the West, Ahn (1982) examined this relationship among Korean wives. Her results also confirmed the association, although not as strongly as the studies in the West. The associations were strongest in the Korean sample among those wives who were younger, better educated, and whose husbands were professionals or technicians.

Another consistent finding in the literature is the negative impact on marital satisfaction of high concentrations of independent, individual activities. All of the studies reviewed found that spending time alone was associated with lower levels of marital satisfaction. This finding is consistently more true for wives than husbands, suggesting that women may be more likely to interpret their larger amount of individual activity time as rejection or lack of concern by their marital partner. This is not to say that individual activities are by themselves aversive to family bonding. Rather, it is only when these activities become significantly greater than the norm that they indicate weakness in the marital relationship.

A third type of family leisure behavior that has been hypothesized to impact on families is parallel leisure activities (Orthner 1975) which involve sharing time but do not include substantial amounts of interaction. Examples include watching television or going to movies. Orthner (1975) found that these types of parallel activities have a positive but somewhat modest impact on the marital satisfaction of husbands and wives. Palisi (1984) found similar results in his three-nation study with positive but lower associations between parallel leisure activities and marital satisfaction, when compared to joint activities. Both of these studies, however, used a priori, investigator definitions of parallel and joint activities. More recently, Holman and Jacquart (1988) used respondent self-definitions of the level of interactions and found that "low-joint," parallel activities were negatively associated with martial satisfaction for both husbands and wives. They conclude that leisure activities that involve little or no communication provide little benefit to families and may actually hurt the relationship. They represent a false front that suggests togetherness when the reality in the relationship is quite the opposite.

Leisure and Marital Interaction

Various studies have examined the relationship between leisure activity patterns and marital or family interaction. While this linkage has been theoretically derived and suggested by a number of writers (Carisse 1975, Orthner 1976), research on family interaction is much less common. Family interaction includes communication, conflict, and the distribution of household tasks and roles.

The relationship between shared leisure activities and marital communication is commonly reported in the research literature. Using a marital communication scale, Orthner (1976) found a very strong relationship between joint leisure activities and positive husband and wife communication, as well as a strong negative relationship between individual activities and marital communication. A study of marital activities in Belgium also indicated that frequency of joint leisure activities was positively related to marital communication, especially the nonverbal communication of caring (Presvelou 1971).

The potential impact of leisure participation on relational conflict has not gone without notice (Kaplan 1975, Orthner 1985, Orthner and Herron 1984, Orthner and Mancini 1980). In a national survey, it was found that one-third of American families experience stress from leisure conflicts (Strauss et al. 1980). Only household roles and sex were more likely sources of family conflict. Similar findings occurred in a world-wide study of military families (Orthner 1980). Conflicts over the use of leisure time and opportunities for companionship were found to be more stressful than child rearing or finances.

Among newly married husbands and wives, Holman (1981) found that the amount of companionship was positively related to the amount of verbal aggression, although the data for the husbands was not statistically significant. He interpreted these findings to mean that the more these couples did things together the more likely they were to communicate and as part of that communication, to argue. Verbal disagreements are viewed by Holman (1981) and Orthner and Mancini (1980) as indicators of healthy mechanisms for reducing family tension and disagreements.

It was suggested by Orthner that parallel activities, such as television watching, can reduce family tension by anesthetizing negative interactions and minimizing communication levels which might lead to conflict (Orthner 1975). This hypothesis was somewhat confirmed by Rosenblatt and Cunningham (1976) in their study of television watching and family tension. These researchers found higher levels of tension in families with higher levels of television watching, but they also noticed a stronger association between more watching and less direct family conflict, especially in higher density families. Thus, the parallel leisure activity diminished communication and reduced overt conflict, even though the under-the-surface tension levels remained relatively high.

Leisure and Family Stability

One of the more common phrases used to promote family recreation is the adage, "The family that plays together stays together." This phrase suggests that leisure experiences do more than promote family satisfaction and interaction, they also promote family stability. In this sense, family stability represents something significantly stronger and of longer duration than relational happiness. Stability implies relational continuity and a reduction in the probabilities for marital separation and divorce. Social scientists have known for some time that relational satisfaction and stability are somewhat independent (Lewis and Spanier 1979). In part, this is a function of the fact that satisfaction is a transitory event while stability is a longitudinal event. Couples may be quite satisfied at one time, but, for a variety of reasons, their relationships might still terminate. Therefore, the ultimate test of the ability of leisure experiences to promote family bonding is perhaps through their impacts on relational stability.

Only two research studies have examined the relationship between use of leisure time and divorce. In the first study, Varga (1972) examined divorce rates among persons from countries participating in a multinational study of leisure time use. Depending on ecological correlations, that study found that countries with higher rates of marital companionship also tended to have higher divorce rates. If taken at face value, this would suggest that shared leisure experiences and marital stability are inversely related. However, there are many other factors that could affect marital stability at that level of analysis and such an interpretation would be spurious, at best. More than likely, higher national rates of companionship are also associated with divorce laws that permit unhappy marriages to terminate.

In a more recent study, Hill (1988) directly tested the hypothesis of linkages between spouses' shared time and marital stability. This study used the 1975-1981 Time Use Longitudinal Panel Study as the data base for the analysis. She found a significant association between shared leisure experiences with the spouse at the beginning of the longitudinal study and marital stability over the next 5 years. This relationship held even when controlling for the presence and age of children in the household. Hill also reported that participation in recreational activities had the strongest contribution to marital stability. Also, in contrast to some of the earlier findings on parallel activities such as TV watching, marital stability was also related to joint TV watching.

Because of the longitudinal nature of Hill's investigation, it is possible to partially confirm the direction of the relationship from leisure activities to marital stability. Included in the analysis was a partial test of the hypothesis that joint leisure activities directly influenced marital satisfaction in the short run, and thereby improved marital stability in the long run. Even though the measures of marital satisfaction and interaction in this study are somewhat weaker than the earlier studies reviewed, the data suggest that family bonds are indeed improved by the sharing of leisure time.

BARRIERS, CONSTRAINTS, AND LEISURE BENEFITS

Thus far we have discussed the leisure-family nexus and have examined the range of benefits that family members may experience by virtue of spending time together in leisure. Our next task is to suggest and elaborate the area of barriers and constraints, that is, those conditions and events that may preclude beneficial family leisure experiences or that modify the range of benefits. With few exceptions, family and leisure researchers have been more concerned

with extolling the virtues of family leisure participation than with empirical examinations of factors which preclude such participation (Crawford and Godbey 1987, Holman and Epperson 1984, Orthner and Mancini 1980). Leisure constraints, however, serve as critical access and opportunity factors. For example, depending on where a family falls on a continuum of degree of work demands, the access to a beneficial leisure experience will vary. Underlying this entire discussion are the dimensions of obligation and of choice. Interwoven with obvious constraints and barriers is a person's desire for spending time with family members, as well as feelings of family duty (Kelly 1978). First, we will refer to several studies which have dealt to some degree with leisure constraints. Second, we will refer to several sources which discuss general classes of constraints.

Specific Studies of Constraints

One of the earliest research studies that specifically focused on barriers to family leisure is reported by Witt and Goodale (1981). In all, 18 barriers were examined, some pertaining to individual competence, others to information deficits, and yet others to competing obligations. It was found that family life cycle stage had a small effect on leisure barriers, but that barriers changed over the life of a family. A number of studies have focused on one or more child-related variables. Bollman et al. (1975) found that more frequent home-centered activity occurred when mothers were not employed outside of the home and when a child was a preschooler. Orthner and Axelson (1980) found that the presence of a preschool child significantly depressed the amount of time husbands and wives spent together in leisure time. Hill (1988) reports that children can contribute to marital dissolution in situations where the spouses have less shared leisure time.

Work issues have also been noted as barriers to shared leisure experiences. Nock and Kingston (1988) indicated that fathers' employment has a more pronounced effect on time spent with children than does mothers' employment, and that parents in a single-earner family are more likely to spend time with children than those in a dual-earner family. Firestone and Shelton (1988) found that women's involvement in work inside and outside of the home occurs at the expense of leisure time. Searle and Jackson (1985) report that major barriers are work commitments, facility overcrowding, and lack of coparticipants. They also state that older people, poor people, and single parents are those most likely affected by leisure participation barriers.

While the studies just mentioned tend to focus on structural and demographic factors, characteristics of the quality of the relationship also function as barriers. Rosenblatt et al. (1979) report that couples who are prone to physical violence have differences in their respective values, and those who exhibit disrespect have lower marital quality (and higher marital tension) the longer that they spend time together.

General Typologies of Constraints

For the most part, discussions of barriers and constraints to family leisure take the form of conjecture and theorizing rather than result from empirical studies. Still, there are a number of general typologies that focus on constraints and provide important roadmaps for constraint-oriented research on leisure experiences and family outcomes.

One such typology which is quite useful and comprehensive discusses intrapersonal, interpersonal, and structural barriers to positive family leisure experiences. Crawford and Godbey (1987) indicate that intrapersonal barriers include stress, depression, anxiety, religiosity, kin and nonkin reference group attitudes, socialization influences, sense of competence, and personal evaluations of the appropriateness and availability of leisure activities. These intrapersonal factors, for the most part, involve internal states. They are said to interact with leisure preferences, and are considered unstable and amenable to change. Interpersonal barriers mainly include aspects of the marriage relationship (sex role attitudes, general quality of the relationship, spousal conflict, decisionmaking abilities, and power in the marital dyad). Also included are factors that relate to the parent-child relationship. Crawford and Godbey say that interpersonal variables may be the products of individual barriers that people bring into the marriage relationship, or the products of the interaction between spouses. Structural constraints include family life cycle stage, financial resources, season, climate, the nature of work time, availability of leisure opportunities, and reference group attitudes regarding activity appropriateness.

Another recent discussion of leisure constraints is offered by Henderson (1989) and oriented specifically to women. These constraints are related to paid and unpaid work, families and the ideal of care, perceived lack of entitlement to leisure, gender-defined personality traits, socioeconomic status, and health and safety concerns. However, many of these constraints can be applied to other family members as well. At the least, constraints said to be more particular to women become constraints to other family members because the family is an interdependent system. The constraints discussed by Henderson fall generally into two categories, external and internal, and parallel the categories offered by Crawford and Godbey (1987).

Iso-Ahola and Mannell (1985) have conceptualized leisure constraints that are social and psychological in origin, and suggest three categories: social-personal, social-cultural, and physical. In the course of discussing constraints, they suggest that we need to know about the perceived causes of constraints, the types of constraints, and whether or not they are enduring. In their discussion of social-cultural constraints they include familial, marital, and parent-child factors. They note that parents and their children can constrain one another, although parents, by virtue of their power and control, are more likely to constrain children than vice versa. Constraints imposed by children have to do with their developmental needs at younger ages. The constraints that relate to the marital relationship involve whether spouses get along with each other, and whether their leisure interests are compatible. The ideas of Iso-Ahola and Mannell (1985) are compatible with others that we have already cited, and they provide a more substantive focus on the parent-child relationship.

In summary, this review suggests that the hypothesized benefits of leisure experiences for families must be tempered somewhat by personal, relational, and structural conditions. Even though the research findings on the benefits of leisure experiences appear to be relatively consistent, the relationships are quite complex. Our understanding of the consequences of leisure behavior must take into account potential factors which can inhibit or block the effects that are predicted. We also need more complex explanatory models to predict the variables that are likely to increase or suppress the effects of leisure on family outcomes.

MODELS OF LEISURE AND FAMILY BONDING

While the studies reviewed appear to be relatively consistent in demonstrating a positive impact of shared leisure experiences on the quality of family relationships, the theoretical underpinnings of this research remain very weak. Very few of the studies reviewed have explicitly stated their theoretical rationale and even fewer have subsequently revised their theoretical position as a result of the investigation. A common complaint in this research is the absence of clearly defined theoretical justification. As a result, the accumulation of findings is less systematic than we would hope and it is difficult to project a logical research track for the future.

In the review that follows, the strength of the family bond is conceptualized through the eyes of several of the major theoretical frameworks now predominating in family research. The role that leisure experiences can play in facilitating relational quality is then described. The frameworks reviewed are exchange theory, family development theory, symbolic interaction theory, and systems theory.

Exchange Theory

Exchange theory is a very useful framework for examining the relationship between leisure activities and family relationships. Principles of exchange are frequently used in both recreation and family social science. It is a major theoretical framework in the field of psychology, sociology and economics (Blau 1964, Homans 1961, Nye 1979). The theory is oriented toward predicting behavior based upon individual motivation to maximize those actions that increase rewards and decrease costs. The theory posits that all individuals seek gratification for their actions and wish to do so with a miminal level of costs they must incur in order to accumlate rewards (Burgess and Huston 1979). The theory is labeled exchange because of this element of explicit and implicit negotiation that goes on between individuals as each seeks to maximize benefits and minimize costs.

Exchange is a dynamic theory suggesting that relationships are being continually negotiated and that the strength of the relationship comes from its ability to negotiate equitable, balanced exchanges on an ongoing basis. In this sense, exchange theory confirms some of the findings from the research reviewed earlier which notes that temporary gratifications are just that—temporary—and that long-term relational stability comes from the continued ability of a relationship to maintain the process of successful negotiation and not rest on previously negotiated settlements.

Implications for Leisure Interactions and Research

How do leisure experiences fit into this exchange perspective of family solidarity? First of all, leisure activities provide opportunities for couples and families to interact and negotiate individual and collective interests. Communication about individual and family needs most often occurs during discretionary time and this probably explains the relatively strong association between joint participation in leisure activities and high levels of communication and conflict. From an exchange perspective, the conflict that is associated with leisure experiences is not bad; instead, it represents opportunities to work out differences, as some of the researchers have noted.

Second, leisure experiences promote opportunities for developing equity. Unlike many other environments within which people interact, leisure experiences promote opportunities for each individual to maximize her or his own

interests and minimize competition. Competition in family recreation is uncommon and this may explain why family activities are so highly regarded by respondents in surveys. It is during leisure time when husbands and wives, and parents and children, are most apt to practice by negotiating family roles and reaching new definitions of consensus.

Third, leisure experiences should increase the opportunity for enhancing family bonds through promoting a positive history of exchange interactions. Relationships characterized by limited interactions may tend to promote individual interests over joint interests yielding more negative negotiations and heated bargaining. When individual interests are promoted over maximum joint interests, family bonds are weakened. Shared leisure experiences encourage opportunities for negotiations and improve the historical comparisons upon which subsequent negotiations are based.

Fourth, shared family experiences reduce opportunities for developing positive comparisons with other relationships. Relational bonds are substantially weakened when attractions to other relationships, either family or friends, become stronger than attractions within the family relationship. The research studies reviewed suggest that couples who spend substantial portions of their time apart feel less satisfaction with their marriages and are less likely to continue their marriage relationships. In this case, individuals feel that they are more likely to achieve more benefits from another relationship than their marriage or family, thus weakening their commitments and desires for continued interactions.

On balance, it would appear that exchange theory offers some major insights into the nature of the leisure interactions and family solidarity relationship. Exchange theory has been proposed by a number of behavioral scientists interested in leisure behavior (Carlson 1979, Hill 1988, Holman and Epperson 1984) as a particularly useful theoretical framework. To date, there has not been a fully developed study utilizing the above exchange principles to fully articulate these relationships.

Family Development Theory

Family development theory describes the process of change (Aldous 1978, Mattessich and Hill 1987). Concepts in this approach fall into three general categories: those concerning the systemic aspects of family life, concepts relating to structure, and concepts pertaining to orderly sequences.

From a developmental perspective, a family is described in terms of interdependence, selective boundary maintenance, ability to adapt to change, and task performance. No family member either lives or acts separate from others in the family; each is involved in a web of relationships. A family is partly receptive to outside influences and develops its own identity and its own history. A family adapts both to the needs of its individual members, as well as to those of society; in the process of adaptation a family makes new behavior patterns and adjusts old patterns. A family must behave in certain ways in order to ensure its survival; the performance of critical tasks is functional for that family and for the society. Critical tasks discussed in the family development framework are: physical maintenance, socialization for roles inside and outside of the family, and maintenance of family morale and of motivation of family members to perform roles.

Family structure concepts are position (a location within a group), role (expectations of behaviors and feelings that accompany a position), and norms (rules for behavior that guide conduct). Three concepts pertain to orderly sequence: positional career, role sequence, and family career. Over time, the role content of a family position changes (positional career), and the normative content of a role changes (role sequence). In addition, the positional careers of family members combine to form a family career.

Implications for Leisure Interactions and Research

First, if family members are interdependent, then studies on how families use time must attend to the web of relationships that are found in a family. If we are to document the range of beneficial experiences that come from playing together, or are to note, for example, cooperation and competition in family recreation, then we ought to research the system rather than particular players in the system.

Second, if families develop a distinct history and create a family identity, it is clear that time use is a major vehicle for that development. For research on beneficial aspects of leisure, it is important to understand how a family's view of itself is enhanced or limited by leisure experiences.

Third, one of the core understandings of the ability to adapt to change involves the ability to create new behavior patterns and to perhaps discard older patterns. An important research activity would be to examine how the leisure experiences alter family behavior patterns and how that change addresses the needs of various family members.

Fourth, the task performance system concept has implications for the role that family leisure plays in socialization. If we view time spent together as a forum in which members learn how to interact with others (including cooperation and competition), then one of the benefits of such an experience has to do with teaching the young social skills. These skills would have applicability to roles outside the family, such as those involved in work, and to responsibilities inside the family, such as working together on family projects.

Fifth, the focus in developmental research should not be on a static variable that places a family in time because of the age of one of its members. Rather, the changing nature of family positions and roles over time is the focus. Research on leisure benefits would examine how change in position and role interacts with what families and their individual members receive from spending time together. Studies of conflict in family leisure could benefit from attending to how role expectations change.

Overall, the family development framework contends that studies of leisure benefits and the family could be placed in a societal, group, or individual context. For example, in the study of barriers and constraints, attention should be given to how work roles and obligations influence family leisure. As a second example, the interplay between family roles and subsequent socialization regarding one's leisure orientation would also be an important object of research. Third, benefits will accrue in part because of what individuals bring to their relationships and to their leisure experiences, which may be related to personality.

Symbolic Interaction Theory

The symbolic interaction framework suggests that we live in a symbolic environment, that we "value" and assign worth, that we define who we are, that the self is multidimensional, that behavior is influenced by the meaning of ideas, and that people are actors as well as reactors. Symbolic interaction is a general theory and from it a number of middle-range theories of the family have been derived (for example, a theory of interpersonal competence, a theory of role strain, and a theory of role transition).

Burr et al. (1979) have provided the most complete discussion of symbolic interaction theory as it applies to families. We have chosen to discuss eight pivotal terms from the symbolic interaction framework; role making, organismic involvement, role strain, quality of role enactment, number of roles, ease of role transitions, consensus on role expectations, and clarity of role expectations.

Role making takes into account that people define situations and posits that roles are fluid. Family members improvise their role behavior and make judgments about what is appropriate role performance. Organismic involvement pertains to the amount of an individual's effort that a particular role requires (ranging from noninvolvement to being engrossed). The "self" is involved in differing degrees, and consequently the meaning of that involvement is tied to one's definition of self and its evaluation. Role strain relates to the difficulty people have in meeting their obligations. It is the stress generated when one cannot meet the expectations attached to a role or to a set of roles. The quality of role enactment suggests that individuals get a sense of how well they are enacting a role within the context of an arbitrary standard or when compared to how others perform.

This approach also accounts for the number of roles that a person concurrently has in aggregate. The ease of role transitions concept notes that some people move easily from one role to another, while others have great difficulty making the transition. Consensus on role expectations is also important. In a family group it is necessary to examine the expectations that individuals have about roles and behaviors, and to what degree there is agreement. The final concept that is relevant for our discussion on family benefits and leisure is the clarity of role expectations. One of the more interesting areas of family research is in regard to how muddled or how identifiable expectations are.

Implications for Leisure Interactions and Research

First, the idea of role making appears consonant with those views of leisure that address discretion and choice. One area of future research could connect role making opportunities in the family with both individual benefits, such as self-esteem, and with family group benefits, such as solidarity.

Second, family leisure activities require varying levels of involvement. Numerous sports have brief periods of intense involvement preceded and followed by inactivity. Involvement may be quite casual, in that a person activates a role with little attention. For some family members the intensity of the involvement (and the interest) is quite low and of little importance for the self, whereas for others the same leisure experience is intense and very meaningful for identity. Conflict and cohesion in family leisure may focus on the question of intensity level differences between family members.

Third, if we are to understand how families are differentially involved in leisure experiences we could examine the range of specific roles that various individuals play. Information on the number of roles should be compared with the relative importance of those roles. If the value placed on family leisure involvement is lower than that placed on other uses of time, then it may be expected that family leisure would not be as beneficial.

Fourth, we should ask how readily family members move from more constrained roles (such as that of worker or of authority figure in the family) to those where people participate more as equals. We may research to what degree families having traditional sex roles are more egalitarian in a leisure context.

Fifth, even as there may be disagreement about marital and child roles generally, there may be disagreement about these roles in conjunction with leisure roles. One example involves planning a family vacation. In any particular family, how are the decisions made regarding why, where, and how to vacation? Who is expected to decide? Is there general agreement on who will make decisions and general agreement that those decisions will be honored?

Sixth, family conflict may be less when the expectations are clear. When we are at play, what amount of freedom do we have to interact as equals, or are play relationships based on the positions of mother, husband, or child? An interesting line of research would examine the clarity of expectations that are held of the leisure experience and that are held of one another in the family.

We have described parts of a social science framework that appears quite amenable to conducting theory-based research on leisure benefits and the family. The approach is based on interpersonal interaction, defining situations and behaving accordingly, the role that the self plays in interaction, and the multifaceted idea of role. Perception, evaluation, and action are the terms that typify the approach.

Systems Theory

Systems theory also offers some potentially useful insights into relationships between leisure and family variables. While social and behavioral scientists have seen systems theory concepts growing and waning in popularity over the last several decades, principles of systems theory have increasingly dominated family oriented theories of clinical intervention. Today, the primary assumptions of marriage and family therapy are largely based on systems theory (Olson et al. 1983). In addition, a recent paper on leisure counseling with families was largely based on the ideas from systems theory (Orthner and Herron 1984).

The chief assumption of general systems theory is that actors are goal-seeking and that, in concert with others, they seek to change social conditions in order to achieve their desired goals or purposes (Orthner and Scanzoni[1]). The primary issue for families from the perspective of systems theory is finding the balance between mutuality and differentiation. Systems are made up of different members, each with their own needs, and this leads to a tendency for systems to spin off differentiation of the system elements. At the same time, systems have boundaries that define the extent to which the system will permit members to exit from the system or system products to merge with those of other systems.

Family bonding from the systems perspective consists of a complex and dynamic balance between cohesion and adaptability between family members. Cohesion represents an emotional bonding between family members that is ideally balanced between the one extreme of "enmeshment" in which individual autonomy is limited, and the other extreme of "disengagement" in which there is very little bonding to the family. Adaptability also lies on a continuum between the extremes of rigid adaptation, in which alternative roles and patterns of behavior are strictly forbidden, and chaotic patterns in which "anything goes."

A family bond from this perspective accommodates some differentiation between family members and encourages mutuality of interests. In order for this balance to be achieved, systems theory suggests that communication is extremely important for system maintenance. In addition, it is important for systems to have stimulation so that new sources of excitement and energy can encourage the system to make changes for the betterment of the system over time.

Implications for Leisure Interactions and Research

From a systems theory perspective, leisure activities contribute to family bonding in several important ways. First, common leisure activities and interests enforce boundaries around the family relationship. Activities that maintain boundaries are particularly important to the family from a systems perspective since it is the uniqueness of the family that yields attachments and bonding to this relationship. In his recent work on systems theory and the family, Marks (1989) makes a significant point of noting that shared interests and activities may be one of the more salient forces establishing and maintaining boundaries in the contemporary family system. Families that do not take the opportunity to share leisure activities weaken their boundaries, thus making the family and other relationships more competitive for the allegiance of family members.

A second contribution that leisure activities provide to the family system is their contribution to developing collective interest and identity. Systems theory suggests that individuals within systems are constantly receiving new inputs that pull members away from collective interests. Shared leisure experiences serve as a countervailing force and strengthen the attachments of system members to the family relationship.

A third contribution that this theory makes is its emphasis on family cohesion. Leisure experiences, as the research reviewed earlier suggests, offer new and continuing sources of cohesion for families. Unlike most of the other theoretical perspectives reviewed, cohesion is a central concept to systems theory. Systems that are not cohesive do not tend to persevere. In order for family systems to remain viable, they must share common interests. In our contemporary society, leisure activities are the major mechanisms for deriving these common interests.

Fourth, systems theory suggests that communication is a critical element in family change or morphogenesis. Since most of the unstructured communication within families that contributes to cohesion occurs during discretionary time, leisure experiences are very important to opening opportunities for and providing the mechanisms through which communication between family members can occur.

Lastly, leisure experiences foster system adaptation to new inputs. The family system is not a static entity; it must constantly adapt to new circumstances in order for it to survive. System adaptation is one of the central requirements for family solidarity and leisure experiences often provide the new inputs that give energy for maintaining a relationship.

Overall, a systems theory perspective offers a useful window into the family and leisure relationship. From a clinical perspective, systems theory has a great deal of intuitive appeal because it describes the nature of the family and provides useful imagery that can help interpret why some families may not be functioning as well as others. From a research perspective, the theory stresses the importance of balance in relationships, but does not do so at the expense of promoting family change. The key concept in family behavior and bonding appears to be family adaptation to changing environmental circumstances. Systems theory is particularly useful in providing cues as to how leisure experiences can promote healthy adaptation.

FUTURE RESEARCH STRATEGIES

It is clear from the research and theories that have been reviewed that much more work is needed to clarify the benefits that leisure experiences have for family bonds. Only the most elementary hypotheses have been tested, and few of the constraints which have been proposed have been systematically examined. In this section of the paper we propose two research strategies which are clearly needed in order to advance both our theoretical reasoning and our hypothesis testing: qualitative research and short-term longitudinal research.

Qualitative Research

Qualitative research methods are especially appropriate in cases in which the area of interest cannot be adequately understood outside of its natural setting, such as the leisure context (Blieszner and Shea 1987). Much of what families do is tied to the setting in which a family finds itself. The leisure setting is an excellent example wherein families ought to be assessed as much as possible while activities are occurring. Observation may be structured, the researcher may actively participate in family life, or ethnographic interviews may come into play (these are important when we want to know what family members think and feel, in addition to what they are doing).

A qualitative approach reveals aspects of family life which are not apparent (Lofland and Lofland 1984). This often involves "meaning"—in the case of leisure issues, the meaning that is attached to spending time with one's family. The qualitative approach helps to generate theory (Glaser and Strauss 1967). This is especially important for our purposes, since we have already said there is a need for more theoretical work in the domain of family leisure. A noticeable amount of the discussion on the benefits of family leisure is speculative, as is the discussion of the range of constraints. While these informed speculations may not be entirely inaccurate, many of them await empirical examination. Factors which contribute to beneficial family leisure experiences have not been fully specified and the range of benefits has not been fully elaborated. Methodologies which allow family members to behave freely or to talk freely without constraint of researcher biases (that is, the structure imposed by some research designs) would be most helpful at this stage of the understanding of family leisure. Qualitative methods invite hypothesis generation and are more likely to enable researchers to uncover the nuances of family interaction.

As an illustration, a qualitative study of family weekend outings may help us better understand how leisure experiences are interpreted by different family members. Families can be observed in the leisure setting and periodically queried as to their perceptions and motivations. Patterns of interaction and their consequences are then realized as they occur and are less dependent on reconstructions or statistical associations based on measures defined by researchers.

Short-Term Longitudinal Research

A second important research strategy that needs to be used more frequently is the short-term longitudinal study. Nearly all of the research that has been conducted on leisure and family variables has been cross-sectional, usually through surveys of one population or another. While the evidence from cross-sectional research consistently demonstrates a relationship between leisure behavior and family bonds, the direction of that relationship is often questioned (Holman and Jacquart 1988). The only way that the direction of effects can be appropriately defined is through longitudinal research.

Two studies which have partially demonstrated the potential value of longitudinal research are the recent study of leisure behavior and family stability by Hill (1988) and the earlier exploratory study of leisure behavior and marital quality by West and Merriam (1970). Both studies suggested that the direction of influence is appropriately from leisure interaction to family interaction and solidarity. The Hill study, however, required a longer term investigation in order to detect leisure effects on marital separation and divorce. While this is very valuable, it is also very demanding on personal and financial resources.

In contrast, shorter term longitudinal investigations have the benefit of demonstrating changes in individuals or relationships as a result of leisure experiences or interventions. These are more practical for most investigators to carry out and the findings can be made available more quickly. The West and Merriam (1970) study is an excellent case in point. They assessed family interaction and relational quality at three points in time: before a camping experience, immediately afterwards and again, several months later. While they admit that their study is exploratory and their measures somewhat crude, nearly everyone who reviews the literature on leisure and family behavior points out how interesting their findings are and how useful it would be to replicate their results. To date, no one has done so.

Since leisure experiences such as family vacations, weekend outings, or even enjoying a game together are often event oriented, they lend themselves methodologically to short-term longitudinal research. While the major question that continues to be asked in the field is the consequence of these leisure events for participants, relatively more longitudinal research (although still very little) has been done on individual recreation experiences. There is now a need to shift toward the examination of family experiences in the same way. Until we do so, it will be increasingly difficult to sort out the complex web of interactions between leisure experiences, family experiences, and outcomes such as family solidarity and bonding.

CONCLUSIONS

The good news from this review of research and theory is that much has been learned thus far and that hypothesized benefits of leisure experiences for family bonding have been demonstrated. Whether the outcome variable is family satisfaction, family interaction, or family stability, leisure activities do appear to be associated with positive outcomes and this is a relatively consistent finding.

The bad news is that the quality and quantity of this research is still somewhat deficient. Samples tend to be relatively small, the measures of family variables are often difficult to compare, the measures of leisure variables are similarly wide-ranging, the populations from which the samples are drawn tend to be urban and middle class, and there has been little replication. Few investigations have used multiple methods to assess interactions, and even fewer studies have used longitudinal methods which can help sort the direction of influence between hypothesized independent and dependent variables. The lack of theoretical frameworks being explicated and consistently used also handicaps the research by limiting the findings to the idiosyncrasies of the investigation at hand.

Much has been accomplished, yet much needs to be done. There is an urgent need for a research agenda for the future to answer the basic question of whether family leisure experiences indeed contribute to family bonding and, if so, under what conditions, for what types of families, and how can this be promoted? A systematic series of research investigations are needed in order to be able to accomplish this agenda. With the fragility of family bonds so evident in our society today, the need for this research is readily apparent.

ENDNOTES

[1] Dennis Orthner and John Scanzoni in a paper on a theoretical framework linking family factors with work commitment prepared for the NCFR Annual Meeting, Theory Construction and Research Methodology Workshop, Philadelphia, 1988.

LITERATURE CITED

Ahn, D. S. 1982. A study of the relation between leisure activity patterns and marital satisfaction of urban housewives. Korea: Srokmyuns Women's University. Ph.D dissertation.

Aldous, J. 1978. Family careers: Developmental change in families. New York, NY: Wiley. 358 p.

Bell, R. R. 1975. Significant roles among a sample of Australian women. Australian and New Zealand Journal of Sociology. 11: 2-11.

Bellah, R. N.; Madsen, R.; Sullivan, W. M., et al. 1985. Habits of the heart: Individualism and commitment in American life. Berkeley, CA: University of California Press.

Blau, P. 1964. Exchange and power in social life. New York: Wiley.

Blieszner, R.; Shea, L. 1987. Designing a research project. In: McAuley, W. J. Applied research in gerontology. New York, NY: Van Nostrand Reinhold: 59-76.

Bollman, S. R.; Moxley, V. M.; Elliott, N. C. 1975. Family and community activities of rural nonfarm families with children. Journal of Leisure Research. 7: 53-62.

Burgess, E. W. 1923. The family as a unity of interacting personalities. The Family. 7: 3-9.

Burgess, E. W.; Locke, H. J. 1945. The family: From institution to companionship. New York, NY: American Book Company.

Burgess, R. L.; Huston, T. L., eds. 1979. Social exchange in developing relationships. New York, NY: Academic Press.

Burr, W. R.; Leigh, G. K.; Day, R. D.; Constantine, J. 1979. Symbolic interaction and the family. In: Burr, W. R.; Hill, R.; Nye, F. I.; Reiss, I. L., eds. Contemporary theories about the family, Vol. II, General theories/theoretical orientations. New York, NY: Free Press: 42-111.

Caplow, T.; Bahr, H. M.; Chadwick, B. A., et al. 1982. Middletown families. Minneapolis, MN: University of Minnesota Press.

Carisse, C. 1975. Family and leisure: A set of contradictions. Family Coordinator. 24: 191-210.

Carlson, J. E. 1979. The family and recreation: Toward a theoretical development. In: Burr, W. R. et al., eds. Contemporary theories about the family. New York, NY: Free Press: 339-452.

Crawford, D. W.; Godbey, G. 1987. Reconceptualizing barriers to family leisure. Leisure Sciences. 9: 119-127.

Decision Research. 1987. 1987 Leisure Study. Lexington, MA: Decision Research Corporation.

Fallding, H. 1961. The family and the idea of cardinal role. Human Relations. 14: 220-246.

Firestone, J.; Shelton, B. A. 1988. An estimation of the effects of women's work on available leisure time. Journal of Family Issues. 9: 478-495.

Glaser, B. G.; Strauss, A. L. 1967. The discovery of grounded theory. Chicago, IL: Aldine. 271 p.

Henderson, C. 1989. A leisure of one's own. State College, PA: Venture Publishing, Inc.

Hill, M. S. 1988. Marital stability and spouses' shared time. Journal of Family Issues. 9: 427-451.

Holman, T. B. 1981. A path analytic test of a model of early marital quality: The direct and indirect effects of premarital and marital factors. Provo, UT: Brigham Young University. Ph.D. dissertation.

Holman, T. B.; Epperson, A. 1984. Family and leisure: A review of the literature with research recommendations. Journal of Leisure Research. 16: 277-294.

Holman, T. B.; Jacquart, M. 1988. Leisure activity patterns and marital satisfaction: A further test. Journal of Marriage and the Family. 50: 69-78.

Homans, G. 1961. Social behavior: Its elementary forms. New York, NY: Harcourt Brace Jovanovich.

Iso-Ahola, S. E.; Mannell, R. C. 1985. Social and psychological constraints on leisure. In: Wade, M. G., ed. Constraints on leisure. Springfield, IL: Thomas: 111-151.

Juster, F. T.; Stafford, F. P. 1985. Time, goods, and well-being. Ann Arbor, MI: Institute for Social Research.

Kaplan, M. 1975. Leisure: Theory and policy. New York, NY: Wiley.

Kelly, J. R. 1978. Family leisure in three communities. Journal of Leisure Research. 10: 47-60.

Kelly, J. R. 1983. Leisure identities and interactions. Winchester, MA: Allen & Unwin.

Levinger, G. 1964. Tasks and social behavior in marriage. Sociometry. 27: 433-448.

Levinger, G. 1965. Marital cohesiveness and dissolution: An integrated review. Journal of Marriage and the Family. 27: 19-28.

Lewis, R. A.; Spanier, G. B. 1979. Theorizing about the quality and stability of marriage. In: Burr, W. R., et al., eds. Contemporary theories about the family. New York, NY: The Free Press: 268-294.

Lofland, J.; Lofland, L. H. 1984. Analyzing social settings. Belmont, CA: Wadsworth. 186 p.

Lynd, R. S.; Lynd, H. M. 1929. Middletown: A study in American culture. New York, NY: Harcourt and Brace.

Mattessich, P.; Hill, R. 1987. Life cycle and family development. In: Sussman, M. B.; Steinmetz, S. K., eds. Handbook of marriage and the family. New York, NY: Plenum: 437-469.

Marks, S. R. 1989. Toward a systems theory of marital quality. Journal of Marriage and the Family. 51: 15-26.

Nock, S. L.; Kingston, P. W. 1988. Time with children: The impact of couples' work-time commitments. Social Forces. 67: 59-85.

Nye, F. I. 1979. Choice, exchange, and the family. In: Burr, W. R.; Hill, R.; Nye, F. I.; Reiss, I. L., eds. Contemporary theories about the family, Vol. II, General theories/theoretical orientations. New York, NY: Free Press.

Olson, D. H.; McCubbin, H. I.; Barnes, H. L., et al. 1983. Families: What makes them work. Beverly Hills, CA: Sage.

Orthner, D. K. 1975. Leisure activity patterns and marital satisfaction over the marital career. Journal of Marriage and the Family. 37: 91-102.

Orthner, D. K. 1976. Patterns of leisure and marital interaction. Journal of Leisure Research. 8: 98-111.

Orthner, D. K. 1980. Families in blue: A study of U. S. Air Force married and single parent families. Washington, DC: U.S. Air Force.

Orthner, D. K. 1985. Leisure and conflict in families. In: Gunter: B. G., Stanley, J.; St. Clair, R., eds. Transitions to leisure: Conflict and leisure in families. New York, NY: University Press.

Orthner, D. K.; Axelson, L. J. 1980. The effects of wife employment on marital sociability. Journal of Comparative Family Studies. 11: 531-543.

Orthner, D. K.; Herron, R. W. 1984. Leisure counseling for families. In: Dowd, E. T., ed. Leisure counseling concepts and applications. Springfield, IL: Thomas Books: 178-197.

Orthner, D. K.; Mancini, J. A. 1980. Leisure behavior and group dynamics: The case of the family. In: Iso-Ahola, S. E. Social psychological perspectives on leisure and recreation. Springfield, IL: Thomas Books: 307-328.

Palisi, B. J. 1984. Marriage companionship and marriage well-being: A comparison of metropolitan areas in three countries. Journal of Comparative Family Studies. 15: 43-56.

Presvelou, C. 1971. Impact of differential leisure activities on intra-spousal dynamics. Human Relations. 24: 565-574.

Roper Organization. 1974. The Virginia Slims American women's opinion poll. New York, NY: The Roper Organization.

Rosenblatt, P. C.; Cunningham, M. R. 1976. Television watching and family tension. Journal of Marriage and the Family. 38: 103-111.

Rosenblatt, P. C.; Titus, S. L.; Nevaldine, A.; Cunningham, M. R. 1979. Marital system differences and summer-long vacations: Togetherness-apartness and tension. American Journal of Family Therapy. 7: 77-84.

Searle, M. S.; Jackson, E. L. 1985. Socioeconomic variations in perceived barriers to recreation participation among would-be participants. Leisure Sciences. 7: 227-249.

Strauss, M.; Gelles, R.; Steinmetz, S. 1980. Behind closed doors. New York, NY: Doubleday.

Sussman, M. B.; Steinmetz, S. K. 1987. Handbook of marriage and the family. New York, NY: Plenum: 437-469.

United Media Enterprises Report on Leisure in America. 1982. Where does the time go? New York, NY: United Media Enterprises.

Varga, K. 1972. Marital cohesion as reflected in time budgets. In: Szalai, A. The use of time. The Hague: Mouton.

West, P. C.; Merriam, L. C., Jr. 1970. Outdoor recreation and family cohesion: A research approach. Journal of Leisure Research. 2: 251-259.

Witt, P. A.; Goodale, T. L. 1981. The relationships between barriers to leisure enjoyment and family stages. Leisure Sciences. 4: 29-49.

Organizational Wellness

Taylor Ellis
Hospitality Management Department
University of Central Florida
Orlando, Florida

Glenn Richardson
Department of Health Education
University of Utah
Salt Lake City, Utah

The term organizational wellness has many meanings in corporate America. It can be applied to both economic wellness and employee wellness. This paper is concerned with the latter terminology. The intent of this document is to assess the economic and psychological impacts to an organization that can result from increased employee wellness.

OBJECTIVES

What is organizational wellness? There are numerous ways to describe programs that are concerned with the wellness of employees. Currently, many businesses provide programs which attempt to improve the overall health and well-being of employees. For example, some of these programs are: employee services, fitness classes, clubs, employee assistance programs and wellness.

Most commonly, the employee services branch is designated in a company to provide services to employees. The consensus of opinion derived as a result of all of the information reviewed pertaining to organizational wellness is that the employee and the company are both winners when programs are provided that promote wellness. According to the articles reviewed, no matter how you approach corporate wellness, it all adds up to the same thing—happier, healthier more productive employees, and economic benefits for the company.

In this paper we will be discussing the concept of organizational wellness as it applies to both employees and employers. It will be divided into the following sections: history and background of employee services, benefits of organizational wellness programs, status of existing theory, methodological constraints, and summary.

HISTORY

Recreation Prespective

The history of employee assistance programs is long and varied. According to Brody (1988), the first half of the nineteenth century was characterized as one where workers often drank while on the job; in some cases, even at the expense of the employers. This was the accepted practice prior to the enactment of workers compensation laws which required employers to address alcohol-related problems. The industrialization of the American work force during the 19th century had a profound impact on the lifestyle of the American people. As workers left the farms to work in automated factories in the cities, the social workers of the time lamented the problems of urbanization. The concerns focused on the poor working conditions of the employees and their inability to obtain "wholesome" recreation.

The development of the labor movement and management's increased interest in providing employee recreational activities were a result of increased urbanization and poor working conditions. As early as 1820, trade unions were beginning to be organized in the larger industrialized cities. As a result, the 10-hour work day was mandated for federal employees during the 1840s by President Van Buren. States began to follow the federal model as early as 1847. By 1854, some of the more progressive companies in the United States were providing recreational activities for not only their employees, but for entire communities.

The apparent interest in public recreation was really the result of economics. The dominant manufacturing companies owned their towns and all of the residents were employees. This resulted in companies providing programs to benefit entire communities. For example, by 1854, the Peacedale Manufacturing Company, of Peacedale, Rhode Island opened a small library for use by the entire community (Murphy 1984).

Labor unions continued to increase in size and power. The Noble Order of the Knights of Labor was formed as a secret organization in 1869 as a reaction to the monopolies of businesses and their interlocking boards of directors who controlled the workers' lives. The railroad strikes of 1873 were a result of overexpansion in the railroad industry and resulting bankruptcies. A panic due to layoffs was blamed on the Noble Order of the Knights of Labor by management. As a result of railroad consolidation, numerous employees were fired from their positions, and the remaining employees were forced to take pay cuts resulting in increased labor/management strife.

For a short while during the 1880s, working conditions again enjoyed a favorable period. The 8-hour day, wage increases, and recognition of unions had begun. Companies were beginning to provide recreational activities for employees in the form of sports and sports leagues. For example, the Warner Brothers Company erected a club house for 500 of its employees in 1887.

Strikes became rampant during the 1880s with employees demanding increased salaries and better working conditions. Management began to provide employees with recreational activities in an attempt to promote employee loyalty, fellowship, high moral standards, and physical and intellectual development. Tolman (1909) documents numerous instances of companies providing recreational facilities for their employees. One aspect of industrial recreation began out of corporate interest in competitive sports. Companies hired individuals for their abilities as athletes to help company sports teams. This resulted in amateur/pro-

fessional athletic leagues. In fact, two professional football teams, the Chicago Bears and the Green Bay Packers, were originally company teams for the A. E. Stanley Company and the Acme Packing Company. The development of athletics continued throughout World War I and II and into the 1950s. Since the 1950s and 1960s, corporate athletics has become more of an intracompany competition rather than extracompany competition, although there are still instances where employees are being hired for their ability to help the athletic team.

Another major purpose of industrial recreation was to integrate immigrants into the American lifestyle. This resulted in company sponsorship of reading classes, social clubs, and cooking activities so that employees could learn how to be "better Americans." In order to accomplish these objectives, meeting rooms and libraries were the most frequently targeted facilities. There were many instances of companies building extremely expensive facilities. For example, in 1899 the Juliet Steele Company built a club house for its employees at a cost of $75,000.00 (Tolman 1909).

By 1896, the first incorporated recreation association was developed by the Ludlow Manufacturing Associates when they created their athletic and recreation society. This society became the home for cooking, dressmaking, millinery, laundry, classical culture, swimming, and dancing classes; dramatic, orchestral, choral, football, and baseball clubs. The facilities operated by the society also had a bowling alley and poolroom. In order to run these facilities, the club had a social secretary who worked as a full-time manager. This was probably the first documented case of a full-time employee running an industrial recreation program (Tolman 1909).

Numerous recreational programs have been developed to benefit employees throughout the 20th century. Frankel and Fleisher (1920) and Anderson (1955) indicated that educational programs were a product of the 19th century and were deemphasized during the 20th century. Educational programs were replaced by social programs between 1916 and 1926. Musical activities such as public bands and choruses were emphasized during the first half of the 20th century and were used mainly for "esprit de corps," advertising campaigns, and cultural activities. Both social programs and musical activities were casualties of the depression.

Physical fitness programs have increased tremendously, particularly those that were begun during the later part of the 20th century. It was not until the 1960s that management began to recognize the importance of the individual employee and the impact that activities for his/her well-being could have on the productivity of the whole company. As a result, numerous programs are being developed to improve employee health.

One of the reasons for the increased development of industrial recreation programs can be attributed to the inception of the Recreation Association for American Industry. This association was born at the 1939 National Recreation Association meeting in Baltimore, Maryland. During this convention, 17 prominent industrial recreation leaders met to form the new organization. Because of the tremendous importance of athletics in industrial recreation programs, the majority of the funding for this new association came from athletic equipment manufacturers. In 1944, the association changed its name to the Industrial Recreation Association. It entered a new era in 1949 when it merged with a western industrial recreation association to become the National Industrial Recreation Association.

Recently, the association has undergone another name change and is referred to as the National Employees Services Association. This new name reflects the de-emphasis on recreation that is apparent in the industry. Their magazine, *Recreation Services Management*, is an important source of information for individuals working in the field of industrial recreation or employee services.

Wellness from a Health Prespective

The wellness movement began in the early 1970s as a delayed response to a concept that was forwarded a decade earlier when Halbert L. Dunn (1961) wrote the book *High Level Wellness*. Dunn promoted the concept that people need to stay as far away from illness as possible and reach optimal states of health. Although there were many key figures in the 1970s that helped to advance the notion of wellness, three will be mentioned.

Bill Hettler at the University of Wisconsin in Steven's Point spearheaded an innovative campus wellness program in the early 70s. Later he formed the Institute for Lifestyle Improvement and sponsored annual wellness conferences which attracted people from across the country and around the world. Later the institute was changed to the National Wellness Institute and the tradition continues.

Don Ardell was and currently is an active promoter of the wellness movement through speaking engagements across the country, writing books and articles, and editing and publishing a newsletter in the name of wellness. Ardell defined wellness as "a conscious and deliberate approach to an advanced state of physical and psychological/spiritual health . . . a dynamic or ever changing, fluctuating state of being" (Ardell 1984).

Ryan and Travis's Wellness Workbook became the "wellness bible" in the early 1980s, and John Travis's health center has become one of the most innovative treatment and high level health promotion centers in the country. Ryan and Travis (1981) defined wellness a number of ways including:

- Wellness is a choice—a decision you make to move toward optimal health.
- Wellness is a way of life—a lifestyle you design to achieve your highest potential for well-being.
- Wellness is a process—a developing awareness that there is no end point, but that health and happiness are possible in each moment, here and now.
- Wellness is an efficient channelling of energy— energy received from the environment, transformed within you, and sent on to affect the world outside.
- Wellness is the integration of body, mind and spirit—the appreciation that everything you do, and think and feel, and believe has an impact on your state of health.
- Wellness is a loving acceptance of yourself.

In an attempt to objectify and measure the wellness process, Richardson and Felts (1985) defined wellness as follows:

Wellness is the active process of improving one's health status as measured subjectively (by feeling better or resolving problems) or objectively (improved physiological, lifestyle, strengths, or psychological indicators) in any dimension of health.

Reflective of these definitions of wellness, our definition of organizational wellness is:

Pragmatic and systematic planning, implementing, marketing, and evaluating programs for a selected group of individuals that will, through environmental, educational, and counseling stimuli, enhance the health status of individuals in the social, physiological, spiritual, emotional, and mental domains of health which can be measured either directly or indirectly, subjectively or objectively.

The assumption upon which this definition is based is that individuals experience some common stages of progression as they approach, attempt, and ultimately change their wellness behaviors. As shown in Figure 1, the individual will enter a program with some preadopted behaviors and preconceived perceptions and knowledge about the value of health and recreation. Through various environmental promptings (i.e., media, friends, etc.) individuals become aware or conscious of wellness needs. They may seek and

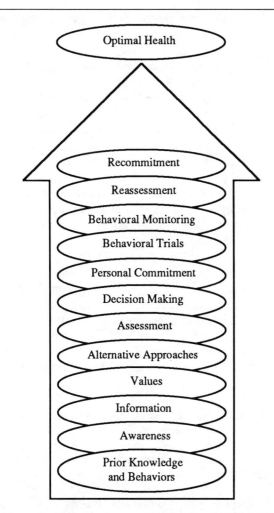

Figure 1. Individual progress toward optimal health.

receive additional information about a variety of health or recreational behaviors. Based on the information, the individual will consider how important the adoption of the behavior(s) is (are) or clarify their values regarding health and recreational behaviors. If deemed important, individuals will look at alternative approaches to adopting the behaviors. They may join an organized program or attempt to do something on their own.

Critical for evaluation as well as providing a motivation force is the individual assessment of health status. Assessment from a multidimensional leisure and health perspective helps clients to understand what their status is and what is attainable. The clients then make decisions and personal commitments to adopt behaviors that will promote wellness or to eliminate behaviors that block wellness progress.

Clients may then set times when they will begin to incorporate the behavior change and start making behavior attempts or trials. Once comfortable with the behavior, careful self or external monitoring is vital to success in objectively measuring the wellness process or subjectively feeling better. After an appropriate period of time, clients are reassessed with the same measures that were used at the beginning of the program. The behavioral commitments and improvements are noted for program efficacy and individual intrinsic rewards. The reassessment triggers additional commitments for continuance toward optimal health and leisure time activity.

It is highly unlikely that all clients experience each of the stages described in Figure 1, but from an organizational wellness perspective, it is likely that these stages are evident in varying degrees or in varied orders. The environmental and organizational influences necessary to facilitate the wellness process are evident. To generate increased awareness, some initial information is needed to promote the values of wellness as a function of marketing or promotion. Providing detailed information, further clarifying values, exploring alternative approaches to change, offering initial or general assessments, facilitating decisionmaking, and even encouraging personal commitments are all potential functions of health and leisure education.

Assuring lifestyle change, which includes in-depth assessment, facilitating decisionmaking, detailing and facilitating personal commitments (lifestyle contracting), helping with behavioral trials, monitoring behavioral progress, reassessing, and recommitting are all functions of health and leisure counseling (Fig. 2).

In consideration of this potential progress toward optimal health, organizational wellness programs should be complete with all planning, marketing, intervention, and evaluation processes. Figure 3 represents an organizational model for a wellness program. Note in the model that there is a cyclic process for the individual that, in concept, never ends. The assessment-feedback-education-commitment-behavioral monitoring, and reassessment process is essential to any wellness program if individual benefits are to occur and be measured. Plugging into that cyclic process is continual planning, refining, and updated marketing. Stemming from the assessment experience is individual, program, and organizational evaluation.

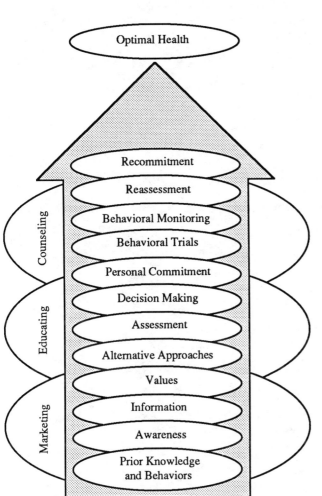

Figure 2. Facilitating wellness.

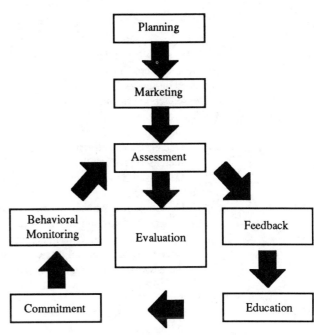

Figure 3. Components of a wellness program.

BENEFITS OF ORGANIZATIONAL WELLNESS PROGRAMS

A recent survey by Hollander and Lengerman (1988) of the Fortune 500 companies found that two-thirds of the companies responding reported having employee recreation programs. The same study found that one-third of the companies without industrial recreation programs planned to start one. Hollander and Lengerman (1988) compare this to a survey which was conducted in 1986 in which only 29 % of the Fortune 500 companies reported having industrial recreation.

The perceived benefits of industrial recreation programs are highlighted in Table 1. It is interesting to note that the Fortune 500 companies surveyed identified the activities provided in order of importance as: hypertension screening and control (offered by 83% of all companies with programs), health risk assessments (78%), alcohol or drug issues (76%), smoking cessation (75%), accident prevention (75%), fitness and exercise (75%), weight and nutritional management (65%), stress management (61%), and cancer screening (61%) (Hollander and Lengerman 1988).

When asked about organizational support for these activities, 72% of the companies indicated that they offer activities after work, with another 71% offering them during lunch time. Only 20% of the companies allowed their employees to participate in the programs on company time (Hollander and Lengerman 1988.) When asked about financing of employee recreational activities, 53% of the companies paid all of the cost, 80% paid for 80% or more of the cost, and only 3% of the responding companies said that their organization paid none of the cost of running a program (Hollander and Lengerman 1988).

It should be noted that the programs reported by the Fortune 500 companies are not recreational in nature. Reviewing the list of activities provided reveals that other

Table 1. Perceived benefits of organizational wellness.

Advantages for Employers
- Reduced disability and death benefits
- Reduced treatment costs
- Reduced on-the-job accidents
- Increased worker health and quality of life
- Economic Benefits
  - Decreased health care costs
  - Decreased absenteeism
  - Increased productivity
  - Decreased turnover and premature death
- Psychosocial Benefits
  - Decreased interpersonal barriers between labor and management
  - Better work atmosphere and work morale
  - Increased ability to recruit talented employees
  - Decreased turnover and increased continuity within company
  - Increased ability to retain talented employees

Advantages for employees
- Reduced health-related costs
- Reduced transportation and waiting time for health
- Reduced sick leave
- Increased co-worker and employer support for positive health behaviors
- Increased morale based on management's concern for health
- Increased satisfaction with health activities
- Improved health and quality of life
- Physiological benefits
  - Increased maximum volume of oxygen (MVO_2)
  - Reduced body weight
  - Reduced percent body fat
  - Reduced resting heart rate
  - Reduced blood pressure
  - Reduced incidence of orthopedic spinal problems
  - Reduced stress-related indicators
- Epidemiological benefits
  - Reduced long-term risk of disease or death
  - Demonstrated relationship between physical activity and longevity
- Psychosocial benefits
  - Increased morale
  - Increased personal satisfaction
  - Improved intrapersonal relations
  - Increased sense of self-worth
  - Better mental health
  - Lowered levels of anxiety
  - Improved self-image

Advantages to society
- Reduced health costs
- Improved health and quality of life
- Adoption of health promotion emphasis

than fitness and exercise, none of the activities even remotely resemble recreation. It is true that these programs are offered through the industrial recreation program but that is the only connection. It appears that in this instance employee well-being has replaced recreation as the driving force behind these programs. Table 2 provides a brief summary of the different types of activities and the program goals that were found or discussed in the literature as provided by organizational wellness programs.

Based on Tables 1 and 2, organization wellness appears to be a panacea for employees and businessmen. The subjective items identified can readily serve as justification for the development of corporate programs by businesses. However, these pale in comparison to the purported economic benefits as identified in Table 3. If all of the purported economic benefits actually exist, it would stand to reason that the American worker is the best taken care of and the most highly productive worker in the world. This does not appear to be the case.

A further breakdown of the evidence of recreation, fitness, and lifestyle program benefits can be seen in Table 4, where the social, psychological, and tangible benefits are also included in reference to each of the activities. The literature is full of testimonials and claims concerning the benefits derived from these programs. However, the hard data to support them is missing. In most cases, the literature is unsubstantiated by research studies that indicate how the benefits were determined.

Individual Evaluation

Health and leisure assessment is a complex and multidimensional experience. Remembering that health and leisure can be interpreted as a social, spiritual, emotional, mental, or physical phenomenon, assessments for health or leisure behavior should be measured from a multidimensional perspective. An activity such as aerobic exercise can have positive results manifested objectively as physical (increased maximum volume of oxygen—MVO_2), social (significant other support), emotional (facilitates coping with anger), mental (coping mechanism for stress), or spiritual (an opportunity for meditation) improvement. Many instruments and protocols have been developed to conduct health and leisure assessments, but the future is rich for further developments in some dimensions. Table 5 is a listing of assessment tools that are currently available for wellness assessment. Again, the function of assessment is to help demonstrate the efficacy of wellness programs and to provide the client with an intrinsic reward demonstrating improvement of health status through objective means.

Program Evaluation

Wellness programs are far from effective at this point in time. Program evaluation is defined as determining the efficacy of the intervention (education, feedback, commitment, and behavioral monitoring) process. In a general sense, the average wellness program results in less than 50% participation in the program, and participation rates after a year are often below 25% of those orginally participating. Program evaluation then identifies the more successful approaches and allows for the elimination of less effective approaches to wellness. It will be through the development and refinement of new health and leisure programs and approaches that program efficacy will be attained.

Organization Evaluation

Evaluation of an organization's wellness program can be viewed from two perspectives, namely, cost effectiveness and cost-benefit. Cost effectiveness is a subjective decision as to whether the cost of implementing a program is worth the outcome. Cost-benefit is an objective evaluation comparing the amount of dollars put into a program to the money that is saved by its implementation over a designated period of time.

Table 3 represents the potential elements that can be measured to determine the health of a company and evidence to facilitate judgments as to cost effectiveness and cost-benefit.

STATUS OF EXISTING THEORY

A serious researcher must question the economic and intangible results that are identified in Tables 3 and 4. Kittrell (1986, 1988) investigated how companies measure the economic impact of organizational wellness programs. His results indicate that only 3.4% of the respondents in 1986 were collecting cost-benefit or savings data for employee organizational wellness programs in their companies. The 1988 survey found that only 11.2% of the companies responding were collecting cost-benefit data. The results of these two studies lead one to question the economic benefits identified in previous studies (Table 3).

It appears from this literature review, that the majority of the economic benefit information provided was generated simply by estimating what would happen in a large company based upon a relatively small sample of respondents. The

Table 2. Goals, content and benefits of wellness programs.

Program Goal	Content of the Program	More Tangible Benefits	Less Tangible Benefits	Reference
Increase job attendence	Well-pay concept, reinforcing employees for not being absent or sick. Give bonus to employees that stay well for four weeks and discontinue sickpay	- Incentives to employees if stay well - Lower absenteeism rate - Improve productivity		Harvey et al. 1984
Health promotion	Exercise programs, nutrition workshops, weight control programs, stress and time management, safety, cancer prevention, smoking cessation, substance abuse control	- Reduce life insurance costs - Reduce health insurance costs - Reduce workmen's compensation costs - Reduce workmen's disability - Decrease absenteeism - Decrease turnover - Increase productivity	- Company visibility - Social responsibility - Improve morale - Improve work environment	Finney 1985 Edington 1983
Increased task/ job performance	Furnish participants with activities they perceive as supplying high levels of control	- Increase job performance	- Decrease the post stress performance	Finney 1984 Finney 1985 Wang et al. 1987
Fitness	Exercise programs, recreation programs, meditation and relaxation programs, education, counseling, and assessment	- Decrease absenteeism - Increase productivity - Decrease health insurance costs - Reduce disability costs	- High morale - Low burnout - Low lack of focus	Harris and Gurrin 1985 Kondrasuk 1980 Berger et al. 1984
Fitness progam	Nutrition awareness, stress management, smoking cessation, alcohol and substance abuse	- Reduce absenteeism - Health costs - Long term disability - Productivity	- Improve worker morale	Harris and Gurrin 1985 Berger et al. 1984 Mobily 1984 Thomas 1983
Attract new employees, recruiting tool, reduce turnover	Recreation programs, discount company store, fitness center, country clubs		- Eye catcher - Magnet to lure employees away from other companies - The company cares about its employees - Presented as part of the company's overall philosophy -Environment conducive to job satisfaction -Transcends beyond job levels and workforce links	Cramer 1984

Table 2. Goals, content and benefits of wellness programs. (continued)

Program Goal	Content of the Program	More Tangible Benefits	Less Tangible Benefits	Reference
Corporate managers' view	Employee recreation programs		- Better employer/ employee relations - Community spirit - Good sportsmanship in employees	Lamke 1984 Phelps and Roys 1983
Improve employee health and physical fitness	Fitness programs, health clubs, health spas. Companies pay 4 cents every mile employees bicycle and 64 cents for every mile they swim	- Better health - Reduce overweight - Greater productivity - Less absenteeism - Lower medical costs - Decrease turnover - Fewer accidents/ injuries - Fewer health/life insurance problems - Lower workers compensation costs	- Reduce dysfunctional stress.	Edington 1983 Mobily 1984 Thomas 1983
Social interaction of employees, Improve employee health practices	Recreational sports, program activities that support health (e.g., basketball, volleyball, racquetball, etc.)	- Better health of the employee	- Social cohesiveness	Edington 1983 Mobily 1984 Price 1987 Streitz 1986
Corporate managers' corporate benefits from recreation programs		- Productivity - Recruitment and retention - Retirement	- Communication - Leadership - Community service - Family participation - Employee morale - Physical fitness	Lamke 1984 Mobily 1984 Phelps and Roys 1983

Table 3. Examples of annual economic benefits for corporations from wellness programs.

Benefit Area	Annual Savings/Reduction	Reference
Absenteeism	1.25 days per employee	Blair et al. 1986b
	$149,578 savings	Blair et al. 1986b
	46% decrease in days	Harvey et al. 1984
	50-400% reduction in days	Kocolowski 1986
	42% reduction in days	Ryval 1984
	$175,000 savings	Ryval 1984
	2.6% reduction in days	Tonti et. al. 1987
Medical Costs	$903 savings	Blanchard et al. 1985
	45.7% decrease in costs	Bowne et al. 1984
	14% reduction in utilization of medical benefits	Edington 1986
	37.5% decrease in costs	Edington 1986
	24% decrease in costs	Gibb et al. 1985
	$140 per employee	Harrington 1987
	$49.74 per year	Kittrell 1988
	$2.51 savings for each dollar spent on program	Kocolowski 1986
	30% decrease in costs	Lenchus 1986
	45% decrease in costs	No author cited 1985
	$700 per employee	Shephard 1983
	$897 per female employee	Smith 1986
	$442 per male employee	Smith 1986
	$232 per program participant	Smith 1986
	17-35% decrease in costs	Vickery et al. 1983
	$2.50-$3.50 savings for each dollar spent on program	Vickery et al. 1983
	$1,284,000 savings	Harris 1986
Disability	20.1% reduction in disability days	Bowne et al. 1984
	31.7% reduction in dollars spent	Bowne et al. 1984
	$232 savings per person	Bowne et al. 1984
	20% reduction in disability days	Edington 1986
Stress	$5.52 savings for each dollar spent on program	Jaffe et al. 1986
	27.3% reduction in stress levels	Harris 1986
	$7,005 monthly savings	Jones et al. 1986
	$22,082 monthly savings	Jones et al. 1986
	$988 monthly savings	Jones et al. 1986
	5-85% reduction in stress levels	Pelletier 1988
Smoking	$200-$500 savings per employee	Koop 1986
	$336-$601 savings per employee	Kristein 1983
	$400-$1000 savings per employee	Voluck 1987
	4.5% reduction in smoking	Harris 1986
Cholesterol	$3 to $208 savings in medical costs per employee	Oster and Epstein 1986
Turnover	1.5% reduction	Ryval 1984
	$500,000 savings	Ryval 1984
Injuries	34% reduction in number	Stamper 1987
	50% reduction in number	Tonti et al. 1987

Table 4. Evidence of benefits of specific fitness, recreation, or lifestyle programs.

Program	Goals	More Tangible Benefits	Less Tangible Benefits
Exercise	- Health of employees, more productive, less absenteeism	- Reduce insurance costs (Sparks 1983)	
	- Improve employee health and physical health	- Financial benefits rated unknown by majority of respondents	
		- 54% of respondents rated their programs somewhat helped meet these goals, 31% helped greatly (Berger et al. 1984)	
	- Improve employee health	- Reduce insurance costs (. . . insurance companies offer lower group insurance rates to industrial firms which have established fitness programs), productivity, less fatigue (Brewn and Wilson 1979)	
	- Reduce illness, accidents, heart attacks, back problems, injuries, death, stress	- (NASA study/Russia studies) - Improve work performance (Kondrasuk 1980)	
	- Health promotion	- Reduce health costs, reduce absenteeism, enhance recruitment, increase productivity (Boyd 1985)	
	- Improve health, mental functioning, reduce stress	- 95% respondents answer to increase health; Canada Life Insurance saved $35,975 in health care costs the first year; no evidence of fitness programs affecting productivity, absenteeism (Kondrasuk 1985)	
	- Promote physical fitness, motivation	- Safety, reduce injuries - Reduce absenteeism, sickness, attract new employees; retention of employers (Yuhasz 1979)	- Communication among employees - Balance between work, family and health - Reduce stress - Social interaction

Table 4. Evidence of benefits of specific fitness, recreation, or lifestyle programs. (continued)

Program	Goals	More Tangible Benefits	Less Tangible Benefits
Exercise (continued)	- Preventive health, alcoholism, obesity	- Reduce illness, injuries - Employee turnover dropped 1.5%, saving the company $500,000 - Absenteeism was reduced by 42%, saving $175,000 (Ryval 1984)	- Motivational - Educational
Recreation	- Increase program adherence to a fitness program		- Social interaction (Ryval 1984)
	- Organization benefits, increase profits	- Reduce absenteeism, turnover, increased performance, health cost reduced, Canada Life Insurance report reduce absenteeism 22%, saving $300,000; turnover rate reduce 13.5% (Finney 1984)	- Reduce stress - Job satisfaction
	- Increase awareness of health habits	- Changes in the parameters of physical activity, maximum oxygen consumption, body weight, resting heart rate, blood pressure, decrease health care costs; absenteeism, productivity, turnover (Hill et al. 1988)	- Increase morale - Satisfaction - Better mental health - Lower anxiety - Better work atmosphere
	- Corporate image	- Marketing of products (Taylor and Silverman 1984)	- Public relations
	- Public relations	- Recruiting, sales (Mihalik 1984)	- Interact with local community, good communication
	- Increase productivity	- Cost benefits, performance (Fain 1983)	- Worker expectation
	- Enhance productivity, improve mental and physical fitness (Howe 1983)	- Productivity	- Job Satisfaction - Worker cohesiveness

Table 4. Evidence of benefits of specific fitness, recreation, or lifestyle programs. (continued)

Program	Goals	More Tangible Benefits	Less Tangible Benefits
Recreation (continued)	- Socialization among workers	- Improve physical fitness - Competition - Convenience (Streitz 1986)	- Social interaction - Personal growth
	- Expand the sense of community	- Reduce absenteeism, turnover rate, accident rates, workers compensation; increase test performance, general health (Finney 1987)	- Reduce stress - Job satisfaction - Morale
	- Increase task performance	- Increase productivity (play activities were provided between stressful work tasks) (Finney 1984)	
	- Increase productivity, reduce stress	- Reduce absenteeism (Nudel 1984)	- Employee loyalty - Reduce tension
	- Health promotion	- Reduce absenteeism, turnover; increase productivity (Coffey 1984)	
Lifestyle Management	- Reduce alcohol consumption, smoking, and drug use among corporate employees	- Health maintenance - Create healthier lifestyles (Kaman 1988)	
	- Health promotion	- Increase productivity (Shaw 1988)	- Happier employee
	- Health promotion	- Reduce health care costs, absenteeism, turnover; productivity (Rosen 1984)	- Job satisfaction, healthier corporate culture
	- Health promotion; health awareness	- Lower disability costs (cost declined 45.7%) (medical costs declined 31.7%) (Elias and Murphy 1987)	
	- Reduce stress	- Reduce health care (Wang et al. 1987)	
	- Improve workers	- Reduce absenteeism; increase productivity (Villeneuve et al. 1983)	- Increase workers' morale
	- Health promotion	- Increase productivity; decrease absenteeism, reduce health costs, burnout (Mobily 1984)	- Increase morale - Reduce stress

Table 5. Health assessment tools available for multidimensional assessment.

Name	Measure	Source
COGNITIVE		
Adaptive Behavior Inventory	Cognitive/Ability	PRO-ED
Arlin Test of Formal Reasoning	Stage of cognitive development	Slosson Educational Publications, Inc.
Stanford-Binet Intelligence Scale	Intelligence test	Nfer-Nelson
Kendrick Cognitive Tests for the Elderly	Cognitive assessment in the elderly	Nfer-Nelson
Wechsler Intelligence Scale for Children	Cognitive assessment for children	Psychological Corp.
Test of Academic Progress	Academic achievement for the grade level	Psychological Corp.
Multilevel Academic Survey Tests	Academic performance	Psychological Corp.
NEUROPSYCHOLOGICAL		
Bender Visual Motor Gestalt Test	Visual motor perceptions	Nfer-Nelson
Quick Neurological Screening Test	Learning problems	Nfer-Nelson
PERSONALITY		
Adjective Check List	Personality/Motivation	Consulting Psychologists Press
Adolescent Multiphasic Personality Inventory	Personality	Pacific Psychological Precision People
Adult Personality Inventory	Personality	Institute for Personality and Ability Testing

Table 5. Health assessment tools available for multidimensional assessment. (continued)

Name	Measure	Source
PERSONALITY (continued)		
16 Personality Factor Questionnaire	Personality	Nfer-Nelson
High School Personality Questionnaire	Personality	Psychological Corp.
California	Normal personality	Psychological Corp.
Psychological	Consulting inventory	Psychologists Press
Jackson Personality Inventory	Normal personality average to above average intelligence	Psychological Corp.
Defense Mechanism Inventory	Five styles to responding to conflict and stress	Psychological Corp.
Beck Hopelessness Scale	Expectations for the future	Psychological Corp.
Minnesota Multiphasic Personality Inventory	Personality	Nfer-Nelson Weathers Reports, Inc. Sienna Software
Eysenck Personality Inventory	Personality	Nfer-Nelson
RISK TAKING		
Alcohol Assessment and Treatment Profile	Drinking behavior and beliefs	Psychologists, Inc.
Eating Disorder Inventory	Anorexia or bulimia	Nfer-Nelson
Alcohol Use Inventory	How and why a person uses and abuses alcohol	National Computer Systems/PAS Division
Suicidal Ideation Questionnaire	Accompanies depression tools for suicide risk	Psychological Corp.
Life Orientation Inventory	Suicide risk	Pro-ed

Table 5. Health assessment tools available for multidimensional assessment. (continued)

Name	Measure	Source
BEHAVIOR		
Comprehensive Behavioral Rating Scale for Children	Cognitive, emotional, and behavioral functioning	Psychological Corp.
Child Behavior Checklist	Ages 4-16, children's competencies and problems	Psychological Corp.
Youth Self Report	Competency and problems for ages 11-18	Psychological Corp.
The Eating Inventory	Three dimensions of eating: cognitive, disinhibition, hunger	Psychological Corp.
Jenkins Activity Survey	Type A Behavior	Psychological Corp.
FACILITATING/MOODS		
Grief Experience Inventory	Bereavement process	Consulting Psychologists Press
Lewis Counselling Inventory	Adolescent behavior on relationships, social confidence, health	Nfer-Nelson
Motivation Analysis Test	Primary behavioral dimensions	Nfer-Nelson
Myers-Briggs Type Indicator	Personality dispositions and interests	Nfer-Nelson
Beck Depression Inventory	Degree of depression	Psychological Corp.
Reynolds Adolescent Depression Scale	Symptoms of depression	Psychological Corp.
Culture Free Self-Esteem Inventory	Self-esteem in children	Nfer-Nelson

Table 5. Health assessment tools available for multidimensional assessment. (continued)

Name	Measure	Source
FACILITATING/MOODS (continued)		
Coopersmith Self-esteem Inventories	Self-esteem	Consulting Psychologists Press
Profile of Moods States	Mood states	Nfer-Nelson
Personal Questionnaire Rapid Scaling Technique	Objective reports of subjective experiences	Nfer-Nelson
Children's Depression Scale	Nature and extent of childhood depression	Nfer-Nelson
Children's State-Trait Anxiety Inventory	Anxiety	Nfer-Nelson
CDS Stress Profile	Multidimensional stress	Computer Diversified
Hassles and Uplifts Scale	Stressors	Consulting Psychologists Press
Coping Operations Preference Enquiry	Defensive or coping mechanisms	Consulting Psychologists Press
Ways of Coping Questionnaire	Eight coping strategies	Consulting Psychologists Press
Coping Resources Inventory	Personal resources to cope	Consulting Psychologists Press
Problem Solving Inventory	Individual's perception of own problem solving behaviors and attitudes	Consulting Psychologists Press
SOCIAL		
Areas of Change Computer Program	Desired change in relationship by a couple	Multi-Health Systems
Elements of Awareness	Interpersonal relationship structures	Nfer-Nelson

Table 5. Health assessment tools available for multidimensional assessment. (continued)

Name	Measure	Source
SOCIAL (continued)		
Social Style Profile	Identifies several social styles	Tracom
FIRO	Behavior and feelings towards others	Nfer-Nelson
Golombok Rust Inventory of Marital State	Quality of heterosexual relationship—areas of conflict	Nfer-Nelson
Golombok Rust Inventory of Sexual Satisfaction	Sexual functioning	Nfer-Nelson
Occupational Stress Indicator	Stress	Nfer-Nelson
Computerized Stress Inventory	30 plus lifestyle stressors	Preventive Measures
Bristol Social Adjustment Guides	Behavioral disturbance in children in school	Nfer-Nelson
Family Relations Tests	Feelings about families	Nfer-Nelson
Family Environment Scale	Social/environmental characteristics of families	Nfer-Nelson
Social Reticence Scale	Shyness	Consulting Psychologists Press
Scale of Social Development	Social skills	Pro-ed
Walker-McConnell Scale of Social Competence and School Adjustment	Social skills	Pro-ed
Waksman Social Skills Rating Scale	Social Skills	Pro-ed

Table 5. Health assessment tools available for multidimensional assessment. (continued)

Name	Measure	Source
SPIRITUAL/VALUES		
Porteous Checklist	Degree and focus of adolescent concerns and problems	Nfer-Nelson
EMOTIONAL		
Children's Apperceptive Story Telling Test	Emotional functioning for school age children	Pro-ed
Index of Personality Characteristics	Test of emotional disturbance	Pro-ed
Social-Emotional Dimension Scale	Risk of conduct disorders, behavior problems or emotional disturbance	Pro-ed
Test of Early Socioemotional Development	Social emotional development	Pro-ed
OCCUPATIONAL		
Employment Productivity	Potential productivity based on dependability, cooperation, and drug avoidance	London House
Employee Attitude Inventory	Job satisfaction and honesty	London House
Staff Burnout	Work burnout and stress	London House
Life Styles Inventory	Personal effectiveness	Human Synergistics
Work Personality Profile	Capabilities to satisfy fundamental work role requirements	The Arkansas Connection
Hilson Career Satisfaction Index	Job satisfaction	Hilson Research Inc.
Occupational Aptitude and Interest Scale	Career development	Pro-ed

fallacies of this methodology are rampant. In fact, Warner (1987) identified five flaws in conventional perceptions pertaining to the economic benefits of industrial recreation:

- What would the increased pension costs be when they are incurred by participants of these programs who may live longer into their retirement years and what are the health care, disability, and other costs that are incurred because these same participants live to be older? These costs have not been included in the calculations.
- The kinds of analysis often used are usually based on the most optimistic estimates in projecting the long-term success rates of health promotion programs, rather than on average or common figures.
- It is important to note that compliance with a behavioral change regime is sometimes treated as synonymous with the elimination of the risk associated with the undesirable behavior; this is clearly not true.
- Many studies fail to even attempt to project program consequences into the future.
- A more sophisticated analytical issue involves how consequences occurring beyond the first year of a program are handled.

Warner et al. (1988) evaluated research pertaining to what he calls "health promotion programs." These programs are similar, if not identical, to organizational wellness or industrial recreation programs. Warner and his associates reviewed the literature on the economics of work place health promotion with an emphasis on characterizing the substantive and structural nature of these programs and their scientific quality. Warner and his associates obtained a listing of 650 bibliographical items dating from 1974 to 1985. Of those 650 articles, 400 were ranked as deserving examination. After review of the 400 articles, 289 required intensive review to evaluate the research methodology on the following health items: hypertension control, employee assistance programs, smoking cessation, work-site smoking restriction policies, nutrition and weight loss, exercise, stress reduction, motor vehicle safety belt use, back injury prevention, and health risk appraisals.

Each article was read and coded based on the type of research conducted, problem addressed, outcome sought, methodological rigor, and findings. The results of their study are reproduced in Table 6.

In summarizing their research, Warner (1988) stated, "In essence, based on work published through early 1986, we conclude that conceptually and empirically sound understanding of the basic behavioral effects of work place health promotion programs is sorely lacking. In the majority of the program areas, assessment of the behavior impact of interventions is primarily anecdotal or based on research that cannot meet minimum standards of scientifically valid evaluation." The authors of this study were able to obtain an additional 106 articles published since the 1986 date covered by Warner. This brings the literature review current through December of 1988. We cannot add much to Warner's finding other than to indicate that research in the areas of organizational wellness or employee wellness programs appears to be increasing.

There has been increased emphasis on research regarding employee wellness programs by individuals in the medical fields. There are a relatively large number of articles now being published in journals such as: The Journal of the American Medical Association, Canadian Medical Association Journal, Preventive Medicine, Journal of Occupational Medicine, Social Science and Medicine, etc. The articles in these journals are theoretically strong; however, the subject matter focuses on health intervention and not recreation. These articles should help to provide a sound basis for further research which will address the role of recreation in developing desired health changes. In contrast to the medical articles, traditional articles in Employee Services Magazine and in parks and recreation literature are, for the most part, self-serving. They only identify programmatics or tell individuals how well the programs are doing.

Most of the current literature provides extremely strong support for the impact of fitness activities on physiological changes such as maximum oxygen intake, weight reduction, and blood cholesterol. However, support for the positive impact of recreational activities is sorely lacking. The literature does not substantiate widespread belief that work place health promotion programs or occupational wellness programs are cost saving or even cost effective. In order to accomplish this goal, research must be undertaken which would consider all of the economic parameters of interest including health care costs, life insurance, short- and long-term workers disability, workers compensation, sick pay, turn over, absenteeism, productivity, and pensions. The long-term implications of wellness programs need to be analyzed in conjunction with the short-term implications for all of these variables.

Table 6. Research-based knowledge of the health and economic effects of workplace health promotion programs.*

HP Program	Articles Reviewed	Epidemiology: Prevalence & Health Impact	Structure of Workplace Interventions	Effectiveness of Interventions (Behavior Change)	Health Effects (Behavior Change)	Cost Information (Types, Measurement Etc.)	Cost-Benefit or Cost-Effectiveness
Hypertension	38	+	+	±	+	±	§
EAP	33	±	±	§	●	§	%
Individual smoking cessation	48	+	±	±	±	§	§
Workplace smoking restriction policies	6	±	§	%	%	●	#
Nutrition and weight control	48	±	●	●	§	%	%
Exercise	28	§	±	§	§	●	%
Stress	35	§	§	●	●	%	#
Motor vehicle safety belts	13	+	§	●	+	±	%
Back injury prevention	26	§	●	●	§	§	#
HRA	14	NA	+	●	●	+	%

* Symbols used are as follows:
+ well understood, solid research base
± generally understood, some good research but limited
§ some good information but more suggestive than definitive, category implies either a very few good studies or substantial number of scientifically weak studies

● very little research
% almost no research base, one or two relevant items
# no research base
NA not available

METHODOLOGICAL CONSTRAINTS

A noted health promotion evaluation specialist, Larry Green, has proposed a model for health promotion programs that is applicable for both health and recreation program evaluation. Green's model (Green 1986) included both individual and organizational considerations. According to the model, interventions should be evaluated through the process of change with identified targets for change. As a result there can be some immediate outcomes, intermediate outcomes, and ultimate outcomes. In Green's model, individual change is a function of health education and promotion efforts for the individual. The process considers direct intervention to the individual's regulatory mechanisms (e.g., smoking policies), organizational considerations (flex-time), and environmental influences (work atmosphere) (see Fig. 4).

Green suggests that three primary questions need to be answered to determine if interventions should be included in a health promotion program. The questions determine if there is good, fair, or poor evidence of effectiveness of interventions, or good or fair evidence that the interventions should not be included. The three questions are:

1. Do actions (behavior, lifestyle) produce positive outcomes?

2. Do health promotion programs produce positive actions (behavior, lifestyles)?

3. Do people who change their behavior or lifestyle as a result of exposure to health promotion programs have positive outcomes compared to others?

Remembering that health promotion programs generally use a medical model for their philosophical basis (e.g., health risk reduction), wellness programs focus more on quality of life. The outcomes of less disease, decreased premature death, and less absenteeism reflect the measurements of success of those programs. Wellness programs often deal with more abstract and less tangible outcomes (i.e., increased energy, better quality of life, reduced stress, and job satisfaction). Contemporary health promotion programs include both wellness and risk reduction components. Most programs do not really distinguish between risk reduction and wellness efforts. Using the Green model as a basis for evaluation of wellness programs, the following procedure is suggested.

Wellness Assessment

A simplistic perspective of efficacious health and recreation programs is capsulized by an "assessment-intervention-reassessment" process. Assessment and reassessment for both the individual and the organization is critical for several reasons. First, assessment is necessary to provide the baseline or starting point for an individual or corporation. For individuals, the baseline data acquired provides both the

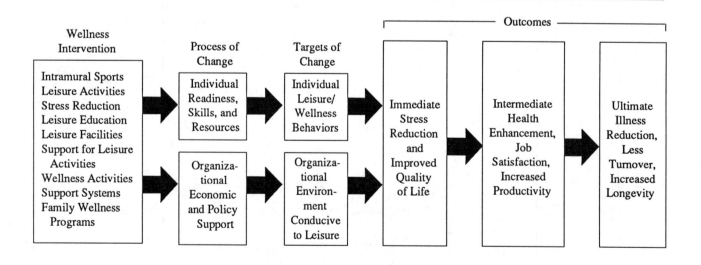

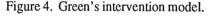

Figure 4. Green's intervention model.

wellness facilitator and the individual a portrait of the individual's health status. The assessment provides directional indicators for lifestyle change that can be treated through intervention. Health enhancement over time can be confirmed with reassessment. For corporations, the baseline information provided by assessments describes a corporate picture of health behavior that has potential for improvement.

A second use of assessment is to provide a means for accurate feedback and motivation for change. Rather than suggesting that "most people" have a need to perform a particular behavior, the assessment will determine if the individual falls under the "most people" category. Personalization allows the individual to know exactly what his health status is and allows for choice in lifestyle modification. It generally functions as a motivation tool, allowing the person to set a goal, make modifications, and work toward improvement that could be felt subjectively or validated by a reassessment.

The evaluation model will include a discussion on corporate assessment instruments and protocols. A holistic perspective of health and recreation would necessitate measurement in a variety of human domains. Well-being, quality of life, and health have physical, social, emotional, mental, intellectual, spiritual, and occupational components. The degree to which valid and reliable measurements can be made in each of these domains varies dramatically. Physical health, supported by medicine and exercise physiology is an extremely sophisticated process whereas a domain such as the spiritual is difficult to define, much less measure, although attempts have been made to do so.

Table 7 provides a listing of physical instruments and protocols that are currently available to measure an individual's physical health and well-being.

Given Green's model and the instruments and protocols identified, research must be undertaken which attempts to look at any of five potential outcomes for organizational wellness or employee programs. These potential outcomes can serve as hypotheses for future research. The potential hypotheses are:

- the program is effective in altering behavior in general at genuine net cost savings to the firm,
- the program is successful in altering behavior and does so in a manner that is cost effective but not necessarily cost saving,
- the program achieves some desired behavior change but at a cost that is excessive,
- the program can be relatively effective in changing behavior and in improving the firm's financial situation,

Table 7. Protocols and instruments available for measuring well-being.

PHYSICAL PROTOCOLS

  Body Composition
      Underwater weighing
      Skin Fold Calibration
      Girth measurements
      Electronic Impedance

  Blood Profiles
      Low density lipoprotein
      High density lipoprotein
      Total Cholesterol
      Triglycerides

  Cardiopulmonary Fitness Levels
      Submaximal MVO_2 estimates
      Maximum MVO_2

  Flexibility
  Strength
  Medical examination

HEALTH AND RECREATIONAL LIFESTYLE

  Lifestyle Improvement Instruments (See Table 5)
  Health Risk Appraisals (See Table 5)
  Leisure Inventories

- the program does not affect the desired change but produces economic benefits by increasing employee morale.

These five questions must be answered for each individual program activity or proposed benefit in order to determine whether or not employee wellness programs or organizational wellness programs are effective. Only one of the above considerations can be true for any existing program or perceived benefit within a company.

To determine whether or not employee recreation or organizational wellness programs are effective in providing economic benefits to a company, it is imperative that research be undertaken which attempts to specify the impact of any item. This can be accomplished through the use of a field experiment design. The design must take into consideration the 16 items listed below as major concerns of previous studies. It is also important to determine long-term impacts of wellness programs. A time series design would be effective for this portion of the study.

The following represent major concerns that must be addressed in any truly methodologically correct research on wellness.

1. Specific and consistent definitions of risk factors or interventions must be developed and used consistently in all research concerning wellness.

2. All outcome measures must be defined in such a way that conclusive, measurable changes can be identified.

3. It is recommended that input measures be used as an index of program effectiveness whenever possible. These input measures should be such that differences between beginning and ending results can be tested for significance.

4. Any study is stronger if multiple measures can be used to collaborate changes that may occur. Because of this it is suggested that multiple divergent outcome measures be used not only in single studies but across different studies of similar topics.

5. Reliance on program participant self-reports as measures of program-related behavioral change should be de-emphasized. Whenever possible, objective measures by nonparticipants is suggested.

6. Important outcomes must be identified before the study begins and an assessment of these outcomes must be evaluated objectively, not by biased individuals.

7. Prior to any study taking place reliable baseline measures must be available for comparison purposes.

8. The use of control groups is a must to accurately evaluate any change and the assignment of causes for these changes.

9. The vast majority of studies have violated the assumption of independence. This failure to assess the implications of self-selection has invalidated the results of numerous studies. Attempts must be made to eliminate this weakness of existing studies.

10. In order to generalize the results of any research it is imperative that the sample be drawn randomly for the population. Because of poorly designed or nonexistent sampling strategy the results of current studies are not generalizable. This makes it impossible to see if similar results can be obtained in other businesses.

11. Because of the nature of wellness research and sampling problems, inadequate sample size must be addressed.

12. As indicated earlier in this paper, numerous long-term effects of wellness should be considered when attempting to establish the economic impact of these programs. Factors such as recidivism, increased cost due to longevity, and retirement costs are just a few factors to be considered.

13. Short-term impacts have not been fully addressed. Factors such as decreased productivity while making major changes in one's life, and time lost to participation, need to be in cluded in the cost-benefit calculations.

14. Research in the area of wellness should not be conducted by advocates of the programs being evaluated. When advocates conduct research on their own programs considerable doubt and methodological concerns are cast on the results.

15. Statistical and methodological techniques are available to address problems of uncertainty. These methods need to be incorporated into wellness research.

16. Researchers must be aware of the scope of generalizability of findings in any study. These considerations must be respected when generalizing findings of wellness research.

If all of these concerns were addressed, research concerning wellness would be substantially improved. It may be impossible to address all of these concerns in one study, but any improvement would be a step in the right direction.

SUMMARY

Wellness research has been conducted in three phases: subjective evaluations, testimonials, and objective measurement of selected portions of the entire concept. The first two phases have predominated in the literature. Only recently has objective research on selected aspects of wellness been undertaken. This objective research for the most part is being conducted by medical personnel, and in situations that are not related to recreation. The concept of wellness seems to have grown out of the social movements spawned by industrialization. As such, the major emphasis was on recreational activities. The field of recreation either was unable or unwilling to prove that the programs provided were beneficial to either the company or the employee. As a result, the wellness movement was taken over by health education professionals who stressed behavioral modification techniques such as smoking cessation. These programs have been justified by comparing national data on the effects of the behaviors being eliminated. The resulting data was limited at best, but at least the results pointed to positive trends, and the potential cost savings for both employers and employees. Currently the movement seems to have been taken over by the medical profession. The majority of the research being done is concerned with physiological changes due to reduction of health risk factors.

In any case, the emphasis on research in the area of wellness has moved away from recreation. Participating in an activity for enjoyment has not been shown to create any positive economic impact for either the company or the employee. There is a similar lack of research pertaining to the effect of the setting on positive changes for the employee. This statement is not to be misconstrued to include such factors as ergonomics. The studies reviewed in this paper did not evaluate differences between exercise performed in a gym versus exercise performed in a natural setting. Likewise, research on running has not compared jogging with participation in a basketball game or other recreational activity.

The final result of this is that no valid empirical evidence could be found to justify the statement that "recreational activities provide an economic benefit to either the employer or the employee." Hopefully this paper will spur someone to eliminate this oversight in the literature.

LITERATURE CITED

Anderson, J. M. 1955. Industrial recreation: A guide to its organization and administration. New York, NY: McGraw-Hill Book Co.

Ardell, D. B. 1984. The history and future of the wellness movement. In: Opatz, J. P., ed. Wellness promotion strategies: Selected proceedings of the eighth annual National Wellness Conference, Dubuque, IA: Kendall Hunt.

Berger, D.; Houston, B.; Johnson, P.; Kondrasack, J. 1984. The present strength of corporate physical fitness programs. Employee Services Management. 27(1): 32.

Blair, S. N.; Piserchia, P. V.; Wilbur, C. S.; Crowder, J. H. 1986a. A public health intervention model for work-site health promotion. Journal of the American Medical Association. 255(7): 921-926.

Blair, S. N.; Smith, M.; Collingwood, T., et al. 1986b. Health promotion for educators: Impact on absenteeism. Preventive Medicine. 15(2): 166-175.

Blanchard, E. B.; Jaccard, J.; Andrasik, P. G.; Jurish, S. E. 1985. Reduction in headache patients' medical expenses associated with biofeedback and relaxation treatments. Biofeedback and Self-Regulation. 10(1): 63-68.

Bowne, D. W.; Russell, M. L.; Morgan, J. L., et al. 1984. Reduced disability and health care costs in an industrial fitness program. Journal of Occupational Medicine. 26(11): 807-16.

Boyd, S. 1985. Fitness and health promotion: Big business and good business in Dallas: What, where, why, and how. Health Marketing Quarterly. 2(3): 75-89.

Brewn, W. C.; Wilson, T. B. 1979. An introduction to industrial recreation. Chicago: National Industrial Recreation Association: 37-58, 195-230.

Brody, B. E. 1988. Employee assistance programs: An historical and literature review. American Journal of Health Promotion. Winter: 13-19.

Coffey S. 1984. Lockheed's employee recreation program. Parks and Recreation. 19(8): 8-10.

Cramer, J. 1984. Employee services and recreation as a recruiting tool: Attracting new employees. Employee Services Management. 27(10): 7-19.

Dunn, H. L. 1961. High level wellness. VA: R.W. Beatty.

Edington, D. W. 1983. Models of validity. CF&R. Oct/Nov: 44.

Edington, D. W. 1986. Health promotion programs and health-care expenditures. Optimal Health. 1: 33-34.

Fain, G. 1983. Why employee recreation? Journal of Physical Education, Recreation, and Dance. October: 32-33.

Finney, C. 1984. Corporate benefits of employee recreation programs. Parks and Recreation. 19(8): 44-46.

Finney, C. 1985. Further evidence. Employee Services Management. 28(8): 8.

Finney, C. 1987. The emergence of corporate sponsored recreation programs as a primary recreation delivery system and its impact on the sponsoring organization, employees and local community. President's Commission on Americans Outdoors. Washington, DC: Government Printing Office: 45-53.

Frankel, L. I.; Fleisher, A. 1920. The human factor in industry. New York, NY: The MacMillan Co.

Gibb, J. O.; Mulvaney, D.; Henes, C.; Reed, R. W. 1985. Work-site health promotion. Journal of Occupational Medicine. 27(11): 826-830.

Green, L. W. 1986. Evaluation model: A framework for the design of rigorous evaluation of efforts in health promotion. American Journal of Health Promotion. Summer: 77-79.

Harrington, H. 1987. Blue Shield of California. Corporate Fitness. 6(3): 9-11.

Harris, J. S. 1986. Northern Telecom: A million dollar medically based program in a rapidly changing high tech environment. American Journal of Health Promotion. Summer: 50-59.

Harris, G.; Gurrin, J. 1985. Gallup survey reveals second fitness revolution. Employee Services Management. 28(1): 26-29.

Harvey, B. H.; Rogers, J. F.; Schultze, J. A. 1984. Sick pay vs. well pay: An analysis of the impact of rewarding employees for being on the job. Employee Services Management. February: 15-17.

Hill, R.; Glassford, G.; Burgess, A.; Rudnick, J. 1988. Employee fitness and lifestyle programs: Introduction, rationale, benefits. CAHPER. January/February: 10-14.

Hollander, R. B.; Lengerman, J. J. 1988. Corporate characteristics and worksite health promotion programs: Survey findings from Fortune 500 companies. Social Science & Medicine. 26(5): 491-501.

Howe, C. 1983. Establishing employee recreation programs. JOPERD. 34: 52.

Jaffe, D. T.; Scott, C. D.; Orioli, E. M. 1986. Stress management: programs and prospects. American Journal of Health Promotion. 1(1): 29-37,84.

Kittrell, A. 1986. Wellness efforts interest employers. Business Insurance. 20(13): 23.

Kittrell, A. 1988. Wellness plans can save money: Survey. Business Insurance. 22(13): 3,10.

Kocolowski, L. 1986. Wellness program pays off for Indiana Blues. National Underwriter Life and Health Insurance Edition. 23(17).

Kondrasuk, J. 1980. Company physical fitness programs: Salvation or fad? Personnel Administrator. 25(11): 47-50.

Kondrasuk, J. 1985. Business and health: Should your company have a physical fitness program? Business. 35(3): 51-53.

Koop, E. C. 1986. Smoking and the workplace. Corporate Fitness and Recreation. 5(4): 35-40.

Kristein, M. M. 1983. How much can business expect to profit from smoking cessation? Preventive Medicine. 12(2): 358-81.

Lamke, Gene C. 1984. Perceptions on corporate recreation. Employee Services Management. May/June: 34.

Lenchus, D. 1986. Benefit cost control—risk management techniques can reduce health claims. Business Insurance. February: 3-4, 6-7.

Mihalik, B. 1984. Sponsored recreation. Public Relations Journal. 40(6): 22-25.

Mobily, K. E. 1984. Wellness in corporate recreation. Employee Services Management. July: 31-33.

Murphy, M. T. 1984. The history of employee services and recreation. Parks and Recreation. 19(8): 34-39.

No author cited. 1985. Wellness programs—insurers uncommitted? National Underwriter Life and Health Insurance Edition. 11: 12.

Nudel, M. 1984. Employee recreation around the country. Parks and Recreation. 19(8): 40-43.

Oster, G.; Epstein, A. 1986. Primary prevention and coronary heart disease: The economic benefits of lowering serum cholesterol. American Journal of Public Health. 76(6): 647-656.

Pelletier, K. E., ed. 1988. DataBase. American Journal of Health Promotion. Fall: 53-58.

Phelps, D.; Roys, K. B. 1983. Views from the top: Employee recreation perceived by chief executive officers. Employee Services Management. 26(10): 14.

Price, J. E. 1987. Here's looking at you. Employee Services Management. 29(10): 20.

Richardson, G. E.; Felts, W. M. 1985. Philosophical and methodological differences: Health promotion, wellness, and health education. Wellness Perspectives. 2(4): 3-8.

Rosen, R. H. 1984. The picture of health in the work place. Training and Development Journal. 38(8): 24-30.

Ryan, R. S.; Travis, J. W. 1981. The wellness workbook. Berkeley: Ten Speed Press.

Ryval, M. 1984. Getting fit on the company. Executive. 26(7): 20-24.

Shaw, D. 1988. Estimating potential savings of corporate health promotions. Fitness Management. February: 20-21.

Shephard, R. J. 1983. Employee health and fitness: The state of the art. Preventive Medicine. 12(5): 644-53

Smith, K. K. 1986. Cost-effectiveness of health promotion programs. Fitness Management. 2(3): 12-15.

Sparks, J. 1983. Arco's ambitious program to promote employee fitness. Parks and Recreation. 18(12): 44-46.

Stamper, M. T. 1987. Good health is not for sale. Ergonomics. 30(2): 199-206.

Streitz, T. M. 1986. The employee perspective. Employee Services Management. July: 9-10.

Taylor, A.; Silverman, I. 1984. Sports sponsorships. Public Relations Journal. 40(6): 28-29.

Thomas, K. A. 1983. Employee health and fitness: The corporate view. Employee Services Management. 26(4): 21.

Tolman, W. H. 1909. Social engineering. New York, NY: McGraw Hill Publishing. 384 p.

Tonti, D. G.; Trudeau, T.; Daniel, M. 1987. Linking fitness activities to rehabilitation. Business and Health. 4(11): 23,26,27.

Vickery, D. M.; Kalmer, H.; Lowry, D., et al. 1983. Effect of a self-care education program on medical visits. Journal of the American Medical Association. 250(21): 2952-2956.

Villeneuve, K.; Weeks, D.; Schwied, M. 1983. Employee fitness: A bottom line payoff. JOPERD. October: 35-36, 49.

Voluck, P. R. 1987. The work environment—burning legal issues of smoking in the workplace. Personnel Journal. 66(6): 140,142-143.

Wang, P.; Springen, K.; Bruno, M. 1987. A cure for stress? Newsweek. October: 64-65.

Warner, K. E. 1987. Selling health promotion to corporate America: Uses and abuses of the economic argument. Health Education Quarterly. 14(1): 39-35.

Warner, K. E.; Wickizer, T. M.; Wolfe, R. A., et al. 1988. Economic implications of workplace health promotion programs: Review of the literature. Journal of Occupational Medicine. 30(2): 106-112.

Yuhasz, M. 1979. Physical fitness in Canadian business and industry. Business Quarterly. 44(1): 72-75.

Benefits of Leisure Services to Community Satisfaction

Lawrence R. Allen
Department of Parks, Recreation, and Tourism
Management
Clemson University
Clemson, South Carolina

The technical and professional literature is replete with suppositions regarding the benefits of recreation and leisure services to one's community (Murphy and Howard 1977, Sessoms 1979, Tindell 1984). Only in limited cases, however, has there been any documentation to support these assertions. Research regarding the efficacy of recreation and leisure services has not been a high priority among leisure researchers, and the research that does exist has focused primarily on well-being regarding one's personal accomplishments and circumstances, rather than well-being associated with the services, characteristics, and opportunities of one's community. Therefore, any attempt at identifying the role of recreation and leisure attributes in relation to the quality of one's community must draw upon literature from a variety of disciplines where recreation and leisure services and opportunities have been peripheral to the primary research question.

This limitation notwithstanding, this chapter will attempt to identify the benefits of recreation and leisure attributes in relation to one's satisfaction with community life. The discussion will first address the various conceptualizations of community and then identify a paradigm interrelating recreation and leisure attributes, community, and quality of life. The discussion will move to a presentation of research findings relative to the role of recreation and/or leisure services in determining community satisfaction. And finally, recommendations relating to future research needs will be discussed.

CONCEPT OF COMMUNITY

The concept of community remains an elusive but frequently studied social phenomenon. Since the earliest records of civilization, humanity's existence and development have been influenced by and a response to the collective functioning of individuals. People have banded together for sustenance and safety; the patterns of relationships that have evolved through the centuries to ensure human existence have been the essence of community (Hassinger and Pinkerton 1986).

The earliest efforts at conceptualizing these patterns of existence are credited to Ferdinand Tönnies in 1887 with the publication of *Gemeinschaft und Gesellschaft* (translated Community and Society). This seminal work in community sociology viewed community on a rural-urban continuum. Tönnies contrasted the human relationships of traditional feudal societies with those of the new capitalist-industrial societies resulting from the industrial revolution. Gemeinschaft relationships of feudal societies, involving extended families and rural villages, were based upon natural will—

a more emotional, creative, and impulsive response to individuals and conditions. A sense of loyalty, tradition, and a respect for the individual, regardless of status or significance, were characteristic of Gemeinschaft interactions and were considered the essence of community. Today, we consider this the establishment of a psychological sense of community (Glynn 1981). Gesellschaft relationships, on the other hand, were based upon rational will where interactions were weighed as to their ability to assist one in surviving and achieving desired goals. Tönnies viewed urban, industrial societies as perpetuating emotional disengagement, lack of respect for the individual, and a limited concept of social bonding.

The rural-urban continuum analysis is known as the typological approach to the study of community. This conceptualization has played a major role in the theory of community and has been supported by several philosophers, political analysts, and sociologists including Weber, Durkheim, and Simmel. These theorists have differed regarding the cause of movement from a Gemeinschaft to Gesellschaft environment, but the nature of the relationship as espoused by Tönnies has remained consistent.

A second approach to the understanding of community evolved from the work of Robert Park, chairman of the sociology department at the University of Chicago during the early 20th century. Drawing from the work of Darwin and the science of ecology, he conceptualized community around the principle of competition for supremacy. Park hypothesized that individuals and groups in a territorially localized population compete for resources to enhance human existence. An interrelated web of spatial forms and function arises through the competitive process, and symbiotic relationships develop based upon the interdependence among various groups (Lyon 1987). The designation of physical environments to fulfill various subsistence functions is a natural outgrowth of the ecological development of population concentrations. This preoccupation with spatial patterns and function has remained a dominant thrust of community analyses in the later 20th century. There have been, however, several modifications of this approach in recent years with community viewed as an ecological system of interdependence among groups and organizations attempting to adapt to their local environment.

Systems theory has provided the basis for a third major approach to the study of community. Talcott Parsons (1951: 5-6) defines a social system as a

. . . plurality of individual actors interacting with each other in a situation which has at least a physical or environmental aspect, actors who are motivated in terms of a tendency to the "optimization of gratification" and whose

relation to their situations, including each other, is defined and mediated in terms of a system of culturally structured and shared symbols.

From this perspective, the tie to geographical space is incidental. The focus is on individual and group values and the interactions that take place among these social units to link them to the larger society.

The various perspectives from which community has been studied have given rise to a multitude of definitions. In fact, in a review of definitions Hillery (1955) found 94 descriptions of the concept. Among the variations, some support the primacy of social interaction while others relate to geographical space and the functionality of community. However, three elements continue to dominate the conceptualization of community. These are a spatial consciousness, commonly shared ties, and interaction with one another (Hillery 1955, Sutton and Munson[1]). Although acceptance of these characteristics reduces the confusion regarding community, there still remains considerable debate regarding these elements. For example, spatial consciousness may be politically, economically, or psychologically defined. Each may provide quite a different set of boundaries and relationships. Additionally, the type of ties and the quality of social interaction have not been specifically delineated (Lyon 1987).

More recent definitions of community have acknowledged the dominant elements identified by Hillery (1955) and Sutton and Munson,[1] but have reinstituted a functional element (Lyon 1987). This involves the establishment of roles and relationships for survival and sustenance. It is an adaptation of the more narrowly focused ecological concept of community. The modern ecological approach recognizes that community involves a collection of people organized in a social system to adapt and modify their environment for well-being and mutual benefits. It suggests a search for community that brings the functional ecological concept into relation with the more social and interactive concept of community (Wilkinson 1986). Therefore, the community is defined as an area in which individuals and groups regularly interact to integrate various attributes, opportunities, and services for the fulfillment of subsistence needs and the establishment of a sense of community. This definition provides the basis for the discussion of the role of recreation and leisure services in relation to community satisfaction.

COMMUNITY AND QUALITY OF LIFE

Quality of Life and Community Satisfaction, As Concepts

The relationship between community and quality of life is not clearly delineated in the literature primarily because of the variety of conceptualizations advanced for both terms. The difficulty of understanding community has been presented, but quality of life is an equally difficult concept to articulate.

Gerson (1976) suggests three approaches to the study of quality of life. The first, the individualist approach, addresses individual accomplishments as they relate to personal desires and expectations. This approach stresses the dominance of the individual over his environment or society. Perceptions of freedom, individual achievement, friendships, marriage and family, personal health, and success are primary factors of this approach. Little reference is made to external forces or environments influencing one's quality of life. Although there are many variations, several researchers have subscribed to this individualistic perspective. The concepts of subjective well-being, life satisfaction, and happiness all reflect a very personal assessment of quality of life and, in fact, the terms have been used interchangeably in many cases (Diener 1984, Kennedy et al. 1978, Larsen et al. 1985, Okun and Stock 1987).

A second transcendental approach stresses the primacy of the external environment over the individual (Gerson 1976). Quality of life is achieved as order and maintenance of the larger community is established. This conceptualization is considered very restrictive because it supplants individualism for the greater good of the community and society. It ignores individual freedom and importance and therefore has never received strong support from social scientists or social planners. It is from this perspective that government generally functions with the thought that jobs, education, health, and safety equate with quality of life.

Recognizing the limitations of only addressing quality of life from an individualistic perspective or the perspective of the external environment, a third approach combining these perspectives has been suggested (Gerson 1976, Kennedy et al. 1978). Each area, viewed independently, is too narrow to provide a total assessment of one's quality of life. The assumption that one area, either the individual or the community, takes precedence over the other is not supported, but rather there is an ongoing process of negotiation and interchange between the two areas, with each being influenced by and influencing the other.

Density of population appears to affect one's perception of community. Especially within an urban setting there is a need to further delineate the external environment. The residential neighborhood, the area immediately adjacent to a residential dwelling, must be assessed in concert with the community. Whereas the residential neighborhood may not fulfill some of the functional needs of the individual, as suggested within the definition of community, it does allow for a more relevant assessment of attributes and characteristics related to social interaction, safety issues, quality of housing, and convenience that lack meaning on a community level. Community and neighborhood are not independent environments, but they do represent different perspectives from which people view the quality of their lives. There is overlap and interdependency between them but not to the point where they should be considered equivalent (Deseran 1978, Marans and Rodgers 1975).

Therefore, for the purposes of this discussion, quality of life is defined as a composite rating of various life experiences relating to the individual and the environment around him. For simplicity these life experiences are organized into three primary domains of satisfaction: personal, neighborhood, and community (Fig. 1)—with each domain consisting of several subdomains as mentioned earlier in this section. This is a bottom-up approach suggesting that quality of life is an additive and/or interactive measure corresponding to one's satisfaction within each of these domains. The exact nature of the relationship among these domains is unresolved in the literature (Marans and Rodgers 1975). The domains are not mutually exclusive, since each domain influences and is influenced by the other, but they do suggest areas of one's life that are sufficiently unique to be studied independently. Therefore, an integrated lifestyle is viewed as essential to enhancing one's quality of life.

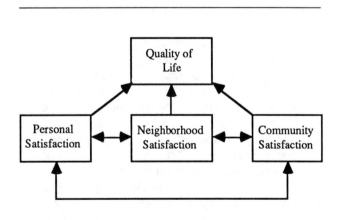

Figure 1. Primary domains of quality of life.

THE STUDY OF COMMUNITY SATISFACTION

What constitutes satisfaction with one's community? Certainly the work of Tönnies provides a basis of understanding; however, his thoughts regarding Gemeinschaft relationships only suggest one approach to addressing community satisfaction. The definition of community presented previously suggests other aspects of community that must be addressed to obtain a comprehensive understanding of one's satisfaction.

In addition to establishing a definition to adequately assess community life, the concept of satisfaction also must be understood. Unfortunately, there has been little theoretical development as it relates to understanding satisfaction with one's community. One study by Miller et al. (1980), however, has suggested three approaches to studying neighborhood satisfaction: belief-affect, commitment, and availability. Although neighborhood cannot be directly equated with community, the methodological discussion has relevance in a community context.

The belief-affect approach suggests that satisfaction is a subjective response to a set of beliefs about an object. Overall satisfaction is a summation of satisfaction with various facets of the object, in this case the community. One must be able to identify the facets or aspects of community for which individuals have an attitude. It also assumes that individuals, through their cognitive processing, will assign a weighting of importance to each facet and take this into account when they are determining their subjective response. Further, it suggests that individuals compare their perception of each facet's quality against some personal standard or expectation (Miller et al. 1980). Campbell et al. (1976) and Marans and Rodgers (1975) utilized this basic approach in their studies of residential and life satisfaction, respectively.

A second model for explaining satisfaction has been referred to as the commitment approach. This approach suggests that people's satisfaction with a neighborhood will be related to their economic and emotional commitment to it. This approach stresses objective measures including employment, number of relatives and friends in the community, the dependence on public services, and factors constraining mobility such as children in school, job skills, income level, and age (Miller et al. 1980).

The third approach, availability, proposes that few evaluations are particularly important and available to the individual; available in the sense that the individual consciously considers these characteristics. These are not necessarily tied to a specific aspect of community, but are more generalized beliefs about the community. Perceptions relating to the neighborhood's future or general feelings of optimism would be indicative of the availability approach. Some of the work of Goudy (1977) and Goudy and Tait (1979) reflects this approach to assessing community satisfaction.

In addition to the neighborhood context, satisfaction has been addressed in other settings such as the work environment which may have application to the community. Lawler (1973) has suggested four basic theories of satisfaction: fulfillment, discrepancy, equity, and two-factor.

The fulfillment theory suggests that satisfaction is simply a measure of how much of a given facet or outcome or group of outcomes an individual perceives he is receiving. It assumes that individuals inherently weigh the importance of each facet and overall satisfaction is a summation of satisfaction with each facet. This approach is quite consistent with the belief-affect approach of Miller et al. (1980). The discrepancy model, although it has several variations, generally maintains that satisfaction is achieved as the discrepancy between real and expected outcomes is minimized. The variations relate to whether one is addressing real or perceived discrepancies.

The equity approach is similar to the discrepancy approach except emphasis is placed on the importance of social comparisons. Individuals assess their own situation in comparison to some standard of reference. In community analysis it may relate to services and characteristics of surrounding communities. The fourth approach, the two-factor, suggests that satisfaction and dissatisfaction do not exist on a continuum but rather are two separate dimensions operating simultaneously (Lawler 1973). This approach has been suggested in the community analysis literature with the understanding that some services and characteristics are necessary for subsistence and others are viewed as contributing to one's satisfaction with community life (Allen and Beattie 1984).

The lack of consensus regarding the concept of community and the lack of theoretical development of satisfaction present difficulties in attempting to accurately assess one's satisfaction with community life and more specifically the relative contribution of recreation and leisure attributes to community satisfaction. There remain, however, several other issues that have restricted the theoretical development and understanding of community life satisfaction.

Other Methodological Issues

As with the study of quality of life, there continues to be an ongoing debate related to the use of objective or subjective measurements of community satisfaction. Physical-ecological determinists have emphasized objective measures of local conditions, on the assumption that indicators such as unemployment rate, population size, density, education level, crime rate, medical professionals, and community layout and design, to name but a few, would provide an adequate measure of the quality of community life (Bardo and Bardo 1983). Obviously a variety of services and characteristics of one's community could be assessed using various standards and/or norms established by experts in the respective areas. Within a few of these studies, availability of park lands and the provision of recreation services have been included in the analysis.

One popular effort in recent years has been an attempt to rate metropolitan areas as to their quality of life using objective indicators of the social, economic, and physical environment. The Boyer and Savageau (1985) study published by Rand McNally is probably the most popular example of such an effort. They used over 50 indicators to establish a quality of life index for 329 metropolitan areas in the United States. The indicators were grouped into 10 major categories: the arts, climate, crime, economics, education, health care, environment, housing, transportation, and recreation. Using objective data relating to each category, summative scores were established and metropolitan areas were ranked from most to least livable.

This approach, although very popular, has been strongly criticized for several reasons. First, there is no consideration of personal values or preferences regarding each of the areas (Pierce 1985, Wish 1986). For example, individual preferences for cultural amenities or specific types of climates are not taken into consideration. It is assumed that all people have the same preference for each of the 50 indicators. This leads to the second issue of the appropriateness of using objective indicators as valid indices of quality of life (Wish 1986). This issue will be discussed later in this chapter. Third, there is no sensitivity to individual well-being, satisfaction, or happiness as it relates to overall quality of life (Gerson 1976, Myers 1987). And, finally, all indicators are weighted equally. Individuals do differentiate the importance among the various indicators, but this approach precludes any individual weighting (Pierce 1985, Wish 1986).

In general, the objective indicators approach has met with disfavor primarily because it does not address individual preferences or reactions to the environment that are based on attitudes, beliefs, group affiliations, and background experiences. Consequently, this approach has not been found to be an adequate predictor of satisfaction with community life (Bardo and Bardo 1983, Ladewig and McCann 1980, Rojek et al. 1975).

More recently, scholars have found that an individual's subjective evaluations better predict satisfaction with community life than do the more traditional objective indicators or social statistics (Bardo and Bardo 1983, Marans and Rodgers 1975, Rodgers and Converse 1975, Russ-Eft 1978). Subjective assessments include individual perceptions of community attributes and an implied reference against which the attributes are judged (Rojek et al. 1975). They give human meaning to otherwise lifeless measures (Rodgers and Converse 1975). For example, Myers (1987) stresses that "community quality of life" is primarily a subjective response to conditions and it must be assessed from a local perspective allowing individual differences in terms of preferences for specific environments and the importance attached to various dimensions. Thus, he acknowledges the value of measuring the subjective experience in relation to the objective condition. Additionally, in terms of facilitating community change, individual perceptions are much stronger catalysts for action than are external references to community conditions (Weigel and Busch-Rossnagel 1984). In using a subjective approach, residents are asked to give their perception of the importance, adequacy, and/or satisfaction with various attributes of community life.

Although subjective assessments have been supported in the literature, there is a related concern regarding the lack of consistency between global measures of community satisfaction and item-specific measures of community opportunities, conditions, or services (Diener 1984, Kennedy et al. 1978, Sofranko and Fliegel 1984). Individuals tend to be very positive when responding to a global question of community satisfaction, but are less satisfied when assessing specific attributes. Further, it has been found that the assessment of specific community attributes explains a limited portion of the variation in the global measures (Sofranko and Fliegel 1984).

One explanation of the disparity between item-specific and global measures involves multiple reference levels. On a general level, taking all things into consideration, one may be quite satisfied with his or her community. However, on an item-specific level, there may be several conditions or services with which the individual is quite dissatisfied. The weighting, or salience, of specific attributes varies from individual to individual, and therefore a lack of relationship between global and item-specific measures becomes more feasible (Kennedy et al. 1978). A second explanation of the disparity relates to the specific nature of the global measure. Previous research suggests that subjective measures involve at least two components: cognition and affect (Andrews and

McKennell 1980, Connerly and Marans 1985, Horley and Little 1985). A cognitive orientation reflects a more rational evaluation of conditions and attributes in relation to an individual's expectations and desires. This type of assessment is associated with one's feeling of satisfaction. The affective orientation, on the other hand, is a more emotional response. A sense of emotional involvement, not so much an evaluation of services and opportunities, provides an affective response to one's community. This response heightens one's sense of attachment or happiness with one's community. Global measures may focus on either orientation or a combination of both orientations. If the item-specific measures do not reflect the global orientation, there certainly will be disparity between these assessments. Therefore, global measures must be directly related to the orientation of the community attributes.

An outgrowth of this previous discussion relates to the relevance of various aspects of community in relation to general satisfaction. Some authorities strongly support residents' assessments of community opportunities and services as good predictors of community life satisfaction (Murdock and Schriner 1979, Rojek et al. 1975). These may include health, education, public safety, and recreation services, as well as physical attributes relating to open space, climate, and topography (Flanagan 1978, Ladewig and McCann 1980). Others have emphasized the need to focus on the social and psychological dimensions of community relating to social networking, bonding, and residential control. For example, Warren (1970: 14) identified nine characteristics of the good community: primary group relationships, autonomy, viability, power distribution, participation, degree of commitment, degree of heterogeneity, extent of neighborhood control, and the extent of conflict. None of these relate directly to services or physical attributes, but they are considered essential factors contributing to satisfaction with one's community. A major question exists as to the potential of various human services, including recreation and leisure services, for providing social opportunities and experiences that facilitate the development of these affective feelings of one's community. Thus, a social dimension relating to the psychological sense of community should be included with the direct assessment of community services and opportunities in developing a comprehensive understanding of community life satisfaction (Goudy 1977).

Figure 2 provides a conceptual framework for investigating the contribution of recreation and leisure attributes to one's satisfaction with community life. As suggested in Figure 1, satisfaction with one's neighborhood and community as well as personal satisfaction directly influence one's quality of life. Each of these consists of several domains or dimensions. The community satisfaction area involves two

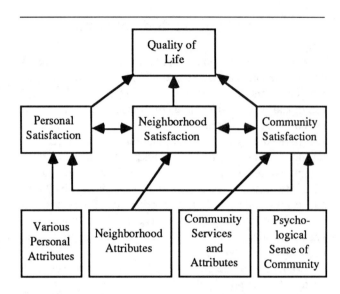

Figure 2. Primary domains and specific attributes contributing to quality life.

broad sets of dimensions; one consists of various dimensions related to community services and opportunities, while the second addresses the psychological sense of community. Further, it is assumed that interaction takes place among the dimensions of community life as well as among the three primary areas of quality of life. The nature of this interaction, however, cannot be clarified at this time.

It is within this framework that the contribution of recreation and leisure attributes to community satisfaction is addressed. Although recreation and leisure experiences impact one's personal and neighborhood well-being, it is left to others to explore this relationship.

THE ROLE OF RECREATION IN COMMUNITY DEVELOPMENT

The urban reform movement of the late 19th century provided some of the earliest documentation of the link between recreation services, residential patterns, and community development. Industrialization and, consequently, urbanization created new residential patterns that were fraught with social and physical problems. Tenement housing grew up rapidly creating poor living environments that resulted in higher rates of morbidity, disease, and crime. Poverty and illiteracy became common, and congestion and unsanitary conditions also prevailed in urban settings (Rohe and Gates 1985). One response to this urban crisis was the social settlement movement. Settlement activists believed science and fellowship could function in an integrated manner to solve the problems associated with industrialization. They believed the problem was the inability of low-income and immigrant groups to adapt to modern industrial society. Through education and an understanding of middle-class values, many of the problems of urbanization could be ameliorated. The local community or neighborhood was viewed as central to addressing crime, disease, illiteracy, and poverty (Rohe and Gates 1985).

Physical activity and culture programs were a mainstay of the settlement movement. Classes in art, literature, dance, and music were commonly offered at settlement houses. Additionally, social activities, athletic experiences, and a variety of classes were scheduled to help new residents understand and integrate into middle-class industrial society. Physical recreation and the appreciation for "the finer things in life" were important values stressed by the settlement leadership (Rohe and Gates 1985).

Although the settlement movement was sometimes criticized for being paternalistic, it did clearly support recreation and leisure services, as we understand them today, in reference to community development. Leisure experiences were viewed as having a social value. They were a medium for addressing certain social problems, as well as a means of assimilating individuals into the new industrial society (Sessoms 1979, Tindell 1984). A second response to industrialization focused on enhancement of the physical environment, as opposed to dealing with social issues through education and services. Ill health, crime, delinquency, congestion, and poor sanitation would best be solved through physical redevelopment. The basic orientation was physical determinism; that is, urban problems were created by poor physical development and they could be resolved through proper redevelopment (Gerckens 1988, Rohe and Gates 1985). Advocates of the physical development movement were concerned with establishing a sense of community—a feeling of pride, cohesiveness, and stability with one's residential area.

Perry (1939), in his classic work—*Housing for the Machine Age*—stressed the concept of neighborhood, the area immediately surrounding an elementary school, as the primary area of an individual's life. The school became the community center—the center for social, political, recreational, and cultural life. As Perry pointed out, recreation areas played a major role in establishing a sense of community. Within each neighborhood, adequate open space, recreation areas, residential areas, and commercial facilities had to be laid out in an integrated fashion to allow for enhanced social interaction and service with minimal congestion or overcrowding. Again, recreation facilities and services were seen as an integral component of community

enhancement or well-being. Many of the principles of physical planning that evolved during this time related to park and open space development and are still adhered to today.

The early 20th century saw a continuation of the social and physical value of recreation areas and services, but during the later years of this century, the emphasis in these areas has been on the wane. There has been a continued concern for the physical development of park and recreation areas, but recreation and leisure services have taken on a connotation of frivolous or merely diversionary activities. They have lost their significance as a developmental service or as a medium for addressing social and individual problems.

RECREATION AND LEISURE SERVICES AND THE GOOD COMMUNITY

Basic Concepts

In recent years there has been an attempt at identifying the good community. The good community can be equated with a psychological sense of community rather than specifically with the services, opportunities, and characteristics of the community. The majority of literature relating to this concept of community takes a sociopsychological approach focusing on primary group relationships, autonomy, viability, power distribution, participation, commitment, heterogeneity, and control (Goudy 1976, Warren 1970, Wilkinson 1979).

Although there is virtually no research addressing this concept of community in relation to recreation and leisure services, there is a conceptual basis for suggesting that recreation or leisure services contribute to one's perception of the good community as defined by Warren (1970) and others. Leisure or recreation services can be considered as one medium through which these feelings of community are established. The literature suggests that as much as 80% of all recreation activity is engaged in within a social setting (Allen and Donnelly 1985). More specifically, as much as 50% of all recreation activity is carried out with family and friends. These experiences provide an opportunity for developing one's primary group relationships, which is one of the major factors in determining the quality of one's community (Goudy 1976, Warren 1970).

The second component of the good community, autonomy—the extent to which community residents control their own destiny, is achieved through public input and control, which has been a mainstay of the leisure service delivery system. Through recreation councils, comprehensive recreation participation assessments and the development of "self-initiated" recreation programs, residents have an opportunity to develop a stronger sense of autonomy. Additionally, viability—the extent of effectiveness in confronting community problems, power distribution—the extent of distribution of power in the community, and participation—the extent of participation in community affairs, are elements of the good community that are directly enhanced through the leisure services delivery system as it has evolved over the last 25 years (Benest et al. 1984, Murphy and Howard 1977).

The concept of commitment—the extent to which the community is an important focus for the lives of the residents—can also be developed through the medium of recreation or leisure services. There are many examples where the development of recreation services or facilities has become the rallying point for a community. McNulty et al. (1985) have suggested that the development of amenities, many of a recreational nature, has both economic and social implications for a community. Individuals are committed to communities that display a sense of change and dynamism; and in many cases, recreation, cultural, and historical amenities become the basis for community action.

Heterogeneity, the seventh element of the good community, relates to the degree of ethnic, racial, and economic diversity in a community. Each community has different levels of acceptance, but it is generally believed that homogeneous communities are not the most satisfying for the residents. There is, however, an optimal point of diversity beyond which disengagement and dissatisfaction will arise. The value of recreation services is in their ability to assist in successful integration of subgroups. By enhancing communication and participation within a nonthreatening setting, they aid the understanding and acceptance of diverse beliefs and values.

The eighth element suggests that neighborhood control is a critical ingredient to one's perception of the good community. The basic philosophy of leisure and recreation services supports decentralization, which contributes to the sense of neighborhood control. The recreation delivery system has subscribed to a decentralized approach.

The final element of the good community is community conflict. As with heterogeneity, it is accepted that a certain level of conflict is best for developing and maintaining a strong and dynamic community. Strategies based upon consensus can result in the support of gross injustices, whereas acceptance of conflict and the development of strategies that acknowledge conflict are viewed as a more productive form of community action. Although recreation and leisure services are not a medium for major social change movements, they are one aspect of the community where conflict will arise and strategies for successful mediation of differences can be achieved. Recreation services do play a minor but consistent role in this area.

Although the role of recreation and leisure services in addressing the elements of a good community have not been substantiated by empirical research, there is a sound philosophical basis suggesting that these services do contribute to the good community in substantive ways. The direct contributions will vary from element to element and community to community, but recreation and leisure services have the potential to substantially impact the quality of one's community if professionals recognize and accept their role in this area.

Recreation and Leisure Services and Community Satisfaction— Empirical Efforts

Most investigations of community that involve recreation and leisure attributes have taken a functional-ecological approach suggesting that "the community" is the social structure through which "community" is achieved (Wilkinson 1986). Community as opposed to "the community" refers to the psychological sense of community referred to previously. These investigations generally assess services, opportunities, and social aspects of one's community. The nature of the elements within a recreation and/or leisure dimension, however, vary tremendously. Some researchers conceptualize the dimension as merely park or recreation facilities (Christenson 1976, Vreugdenhil and Rigby 1987); others address recreation services for specific subgroups (Goudy 1977, Ladewig and McCann 1980). Additionally, some investigators have viewed recreation and leisure attributes as a separate dimension (Allen and Beattie 1984, Blake et al. 1975, Murdock and Schriner 1979); while others have included it within a broader category of community life (Goudy 1977, Ladewig and McCann 1980, Rojek et al. 1975).

Given the variety of descriptors used, it is natural that the findings regarding the relative importance of recreation and leisure services to community life satisfaction have varied greatly. The remainder of this section will attempt a synthesis of the findings from more recent research since 1969. Studies conceptualizing recreation and leisure attributes as a separate dimension of community life will be presented first. Then those studies in which recreation and leisure attributes have been included within a broader dimension of community life will be discussed.

Independent Dimensions

As discussed earlier, the Marans and Rodgers (1975) study of residential environments developed a conceptual model that placed community satisfaction within the context of one's quality of life. Community, macro-neighborhood, micro-neighborhood, residential dwelling, and more personal elements of life were viewed as primary components of overall quality of life. Attributes were identified for each component that clearly differentiate among them. The macro-neighborhood was generally defined in relation to an elementary school area or by major thoroughfares. The micro-neighborhood was identified as the immediate cluster of dwellings adjacent to one's residence, and personal elements related to such areas as marriage, family, work, and finances.

From a national sample the investigators collected data relating to nine attributes of community life and overall satisfaction with the community. The nine attributes related predominantly to community services and characteristics such as public schools and local taxes. One attribute entitled parks and playgrounds was also included in the investigation. A regression analysis revealed that only 19% of the variation in the global measure of community satisfaction was explained by the attributes. The parks and playgrounds attribute (.13) tied for third with streets and roads (.13), behind public schools (.17) and climate (.17), in contributing significantly to the model (beta coefficients are in parentheses). In a subsequent analysis involving sociodemographic characteristics, the parks and playgrounds attribute dropped to eighth in terms of its contribution to the explained variance, which increased to 21%. Several reasons for the low predictability of the model included: 1) possible nonrepresentativeness of the attributes; 2) varying, and therefore unreliable, interpretations of attributes among respondents; and 3) lack of opportunity for respondents to weight importance of the attributes. Further analysis also revealed that the differences in results for the community and macro-neighborhood satisfaction assessments were negligible, therefore suggesting that these components be treated as conceptually equivalent.

Other findings of the Marans and Rodgers study had additional implications for recreation and leisure attributes. In an analysis of the relationship among community satisfaction; macro-neighborhood satisfaction; personal areas of one's life relating to family life satisfaction, financial satisfaction, work satisfaction and marriage; and a life-quality index, they found nonwork activities and family life satisfaction to be the best predictors of life quality, whereas community and housing satisfaction were found to be relatively unimportant. Nonwork activities were not defined further but were assumed to relate to recreation and leisure experiences. These findings support the primacy of personal relations in assessing all areas of one's life, as well as give credence to recreation and leisure experiences (but not necessarily those offered by formal recreation or leisure services agencies) as major contributors to one's quality of life. Blake et al. (1975), using a discrepancy model, assessed individuals' perceptions of the ideal community. They hypothesized that attributes of one's community would receive varying levels of importance depending upon the size of the community. Individuals' perceptions of the importance of 11 community attributes were collected, and 3 dimensions of community life were identified for small, medium, and large communities using factor analysis. The first dimension, system maintenance and change, consisted of services and opportunities necessary for subsistence: medical services, employment opportunities, schools, and the availability of stores and businesses. The second dimension, personal relations, approximated a social dimension consistent with the concept of the "good community," or a psychological sense of community. The two attributes included in this dimension were proximity to friends and proximity to immediate and extended family. The third dimension, recreation, consisted of clubs and organizations, outdoor recreation, and entertainment facilities. These dimensions remained fairly consistent across the three different-sized communities.

The variation in importance of each dimension was assessed by conducting a regression analysis among the three dimensions and a criterion variable relating to one's attachment to the community. Community attachment is generally considered an affective response to one's community, whereas community satisfaction is viewed as a cognitive response. Both approaches, however, have been generally accepted in the literature in relation to community well-being. The findings revealed that within small communities (10,000 or less) greater attachment was shown by residents with stronger personal relations and weaker recreation orientations. This same pattern held for medium-size communities (10,000 to 50,000); but within larger communities (50,000 or more), stronger personal relations and marginally stronger maintenance scores were related to a higher level of attachment. The recreation dimension had no relationship in larger communities. These findings support the identification of a unique dimension of community life relating to recreation, but it is interesting to note that the relationship between the recreation dimension and one's level of attachment with small and medium communities was inverse. Thus, as one's orientation toward recreation decreased, community attachment increased. Although the results relating to the recreation dimension were confusing, the findings did support the primacy of personal relations over economic and maintenance services in defining one's attachment to a community.

Knox (1976), citing the weakness of economic indicators and other objective measures of community life, investigated the use of subjective social indicators as an index of social well-being. An analysis of the eight life domains under investigation suggests that Knox viewed social well-being primarily from a community rather than personal perspective. Since he was interested in looking at changes in perceptions in relation to oil development, respondents' perceptions of life in general were collected from a past, present, and future perspective. Further, the eight domains of community life were collected from the past and present temporal perspectives. The domains included: bus services, health services, educational services, housing conditions, entertainment, outdoor recreation facilities, freedom from crime, and employment opportunities. A regression analysis revealed that 33.8% of the variance in respondents' past level of satisfaction with life in general could be explained by the past level of satisfaction on each of the eight life domains. The three domains of housing conditions, employment opportunities, and health services accounted for over 80% of the explanatory power in the model. A second analysis involving respondents' present perceptions of satisfaction explained 30.4% of the variance. All life domains except outdoor recreation facilities contributed significantly to this model. The third model, which attempted to predict future level of satisfaction with life in general from present levels of domain satisfaction, was unable to explain more than 8% of the variance in the dependent variable. The specific domains contributing significantly to this model could not be gleaned from the article. Knox suggests that the relatively poor explanatory power of the three models may have been caused by an unrepresentativeness of life domains. Another equally feasible explanation may relate to one's interpretation of the criterion variable; it could have been viewed as a question relating to personal well-being or satisfaction, while the life domains primarily addressed community, not personal, issues. The methodological issues notwithstanding, the recreation domain had little relationship to one's social well-being.

Kennedy et al. (1978), using an approach similar to Knox, studied social well-being in Edmonton, Canada. Overall social well-being was measured by a single item asking "How satisfied with life are you these days?" Residents' satisfaction with six different life domains were also assessed. They included: 1) an economic domain consisting of perceived standard of living, estimated financial position relative to previous years and one year hence, employment satisfaction, and housing satisfaction; 2) satisfaction with

health; 3) neighborhood, assessed as a place to live and in terms of satisfaction; 4) interaction relating to quality of family life and friendship; 5) recreation satisfaction in terms of time, participation, and facilities; and 6) quality of children's education. A regression analysis, using each individual item within each domain as independent variables and the single item relating to social well-being as the criterion variable, explained 45% of the variance. The recreation activities domain was the fourth best predictor of social well-being, while quality of friendships, standard of living, and health were the first, second, and third best predictors, respectively.

Fitzsimmons and Ferb (1977) also took a social indicators approach to investigate residents' attitudes toward their community. Fifteen life areas were measured on four attitude dimensions: importance of each area, equality of opportunity in each area, personal influence in decisions regarding each area, and satisfaction with each area. The 15 domains included: schools, jobs, public welfare, local government, health services, protection of natural environment, housing, economic strength, social services, mass media, mass transportation and roads, police and courts, recreation and leisure activities, churches, and family life. All responses were on a 5-point Likert scale. Recreation and leisure activities tied for the lowest importance rating (3.6) along with social services, housing, and transportation. Family life (4.8) received the highest rating, followed by education (4.6). In terms of personal influence regarding decisions in each area, recreation and leisure activities (2.8) rated sixth out of the 15 areas; again family life (4.2) was rated the highest, followed by religious life (3.4). Recreation and leisure activities (4.1) tied for fourth place with mass media and employment opportunities in reference to equality of opportunity. Family life (4.6) and religious life (4.5) received the highest ratings on this attitude. Recreation and leisure activities (3.3) tied with housing and economic strength for fifth place in reference to one's satisfaction with each of the areas. Family life (4.1) and religious life (3.8) once again had the highest rating. The design of this study did not allow a direct analysis of the impact of each life area on the overall assessment of community life; however, a synthesis of the results suggests that family and religious life had the greatest impact upon one's perception of community life. Recreation and leisure activities clearly were not viewed as important to community life, but individuals did have a moderate degree of satisfaction with this area. The study does suggest that to attain a comprehensive understanding of community life, it must be assessed from a variety of perspectives. Later studies indicate that importance and satisfaction ratings are equally important in understanding individuals' perceptions of community life.

Murdock and Schriner (1979) conducted a study methodologically similar to Fitzsimmons and Ferb (1977) but measured community satisfaction in relation to three different stages of community development and length of residency. Mean scores for 17 community services were calculated for predevelopment, currently developing, and postdevelopment communities. Four recreation-related items were included: indoor recreation, outdoor recreation, other amusements, and clubs and organizations. The other service areas included: law enforcement, fire protection, water supply, sewer service, garbage collection, streets and sewers, medical, shopping, city government, schools, mental health services, housing availability, and housing quality. Generally, levels of service dissatisfaction were higher for currently developing communities than for either pre- or postdevelopment communities. Further, differences in satisfaction were not found to be influenced by population characteristics, including length of residency. Across each of the three stages of community development, the recreation-related items generally were among the lowest in terms of service satisfaction. Support for a distinct community dimension of recreation services was supported through a factor analysis of the 17 services conducted for each stage of community development. For the predevelopment and currently developing communities, a recreation dimension consisting of indoor and outdoor recreation services was identified. For the postdevelopment communities, other amusements and indoor recreation services comprised the recreation dimension. Although the direct influence of the recreation dimension on overall community satisfaction could not be determined, this study did point out that residents living in communities at various stages of development view recreation services as a distinct component of community life.

Extending the general approach of Murdock and Schriner (1979), Trent et al. (1984) investigated the relationship between life course, using age and lifecycle stages as indicators, and satisfaction with 20 community services. Many of the services were directly related to the Murdock and Schriner study, but only indoor and outdoor recreation services were used in this study. No attempt was made to identify which services were most directly related to overall community satisfaction. Although the findings did little to further the understanding of recreation services in relation to community satisfaction, the researchers did find that indoor recreation services were positively correlated with both life cycle stage and age, whereas outdoor recreation services had a curvilinear relationship with life cycle stage. Since age did not reveal a significant relationship and life cycle stage took into account the presence of children, it appears that this is the critical factor in determining satisfaction with outdoor

recreation services. Basically, as children get older one's satisfaction increases, but once they leave the home, one's satisfaction generally decreases. If outdoor activities are perceived as positive outlets for youth, perceptions of satisfaction may be related to perceived importance.

Sofranko and Fliegel (1984) conducted an interesting study asking migrants to assess satisfaction with their present and previous community residence from a global and an item-specific perspective. They were especially interested in determining if respondents had a generalized response to community satisfaction or if they actually did differentiate among community attributes. To specifically address this issue, migrants indicated their level of satisfaction with 10 community attributes using a 4-point Likert scale and their global satisfaction using a single-item scale. A regression analysis revealed that 35% of the variance in the global measure could be explained by a model involving five of the community dimensions. This finding suggested that people did not have a generalized community response but did differentiate among dimensions. The availability of outdoor recreation was the third best predictor of global satisfaction. Friendliness of neighbors and shopping facilities were the two best predictors, respectively, and quality of schools and maintenance of streets/roads were the fourth and fifth best predictors, respectively. The findings also revealed that residents could distinguish among community attributes of two different communities. Eight of 10 mean ratings differed between respondents' current and former community. It is interesting to note that even though the recreation dimension was narrowly defined, it still contributed significantly to the regression model; the influence of the recreation dimension, however, could be severely altered by the inclusion of a more comprehensive list of community services, opportunities, and attributes. Vreugdenhil and Rigby (1987), in a study involving two Australian communities, attempted to establish a global measure of community satisfaction that comprehensively addressed overall satisfaction with community. Previous single-item global measures were viewed as inadequate in assessing general satisfaction with community life.

Community satisfaction was viewed primarily as a social-affective response to local conditions. They developed a 24-item scale to assess this response and an additional 36-item scale to assess direct services, characteristics, and opportunities within the study communities. A factor analysis of all 60 items revealed a factor structure that supported their hypothesis of a generalized community satisfaction factor. The first factor contained all 24 items relating to a generalized response to community satisfaction. Two other factors emerged: one consisting of 11 items was referred to as recreation facilities, and a second consisting of 5 items was referred to as work of the councils (local government). Other factors were identified, but they were neither easily interpretable nor consistent across the two communities. A correlation analysis revealed a very strong relationship between the generalized community satisfaction factor and both recreation facilities (r = .59) and work of the councils (r = .58). A multivariate analysis was not conducted to determine the unique contribution of the two factors, but the findings did suggest that a recreation factor was worthy of further consideration. As with other studies, however, the recreation factor was determined from a very narrow perspective.

The previously cited research clearly suggests that there is a lack of consensus regarding the community attributes that appropriately represent community life. Some studies have focused entirely on community services, while others have stressed social and environmental issues relating to one's community. Given this situation, the relative importance of certain aspects of community life to overall community satisfaction remains unclear. As suggested by the literature, this situation appears to be especially true with regard to recreation and leisure attributes. The contribution of recreation and leisure to overall satisfaction with community life has not been addressed in a comprehensive manner. This may result from a lack of understanding by the researchers or a lack of interest in the leisure domain.

In an effort to directly address the relationship between a leisure dimension and community life satisfaction, a series of studies have been undertaken by Allen and Beattie (1984), Allen et al. (1987), and Long et al. (1988). Although each study attempted to address a unique research question, the basic design and the majority of variables remained consistent. Initially, Allen and Beattie (1984) attempted to establish a comprehensive framework for assessing one's community primarily focusing on services, characteristics, and opportunities. A total review of instrumentation and previous literature resulted in the development of a 25-item questionnaire covering 7 major dimensions of community life. These included: health and safety services, formal education opportunities, environmental issues, economic characteristics and opportunities, public administration services, opportunities for community involvement, and leisure services. Respondents were asked to rate the importance of and their satisfaction with each dimension as it related to community life. A single-item global measure of overall community satisfaction was also identified for each respondent.

In the Allen and Beattie study, the leisure dimension was conceptualized around the broader concept of leisure life-space. This included the availability of public and private recreation facilities and services, as well as the availability of parks and open space and opportunities to socialize with others. It was believed that the more comprehensive interpretation of the leisure dimension might result in responses dissimilar to those given in previous investigations. Mean ratings for the importance of each dimension revealed that the economic dimension was considered most important followed by education, health and safety, environment, leisure, public administration, and community involvement. Although all dimensions were considered relatively important, the leisure dimension was only ranked fifth on a comparative basis. The satisfaction ratings revealed that individuals were most satisfied with the environment followed by community involvement, health and safety, education, leisure, public administration, and the economic dimension, respectively.

Two separate regression analyses were conducted. The first involved the seven importance ratings and the global measure of satisfaction as the criterion variable. This analysis explained a very small proportion of the variance in the criterion measure (R^2=.07) and therefore will not be discussed further because of the limited utility of this analysis.

The second regression analysis was conducted involving the seven satisfaction ratings and the same global measure as the criterion variable. Preliminary analyses revealed that the sex of the respondent had an interactive effect with the leisure dimension; therefore, this variable was included in the final analysis. The results revealed a moderate relationship with 4 variables that explained 21% of the variance in the criterion variable. The leisure (.23), environment (.13), and economic (.13) dimensions, as well as the sex/leisure (.10) interaction, all had significant beta coefficients. The sex interaction, however, only had an effect on overall satisfaction if the subject were female, since the interaction term was zero for males.

The findings suggest that all dimensions were perceived as important to overall satisfaction with community life. However, in terms of explaining the relationship between the dimensions and global satisfaction, the importance ratings had little meaning as suggested by the regression analysis. In fact, leisure, which was rated fifth in both importance and satisfaction, was the strongest predictor of overall community satisfaction when the satisfaction ratings were utilized.

Although the authors acknowledged the need for further investigation to substantiate the findings, they did suggest an interesting conception of community satisfaction. Using Maslow's (1954) hierarchical theory of personality and Herzberg's (Herzberg et al. 1959) motivation/hygiene theory of work satisfaction as a theoretical basis, the authors suggested the possibility that certain community dimensions relate predominantly to subsistence needs, while others relate more to one's affective and cognitive perceptions of satisfaction. People's ratings of importance appear to tap a sense of subsistence where economics, education, and health and safety issues predominate. The regression analysis involving the satisfaction ratings, on the other hand, suggests that the dimensions most related to community satisfaction are leisure, economics, and environmental concerns. This conceptualization suggests that overall community satisfaction is a composite evaluation of elements of community life that are considered essential for subsistence combined with other elements that are more directly related to satisfaction. Clearly, the leisure dimension falls into the latter category, while a dimension such as economics contributes in both areas. The authors emphasize that this conceptualization needs empirical validation, but it does suggest a theoretical model that helps clarify some of the inconsistencies in previous research. Lastly, the results indicate that the leisure dimension, viewed in a comprehensive manner, may have a significant contribution to one's perception of overall community satisfaction.

A subsequent study expanding upon the work of Allen and Beattie (1984) was conducted by Allen et al. (1987). Several revisions of the initial questionnaire resulted in an expanded instrument containing 33 elements primarily focusing on community services and opportunities. Table 1 presents the elements organized into seven dimensions of community life. The dimensions were created a priori, grouping elements that fit logically together either in content or from an administrative point of view. It should be understood that the focus of these investigations was on direct services and opportunities and aspects of community life that could be directly affected by policymakers. The elements contained within these investigations only minimally addressed the psychological elements of community suggested by Goudy (1976), Warren (1970), or Wilkinson (1986). Further, since single-item global measures have been criticized for low reliability and the focus of this study was on services and opportunities, a multi-item global measure of community life was selected to correspond more directly with the authors' orientation and design. A modified form of Goudy's (1977) community evaluation scale was selected for inclusion as the criterion variable.

Mean scores for the seven importance ratings and seven satisfaction ratings revealed that the recreation dimension was ranked sixth in both cases. Thus, respondents did not view recreation services and opportunities as important, nor were they very satisfied with the services in relation to the other dimensions. One would logically conclude that the recreation dimension had little relationship to overall community satisfaction. A subsequent regression analysis, however, revealed quite divergent results. Forty percent of the variance in the criterion variable was explained by the

seven satisfaction ratings with the public services (.28), environment (.24), and recreation (.12) dimensions being the only significant contributors to the model.

These results were similar to the previous study by Allen and Beattie (1984). However, the amount of variance explained increased by 90%, and the dimensions contributing to the relationship changed moderately. The increase in explained variance suggests that this conceptualization of community satisfaction had a better fit between the community attributes and the global perception of satisfaction. The environment and recreation dimensions continued to make a significant contribution, but the economic dimension was displaced by the public services dimension. These changes can be attributed to several factors: 1) the elements of community life were expanded from 25 to 33, 2) the 7 dimensions were modified somewhat from the 1984 study (Allen and Beattie 1984), 3) the criterion variable was changed to reflect a global evaluation of community services and opportunities, and 4) the population changed.

The variations in the results emphasize that one must be sensitive to the nature of the community attributes and global measures used in the study of community satisfaction. The literature clearly suggests that different global measures tap varying components of one's perception of community life and therefore may reveal different patterns of relationship with various community services, opportunities, and characteristics (Andrews and McKennell 1980, Connerly and Marans 1985).

Integrated Dimensions

Additional studies have not included recreation and leisure attributes as a distinct dimension, but have included them within a broader dimension of community life. Such efforts make it impossible to single out the contribution of recreation and leisure attributes to satisfaction with community life. They do, however, provide a general understanding of these attributes in relation to other attributes of community life. For example, Rojek et al. (1975) factor analyzed 15 elements of community life and identified a commercial dimension that contained the attributes of recreation facilities, shopping facilities, job opportunities, and education services for the handicapped. They found this dimension to be the second best predictor of overall community satisfaction although the amount of variance it explained in the criterion variable was rather small. Goudy (1977) identified an opportunities dimension that contained four elements relating to recreation opportunities along with employment, education, religious, and public involvement opportunities. This dimension also was found to be the second best predictor of three different global measures of community

Table 1. Dimensions of community life.

PUBLIC SERVICE
    Fire protection
    Welfare and social services (public assistance)
    Public transportation to and from other communities
    Police protection
    Local government
    Roads and highways
    Public health services

FORMAL EDUCATION
    College/university courses (for credit)
    Public schools (K through 12 programs)
    Technical and/or vocational training for career development

ENVIRONMENT
    Physical geography or terrain
    Environmental cleanliness (air, water, soil)
    Climate and weather
    General appearance of your area of town
    General appearance of your town/community

RECREATION OPPORTUNITIES
    Private/commercial recreation (health clubs, movies, bowling)
    Publicly funded recreation (social, cultural, and
        sports/fitness programs for youth and adults)
    Adult education (noncredit classes)
    Parks and open space

ECONOMICS
    Shopping facilities
    Cost of living
    Housing (cost and availability)
    Utilities (water, gas, electricity, sewage)
    Job opportunities

CITIZEN INVOLVEMENT AND SOCIAL OPPORTUNITIES
    Opportunities to be with friends and relatives
    Citizen input into community decisions
    Churches and religious organizations
    Opportunities in civic and fraternal organizations
    Opportunities to become familiar with other residents

MEDICAL
    Hospital and medical facilities
    Medical doctors
    Dentists
    Emergency services

satisfaction. A social dimension, however, containing items relating to a psychological concept of community similar to Warren's (1970) good community, was the best predictor in all three cases. Ladewig and McCann (1980), using factor analysis, identified an institutional dimension containing recreation opportunities, church and religious services, medical services, public schools, physical environment, assessment of law and order, spendable income, welfare programs, and agriculture and land use. This dimension was found to have no relationship to overall satisfaction with community life.

Although these findings provide limited understanding of the contribution of recreation and leisure services to community life, they do suggest that the manner in which the various attributes of community are operationalized will significantly affect the nature of the relationship among the elements. Clearly there is limited consistency in the relationship between recreation and leisure attributes and other aspects of community life.

SUMMARY OF FINDINGS

Although the methodologies and findings vary considerably, there is conceptual and empirical support for recreation and leisure areas, services, and opportunities as contributors to community life satisfaction. Early efforts to address urban issues in the late 19th century and early 20th century found, at least ideologically, recreation services and facilities central to combating many of the maladies associated with urbanization (Rohe and Gates 1985). During the settlement movement it was believed that recreation and cultural programs were a means of integrating individuals into modern industrial society. Additionally, advocates of physical determinism supported the development of parks and open space as a means of overcoming social and physical problems. Many of the physical planning principles (Perry 1939) developed in the early part of this century were based upon the proper and adequate development of recreation areas and open space.

The continued concern for enriching community life led to more empirical efforts to define the good community and articulate those elements of community that contribute most to an individual's sense of well-being or satisfaction. Objective measures of community have recognized recreation services and areas as a component of community life (Myers 1987, 1988). However, because there has been no effort to weight various components of community, recreation's contribution to community satisfaction has been viewed as no more or less important than any other

component of community life. This approach has been strongly criticized for its lack of sensitivity to individual and regional differences, which gives it little value in identifying the direct contribution of various attributes to satisfaction with community life.

On the other hand, subjective measures of community have provided a basis for weighting community elements in relation to overall satisfaction. This approach has provided a more substantive understanding of the contribution of recreation and leisure attributes, but it remains difficult to provide any definitive answers because of the variety of methods and designs used.

In their comprehensive study of quality of life, Marans and Rodgers (1975) found parks and playgrounds to be the eighth ranked predictor of community satisfaction where various sociodemographic characteristics were included with the analysis of nine community attributes. In an expanded analysis of quality of life, they found nonwork activities and family life to be the best predictors of life quality. This supports the importance of leisure experiences, but formal recreation and leisure services may not be perceived as an important medium for providing these experiences.

Additionally, Blake et al. (1975) found a recreation dimension defined as clubs and organizations, outdoor recreation, and entertainment facilities to be the second best predictor of community attachment for small and medium-size communities, but it had little influence in large communities. The nature of the relationship between the recreation dimension and community attachment, however, was inverse. Kennedy et al. (1978) and Knox (1976) assessed six and eight components of community life, respectively, in relation to explaining one's sense of social well-being. Both efforts identified a recreation dimension; however, the dimensions were conceptually quite different as well as very limited in scope. The Knox study suggested that the recreation dimension had no relationship to social well-being, while Kennedy et al. (1978) found the recreation domain had a positive relationship with social well-being and was the fourth best predictor.

Fitzsimmons and Ferb (1977) and Murdock and Schriner (1979) investigated the various attitudes residents had toward community services. Fitzsimmons and Ferb (1977) found recreation and leisure services to be the least important dimension in terms of residents' attitude toward their community. However, they did find that residents were moderately satisfied with the recreation and leisure services dimension. Murdock and Schriner (1979) found residents in communities at three different stages of development to be very dissatisfied with the four elements relating to recreation and leisure opportunities in their communities. Although their research design did not provide an assessment of recreation's contribution to overall community satisfaction, they did find empirical support for a distinct recreation dimension involving indoor and outdoor facilities.

In a study of two Australian communities, Vreugdenhil and Rigby (1987) also found empirical support for a recreation dimension. A factor analysis identified a dimension containing 11 recreation-related services and facilities. They also found this dimension to be highly correlated with a generalized community satisfaction index. Additionally, the study by Trent et al. (1984), using similar community attributes to the Murdock and Schriner study, found that indoor recreation services were positively correlated to lifecycle stage and age but outdoor recreation services had a curvilinear relationship with lifecycle stage.

Sofranko and Fliegel (1984), using only 10 community attributes, found that the availability of outdoor recreation was the third best predictor of how satisfied an individual was with his/her community as a place to live. In a study using a similar research design, Allen and Beattie (1984) found a recreation dimension to be the best predictor of one's overall satisfaction with community life even though this dimension was rated very low in terms of importance and satisfaction. A subsequent effort using an expanded list of community attributes found the recreation dimension to be the third best predictor of community life satisfaction (Allen et al. 1987).

In summary, recreation and leisure services, opportunities, and areas do play a substantive role in enhancing community life. From a social and physical planning perspective, recreation services and development have received continuous attention and support. More recent empirical investigations of community satisfaction have displayed relatively strong support for a recreation domain, but the lack of conceptual and methodological consistency has impeded the development of a clear understanding of the role of recreation and leisure attributes in determining satisfaction with community life.

Clearly, methodological and conceptual issues have limited the understanding of recreation and leisure attributes, but the interpretive approach used in several studies also has contributed to this situation. The studies by Marans and Rodgers (1975), Fitzsimmons and Ferb (1977), Murdock and Schriner (1979), Allen and Beattie (1984), and Allen et al. (1987) acknowledge that respondents do not perceive recreation and leisure attributes as very important and are not very satisfied with these attributes based upon mean ratings. These mean importance and satisfaction ratings rather than relational analysis are commonly used to interpret the findings. This being the case, policymakers generally view recreation and leisure attributes as having no

relationship to community satisfaction. Clearly, this is incorrect, but the relationship is only detected if some form of more insightful interpretation is conducted beyond the mere reporting of mean rankings.

RECOMMENDATIONS

Before a comprehensive understanding of the benefits of recreation and leisure attributes to community life satisfaction can be achieved, a number of conceptual and methodological issues must be addressed. First and foremost, researchers must provide a more thorough conceptualization of community in their investigations. Community needs to be studied from various perspectives but the conceptual basis must be clearly developed by the researcher. For example, community can be viewed from a social-psychological perspective focusing on the more abstract psychological sense of community. Or, as has been the common approach, community can be viewed from an ecological-functional perspective focusing on a set of services, opportunities, and characteristics. Additionally, these perspectives can be integrated into one conceptualization as has been implied by Wilkinson (1986). Regardless of the perspective, there needs to be a more concentrated effort to establish a strong conceptual base. Further, the relationship between community and neighborhood must be more clearly delineated. Presently, these terms are used interchangeably in much of the literature, but some would suggest that neighborhood is a subunit of community that is primarily geographically defined (Deseran 1978, Marans and Rodgers 1975).

An equally important area of concern is the development of theoretical models for the study of community satisfaction. Authors have identified a variety of models (Lawler 1973, Miller et al. 1980, Myers 1988), but their use in a community context has not been substantiated in the literature. As revealed in this chapter, very few investigations provided a theoretical basis for the study of community satisfaction. Parenthetically, there needs to be greater sensitivity to the subtle differences among terms that are now used interchangeably. These include primarily: quality of life, community well-being, community satisfaction, social well-being, neighborhood satisfaction, life satisfaction, subjective well-being, and happiness.

Third, there needs to be a concerted effort to identify appropriate indicators of community life. This author identified only two studies where the attributes of community life remained consistent across populations and time. As stated in the Allen and Beattie (1984) study, there is little effort to systematically determine the attributes of community life. This is a critical issue that, if continued to be neglected, will severely limit the development of a comprehensive understanding of community life. Obviously, the diversity of findings relating to recreation and leisure attributes are partially caused by the various conceptualizations of these attributes as well as the other attributes used as indicators of community life.

In addition to the need for consistency among the indicators or elements of community life, the same need arises in relation to the global measures of community life. Affective and cognitive measures tap different responses by individuals, but until recently there has been little regard for the nature of the global measure. Differences resulting from the use of a particular measure must be acknowledged and addressed in subsequent studies of community life. The weak relationship between community indicators and global measures has resulted, in part, from the lack of conceptual consistency between the two variable sets. A question that arises is whether recreation and leisure attributes tap an affective or cognitive response relating to community satisfaction. Further, are we most interested in predicting community satisfaction, community competence, or community attachment?

The existing literature on community life satisfaction has been fairly responsive to the potential influences of intervening variables on one's perception of community life. The identification of social and demographic characteristics that influence perceptions must continue to be integrated into the research design on a consistent basis.

The relationship between community services and opportunities and a psychological sense of community has been virtually ignored in the research literature even though this connection has received strong philosophical support from several authors (Deseran 1978, Glynn 1981, Wilkinson 1986). Since the literature supports the primacy of primary group relationships, mutual support and trust, group control, and commitment as the dominant factors contributing to satisfaction with community, it is essential that the etiology of these factors be more clearly articulated. Do direct services and opportunities have a role in the development of these attributes and feelings, and if so, which ones have the greatest contribution? This is an extremely important area of investigation in relation to recreation and leisure attributes since they are purported to contribute to social and emotional development of the individual and group.

Lastly, the most effective research design for establishing the contribution of various aspects of community life to overall community satisfaction has not been articulated. Most studies have used an ex post facto design involving some form of correlation or regression analysis. Other research designs including experimental efforts and qualitative approaches need to be explored. There is a need to conduct longitudinal studies which can address changes over time. A strong case can be made for qualitative designs since much of the literature provides virtually no understanding of why a particular set of results were achieved. A recent study by Hood (1989) suggests that qualitative assessments of community satisfaction will be quite divergent from the more traditional survey efforts used.

Although the study of community has a long tradition, it appears that the study of community satisfaction has suffered from a need for applied answers at the cost of theoretical development. Much of the impetus for the study of community life satisfaction has come from social planners and local decisionmakers (needing information to assist them in responding to rising expectations in an environment of decreasing resources) who have not insisted on a strong conceptual or theoretical base. This situation, however, appears to be changing somewhat because of the growing interest in quality of life issues and the inconsistencies and inaccuracy of findings that have affected communities in recent years. Hopefully, future efforts will be more sensitive to some of the recommendations made in this chapter. And, as the study of community satisfaction develops a stronger theoretical basis, the relative importance and/or benefits of recreation and leisure attributes will be articulated. It is, however, incumbent upon the leisure researcher to ensure that the leisure component of community life is accurately portrayed in these efforts.

ENDNOTES

[1] Willis Sutton and Thomas Munson gave a presentation titled "Definitions of Community: 1954 through 1973" at the 1976 American Sociological Association Annual Meeting in New York, New York.

LITERATURE CITED

Allen, L. R.; Beattie, R. J. 1984. The role of leisure as an indicator of overall satisfaction with community life. Journal of Leisure Research. 16(2): 99-109.

Allen, L. R.; Donnelly, M. A. 1985. An analysis of the social unit of participation and the perceived psychological outcomes associated with most enjoyable recreation activities. Leisure Sciences. 7(4): 421-441.

Allen, L. R.; Long, P. T.; Perdue, R. R. 1987. Satisfaction in rural communities and the role of leisure. Leisure Today: Journal of Physical Education, Recreation and Dance. April:33-36.

Andrews, F. M.; McKennell, A. C. 1980. Measures of self-reported well being: their affective, cognitive, and other components. Social Indicators Research. 8: 127-155.

Bardo, J. W.; Bardo, D. J. 1983. A re-examination of subjective components of community satisfaction in a British new town. Journal of Social Psychology. 120: 35-43.

Benest, E.; Foley, J.; Welton, G. 1984. Organizing leisure and human services. Dubuque, IA: Kendall/Hunt Publishing Company. 227 p.

Blake, B. F.; Weigl, K.; Perloff, R. 1975. Perceptions of the ideal community. Journal of Applied Psychology. 60(5): 612-615.

Boyer, R.; Savageau, D. 1985. Places rated almanac (revised edition). Chicago, IL: Rand McNally. 448 p.

Campbell, A.; Converse, P. E.; Rodgers, W. L. 1976. The quality of American life: perceptions, evaluations and satisfactions. New York, NY: Russell Sage Foundation. 583 p.

Christenson, J. A. 1976. Quality of community services: a macrounidimensional approach with experiential data. Rural Sociology. 41(4): 509-525.

Connerly, C. E. 1985. The community question—an extension of Wellman and Leighton. Urban Affairs Quarterly. 20(4): 537-555.

Connerly, C. E.; Marans, R. W. 1985. Comparing two global measures of perceived neighborhood quality. Social Indicators Research. 17: 29-47.

Deseran, F. A. 1978. Community satisfaction as definition of the situation: some conceptual issues. Rural Sociology. 43(2): 235-249.

Diener, E. 1984. Subjective well-being. Psychological Bulletin. 15 (May): 542-573.

Fitzsimmons, S. J.; Ferb, T. E. 1977. Developing a community attitude assessment scale. Public Opinion Quarterly. 41: 356-378.

Flanagan, J. C. 1978. A research approach to improving our quality of life. American Psychologist. February: 138-147.

Gerckens, L. C. 1988. Historical development of American city planning. In: So, F.; Getzels, J., eds. The practice of local government planning. Washington DC: International City Management Association: 20-59.

Gerson, E. M. 1976. On "quality of life." American Sociological Review. 41: 793-806.

Glynn, T. J. 1981. Psychological sense of community: measurement and application. Human Relations. 34(7): 789-818.

Goudy, W. J. 1976. Perceptions of the good community. Journal of Community Development Society. 7(1): 70-87.

Goudy, W. J. 1977. Evaluations of local attributes and community satisfaction in small towns. Rural Sociology. 42(3): 371-382.

Goudy, W. J.; Tait, J. L. 1979. Integrating research with local community development programs. Journal of the Community Development Society. 10(2): 37-50.

Hassinger, E. W.; Pinkerton, J. R. 1986. The human community. New York, NY: Macmillan. 474 p.

Herzberg, F.; Mausren, B.; Synderman, B. 1959. The motivation to work. New York, NY: John Wiley and Sons, Inc. 157 p.

Hillery, G. A., Jr. 1955. Definitions of community: areas of agreement. Rural Sociology. 20:779-91.

Hood, R. 1989. Perception of factors contributing to community satisfaction: a comparison of methodologies. Champaign, IL: University of Illinois. Masters thesis.

Horley, J.; Little, B. R. 1985. Affective and cognitive components of global subjective well-being measures. Social Indicators Research. 17: 189-197.

Kennedy, L. W.; Northcott, H. C.; Kinzel, C. 1978. Subjective evaluation of well-being: problems and prospects. Social Indicators Research. 5: 457-473.

Knox, P. L. 1976. Social well-being and North Sea oil: an application of subjective social indicators. Regional Studies. 10: 423-432.

Ladewig, H.; McCann, G. C. 1980. Community satisfaction: theory and measurement. Rural Sociology. 45(1): 110-131.

Larsen, R. J.; Diener, E.; Emmons, R. A. 1985. An evaluation of subjective well-being measures. Social Indicators Research. 17: 1-17.

Lawler, E. 1973. Motivation in work organizations. Monterey, CA: Brooks/Cole Publishing Company. 224 p.

Long, P.; Allen, L.; Perdue, R.; Kieselbach, S. 1988. Recreation systems development in rural communities: a planning process. Journal of the American Planning Association. 54(3): 373-378.

Lyon, L. 1987. The community in urban society. Chicago: Dorsey Press. 276 p.

Marans, R. W.; Rodgers, W. 1975. Toward an understanding of community satisfaction. In: Hawley, A.; Rock, V., eds. Metropolitan America in contemporary perspective. New York, NY: John Wiley and Sons: 299-352.

Maslow, A. 1954. Motivation and personality. New York, NY: Harper and Row, Inc. 411 p.

McNulty, R. H.; Jacobson, D. R.; Penne, R. L. 1985. The economics of amenity: community futures and quality of life. Washington, DC: Partners for Livable Places. 157 p.

Miller, F. D.; Tsemberis, S.; Malia, G. P.; Grega, D. 1980. Neighborhood satisfaction among urban dwellers. Journal of Social Issues. 36(3): 101-117.

Murdock, S. H.; Schriner, E. C. 1979. Community service satisfaction and stages of community development: an examination of evidence from impacted communities. Journal of the Community Development Society. 10(1): 109-123.

Murphy, J.; Howard, D. 1977. Delivery of community leisure services: an holistic approach. Philadelphia, PA: Lea & Febiger.

Myers, D. 1987. Community-relevant measurement of quality of life—a focus on local trends. Urban Affairs Quarterly. 23(1): 108-125.

Myers, D. 1988. Building knowledge about quality of life for urban planning. American Planning Association Journal. Summer: 347-358.

Okun, M. A.; Stock, W. A. 1987. The construct validity of subjective well-being measures: an assessment via quantitative research syntheses. Journal of Community Psychology. 15 (October): 481-492.

Parsons, T. 1951. The social system. Glencoe, IL: Free Press. 575 p.

Perry, C. 1939. Housing for the machine age. New York, NY: Sage Foundation. 261 p.

Pierce, R. M. 1985. Rating America's metropolitan areas. American Demographics. July: 21-25.

Rodgers, W. L.; Converse, P. E. 1975. Measures of the perceived overall quality of life. Social Indicators Research. 2: 127-152.

Rohe, W. M.; Gates, L.B. 1985. Planning with neighborhoods. Chapel Hill, NC: The University of North Carolina Press. 238 p.

Rojek, D. G.; Clemente, F.; Summers, G. F. 1975. Community satisfaction: a study of contentment with local services. Rural Sociology. 40(2): 177-192.

Russ-Eft, D. 1978. Identifying components comprising neighborhood quality of life. Social Indicators Research. 6: 349-372.

Sessoms, D. 1979. Community development and social planning. In: Lutzin, S., ed. Managing municipal leisure services. Washington DC: International City Management Association: 120-131.

Sofranko, A. J.; Fliegel, F. C. 1984. Dissatisfaction with satisfaction. Rural Sociological Society. 49(3): 353-373.

Tindell, J. 1984. "Grass roots" community development of leisure opportunity. Journal of Park and Recreation Administration. 2(1): 64-72.

Trent, R. B.; Stout-Wiegand, N.; Furbee, P. M. 1984. The nature of the connection between life course and satisfaction with community services. Social Indicators Research. 15: 417-429.

Vreugdenhil, A.; Rigby, K. 1987. Assessing generalized community satisfaction. The Journal of Social Psychology. 127(4): 367-374.

Warren, R. L. 1970. The good community—what would it be? Journal of Community Development Society. 1(1): 14-23.

Weigel, D. J.; Busch-Rossnagel, N. A. 1984. Measuring change in rural communities: objective and subjective approaches. Journal of the Community Development Society. 15(1): 1-13.

Wilkinson, K. P. 1979. Social well-being and community. Journal of the Community Development Society. 10(1): 5-16.

Wilkinson, K. P. 1986. In search of the community in the changing countryside. Rural Society. 51(1): 1-17.

Wish, N. B. 1986. Are we really measuring the quality of life? Well-being has subjective dimensions, as well as objective ones. American Journal of Economics and Sociology. 45(1): 93-99.

Leisure Resources, Recreation Activity, and the Quality of Life

Robert W. Marans
College of Architecture and Urban Planning and
Institute for Social Research
University of Michigan
Ann Arbor, Michigan

Paul Mohai
School of Natural Resources
University of Michigan
Ann Arbor, Michigan

INTRODUCTION

William K. Kelly, President of the World Wildlife Federation and the Conservation Foundation, states in his forward to the report of the President's Commission on American Outdoors (1987) that the "Commission has a great deal to say about the enormous contribution the outdoors makes on the quality of our lives, our sense of community, and our economy." This proclamation is not surprising since organizations and professionals associated with the outdoors and the leisure opportunities it affords have accepted as gospel the importance of outdoor recreation to the quality of life of those who engage in such pursuits. Findings from the report of the President's Commission indicate that Americans indeed place high value on the outdoors, implying that it is central to their quality of life and the quality of their communities. At the same time, the Commission reports that high-quality resources of land, water, and air (environmental quality) are essential to outdoor recreational activity.

While the contributions of the outdoors and recreation to individual well-being have been the topic of exploration among researchers over the past 20 years, few investigators have systematically examined their significance in characterizing the relative goodness of communities. In recent years, rankings of communities have appeared in the popular press, with cities being compared along dimensions of environmental quality and designated as high and low in urban stress and as excellent or bad places to live (Boyer and Savageau 1985, *East-West* 1989, Levine 1988). As we discuss below, the degree to which the outdoors, recreational resources, and environmental factors are included in such rankings varies greatly.

The importance of outdoor recreation and leisure to the quality of communities has been recognized by urban planners and community builders for some time. The post-war era of rapid suburbanization, so highly criticized by planners, gave way to better planned, amenity enriched residential environments in the 1960s and 1970s. The standard bearers of such communities have been Reston, Virginia and Columbia, Maryland, two highly planned residential environments that purportedly could enhance the quality of life of the residents who chose to live there. A key ingredient of such communities was the array of leisure resources available to residents of all ages—golf courses, tennis courts, biking and hiking trails, swimming pools, lakes, community centers, and so forth. These resources and facilities have been a major part of the physical infrastructure of such communities and were important in the choice of early residents who elected to live there (Lansing et al. 1970, Zehner 1976). They are also important in the planning and marketing of many residential environments today.

Over the same period, a number of retirement communities, aimed at a growing elderly population, have appeared on the American landscape. Communities such as the Leisure Worlds and Sun Cities have prided themselves on their array of opportunities for pursuing leisurely activity, implying that such participation enriches the quality of life of community residents, while prolonging the quantity of life (Hunt et al. 1983, Marans et al. 1985).

Older, established communities near natural resources, suitable for recreation, have also capitalized on their location by attracting year-round as well as seasonal residents seeking an environment rich in leisure opportunities. Emerging leisure environments along the Atlantic coastline as well as in the Ozarks and the Rockies have turned one-time sleepy hamlets into leisure boom towns.

In this paper, we systematically explore the issue of leisure and recreation as they contribute to the quality of life of the individual and to the quality of communities in new "leisure environments" and in places not established for leisure purposes. We do so by first discussing various recreational and leisure resources which can be used to describe communities in terms of their leisure potential. We refer to these resources as the urban and environmental amenities of a community. We then review empirical research relating recreation and leisure to the quality of life of the individual as well as to the quality of communities. Next, a conceptual framework for linking leisure resources, the quality of life of the individual, and the quality of communities is presented as a means of guiding future research on the topic. Finally, we suggest how this model might be tested and outline additional topics for new research.

OPERATIONAL DEFINITIONS

In this paper, we identify three categories of leisure resources: 1) natural (nature-based) recreation resources, 2) man-made (sports-related) recreation resources, and 3) cultural resources. We take the position that these resources not only collectively contribute to people's quality of life but also characterize the leisure environment of communities.

Natural (nature-based) recreation resources are those which provide opportunities to experience and enjoy nature during the course of a recreation activity. Such resources can include natural settings (forests, lakes, and streams, etc., see Table 1) and/or the objects contained in them (plants, fish, and wildlife, etc.). Activities which use these resources include hiking, mountain climbing, canoeing, whitewater rafting, hunting, fishing, birdwatching, snowmobiling, and car touring. These activities usually involve physical movement and may or may not promote physical fitness.

Man-made (sports-related) recreation resources are facilities which have been artificially created to house activities that promote health and physical fitness. Such facilities can be located in buildings or out-of-doors and include gymnasiums, swimming pools, tennis courts, and jogging trails. Activities which take place within them include weight lifting, swimming, jogging, and sports of all kinds such as tennis, racquetball, basketball, etc. (see Table 1). Nature appreciation is not considered an important benefit of these activities.

Cultural resources are also artificially created for pursuing leisure activities that offer psychological and social benefits exclusive of physical fitness, health, or nature appreciation. Such resources can include museums, theaters, libraries, and restaurants. Activities employing these resources usually involve minimal physical movement and include such endeavors as reading, listening, watching, and eating and drinking.

These leisure resources exist in varying degrees and varying combinations in or around a given community. The urban amenities of a community represent its unique set of man-made recreation and cultural resources. A community's environmental amenities are characterized by the natural recreation resources within or surrounding its borders. They are also characterized by the quality (i.e., the "cleanliness") of the environment in or around the community as well as climate. Environmental amenities include clean air; clean water; freedom from noise, litter, congestion, and hazardous wastes; and climatic factors such as temperature, humidity, and wind speed. The unique urban and/or environmental amenities of a community often distinguish it from other places. For example, New York City (the "Big Apple") is known for its museums, theaters, and restaurants (i.e., cultural resources); while Vail, Colorado is known for its spectacular scenery and unique skiing opportunities (the environmental amenities).

We note that much of the recent literature, both popular and scholarly, has included various environmental and urban amenities in ranking U.S. communities in terms of their quality of life. But the inclusion of these leisure and recreation resources has been less than systematic and less than complete. One of the purposes of this paper is to achieve a more systematic treatment of such resources in their relationship to quality of life.

Table 1. Examples of environmental and urban amenities.

Environmental Amenities		Urban Amenities	
Environmental Quality	Natural Recreation Resources	Man-Made Recreation Resources	Cultural Resources
Air Quality	Lakes	Swimming Pools	Museums
Water Quality	Rivers	Gymnasiums	Theaters
Population Density	Coastline	Ball Fields	Restaurants
Solid Waste	Forests	Tennis Courts	Zoos
Hazardous Waste	Mountains	Jogging Trails	Aquariums
Noise	Wilderness/Scenic/ Natural Areas	Bicycle Trails	Libraries
Climate	(National Parks, National Forests, State/Local Wilderness Parks, Wildlife Refuges, Other Public Lands)	Bowling Lanes	Orchestras
		Golf Courses	Opera Companies
			Dance Companies
			Professional Sports Teams

LITERATURE REVIEW

The above definitions have focused on specific urban and environmental amenities that can contribute to individual well-being and community quality. Individual well-being has been used as a synonym for quality of life, a phrase used with regularity in the popular press and among local and national political leaders in the United States and abroad since the 1950s. Similarly, quality of life indicators have been used to rank and assess community quality. Unfortunately, quality of life has been rarely defined. With respect to the individual, it is assumed that people who have it are "well off" in financial terms, and at the same time, experience a sense of wholeness or psychological well-being.

Perhaps the earliest empirical research attempting to measure and assess quality of life as experienced by individuals was conducted in the late 1950s by Gurin, Veroff, and Feld at the University of Michigan's Institute for Social Research (1960). Their national study was based on a probability sample of America's population and attempted to measure the mental health of the nation and investigate "the level at which people are living with themselves—their fears and anxieties, their strengths and resources, and the problems they face and the ways they cope with them." While the study focused on mental health issues, it also asked people to report on the degree to which they were happy with their lives.

Subsequent work by Bradburn and Caplovitz (1965) and Bradburn (1969) used sample surveys to pursue the issue of individual happiness by examining the concept of positive and negative affect with respect to people's life as a whole and the domains of marriage and work. Bradburn's theory of psychological well-being was based on the notion of "emotional balance," i.e., the presence of positive feelings about life and the absence of negative feelings.

These pioneering studies formed the intellectual foundation for Campbell, Converse, and Rodgers' examination of the quality of American life in terms of people's perceptions, evaluations, and satisfactions (1976). The study used questionnaires administered to a probability sample of over

2,000 U.S. residents. In focusing on the holistic experience of life rather than the conditions of life, Campbell and his colleagues chose to address the concept of satisfaction rather than happiness considered in earlier studies. Satisfaction was viewed as more definable to researchers and implied a judgmental or cognitive experience, whereas happiness reflected relatively short-term moods of elation or gaiety. Level of satisfaction was defined as the perceived discrepancy between aspiration and achievement, ranging from the perception of fulfillment to that of deprivation (Campbell et al. 1976: 8).

Satisfaction of individual and societal needs also was considered a more plausible and realistic objective for policymakers than that of creating happiness (gaiety), and the researchers were interested in generating data that could potentially influence public policy. Finally, Campbell et al. felt that "satisfaction" was more appropriate to the goals of their study than "happiness." Their intent was to measure and compare people's assessments of several domains of life rather than simply ask people about "life as a whole"; and inquiring about the extent to which people were happy with their health, housing, and so forth, was viewed as less meaningful to both respondents and researchers. Besides these domains, Campbell and his colleagues asked people about their satisfaction with marriage, family life, friendships, community, and nonwork activities. Nonwork activities included hobbies and other leisure pursuits.

Contributions of Leisure to Individual Well-Being (Quality of Life)

In addition to a single life satisfaction question aimed at capturing people's overall assessment of their lives, Campbell et al. developed a second quality of life indicator referred to as a composite index of well-being. The composite index of well-being consisted of people's responses to eight semantic differential items and an overall life satisfaction question. The semantic differential items tapped people's views on the following dimensions of life: enjoyable vs. miserable, full vs. empty, rewarding vs. disappointing, interesting vs. boring, hopeful vs. discouraging, friendly vs. lonely, worthwhile vs. useless, and brings out the best in me vs. doesn't give me much chance.

When the index of well-being was used along with the several domain satisfaction scores in a small space analysis, satisfaction with nonwork activities was most closely associated with this second composite quality of life index. However, in subsequent analyses, the researchers reported that the role of leisure was less central to the quality of life experience of individuals (overall life satisfaction) than

other life domains such as family life and health. Following a model suggesting that an individual's assessment of one's life is dependent upon one's assessment of several differentially weighted domains of life, the importance of nonwork activities ranked only ninth among 12 predictors used to explain variation in life satisfaction. While Campbell et al. offer a plausible explanation for this discrepancy, their findings with respect to the role of leisure in the quality of life as experienced by people were inconclusive.

Using data from several national and local area surveys, Andrews and Withey (1976) also examined Americans' perceptions of life quality and a number of psychological factors most closely associated with it. One factor was leisure, defined as "the way you spend your spare time, your nonworking activities." Responses to the leisure question and its relatively limited power in predicting life quality were comparable to those reported in the Campbell et al. study.

In still another empirical study using national survey data, London, Crandall, and Seals (1977) found that feelings about leisure predicted perceived quality of life and were more important than job-related feelings. When relationships were examined for subgroups of the population, however, leisure satisfaction was less important than job satisfaction among male respondents. Contradictory findings were reported by Haavio-Mannila (1971) who showed that for single women, work was more central to their life satisfaction than leisure; whereas for single men, the opposite was true. For both married men and women, work was more important to life satisfaction than feelings about leisure. Most important to the life satisfaction of married people, however, was their satisfaction with home and family life, suggesting that leisure, if it were defined to include time with family, may be the most important predictor of life satisfaction.

Numerous studies have also examined the role of leisure in the psychological well-being of older people living in a variety of settings (Bull and Aucoin 1975, Delgado,[1] Ragheb and Griffith 1982, Riddick and Daniel 1984, Romsa et al. 1985, Sneegas 1986). Using survey data covering Florida residents 55 years of age and over, Ragheb and Griffith found that leisure satisfaction was a strong predictor of life satisfaction. When satisfaction with standard of living, health, leisure, family relations, and leisure participation were used in a regression analysis, 39% of the variance in life satisfaction was explained, with leisure satisfaction accounting for more than half of the explanatory power. Leisure satisfaction was measured through a multiple-item index, capturing feelings about several dimensions of leisure.

In a study of the quality of life of adults throughout the Detroit metropolitan area, Marans and Fly (1981) reported that older people were generally more satisfied with their leisure time and their lives than younger adults. The relationship between leisure satisfaction and feelings about life as a whole was particularly strong for women, people over 64, and those without a college degree. However, Bull and Aucoin (1975) in their study of elderly Kansas City residents found no relationship between one form of leisure—volunteerism—and life satisfaction. Finally, Sneegas (1986) reports that among older Americans, the links between leisure satisfaction and life satisfaction are complex and are influenced by both the degree of participation in leisure activities and social competence.

The complex relationships between leisure attitudes, leisure participation, and quality of life are also discussed by Iso-Ahola (1980) who reviews several empirical studies. In a study which takes a longitudinal perspective, Brooks and Elliott (1971) show that those who learned to derive satisfaction from their active leisure while young were better adjusted in later life than those deriving their leisure satisfaction from more passive activities such as watching TV.

Finally, several studies have addressed the role played by recreation participation and other leisure pursuits in the quality of life experience of individuals and in their leisure satisfaction. Flanagan (1978), using national survey data, showed that one form of leisure (i.e., active recreation) was highly correlated with overall quality of life. Marans and Fly (1981), on the other hand, showed that the extent of involvement in several recreational activities had no bearing on feelings about life and leisure except for individuals between 45 and 54 years of age. No relationship was also reported between socializing activities and the life satisfaction of a sample of community residents except for males between 40 and 65 years of age (Steinkamp and Kelly 1987). However, the researchers showed that the total bundle of leisure activities for all adults 40 and over contributed significantly to their life satisfaction. Similar findings were reported by Romsa et al. (1985) in their study of older Canadians which examined relationships linking Maslow's psychological needs to recreation participation and life satisfaction.

Leisure and the quality of life have also been examined in studies of U.S. new towns and highly planned residential communities. These communities, designed to enhance the quality of life of their residents, were viewed as alternatives to the suburban sprawl of the 1950s and 60s. Indeed, many advocates of residential planning and new towns since the turn of the century (see Howard 1965) have suggested that people living in a planned setting would be happier and more satisfied with their overall lives. Implicit in this assertion was the contention that new town residents would have greater access to recreational resources, would participate more in recreational pursuits, and would consequently be more content with their leisure and their lives.

As part of a study of these highly planned residential environments in the U.S., Lansing et al. (1970) found that recreational facilities were indeed closer to the homes of new town residents than a comparable group of residents from more traditional communities. At the same time, there was a tendency for people having facilities near their homes to participate more in a number of outdoor recreational activities. However, the magnitudes of the effects of proximity were small. Moreover, life satisfaction did not differ across the 10 sample communities which varied in the degree to which they were planned. In fact, several communities that had numerous recreational facilities contained residents who were the least satisfied with their lives and their community as a place to live.

In a subsequent study of new communities, Zehner (1971, 1976) examined the quality of life issue in greater depth and found little difference in life satisfaction ratings between new community and conventional community residents. The study also found that satisfaction with leisure was not widely associated with either the new community continuum or the extent to which recreational facilities were available. Communities which had extensive facilities were rated highly by their residents but ranked fairly low on a measure of leisure satisfaction (Zehner 1976: 109). However, the study demonstrated that in both new and conventional communities, proximity to nature and the outdoors and the convenience of recreational facilities were factors contributing to residents' satisfaction with the community as a place to live; and among those in the new communities, use of leisure time ranked second among 10 predictors of life satisfaction.

In sum, the previous research suggests that relationships between leisure attitudes and activities and quality of life are complex. In part, relationships are influenced by selected characteristics of respondents (i.e., age, gender, marital and employment status) and the particular setting within which the respondents live. Moreover, conflicting findings may be attributable to different ways of conceptualizing and measuring leisure and life quality (i.e., the questions that are asked) and the leisure activities considered by researchers. Yet, there are strong threads throughout the literature indicating that feelings about one's leisure and the particular activities one engages in bear on one's overall quality of life.

Contributions of Recreation/Leisure to Community Quality

In addition to assessing the benefits of leisure and recreation to the quality of life of the individual, we examined recent literature on the quality of communities and the role played by leisure resources in contributing to that quality (also see Allen in this volume). Community quality has been considered as either a function of objective community attributes or in terms of people's subjective assessments of those attributes or the community as a whole. Few investigations, however, combine the objective approach and subjective assessments. Our contention is that community quality (the quality of place) is the sum total of attributes which characterize a place and the goodness or badness of the attributes as defined by the residents. As we discuss momentarily, no clear consensus on how to measure community quality exists and current approaches contain numerous and varied methodological problems.

Alternative Approaches to Assessing Community Quality

Myers (1988) has referred to three approaches to assessing community quality as: 1) the livability-comparison approach, 2) the wage-differential approach, and 3) the personal well-being approach.

The livability-comparison approach attempts to rank communities on quality based on an evaluation of a list of objectively measurable attributes (see, for example, Boyer and Savageau 1985, East-West 1989, Haupt 1989, Levine 1988, Liu 1975, Pierce 1985). Perhaps the best known of such studies is the Places Rated Almanac (Boyer and Savageau 1985) which contains data on attributes for 329 metropolitan areas organized into 9 categories: climate and terrain, housing, health care and environment, crime, transportation, education, the arts, recreation, and economics. Within each category, specific attributes are evaluated. In the category of recreation, Places Rated includes the number of public golf courses; zoo size; number of movie theaters; percent of metro area classified as national park, forest, or wildlife refuge; and other leisure amenities. In the category of the arts, it includes the number of museums, universities, symphonies, opera companies, and other cultural amenities. Each of these specific attributes are given a weight and based on a weighted sum of these attributes, the metropolitan area is ranked for each of the nine larger categories. The ranks of the nine categories are then summed and an overall ranking of the metro area is obtained. The relative rank of each place is taken to be a composite measure of the quality of life it has to offer.

Other livability-comparison studies take the same basic approach of ranking communities based on the objective measurement of a range of community attributes. The greatest difference among these studies is with the community attributes that are included in the assessments. For example, Places Rated examines only one environmental hazard in the community: air pollution. East-West (1989) examines five: air and water pollution, hazardous wastes, radon, and nuclear facilities. Liu considers air quality, noise, solid waste, and water pollution; and Levine (1988) measures no community attributes other than rates of alcoholism, crime, and suicide. Likewise, there is wide variation in what recreational attributes are considered in the ratings. Not surprisingly, community rankings vary considerably from study to study.

There are a number of methodological problems with the livability-comparison approach to measuring community quality (Landis and Sawicki 1988, Myers 1988). First, decisions about which attributes to include in the assessments are made rather arbitrarily by each investigator. For example, East-West declares that: "We started by compiling a list of as many factors that came to mind that might indicate whether an area is healthful to live in." As noted, one result of this approach is inconsistency in the rankings from study to study. A more critical problem, however, is that there is little information about how important the attributes being assessed are to residents, community leaders, and community planners. Thus, the resulting quality of life rankings may have little meaning to those most interested in community quality.

Another problem is that little theoretical basis exists for assigning weights and summing the ranks of attributes to arrive at a composite score. The relative rank of the community's quality of life can change dramatically with a different system of weights assigned in the aggregation. Thus, a dramatic change can occur simply as a result of the researcher changing his or her mind, rather than as a result of any actual change occurring in the community (see, for example, the discussion by Landis and Sawicki 1988). Pierce (1985) obtained dramatically different rankings from Places Rated after assigning differential weights to the nine community attributes based on opinions of a random sample of New York State residents. Some have questioned the appropriateness of rankings altogether in making evaluations such as those involved in the livability-comparison studies (Nagel 1988).

The wage-differential approach attempts to measure community quality by relating a list of objectively measurable attributes to the wage level and cost of living of the community (Berger et al. 1987, Hoch 1977, Roback 1982, Rosen 1979). The assumption made is that low community quality must be compensated for by offering higher wages in order to attract people to move and live there. Thus, it is assumed that community quality and wage levels are inversely related. Regression analysis is used to determine the strength of the relationship between the attribute and the inverse of the wage level and, hence, the importance of the attribute's contribution to community quality of life. Weights derived from the regression for each attribute are used to build a composite "quality of life" index. A value on the index is obtained for each city. These values are then used to rank the cities in much the same manner as the livability-comparison studies have done.

As an example, Berger et al. (1987) relate wage levels and the cost of housing to the following categories of community attributes: climate, crime, coastline, teacher-pupil ratio, and environmental quality. For climate, such factors as precipitation, humidity, and percent of possible sunshine were measured. Environmental quality measures included ambient concentration of total suspended particulates, visibility, number of high risk abandoned hazardous waste sites (i.e., Superfund sites), and number of licensed hazardous waste landfills. Regression analysis was used to determine which attributes were most strongly related to wage levels and cost of housing, and to construct a quality of life index. The index was then used to rank 185 metropolitan areas in the U.S.

As in the case of livability-comparison studies, considerable variation exists among the wage-differential studies as to which community attributes are included. Thus, as before, rankings are not consistent from study to study. Also, since the attributes used in an assessment are limited to the objectively measurable data available from government and other sources, it is unknown whether community attributes not included in the assessment are of greater importance to residents, community leaders, and planners. Another disadvantage with the wage-differential approach is that the wage level and cost of living of the community cannot be directly included in the quality of life assessment as they are used as indirect indicators of that quality (Myers 1988).

In spite of these difficulties, the wage-differential approach has two advantages over the livability-comparison approach. First, it provides a theoretical basis for including or excluding various attributes as indicators of community quality (Myers 1988). Second, it provides a theoretical basis for weighting and combining the relative contributions of each attribute in determining an overall rank of community quality.

Unlike the previous two approaches, the personal well-being approach has not been used to rank communities. Nevertheless, it has important implications for assessing community quality. As noted earlier, this approach is best

reflected in the work of Campbell et al. (1976) which focuses on domains related to life satisfaction and well-being, e.g., marriage, nonwork activities, family life, community (city or county), housing, and so forth. Most significantly related to life satisfaction were the domains associated most closely with the personal lives of respondents, including their family life, standard of living, work, and marriage. Less significant, but still related to life satisfaction and well-being, were factors related to the residential environment (e.g., home, neighborhood, community). Myers (1988) has observed that such an outcome has raised doubts about the ability of planners to influence the quality of life experience. He cautions, however, that such results by personal well-being researchers are the consequence of focusing questions on the state of the individual rather than focusing on assessments of shared community factors, and that quite different results may be obtained when questions are focused on aspects of the latter. In another context, Burch (1987) has agreed that the community contributes significantly to people's sense of well-being but that its contributions are often taken for granted and unrecognized by community residents. Such benefits include the opportunities communities offer for social interaction, social cohesion, continuity and stability, and sense of place.

Another important distinction between personal factors and shared community factors is that community factors (and, hence, community quality) can be addressed by public policy more easily than the state of the individual. In other words, the quality of life of the individual must necessarily be left in the hands of the individual, while the quality of the community is something that can be effectively managed by government.

In spite of the cautions to distinguish individual quality of life from community, it may be incorrect to conclude that the personal well-being approach has little value in assessing the latter. In addition to assessing respondents' satisfaction with life and well-being, Campbell et al. (1976) and Marans and Rodgers (1975) directly assessed people's overall satisfaction with their communities and correlated these with assessments of nine community attributes: streets and roads, public schools, garbage collection, parks and playgrounds, police protection, police-community relations, climate, public transportation, and local taxes.[2]

Assessing community satisfaction may be a more appropriate and direct indicator of community quality than assessments of individual well-being. Moreover, unlike the livability-comparison and wage-differential approaches, this approach has the advantage of taking into account the evaluations of *the residents themselves* of the quality of their communities and specific community attributes, rather than limiting such judgments to the researcher or relying on indirect indicators.

Since community quality, in our view, is a function of both the objective conditions of a community *and* residents' assessments of these conditions, community quality can change as the result of changes in either the conditions or in the population (or subpopulations) residing within the community. As discussed in the next part of this chapter, we suggest that an appropriate measure of community quality include the aggregate assessment of the population living within the community. We also suggest that various subpopulations within the community may assess its quality differently (e.g., blacks versus nonblacks, young versus old, etc.). Over time, community quality may change because the objective conditions of community attributes change, because the community population and its needs change, or both.

The Role of Environmental and Urban Amenities

Regardless of the type of approach used to measure community quality (and the range of attributes included in the analysis), environmental quality, recreation (natural and man-made), and cultural resources have generally been viewed as significant correlates of community quality. For example, of the nine categories ranked in *Places Rated*, four (climate, health care and the environment, the arts, and recreation) deal in varying degrees with these environmental and urban amenities. Since the overall rank of each community is based on the unweighted sum of the ranks of each of the nine categories, it is clear that these amenities contribute significantly to the overall rank and, hence, to the quality of the community. Likewise, enviromental and urban amenities play a significant role in the rankings of Liu (1975) and *East-West* (1989). Although the priorities placed on these attributes reflect Boyer and Savageau's views, other studies have confirmed the apparent importance of environmental quality and recreation factors to residents. For example, from a multivariate analysis, Herzog and Schlottmann (1986) found recreation along with crime, education, and housing costs to be significantly related to migration. Landis and Sawicki (1988) found from a survey of 32 city planning directors that environmental quality along with jobs were the most frequently mentioned concerns. Also, "four [planning directors] noted that maintaining and improving local recreational opportunitites had emerged as recent priorities" (Landis and Sawicki 1988: 343).

In addition, wage-differential and personal well-being approaches have generally found environmental and urban amenities to be significantly related to community quality. For example, Berger et al. (1987) found climate along with the teacher-pupil ratio to be most significantly related to

wage levels and cost of living. Although less significant, they also found the number of Superfund sites in the community to be statistically related. Likewise, Rosen (1979) found climate and air pollution to be significantly related to wage levels, as did Roback (1982). Hoch (1977) found cultural resources such as number of museums, "good" restaurants, and "things to do" to be significant. Campbell, Converse, and Rodgers (1976) found respondents' assessments of climate along with assessments of the public schools to be significantly related to community satisfaction. Although less significant, assessments of parks and playgrounds were also statistically related to community satisfaction.

Future research needs to refine methods and to examine in greater detail the relative contributions of a range of environmental and urban amenities to community quality and the quality of life experience of individuals.

A CONCEPTUAL FRAMEWORK

The previous discussion reports on research that examines relationships between the quality of life or individual well-being on the one hand, and leisure, recreation, and community quality on the other. It also considers the contributions of environmental and urban amenities as indicators of community quality. While several individual studies suggest relationships of recreation and leisure to the quality of life of individuals, others do not. Taken as a whole, the studies do not present a complete picture of the value of recreation resources to individual well-being. Nor do they clearly demonstrate the role of such resources in ranking communities in terms of their quality. In this part of the paper, we present a conceptual model suggesting multiple relationships among recreation resources, individual well-being, and the quality of communities.

The model can be viewed as an organizational framework for guiding future research on the subject, including the nature of empirical data that should be collected and the manner in which it might be analyzed. Specifically, the model shows how different sets or classes of variables covering people and their actions, thoughts, and environmental surroundings might be interrelated. By environmental surroundings, we mean the individual's community, including its natural, recreational, and cultural resources, and the environmental quality associated with those resources. The model also shows how these resources, classified as environmental amenities and urban amenities, can be indicators of community quality. Our conceptual model, shown in Figure 1, builds on a framework initially developed in Campbell et al. (1976) and expanded upon in Marans and Rodgers (1975) and Marans and Fly (1981).

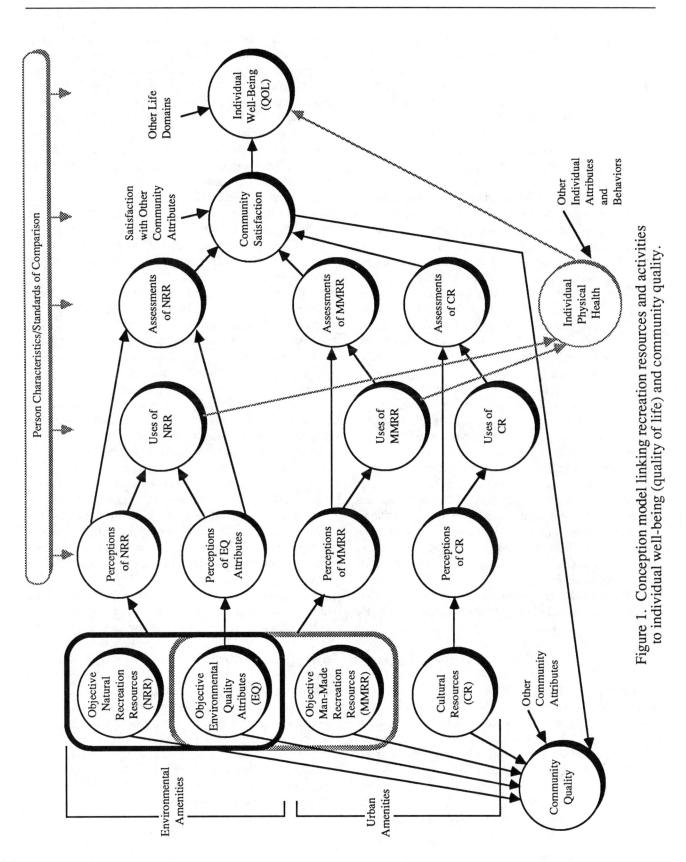

Figure 1. Conception model linking recreation resources and activities to individual well-being (quality of life) and community quality.

The model is organized into two parts. In one part, we deal with environmental and urban amenities as they affect the well-being of the individual. This portion of the model takes an ethnocentric approach and considers the individual as the unit of analysis. In the other, we consider the role of these amenities in contributing to community quality and, correspondingly, in defining a community as a leisure environment. This portion of the model takes a more macroscopic view by considering the community as the unit of analysis. It is important to note that each element in Figure 1 represents a set of variables rather than a single variable. For example, the circle labeled "objective man-made recreation resources" depicts the bundle of discrete resources existing in an individual's community. Similarly, "uses of MMR" is intended to represent the extent of use of each resource by an individual. Likewise, "community satisfaction" may be a composite of several responses to general questions posed about an individual's community.

The model also reflects the thinking of Campbell et al. who suggest that an individual's assessment of his or her life is dependent upon his or her assessment of specific domains of life. Their research demonstrated that for the population in the United States, family life, health, and financial well-being are the main contributors to overall life satisfaction. Also related to the individual's quality of life is his/her assessment of the physical surroundings, including assessments of the dwelling, neighborhood, and the community within which the individual resides, as well as the climate of the place. Campbell et al. and others have further suggested that other factors need to be considered in understanding people's assessments of these specific domains, including the characteristics of the individuals themselves, the standards against which they make the assessments, and the objective conditions of the individual's life with respect to a particular domain.

The model in Figure 1 reflects this line of thought and suggests that there are many domains contributing to the well-being of individuals, including their satisfaction with the community in which they live. How people feel about their community, in turn, is colored by their satisfactions with a bundle of specific community attributes, including the environmental and urban amenities which surround them. Satisfaction with a community's environmental amenities is represented in the figure by the circle "Assessment of NRR" (natural recreation resources), whereas "Assessments of MMRR" (man-made recreation resources) and "Assessments of CR" (cultural resources) represent people's satisfaction with a community's urban amenities. Furthermore, an individual's assessments of these environmental and urban amenities are a function of the individual's

uses and perceptions of them. In turn, individual perceptions are based on the reality of the situation or the extent to which the amenities are available in one's community.

The model also classifies "objective environmental quality attributes" together with "objective natural recreation resources" as "environmental amenities." Our contention is that the objective environmental quality attributes of a place, such as its air and water, act in combination with both the natural recreation resources and the man-made recreation resources to influence people's perceptions and use of these resources. For instance, people are more likely to be aware of (and ultimately use) a pristine mountain stream (a natural recreation resource) than one which is heavily polluted. Similarly, a playing field is more likely to be recognized and used when the quality of the ambient environment (smog-free air) is good.

The model also suggests that perceptions or awareness of these resources will influence both people's use and evaluation of them. One cannot be expected to engage in a recreational activity when one is unaware of the availability and condition of the recreational resource where that activity can be pursued. Similarly, awareness of the existence of the resources can influence people's assessments of them, whether or not they actually use them. It is not uncommon to hear about the abundance of parks, playgrounds, restaurants, and other leisure opportunities within a community from people who never avail themselves of them.

Besides use of natural and man-made recreation resources being a factor in people's assessments and ultimately their psychological well-being, resource use is shown in the model as contributing to the physical health of the individual. That is, physical activity that occurs in recreational settings (and, of course, elsewhere) has a direct bearing on one's physical condition as well as one's mental state.

In the second part of the model we suggest, as has Allen (this volume), that environmental and urban amenities can contribute to the overall quality of communities. That is, the objective natural and man-made recreational resources, the cultural resources, and the objective quality of its air and water should be taken into consideration in labeling a community in terms of its relative goodness. While these objective indicators are viewed as important to researchers and planners interested in monitoring and assessing community change over time, the model also suggests that collective community satisfaction measures can be used as additional indicators of community quality. In other words, how the residents of a community feel about living there should also be an indicator of community quality.

DIRECTIONS FOR FUTURE RESEARCH

Our review of the literature on the contributions of leisure and leisure resources to the quality of life experience of individuals and to community quality, together with our conceptual model, suggest several avenues for future study that might be pursued by researchers and policymakers. These deal with broad definitional issues, measurement and research design issues implied by our model, and issues of applicability of what we now know and what future research will tell us.

Research aimed at understanding the role of leisure in life quality has measured either active and passive recreational pursuits, family and friendship patterns, or voluntary activity; but few studies have considered a full spectrum of behaviors that could be construed as leisure. There is a need to systematically sort out the various components of leisure identified in the literature and explore their interactions and substitutability vis-à-vis quality of life within the context of a single study. One approach, for example, is to consider leisure behavior as nonwork and measure it through individual and household time budgets using survey research (Hill 1985, Marans and Wellman 1978).

Explorations into the meaning of leisure, quality of life, and community quality among various population groups are also needed. While empirical studies utilizing established definitions of these concepts should be pursued through survey research, in-depth interviewing, focus groups, and other qualitative approaches can be an effective means of better understanding and ultimately measuring them.

Related to the issue of concept definition is that of measurement. For instance, differences in question wording, written to measure a single concept such as leisure satisfaction, may result in conflicting findings in studies aimed at identifying concept correlates. This was demonstrated in our review of the literature. Methodological studies are needed which first consider alternative measures of the same concept and then examine these measures vis-à-vis the same variables. Similarly, objective statistics such as crime and suicide rates, measures of physical and mental health, and other "hard" indicators of life quality need to be examined as possible correlates of various subjective quality of life measures.

Alternative ways of measuring each type of urban and environmental amenity, as depicted in our model and in Table 1, should be explored. Is it simply the quantification of each of the attributes such as whether or not it exists, the quantity of it (e.g., acreage), or the time required to reach it, or does its measurement include such things as cost, secu-

rity, and other quantifiable qualities of the attribute? Although a number of studies have measured physical and environmental amenities and considered them along with socioeconomic, attitudinal, and behavioral variables in relation to quality of life or community satisfaction measures, the contributions of these objective measures to the predictive power of the models being tested has been relatively small. A fruitful strategy for future research might be to initially focus on only the environmental amenity measures as correlates of, say, community quality. Small sets of such measures could be examined vis-à-vis community quality and, gradually, the number of physical measures could be expanded in efforts to maximize their predictive power.

The model presented in this chapter offers a framework for examining the complex interrelationships that exist between leisure resources, recreation activity, and individual well-being. Testing of the model and its components is needed in a variety of settings and with different population subgroups. For example, three or four communities of comparable size and population mix could be selected which purportedly differ in their amenity package and attractiveness as a place to live (i.e., community quality). Within each community, amenities could be measured and data could be obtained on leisure use and attitudes, community satisfaction, and individual well-being. This study design could be helpful in identifying the consequences (positive and negative) of having (or not having) urban and environmental amenities. Furthermore, the study could be designed so that comparisons could be made between different sectors (i.e., neighborhoods) within each community. At the same time, a longitudinal perspective would enable researchers and policymakers to better understand the impacts of changing amenity packages on community quality.

Finally, the extent to which current knowledge about the benefits of leisure to quality of life and community quality is understood and used by policymakers and the public needs to be explored. Specifically, a forum is needed to determine the relevance of quality of life research and community quality rankings in addressing numerous public policy issues at the local, state, and national levels. Similarly, there is potential for individuals and households who plan to move within and between communities to benefit from the research discussed in this chapter. While community rankings suggesting different levels of quality may contribute to the decision to move, specific aspects of the rankings such as those covering environmental amenities can lead to more informed decisions. Other aspects need to be identified and tested as to their use in the marketplace.

In addition to their use by individuals and households, rankings of urban and environmental amenities can contribute to public and private decisionmaking and planning with respect to tourism and industrial location. Types of urban and environmental amenities which are important to these activities might be gleaned from discussions with planners in the public and private sector. Such information could then be used to modify the list offered in Table 1. Finally, the question of whether community quality and, indirectly, the quality of life should be managed for specific segments of the population through the distribution of amenity packages needs to be examined.

ENDNOTES

[1] N. Delgado in a study of the relationship between leisure satisfaction and life satisfaction based on older adults' participation in selected recreation centers in St. Petersburg, Florida, 1979.

[2] They found that assessments of nine attributes explained about 19% of the variation in people's expressed satisfaction with their community. Although this appears to be a rather low correlation, it was noted that the predictive strength of the model could improve dramatically as assessments of other community attributes, such as the amount of air and water pollution, fire protection, and quality of stores, are included.

LITERATURE CITED

Andrews, F. M.; Withey, S. B. 1976. Social indicators of well-being. New York, NY: Plenum Press.

Berger, M. C.; Blomquist, G. C.; Waldner, W. 1987. A revealed preference ranking of quality of life for metropolitan areas. Social Science Quarterly. 68(4): 761-778.

Boyer, R.; Savageau, D. 1985. Places rated almanac. New York, NY: Prentice Hall Press.

Bradburn, N. M. 1969. The structure of psychological well-being. Chicago, IL: Aldine.

Bradburn, N. M.; Caplovitz, D. 1965. Reports on happiness. Chicago, IL: Aldine.

Brooks, J. B.; Elliott, D. M. 1971. Prediction of psychological adjustment at age thirty from leisure time activities and satisfactions in childhood. Human Development. 14: 51-61.

Bull, C. N.; Aucoin, J. B. 1975. Voluntary association participation and life satisfaction: a replication note. Journal of Gerontology. 30(1): 73-76.

Burch, W. R. 1987. Ties that bind—the social benefits of recreation provision. Literature Review: The President's Commission on the American Outdoors. Washington, DC: U.S. Government Printing Office: 81-91 of Values Section.

Campbell, A.; Converse, P. E.; Rodgers, W. L. 1976. The quality of American life. New York, NY: Russell Sage Foundation.

East-West. 1989. Best and worst places to live: East-West ranks America's most and least healthful states and cities. East-West. 19(5): 47-55.

Flanagan, J. C. 1978. A research approach to improving our quality of life. American Psychologist. 33: 138-147.

Gurin, G.; Veroff, J.; Feld, S. 1960. Americans view their mental health. New York, NY: Basic Books.

Haupt, A. 1989. Rating U.S. urban stress. Population Today. 17(1): 9.

Haavio-Mannila, E. 1971. Satisfaction with family, work, leisure and life among men and women. Human Relations. 24: 585-601.

Herzog, H. W., Jr.; Schlottmann, A. M. 1986. The metro rating game: what can be learned from the recent migrants? Growth and Change. 17(1): 37-50.

Hill, M. 1985. Patterns of time use. In: Juster, F. T.; Stafford, F. P., eds. Time, goods, and well-being. Ann Arbor, MI: The University of Michigan Institute for Social Research: 133-176.

Hoch, I. 1977. Variations in the quality of urban life among cities and regions. In: Wingo, L.; Evans, A., eds. Public economics and the quality of life. Baltimore, MD: Johns Hopkins University Press: 28-65.

Howard, E. 1965. Garden cities of tomorrow. Cambridge, MA: MIT Press (originally published in 1898).

Hunt, M.; Feldt, A.; Marans, R. W., et al. 1983. Retirement communities: an American original. Boston, MA: Haworth Press.

Iso-Ahola, S. E. 1980. The social psychology of leisure and recreation. Dubuque, IA: Wm. C. Brown Company Publishers.

Landis, J. D.; Sawicki, D. S. 1988. A planner's guide to the places rated almanac. Journal of the American Planning Association. 54(3): 336-346.

Lansing, J. B.; Marans, R. W.; Zehner, R. B. 1970. Planned residential environments. Ann Arbor, MI: The University of Michigan, Institute for Social Research.

Levine, R. 1988. In search of Eden: city stress index. Psychology Today. November: 53-58.

Liu, B. 1975. Quality of life indicators in U.S. metropolitan areas, 1970. Washington, DC: U.S. Environmental Protection Agency, Washington Environmental Research Center.

London, M.; Crandall, R.; Seals, G.W. 1977. The contribution of job and leisure satisfaction to quality of life. Journal of Applied Psychology. 62: 328-334.

Marans, R. W.; Fly, J. M. 1981. Recreation and the quality of life: recreational resources, behaviors, and evaluations of people in the Detroit region. Research Report Series No. 9013. Ann Arbor, MI: The University of Michigan, Institute for Social Research, Survey Research Center, Urban Environmental Program. 234 p.

Marans, R. W.; Hunt, M. E.; Vakalo, K. L. 1985. Retirement communities. In: Altman, I.; Lawton, M. P.; Wohlwill, J. F., eds. Elderly people and the environment. New York, NY: Plenum Press.

Marans, R. W.; Rodgers, W. L. 1975. Toward an understanding of community satisfaction. In: Hawley, A.; Rock, V., eds. Metropolitan America in contemporary perspective. New York, NY: Halsted Press: 299-352.

Marans, R. W.; Wellman, J. D. 1978. The quality of nonmetropolitan living: evaluations, expectations, and behaviors of northern Michigan residents. Ann Arbor, MI: University of Michigan Institute for Social Research.

Myers, D. 1988. Building knowledge about quality of life for urban planning. Journal of the American Planning Association. 54(3): 347-358.

Nagel, S. S. 1988. Evaluating cities, multidimensionality, and diminishing returns. Evaluation Review. 12(1): 60-75.

Pierce, R. M. 1985. Rating America's metropolitan areas. American Demographics. July: 20-25.

Ragheb, M. G.; Griffith, C. A. 1982. The contribution of leisure participation and leisure satisfaction to life satisfaction of older persons. Journal of Leisure Research. 14(4): 295-306.

Report of the President's Commission on Americans Outdoors. 1987. America's outdoors: the legacy, the challenge. Washington, DC: Island Press.

Riddick, C. C.; Daniel, S. N. 1984. The relative contribution of leisure activities and other factors to the mental health of older women. Journal of Leisure Research. 16(2): 136-148.

Roback, J. 1982. Wages, rents, and the quality of life. Journal of Political Economy. 90(6): 1257-1278.

Romsa, G.; Bondy, P.; Blenman, M.. 1985. Modeling retirees' life satisfaction levels: the role of recreational, life cycle, and socio-environmental elements. Journal of Leisure Research. 17(1): 29-39.

Rosen, S. 1979. Wage-based indexes of urban quality of life. In: Mieszkowski, P.; Straszhein, M., eds. Current issues in urban economics. Baltimore, MD: Johns Hopkins University Press: 74-104.

Sneegas, J. J. 1986. Components of life satisfaction in middle and later life adults: perceived social competence, leisure participation, and leisure satisfaction. Journal of Leisure Research. 18(4): 248-258.

Steinkamp, M. W.; Kelly, J. R. 1987. Social integration, leisure activity, and life satisfaction in older adults: activity theory revisited. International Journal of Aging and Human Development. 25(4): 293-307.

Zehner, R. B. 1971. Neighborhood and community satisfaction in new towns and less planned suburbs. Journal of the American Institute of Planners. 37 (Nov): 379-385.

Zehner, R. B. 1976. Indicators of the quality of life in new communities. Cambridge, MA: Ballinger Publishing Company.

Parks and Recreation: More than Fun and Games

Charles R. Jordan
Bureau of Parks and Recreation
City of Portland
Portland, Oregon

Every spring we tune into the Academy Awards and all evening long we hear:

"The nominations for the best in this category are . . ."

"Nominations for the best in that category are . . ."

"And the winner is . . ."

But we also hear:

". . . and for the best supporting role, the nominations are . . ."

I would like to draw your attention to the unsung value of the supporting role.

I am ashamed to admit it, but here we are, in the midst of the "information age" and I come to you without charts, computer print-outs, or statistics. In their stead, I must ask you to trust in plain, old, common sense. Because at this time, there are no statistics to substantiate the real value of parks and recreation to society.

In October of 1956, I was invited to keynote the closing session of the National Recreation and Park Association's annual congress. I brought to light the fact that year after year, parks and recreation funding goes under the ax with no substantial defense; at every budget hearing we find ourselves immersed in a nuclear war armed only with conventional weapons. We are ill-prepared to compete with the established "essential services," i.e., police, fire, and public works. It's not difficult, when armed with the right statistics and charts, to convince decisionmakers that without an adequate police budget, crime will run rampant; without an adequate fire budget, people will burn alive in their beds; and without an adequate public works budget, garbage will pile up and create a serious health hazard.

At that congress I also questioned my colleagues: How did we allow ourselves to get into such a weak position? Where are our visionaries? Who is reading the signs? Where is our Paul Revere?

As we move into the 90s, our competitive position has improved. However, our arsenal still lacks essential weapons—proof that we are who we say we are, and proof that we do what we say we do!

Yes, you can make statistics reflect what you want them to support. But the truth is, statistics do have a way of convincing others and could make believers of them that parks and recreation make a difference! It's also clear that if we trust our common sense as much as we trust our statistics, the importance of parks and recreation as a valuable team member, and even leader, would not be questioned.

During difficult economic times, we tend to be a little too bottom-line oriented. You just can't look at the bottom line when it comes to parks and recreation. What we do changes people's lives, so there must be a strong social ethic governing our actions.

Most of the methods used today to assess the value of parks and recreation focus on economics. But our parks and the leisure services we provide means more than that to our participants. John R. Kelly of the University of Illinois states, "recreation is a complex . . . phenomenon, not . . . simple behavior. Recreation participants bring . . . a variety of intentions and personal resources . . . and their anticipated benefits are usually multiple rather than simple." Recreation is the business of recreating one's mind, body and soul—that is one of the few remaining pursuits where the real benefits do not come in the form of material success. Rich and poor alike can benefit from what recreation does for a person. But the idea of what recreation does and what it should do has changed over the years. Galen Cranz (1982) identified four eras of development of the idea of parks and recreation. In the Pleasure Ground Era, prior to 1900, large tracts of land were designed to recreate a rural countryside in the middle of a city. Parks were designed for all-day use and intended to represent, in the words of park designer and landscape architect Frederick Law Olmstead, "a class of opposite conditions from urban life."

The Reform Park Era, 1900-1930, focused on children and their play needs. The play movement, under the leadership of Joseph Less, was based on the idea that play could help develop character and that children playing needed guidance from qualified play leaders of good character. Playgrounds became a standard feature of parks and slowly evolved into recreation centers that were a combination of playgrounds and settlement houses. Our organized recreation programs of today evolved from such centers.

In the Recreation Facility Era, 1930-1965, urban parks and recreation administrators began to abandon efforts to use parks and recreation services as devices for reform, and instead were driven by the concept of demand—giving people what they want.

Finally, the Open Space System Era, 1965 to present, has been characterized by Galen Cranz as a "philosophical vacuum" dedicated to cataloging all the public and private land not covered by buildings, and experimenting with ways to meet the needs of an increasingly varied population. What I'm proposing, in this fourth era of parks and recreation development, is that we remember the previous eras and conclude that the field of parks and recreation is all of those things today. We create pleasure grounds, playgrounds, recreational facilities, and nature preserves. Our love of nature may guide us and the parks we create can be urban oases. But in addition to preserving the natural world, we are serving our clients, especially the young people, whose lives can be radically changed by our programs and facilities.

As early as 1918, there were studies underway on how recreation might reduce crime and delinquency. H. W. Thurston (1918), in *Delinquency and Spare Time,*

concluded that the delinquents he studied were delinquent because of habitual misuse of their leisure time. Play is one of the most important forces in the world. Bottle-up the playlife of boys and girls, and the energy that should be released in playing can be redirected to evil ends.

Lewis E. Laws, warden of Sing Sing prison stated, "It is my experience that a person's environment has caused the trouble. Boys do not get into trouble during school hours or when they are home, but in their spare time. Leisure is one of the major problems of youth and the way to cut down the number of delinquents is to see that these boys spend their time under good leadership." Recreation at its best prohibits delinquency by providing healthful activities, developing social relationships, and promoting the idea that success is the result of one's own efforts (Thurston 1918). Now we can understand why most parks and recreation departments have reduced fees for young people. It's not because they lack disposable income, because a weekend at the shopping mall would lead one to believe that disposable income is one thing they have in abundance. So common sense would dictate that we offer them a special rate as an incentive to encourage their participation and thus ensure proper guidance while they are at play.

In Frederic Thrasher's 1936 book, *The Gang,* he concluded that only through a community-wide approach encompassing all phases of the predelinquent period could delinquency be prevented. He found that, in general, fewer delinquents participated in supervised programs than did nondelinquents, and that delinquents who attended recreation agencies were less likely to commit delinquent acts than those who did not attend. On the basis of those findings, the main recommendation of the Chicago Recreation Commission was that ". . . more supervised recreation should be provided" (Thrasher 1936).

But saving kids who might otherwise be lost isn't all we do in parks and recreation. We are also the caretakers of those bits of the natural world closest to city dwellers, and oftentimes responsible for translating the natural world to our clients.

In 1985, President Reagan asked 15 people to serve on the President's Commission on Americans Outdoors. I was fortunate to be one of those given the opportunity to serve. President Reagan asked us to look ahead a generation and see what Americans will need and identify what they want to do outdoors. In addition, we wanted to find out what outdoor recreation meant to the American people so that we could recommend ways to make sure our government, our communities, and our actions as individuals reflect the value we attach to outdoor recreation.

Given that charge, where did we go? We went to the people. We listened to Americans, more than a thousand, who testified at 18 public hearings in every region of the

United States; as well as to people who wrote, called, or met with us. We visited public and private recreation sites in communities across the country, and we listened to those who operate, as well as to those who use these areas. The people shared their ideas, their concerns, and their hopes for the future with us.

And what did we find? More than anything else, we found in Americans a love of the land and a shared conviction that it is our legacy for the future. We learned that recreation is important to people in their daily lives, and that most of us cannot imagine a world in which we do not have access to the outdoors. We found that Americans are willing to work and pay to see that quality outdoor opportunities continue to be available to us and to our children's children.

I quote from the report of the President's Commission on Americans Outdoors (1986): "The total value of the outdoors for recreation is difficult to describe, let alone price . . . price denotes short-term value . . . a sunset, a rainbow, an ocean wave, a 500-year-old tree are priceless commodities . . . the real value of the outdoors lies in its vitality . . . the way it enhances our lives. When a sport program keeps a teenager away from drugs, when a neighborhood park offers a friendly gathering place for older people, when families learn to appreciate each other on a camping trip, when a jogger adds years to her or his life, how do we place a price on it? The value is life itself."

It is not my intent to tell you that parks and recreation is *the* panacea, because it isn't! But it is my intent to cause you to pause and reflect on all I've said, using your plain, old, common sense, and then ask yourself: Is it possible? Is it possible that daily engagement in positive and constructive activities by thousands of young people can be a deterrent or replacement to not so positive or not so constructive activities?

Is it possible that winning does contribute to building self-esteem? And that creating games, no matter how silly, ensures that every kid has a chance to taste victory, a chance to run home and tell Mom that today, she or he was number one! The majority of kids may not hit a home run, dunk a basketball or run for a touchdown, but with a little imagination on our parts, victory may be experienced by every child.

Is it possible that lasting friendships have gotten their start on the playing fields and gym floors of our parks and recreation departments, where people of different backgrounds, different colors, and different races have come together as a team and only tasted victory after they set aside those differences? Common sense has to make us pause and wonder. If we can do it on playing fields and the gym floors, then maybe, just maybe, we can do it on our jobs, in our churches, and in our communities.

Is it possible that all those people who spend hours on our jogging trails, running up and down our courts, and running around our bases, are adding years to their lives and reducing the cost for medical services? Is it possible that we could put an economic value on our contribution to the wellness of our communities? Is it possible that the 350 billion dollars Americans spend annually on leisure is more than just a drop in the bucket and that it could have an impact throughout our society in terms of crime prevention, health maintenance, improved social relations, increased awareness and sensitivity to environmental protection, and even economic development? But remember, we're not claiming stardom, we're only asking for recognition of our contributions.

So, since all the starring roles have been delegated to others—crime prevention, starring the police department; economic development, starring the chamber of commerce; well-being, starring the medical profession; building self-esteem, starring the professional counselors; harmonious community relations, starring the human relations commission—since all the starring roles have been ear-marked, what's left is the all-important supporting role. On behalf of the parks and recreation profession, I gladly accept the nomination. We don't have to be the quarterback, we are happy being the lineman. We don't have to be the basketball shooter, we are happy being the rebounder. If not the egg, we'll be the salt. If not the bread, we'll be the butter. We just want to be what we are and be recognized for what we do, in our supporting role.

One of Webster's definitions of "support" is to "keep from sinking or falling." But the definition I like best is "to help overcome a challenge." We are soon to leave behind a most challenging decade, and the 90s will demand no less than the best from all of us—public and private, the minorities and the majorities, young and old, academicians and practitioners. Many of the social challenges that we failed to address in the 80s—juvenile delinquency, teenage pregnancy, and drop-out rates, just to mention a few—all of these ills will defy any solution that is not holistic. We must see the problem's whole, and deal with the whole problem.

For those of us in the field of parks and recreation, it has to be business *not* as usual. We have to add new hats to our wardrobe and become social scientists, therapists, big brothers and sisters, and even parents when we must. We have to become brokers as well as providers. We must recognize and join with the private sector to ensure that Americans have access to a variety of leisure pursuits, regardless of who provides them.

But as we plan, compute our cost-benefit ratios, and sharpen our pencils, let us be ever mindful that today, one out of every five children in America live in poverty or on the edge of poverty. By the time that generation reaches the age of 18, one-third will have lived beneath the official poverty line, and FBI records show that crime continues to rise. We need to factor these kinds of realities into our planning because what those youth do, and what is done to them at home, may determine their needs and affect their behavior when they are with us.

To our colleagues in the halls of higher learning, the philosophers, sociologists, economists, psychologists, behavioral scientists, and to all in our laboratories exploring the all important question *why*—we need your assistance in providing us with the missing statistics and charts needed to convince decisionmakers that the supporting role of parks and recreation is an essential part of the holistic solution to the challenges of the 90s that are facing our society. You can provide us with the indisputable facts that we are who we say we are. You can provide our arsenal with comparable weapons that attest to the fact that we do what we say we do. You can lay to rest, once and for all time, the idea that parks and recreation is nothing more than fun and games.

Let there be no doubt that we provide a positive, vital, and basic service. For many of America's children, we can be the difference between a productive future and no future at all. So, for the best supporting role . . . the winner is . . . Parks and Recreation!

LITERATURE CITED

Cranz, G. 1982. The politics of park design: A history of urban parks in America. Cambridge, MA: MIT Press.

President's Commission on Americans Outdoors. 1986. Report and recommendations to the President of the United States. Washington, DC: U.S. Government Printing Office.

Thrasher, M. F. 1936. The gang: A study of 1,313 gangs in Chicago. Chicago, IL: University of Chicago Press. 494 p.

Thurston, H. W. 1918. Delinquency and spare time: A study of a few stories from the court records in Cleveland. Cleveland, OH: The Survey Committee of the Cleveland Foundation.

Mapping a New Frontier: Identifying, Measuring, and Valuing Social Cohesion Benefits Related to Nonwork Opportunities and Activities

William R. Burch, Jr.
School of Forestry and Environmental Studies and
Institute of Social and Policy Studies
Yale University
New Haven, Connecticut

Elery Hamilton-Smith
Department of Leisure Studies
Phillip Institute of Technology
Bundoora, Victoria
Australia

The authors acknowledge the valuable contributions of Christian Gallup who assisted in the organization and research for this paper.

This paper provides a partial synthesis and state-of-the-art analysis of the literature on the social cohesion benefits of leisure. Though there is an emerging literature on the health, psychological, and economic benefits of leisure (defined in various ways), the available systematic knowledge of the potential and actual social benefits of leisure is very thin, and empirical evidence is especially lacking. The situation is even worse when one focuses on benefits related to social cohesion, which was our assignment. Even the anecdotal and other evidence is scattered over a wide array of sources and is often speculative rather than established. Our task in this paper, therefore, is to explore the possible identification of social cohesion benefits, ways to measure such benefits, and hence to map some patterns of future research. We will begin by considering the social benefits of leisure generally and end with a focus on social cohesion.

METHOD

We examined the major textbooks in leisure, recreation, tourism, play, and sport. We interviewed colleagues in the "invisible" college of the recreation field. We made major literature searches of two electronic databases—Sociofile and Public Affairs Information Services—and the Leisure and Tourism Abstracts, volumes 2 to 13. We searched with 16 keywords such as parks, forests, stability, and so forth. From these searches we identified 160 items that might shed light on the social benefits of leisure. Of the 160, 30 had some indirect or direct relevance to our topic.

Most of the studies on benefits of leisure considered health (House et al. 1988), economic (Peterson and Brown 1985), or psychological (Williams 1985) variables. The social aspects considered broad structural matters such as the evidence that working class communities give more emphasis to infrastructure items, while richer communities give more attention to parks and environmental matters. Such findings seem to offer an indirect measure of the perceived benefits of leisure settings.

Our findings suggest that it will be possible to achieve steady improvement in the identification, measurement, and evaluation of broadscale social benefits of leisure. Specifically, since little has been done in this arena, the field is a relatively open one. So we can draw upon some broad theoretical traditions to suggest possible approaches to identification and measurement of the benefits.

SOME PROBLEMS, APPROACHES AND CONSTRAINTS

The identification, measurement, and valuation of social benefits has various dimensions of possible gain and loss that current research designs tend to separate. Many of the studies reviewed elsewhere in this volume demonstrate this segmentation into categories defined in terms of targeted beneficiaries—individuals, families, or communities—or types of measures used, such as economic and noneconomic. Yet, a full picture of social benefit cannot separate all these dimensions. It is a reasonable notion that if all economic gains of the skiing and camping service industries using the Rocky Mountain Region public lands were measured, they would equal or exceed the net returns of timber sales and sales from water impoundments. Certainly, areas such as Waterville Valley in the White Mountains of New Hampshire or Vail in the Colorado Rockies are locally significant activities that dwarf the economic returns of logging and stock raising.

One could examine a wide range of nature-based recreation activities in primary producing regions and find equally useful economic benefits. However, the important *social benefit* is that these local communities have diversified their economic base and thereby their ability to better balance fluctuations in their several primary activities. Consequently, the communities have a more solid and continuous base from which to sustain themselves. In such diverse communities, institutions can establish roots with a high expectation that they are building for a more certain future. The social benefit research question would consider these stabilizing patterns associated with certain economic activity mixes. It might consider the "threshold" level when the mix moves toward a destabilizing pattern of dominance, say from 40% tourism-dependent employment to 85% tourism-dependent employment.

Turning to the individual dimensions, one finds a range of psychological studies pointing to benefits from participation in outdoor recreation activities, as indicated by many chapters in this volume. Yet, these activities also provide substantial social benefits. Perhaps the clearest is that in the current climate of rapid and turbulent social change, with accompanying townscape changes, natural settings are a place of seeming stability (Rossman and Ulehla 1977). There seems to be a rising genre of literature which gives specific attention to the value placed upon this sense of stability and its relationship to individual identity (for instance, Doig 1978, Maclean 1976). Even the anarchy of Edward Abbey (1988) builds upon a sense of identity rooted in a particular relationship to the stability of the natural

environment. The rise and popularity of this kind of writing is in itself indicative of at least a widely held perception of broad social benefit centered on the notion of perceived stability.

Perhaps that sense of stability helps explain why people become so upset when a natural area is dramatically altered. Keith McCafferty, writing about hunting activities, gives a good summary of this social benefit.

> I looked over at the man who sat beside me and thought: He may no longer be able to recognize the streets he grew up on. But here is the one place that has not changed during his life. He can tell an old story without any need for explaining how things used to be. I hoped that might be me someday, sitting with my boy. One more generation, I could wish for that much (1985: 122).

We know intuitively and empirically that certain outdoor recreation settings are highly valued by people. The change of a recreation area from less developed to more developed, from passive to active sports, the conflicts between motorized recreationists and nonmotorized users of the same land, fly fishing versus bait fishing, and so forth, all attest to the fact that Americans care a great deal about what happens to their outdoor recreation heritage.

The social benefits of recreation have a strong political specification, measurement, and determination of relative worth. Outcomes are the results of political struggle. One but needs to reflect upon loggers and lumber companies specifying the relative worth of publicly owned old growth timber in the Pacific Northwest of the United States and how those specifications differ from ecologists' and environmental advocacy groups'. So political change and political struggle shape which benefits will be specified and how they will be measured and allocated.

In spite of such obvious political struggles over the nature, type, and distribution of recreation resources and their perceived benefits, we have little theoretical and empirical knowledge as to the nature, type, and distribution of such benefits. Perhaps most persons involved in supplying, managing, and using recreation resources have simply assumed that recreation resources and uses were obviously of great benefit to society. Consequently, we have not asked what those social benefits are, or how they match up to the benefits that might be produced from alternative uses of the land and public investment. Such intuitive appreciation has been much like our faith that there are inherent social benefits from a variety of public investments: libraries, museums, schools, public plazas, coffee breaks, the provision of high-tech weapons, and the conferring of large amounts of money upon various vague insurgents in foreign countries who claim to be "freedom fighters."

A variety of factors have combined to make us question the intuitive value of recreational provision. The Renewable Resources Planning Act of 1974 compelled the USDA Forest Service to strive for some equivalency of measure for its various uses so that tradeoffs between timber, recreation, and other products, goods, and services could be made in the planning process. The national administrations since Nixon have been attempting to deal with the debts coming due on the Vietnam War, the War on Poverty, various energy crises, and the rising fiscal conservatism of voters. Hence, many of the public goods and services that had been taken for granted are being more closely examined for their beneficial returns on public investment. Yet, with a few notable exceptions, there is little theoretical and empirical work on the social benefits of various recreation services.

This paucity of systematic research on the benefits can be attributed to a variety of factors. As noted above, there was little demand from the management agencies that fund research. In the early 1970s, the U.S. Forest Service provided a modest grant to Burch to do a literature search on the "benefits" of recreation for urban people. He gave most attention to children's programs and census tract analyses (Burch 1977). A pioneering paper by Driver (1976) sought to call attention to the need for measuring the social benefits of publicly provided recreation opportunities. Yet, after more than a decade, the challenge he offered has only marginally touched the involved agencies, funding, and the research communities.

Partial explanation for the less than overwhelming response by the recreation research community to Driver's challenge can be found in the limitations of conventional research techniques. The favored techniques of demand analysis are based on large population samples who receive attitude questionnaires or are interviewed by trained interviewers with set schedules. Behavioral studies have been equally confined to on-site observations, questionnaires, and interviews with more open-ended response opportunities. Consequently, we can gather useful information on what people do, who they do it with, when they do it, how often they do it, their willingness to pay for certain services, and other self-reporting of the respondents' behavior. Yet, any interest in social benefits derived from recreation activity can only be inferred from data collected by such techniques. We really do not know whether benefits could have occurred as easily from a stroll through a slum, or a large shopping mall, or through no activity whatsoever. Nor do these techniques permit separating perceived, invented, or actual social benefits from the provision of outdoor recreation opportunities.

Our issue is extremely complex. There is the problem of how do we know a social benefit when we see it, and how do we gain consistent measures of something whose perception has such high variability of "worth" depending upon whether it is anticipated, is actually being acted out, or is part of recall. We are certainly unlikely to tap such a complex factor with conventional techniques. We are most likely to gain such understanding through in-depth interviews of panel groups studied over a reasonably substantial time period of several decades. These kinds of studies are costly and seldom fit the usual budgetary cycles and the career cycles of scientific investigators who need rather direct payoff in terms of publications with more frequency than possibly every 30 years.

Consequently, a variety of factors have worked against the production of a substantial corpus on the social benefits of recreation opportunities. We have treated recreation as an unexamined good. Much like freedom, it was assumed to have benefit because we made it part of public provision. Secondly, management agencies have more often seen recreation as a cost rather than a return on investment. Therefore, they have been more interested in research that could help them identify demand trends and to meet them with a minimum of political fuss so they could get on with the important things like cutting timber, grazing cattle, pumping water, and protecting natural habitats. The idea of a recreation clientele who had a variety of demands for services that could be poorly or well-marketed and management interventions that could serve those clients poorly or well is still not widespread in the management of wild lands. Thirdly, we have conceptual approaches that are not the best guides in sorting the necessary and sufficient causes of social benefit that can be attributed to certain outdoor recreation services. We think our scales measure the improvement in the behavior of delinquents who have spent a week in the wilderness, or executives who have rafted down wild rivers, or parents and children who have pulled their trailer into a campground. Yet, we have no systematic theory to explain and to direct the testing of such ideas.

More often, the inquiry into benefits of leisure seems to have been driven by either moral philosophizing or a dedication to collecting visitor statistics. That is, rather than being driven by an established body of theory, there has been a search to sustain the essential goodness of nonwork time. Quite understandably, there has been little attention given by leisure researchers to less beneficial aspects of "free" time such as the consequences of recreational drug use, the drunkenness and child abuse associated with week-long camping trips, the malaise of family vacation travel by auto, the divorces provoked by wilderness river runs, and the bigotry and hate expressed by park and wild land managers toward many client groups.

However, the entrepreneurs of illicit drugs and tolerated but severely damaging drugs (tobacco and alcohol), pornography, prostitution, and other such commodities doubtless see their activities as parallel to that of the amusement park owner or the resort operator, and they certainly have a greater social responsibility than the individual whose behavior is labeled as deviant. Perhaps more importantly, there are a range of hidden but important symbiotic interrelationships between these entrepreneurs and the institutions of mainstream society. In addition to these infrastructural issues, there are questions about the social construction of deviancy and the differing perceptions held by various individuals. But essentially, the difference between these forms of behavior and others commonly recognized as recreational is one of moral judgment. This judgment often, but not necessarily, coincides with negative outcomes. The implications are clear; we need to examine both the benefits and disbenefits of the array of uses of free time, whether as "good" or "bad" leisure. The broader issue thus arises here of the failure to develop operational concepts of leisure and/or recreation which have a sound ontological basis. Much of the current research has been clouded because these key concepts have been fuzzy. This problem leads us to the first of a series of proposals for future research.

Definitions

It is clear that the definition of work drives our definition of nonwork. Work has generally been seen as clearly defined, so that all persons would know when they are working and when they are off duty. This clarity is now being challenged on a number of fronts: the people whose work, like Gilbert and Sullivan's policemen, spills over into their nonwork time and even their sense of leisure; the growing hidden economy, and its implications for how we define work and productivity; and the feminist movement, with its emphasis upon the significance of the unpaid labor of women (Waring 1988).

Nonetheless, work exhibits a different pattern of organization. Participation reflects a necessity or obligation imposed by others; the selection, timing, and sequence of action is often determined by others, and there is usually both an obligation to produce (in whatever mode) and a tangible, or at least explicitly valued, outcome. Generally, this difference can be demonstrated in both conceptual and empirical terms. A potential source of confusion here is that much of women's work has been socially constructed as falling within the leisure domain, so that its real organizational

structure is clouded. However, if we clear away such confusions, then it is reasonable to claim that as we move from the work domain to the nonwork domain, our behavior is guided by quite different patterns of social organization and social relationships. For example, fishing practiced as a work activity requires a different organizational pattern, system of normative constraints, and involvement of the individual than is found in fishing as a nonwork activity. Thus, the social organization of fishing for a Maine guide is very different than it is for his Boston client. The incentives, the payoffs, the state mandated certification of the guide, and the three-day license of the "sport," and all the other ways of doing things, are perceived and acted upon in quite a different manner, though the actual fishing behavior of the two persons might seem very similar.

Within the broad categories of work and nonwork there are many subdivisions. For work we have subdivisions such as wage earners, professionals, and craftspersons, or primary, secondary, and tertiary production activities of agriculture, manufacturing, and service. For nonwork we have leisure, play, games, sport, and recreation as a few possible subdivisions. Leisure—in the classical sense—reflects socially mandated freedom from daily routines to create and sustain ideas, myths, visions, and hopes. Universities, art colonies, monasteries, think tanks, and other organizations contain leisure. Play is organized by close knit associations to permit individuals to "try on" and to prepare for shifts in their life cycle, status (unmarried to married), and so forth. The play of children is only the most obvious preparation for understanding the normative rules for future anticipated social roles; however, we all prepare for rites of passages throughout our lives. Participation in games occurs when an individual begins to adopt the expectations and norms of the larger community organization. We participate in games at work and with the local softball club. We consider our particular role and the norms governing its performance in relation to all the other impinging roles in the organized network. Sport demands spectators and is organized to serve their needs and the larger myths of the supporting organization—be it a local high school or the city of Seattle with its Mariners or Seahawks. And finally the most worklike, nonwork activity is recreation done purposefully by people to refresh and re-create themselves so they can be more productive on the job. That and other forms of recreation are frequently organized by professionals and others whose job (work) is to ensure that their clients are "re-created." Of course, individuals, family groups, or friendship groups may be the primary behaving units. However, they are organized by professionals who sell them recreation means; provide, manage, and establish rules for playing fields such as wilderness areas and campgrounds; and organize leagues, flea markets, and other collective activities and indicators so that participants are assured they are having a "good time." The point is that each of these nonwork activities can be separated from the other by an empirically measurable means—the organizational pattern that shapes the observed, expected, intended, and perceived normative behavior.

Consequently, when we talk about the social benefits of leisure, we need to specify which nonwork organizational system we are considering. The nature, types, and measures of benefits related to leisure for a group of Trappist monks will be very different than the nature, types, and measures for a family in its Winnebago, doing recreational camping at the Good Sam campground. Table 1 illustrates our social-organizational approach to nonwork domains.

Table 2 takes an activity approach to nonwork. Here, rather than talk about how variation in benefit output is related to the social organization, we offer different "behavioral clusters," example associated activities, and their likely social benefits.

The point in both of these tables is that as one varies or refines the analysis of the independent variables (types of nonwork), we are more likely to approach a better specification of possible social benefits. Neither the social organization nor the activity approaches should be seen as final solutions. They are illustrations of ubiquitous and universal nonwork possibilities in all human societies. The variation between societies and over time would be shifting proportions of person days or hours devoted by a whole society to one or more approaches.

It is important for our ensuing discussion to emphasize that shifts in the political and social system will greatly transform the nature of the work-nonwork mix and the associated state of benefits, perception of them, access to

them, and the final state of evaluation by the participating unit—individual, family, institution, or community. That is, changes in the political economy—the restructuring of political struggles from a central concern with access to the means of production, to a concern over means of access to the means of consumption—will have significant impact upon specification, measurement, and valuation of the benefits of various social pursuits. In the next section, we will consider some of the emerging social structural changes as we move from an industrial to a "post-industrial" political economy.

SOME TRENDS IN THE POLITICAL DEFINITION AND ALLOCATION OF NONWORK BENEFITS

The polar values of hedonism (indulgence) and asceticism (denial) are at the base of any discussion concerning lifestyle, leisure, recreation, and their provision. After more than two decades of our publicly proclaimed arrival at a "leisure-consumer" society, we are still uncomfortable when we begin to enjoy ourselves. Sport is more work-like than ever. Play is to "train" children for careers or other social ambitions of the parents. Art, science, and religion seem to be more corporate structure and social therapy than the lonesome quest of impoverished and eccentric dreamers expressing creative freedom from regular work. Recreation has become its own political economy of diversion produced by competing bureaucracies.

Table 1. Ways to consider types of nonwork and example social benefit output.

Nonwork Domain	Organized By	Function	Example Social Benefit Output
Classical leisure	Individual	Creating	Knowledge/myth
Play	Intimates	Anticipating	Better future role performance
Games	Team	Participating	Better social awareness, behavior
Sport	Corporate body	Spectating	Collective release
Recreation	Professionals	Re-creating	Efficient production

Table 2. Example outdoor recreational behavioral clusters, activities, and social benefits.

Behavioral Clusters	Recreaction Activities, Segmented by Amount of Capital Investment			Example Social Benefit Output
	High	Moderate	Low	
Movement	Driving for pleasure	Wilderness hiking	Walking for pleasure	Shared experience
Vertigo	Sky diving	River running	Diving from a cliff	Pride in self and group
Nesting	Second home	Camp trailer	Tent	Social stability
Spectacle	Royal wedding	Tickertape parade	Local fair	Sense of belonging to large social forces
Agon	NY Yankees	AAA baseball	Pigtail league	Social catharsis
Collecting	Big game hunting	Rock-hounding	Collecting stones	Social continuity
Curiosity	NPS Interpretive Center	Bird-watching	Amateur botanizing	Knowledge sustainability
Consuming	Stockcar demolition derby	Shopping	Eating and drinking	Social class stability
Sociability	Commercial campground	Sidewalk cafe	Roadside rest area	Social bond sustained
Woolgathering	Defining what cloud formations look like	Counting cloud formations	Watching clouds pass by	New visions of social order

With all this change, however, we may be certain that the many peoples of the Anglo democracies have never been comfortable with hedonism—which is nonwork unmanaged—whilst remaining comfortable with asceticism because it is closer to the externally controlled confines of work. We write books on the "problem" of leisure, but seldom do we consider work as a "problem." Work is something that we never seem to have enough of to go around, while leisure sits heavy and is too much with us. We treat the play of children as work, which if it is of the right sort, will lead them to a "productive" adulthood. Sport is to prepare us for victory on some future battlefield. Indeed, it is claimed that men have an advantage in the corporate world of work because they have more often played team sports than women, so they can function more easily as "team" players. We tolerate public and corporate recreation departments as their rightful function is to have us return to work refreshed and more productive. In all of this we view nonwork as too much amenity and not enough sacrifice, too much personal pleasure and not enough collective responsibility. It is unregulated and not within the purview of professional guidance and managerial discipline.

Despite all these attempts to avoid enjoying nonwork, we face major questions about the role of work in the predicted "post-industrial" society. A variety of scenarios have been held up, but the majority predict that either there will be much less opportunity for people to work at all (Veal 1987), or alternatively, that work will increasingly be routinized as technology and restructuring of the labor force come increasingly into play (Abercrombie and Urry 1983, Braverman 1974). Either of these suggest that work will be less likely to be seen as a central life motive. However, whether one will find leisure providing a central interest for people in the mature industrial society remains problematic. Although often predicted, the failure of compensation theories of leisure in contemporary society surely questions whether leisure activities will become central. More complex scenarios point to contradictions in the emerging work processes. For various reasons, including increasing working hours for a large sector of the population, work for many of these people is all-absorbing and very much a central life concern, while opportunities for nonwork activities are diminishing (Godbey 1989). One of the more perceptive social forecasts of the 1950s predicted that "people will become increasingly divided into those who have more leisure and those who have less; perhaps one of the worst features is that the leisure of those who have more will be planned and managed by those who have less" (source now lost).

Parallel to all of this, and of much more importance, leisure activities are becoming increasingly visible and are now upheld as a new economic sector. Thus, the so-called leisure industries are seen as a way of providing employment opportunities and sustaining flagging economies. To pile one contradiction on top of another, it seems that the new leisure industries are among those which are developing especially routinized and even exploitive work practices with little chance of worker satisfaction (Seabrook 1988). But leisure as expressed through or shaped by this new industrialization is now entering into the arena of economic and hence political struggle. Furthermore, its very visibility is heightening the leisure aspirations of the work population.

The present era is not unlike the incipient phases of industrial capitalism as labor and management struggled to establish relevant spheres of influence. Leisure decisions are being shaped by markets, by pressure groups, by mass media campaigns, by professionals seeking to expand their turf, and by governments hoping to buy some time in office. This struggle does not seem to have the drama of earlier "class struggles" because it does not fit the comfortable rhetoric of academic Marxism. Indeed, when it comes to play and work, it is hard to find a more pure ascetic than an academic Marxist. Yet, all the elements of a classic class struggle are here. How will the mature industrial order allocate certain scarce collective resources—time, space, wealth, land, people? And how equitable will that allocation be?

In short, the struggle for access to work will continue to be important. However, the central class struggle of "post-industrial" societies will be over the nature, types, and provision of nonwork amenities and services. This struggle will take a variety of forms:

- Struggle over whose perceptions of nonwork amenity will prevail.
- Struggle over who pays and who gains from the nonwork amenity.
- Struggle over the moral consequences of amenity provision. Where are the shifting margins of sin and how do we tax or regulate it? (e.g., current proposals to solve United States drug problems by making such use legitimate rather than deviant).
- Struggle between professional groups managing different amenity institutions as to which is to receive the largest share of public and private support—museums or libraries, parks or human services, etc.
- Struggle over the relative worth of publicly and privately provided services.
- Struggle over private opulence of services (e.g., private swimming pools, etc.) and public poverty (e.g., inner city children punished for opening fire hydrants to cool off because there are no nearby swimming pools).
- Struggle over most effective and efficient provider of nonwork services—public, private for profit, or private nonprofit volunteer organization.
- Struggle between localities that want to control the nature and access to nonwork amenities, with the central government providing financial resources; which, in turn, thinks that if it pays, then its professionals should determine how "national" interests are to be served. Locals claim that only a government that is closest to the people can be the best means of allocating leisure amenity. National governments think otherwise. The establishment and management of national reserves will become a central focus of such local-national struggles and tradeoffs.

• Struggle within and between voluntary organizations and their volunteers to carry out their leisure political agendas, even though their emphasis will be on "nonpartisan, nonpolitical means." For example, the National Rifle Association and various animal rights groups struggle over property rights and access to state "owned" wildlife populations.

Since all enduring social systems represent some accommodation regarding what are appropriate and inappropriate behavioral expressions of social values, we can expect the postindustrial order to give much attention to nonwork domains or lifestyles. It seems likely that the struggle over appropriate and inappropriate lifestyles will fall somewhere on the continuum of hedonism to asceticism—or indulgence to denial. That is, with a freeing from work as a central life goal, large numbers of people can define benefit by maximizing their indulgence in material and experiential pleasures or maximize benefit by denying such pleasures. The Table 3 matrix suggests some possible market segments or lifestyle types that are emerging in the postindustrial society.

The reader can recall a variety of actual social groups that represent the ideal types of this matrix. Persons who view disequilibrium by legal and illegal drugs as a sin and shopping binges as nearly a patriotic contribution are those who see benefit from material indulgence and experiential denial (e.g., "Puritan consumers"). On the other hand, there are wilderness purists who carry expensive illegal drugs in their backpacks to "heighten the experience" (e.g., ecstatic retreatists) while showing great contempt for the possession of Winnebagos by campers. The point for the present paper is that the independent (causal) variables of type of nonwork are filtered by intervening variables, such as the lifestyle market segment, that define appropriate and inappropriate sources of nonwork benefit.

Even if the more contradictory scenarios about the future of work and nonwork prevail, political struggle over the leisure domain, the increasing visibility of leisure, and heightened leisure aspirations will probably lead many of the leisure-deprived to identify themselves with these potential market directions. Just as at present, those who have limited time opportunity for leisure activities commonly use that time with maximum effect, and have more satisfying leisure lives than the less busy. It is unlikely that this will change.

MEASURES OF RELATIVE WORTH

Even if the social benefits of nonwork activity could be specified and their magnitudes measured accurately, the problem would remain of determining their relative worths. Social ecology suggests that four budgets should be used in such valuations—time, space, energy, and materials.

Social ecology has always given a great deal of attention to how the time-space nexus affects the production of certain socially desired benefits from combinations of land, labor, and capital. We consider the time budgets of a household in accomplishing certain tasks, the distance to various agricultural fields, the distance and time to certain markets, and we attempt to manage these variables so that the distance covered may be greater, but the rise of certain institutions and technologies permit a shorter travel time.

Table 3. Market segments that will define appropriate and inappropriate benefits.

		MATERIAL BENEFITS	
		DENIAL	INDULGENCE
EXPERIENTIAL BENEFITS	DENIAL	Ascetics (religious retreat)	Puritan consumers (followers of TV evangelists)
	INDULGENCE	Ecstatic retreatists (hippie communitarian)	Hedonists (playboy market segment)

Like classic sociology studies, social ecology documents how the regularities of human use of space and time map particular social relations, constraints, and opportunities as clearly as they map biophysical patterns. Intimate and distant social relations; high and low social classes; favored and despised ethnic, occupational, and caste groupings all have assigned and clearly regulated measures as to *when* and *where* those relations should and should not occur. Consequently, time and space are not simply physical metrics, but are filtered through a prescribed and predictable cultural metric. (For further details, see Field and Burch 1988.)

Our studies are less clear empirically, but theoretically they suggest that people make tradeoffs between time and space. We see the time spent in a Bangkok traffic jam as a painful cost; though the distance may be short, the time seems forever. Conversely, the time spent with our lover is a benefit that never lasts long enough and any distance apart is too great. As the speed of movement increases, the amount of time we devote to various activities remains about the same (e.g., journey to work) though the distance traveled may be much greater. A poor, landless family has a surplus of time, so time costs may be less crucial than distance costs. In contrast to poor families, wealthier families tend to have more space per capita, have less free time, consume more energy per capita, and spend a higher proportion of their incomes on consumption rather than subsistence.

In sum, all human social systems have predictable, routine patterns of time-space dimensions that overlay those of the biophysical. Social ecology asks how human space-time dimensions overlay or conflict with the necessary ones of ecosystems. Further, as in nonhuman ecosystems, there is a third driving force—energy that operates by certain laws of physics and affects human time-space processes. So, too, in human systems, energy—its nature, types, and amounts— greatly affects patterns and processes of time-space factors. We can direct more energy in certain ways and gain more productivity in a smaller space and for a shorter time. We substitute human energy for fossil energy or for renewable energy (such as wind), and each change reflects changes in human organization. A city has a higher per capita fossil energy consumed than a rural village, and that is part of the attraction of the city, and part of the reason it has a different organizational form. Finally, human social systems have developed the abstraction "money" to try and assign value to energy, time, and space, and their products. Consequently, each person, household, or community has four regularized measures of their structure and functioning—space, time, energy, and material (money). Each can substitute for the other, and each can be enfolded into the other. The relative allocation of proportions of those budgets is a measure of the "relative" worth. In short, money may often be the least

important measure of worth, whilst time expenditure may be the most important. Consequently, managers who use only monetary or surrogate measures are likely to miss the relative values of activities in the postmodern era.

Table 4 summarizes how the four resource budgets might be applied for different social units. It is important to note that the examples provided here are central tendencies from the literature, rather than the specifics of any particular scholar.

A POSSIBLE REFORMULATION AND APPLICATION OF CLASSIC THEORIES

In the postindustrial society, the meaning of social benefits no longer reflects the usual supply and demand models associated with the industrial order. Postindustrial social benefits are likely to reflect a social construction of reality that is some combination of *shared* being, perception, access, and evaluation. For large segments of the population, scarcity of goods and their attendant benefits are less important than scarcity of time and possession of sound relationships and desirable experiences.

The social sciences look to a new century with all the wonder and a good deal less confidence than did the classic theorists of the 19th century—Marx, Simmel, Weber, Durkheim, Freud, et al. They, too, were faced with attempting to explain and understand a fundamental shift in the world's political economy—from agrarian to industrial. They gave the new organization of work their central attention. We suspect that though work remains important as a "means," lifestyle "careers" will be more driven by nonwork patterns. However, the universal concern with how social systems hold together or fall apart will remain central in our investigations. We will still want to know the patterns and processes of functional integration through the division of work and nonwork. We will still want to know how social bonds between intimates are developed, sustained, and altered. We will still want to know how larger symbolic connections of belonging to ethnic and national collectivities emerge and are sustained. In short, we need a reformulation and application of classic theories to understand issues of social benefit.

Cheek and Burch (1976) argued that the large volume of research on work tells a good bit about how the division of labor contributes to social integration. However, it does not really help us to understand the nature of the social bond, especially between gender and generations, nor do we understand the linkages between the basic associations of

Table 4. Illustrative measures of key social budgets for social benefit monitoring and evaluation (examples only).

Measure	Unit of Analysis		
	Individual	Household	Community
Time	- Stage of life cycle - Daily/weekly time allocation to various tasks, e.g., work, play, subsistence - Frequency, duration, and intensity of specific interactions	- Stage of family life cycle - Daily/weekly/ seasonal regularities in time allocation by person to functional tasks	- Stage of social evolution - Celebration and ritual cycles
Space	- Personal location of work, play, rest, etc. Square meters per person and activity - Property rights in certain personal space/objects	- Within residence space allocation, e.g., parents-children/between status and class groups - Distribution of land ownership amounts, type, etc.	- Formal functional spaces, e.g., village square relative to space for commerce, etc. - Informal functional spaces, e.g., village well
Energy	- Kilocaloric intake-expenditure by certain tasks	- Fuel sources by BTU - Per capita BTU consumption	- Total annual BTU by function - Distribution by fuel sources
Material	- Personal income percent spent on various functions - Nonmonetary or in-kind income and its expenditure - Rights and obligations of access to material and spiritual resources of collectivity	- Total household income - Nonmonetary resources, e.g., garden food - Allocation to basic functions	- Total village income (taxes) in-kind; government subsidy, etc. - Total village expenditures by specific function

kinship and friendship to the larger collective representations such as ethnic community or the nation-state. They argued that nonwork permits the conversion of certain biosocial propensities into symbolic structures which sustain social bonds and link smaller human associations to larger ones.

Social ecological theory, as developed by sociologists, concerns itself with understanding the origins, persistence, alteration, or destruction of a particular pattern or web of social relations. Sociological human ecologists have developed a wide range of key metaphors and concepts to delimit the range of observation and analysis. Attention has generally been given to three major structural and three major processional dimensions.

The three common structural dimensions are:

- *Ideologies and values*—as they structure perception and socialization;
- *Social differentiation*—the universal but variable patterns of generation, gender, class, and status which flow from and impact the production and distribution of a given political economy's goods and services and which are overtly expressed through lifestyles; and
- *Community*—the aggregated means by which a collective develops distinctive and routinized patterns of social and spatial interaction which distinguish it from other similar collectives.

The three sets of concepts about key social processes, center on fundamental social achievements related to *social bonding* (ties between intimates), *social integration* (linkages between functional elements such as individuals, families, neighborhoods, etc.), and *social solidarity* (emotional commitment to a larger social whole). We identify these three achievements as the essential dimensions or components of social cohesion. We will now argue that each are necessary for an enduring social system and that each should be promoted by nonwork activity in a post-industrial society.

Social bondings are structured by a household, kinship, friendship, or other intimate human associations' values to create and to sustain loyalty toward that association. Such bonding mechanisms also encourage performance of age, gender, and status roles which are the basic building blocks of larger, more general associations such as the institutions of a community. *Social solidarity* is structured by values that make individuals feel shame, guilt, or pride in their role performance. Since only a small proportion of human behavior is programmed genetically, there is the constant need to inculcate or to coerce conformity. At the community

level, solidarity is sustained by accepted and ritualized collective explanations of the unexplainable (myth). Thus, myth both internally binds and externally differentiates social entities, one from another. *Social integration* is structured by shared values regarding necessary roles and the patterned and legitimate exchanges between these social roles (and clusters of roles of institutions). That is, our streets are cleaned and policed and our garbage hauled away, just as children are schooled and airplanes guided to landings, through a functional division of labor that operates with such effectiveness that we are only aware of such integration during the rare times when there are strikes, accidents, or similar crises. Enduring societies have this base of expected and routine fulfillment of function. Disintegrating societies, such as present-day Lebanon, exhibit none of that predictability.

As in *all* ecological studies, we are operating at the level of whole systems, rather than reducing our analysis to individual particulars. Consequently, like biological ecology, social ecology is an historic and synthetic discipline that deals with collectives rather than individual organisms or their component parts. That is, though we are necessarily dependent upon understanding these component organizations—cells, atoms, genes, individuals—our understanding of them is not sufficient to permit us to understand behavior of the whole.

Like biological ecology, our basic questions revolve around the creation of unity out of diversity, and the relations between structures of order and processes of change. We have shared assumptions: the whole is greater than the sum of its parts; and in the examination of relationships, we cannot understand the behavior of "A" and "B" unless we understand their mutual relationship to "C." And because we have these basic questions and assumptions, much of our attention is directed to the forms of hierarchy which regulate patterns of dominance between species and individuals over access to particular niches. In short, hierarchy is universal and ubiquitous in all ecological systems.

SOCIAL COHESION AS A BENEFIT OF NONWORK ACTIVITIES

Given the foregoing discussion, we can now focus on the social cohesion benefits of leisure. That will be done by examining the linkages between the above three dimensions of social cohesion (social bonding, solidarity, and integration), nonwork activities in a post-industrial society, and freedom. The necessary properties of an enduring social system include how well the social system connects individuals to one another (interpersonal relations); relates institutions to their subelements and to one another (institutional relations); and how the entire set of persons, institutions, and values can sustain predictable patterns (structural relations). Each level folds into the other level. Reciprocity and sharing sustain household bonds which, in turn, are sustained and supported by the continuity of symbols and places that tie us to larger social elements, such as the social structures of functional roles in community and society.

Table 5 helps point out the role of nonwork opportunities and activities in the establishment and maintenance of the broader society. It suggests some potential interconnections, and points to the generation of a range of social processes and possible outcomes of nonwork activity, any of which may be positive, negative, or neutral in nature. Naturally, a society should strive to realize positive outcomes (or capture the social cohesion benefits listed) of nonwork activities.

We contend that there is an extremely strong prima facie case to show the importance of nonwork at the interpersonal and institutional levels, and these in turn are vital preconditions for integration. The question which must be asked then is: To what extent will the nonwork arena provide for the development of those positive outcomes, both currently and in the future mature industrial society?

SUMMARY AND CONCLUSIONS

We have argued that social cohesion, while basic to the effective functioning of any society, remains primarily an abstraction. Furthermore, unlike the cardiovascular benefits of physical activity, methods have yet to be developed for measuring the social cohesion benefits of nonwork behaviors. In fact, theoretical paradigms still need to be refined concerning the complete set of social interactions that explain the multiple processes which nurture and sustain opportunities to realize these benefits. Given this state of

knowledge, we have outlined the sets of variables and processes that we believe must be considered in attempts to relate nonwork activity to social cohesion.

At this time, we cannot propose specific research designs or hypothesize functional relationships beyond those implicit in our discussion of each set of variables as we introduced them. Put simply, the research possibilities are great, but the routes still need to be mapped by creative and integrative scientists. To give direction to those journeys, we will close with a brief summary of the sets of variables that need to be considered in attempts to relate social cohesion to nonwork activity.

- *Nonwork Domain*—or the type of nonwork behavior being analyzed, whether leisure, play, games, sport, recreation, or other nonwork activity.
- *Dependent Variable of Social Cohesion*—which results in these three achievements:
  - *Bonding*—or ties between intimates, as indicated by *reciprocity*.
  - *Solidarity*—or commitment to a larger whole, as indicated by *continuity*.
  - *Integration*—or linkages between social units (see immediately following), as indicated by *consistency*.
- *Social Units*—receiving the benefits, hierarchically covering individuals, households/families (and other bonded small groups of individuals), neighborhoods, communities, and society.
- *Organizational Units*—who organize the nonwork activity, such as individuals, teams, professionals—who might or might not be the same as the social units receiving the benefits.
- *Behavioral Clusters*—or grouping of respondents by different types of nonwork behavior, such as being a spectator or actively engaging in a specific type of activity. Alternatively, these

Table 5. Possible social cohesion outcomes of nonwork opportunities.

Units of Analysis (relationships)	Processes	Outcomes	Elements
Interpersonal	Reciprocity	Bonding	Persons (Values)
Institutional	Continuity	Solidarity	Places (Differentiation)
Structural	Consistency	Integrating	Patterns (Community)

could be defined as Motive Clusters by groupings based on types of motivation (socializing, caring, etc.).

- *Lifestyle Segments*—that define different personal value orientations of the respondents such as ascetics, Puritan consumers, ecstatic retreatists, and hedonists.
- *Social Budgets, of time, space, energy, and materials*—to be used to determine the relative worth of the benefits.

In their introductory chapter to this volume, Driver, Brown, and Peterson describe three necessary analytical stages of leisure benefit research as follows:

- *Qualitative* studies to define possible benefits and the variables and their parameters to be used to quantify the magnitude of a particular type of benefit and to estimate its relative worth.
- *Quantification* of the magnitudes of the benefits.
- *Valuation* of the relative worth or importance to determine the value individuals and/or society assign a benefit, realizing that benefits of large magnitudes might have small values and vice-versa.

Some of the above listed sets of variables will help promote tighter specification of the social cohesion benefits of nonwork activity, especially the definition of which social groups, lifestyle types, etc., might benefit in differential ways. Other sets will mostly facilitate measuring the magnitudes of the benefits and controlling for differences between different social units, organizational units, and groups comprising other segments. The social budgets of time, space, energy, and material should help guide valuation efforts.

Although we have sketched some possible variables, we have not indicated how they might line up to test solid causal patterns. We make no claim that these are mutually exclusive or necessary and sufficient variables. Rather, our whole intent has been the provision of illustrations as to how we might *start* some theoretically driven, systematic research on the relations between nonwork possibility and opportunity to enhance social cohesion. It is clear that research is complex: many factors influence the creation and maintenance of social cohesion, many intervening variables exist, and longitudinal studies are needed.

Our effort is akin to the broad, almost mythical, map of the Western United States that President Jefferson gave to Lewis and Clark before they began their lengthy exploration of that vast area in the early 1800s. We are certain that much of importance is out there, that it is our destiny to explore it, that we know the means for discovery. We are equally certain that most of the contours we have so confidently sketched will be inaccurate, in the wrong place, or poorly shaped. Yet, the contour of provocative possibility, if it stimulates future correction of present error, may be the right map for our time.

In conclusion, we must point to the difficulty and contradictions of assessing broad social benefits of leisure. On the one hand, we must identify and define our concepts more tightly than has often been the case, and we must strive for research based on specific situations and related to the context within which the research occurs. On the other hand, we must look at the global impacts of the phenomena we study—how much does the nonwork domain provide for the furthering of reciprocity and social bonding, the transmission of cultural traditions in a way which optimizes continuity and solidarity, and the development of a consistent and integrated society with its appropriate sense of place for its people? These may seem like sociological abstractions, but these three components of social cohesion are the dynamic social infrastructure that gives substance, meanings, and fiber to a society. Without these "macrocosms," freedom for the "microcosms" (we individuals) has little meaning because of the lack of vertical integration.

Having emphasized these elements of social cohesion, we conclude, appropriately enough for a volume concerned with research, with a series of questions. Our rhetoric tells us that leisure is about the expression of freedom, and we know that freedom requires a stable and integrated society. In mature industrial societies, we need to look much more critically at the extent to which freedom is fostered and built through the proper functioning of the nonwork domain. Is the furtherance of freedom one of the benefits which accrue from our leisure? Does social conformity arise from a positive commitment to valued social continuity, or does it arise from mindless subservience to market forces, recreation professionals, or some other constraining force?

The fundamental problem is that we do not have good detectors of the incremental loss of any of the three components of social cohesion or good predictors of what facilitates and nurtures each. We thus know that something vital is missing but don't yet understand what it is. Further research on these benefits of nonwork activity related to social cohesion will help promote that understanding and improve our grasp of the linkages between these benefits and freedom.

LITERATURE CITED

Abbey, E. 1988. One life at a time, please. New York, NY: Henry Holt & Co. 225 p.

Abercrombie, N.; Urry, J. 1983. Capital, labor and the middle classes. London: Allen and Unwin. 169 p.

Braverman, H. 1974. Labor and monopoly capital: the degradation of work in the twentieth century. New York, NY: Monthly Review Press. 465 p.

Burch, W. R. 1977. Urban children and nature: a summary of research on camping and outdoor education. In: Stillman, C., ed. Children, nature and the urban environment. Gen. Tech. Rep. NE-30. Broomall, PA: USDA Forest Service, Northeastern Forest Experiment Station: 101-111.

Cheek, N. H.; Burch, W. R. 1976. The social organization of leisure in human society. New York, NY: Harper & Row Publishers.

Doig, I. 1978. This house of sky: landscapes of a western mind. Orlando, FL: Harcourt, Brace, Jovanovich. 314 p.

Driver, B. L. 1976. Quantification of outdoor recreationists' preferences. In: Smissen, B. V.; Myers J., eds. Research: camping and environmental education. HPEP Series, No. 11. University Park, PA: Pennsylvania State University: 165-187.

Field, D. R.; Burch, W. R. 1988. Rural sociology and the environment. New York, NY: Greenwood Press.

Godbey, G. C. 1989. The future of leisure services: thriving on change. State College, PA: Venture Publishing, Inc. 112 p.

House, J. S.; Landis, K. R.; Unberson, D. 1988. Social relationships and health. Science. (July) 241: 540-545.

Maclean, N. 1976. A river runs through it. Chicago, IL: University of Chicago Press. 217 p.

McCafferty, K. 1985. Close to home. Field & Stream. (November) 80:54-55, 122.

Peterson, G.; Brown, T. A. 1985. The economic benefits of outdoor recreation. In: President's Commission on America's Outdoors: A Literature Review, values, 11-18.

Rossman, B. B.; Ulehla, J. 1977. Psychological reward values associated with wilderness use—a functional-reinforcement approach. Environment and Behavior. 9:41-66.

Seabrook, J. 1988. The leisure society. Oxford: Blackwell. 195 p.

Veal, A. J. 1987. Leisure and the future. London: Allen and Unwin. 201 p.

Waring, M. 1988. Counting for nothing: what men value and what women are worth. Wellington, New Zealand: Allen and Unwin. 290 p.

Williams, D. 1985. Psychological perspectives on the environment-experience relationship: implications for recreation resource management. In: President's Commission on America's Outdoors: A Literature Review, motivation, 17-32.

II.

STATE-OF-KNOWLEDGE CHAPTERS

D. Economic and Environmental Measures

Beneficial Economic Consequences of Leisure and Recreation

Rebecca L. Johnson
Department of Forest Resources
Oregon State University
Corvallis, Oregon

Thomas C. Brown
Rocky Mountain Forest and Range Experiment Station
USDA Forest Service
Fort Collins, Colorado

A "beneficial consequence" has been defined as "a consequence that improves the state or condition of a person or society, or prevents a worse state" (Driver, Brown, and Peterson, this volume). What would distinguish a beneficial consequence that is economic in character from other types of beneficial consequences? Some might say that monetary rewards are a necessary ingredient of beneficial economic consequences. But economists are careful to distinguish between financial benefits (monetary rewards) and economic benefits—they are often different. The important difference between "beneficial consequences" and the economists' notion of "benefit" is that the former focuses on the physical or emotional *state* of individuals or society, while the latter focuses on the importance or value of the goods, services, and activities that contribute to that state of being.

In this paper, we first describe more fully this distinction between the economic definition of benefits and the broader definition of benefits used in this book. If some common understanding about terminology can be developed, it will facilitate discussion across disciplines. We also will identify beneficial consequences of leisure activities which are "financial" in character. These activities would improve the financial situation of either the participant or someone directly related to the participant. Finally, we will discuss the uses of economic benefit measures, and the implications for future research.

ECONOMIC BENEFITS OF LEISURE ACTIVITIES

"Economic benefit" has a specific meaning in neoclassical economic literature, and apparently economists' narrow definition of the term "benefit" has caused some confusion among members of other disciplines (Bishop 1987). The economic definition of benefits really concerns the measurement of the value of goods and services which contribute to an individual's utility or well-being. For example, Dwyer, Kelly, and Bowes (1977) state that "benefits represent the value of the goods and services . . ." and "benefits . . . are to be measured in terms of willingness of users to pay for each increment of output provided." Bishop (1987) states that "...the benefits of a proposed policy or project are defined in theory as the maximum amount that gainers would be willing to pay in compensation to losers."

Applied welfare economics attempts to measure the value, in monetary terms, of alternative states of the world so that choices can be made among alternative resource allocations. Economic theory postulates that people derive different "utility" levels from different states of the world. "States of the world" are defined broadly to include not only the allocation of goods and services, but also "political conditions such as freedom of speech and nondiscrimination, physical characteristics such as the weather, and so on" (Boadway and Bruce 1984).

The utility level that people derive from states of the world is not considered to be measurable. Rather, it is simply an index of the individual's (the consumer's) understanding of his or her well-being. If, according to the consumer, something makes an individual better off, then utility has increased. As Hicks (1946) said, "Utility is not a quantity, but only an index of the consumer's scale of preferences," or as Hirshleifer (1980) wrote, "In finding the most preferred position, the individual maximizes utility." That is, utility is just that which we assume people attempt to maximize as they go about their lives.

It is important to note here that economic benefits are strictly the result of the consumer's choices, regardless of what someone else may think the consumer should choose, do, desire, etc. The economist takes the consumer's choices as given, not questioning the wisdom of those choices. The "sovereign" consumer reigns.

The consumer, in the economic paradigm, utilizes a "production technology" that requires inputs consisting of goods, services, and other elements of the state of the world, to produce outputs desired by the consumer. Within this production technology are activities of all sorts, including leisure activities. The consumer is assumed to be efficient in use of available inputs, producing the mix of outputs of greatest value to the consumer, within the constraints that he or she faces. That is, the consumer is assumed to maximize utility. The inputs are generally measurable entities, and are called "arguments" of the consumer's utility function.

Economic theory does not focus on the production technology by which goods and services are used to produce desired outcomes, and therefore, to affect well-being. Economists observe participation in activities, such as leisure activities; such participation is data for economic analyses. But economists don't tend to study the activities themselves, or the changes in the states of the human being that such activities create. The economists' lack of interest in personal production technology follows from the capability of neoclassical economic methodology to measure economic benefit without ever knowing about that technology, and from a philosophical willingness to let the consumer decide what is best for him or her (the consumer sovereignty assumption).

Economists also do not focus on the types of well-being, such as health or happiness, that are outcomes of the personal production technology. Economics is a study of choice in a world of scarcity, and most investigations are concerned with resource allocation among competing demands. To the extent that there is a common metric by which all goods and services can be measured, it is not necessary to know *why* an individual values one good more or less than another. Resource allocation is facilitated simply by knowing the magnitudes of the relative values of goods and services. For example, suppose that two individuals with equal and substantial incomes want to fish in the same location. If one individual is willing to give up fifty dollars worth of other goods and services for the right to that location and the other is willing to give up only twenty dollars worth of goods and services, the economist has the information needed for deciding the economically efficient resource allocation. Should it matter if the first angler's value is derived from the fact that fishing is "fun" while the second angler's value is derived from the fact that he or she likes to eat fish?

But what if resource allocation isn't the important question? Are there management and/or policy questions where it matters *why* people value leisure activities? There are probably many, and other chapters will discuss these. One which has relevance to economics is the availability of substitutes. Using the fishing example, the angler who likes to eat fish might be happy with fresh fish from the store. But if the fishing opportunity were taken away from the other angler, a different fishing site may be the only alternative. In these cases, it is necessary to know the motives of the individual in order to determine substitutes.

Recall that Driver, Brown, and Peterson (DBP) (earlier in this volume) define "beneficial consequences" as the improvements in the state or condition of a person or society. Within this broader context, the economists' focus on benefits as monetary measures of the value of goods and services from the consumer's point of view may seem overly narrow. There are at least three important differences between the DBP and the economists' notions of benefit. First, the DBP definition of beneficial consequences seems to encompass both the supply of goods and services that are the focus of economics, and the states and conditions of humans that are the focus of psychology, medicine, philosophy, and other disciplines. The former are arguments in the utility function, while the latter are not. For example, the availability of an area of forest could be the consequence of road construction. The new opportunity for forest recreation created by the road would be external to the individual and could be an argument of the utility function. However, a change in the condition of a human being, such as a drop in blood pressure as a consequence of exercise is internal to the individual, and not an argument of the utility function. The DBP notion focuses on the personal production technology that the economist takes for granted.

There are numerous states or conditions of human existence that contribute to greater well-being/utility, such as health, happiness, spiritual depth, sense of purpose, and sense of belonging. There also are objective measures that indicate the degree of some of these states or conditions. For example, measures of health include blood pressure level and days without symptoms of bacterial or viral infections. And measures of happiness include, perhaps, a smile index or deepness of sleep. But these measures are only partial. Further, there may not be any behavioral measures of some conditions, such as a sense of belonging.

In any case, it should be clear that some types of "beneficial consequences" can be considered arguments of the utility function, and are traditionally subject to the economists' attempts at monetary valuation, while other types are really internal human states that are closely tied to utility, and not an object of measurement in standard neoclassical economics. The question arises, can economic theory be extended to also directly estimate the economic benefit of alternative states or conditions of individuals?

The second difference between the economists' notion of benefits and the more general DBP notion is that economists focus on measuring the value or importance of a beneficial change, while the DBP notion focuses on the actual change in human or societal states or conditions. The latter attempts to measure changes in physical or emotional conditions, while the former attempts to measure the value that people place on the goods and services that produce those changes.

The third difference is that economists take the sovereign consumer's preferences and choices as given, while the DBP notion of beneficial consequences seeks to provide information that may influence those preferences and choices. It is possible that new knowledge of beneficial consequences may change demand for goods and services (via new knowledge of the value of activities using those goods and services), but estimating the demand for goods and services will not help explain the beneficial consequences of activities.

BENEFICIAL CONSEQUENCES THAT ARE FINANCIAL IN CHARACTER

The economic definition of benefits is different from the financial definition of benefits. The economic approach measures benefits as the net gain in welfare to an individual or society from some change. The financial measure only incorporates monetary flows. Both approaches measure

benefits in monetary terms, but the financial approach makes no attempt to include the value of changes in welfare that do not result in monetary flows. A classic cause of differences between financial and economic benefit measures is the presence of "externalities." For example, air pollution is a common externality of manufacturing. Production processes which create air pollution may result in financial profits and an increase in GNP. However, the net benefits to society—i.e., the economic measurement of net benefits of production—may not even be positive when the decrease in individual or societal welfare from reduced air quality is included in the net benefit measure.

Since financial benefits can diverge from economic benefits, simply measuring the flow of dollars in the economy that results from participation in leisure activities would not be a good method for assessing economic benefits. Nevertheless, many people are interested in financial benefits, and those flows of dollars often carry an inordinate amount of weight in decisionmaking. For that reason, it may be useful to look in more detail at the types of financial benefits which can arise from participation in leisure activities. There is already a body of literature that addresses the measurement of some of these benefits, and research is continuing into the refinement and extension of those methods.

Types of Financial Benefits

While there are many elements that influence the state or condition of a person, certainly one's wealth or income is one of those elements. Leisure activities may enhance the financial situation of participants (income or wealth is increased) or of nonparticipants. We define the former case as one where the participant is in a superior financial position after engaging in the leisure activity than without the activity.

Financial Benefits to the Participant

There are at least three types of beneficial financial consequences to participants.

1. Some leisure activities improve health or fitness, which increases the wage-earning potential of the participant. For example, activities that are strenuous and increase the participant's strength and endurance will allow the individual to be more productive at jobs that require physical labor. Improved health and fitness have also been found to increase the productivity of workers whose jobs do not require physical labor, and to reduce health costs (see Ellis and Richardson, this volume).

2. There are cases where the participant is paid directly for engaging in a leisure activity (sport). The most obvious examples are professional athletes. However, there are many other examples such as river and fishing guides; exhibitions; fishing and hunting contests; and payments for photographs, film, or accounts of leisure activities. We note, however, that it might be argued that if the individuals are paid for participation, it is no longer "leisure."

3. A more indirect form of financial gain is when the participant is paid for the experience or skills aquired from participation in a leisure activity. An example would be an outdoor leader/teacher who learned the necessary outdoor skills from previous participation. Another example is a strength and conditioning coach who gained experience from previous participation in bodybuilding.

The above categories are not thought to be exhaustive or mutually exclusive. Empirical estimates of these benefits have been reported by businesses that offer fitness programs for their employees (Baun and Williams 1985, Driver and Ratliff 1982, Falkenberg 1987, Klock 1985, Kondrasuk 1985). However, these results don't show that the *participants* always reap the financial benefits associated with increased productivity in the workplace. Future research could focus on the degree to which employees gain financially from improved health and fitness. There also is reason to believe that the same benefits could be gained from leisure activities other than fitness programs that improve health and fitness. Since corporations have invested substantial sums in fitness programs, it stands to reason that they would have the incentives to research the benefits of those programs. The results of that research could be extended to other types of leisure activities which also improve health and fitness.

Financial Benefits to Nonparticipants

Nonparticipants may also gain a superior financial position from participation in a leisure activity. There are at least three types of financial benefits to nonparticipants.

1. It was noted in the previous section that participation in some leisure activities leads to more healthy, productive workers. Since labor is a factor of production, when that factor becomes more productive, the costs of production decrease. The actual financial gain to employers from this extra productivity from healthy workers will depend on the characteristics of the industry and the market (e.g., cost structure and degree of competition).

2. A second group that can gain from the increased productivity of workers are consumers who gain from decreases in prices. Again, this will depend on the characteristics of the industry and market.

3. Another obvious economic impact of leisure activities is the gain by businesses from participants' expenditures. While these expenditures are not a measure of the economic benefits of the leisure activity (economists distinguish between economic benefits and economic *impacts*), the businesses that receive these expenditures (e.g., restaurants, gasoline stations, hotels and motels, etc.) have certainly gained from the participation of others.

Empirical estimates of gains by businesses from the fitness of employees have been widely reported (B.E.R. 1985, Baun and Williams 1985, Driver and Ratliff 1982, Falkenberg 1987, Klock 1985, Kondrasuk 1984, Pechter 1986, Perham 1984). Whether these savings are passed on to consumers in the form of lower product prices (the second category above) is not clear. A market analysis of the employers that realize lower costs could determine whether those costs result in lower product prices. To our knowledge, this has not been done.

The financial benefits described above could be measured as economic benefits. That is, the willingness to pay of individuals to obtain those benefits is theoretically measurable. For example, if participation in leisure activities improves the health of an individual, then insurance companies should be willing to pay individuals (in the form of decreased premiums) up to the amount that the insurance company benefits from lower claims. The problem with assuming that the financial benefits are equal to the economic benefits is that the "market" for exchanging these services is very imperfect. Health insurance companies do not have perfect information about the decrease in claims that result from increased participation in fitness programs. Individuals do not always recognize that their participation in fitness programs results (or could result) in decreased premiums. In addition, group health insurance masks the relationship between individual participation and individual premiums. As a result, the financial benefits of participation should be clearly distinguished from the (unmeasured) economic benefits.

With respect to the third category above, there is a growing literature on the measurement of economic impacts of recreation and tourism spending. Past studies have estimated the economic impacts of different components of the tourism industry, such as state parks (Dean et al. 1978), ports (Yochum and Agarwal 1987), recreational boating (Stoll et al. 1988), coastal tourism (Johnson et al. 1989), and hunting, fishing, and camping (Polzin and Schweitzer 1975). However, the lack of a generalized system for estimating the economic impacts of tourism and recreation was noted in a conference and workshop on the topic in 1984 (Propst 1985).

Economic impact can be measured in terms of income, output, or job changes resulting from participation in the leisure activities. If expenditures are known, input-output models such as the U.S.D.A. Forest Service's IMPLAN model (Alward and Palmer 1983, Alward and Lofting[1]) can be used to estimate the effects in any of these units. The IMPLAN sectors are not always conveniently defined for recreation expenditures, but these problems can usually be solved by combining some primary data with the IMPLAN model.

A more difficult problem, one where more research is needed, is estimating the change in expenditures that may occur from a change in management or policy (Leiber et al. 1989). For example, if an interpretive trail is developed at an historical site near a small town, how many new visitors will travel there? How many people passing through the area would be enticed to stay an extra day at the local motel? How many of them will eat an extra meal even if they don't stay an extra night? Even though we know a fair amount about the expenditures of visitors engaged in particular leisure activities, we don't know very much about how to predict the change in numbers of visitors and/or their expenditures from changes in management or policy.

Investigations into the economic impacts of leisure activities can address the distributive consequences of management and policy changes. At the local level especially, those impacts are often of considerable interest. For that reason, research on economic impacts should continue and add to our knowledge of distributive effects. We also expect research into the financial benefits of leisure activities to continue because local policymakers are generally more interested in cash flows than in willingness to pay. However, we caution against relying on financial analysis for making policy and management decisions because the outcomes may not maximize society's benefit. In order to make sound economic decisions, information on economic benefits is needed.

USES OF ECONOMIC BENEFIT MEASURES

Efficient use of scarce resources is a basic social concern. Efficiency in economics has a specific meaning. A project is economically efficient if there is greater aggregate wealth with than without the project. Benefit-cost analysis was developed to measure the change in aggregate wealth from specific changes in resource allocation. The results of a benefit-cost analysis may facilitate public resource allocation decisions, and are often useful input in setting public policy.

For the conclusions of a benefit-cost analysis to be correct, all gains and losses must be measured, regardless of to whom they accrue, and the measurements must be in terms of commensurate monetary units. The gains and losses are measured in terms of willingness to pay and compensation demanded. For institutional reasons, economic efficiency is generally analyzed at the level of concern of the government entity evaluating the proposed project.

The economic values that are measured in benefit-cost analyses are a function of consumer behavior. Consumer choices are taken as given. Thus, economic values derived from consumer choices look backward to what has happened. These value estimates are then used to evaluate the social worth of new projects. There is undoubtedly some lag between the discovery and initial dissemination of new information about the consequences of human decisions (such as the effects of exercise on human health) and the use of this information by people. Thus, the behavior-based estimates of economic value that we obtain today may not fully reflect recently published information relevant to those estimates. This lag is a problem during periods when consumer preferences are rapidly changing.

The link between information, consumer behavior, and economic value highlights the importance of new information about the benefits of participation in recreation activities. Improved knowledge may lead to more successful personal behavior, which will be reflected in future measures of economic value to the extent that consumers incorporate the knowledge in their behavior. Two classes of information are very important in influencing consumer behavior and, therefore, the economic value of recreation goods and services. The first is the specification and measurement of the personal and social benefits of participating in recreation activities, which is the principal theme of this volume. The second is about the degree of substitution among recreation goods, services, and activities in providing those personal and social benefits. We know little about how specific recreation activities can substitute for each other in maintaining or enhancing human health and well-being. For example, how do backpacking and jogging compare in providing the cardiovascular benefits of exercise, or how do a natural forest and a carefully planned public garden or arboretum compare in providing an environment for contemplation of and communion with nature? What is unique about each environment and activity in the provision of benefits of recreation and leisure activities? The answers to such questions will help consumers make wise personal decisions, leading to new estimates of economic benefit, thereby affecting future assessments of public projects.

CONCLUSIONS

The economists' definition of benefits differs fundamentally from the definition of "beneficial consequences" put forth by Driver, Brown, and Peterson. Economists focus on measuring the *importance* (the relative value) of goods and services, including leisure activities, as opposed to directly measuring changes in physical and emotional well-being. Both approaches can provide useful information for personal and societal decisionmaking.

Information about beneficial economic consequences is especially needed in the evaluation of public expenditures which facilitate leisure activities. For example, the Forest Service must evaluate the relative benefits of alternative uses of Forest Service lands in order to allocate resources. The benefits of leisure activities on those lands is often unknown, while the economic benefits of timber and grazing uses are readily available. It is critical that all resources be evaluated consistently in the decisionmaking process, even though the economic benefit calculation is only one piece of the information necessary for public resource allocation.

Financial benefits, economic impacts, and economic benefits are distinct measures of the importance of leisure activities. There is a great interest in financial benefits and economic impacts (distributive consequences) of leisure activities. Much of the empirical work on financial benefits has been done in the area of corporate returns from employee fitness programs. To our knowledge, that research has rarely been extended to other types of leisure activities. There is clearly a need for researchers in the leisure and outdoor recreation fields to interface with researchers in the health and fitness fields.

The research into *types* of benefits reported elsewhere in this book can affect measurements of economic benefits. Information about human effects of leisure activities will surely affect consumer choices. Those choices, in turn, affect the economic value of goods and services related to the leisure activities. So, while economists do not focus on types of well-being, the outcomes of economic analyses will be affected by research into the types of well-being that occur from leisure activities.

ENDNOTES

[1] Gregory S. Alward and Everard M. Lofting in paper on opportunities for analyzing economic impacts of recreation and tourism expenditures, presented at the 30th Annual Meeting of the Regional Science Association in Philadelphia, Nov. 14-16, 1985.

LITERATURE CITED

Alward, G. S.; Palmer, C. J. 1983. IMPLAN: An input-output analysis for forest service planning. In: Seppala, R.; Row, C.; Morgan, A., eds. Proceedings, First North American Conference on forest sector modeling; 1981, 30 November-4 December; Williamsburg, VA: 131-140.

B.E.R. 1985. Executive fitness: exploring the new corporate lifestyle. Dun's Business Month. 126(6): 64-70.

Baun, B.; Williams, K. 1985. Productivity through fitness (Tenneco: Building on corporate quality through good health). Management Review. 74(6):51-53.

Bishop, R. C. 1987. Economic values defined. In: Decker, D. J.; Goff, G. R., eds. Valuing wildlife: economic and social perspectives. Boulder, CO: Westview Press: 24-33.

Boadway, R.; Bruce, N. 1984. Welfare economics. Oxford: Basil Blackwell Publisher Limited. 344 p.

Dean, G.; Getz, M.; Nelson, L.; Siegfried, J. 1978. The local economic impact of state parks. Journal of Leisure Research. 10(2): 98-111.

Driver, R. W.; Ratliff, R. A. 1982. Employers' perceptions of benefits accrued from physical fitness programs. Personnel Administrator. 27(8): 21-26.

Dwyer, J.; Kelly, J.; Bowes, M. 1977. Improved procedures for valuation of the contribution of recreation to national economic development. Research Report No. 128. Urbana-Champaign, IL: Water Resources Center, Univ. of Illinois. 218 p.

Falkenberg, L. E. 1987. Employee fitness programs: their impact on the employee and the organization. Academy of Management Review. 12(3): 511-522.

Hicks, J. R. 1946. Value and capital. 2nd edition. Oxford: Oxford University Press. 340 p.

Hirshleifer, J. 1980. Price theory and applications. Englewood Cliffs, NJ: Prentice Hall. 506 p.

Johnson, R.; Radtke, H.; Obermiller, F. 1989. The economic impact of tourism sales. Journal of Leisure Research. 21(2): 140-154.

Klock, H. S., III. 1985. Outlook on compensation and benefits. Personnel. 62(7): 13-16.

Kondrasuk, J. N. 1984. Corporate physical fitness programs: the role of the personnel department. Personnel Administrator. 29(12): 75-80.

Kondrasuk, J. N. 1985. Should your company have a physical fitness program? Business. 35(3): 51-53.

Leiber, S. R.; Fesenmaier, D. R.; Bristow, R. S. 1989. Recreation expenditures and opportunity theory: the case of Illinois. Journal of Leisure Research. 21(2): 106-123.

Pechter, K. 1986. Corporate fitness and blue-collar fears. Across the Board. 23(10): 14-21.

Perham, J. 1984. Fitness programs down the line. Dun's Business Month. 124(4): 106-107.

Polzin, P. E.; Schweitzer, D. L. 1975. Economic importance of tourism in Montana. Research Paper INT-171. Ogden, UT: USDA Forest Service, Intermountain Forest and Range Experiment Station. 19 p.

Propst, D. B., ed. 1985. Assessing the economic impacts of recreation and tourism. Asheville, NC: USDA Forest Service, Southeastern Forest Experiment Station. 64 p.

Stoll, J. R.; Bergstrom, J. C.; Jones, L. L. 1988. Recreational boating and its economic impact in Texas. Leisure Sciences. 10: 51-67.

Yochum, G. R.; Agarwal, V. B. 1987. Economic impact of a port on a regional economy: Note. Growth and Change. Summer: 74-87.

Creation and Recreation: Environmental Benefits and Human Leisure

Holmes Rolston, III
Department of Philosophy
Colorado State University
Fort Collins, Colorado

The way in which nature-based recreation and preservation are inseparably entwined is suggested by the word *creation* embedded in the word *recreation*. This is partly an etymological accident, but not totally. Persons off the job are re-created, in the environment of creation. Other recreation involves artifacts, but this kind requires natural history; these connections are not accidental, but biologically and psychologically profound. Persons turn to the natural environment, preserved by humans perhaps as a park, a wilderness, a wildlife refuge, for something they cannot get in the built environment. This "recreation" (if that is the proper word for this re-contacting of creation) demands natural history; such recreation presupposes and results in nature preservation. We shall find these connections deceptively simple, finally profound.

The subtitle also needs exploring. How the adjective "environmental" operates on the noun "benefits" needs to be clarified, as does the meaning of the other noun "leisure." How is human leisure tied to environmental benefits? Exactly what are environmental benefits? To whom do they accrue? How significant are they? Some of this logic of leisure and environment will strain, even explode the words "leisure" and "benefits."

RECREATION AND CREATION

Though some persons work outside, the only time that most of us spend with the sky over our head or the ground under our feet is when we are at leisure. Even those who work in and on nature may also recreate there. We may first seek field and stream to "get away from it all," frustrated with office or factory. But later we discover that we are getting back to it all. In the country, we touch base with something greater than can be found in town. We recontact the natural givens, the archetypal world that runs itself, surrounding and supporting us.

At work we are usually too busy to think about these things, but with more leisure, and a reflective turn, we sometimes want to participate intimately in our ecology. When we are at work we are surrounded by artifacts, using or producing them. We use natural things as resources. In that sense, culture always reworks nature; an artifact produced by work interrupts rather than preserves spontaneous nature. At leisure in nature, we are reminded of what we tend to forget when at work in culture. We are re-created by the creation.

Outside of the work context and in pursuit of a recreation environment, humans now defer to what was there before. As expressed by Congress in the Wilderness Act of 1964, we want regions "where the earth and its community of life are untrammeled by man, where man himself is a visitor who does not remain" (U. S. Congress 1964, sec. 2c). The resolution to be only a visitor who does not remain and to leave natural history untrammeled is ipso facto a resolution to preserve nature. Wildernesses, national parks, and sanctuaries are where humans go on vacation. Such areas are unique in seeking to limit humans to nonconsumptive, nondisruptive uses of the land. Humans resolve that they will not divert significant amounts of energy and materials from these systems of wild nature; they will neither alter natural processes, nor cause the extinction of native species from such natural systems, nor impose artificial materials, energy, processes, and exotic species on them. They will protect them from and prevent or compensate for human alterations.

In the original legislation of 1872, Yellowstone Park was set aside as "a pleasuring-ground for the benefit and enjoyment of the people" (U. S. Congress 1872, Chap. 24). Our park-founding fathers carved that on the gateway arch, designating a place of leisure. But Disneyland, too, is a pleasuring ground for people, and we need to say more today than our fathers about natural pleasuring grounds or we have only a shallow, inadequate description focusing on humanistic benefits and careless about natural preservation. Yellowstone is and ought to be a pleasuring ground for people only insofar as this is commensurate with the preservation of natural history there. The *recreation* there has *creation* embedded in it; the leisure benefits permitted are constrained by environmental preservation.

Two prominent Yellowstone officials have, in modern days, stated a deeper policy. Preservation comes first, and leisure afterward. Douglas Houston says, "The primary purpose of the National Park Service in administering natural areas is to maintain an area's ecosystem in as nearly pristine a condition as possible" (Houston 1971). Glen Cole insists, "The primary purpose of Yellowstone National Park is to preserve natural ecosystems and opportunities for visitors to see and appreciate scenery and native plant and animal life as it occurred in primitive America" (Cole 1969). That is the better order: to preserve nature and for humans to take pleasure in it.

This presumes that humans can and will find pleasure in appreciating spontaneous natural history. Now we do have a critical difference between Yellowstone Park and Disneyland. Both are pleasuring grounds—one takes pleasure in human artifacts and fantasy, in fairy castles and roller coasters; the other takes pleasure in wild nature. Much of our leisure is technology-based, and we require technology to get to Yellowstone. But once there, we want nature-based leisure. If some persons there fail to find pleasure in pristine natural history, so much the worse for them; they need to change their sensitivities, not to alter the state of nature. The sort of recreation encouraged and allowed is constrained by natural history. In Disneyland we rebuild nature to amuse ourselves with artifacts; in Yellowstone we reeducate ourselves to appreciate natural history.

Sometimes when humans recreate they interrupt nature. They hunt and fish, cut firewood, and "harvest" these resources, as we like to put it. It may seem that this type of leisure is no longer entwined with preservation. Even in consumptive recreation, there must be renewability, and so the integrity of the resource is necessary for the recreation. Further, the quality of recreation is often entwined with the preservation of native wildlife. Put-and-take fishing is reduced quality angling; one is catching only hatchery artifacts. A wild trout is a real prize. Quality angling, as opposed to quantity of catch, will want native cutthroat trout on a catch-and-release basis, rather than rainbows in the creel. Some of us think that recreational angling in Yellowstone Park is really not commensurate with streams stocked with exotic, hatchery-bred species. Angling ought to defer to the native species. A fishing pond is one thing; wild nature is something else.

Only about 2% of the contiguous United States remains wilderness, 98% is worked over—farmed, grazed, timbered, hunted, dwelt upon, paved, or otherwise possessed. If we have only a work ethic, then failing to put the remaining wildlands to some use can seem anti-American. But a benefit of leisure is that the work ethic is exploded for the relict wildlands. Not all that we value is labored over. We want to preserve and to enjoy at leisure this pristine 2%. Likewise, when we recreate in rural woodlots, fields, and fencerows, in the semiwild lands of state parks or nature conservancies, we value at leisure what we have not worked to make: wild nature.

Both we and nature must be unoccupied—we from our work and nature from our works. In this kind of recreation, we are free to be ourselves only if natural things are free to be themselves. The preservation of nature and the presence of nature-based nature are, again, empirically and logically inseparable. If such recreation is to be realistic, the nature encountered cannot be an illusion, a fake (though it may perhaps be restored). The historical genesis of the landscape is requisite if the recreational, re-creational experience is to be authentic. We go to Disneyland when we are at leisure, but Disneyland is unreal, a fantasy land. That make-believe recreation is something different.

BENEFITS, ENVIRONMENT, AND LEISURE

Coming at these issues another way, we can explore the connections between benefits, environment, and leisure.

What is an Environmental Benefit?

In human terms, a benefit is an outcome that improves a person's quality and quantity of life, perhaps by improving the society he or she inhabits, perhaps by preventing a harm. If nature-based recreation brings health benefits, economic benefits, social benefits, aesthetic benefits, spiritual benefits, and so on, it is humans who receive these benefits. Following that logic, if nature-based recreation brings environmental benefits, this too is a humanistic benefit. Humans are helped or hurt by the condition of their environment, and thus an environmental benefit is one where an improved environment helps persons; an environmental cost is one where a worsened environment hurts persons.

But notice again (just as recreation was entwined with creation) that an environmental benefit, before it can accrue to persons, first has to happen so as to maintain or improve, or prevent degradation of the natural world. Environmental benefits differ from other outcomes affecting health, society, economics, and spirituality because the immediate beneficiary is not humans. The environment is the direct beneficiary; humans are the secondary beneficiary.

Wild animals can be better or worse off; they have a welfare, as surely as do humans. Trees can be in good or bad condition; forests are made worse by acid rain. A species can be flourishing or in danger; ecosystems can be stable or degraded. Human behaviors can hurt or help the vitality of all these things. So the environment in a generalized sense can be benefited, and the detail of this has to do with the welfare of individual animals and plants, of species populations, of ecosystems, and so on.

Human well-being is tied into the condition of these natural things. These ties are diverse and differ when humans are at work and at leisure. Often when at work, humans take natural resources by value capture. In this sense human welfare and the welfare of animals and plants is negatively correlated. To be better for humans, it must be worse for a deer or a tree—the deer is shot for food and the tree cut for shelter. The grasslands ecosystem is plowed and destroyed when humans plant wheat. In resource use in the everyday sense, when resources are taken for human benefits, wildlife, forests, species, and ecosystems suffer. In an economic sense, when humans labor, natural things must be destroyed. Industry, agriculture, and business are in conflict with preservation.

Even in the economic context, we want renewability. Minerals once mined are gone forever, though they can to some extent be recycled in the economy. Plants grown, animals raised in agriculture, forests clearcut, and water diverted for irrigation are resource uses that require conservation. Mineralogical capital has to be spent, but there is no need to spend biological capital at all. When humans labor in and on the biological world, the human use of natural resources can be by value complementarity as well as by value capture. For it to be well with humans, it must be well with at least the useful trees, and even with the whole forest system in which they grow. In this economic sense, human well-being and the well-being of natural things, so far as these are resources for labor, are positively correlated. It is hard to have an economy doing well in a sick environment. Still, there is not yet *preservation*, only *conservation*.

Preservation comes with humans at leisure. The only sort of "resources" that will be *preserved*, as distinct from being *conserved*, are those "used" at leisure. They are not really used up at all; they are not converted to anything else by labor. They are loved at leisure. Even leisure can sometimes destroy resources; wildlife can be hunted until gone, wildflowers picked until extinct, mineral specimens collected, trails and lakeside campsites trampled and trashed until degraded. So recreation has to take care that it is constrained by preservation. Nature-based recreation that really loves the creation will defer to its integrity. Meanwhile, humans at labor destroy, modify, or at best conserve. Only humans at leisure preserve their environment. Environmental benefits and leisure are more closely connected logically and practically than first appears.

At first it seems odd to suggest that human leisure benefits nature. Rather, it is the other way around. The natural world benefits humans in multiple ways, both when taken as a resource and enjoyed recreationally. Human recreation is epiphenomenal to the natural world, a world that was in place for millennia before humans arrived. The natural world is what it is without benefit of humans. The "benefit" (to strain the word) is a laissez faire benefit. When humans are at this kind of leisure, they by conviction do nothing to interrupt spontaneous nature and may take pains to restore it. They limit their industry, labor, and development so as to leave place for wild nature. Environmental preservation results.

Leisure and Work

We cannot live by leisure alone. Every organism in nature must earn its way; and agriculture, forestry, and industry follow the natural imperative that humans must labor for food and shelter. This much of what is the case we can also endorse as what ought to be. What nature requires (that humans work), and what is the case (that humans must work), we also command (humans ought to work). Otherwise humans cannot flourish and, in extremes, we die. That much of a bread-and-butter work ethic properly opposes a romantic naturalism that wants to leave nature untouched and enjoyed only at leisure. Natural resources must and should be put to multiple uses for the benefit of humans in their culture. Seeking goods of their kind, humans must modify the natural kinds.

But labor, industry, and business form only a part of our manifold human relations with nature. Nature as a resource to work on should not entirely preempt these other relations that are also important. After business hours, when we are at leisure and no longer consuming nature, we pursue our quality of life in ways that are recreational, residential, aesthetic, appreciative, pastoral, scientific, philosophical, and religious. Some areas should be absolutely free and others relatively free of human management and intervention. Some spaces should remain rural, some wild. There should be mockingbirds and cottontails, bobwhites and pristine sunsets, mountain vistas and canyonlands. The preservation of these things is valued for what they spontaneously are, not less than the transformation of other things into our artifacts.

Leisure and work are opposites, but not mutually exclusive categories. When we are not at work for pay, we may still be doing the chores. On vacation, we may work hard chopping wood or carrying a pack uphill. Much work has been spent on mountain cabins. Is a vacation with Outward Bound spent at leisure? Some persons do at work what they would nevertheless do if independently wealthy; and the really fortunate, such as an enthusiastic interpretive naturalist, or, to take my own case, a philosopher, can hardly distinguish between their leisure and their work. Leisure does not always mean pleasure, as hunters caught in a snowstorm can testify. Still, we are typically said to be at "leisure" when we are not at work drawing pay, not exploiting resources, not producing any product or service. In that sense, we can only appreciate something "for its own sake" when at leisure. If I am making a resource out of it, I am too otherwise occupied to consider it freely, objectively.

In certain respects, leisure time is superior to work time. A bumper sticker reports that a bad day fishing is better than a good day at work. Sometimes we are lazy and dislike work. But going deeper, in leisure time we are free for self-expression. At work we must do what the boss says, turn out what the customers need; but off duty we can be ourselves, self-motivated. The fortunate in work find it a vehicle of their self-expression, but even those persons also are who they are as much in their leisure as in their work. When such

self-expression occurs in enjoyment of the natural world, we must resist a tendency to think that the benefits associated with leisure must be soft. Some will say that they cannot be hard benefits, since one is not at work. One is off-duty, idle, not contributing to the gross national product. But all work and no play makes Jack a dull boy; at worst, it also degrades environments, and at best can go no further than conserving them.

At leisure we do not utilize; rather, we participate. We figure out who we are and where we are. This benefit of leisure is, if you like, mature character coupled with environmental appreciation and thus environmental protection. Those who join the Audubon Society, the Wilderness Society, the Sierra Club, or the National Wildlife Federation do so not to work on wildlands but to enjoy them, entwined with the preservation of the wild for us and for what they are in themselves. Leisure and preservation are entwined.

LIFE SUPPORT BENEFITS

When humans recreate in nature in pensive moods, they learn again that culture remains tethered to the biosystem. The technosphere of their work is coupled with the biosphere they enjoy at leisure. The options within their built environments, however expanded, provide no release from nature. Our economic wealth may be labored, but our ecologic welfare has deeper, natural roots. Humans depend on airflow, water cycles, sunshine, nitrogen fixation, photosynthesis, food chains, decomposition bacteria, fungi, the ozone layer, insect pollination, earthworms, speciation and reproduction, climates, polar ice caps, oceans, and genetic materials.

Forests and soil, sunshine and rain, rivers and sky, the everlasting hills, the rolling prairies, the cycling seasons—these are superficially pleasant scenes in which to recreate at depth the surrounding creation that supports life. The central goods of the biosphere were in place long before humans arrived. They are the timeless natural givens that support everything else. An ecology always lies in the background of every culture. Some sort of inclusive environmental fitness is required of even the most technically advanced civilization.

These ecological values contribute positively to human experiences, and so humans want to preserve them for their beneficial consequences. But the ecological processes also are there apart from humans being here. Nature is an evolutionary ecosystem, with humans a late add-on. Nature is an objective value carrier; when humans work they cash in on, and spend, what is naturally given. Earth is a fortunate, fertile place, a place where life has been nourished. This concept begins to value nature not simply as a resource for human life support, but for nature's exuberant support of all the fauna and flora. Earth can seem a satisfactory place because humans have found it a prosperous place to reside and work, but also because a myriad of species have found satisfactory environments, life-supporting niches into which they are well-fitted.

The "benefits," the good consequences, within this earthy life-support system are not really just matters of late-coming human interests (though it may seem so when we are actively on the job). At leisure, we are less naive. We are able to consider the living landscape for what it is without human labor. Earth is historically a remarkable, valuable place prior to the human arrival, culture, and industry. The human part in the drama is perhaps the most valuable event of all, and human labor does produce things of value unprecedented in spontaneous nature. But it seems parochial, as well as uninformed ecologically, to say that the human part alone in the drama establishes all its worth and is the only benefit to consider. Ecology is not something subjective, not something that goes on in the human mind. It is not something produced by human agriculture or business. Ecology is objective in the world; it must and ought to be preserved as the foundational support of all life, both human and nonhuman.

At work, one needs to be in the black; but at leisure, one knows that the most important color on Earth is green.

AESTHETIC BENEFITS

What is preserved in a park, a wilderness, a wildlife refuge, a water gap, an offshore island, a mountain on the skyline is not merely the life-supporting environment; we preserve the natural world with its possibility for dynamic aesthetic encounter. There is a large aesthetic component in all preservation of landscapes and wildlife. We want clean air not simply to breathe for life support but also to see through when enjoying scenery, and hence we amended (in 1977) the Clean Air Act to set air quality standards higher in scenic areas. Recreation and preservation are entwined again.

Sometimes people recreate in nature to show what they can do; they want game to shoot, a cliff sound enough for pitons, a snow-packed trail to ski. Sometimes they recreate to be let in on nature's show; they want to enjoy the aerial skills of the hummingbird at the bergamot, the scenic beauty of the Grand Tetons, to listen to wolves howl. The one activity uses nature as an outdoor gymnasium; the other activity—really more contemplation—uses nature as an outdoor theatre. Now it is not life's support in the landscape so much as it is beauty in life and landscape that recreates. Nature's show must be there to be enjoyed.

A critical difference between aesthetic appreciation of art objects and of natural history is that the one is of human craft and the other of spontaneous nature. We are enjoying aesthetic creativity in nature, and if we discover that the supposed natural spontaneity has in fact been engineered by human ingenuity, the aesthetic experience collapses. At the cinema, the play, the symphony, the audience response is carefully controlled. In the field, the wildlife is organic form in locomotion, on the loose, without designs on the human beholder. The animal does not care to come near, sit still, stay long, or please. At this theatre we are not beholders of a programmed performance but of spontaneous nature—an eagle soaring, a snake slithering, a coyote on the run, the fiddleheads of ferns, purple mountains' majesties, the roar of cataracts, expansive seascapes.

At leisure, we may enjoy television wildlife programs and wildlife art and photography. Compared with direct experience in the wild, these are poor substitutes for the real thing, because we begin to admire the artist's brush strokes, and the photographer's skill as they have captured the wildlife. The event in nature is not presented but represented. Interest in the art form mingles with interest in the wildlife or scenery depicted. We admire the workman who entertains us in our leisure. Aesthetic experience of spontaneous nature requires the preservation of the wild in itself. We cannot benefit aesthetically on the scene, unless the integrity of natural history is maintained.

At leisure we may visit the zoo, but, again, compared with direct experience in the wild, zoos do little to preserve wildlife aesthetically. We may forget the bears we have seen in a zoo; we do not forget bobcats we by chance encounter in the wild. At leisure in the city park, we may enjoy a walk with our dog, but a thousand such walks are less than the howl of a wolf heard when returning to camp at dusk.

At leisure in wild nature, we sometimes enjoy a sense of the sublime. The sense of abyss overlooking a gorge is aesthetic, as is the eerie chill when, nearing a stormy summit, one's hair stands on end in the charged air. Such experiences are unlikely to be had in built environments, whether at work or at leisure. They are unlikely to be had in factories, or even at the Metropolitan Museum. For such experiences, we must have environments that are primeval and pristine.

After seeing the mating dance of the woodcock, Aldo Leopold concluded, "The woodcock is a living refutation of the theory that the utility of a game bird is to serve as a target, or to pose gracefully on a slice of toast. No one would rather hunt woodcock in October than I but since learning of the sky dance I find myself calling one or two birds enough. I must be sure that, come April, there will be no dearth of dancers in the sunset sky" (Leopold 1969: 34). His aesthetic experience of the dance demanded the preservation of the birds he so much enjoyed. It constrained how far he could enjoy the hunt.

At such moments of leisure we realize that our economy, benefited so much from what we produce at work, is surely rich enough that we can afford to keep wild things; it is not so rich that we can afford to lose them.

SCIENTIFIC BENEFITS

Most of us think that science is work, not leisure. Certainly professional scientists must work for pay. During their leisure, they produce no scientific benefits. So what can be the connection between leisure and scientific benefits? Sometimes amateur scientists study ferns or birds. We might not want to call such serious concerns recreational at all. Such pursuits are perhaps not for pay, but neither are they exactly play. They involve curious humans at work figuring out what goes on in the natural world. They are a kind of recreation gone in pursuit of creation. In that sense, persons at such leisure studies produce scientific benefits. Kenneth Kent Mackenzie, who produced the major taxonomic study of *Carex*, was a New York City corporation lawyer by trade (Mackenzie 1940). Fred Hermann made some of the major moss collections in Colorado on weekends and after he retired as Curator of the Forest Service Herbarium in Fort Collins.

Recreation, since it requires creation, is compatible with those sciences that are conducted in the field. Professional biology also requires the natural world. Although much activity in recent science requires elaborate instrumentation and analytical equipment in indoor laboratories (electron microscopes and ultracentrifuges), the subject matter of all natural science lies first and fundamentally in field natural history. Any big scale biology still requires its laboratories outdoors. When and where humans at leisure resolve to leave the natural world as it spontaneously is, we have such an outdoor laboratory. The great primeval theatre of nature, which provides life support, which is enjoyed aesthetically, can also be studied scientifically; and no matter whether this is done by persons at work or at leisure.

The answers to great unanswered questions lie hidden in the spontaneous natural environment. Despite ecology's progress in recent decades, it is still the most juvenile natural science. Scientists have little idea how evolution takes place at ecosystem levels. Successive levels of biochemical organization have properties that cannot be predicted from simpler levels, and the least known level of biological organization is that of landscape ecology. We are not yet clear about what the natural successions were, or are, over a few hundred years in many regional systems. We do not yet know all the effects of the big predators on their ecosystems, the extent to which wolves regulate the ungulates which regulate the condition of the range.

Scientists do not know why the balds in the Southern Appalachians are there or why treeline in the alpine Rocky Mountains varies as it does. Scientists debate whether and how insects regulate forest productivity, uncertain whether insects are detrimental to trees or have coevolved with them to the mutual benefit of both. In analogous ways, insect outbreaks may provide beneficial effects such as those of fire that we have only lately come to recognize. The answers to these questions are likely to come from the same wild lands as those on which people recreate, where preservation simultaneously serves recreational and scientific needs.

Nor are the connections between recreators at leisure and scientists at study simply from the happy coincidence that both want pristine nature. The kinds of recreational experience that humans enjoy on wild lands is often more or less science-based. Everyone who stands on the rim of the Grand Canyon is at leisure, and not one of them understands the Grand Canyon unless it is seen through a scientist's eyes. We learn that the Canyon is five thousand feet deep and was within fifty feet of its present depth when *Homo sapiens* arrived on the planet. That kind of experience endorses Teddy Roosevelt's plea, "Leave it as it is. You cannot improve on it. The ages have been at work on it, and man can only mar it" (Roosevelt 1903).

Tens of thousands of persons drive over Trail Ridge Road in Rocky Mountain National Park each season and visit the interpretive center there, with their experiences enriched by what each learns from scientists about the alpine life and its harsh processes. Experience of such tenacious and fragile life, aided by interpretive naturalists, feeds in turn a resolution to preserve the tundra. The recreational experience and the scientific interpretation team up to produce preservation of the natural system; and the natural system, preserved, feeds back to produce future benefits for science and recreation alike.

HISTORICAL BENEFITS

These scientific benefits are entwined with historical benefits of two kinds: cultural and natural. Few persons are professional historians. History is something most of us learn at leisure. But without history we cannot know who we are and where we are. As we first learn it, history is cultural history, that of politics and kings, of the wars and migrations of peoples. Even this cultural history can benefit from preserving wild lands. New World cultures remain close to the memory of a primitive landscape. Forests, prairies, and ranges ought to be preserved as souvenir places for each generation's learning (however secondarily or critically) our forefather's experiences, learned there quite as much as in the Minuteman Historical Park. They provide a lingering echo of what we once were, of a way we once passed. There is nothing like the howl of a wolf to resurrect the ghost of Jim Bridger. Experience of the wild mixes the romance and the reality of the past in present experience. It is impossible to understand American history without an appreciation of the continent that Americans settled; and some of that continent, preserved, yet wild, will feed this sense of history.

History is natural history—not as we first learn it, but as history really first took place. Beyond cultural history, wild lands as natural history provide the profoundest historical museum of all, a relic of the way the world was in 99.99% of past time. The natural tale, how things are, how they came to be, is a story worth telling, and natural history is the textbook from which it can be deciphered and taught. Human roots lie in it and humans find the story a delightful intellectual pursuit. That history too has an epic quality—the eras of the dinosaurs, of the glaciers, of the inland seas, of the Appalachian miogeosyncline, of Lake Bonneville, of the Rocky Mountain orogeny, of bison ranging across the plains.

Tourists at Yellowstone learn that anaerobic bacteria still present in those steaming pools exist in an optimal thermal habitat that survives little changed from the time when life evolved in an oxygen-free atmosphere, and that further studies might furnish clues to the origins of life on Earth. Such recreation has touched creation, touched history, and, after vacation, we return to work with a better sense of place and perspective. We need more than a little leisure to think across a billion years, and, afterward, we return to our own work with less hurry and more patience.

ENDANGERED SPECIES/ ECOSYSTEMS BENEFITS

When recreation takes place in the presence of endangered species (and few pristine areas are without their rare species), leisure mixes with serious preservation. Recreation again touches creation. Such concerns appear in the Endangered Species Act of 1973, where Congress lamented the lack of adequate concern for and conservation of "threatened and endangered species" and mixed this with "esthetic, ecological, educational, historical, recreational, and scientific value to the Nation and its people" (U. S. Congress

1973, sec. 2). National parks, wildlife refuges, forests, wildernesses—for whose benefit are these preserved? An old and still good answer is that they are for the multiple uses of the people, including their recreational use. A new and powerful answer is that these are the habitats of grizzly bears and whooping cranes, of *Trillium persistens* and the palila, and that these endangered species have something like a biotic right to exist. The deeper good being preserved is life itself, indeed the highest of priorities.

The order of priority is preservation first, which ipso facto benefits the wild species, and, secondly, recreation (or education, aesthetics, science), as it may benefit humans. These types of recreational benefits are unavailable unless these rare species are there, but such recreational benefits defer to the preservation of species. In Rocky Mountain National Park, at lakes containing mineral salts frequented by bighorn sheep, a Park Service sign cautions visitors not to approach too closely because harassment of the sheep can result in their death; it concludes, "Respect their right to life." Visitors enjoy seeing the bighorns, but only at more distance than they might otherwise prefer, because such distance respects their life. Indeed, the Specimen Mountain trail is closed entirely during lambing season. Mountaineers have long enjoyed climbing Lumpy Ridge there, but no longer during nesting season. The area is closed as prime habitat for endangered peregrine and prairie falcons.

Unfortunately, those who recreate outdoors in the United States no longer see 500 species and subspecies that have become extinct since 1600 (Opler 1976). Unfortunately, they rarely see another 500 species that are (officially or unofficially) threatened and endangered. People enjoy seeing these things of course, and they do so at leisure. No one is paid to go and visit the Devil's Hole with its pupfish, or to take a field trip to the endangered Arizona hedgehog cactus, *Echinocereus triglochidiatus* var. *arizonicus*. We do not save these things because they are of economic benefit. They are of no use to anybody at work. To the contrary, the list in the Endangered Species Act does not even mention economic benefits. It blends such things as recreation, science, aesthetics, ecology, and history. If anyone wants to plead economic benefits against the preservation of an endangered species, that case must be argued before a special high-level committee.

A birdwatcher spots a pair of whooping cranes in a flock of sandhill cranes and never thereafter forgets the rare birds, a vanishing life form of beauty. In the months and years following, reading of an increase or decrease in their numbers, he hopes for their recovery and fears their extinction, hopes above all that humans will not cause their extinction. An ingredient in this hope is the memory of how once he shared aesthetically a moment of wonder, of reverence for life. His leisure experience—if "leisure" is the right word for such experience—is inseparably entwined with the preservation of species. Notice always that the preservation comes first and the leisure follows. People want these things there whether they or anybody else sees them or not.

RELIGIOUS/PHILOSOPHICAL BENEFITS

We are having trouble with what counts as leisure activity— studying *Carex,* learning one's ecology, re-contacting the primeval creation. Being religious and philosophizing are not activities that many engage in for pay. A philosophy degree is worthless for getting a job. On the other hand, religion is too vital in life to think of as recreational. Yet rest from work and the sabbath are closely connected in the Judeo-Christian tradition. Six days we are to work, but the seventh is a sabbath for worship and rest. We can think of those who are religious in the out-of-doors as being, if you like, on sabbath. Recreation once more blends with creation.

Nature generates poetry, philosophy, and religion, and at its deepest educational capacity we are awed and humbled by staring into the stormy surf or the midnight sky, by overlooking the canyonlands, or by an overflight of migrating geese. Mountaintop experiences, sunsets, canyon strata, or a meadow of dogstooth violets can generate experiences of "a motion and spirit that impels . . . and rolls through all things" (Wordsworth 1798). The natural environment becomes something like a sacred text, a cathedral. For wilderness purists intensely, and for most persons occasionally, outdoor settings provide religious experiences. The wilderness elicits cosmic questions, differently from town. Some of the most moving experiences attainable are to be had there. Encounter with nature integrates people, protects them from pride, gives a sense of proportion and place, teaches them what to expect and what to be content with, and comforts them with the natural certainties.

Nature is a vast scene of birth and death, springtime and harvest, permanence and change, of budding, flowering, withering away, of pain and pleasure, of success and failure, of beauty giving way to ugliness and again to beauty. From the contemplation of it all there comes a feeling valuing life's transient beauty sustained over chaos. There is a music to it all, even when in a minor key. It is wild lands above all that carry this signature of time and eternity, and their preservation and enjoying these religious experiences are inseparably entwined.

A forest wilderness is a sacred space. "The groves were God's first temples" (Bryant 1825). There we recognize God's creation, or the Ultimate Reality, or a Nature sacred in itself. I become astonished that the forest should be there, spontaneously generated and regenerated on its own, astonished that I should be there, immersed in it and struggling to come to terms with it. There are no forests on Mars or Saturn; none elsewhere in our solar system, perhaps none elsewhere in our galaxy. But Earth's forests are indisputably here, an archetypal expression of the creative process. There is more operational organization, more genetic history, more of interest going on, in a handful of forest humus than in the rest of the universe, so far as we know. The forest is presence and sacrament of ultimate sources. The forest is primal ground, as nearly as we can encounter this in phenomenal experience. The wilderness works on a traveler's soul as much as it does his muscles.

The forest is where the "roots" are, where life rises from the ground. A wild forest is, after all, something objectively there—there without benefit of human subjectivity. The phenomenon of forests is so widespread, persistent, and diverse, appearing almost wherever moisture and climatic conditions permit, that forests cannot be accidents or anomalies, but rather must be a characteristic, systemic expression of the creative process. Some experiences in old-growth forests are simply unavailable elsewhere.

If we must put it so, overworking the term, nature is a philosophical "resource," as well as bringing scientific, recreational, aesthetic, or economic benefits. But, using a better word, a word that combines the protectionist attitude with the religious mood, we want a wildlife or wilderness "sanctuary." At these sacrosanct, holy places we can get near to ultimacy. Humans are programmed to ask why, and the natural world is the cradle of our spirituality. The unexamined life is not worth living, said Socrates, and no one pays us to examine life; that must be done at leisure. Contrary to Socrates—less wise when he lamented that trees and fields could not teach him anything—life cannot be fully examined until examined in its ecology and evolutionary history.

It profanes such experiences and nature alike to see an archetypal natural world and then to take no interest in its preservation. The life that examines itself in its evolutionary ecosystem finds that what we are subjectively experiencing lies within something objectively miraculous. When we argue for preservation, such values will again be said to be "soft" beside the "hard" values of commerce. They are vague, philosophical, subjective, impossible to quantify, or demonstrate. Perhaps. But it does not follow that such values are either unreal in human experience or unreal in the forest. What is really meant is that such values lie deep. We want to keep our roots.

INTRINSIC NATURAL VALUES

Pointed in this direction already by concerns for endangered species and their biotic right to exist, by the wish to leave some wilderness untrammeled by humans, by philosophical and religious experiences in encounter with creation, those who recreate in the natural environment reach beyond human benefits to intrinsic values in the natural order. Wild creatures are of value in themselves, not just as resources for our use and pleasure. Encountering the creation, past concerns of recreation, we discover that values have been created in nonhuman lives. At leisure we resolve to preserve environmental benefits in the nonhuman sense.

The wild creatures defend their own lives, because they have a good of their own. Animals hunt and howl, seek shelter, build nests and sing, care for their young, flee from threats, grow hungry, thirsty, hot, tired, excited, sleepy, seek out their habitats and mates. They suffer injury and lick their wounds. They can know security and fear, endurance and fatigue, comfort and pain. Even plants have biological needs—water, nutrients, sunlight; they can be injured and suffer stress, despite the fact that they feel no pain.

Indeed, in this sense, every organism defends its own life. Every genetic set has a program it is set to execute; a life is a spontaneous motion toward such a goal. Every organism resists dying and assimilates environmental materials to its own needs, struggling for health and resisting disease. Each organism has goods of its kind independently of the question whether these are goods for humankind. Humans recreating outdoors may enjoy being let in on these goods of a nonhuman kind. Beyond this enjoyment, one of the benefits to be preserved outdoors is these nonhuman goods—the flourishing in rural and wild places of these lives other than our own. These creatures, too, prefer their wild outdoors, and we want the natural environment preserved not simply because it is good for us, but because it is good for eagles and bighorn sheep, good for an everglades ecosystem or a salt marsh. Just so far as the environmental integrity is incomplete, the experiences sought are incomplete.

SOURCES AND RESOURCES

The word *source* is embedded in the word *resource,* like the word *creation* is embedded in *recreation.* With soil, timber, or game, the meaning of "resource" is clear enough. Humans tap into spontaneous nature, dam water, smelt ores, domesticate, manage, and harvest, redirecting natural courses to become our resources. We wanted potatoes, but the fields grew worthless brush. We wanted logs dovetailed around us

as a home, but the world gave only standing trees. We rearrange natural properties creatively to meet our needs. Molybdenum serves as an alloy of steel. Vincristine and vinblastine, extracted from a Madagascar periwinkle, are used to treat Hodgkin's disease and leukemia. Such resource use can persuade us that the benefits carried by nature almost always come when humans work at it, make over natural sources into our resources.

But after work, we also find that at leisure we want some nature preserved and pristine. If one insists on the word, we can still think of nature as a resource, but resources now seem to be coming in two kinds: the ordinary kind which are rearranged into artifacts; and the extraordinary, wild type which we impact as little as possible. Contrary to typical resource use, recreational visitors come to the Teton wilderness on its own terms and do not reform it to theirs. Humans ordinarily value resources they can make over, but here value what they will not disturb lest they devalue it, although they do wish to visit it.

Well, some will reply, nature offers some resources that take no redoing or consuming, only looking and enjoying. Most are commodities to be drawn upon, but others are amenities left as is. Everything is a resource, really—if it is worth preserving at all. The argument cites how humans redirect nature to their benefit, and then turns to apparent nonresources. Nevada authorities labor to save the Devil's Hole pupfish, which requires reduced water drawdown for ranching. Southwest developers agree not to build the Marble Canyon Dam, and members of the Wilderness Society contribute money to save wildernesses, some nearby which they expect to visit, and some remote, as in Alaska, which they do not. But some humans are fascinated by the pupfish, run rafts down the Grand Canyon, visit the Indian Peaks, enjoy knowing the Alaskan wilds are there, and hope their children may visit them. What we want is high quality wilderness experience that improves human life.

But perhaps the resource orientation is only a half-truth and afterward logically misguided, because man is the only measure of things. Everything is defined in relation to us. One is not so much looking to *resources* as to *sources,* seeking relationships in an elemental stream of being with transcending integrities. Our place in the natural world necessitates resource relationships, but there comes a point when humans want to know how we belong in this world, not how it belongs to us. We want to get ourselves defined in relation to nature, not just to define nature in relation to us. A powerful emotion when leaving culture and our works to return to nature and its works is the sense of entrance into a natural scene that is there and flourishing independently of any human works, resources, or managerial control. The forces by which these run are not human forces; they are the biological and physical sources that have generated the world. They ought to and must be preserved. This larger appreciation of nature, with appropriate conduct, is what we figure out at our leisure.

PERSONAL RESIDENCE IN NATURAL HISTORY

When free from the demands of work, at leisure we realize an attachment to landscape. Whatever our options in culture, however we rebuild our environments by our labors, the world is not just our resource but also our residence, where we dwell for a lifetime. If our residence is a house, the house must be some place, and even if in a city, the city, too, must lie on a landscape. In wilderness areas humans may resolve to be only visitors who do not remain, but we have to reside somewhere. On the 98 percent of the continent that humans occupy, sooner or later our residence must be and ought to be natural not in the pristine sense but by keeping much of the rural and the wild about the places where we live. There is entwined residence.

The art of life, if we wish to use the term "art" for something we humans make, is to reside with an appropriate culture embedded in the continuing natural world. We enjoy the seasons, the vital regenerative powers of life, the life support, the proportions of time and place. We realize something of the richness and integrity of what is taking place on the landscape. We must not think of leisure as only activities that take place trivially when we are idle; leisure in the broad sense is lifestyle larger than work. Leisure in the ecological sense is our being at home in this world in which we reside. Human habits also need a habitat.

There follows a sample test of your sensitivity in your resident environment. The items are only suggestive; some will apply at particular seasons and places and to particular persons. Notice how again and again this sense of personal residence requires and results in an abiding natural world as well.

- Name a half-dozen wildflowers currently in bloom in a nearby natural environment you frequently visit. Where can violets first be found in the spring? What will be the last flowers of autumn?
- Recall an experience appreciating nature aesthetically—a sunset, a cumulus cloud, a snowflake, the flair of an elm, a flight of geese overhead—within the last week.

- Do you have a sense of seasons passing (beyond calendar dates), a sense of the day passing (beyond o'clock)? Do you ever check time by looking at sun or sky, or think seasons by looking at a flower or bird that has arrived, or disappeared? When was your last experience of geological time?
- Recall a natural place—a swimming hole, a waterfall, a tree or boulder in the meadow, a mountain summit, a country road, a shoreline, a bay—that you enjoyed as a child, one to which you could not return without bringing goose pimples or a lump to your throat.
- Name a half-dozen birds now resident in, or migrating through, your environment. Where is the nearest active bird's nest? What birds now present will leave, come winter or summer?
- What large mammal did you last see in the wild? Small mammal?
- What encounter with an animal, bird, or plant recently took you by surprise, so much so that you turned aside from what you were doing to observe it?
- What fauna and flora inhabited the landscape on which your home is located before humans lived there? Where is the nearest that each of these can now be found? Can you name your native ecosystem?
- What species are especially characteristic of your ecosystem—not found or more difficult to find when you travel further north, south, east, or west? What is your state animal, flower, bird?
- What species are endangered in your state? Which are not officially listed but ought to be?
- What local natural area that you formerly enjoyed has been so much degraded by development that you are disappointed when you return there?
- If all the human-made noises were to cease, what cries, calls, or natural sounds could you expect to hear after dark at your home or in a nearby natural area?
- Where is the nearest wild or semiwild area large enough that it would take a day on foot to cross it? How much time have you spent in this area?
- What part of your local natural environment—birds, flowers, insects, trails, fishing spots, tackle, flies and baits to use, hunting areas, drainage patterns and names of streams, types of flowers and vegetables that grow best in your climate—do you know particularly well, so much so that others seek you out for information?

- Recall a recent newspaper story or television feature dealing with biological or environmental conservation.
- When did you last write a congressman or other official about a matter of environmental concern? Of what conservation group are you a member? Have you made any recent contribution toward environmental conservation?
- What was the most recent natural area in your state to be protected by federal, state, or private designation? For what areas is protection still being sought?
- What is the next outing you plan that will increase your familiarity with your natural environment? What has been your most memorable such outing this year?
- How many hours did you spend last week with your feet on the ground? With the sky over your head?
- When did you last act, or refuse to act, in encounter with nature out of moral conviction?
- When was your last encounter with birth or death in the natural world? When did you last pause with a sense of mystery before nature? With a sense of assurance, or a shudder? Recall a recent experience of the sublime, or religious experience outdoors. Where, if you could, would you most like to be buried?

These are all activities of leisure in that they do not occur when we are at labor; they do not belong to commerce, industry, agriculture, or business. They belong to a proper named person who lives in Montana, Utah, Newfoundland, on the tall grass prairie, or the Cape Cod coastline.

KEEPING LIFE WONDERFUL

We ought to keep life wonderful, and so we must keep a natural wonderland. In more subdued language, we ought to keep life natural, and only by keeping nature around us can we keep life natural. Experiences of wonder take place for most persons when they are at leisure; not many find much that is sublime in the office or at the factory. Since there is no wonder present in nature apart from humans, we could say that humans preserve nature as a catalyst for human wonder, valued for its capacity to elicit these experiences. Humans desire an environment sophisticated enough to match their wonderful brains. From another perspective, we ask whether such wonder (taking place in wonderful brains) can be generated except in the presence of something worthy enough to induce it, which suggests that nature is intrinsically a wonderland. Such a natural wonderland generates not only wonder in humans, but also their resolution to preserve it. Natural wonders keep human life wonder full when humans keep a world full of such wonders.

LITERATURE CITED

Bryant, W. C. 1825. A forest hymn.

Cole, G. F. 1969. Elk and the Yellowstone ecosystem. Yellowstone National Park. 14 p.

Houston, D. B. 1971. Ecosystems of national parks. Science. 172:648-651.

Leopold, A. 1969. A Sand County almanac. New York, NY: Oxford University Press. 226 p.

Mackenzie, K. K. 1940. North American cariceae. New York, NY: New York Botanical Garden.

Opler, P. A. 1976. The parade of passing extinctions: a survey of extinctions in the U. S. The Science Teacher. 43 (9):30-34.

Roosevelt, T. 1903. Address at the Grand Canyon, recorded in The New York Sun. May 7.

U. S. Congress. 1872. Yellowstone Act. 17 Stat 82 (Boston, MA: Little Brown, and Co. 1873).

U. S. Congress. 1964. Public Law 88-577. Wilderness Act. 78 Stat. 891.

U. S. Congress. 1973. Public Law 93-205. Endangered Species Act. 87 Stat. 884.

Wordsworth. W. 1798. Lines composed a few miles above Tintern Abbey.

III.

RESPONSES FROM DISCIPLINARY PERSPECTIVES

A Psychophysiological Perspective, with Emphasis on Relationships Between Leisure, Stress, and Well-Being

Andrew Baum
Uniformed Services University of Health Sciences
F. Edward Hebert School of Medicine
Bethesda, Maryland

The opinions or assertions contained herein are the private ones of the author and are not to be construed as official or reflecting the views of the Department of Defense or the Uniformed Services University of the Health Sciences.

The benefits of leisure—or more properly stated, the necessity of leisure—have been well-documented in this volume. Ranging from the increases in cardiovascular performance discussed by Froelicher and Froelicher, and by Paffenbarger, Hyde, and Dow; to the social psychological benefits noted by Ajzen and psychological need fulfillment discussed by Driver, Tinsley, and Manfredo; the positive effects of leisure are clear. The issues of interest then, are to understand the nature of these benefits, the reasons for them, and the best ways of meeting needs for relaxation, recreation, or rest.

Several barriers to studying leisure are apparent. Among these is the great diversity of potential leisure activities that must be considered. While not intending to be circular, it is very difficult not to classify anything that one considers a leisure activity as a leisure activity. If one spends the weekend writing a book—is this leisure? If so, what makes it different from writing during the week in one's office? Does it need to be done at home to constitute leisure? What if someone freely chooses to work when he or she does not need to—is that leisure? That self-actualization and immense positive affect can be derived from one's work is widely held. Is this also true of leisure?

Such questions abound, and as a newcomer to the area, I have likely pulled out several dusty, old, well-debated issues that do not have very satisfactory answers. But as I read the chapters in this volume and the work I could find on this topic, I was immediately faced with the extraordinarily complex task of studying something I have taken for granted for years. Of course we like leisure, of course it is a need, for why else would we engage in it? Yet, the difficulties inherent in defining and operationalizing it as a workable construct reflect only a small part of the difficulty involved in investigating its occurrence.

My work has focused on stress and ways in which psychophysiological changes due to stress can contribute to health and illness. In many ways the work on leisure discussed in this volume is the antithesis of stress; one can assume and easily defend the notion that one virtue of leisure is stress reduction. Relaxation tends to alleviate many of the symptoms of stress (e.g., Benson 1975, Kiecolt-Glaser and Glaser 1987), and activities that fill leisure time are often done in groups, strengthening social support ties that also appear to negate some negative aspects of stress (Cohen and Wills 1985). These perspectives are clearly reflected in some of the chapters in this book (see, for example, Burch and Hamilton Smith; Hull; or Ulrich, Dimberg, and Driver). However, there are other ways to think of this. Some believe that stress affects the speed at which we age, so one could argue that the reduction of stress by leisure activity could make us live longer. It certainly makes sense that it could make us stay healthier, but we know little of why this might be so. Aside from the clear desirability of understanding the mechanisms by which these benefits occur, we need to establish meaningful outcome measures of these leisure-stress-health relationships beyond ultimate impacts such as longer life. In addition to behavioral and quality of life measures, psychophysiological measures are important in establishing these relationships.

Overlaying the complexity of studying leisure is the question of whether it is a desirable add-on to life or an integral part of life's fabric. Should we proceed as if we are studying something like a vitamin supplement that is a desirable adjunct, or as if we are studying the consequences of spiritual malnutrition? Is this a meaningful issue only because of the ways in which we have evolved? My psychophysiological orientation leads me to think of things in terms of optimal balances (e.g., homeostasis, regulation of positive feedback) rather than absolutes, so that when studying stress, the issue is not how to prevent stress (a task which could be deemed impossible) but how to create a balance of positive and negative experiences that produces optimal mood and well-being. This leads me to view leisure as a central part of life, much like sleeping, and to see our task as maintaining needed activities and researching the consequences of not doing so. It is possible, though seemingly less likely, that increasing one's leisure above a particular level will increase health or activate the body's defenses against illness. It is more likely that not having enough leisure is stressful, exacerbates the consequences of other stressors, or otherwise causes us physical and psychological hardship. Psychophysiological research is needed to test hypotheses such as these.

One way to facilitate the process of understanding leisure and its benefits is to derive overarching theories or perspectives with which it can be viewed. Exercise is leisure for many, but not all, and should not be synonymous with leisure. Many use it as if it were. Natural environments are pleasant, relaxing, and stress-reducing for many, but urban settings cannot be dismissed as not providing such opportunities. In fact, it is again a balance of natural and human-made landscape features and conveniences, of exercise and rest, that may make leisure optimally positive.

Another benefit of considering leisure independent of the specific activity is the irresolvable problem introduced by self-selection. People choose their leisure activities, and while they also exercise some control over how much time is devoted to them, this choice of time spent seems more likely to be externally determined than selection of activities. To think of these choices as unrelated is naive, but it is probably the case that choice of activity reflects a lifetime of preferences, conditioning, and so on. Is it useful to think of leisure as anything, anywhere, that fulfills certain needs and study the effects of having more or less of it? Or should we begin by focusing our attention on the effects of nonurban, serene, or otherwise "picturesque" settings independent of preferences or need?

Let me provide an example. Work can be, and frequently is, stressful. Leisure serves as a balance to work, in part by providing restorative refractory periods in which the pressures of work are less salient. Should characteristics of one's work pressures determine the shape of one's leisure? Short-cycle jobs that yield products quickly and often may place different demands on one than longer cycle jobs, in which products are less frequent and more time is spent on each. Producing machine parts on an assembly line is shorter cycle than manufacturing them by hand; far more products will come from the former, at a much greater rate. The benefits of such a job—quick turn-around and completion of tasks, frequent rewards, etc.—may outweigh costs such as loss of control over one's schedule, or may balance the self-efficacy enhancing aspects of a slower, more craftsman-like situation. But it is likely that the shorter cycle job makes it easier to relax or play—one may be considerably less likely to bring one's work home with them in the shorter cycle situation and choice of distracting or "all-consuming" leisure activities may be more critical in the latter case.

Several of the chapters in this volume reflect assumptions that derive from societal biases. The natural, beautiful, and relaxing is considered conducive to leisure; while the human-made, unaesthetic, and stimulating is not. Leisure appears to be most likely or fully achieved in wilderness environments, parks, or other "therapeutic natural settings" (Ulrich et al., this volume). Certainly, it is true that such settings have great appeal and, for many of us, represent ideal spots for rest and relaxation, play, and the like. Yet this bias potentially ignores an important aspect of leisure: if we assume that one's needs for leisure, be they comfort or restoration, occur more often than do vacations, and we assume that most of us cannot live in the country or in park-like settings with lush vegetation and horses running freely, then we must also assume that a great deal of our leisure time is spent in accommodating our everyday environment, which is neither natural nor therapeutic. It is likely that recreation opportunities which are readily available in our everyday environment provide more benefits than relaxing or recreating in the "proper, natural setting" which may produce optimal benefits. We all can agree that temporary escapes such as daydreaming about a favorite recreation area or actually going to that spot are leisure. Similarly, a picnic in an urban park is readily considered leisure. But what of watching television to achieve the same temporary escape? Are video games restorative without being relaxing? Too many of our concepts and interpretations of measures reflect these biases and may hinder a full understanding of these issues. Heywood's study (1978) bears this out to some extent: activities that were perceived as positive and enjoyable, regardless of what they were, facilitated recovery of skin conductance, muscle tension, and heart rate responses following a stressful experience. Subsequent studies of recovery from brief stressful episodes suggests that natural scenes were more conducive to recovery of these physiological responses than were urban scenes (Ulrich and Simons 1986; Ulrich et al., in press). Yet, these measures might be measuring arousal more than stress, and arousal can reflect either positive or negative states. That sweating, respiration, or heart rate recovered more slowly during viewing of urban settings could reflect excitement or exploration rather than interference with recovery. It is also possible that the activities depicted in the urban scenes (traffic) were responsible for added arousal rather than the urban scape itself. It is difficult to tell from these studies how much of what is being measured is due to the stressor and how much is actually caused by the distraction devices (i.e., the natural and urban scenes), particularly in light of the fact that people adapt very rapidly to acute laboratory stressors and exhibit little arousal beyond a few minutes post-session (e.g., Glass and Singer 1972).

The kinds of interpretational problems noted above are common when nonspecific physiological measures are used as dependent variables. Arousal simply reflects activation: it is used variously to describe increases in the intensity or characteristics of emotions, in the activity of the brain, in the activity of a system (e.g., the sympathetic nervous system), or as a general term for increased organism-wide activity. Measures of arousal are based on these conceptions, and indices such as heart rate, EMG, or sweat gland activity are designed to detect sympathetic activity by assessing responses in several systems associated with it. These measures have gradually become interchangeable in some circles, despite the fact that they are not always correlated. This kind of approach belies the complex relationships among these variables and in the systems they represent, and in the case of nonspecific responses—those that occur in similar fashion as part of several syndromes—interpretation can be murky. If one becomes aroused when very happy events occur, when one is very stressed, when one has just exercised, or when concentrating on a difficult task, how are we to interpret increases in heart rate or skin conductance? Clearly, the social, behavioral, and cognitive contexts in which these responses occur are critical if one is to make any sense of such measures.

Underlying several issues discussed in this volume is the question of mechanism: how does leisure produce benefits or block ill effects of the wear and tear of daily life?

Tinsley and Tinsley (1986) have suggested that leisure provides satisfaction of psychological needs, which in turn enhances both physical and mental health and directly and indirectly facilitates life satisfaction and personal growth. Somehow, having "enough" leisure maintains the status quo in these domains, while less than optimal leisure produces deterioration. Assuming the hypothesized links between leisure and such psychological needs as self-expression, security, and solitude, the question now becomes one of how this need fulfillment or a lack thereof affects our health and well-being. Are we simply considering the mood enhancing effects of rest or are there more complex links to explore?

It is likely that the latter is true, and several different kinds of mechanisms can be postulated. One mechanism that has been discussed in this volume is stress. If unmet needs can cause stress, or if unmet needs fail to reduce stress, there are many ways in which health could be affected. We know that stress has direct physiological effects, such as increased sympathetic activity, cardiovascular activity, and reduced immune function, that can directly affect health. These effects can be quantified fairly accurately with available physiological measures. However, stress can also influence the ways in which we behave when we are ill, reducing the likelihood that we will take care of ourselves and recover promptly. Stress can also increase unhealthy behaviors such as cigarette smoking, drinking, and drug use. If we extrapolate from this to a situation in which needs are not satisfied because leisure activity is not sufficient, some possible mechanisms are indicated. When there is leisure deficit, might we substitute unhealthy behaviors that can be done more quickly and that pack a bigger "punch" when healthier modes of need gratification are not available or the necessary skills or motivations are absent? For example, is it possible that drug and alcohol use, smoking, binge eating, or other activities that can have harmful effects on health and well-being might somehow be used as a substitute for healthier achievement of one's needs, both psychological and physiological?

In this brief response to the chapters in this text, I have tried to raise several questions from my perspective as someone who does psychophysiological research on the relationship between stress and human well-being. Although it seems tautological to say that recreational activities can be "re-creative," the chapters in this text show that much research is needed to document these restorative benefits of leisure, which to me seem directed at health recovery and maintenance. It also seems unnecessary to suggest that psychophysiological research is needed to evaluate the links between leisure and these types of coping-related benefits. Not so self-evident, though, is the important role that psychophysiological research can play in establishing more objectively the more "creative" benefits of recreation such as health promotion (which positively goes beyond health recovery and maintenance), promotion and maintenance of positive affect (see Hull, this volume), and creation and maintenance of optimal states such as self-actualization and flow (see Csikszentmihalyi and Kleiber, this volume)—which probably have psychophysiological correlates.

LITERATURE CITED

Benson, H. 1975. The relaxation response. New York, NY: Morrow.

Cohen, S.; Wills, T. 1985. Stress, social support, and the buffering hypothesis: An integrative review. Psychological Bulletin. 98: 310-357.

Glass, D.; Singer, J. E. 1972. Urban stress. New York, NY: Academic Press.

Heywood, L. 1978. Perceived recreation experience and the relief of tension. Journal of Leisure Research. 10: 86-97.

Kiecolt-Glaser, J.; Glaser, R. 1987. Psychosocial moderators of immune function. Annuals of Behavioral Medicine. 9(2): 16-20.

Tinsley, H. E. A.; Tinsley, D. J. 1986. A theory of the attributes, benefits, and causes of leisure experience. Leisure Sciences. 8: 1-45.

Ulrich, R.; Simons, R. 1986. Recovery from stress during exposure to everyday outdoor environments. In: Winerman, I.; Barnes, R.; Zimring, C., eds. Proceedings of the Seventeenth Annual Conference of the EDRA, April, Atlanta. Washington, DC: EDRA: 115-122.

Ulrich, R.; Simons, R.; Losito, B.; et al. [In press]. Stress recovery during exposure to natural and urban environments. Journal of Environmental Psychology.

Benefits of Leisure: A Social Psychological Perspective

Icek Ajzen
Department of Psychology
University of Massachusetts
Amherst, Massachusetts

It is no small task to provide a social psychological perspective on the papers presented in this volume. For one, the papers represent a diverse set of scientific disciplines, covering a wide range of topics related to the benefits of leisure. For another, there is no single social psychological perspective that can be brought to bear; rather, social psychology is itself a broad field of study, and many different orientations could be adopted. My comments, therefore, represent my own perspective and they focus for the most part on papers in this volume for which this perspective may be of some relevance.

Given these limiting conditions, it is only fair that I comment first on some of the biases inherent in my orientation. As a social psychologist I come from a positivist tradition, with a strong inclination to tie theoretical constructs to empirical operations, especially those constructs that refer to independent and dependent variables. I get a bit uneasy when we consider self-actualization or self-identity benefits of leisure (Haggard and Williams, this volume), mainly because it is so difficult to develop good operations to assess these constructs (see Csiskszentmihalyi and Kleiber, this volume, for a discussion of the difficulties associated with assessing self-actualization). And I have great trouble dealing with benefits of a transcendental or spiritual nature (McDonald and Schreyer, this volume). These kinds of benefits, assuming they indeed result from leisure activities, are almost by definition inaccessible to standard psychometric measurement procedures.

Related to my preference for dealing with leisure activities and benefits that can be validly operationalized, I eschew excessively broad questions and tend to focus instead on specific hypothesized relations that can be subjected to empirical tests. To advance toward the goal of constructing a systematic body of knowledge about the benefits of leisure, we would ideally start with a theoretical model that is articulated well enough to permit us to derive specific hypotheses for empirical investigation. Many of the papers in this volume review areas of research on leisure benefits that fall far short of this ideal. Thus, much of the work on the benefits of leisure for learning (Roggenbuck, Loomis, and Dagostino), organizational wellness (Ellis and Richardson), mental health (Levitt), community satisfaction (Allen), child development (Barnett), and so on, seems to be guided less by systematic theory than by ad hoc hypotheses developed for the purpose of a given investigation. Although such research can be useful in the initial stages of theory development, it is of relatively little value in and of itself. If proof were required, one need only examine the rather pessimistic conclusions reached by many participants in the leisure benefits workshop who were asked to review a particular body of research. Time and time again we are told how little is known conclusively and that we need better methods and more theory to guide the research.

THE NATURE OF LEISURE AND ITS BENEFITS

Definition of Leisure

On reading the chapters in this volume one cannot fail to be impressed by the difficulty of defining *leisure*, the field's central construct (see, for example, Roggenbuck, Loomis, and Dagostino). The discussions of this issue in the present volume make it clear that no single definition of leisure is acceptable to everybody. None seems to capture all that is connoted by this construct, nor would it clearly differentiate leisure activities from all other kinds of behaviors.

It should be noted, however, that most constructs taken from everyday life carry a great deal of "surplus meaning" (MacCorquodale and Meehl 1948) and must be simplified to be useful for scientific purposes. Moreover, all measurement involves abstraction (Thurstone 1931), a condensing of the construct to its essential underlying dimension. Although I am not an expert on leisure, it would seem to me that most investigators in this area probably concur with Csikszentmihalyi and Kleiber (this volume) that leisure activities are freely chosen and pursued for their own sake. The intrinsic motivation dimension may not capture all that we might want to incorporate in the leisure construct, but defining leisure in terms of intrinsic motivation has the distinct advantage of suggesting appropriate operations to assess the construct. Whatever definition is eventually adopted, I would urge that it be a relatively simple, unidimensional definition that lends itself easily to empirical operationalization.

Benefits of Leisure

At the most general level, to ask about the benefits of leisure is not a very meaningful question. Few would deny that there are benefits to be derived from leisure activities (as there are some benefits to most human activities). The more interesting questions have to do with the relations between particular kinds of leisure activities and the specific benefits they produce (see Driver, Brown, and Peterson, this volume). Several papers mention different taxonomies of leisure activities and benefits (for a discussion, see Driver,

Tinsley, and Manfredo, this volume), but few papers try to link particular leisure behaviors to specific benefits.

The authors of most papers in this volume were asked to focus on a particular class of benefits: mental health, family solidarity, self-actualization, and so forth, and to review the evidence as to whether leisure activities can be shown to have benefits of the specified kind. This question is still much too general. We need to ask what kinds of leisure activities are most likely to produce the benefit(s) under consideration. Questions of this kind can easily produce researchable hypotheses. For example, it might be proposed that mental health is facilitated by leisure activities in a social context (because social networks are known to mitigate depression and other psychological difficulties) or that stress is relieved by solitary leisure activities in the natural environment. In this manner it would be possible to compare physical exercise, fishing, reading, hiking, and so forth, in terms of a particular class of benefits and to determine which kind of activity is most useful.

MOTIVATION AND LEISURE

From a social psychological perspective, many of the papers in this volume show a conspicuous lack of concern with people's motivation to engage in leisure activities. At some level, this is perhaps understandable. After all, it seems obvious why people enjoy leisure activities. However, the reasons for choosing one activity rather than another are not at all self-evident, and the choice may be closely related to the benefits people derive, or believe they derive, from engaging in a particular leisure behavior.

For purposes of this volume, benefit was defined as "a gain to an individual, to a group, to society, or to another entity" (Driver, Brown, and Peterson, this volume). However, such a gain can be defined only in relation to a goal, a standard, or a criterion, whether set by the individual or some larger unit. (As a social psychologist, my natural tendency is to consider the individual or a small group as the appropriate unit.) Once the goal has been clearly specified, the benefit of an activity can be operationalized by assessing the extent to which the goal has been attained, as well as the value of the goal to the social unit. Consider for example the goal of losing weight. A program of physical exercise would be a beneficial leisure activity if it resulted in some measurable weight loss. The magnitude of benefit would depend on the amount of weight lost and the value of this outcome to the individual. Of course, any given leisure activity can, and often does, have more than one beneficial outcome. Each benefit, however, can be assessed only with reference to a clearly defined goal.

A Theory of Planned Behavior

Motivation has to do with the psychological factors that propel an individual toward his or her goals. On the pages below, I propose a theoretical framework that may prove useful for the study of leisure activities and their benefits by enabling us to examine the links between them in relation to an individual's goals.

The proposed theoretical framework derives from Ajzen and Fishbein's (1980, Fishbein and Ajzen 1975) theory of reasoned action and from the recent extension of that theory to the prediction of behavioral goals (Ajzen 1985, Ajzen and Madden 1986). As in the original model, a central factor in the theory of planned behavior is the individual's *intention* to perform a behavior. Intentions are assumed to capture the motivational factors that impact on a behavior; they are indications of how hard people are willing to try, of how much effort they are planning to exert, in order to perform the behavior.

The theory of planned behavior postulates three conceptually independent determinants of intentions. The first is the *attitude* toward the behavior and refers to the degree to which the person has a favorable or unfavorable evaluation of the behavior in question. The second predictor is a social factor termed *subjective norm;* it refers to the perceived social pressure to perform or not to perform the behavior. The third and novel antecedent of intention, which was not part of the theory of reasoned action, is the degree of *perceived behavioral control.* This factor refers to the perceived ease or difficulty of performing the behavior and it is assumed to reflect past experience as well as anticipated impediments and obstacles. As a general rule, the more favorable the attitude and subjective norm with respect to a behavior, and the greater the perceived behavioral control, the stronger should be an individual's intention to perform the behavior under consideration.

Intention, in turn, is viewed as one immediate antecedent of actual behavior. That is, the stronger people's intentions to engage in a behavior or to achieve their behavioral goals, the more successful they are predicted to be. However, the degree of success will depend not only on one's desire or intention, but also on such partly nonmotivational factors as availability of requisite opportunities and resources (e.g., time, money, skills, cooperation of others, etc.; see Ajzen 1985 for a review). Collectively, these factors represent people's *actual control* over the behavior. To the extent that a person has the required opportunities and resources, and intends to perform the behavior, to that extent he or she should succeed in doing so.

Of course, in many situations perceived behavioral control may not be particularly realistic. This is likely to be the case when the individual has relatively little information about the behavior, when requirements or available resources have changed, or when new and unfamiliar elements have entered into the situation. Under those conditions, a measure of perceived behavioral control may add little to accuracy of behavioral prediction. The path from perceived behavioral control to behavior is therefore expected to emerge only when there is some agreement between perceptions of control and the person's actual control over the behavior.

The theory of planned behavior also deals with the antecedents of attitudes, subjective norms, and perceived behavioral control—antecedents which in the final analysis determine intentions and actions. At the most basic level of explanation, the theory postulates that behavior is a function of salient information, or beliefs, relevant to the behavior. Three kinds of beliefs are distinguished: *behavioral beliefs* which are assumed to influence attitudes toward the behavior, *normative beliefs* which constitute the underlying determinants of subjective norms, and *control beliefs* which provide the basis for perceptions of behavioral control. Each behavioral belief links the behavior to a certain outcome, or to some other attribute such as the cost incurred by performing the behavior. Based on an expectancy-value model of attitude (Fishbein 1963, Fishbein and Ajzen 1975), an estimate of attitude is obtained by multiplying belief strength by outcome evaluation and summing the resulting products across all salient behavioral beliefs. Normative beliefs, on the other hand, are concerned with the likelihood that important referent individuals or groups would approve or disapprove of performing the behavior. The strength of each normative belief is multiplied by the person's motivation to comply with the referent in question, and an estimate of subjective norm is obtained by summing the resulting products across all salient referents.

Finally, among the beliefs that ultimately determine intention and action there is, according to the theory of planned behavior, a set that deals with the presence or absence of requisite resources and opportunities. These control beliefs may be based in part on past experience with the behavior, but they will usually also be influenced by second-hand information about the behavior, by the experiences of acquaintances and friends, and by other factors that increase or reduce the perceived difficulty of performing the behavior in question. The more resources and opportunities individuals think they possess, and the fewer obstacles or impediments they anticipate, the greater should be their perceived control over the behavior. Specifically, each control belief is multiplied by the perceived facilitating (or inhibiting) effect of the resource or opportunity under consideration, and the resulting products are summed to obtain an estimate of perceived behavioral control. Thus, just as beliefs concerning consequences of a behavior are viewed as determining attitudes, and normative beliefs are viewed as determining subjective norms, so beliefs about resources and opportunities are viewed as underlying perceived behavioral control.

Empirical research over the past 15 years has provided evidence in support of the theory of reasoned action in a variety of experimental and naturalistic settings (Ajzen and Fishbein 1980; Ajzen et al. 1982; Bentler and Speckart 1979, 1981; Fredricks and Dossett 1983; Manstead et al. 1983; Smetana and Adler 1980). The behaviors involved have ranged from very simple strategy choices in laboratory games to actions of appreciable personal or social significance, such as having an abortion, smoking marijuana, and choosing among candidates in an election. Intentions to perform behaviors of this kind can be predicted from attitudes toward the behaviors and from subjective norms, and the intentions in turn correlate well with observed actions. For the most part, however, the behaviors investigated have been behaviors over which people tend to have considerable volitional control. Recent research on the theory of planned behavior has demonstrated that when volitional control is more problematic, the addition of perceived behavioral control significantly improves prediction of intentions as well as prediction of behavioral achievement (Ajzen 1987, Ajzen and Madden 1986, Schifter and Ajzen 1985).

An example in the domain of leisure behavior may be instructive. Consider, first, the question of a goal such as improved family solidarity or family bonding (Orthner and Mancini, this volume). According to the theory of planned behavior, attainment of this goal is facilitated if the individual intends to attain it (i.e., is ready to make an effort to improve family solidarity) and if he or she has the required resources to attain it (as reflected in perceived behavioral control). The intention to improve family solidarity, in turn, is dependent on the person's attitude toward attaining this goal, on perceived social pressure to attain it, and on perceived control over goal attainment. Finally, beliefs concerning the likely outcomes of increased solidarity influence the attitude toward this goal; beliefs that important referents (spouse, children, friends) would approve of making an effort to improve family solidarity influence the subjective norm; and beliefs about likely obstacles (time limitations, resistance on the part of the children) or facilitating factors (availability of professional help) influence perceived behavioral control.

This example shows how the theory of planned behavior can help explain why a person may choose to pursue a particular behavioral goal. In a similar fashion, it is possible to apply the theory of planned behavior to account for the choice of a leisure activity. Consider, for example, a woman's decision to go camping with her family. Figure 1 shows the determinants of camping behavior, as well as some of its possible outcomes, including the goal of increased family solidarity. According to the theory, a person may choose to go camping (or not to go camping) for a variety of reasons. In the present example we assume that the individual has the goal of improving family solidarity and that she anticipates this to be one of the possible outcomes of camping. Of course, she will also hold a variety of other beliefs about camping (that it brings you close to nature, that it involves living under primitive conditions, etc.) which, together, determine her attitude toward this recreational activity.

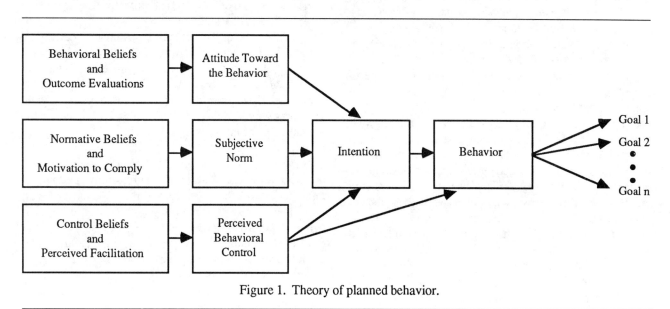

Figure 1. Theory of planned behavior.

In arriving at her intention, the woman also takes into account the normative expectations of such important others as her husband, children, and close friends, thus deriving a subjective norm with respect to camping. Lastly, she considers the required resources (time and money, camping equipment, availability of a desirable campground within driving distance, cooperation of her husband, etc.), all of which result in the formation of perceived control over the behavior in question. The intention to go camping, formed on the basis of all of these considerations, results in performance of the leisure activity to the extent that the woman actually has sufficient behavioral control in the situation.

LEISURE BENEFITS IN A SOCIAL PSYCHOLOGICAL CONTEXT

The above example illustrates the intimate connections between leisure benefits and other social psychological processes. A leisure activity is beneficial to the extent that it helps people to attain one or more of their goals. Goal setting and selection of leisure activities to attain the goals are therefore important issues for investigation.

Subjective Versus Objective Benefits

For a number of reasons having to do with scientific rigor, investigators often see advantages to objective measures of leisure benefits. Physical health and fitness is one area where objective measures can be obtained. However, the paper by Froehlicher and Froehlicher (this volume) makes it clear that cardiovascular benefits are contingent on engaging in a consistent and vigorous program of exercise. Most leisure activities, whether fishing, camping, or playing golf, probably have little discernable impact on cardiovascular health. If we are interested in objectively defined benefits, therefore, it is perhaps more promising to look at other psychophysiological indicators (see Ulrich, Dimberg, and Driver, this volume).

From a social psychological perspective, there is no obvious advantage in objective over subjective measures of leisure benefits. As noted earlier, benefits are defined in terms of goal attainment, and it may often be more important to assess whether people *believe* that a leisure activity helps them attain their goals than it is to assess progress toward the goal in a more objective manner.

In fact, much of the work reviewed in the chapters of this volume relies on subjective, rather than objective, measures of leisure benefits. This is hardly surprising, given that many benefits due to recreational activities cannot be directly observed (see Driver, Tinsley, and Manfredo for a great variety of relevant examples). Thus, engaging in sports is said to produce personal enjoyment and growth, reduce stress and anxiety, and alleviate depression (Wankel and Berger), all benefits of a rather subjective nature. Similarly, mood-related benefits of leisure (Hull) are subjective almost by definition.

Applications and Implications

By way of illustration, the social psychological approach described earlier is, in this section, applied very briefly to a few of the domains reviewed in the state-of-knowledge papers of this volume. Since relevant data are largely unavailable, no attempt is made to derive definite conclusions. This discussion is merely designed to clarify some of the implications of the theory of planned behavior for the study of leisure benefits. In fact, we already considered one type of benefit earlier, namely, family solidarity. We will see how the same set of constructs can be used to analyze two other types of benefits.

Quality of Life

Marans and Mohai (this volume) and Allen (this volume) provide good overviews of the literature on community quality and life satisfaction. Their discussions suggest that individual well-being and community satisfaction are the result of a complicated set of factors that include presence of natural resources, man-made resources, various other community attributes, perception and use of available amenities, and so forth (see Fig. 1 in the Marans and Mohai chapter).

Using the theory of planned behavior, we might define greater life satisfaction as a broad goal and examine perceived relations between recreational activities and goal attainment. To determine whether performance of leisure activities is motivated by a desire for greater life satisfaction, we would elicit salient beliefs about the leisure activities of interest. Examination of these beliefs reveals the contribution of life satisfaction goals to selection of leisure activities. Availability of natural and man-made amenities finds expression in perceived behavioral control: the more amenities that are believed to be available, the greater should be the person's perceived control.

Organizational Wellness

The paper by Ellis and Richardson (this volume) provides a thorough review of the benefits of leisure for the well-being of company employees. Two relevant social units can be considered in this case: the company and the employees. For purposes of illustration, we focus on the company's perspective. Using the theory of planned behavior to approach this issue, we would first assess the extent to which company executives have set employee well-being as an explicit goal. We then elicit their beliefs about the likely effects of providing leisure opportunities to employees, including effects on psychological well-being. In addition, perceived expectations of relevant others (employees, company stockholders, the larger community, etc.) are assessed to get at subjective norms; and perceived availability of requisite resources (money, space, cooperation by the union, etc.) is assessed to ascertain perceived behavioral control. These factors combine to determine whether or not the company's decision-makers will improve the leisure opportunities offered to employees. What then remains to be examined is the effect of providing increased leisure services on employee well-being.

The examples discussed above show how the theory of planned behavior can provide a general framework for research on leisure benefits. Each type of benefit, of course, poses its own problems of identifying relevant antecedent factors and developing appropriate procedures to assess the resulting benefits. However, the theory directs attention to several common issues: the need to clearly identify the social unit's goals in the situation; to assess perceived relations between leisure activities and attainment of those goals; and to consider the attitudinal, normative, and control factors that lead to the performance or nonperformance of those leisure activities.

SUMMARY

Leisure benefits were defined as those outcomes of recreational activities that advance the goals set by an individual or some other social entity. The theory of planned behavior was proposed to provide a conceptual framework for the study of leisure benefits. It involves identification of goals; assessment of perceived relations between leisure activities and those goals; assessment of other beliefs as well as attitudes, subjective norms, and perceived behavioral control; measurement of intentions to engage in leisure activities; and finally, assessment of actual performance of the behavior and of goal attainment. In an attempt to illustrate its generality and potential usefulness, this theoretical framework was applied to several types of leisure benefits discussed in the state-of-knowledge chapters of this volume.

LITERATURE CITED

Ajzen, I. 1985. From intentions to actions: a theory of planned behavior. In: Kuhl, J.; Beckmann, J., eds. Action-control: from cognition to behavior. Heidelberg, Germany: Springer: 11-39.

Ajzen, I. 1987. Attitudes, traits, and actions: dispositional prediction of behavior in personality and social psychology. In: Berkowitz, L., ed. Advances in experimental social psychology. New York, NY: Academic Press: 1-63. Volume 20.

Ajzen, I.; Fishbein, M. 1980. Understanding attitudes and predicting social behavior. Englewood Cliffs, NJ: Prentice-Hall.

Ajzen, I.; Madden, T. J. 1986. Prediction of goal-directed behavior: attitudes, intentions, and perceived behavioral control. Journal of Experimental Social Psychology. 22: 453-474.

Ajzen, I.; Timko, C.; White, J. B. 1982. Self-monitoring and the attitude-behavior relation. Journal of Personality and Social Psychology. 42: 426-435.

Bentler, P. M.; Speckart, G. 1979. Models of attitude-behavior relations. Psychological Review. 86: 452-464.

Bentler, P. M.; Speckart, G. 1981. Attitudes "cause" behavior: a structural equation analysis. Journal of Personality and Social Psychology. 40: 226-238.

Fishbein, M. 1963. An investigation of the relationships between beliefs about an object and the attitude toward that object. Human Relations. 16: 233-240.

Fishbein, M.; Ajzen, I. 1975. Belief, attitude, intention, and behavior: an introduction to theory and research. Reading, MA: Addison-Wesley.

Fredricks, A. J.; Dossett, D. L. 1983. Attitude-behavior relations: a comparison of the Fishbein-Ajzen and the Bentler-Speckart models. Journal of Personality and Social Psychology. 45: 501-512.

MacCorquodale, K.; Meehl, P. E. 1948. On a distinction between hypothetical constructs and intervening variables. Psychological Review. 55: 95-107.

Manstead, A. S. R.; Proffitt, C.; Smart, J. L. 1983. Predicting and understanding mothers' infant-feeding intentions and behavior: testing the theory of reasoned action. Journal of Personality and Social Psychology. 44: 657-671.

Schifter, D. B.; Ajzen, I. 1985. Intention, perceived control, and weight loss: an application of the theory of planned behavior. Journal of Personality and Social Psychology. 49: 843-851.

Smetana, J. G.; Adler, N. E. 1980. Fishbein's value x expectancy model: an examination of some assumptions. Personality and Social Psychology Bulletin. 6: 89-96.

Thurstone, L. L. 1931. The measurement of attitudes. Journal of Abnormal and Social Psychology. 26: 249-269.

Sociological Perspectives on Recreation Benefits

John R. Kelly
Department of Leisure Studies
Office of Gerontology and Aging Studies
University of Illinois
Champaign, Illinois

Sociology has come to be associated with particular methods and questions. Surveys of population samples, demographic indices of social position, and correlational analyses have been applied to questions of the behavior of population aggregates. Popular sociology has become a media segment with graphic reports of polls sponsored by government agencies, advertising and marketing departments, and the media themselves. All of this attention obscures the nature of sociology as a discipline.

Sociology is the study of social action. As such it encompasses the dialectic between the individual actor and the social forces and contexts of action (Giddens 1976, Kelly 1981). Its premise is that action is always from, within, and toward social contexts. Sociological analysis takes regularities of interactional behaviors and meanings as the data to be explained in terms of institutional roles and identifications, group processes, the symbol systems of situated action in a culture and society, and the composition of the social system.

The methods employed are instrumental toward the end of social explanation. As such they include the immediacy of observation and the distance of historical analysis, the singularity of case study and the aggregation of massive data sets, the situated and the abstracted, the narrative and the statistical, the attitudinal and the behavioral, the timeless and the processual.

From a sociological perspective, action is the creation of both individual actors and social forces. Structure, the forms and forces of the society, are integral to any social action and interaction. Leisure, then, is situated freedom, not an absence of constraint or form. It is both existential in its action component and social in its contextual meanings and forms. In this dialectic of action and context, leisure can be approached from a variety of perspectives. Each perspective or metaphor adopts certain premises that direct and limit the issues to be addressed and the phenomena to be included.

THEORETICAL PARADIGMS IN SOCIOLOGY

As a discipline, sociology has encompassed many theoretical perspectives or paradigms (Ritzer 1975). Each is based on certain assumptions about the nature of society and social action. Each focuses on issues identified by the paradigm and adopts research methods that are compatible with its assumptions. Each incorporates its own modes of analysis, vocabularies, and systems of explanation.

Leisure and recreation are like all other kinds of social action in being defined and explained differently within each theoretical metaphor. Therefore, attention to a specific question, such as the nature of the benefits of recreation and leisure, is shaped by the paradigm adopted. Even with the premise that the benefits to be identified are *social*—accruing to groups, collectivities, institutions, and social systems—there are multiple possibilities depending on the perspective.

There are commonly considered to be three high-level classifications of major sociological models: the critical, the interactional or interpretive, and the institutional or functional (Kelly 1976, Ritzer 1975). The critical focuses on the economic and political bases of social cohesion and conflict. The interactional begins with the premise that the social system is the construction of actors whose actions and interactions are within frames of symbolic meaning that are learned, communicated, and reinforced. The institutional approaches the society as a system of interrelated and organized roles with complementary functions. Each paradigm has been employed in the sociological study of leisure. Each has directed attention to issues and answers within its domain assumptions. And each has offered significant modes of analysis to the understanding of leisure and recreation (Kelly 1987). In time, it may be possible to develop a "... new paradigm ... in which group consciousness, differential power, regularities of definition and action, and the creating of new definitions by decisions are all interwoven" (Kelly 1976: 155). Such a paradigm would be both social in the inclusion of resources, environments, communities, and systems, and existential in its attention to interpretive decisions and action (Kelly 1987).

At this time, however, the three main paradigms of sociology each provide distinct perspectives on social issues. The analysis that follows begins with each of the three models and sketches the kinds of benefits and outcomes that each can identify for leisure and recreation. This is not a summary of findings, but an outline of possibilities—most of which have not yet been realized.

Critical Theory

Critical theory is based on the Marxist approach that considers the society to be divided among two or more groups with different powers, interests, and control of resources. Only recently has this paradigm been applied to the analysis of leisure in contemporary society. Underlying the model is the Marxist assumption that leisure should be a realm of freedom for personal development and the building of community. Leisure is a social environment in which developmental and creative action is possible. Its benefits are twofold: in leisure individuals become more human and they are bonded to each other in community—that is the context of being and becoming human.

The critical thrust of this perspective is simply that in modern societies, leisure has become distorted into an instrument of social control that is alienated and alienating. Rather than creative and community-building action, leisure has become tied to the market, to the acquiring, possessing, and displaying of "things." Leisure is seen as the proper reward for acquiescence in the political and economic system. It binds workers and citizens to the system through the market. Such an approach points to evident negative outcomes of leisure and recreation. The particular commodified and competitive modes of recreation may be dehumanizing in their distorted images of possible action. Authentic leisure becomes a struggle against the system to avoid buying the package of marketed entertainment.

On the other hand, the potential benefits of leisure remain possible for those with the courage to take authentic action. Even if limited and distorted, leisure presents environments and orientations that offer possibilities for humanizing action and interaction and that may become a standard of meaning for all the rest of life. The fundamental benefit of leisure from this perspective is the development of creative action and community that may become one element in a consciousness that leads to change in the social system.

Interpretive-Interactional Theory

In this paradigm, the society is understood to be constructed by the common action of those who interpret the symbolic meanings of their social environments and take meaningful action. The focus is on coordinated lines of action, the development of relationships, cultural symbol systems and modes of communication, and the development of personal and social identities. Behavior is understood to be a dialectical process of action *in* social contexts of shared symbols.

From this perspective, leisure and recreation may offer both social and personal benefits. Leisure is a realm of social life in which the meanings of the society and culture are celebrated, communicated, and reinforced. The necessary learning process in which the shared symbols are communicated takes place in the drama of shared celebration, of festival and remembrance.

The personal benefits of leisure from this perspective are developmental. Through the life course, the play of leisure is a crucial context in which individuals take action that contributes to their development. Not only the play of children, but the relatively open action of adults in every life period provides for both the continuity and change of self-definitions and lines of action. Leisure and recreation provide opportunities for self-creation and expression that may be limited in other roles and contexts.

At the same time, in this paradigm life is seen as profoundly social. Individual actors become who they are and would like to be in social interaction. The persistently social nature of most leisure suggests that it is a context for social learning, exploration, action, and interaction crucial to being human. Through interaction in which the outcomes are not prespecified, in which the environments may even foster exploration and risk, communities of interaction may be developed that are central to self-definitions and development throughout the life course. Further, this sociological paradigm provides a framework for the analysis of process—what actually occurs in the action and interaction of leisure and recreation.

Institutional Theory

From a functional or systemic perspective, the society is composed of a set of related institutions that each make certain necessary contributions to the social system. As a consequence, benefits to the society tend to be identified in terms of their contribution to its institutions. When each of the institutions is able to carry out its mission or central functions, then the entire society continues. The premise is that the adaptive survival of the social system is the fundamental benefit to its constituent members.

Leisure and recreation may be identified as an institutional component of the system. More often, however, they are understood as secondary because they have no distinct and necessary function of their own. Rather, they support the functions of the primary institution. It is from this perspective that we will outline possible benefits. And it is from this perspective that most sociologists approach the question of social benefits of recreation.

The economy.—The function of the economy is to produce goods necessary for the survival of the society. Productivity is the central value. The measure is through the market. Therefore, the social benefit of recreation for the economy is to productivity as measured by market valuation.

Leisure and recreation are seen as secondary to the economy. Benefits may be found in ways in which workers are made more fit or prepared for production through recreational participation. Market-sector and public provisions and opportunities are augmented by programs provided by production units, the corporation. Benefit is in the contribution to productivity.

A second economic, but not social, benefit is based on the current postindustrial shift of the economy in which services now account for most employment and a larger segment of the national product. Leisure is a growing sector of the economy which yields a return on investment and employs large numbers whose purchasing power adds to market demand for goods and services.

Education.—Recreation can be said to contribute to education in a narrow sense similar to possible contributions of productivity. The diversion of recreation makes students in educational institutions better able to learn. More comprehensively, however, the relationship between recreation and education includes leisure environments for learning, leisure as a context for the expression of educational achievements, and the close ties of the content of education and leisure, especially in the arts. When leisure is understood as creative action, then it becomes itself a crucial mode of learning and development.

Government.—Social benefits of leisure and recreation for the polity are twofold. First, recreational events provide a means of celebrating and reinforcing the common values of a society. The stability of the government is reinforced in the festivals in which the historic and current values are reenacted and celebrated. Second, recreational venues and activities are for the most part social. As such, they provide a context for common participation that may support and build community. This is seen as especially important in a mass society in which most interactions and relationships tend to be relatively instrumental and anonymous. Leisure, then, may benefit the institution of government through social participation that reinforces common values and a sense of participation.

Religion.—The function of religion from this systemic perspective is to develop and nurture a common set of values for the society. The social benefit of leisure from this perspective is to provide a time and space context for the rituals that dramatize and strengthen those value systems. Further, the church may employ recreation to develop a sense of community that binds constituencies together. Insofar as contemplation is a classic leisure activity and central to religious expression, religion and leisure may be closely related.

The family.—The primary function of the family is the reproduction of the society through the production and nurturing of children. The family is, however, also central to property holding and transmission and to the provision of shelter and care as a unit of consumption. The maintenance of family bonds, then, is essential to the social system. It is in providing a context for such bonding, the expression of solidarity and intimacy, that leisure contributes most significantly to the society (Cheek and Burch 1976). This function has more research support than others as common participation in recreational activity is found to be correlated with the quality of relationships in the family as well as with marital stability. Recreation is also a context in which many nurturing and developmental aims for the family are actualized. Even when "family" is expanded to include other central and stable primary relationships, leisure is critical to developing and maintaining bonds of commitment and sharing.

SOCIOLOGY AND RECREATION BENEFITS

Sociology is not a method. Rather, it is a set of perspectives on society and social interaction that point to certain factors in stability and change and to particular sets of issues. The outcomes identified from any kind of social action, including leisure and recreation, depend on the theoretical paradigm adopted. Each paradigm yields a perspective and framework for analysis. What is common to all is the focus on social action and on regularities within a persistent social context.

Some would like to apply a causal analysis to the examination of social benefits. That would require that leisure and recreation consistently and measurably produced something valued in the consensus of the social system. Evidence of such causality is difficult to obtain, even with complex statistical measures and analytical techniques. The relationships are seldom direct enough for such measurement except on a very small scale. Societies are not amenable to such analysis except when a series of presuppositions sets the framework within clear limits. At best, social benefits may be indicated by some consistent correlations that index a relationship that may not be unidirectional or free of confounding factors.

In the current state-of-the-art, despite a few such circumscribed indications, causal analysis is lacking. The indications, such as those related to family cohesion or productivity, are indirect and partial. In fact, the most commonly cited indications are actually attitudinal rather than behavioral. Such data raise the whole issue of the relationship between consciousness and action.

The ideal model would be a simple causal relationship:

recreation —> specified beneficial outcomes

The actuality is more complex:

recreation —> direct outcomes —> social benefits

Even such a model is based on a whole set of premises about the nature of the social system, the functional relationship of its institutions, and the validity of the social system.

The maintenance of a social system with a high degree of stability is an unexamined premise. The fragility of such a social system as a symbolic construction is developed by interpretive-interactionist theory. The power-differentiated alienation of a social system critiqued in political theory is based on quite a different model.

From any sociological perspective, it is necessary to specify the theoretical framework, consequent issues, and model of society on which the analysis is premised. Then, research may be designed that directly or indirectly indexes outcomes of behaviors, and of social actions that are identified as recreation. Such research may be specific to particular opportunities, contexts, or behaviors, or may encompass a more inclusive range of related actions. In either case, the results may be indicative of actions and outcomes in the larger social system.

The more modest approach is that direct measurement of social benefits is not possible. What is possible, however, is the systematic accumulation of indices of beneficial outcomes. To be persuasive, such research would require a systematic program of integrated strategies and designs.

LITERATURE CITED

Cheek, N.; Burch, W. 1976. The social organization of leisure in human society. New York, NY: Harper & Row.

Giddens, A. 1976. New rules of sociological method. New York, NY: Basic Books.

Kelly, J. R. 1976. Sociological perspectives and leisure research. Current Sociology. 22(1): 127-158.

Kelly, J.R. 1981. Leisure interaction and the social dialectic. Social Forces. 60: 304-322.

Kelly, J. R. 1987. Freedom to be: a new sociology of leisure. New York, NY: MacMillan.

Ritzer, G. 1975. Sociology: a multiple paradigm science. Boston, MA: Allyn & Bacon.

Aging and Leisure Benefits: A Life Cycle Perspective

Barry D. McPherson
Faculty of Graduate Studies
Wilfrid Laurier University
Waterloo, Ontario,
Canada

Ever since Ponce de Leon set out to find the Fountain of Youth, mankind has been interested in extending the life span. Indeed, over centuries the life span has increased to a present theoretical maximum of about 100 years. More importantly, however, there has been an increase in the average life expectancy at birth to about 73 years for men and about 80 years for women. As a result, more people are living longer and societies are experiencing population aging. But are older adults experiencing a higher quality of life during these additional years? This is an important question for scholars, policymakers, and practitioners in the field of leisure studies.

Because of declining birth rates and an increasing life expectancy, adults over 65 years of age now represent about 11% of the total population in North America. It is projected that this segment of the population will increase to 15% by 2011 and 22% by 2031, the latter being a percentage that can be found in some European countries today. Given these demographic facts, this chapter considers the sociological implications and outcomes of population aging for the study of leisure in the later years. Much of this discussion focuses on clarifying the conceptual and methodological approaches that need to be addressed by scholars and policymakers as they seek to understand the role of leisure in the lives of older adults. In addition, in keeping with the theme of this text where possible, the benefits of leisure in the later years are discussed from a sociological perspective. However, whereas psychologists have directed considerable attention to the psychological benefits of leisure for older adults (Tinsley et al. 1985, 1987; Driver, Tinsley, and Manfredo, this volume), sociologists have been more interested in documenting the types of leisure activities pursued by older adults with different sociodemographic characteristics, in describing the use of time for leisure and domestic work in the later years, and in comparing how different cohorts of older adults use their leisure time. That is, sociologists have focused their research on the role of leisure in the lifestyles of older adults, whereas psychologists have focused their research on the beneficial outcomes of that involvement.

POPULATION AGING: DEMOGRAPHIC IMPLICATIONS FOR LEISURE

Clearly, our population is aging. This fact, alone, is no longer surprising. Rather, there are a number of subtle demographic facts within this demographic shift that merit serious consideration by academics and policymakers who work in the leisure field. First, aging is primarily a women's issue. The number of women compared to men in the middle and later years of the life cycle increases with age. In North America, for those 65 to 79 years of age, the current sex ratio is 124 women for every 100 men. By age 80, the ratio increases to 134 women for every 100 men and is projected to increase to over 200 women per 100 men by the year 2000. Most older men are married and most older women are either single (never married or divorced) or widowed. Living arrangements and lifestyles of older women generally differ from those of older men: more older women live alone; more are institutionalized; fewer drive; more live in fear of being victimized; fewer have pension benefits and economic security; and more women, because they live longer, report a lower health status. Thus, from a policy or program development perspective, we must recognize that the elderly population is increasingly comprised of women. Moreover, in the leisure domain it must not be forgotten that the current generation of elderly women had little experience with formal leisure activities throughout the early and middle years of their life cycle. In the near future this will change as some segments of the future generations of older women will have had a variety of work and leisure experiences throughout their lives. Some of the future elderly may even opt to retire from a career to pursue leisure on a full-time basis.

A second important demographic fact is that as life expectancy is increasing, the number of disability-free years are also increasing. Older adults, especially males, are less likely to be physically disadvantaged, housebound or institutionalized than they were two or three decades ago. Moreover, as an outcome of the health, wellness, and fitness movement of the 1970s and 1980s, middle-aged and older adults are generally more physically active during their leisure. To illustrate, following the conference at which the papers in this volume were discussed, Dr. Ralph Paffenbarger, the 66-year-old co-author of the paper on *Health Benefits of Physical Activity* (this volume), competed in an ultramarathon race in South Africa. Most of the other "senior" authors of this book spent their leisure time at the conference hiking, walking, or skiing. Clearly, we are entering an era where the most popular or preferred leisure activities for seniors will likely go beyond the more traditional activities of gardening, reading, watching television, or visiting. Physically and cognitively active lifestyles are becoming the norm for older adults.

A third demographic fact to consider with respect to leisure benefits is that the mobility and migration rates of seniors are increasing, especially on a seasonal basis. This increased mobility has profound implications for travel and tourism, for parks management, for planners, and for community recreation personnel. The needs, interests, and frequency of use patterns for a program site or facility can change dramatically if senior citizens become interested or involved, especially if group usage such as bus tours is promoted by seniors' organizations.

LEISURE AND AGING: CONCEPTUAL AND METHODOLOGICAL ISSUES

To date, there have been few national studies with large, representative samples of older adults across two or three generations. Rather, most studies of leisure and aging have been small local and regional studies of the leisure needs, activities, preferences, and patterns of older adults (McPherson 1983: 119). To arrive at a more complete understanding of the consequences of leisure in the later years, a number of conceptual and methodological issues must be addressed. First, however, when considering the "benefits" of leisure in the later years, we need to seriously address two questions:

1) Are the benefits any different for the elderly than for other age groups?
2) Should the benefits (and thereby policies and programs) be any different for the elderly than for other age groups?

While these questions have yet to be addressed seriously, based on my understanding of aging as a social process (McPherson 1983, 1990), I argue that the potential or ideal benefits of a given leisure experience should not be any different for a 20-, 40-, 60-, or 75-year-old. Certainly, the frequency, format, and duration of a given leisure activity (e.g., tennis, sex, concert attendance) may change, and the basic intrinsic meaning may vary significantly by age group; but the potential benefits (e.g., physical, mental, social) should not change just because someone ages.

From another perspective, those who are somewhat pessimistic about life in the later years might argue that with the onset of retirement, leisure becomes a bane rather than a blessing. For some older adults, the advantages or benefits of leisure disappear because they have too much "free" time, because they are not provided with the resources to use this "free" time in a meaningful way, or because "free" time has not been an integral component of their lifestyle. Therefore, some older adults may have varying degrees of difficulty in managing this "free" time (McPherson 1983: 406-435, 1985, 1986). Ideally, as Kelly (1987: 117) suggests, "leisure is not leftover time, but a context for the expression of personal meaning and for social bonding." Thus, there is a need for more serious study of the use and meaning of leisure, both across the life cycle and at different stages in the later years. This type of study should include older adults who live in semi- or fully institutionalized settings, as well as in the community.

It must be remembered when studying seniors that aging is a lifelong process. Being old does not begin at age 65. Rather, aging, and the product of that process, is characterized by a number of role transitions and adjustments to life events that leave their mark on the individual (e.g., the outcomes of divorce, widowhood, a career change, unemployment, retirement, the empty nest). Most studies suggest that there is a high degree of continuity in behaviors, attitudes, and values after the age of 30, unless a major role transition or life event has a major impact on an individual. However, this does not mean that some individuals or members of a specific age cohort do not change their beliefs, values, or perceptions over time. Some changes can and do occur, and it is for this reason that individual and cohort needs and preferences must be periodically assessed. Thus, any consideration of leisure in the later years must involve a life course or life cycle perspective (Klieber and Kelly 1980; McPherson 1983, 1990; Osgood and Howe 1984). To illustrate, a number of hypothetical alternative participation patterns that could emerge across the life cycle for a given individual, for a given cohort, or for a given type of leisure activity are shown in Figure 1. For example, six older individuals could exhibit six different lifelong patterns for recreational reading. Similarly, the lower-right bimodal pattern could reflect a pattern of high involvement in golf or television viewing during adolescence and retirement, with little involvement in the middle years of the life cycle due to career or child-rearing demands on one's time, or the upper left figure might reflect the typical life cycle pattern of involvement in physical activity and sport by your grandparent's generation, whereas the upper right figure may represent the pattern for your generation. Similarly, the benefits of leisure at any point in the life course could vary according to these patterns for a given individual cohort or activity.

Researchers and policymakers must also recognize that aging does not occur in a vacuum. Within a community, society, or the world, beliefs and values change. Each age cohort and each generation has a unique history and a set of somewhat unique values and norms. For example, a major societal event can have a profound impact on a given cohort that will make that age cohort different from others which follow, or which preceded it through the life course. Some examples of significant events that might influence the leisure values, preferences, or opportunities of a significant segment of a particular age group include wars, depressions, and major social movements (e.g., the radical 1960s, the women's movement).

As a result of social change, we can not necessarily apply the knowledge about seniors in the 1980s to those who will be seniors in the year 2000. To understand the preferences and needs of future generations of seniors, we should be studying the particular age cohorts when they are in the early and middle years of the life cycle. For example, those who will be seniors in the early years of the next century (only 10 years from now!) may very well be healthier, wealthier, and more active than current seniors, and they will have acquired different leisure values and experiences throughout the middle years of the life cycle. This will be especially true of women—many of whom will have had careers, a personal income, and leisure opportunities unknown or not valued by their mothers and grandmothers.

Given the evidence that aging occurs within a changing social, cultural, and economic environment, scholars seeking to understand leisure needs and benefits in the later years must consider the interaction of individual and population aging. An excellent conceptual model is provided by Powell Lawton (1980, 1985) who considers aging as a process of maximizing the "person-environment" fit. In short, researchers and policymakers concerned with leisure must understand that the leisure needs and interests of individuals may interact with such diverse needs and interests as the environment, the life insurance industry, the health care industry, other age groups competing for scarce resources, and the manufacturing sector that produces goods and services for the expanding "maturity" market.

Contrary to popular belief, aging is not just a biological process, but a social process as well. Aging and leisure behavior are influenced by a number of sociodemographic factors that must be included in studies addressing the question of leisure in the later years. These factors include: gender, race, ethnic membership, education, lifelong and present income and assets, marital status (past and present), and type and place of residence (rural vs. urban, north vs. south, east vs. midwest vs. west, etc.). All of these factors, alone or in combination, can influence past, present, or future leisure values, preferences, and opportunities.

As a consequence of the considerable influence of these sociodemographic factors, plus a variety of other social psychological factors (e.g., sociability, number of friends and relatives) and community factors (e.g., availability of public transportation, economic resources, community leadership), heterogeneity prevails when we discuss research on aging and policy matters for the middle and later years of the life cycle. The elderly are not a homogeneous group, as is so often assumed in research studies and in the development of policies and programs. Many studies report only aggregate data wherein all those 65 and older are considered as one group—"seniors," "the elderly," "retirees." In reality, there

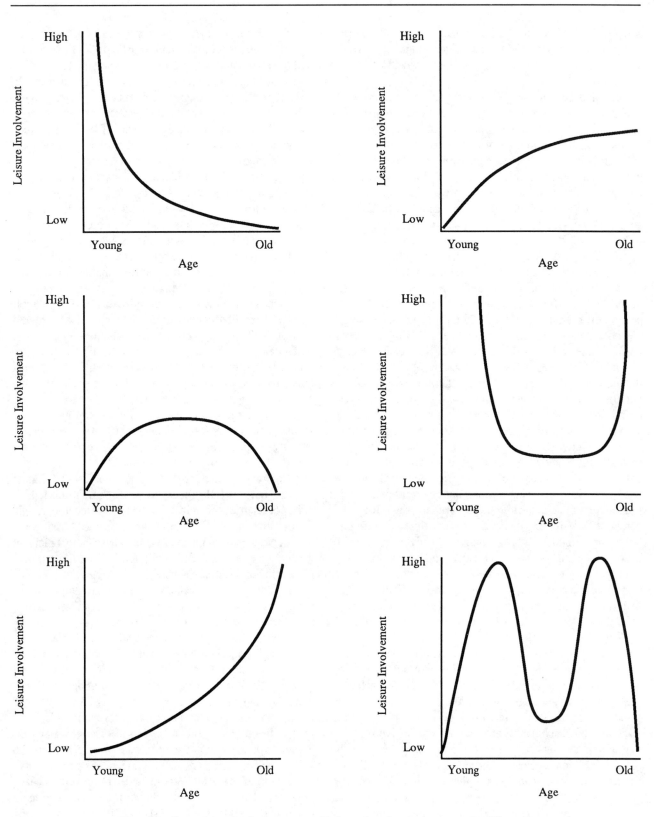

Figure 1. Some hypothetical patterns of leisure involvement across the life cycle.

are at least two or three distinct age groups within the older population: 60-69; 70-79; and 80+. To properly recognize and fully understand this hetrogeinity, we must examine both within and between age cohort variations. For example, there is considerable variation in a number of important variables (e.g., health, economic, employment, or marital status) between and within these three age cohorts. Furthermore, as noted earlier, despite aging being primarily a women's issue, females are usually underrepresented in studies of seniors, while the well-elderly, the white-collar elderly, and the urban elderly are often overrepresented. Finally, such important subcultural variations as race, ethnicity, and social class are seldom considered in studies of leisure and aging. The values, traditions and beliefs about leisure vs. work within these subcultures can vary considerably from those of the dominant or mainstream culture. This is especially true among first generation immigrants who have had different values, experiences, and opportunities than second or third generation members of the same ethnic group. In North America, many of our current seniors are first generation immigrants. Their needs and experiences in the later years are quite different from their nonimmigrant age peers, for both economic and cultural reasons. But, when the children and grandchildren of the first generation reach the later years, their reservoir of experiences and resources will be more similar to others within their age cohort. That is, ethnicity may be of little or no importance in understanding the leisure lifestyles of later generations within a given family.

To date, most studies of leisure and aging have been quantitative studies that focus on the frequency of participation in specific types or groups of leisure activities. While continuity may prevail in the type of leisure pursued across the adult life cycle (that is, there is a set of "core" activities) (Kelly 1987), the meaning and purpose of involvement may change with age, or the activity may provide a number of meanings at the same time. To illustrate, hiking in the mountains may be pursued primarily as a physical fitness activity in early adulthood (how fast can one hike up and down a trail?), as a way to escape job and urban stress in middle adulthood, and as a setting to pursue a hobby (photography or bird watching) in later adulthood. Thus, the preferred type of leisure activity may not change, but the meaning or purpose of the activity may change across the life cycle. Alternatively, the frequency or type of leisure involvement may change, but the meaning may not.

It is for these reasons that scholars and policymakers must consider the quality and meaning of outcomes of leisure in the later years, not just the quantity of leisure involvement. A major conceptual error in the field of gerontology has been the unquestioning acceptance of disengagement theory (McPherson 1983: 137-140). Yes, older adults may disengage from some activities in the later years (but so do many teenagers and young adults disengage or alienate themselves from social activities or from society). At the same time as they disengage from some activities, older adults may become more deeply engaged in a few select activities. Or they may drop activities that no longer have as much meaning to focus on new or continuing activities that are perceived to be more important or meaningful at that stage in life (e.g., family and home-based activities).

Before we can consider the benefits of leisure for a particular individual or cohort, we need to consider whether there are barriers inhibiting the opportunity or potential to attain the possible desired outcomes of leisure (cf., Backman and Mannell 1986, Buchanan and Allen 1985, McPherson 1983: 418). Clearly, as in most other domains, there are both individual and institutional barriers that must be overcome. At the individual level of analysis, there are barriers due to personal factors (e.g., lack of motivation, negative attitudes toward leisure, lack of experience) and to such aging effects as a decline in health and energy, an inability to drive, a reduction in discretionary income if retired or unemployed, and the loss of a partner through death or divorce. There are also barriers due to societal factors: lack of information about leisure opportunities; failure of a community to provide leisure programs, counseling, or facilities for seniors; unavailability of public transportation; prevailing myths or negative stereotypes concerning the supposed interests (or lack of) and abilities of older adults (evidence suggests that they can and are willing to learn new skills); fear of being victimized if they leave their home or familiar neighborhood environment; and local or regional norms or cultural values that discourage the involvement of older adults in certain leisure activities or facilities.

All of these individual and societal barriers are unnecessary and can be reduced or eliminated by the dissemination of scientifically valid information to both policymakers and the general population, and by the initiation of a full-scale program of leisure opportunities for all seniors in every community. This reduction of barriers is especially important for older adults living in rural and inner city environments, for those with health problems, for those who are economically disadvantaged, and for those from different cultural backgrounds.

As a final suggestion to further the quality and quantity of research and policymaking on leisure in the later years, it is essential that the older individual, per se, not be neglected in either the research or policymaking process. For too many years, younger adults have been imposing the research and policy agenda on a passive, uninformed, elderly clientele. I refer to this as the "shuffleboard" syndrome wherein it has been assumed by young and often naive recreation programmers that seniors want to, need to, and enjoy playing shuffleboard (or similar passive activities). Because this is the major activity provided in some settings, some seniors have passively accepted the option and "played the game"—the outcome is a self-fulfilling prophecy whereby the image of the passive, mildly active senior is further perpetuated. This scenario is then often repeated in other communities or settings.

Today, many seniors are no longer passively accepting the status quo, including within the leisure domain. Older adults, individually and collectively (e.g., local and national seniors' organizations), are more vocal and demanding. Creative, sensitive, and wise researchers and policymakers are asking older adults to articulate their needs, preferences and desires, and are including seniors as part of the research or decisionmaking team. For example, in the research domain older adults are enrolling in graduate programs and becoming involved in research on aging issues. Moreover, more valid and reliable quantitative and qualitative data may be obtained if interviews and participant observation studies are conducted by seniors. Similarly, most innovative programs and policies have benefited from the input of seniors serving as members of advisory boards. It is not surprising, therefore, to find that the annual meetings of both the Gerontological Society of America and the Canadian Association on Gerontology are increasingly being attended by senior citizens. Similarly, seniors should be invited to attend and participate in sessions on aging at discipline-oriented meetings concerned with leisure. Serious consideration of the input of seniors will generate and focus more valid and creative research questions, programs, and policies in the leisure sciences and professions.

OUTCOMES OF LEISURE INVOLVEMENT IN THE LATER YEARS

As an outcome of research to describe and explain life satisfaction, happiness, psychological well-being, or the quality of life in the later years (cf., Altergott 1988, Larson 1978, Lawton et al. 1984, Okun et al. 1984), scholars have begun to consider the contribution of leisure to these larger outcome measures (cf., Kelly et al. 1986; Kelly 1987; Larson et al. 1986; Lawton 1985; McPherson 1990; Romsa et al. 1985; Tinsley et al. 1985, 1987; Zuzanek and Box 1988).

These studies, like many in the field of gerontology, are not without conceptual and methodological flaws. For example, most are one-time only, cross-sectional studies that cannot capture the influence of mood or health changes, or the outcomes of recent events in the subjective responses of respondents. That is, a particular mood or perceived feeling of health on a given day may significantly influence a questionnaire or interview response to a question pertaining to well-being, life satisfaction, happiness, or quality of life. It is also important to understand that most of these studies describe the outcome rather than provide an explanation of the underlying mechanisms of why and how leisure involvement influences these larger dependent outcomes. One exception in the field of sociology is the work of Kelly (1986, 1987) who argues that leisure activities provide a social setting for the initiation and development of primary social relations. At a stage in life characterized by social losses (e.g., loss of friends and the social milieu at work upon retirement, death of friends and spouse), leisure activities can provide a social milieu to create new social relationships. Furthermore, Kelly (1987) states that an ability and willingness to engage in leisure demonstrates competence and self-worth.

Notwithstanding the above caveats, a growing body of research suggests that "there is a strong correlation between life satisfaction and rates of leisure participation, but little correlation between life satisfaction and the older adults' uses of free time" (Zuzanek and Box 1988: 180). However, as Okun et al. (1984) concluded, based on 556 sources of data on the relationship between adult social activities and subjective well-being, formal and informal activities only account for between 1% and 9% of the variance in self-reported life satisfaction. The highest levels of life satisfaction are reported by those who engage in activities that provide stimulation and interaction with significant others. But, remember this same finding also applies to younger age cohorts as well.

The impact of leisure activities on life satisfaction, well-being, or happiness is quite likely related to a number of interacting factors, two of which are the type of activity and the meaning of the activity. It is suspected that informal, self-initiated activities rather than formal, organized activities may provide more meaning and satisfaction to the individual, which, in turn, translate into reports of higher life satisfaction and well-being. Similarly, expressive and instrumental activities may provide more or less satisfaction, depending on the needs and preferences of the older individual. A lifestyle characterized by solitary activities may best serve the needs of some older adults; for others, social activities involving other people will be desired; a mix of both types may satisfy still other older adults. In short, there is not a common recipe as to which leisure activities will enhance life satisfaction or well-being in the later years. Again, as with so many other facets of aging, heterogeneity prevails.

SUMMARY AND CONCLUSION

In determining and explaining the outcomes of leisure in the later years, scholars and practitioners must understand that aging involves both continuity and change. Older adults may disengage, voluntarily or involuntarily, from some activities, continue others with varying degrees of frequency and intensity, or substitute for lost activities by starting new activities or increasing the level of involvement in other life-long interests. Tradeoffs are made, and the outcome of these decisions may enhance or inhibit life satisfaction, happiness, or well-being at a given point in time.

As Zuzanek and Box (1988: 179) conclude:

Having more free time does not automatically translate into greater happiness. Being able to fill this time with activities and to structure it in a meaningful and diversified way does! Acquiring a satisfying lifestyle in retirement presupposes an ability to structure one's time.

In short, there is strong evidence that leisure contributes to life satisfaction, and we have some evidence that it provides a context for social interaction, for enhancing personal self-worth, and for testing self-competence. However, we still do not fully understand how or why the relationships prevail, and more importantly, why some older adults are not involved in leisure pursuits, and why others, despite being involved, report low levels of life satisfaction, well-being, or happiness. Herein lies a challenge to those who pursue a career in the field of leisure studies.

LITERATURE CITED

Altergott, K. 1988. Daily life in later life. Newbury Park, CA: Sage.

Backman, S.; Mannell, R. 1986. Removing attitudinal barriers to leisure behavior and satisfaction: a field experiment among the institutionalized elderly. Therapeutic Recreation Journal. 19(3): 46-53.

Buchanan, T.; Allen, L. 1985. Barriers to recreation participation in later life cycle stages. Therapeutic Recreation Journal. 19(3): 39-50.

Kelly, J.; Steinkamp, M.; Kelly, J. 1986. Later life leisure: how they play in Peoria. The Gerontologist. 26(5): 531-537.

Kelly, J. 1987. Peoria winters: styles and resources in later life. Lexington, MA: Lexington Books.

Kleiber, D.; Kelly, J. 1980. Leisure socialization, and the life cycle. In: Iso-Ahola, S., ed. Social psychological perspectives on leisure and recreation. Springfield, IL: Charles C. Thomas.

Larson, R. 1978. Thirty years of research on the subjective well-being of older Americans. Journal of Gerontology. 27(6): 511-523.

Larson, R.; Mannell, R.; Zuzanek, J. 1986. Daily well-being of older adults with friends and family. Psychology and Aging. 1(2): 117-126.

Lawton, P. 1980. Environment and aging. Monterey, CA: Brooks/Cole Publishing Company.

Lawton, P. 1985. Activities and leisure. In: Eisdorfer, C., ed. Annual review of gerontology and geriatrics. Volume 5. New York, NY: Springer Publishing Company. 127-164.

Lawton, P.; Kleban, M.; di Carlo, E. 1984. Psychological well-being in the aged. Research on Aging. 6(1): 67-97.

McPherson, B. D. 1983. Aging as a social process. Toronto, ON: Butterworths.

McPherson, B. D. 1985. The meaning of and use of time across the life cycle. In: Gutman, G.; Gee, E., eds. The challenge of time. Winnipeg, MB: Canadian Association on Gerontology: 110-162.

McPherson, B. D. 1986. Age patterns in leisure participation: the Canadian case. In: Marshall, V. Aging in Canada: social perspectives. Toronto, ON: Fitzhenry and Whiteside: 211-217.

McPherson, B. 1990. Aging as a social process. 2d and rev. ed. Toronto, ON: Butterworths.

Okun, M.; Stock, W.; Haring, M.; Witter, R. 1984. The social activity/well-being relation. Research on Aging. 6(1): 45-65.

Osgood, N.; Howe, C. 1984. Psychological aspects of leisure: a life cycle developmental perspective. Society and Leisure. 7: 175-195.

Romsa, G.; Bondy, P.; Blenman, M. 1985. Modeling retirees' life cycle and socioenvironmental elements. Journal of Leisure Research. 17(1): 29-39.

Tinsley, H.; Teaff, J.; Colbs, S.; Kaufman, N. 1985. A system of classifying leisure activities in terms of the psychological benefits of participation reported by older persons. Journal of Gerontology. 49(2): 172-178.

Tinsley, H.; Colbs, S.; Teaff, J.; Kaufman, N. 1987. The relationship of age, gender, health and economic status to the psychological benefits older persons report from participation in leisure activities. Leisure Sciences. 9: 53-65.

Zuzanek, J.; Box, S. 1988. Life course and the daily lives of older adults in Canada. In: Altergott, K. Daily life in later life. Newbury Park, CA: Sage: 147-185.

Economic Quantification of Leisure Benefits

Mary Jo Kealy
Economic Studies Branch
US Environmental Protection Agency
Washington, District of Columbia and
Department of Economics
Colgate University
Hamilton, New York

THE CASE FOR ECONOMIC QUANTIFICATION

The economic quantification of the benefits of leisure is but one method of measuring the benefits that society derives from leisure. Included are those effects of leisure that increase producer surplus by, for example, decreasing production costs, or those that result in greater utility (i.e., net willingness to pay) for humans. Ultimately, if humans had complete understanding of the contribution of leisure activities to individual, corporate, and societal economic well-being, whether those contributions be in the form of improved life satisfaction, greater muscle tone, higher self-esteem, heightened spirituality, enhanced family life, increased productivity, reduced stress, or decreased recovery time from illness, they would have the wherewithal to choose those activities that generate the greatest net economic benefit subject to their constraints on income and discretionary time. Moreover, faced with the choice between leisure and other goods and services, individuals and businesses, or in the case of external benefits from leisure, society, would be capable of making the necessary trade-offs that would maximize net economic benefits. All would know the personal, corporate, or societal economic worth of leisure.

The concept that leisure can be valued by the revealed preferences of individuals, businesses, and society, renders economic quantification compelling. Economics provides a means of determining how much of which kinds of leisure activities are preferred by the current generation to the alternative uses of society's limited resources, all conditional on the given distribution of income. This is useful because the resources necessary to "produce" leisure services must be diverted from alternative service, unless they would otherwise be idle. Furthermore, economic quantification, as with all methods of quantification, provides a metric for assessing the effectiveness of leisure activities at generating beneficial outcomes.

This particular metric, the economic value of leisure, has implications for policy because it is the relevant metric for efficient allocation of resources. As Darrell Lewis (this volume) observed, to the extent that policymakers are concerned about using society's resources efficiently, it is important that the economic benefits of leisure be quantified, lest they be undervalued. Moreover, the policymaker who must optimize multiple societal goals in addition to economic efficiency (e.g., national competitiveness, income redistribution, preserving natural areas for the enjoyment of future generations, providing recreation alternatives for disadvantaged youths), may be influenced by the implicit price tag of the goals that are (currently) external to the economic system. That is, if the policymaker is acutely aware of the cost of providing leisure services, and the economically quantified benefits do not measure up, she or he may ask whether or not the unquantified benefits are worth the extra cost.

Unfortunately, individuals, businesses, and society do not have a complete understanding of the improvements to individual, corporate, and societal well-being that result from leisure. This means that many of the effects of leisure are not currently quantified either in economic or in any other terms. Indeed, a predominant theme running through the papers in this volume is the necessity for greater quantification for evaluative and improved decisionmaking purposes. Information regarding the consequences of the various facets of leisure is only one of the prerequisites for the optimal flow of resources toward leisure services, but it will be the major focus of this critique. The usual market distortions (e.g., taxes, externalities, and public goods), which may be particularly applicable to leisure services, are impediments as well. Nonetheless, the main objective of this critique is to motivate and facilitate greater quantification, and in particular, economic quantification of the effects of leisure.

At the outset it is important to recognize that beneficial outcomes can be assessed using other metrics (e.g., psychophysiological changes, satisfaction ratings, mood changes, community crime rates, time spent in hospitals, physical endurance, and changes in the immune system, to name just a few). Knowledge of these outcomes can be important in and of itself, and for evaluating program effectiveness, but it is also the prerequisite for any assessment of economic benefits. There can be no economic benefits from leisure if there are no effects or changes that can be attributed to leisure. Moreover, the way in which the effects or consequences of leisure are described by researchers influences the extent to which linkages can be made between those consequences and economic measures of benefits. It is only when the changes affect the willingness to pay of individuals or the production possibilities of firms that they become economic effects.

Therefore, this paper attempts first to illustrate the potential economic measures of benefits of certain leisure activities and services by drawing from a sample of the contributions to this volume, and second, to suggest the linkages that may be necessary for establishing monetary values for the benefits from leisure. This may highlight some possibilities for interdisciplinary research designs. Thus, despite the view that the subset of readily, economically quantifiable benefits from leisure is small relative to the total, it is nonetheless recognized that the economic

benefits of leisure are most directly counterbalanced by the economic costs. It seems that greater economic quantification can only tip the economic balance in favor of a service such as leisure; it will decrease the difference between the monetized costs and benefits of leisure.

ECONOMIC QUANTIFICATION OF BENEFITS USING APPLICATIONS FROM THIS VOLUME

The majority of the contributions to this volume address effects in one of two areas in which economists have had significant valuation experience. The first is health effects and the second is outdoor recreation. Although economics can also play a role in valuing other effects such as quality of life (Marans and Mohai, this volume), organizational wellness (Ellis and Richardson, this volume), this paper concentrates only on health and outdoor recreation for focus. It is not meant to imply that the other areas of effects are not of economic consequence.

The main motivation behind the interest in valuing programs that affect human health is the importance placed on it by Congress and the American people. For example, all regulations to protect the environment are based on achieving certain health standards, and not, for example, preserving ecosystems for the ecosystem's sake. Economists contribute by assessing the relative benefits and costs of various programs intended to reduce health risks, save lives, and the like. This has lead them into the unpopular area of placing a monetary value on a statistical human life, and on changes in morbidity, but economists are quick to point out that this is the only way to ensure that resources are directed to save the most lives, if indeed that is society's objective. The application of the economic literature on valuing health effects to various leisure programs with consequences for human health is straightforward in theory, but difficult in practice.

Outdoor recreation became a major focus of attention by environmental economists because it was and still is believed that the outdoors provides significant national economic benefits that are nonetheless external to the market place. Therefore, resource allocation decisions that are based only on market data drastically underestimate the economic value of recreation uses relative to alternative uses of the same resources (e.g., resource extraction, other development). This paper highlights the national importance of outdoor recreation and some economic approaches to valuing outdoor recreation. It also discusses possible linkages between various types of leisure programs identified in this volume and improved economic modeling of recreation behavior. Finally, some recommendations that can lead to the economic quantification of benefits from certain leisure programs are suggested.

Health Benefits

We can now examine some of the contributions to this volume from an economic perspective. This will involve using the economic framework already established to identify benefits that can be linked to economically quantifiable measures. In practice, many of the identified benefits may be difficult to measure in monetary terms because of lack of information or other market failures, and may require the use of nonmarket economic valuation methods. In the event that even these methods fail to produce monetary measures of benefits, it may still be useful to have an understanding of the conceptual basis underlying the monetary measurement of the benefits from leisure. Then, although the benefit may not be monetarily quantified explicitly, any decision to abandon or support the project would place an implicit monetary "price" on the benefit.

One area of economic inquiry relevant to many of the topics in this volume relates to valuing changes in morbidity or health. The health benefits from leisure identified in this volume include, for example, cardiovascular (and other) benefits of physical activity (Froelicher and Froelicher; Paffenbarger, Hyde, and Dow), stress reducing benefits attributed to natural settings (Ulrich, Dimberg, and Driver), positive mood changes that promote health and positive cognitions and behavior (Hull), and therapeutic benefits from recreation for the mentally ill (Levitt).

To illustrate an economic approach to measuring the monetary benefits of changes in health, let us consider Levitt's discussion of the effects of various types of recreation on the mentally ill. Here, one can view the mental state of the patient as the "product" and leisure as an "input" toward an improved mental state. Then, focusing on therapeutic camping programs, for example, one can compute the measures of improved mental health (e.g., improved physical health, improved school behaviors, shorter hospital stays, reduced recidivism rates, etc.) as well as any negative changes (e.g., increased anxiety and guilt) and compare to a control group as Levitt recommends, and to alternative methods, if any, of achieving similar results. The comparison with the control group is to isolate and quantify the effect of the treatment, whereas the comparison with alternative methods is to determine the relative net present value (i.e., the discounted net benefit stream) or perhaps the cost-effectiveness of alternative treatments.

It may very well be the case that different treatments or programs will be particularly well suited for meeting different objectives so that cost-effectiveness analyses are not sufficient for making the most efficient decision. One also needs to know the relative quantities of the various program outputs in order to perform benefit/cost analyses. The general categories of economic benefits are: 1) lower costs of caring for the mentally ill (e.g., shorter and less frequent hospital stays, lower cost of improving a measure of physical ability, less lost income due to time away from work); 2) the affected individuals' willingness to pay for the shorter and less frequent hospital stays over and above the cost savings from reduced medical bills, lost income, and other expenses; 3) the willingness to pay of family and friends for the patient's shorter hospital stay over and above the cost savings, etc.; and 4) society's willingness to pay for statistical reductions in hospital stays, etc. Alternatively, one can measure total economic benefits by measuring the total willingness to pay of the affected individuals, their family and friends, and society, inclusive of the cost savings, lost income, etc.

The first category is straightforward to compute in theory once each of the effects are quantified. Indeed, until recently, these were the only benefits considered by federal agencies when valuing the impacts of government policies on life and health (Viscusi 1986). Now that it is recognized that the total benefits of health changes include the willingness to pay of affected individuals, their family and friends, and other members of society, the quantification task is much more difficult. These complexities are addressed by Cropper (1981), Viscusi (1986), Berger et al. (1987), and Fisher et al. (1989), to name a few.

For some types of health impacts (e.g., job- or residence-related), it may be possible to infer the individual's willingness to pay for lower risks to health from market data on earning differentials across job categories or places of residence (see Blomquist 1979, Brown 1980, Olson 1981, Portney 1981, Viscusi and O'Conner 1984). However, this valuation method is not an option for illnesses that are not work- or residence-related. Instead, it may be necessary to rely on direct questioning methods that ask the individuals to state their willingness to pay for the health improvement. Such direct questioning methods are called "Contingent Valuation Mechanisms," and they are gaining wide applicability in the environmental valuation area (Cummings et al. 1986, Mitchell and Carson 1989). Also, researchers are now applying these methods to the health area (Acton 1973, Hammerton et al. 1982, Jones-Lee 1976, Tolley and Babcock 1986).

The direct questioning method requires the individual to first, perceive a change in well-being from the program and second, express the change in monetary terms. This is quite a demanding task, especially because illness is a very emotional issue. Nonetheless, this may be the only means to learn the individual's willingness to pay under certain circumstances.

Similar methods can be applied to estimate the third and fourth categories of benefits. In these cases, emotional involvement may not be as significant a problem for valuation as it is for the affected individual; but family and friends, and in particular society, may not be as knowledgeable about the illness. Also, although society members may benefit from the improved mental health of its members, the individuals who comprise society may be reluctant to reveal their willingness to pay. As with public goods in general, individuals may perceive that it is in their interest to either underestimate or overestimate their willingness to pay in order to minimize their personal payment or influence the amount of societal resources devoted to mental health. These and other potential shortcomings of the method are the subjects of research in this fast growing field (Mitchell and Carson 1989).

Outdoor Recreation Benefits

An area of leisure benefits that has received considerable attention from economists is outdoor recreation, particularly as provided in our nation's forest lands and waterways. The attention is warranted given that almost 90% of the American population over the age of 12 engages in some form of outdoor recreation at least once a year (U.S. DOI 1986). In addition, the average American participates in 7 different outdoor recreation activities for a total of 37 activity-days per year (U.S. DOI 1986). When asked to identify the reasons why they enjoyed their favorite outdoor recreation activities, respondents chose enjoyment of nature and the outdoors (68%), getting exercise or keeping in shape (66%), getting away from day-to-day living or problems (56%), chance to be with family and friends (53%), and chance for peace and quiet (47%) as their top selections (U.S. DOI 1986: 32). Many of the contributions to this volume describe the beneficial outcomes of exposure to nature and the outdoors (Ulrich, Dimberg, and Driver), getting exercise or keeping in shape (Froelicher and Froelicher; Paffenbarger, Hyde, and Dow; Wankel and Berger), and leisure time spent with family and friends (Orthner and Mancini). These benefits also emerge in Driver, Tinsley, and Manfredo (this volume) who report that people perceive many of the other benefits that are the subject of research in this volume. Included are learning (Roggenbuck, Loomis, and Dagostino;

Easley), independence (Haggard and Williams), introspection (McDonald and Schreyer), and achievement/stimulation (Hull, and Wankel and Berger) to name a few.

Clearly, outdoor recreation provides benefits that can be measured using a wide array of metrics from the physiological to the perceptual. It is also possible to monetize the benefits of access to outdoor recreation opportunities and changes in the quality of the recreation experience. To the extent that leisure programs offer the abovementioned benefits, it is possible to conceptualize a linkage between changes in the quality of the recreation experience (e.g., enhanced opportunities for introspection or achievement) and the demand for the outdoor recreation experience. In practice, to monetize the benefits from these enhancements it will first be necessary to find objective measures for them. We explore this line of thought in greater depth below. Traditionally, economic valuation methods have been used most often to value access to outdoor recreation opportunities rather than changes in the qualities of the resource. A discussion of the application of these methods to the economic valuation of urban parks (Jordan, this volume) is also included below.

Economic Methods of Valuing Outdoor Recreation

Before continuing, a brief digression is warranted to explain the economic basis for quantifying outdoor recreation benefits to participants. By engaging in outdoor recreation activities, enthusiasts reveal their preferences for outdoor recreation. They demonstrate a willingness to devote the necessary expenditures of time and money to participate. Given this information on the expenditure of valuable resources, it is possible to infer "demand" for outdoor recreation activities. Then, when combined with the supply opportunities, it is a straightforward calculation to determine the monetary worth of the available outdoor recreation resources as well as which types of opportunities are most in demand.

In practice, the majority of outdoor recreation opportunities in natural settings are supplied by the government and the fees charged are not the result of a market process (Cordell 1989). The nonmarket nature of many outdoor recreation activities complicates demand measurement. Nonetheless, economists have estimated the demand for outdoor recreation activities (e.g., hunting, fishing, skiing, swimming, nonconsumptive uses of wildlife, and boating) at numerous recreation sites and systems of sites throughout the country. The two predominant valuation methods used are the contingent valuation method (CVM) in which the individual is asked directly to state her willingness to pay to recreate at the site, and the travel-cost method (TCM), which relates the cost of travel (i.e., "price") to the quantity of recreation trips. (For comprehensive reviews of the CVM, see Cummings et al. 1986, and Mitchell and Carson 1989; for the TCM see Bockstael et al. 1986).

Noteworthy efforts to assess the national economic benefits from recreation are underway by the National Forest Service (Cordell et al. 1987) and the National Oceanic and Atmospheric Administration (Leeworthy and Meade 1989). They have collected pertinent "demand" data on a wide range of recreation sites across the nation using the Public Area Recreation Visitor Survey (PARVS). These data will permit the estimation of participant unit-day values for specific activities at specific sites. When combined with comprehensive population participation rates (not currently available) and resource supply data, these data may enable an overall (albeit aggregate) assessment of the current economic benefits from public outdoor recreation opportunities in America.

This approach to obtaining national economic benefit estimates of outdoor recreation was first implemented by Russell and Vaughan (1982) to estimate the national recreational fishing benefits of water pollution control. They first developed a participation model to predict: 1) the probability of being a fishermen of any sort; 2) conditional on being an angler, the probability of fishing for a particular species; and 3) conditional on seeking a certain species, the average number of days per fisherman per year devoted to fishing for that species. Then the total number of days per year was calculated by taking the sum of the first three figures times the population size. Independent estimates of the value of a fishing day were obtained from two sources. Charbonneau and Hay[1] estimated willingness to pay using the contingent valuation method, and Vaughan and Russell (1982) used an application of a varying parameter type of travel-cost demand model. These per day values were then multiplied by the estimates of increased fishing days resulting from increased fishable water acreage as various phases of water pollution control were implemented.

Modifications of the two predominant economic valuation methods for outdoor recreation are important for characterizing national economic benefits. However, to assess the monetary benefits of particular outdoor recreation resources or changes in their quality, it may be necessary for accuracy to analyze the specific area of interest using either the CVM and/or the TCM.

Application of Economic Valuation Methods

So far this discussion has identified two economic methods for valuing outdoor recreation opportunities. Of interest is whether or not economic valuation methods can be applied to the measurement of improvements in outdoor recreation opportunities along the dimensions of the various contributions to this volume. To address this question, a suggested area of research is to take Driver, Tinsley, and Manfredo's work (this volume) one step further. They already identify the characteristics of outdoor recreation (e.g., exposure to nature, learning, introspection, achievement, etc.) that various types of participants view as important to the recreation experience. A testable hypothesis is whether or not changes in the level or type of learning experience, for example, has an effect on individuals' demands for outdoor recreation. To test such an hypothesis, it remains to find objective measures of program output (e.g., test scores, skill level evaluations, quantity and type of learning programs offered) and then use those objective measures as explanatory variables in predicting the quantity of recreation trips demanded (using the TCM) or willingness to pay (using the CVM). Then, as the improvements in program output increase the demand for outdoor recreation services, economic benefits can be quantified by taking the difference in areas under the new and old demand curves. The underlying assumption is that if the learning programs enhance the perceived quality of the recreation experience, then people will demand more outdoor recreation, all else being equal. For something like educational programs or outdoor learning experiences, it may be possible to estimate demand and economic value more directly by treating units of the program as the dependent variable. The key for economic quantification of program benefits is to find objective measures of program output that should, in theory, influence the behavior of individuals seeking to maximize their well being.

Economic Benefits of Urban Parks

Besides the direct use value that participants gain from participating in outdoor recreation in the nation's federal, state, and local parks, it is recognized that nonparticipants may also attach an economic value to others' uses of the outdoors. Whether out of feelings of altruism or out of belief that outdoor recreation opportunities contribute to a more socially desirable citizenry, nonparticipants may be willing to pay for the provision of outdoor recreation opportunities for others. Thus, to capture the total economic benefits from outdoor recreation opportunities, it may be necessary to tap the willingness to pay of both participants and nonparticipants.

Perhaps nowhere is this more apparent than in the urban parks of Charles Jordan's world. Jordan (this volume) identifies several potential benefits of urban parks, from opportunities for building greater self-esteem and confidence and developing positive role models, to reducing crime rates and contributing to the wellness of our communities. The latter two types of benefits are especially pertinent to nonparticipants.

The economic benefits provided by urban parks have not been studied extensively, however. At least in part, the relative lack of attention is due to a greater demand for economic benefit assessments of national environmental treasures; but also, some of the economic valuation methods are better suited for valuing the more unique resources. For example, the travel-cost method relies upon ever increasing travel costs as the distance from the recreation site increases to relate the quantity of recreation trips to the cost of travel. It is expected that the quantity of recreation trips demanded by people who reside closest to the recreation site will be highest and that the visitation rate will decline as distance from the site increases. For neighborhood parks, however, all visits originate from roughly equal distances from the park so that the necessary variation in the cost and quantity of recreation trips is lacking. In addition, this method completely fails to capture the benefits from outdoor recreation in urban parks that are accrued by nonparticipants as, by definition, these people do not travel to the park at all.

There have been some attempts to quantify the economic value of urban parks using the contingent valuation method (Brookshire and Coursey 1987, Darling 1973, Hoehn and Randall[2]) and this may be a more promising approach for future investigations. As this method directly asks people to reveal their willingness to pay, it does not have the same deficiencies as the travel cost demand model. However, the CVM relies upon well-informed and highly motivated citizens to take the time to formulate and consider their preferences for urban parks. In addition, it is important that the respondents to the contingent valuation survey not perceive an incentive to either underestimate or overestimate willingness to pay and thus invalidate their responses. These special problems are addressed at length in Mitchell and Carson (1989) along with issues involving the crediblity of the valuation scenario and the appropriateness of the sampling method for hypothesis testing and for drawing inferences, to name a few.

SUMMARY

This paper attempts to provide an economic perspective to the contributions to this volume on leisure benefits and to motivate greater economic quantification of leisure benefits. The rationale for greater economic quantification is based on the efficiency principle. To balance the costs and benefits of leisure services one must first quantify them to the extent possible.

Leisure benefits are often external to the normal operations of the market and are thus not quantified by the market. Therefore, in making policy decisions that impact the flow of resources away from or toward the production of leisure benefits, politicians often must act with insufficient and often unbalanced information. Those who are close to the policymaking process, Siehl and Kostmayer (this volume) and Lewis and Kaiser (this volume), warn that leisure benefits can get shortchanged due to insufficient quantification and the corresponding lack of political will to effect change. Economic efficiency is not and should not be the only relevant consideration in making policy decisions, but it clearly is an important one. Other disciplines can contribute to greater and more accurate economic quantification of benefits through interdisciplinary research. Economists have already developed methods to assess the economic benefits associated with improvements in health and outdoor recreation, two areas that span most of the contributions to this volume. It remains for each of the disciplines to develop objective measures of program outputs in conjunction with economists to ensure appropriate linkages between the program outputs and economic behavior or willingness to pay.

ENDNOTES

[1]Jon Charbonneau and Michael J. Hay on determinants and economic values of hunting and fishing—paper presented at the 43rd North American Wildlife and Natural Resources Conference, Phoenix, AZ, March 20, 1978.

[2]John Hoehn and Alan Randall on demand-based and contingent valuation—paper presented at the Annual American Agricultural Economics Association Meetings, Ames, IA, August 1985.

LITERATURE CITED

Acton, J. P. 1973. Evaluating public programs to save lives: the case of heart attacks. Research Report R-73-02. Santa Monica, CA: Rand Corporation.

Berger, M. C.; Blomquist, G. C.; Kenkel, D.; Tolley, G. S. 1987. Valuing changes in health risks: a comparison of alternative measures. Southern Economic Journal. 53:967-984.

Blomquist, G. C. 1979. Value of life-saving: implications of consumption activity. Journal of Political Economy. 87:540-558.

Bockstael, N. E.; Hanemann, W. M.; Strand, I. E. 1986. Benefit analysis using indirect or imputed market methods. In: Measuring the benefits of water quality improvements using recreation demand models, Volume 2. Washington, DC: Environmental Protection Agency, Office of Policy Analysis, CR-811043-01-0, University of Maryland.

Brookshire, D. S.; Coursey, D. L. 1987. Measuring the value of a public good: an empirical comparison of elicitation procedures. American Economic Review. 77(4):554-566.

Brown, C. 1980. Equalizing differences in the labor market. Quarterly Journal of Economics. 94(1):113-154.

Cordell, H. K. 1989. An analysis of the outdoor recreation and wilderness situation in the United States: 1989 - 2040. A Draft Technical Document supporting the 1989 RPA Assessment. Athens, GA: USDA Forest Service, Southeastern Forest Experiment Station.

Cordell, H. K.; Hartmann, L. A.; Watson, A. E., et al. 1987. The public recreation visitor survey: a progress report. In: Proceedings, Southeastern Recreation Research Conference, Feb. 1986, Asheville, NC. Athens, GA: University of Georgia, Recreation Technical Assistance Office, Institute of Community and Area Development.

Cropper, M. L. 1981. Measuring the benefits from reduced morbidity. American Economic Review Papers and Proceedings. May:235-240.

Cummings, R. G.; Brookshire, D. S.; Schulze, W. D., eds. 1986. Valuing environmental goods: a state of the arts assessment of the contingent valuation method. Totowa, NJ: Rowman and Allanheld.

Darling, A. H. 1973. Measuring benefits generated by urban water parks. Land Economics. 49(1):22-34.

Fisher, A.; Chestnut, L. G.; Violette, D. M. 1989. The value of reducing risks of death: a note on new evidence. Journal of Policy Analysis and Management. 8:88-100.

Hammerton, M.; Jones-Lee, M. W.; Abbott, V. 1982. The consistency and coherence of attitudes to physical risk: some empirical evidence. Journal of Transport Economics and Policy. May: 181-199.

Jones-Lee, M. W. 1976. The value of life: an economic analysis. Chicago, IL: University of Chicago Press.

Leeworthy, V. R.; Meade, N. F. 1989. A socioeconomic profile of recreationists at public outdoor recreation sites in coastal areas, Volume 1. Rockville, MD: U.S. Department of Commerce, National Oceanic and Atmospheric Administration.

Mitchell, R. C.; Carson, R. T. 1989. Using surveys to value public goods: the contingent valuation method. Washington, DC: Resources for the Future.

Olson, C. 1981. An analysis of wage differentials received by workers on dangerous jobs. Journal of Human Resources. 16(2):167-185.

Portney, P. 1981. Housing prices, health effects, and valuing reductions in risk of death. Journal of Environmental Economics and Management. 8:72-78.

Russell, C. S.; Vaughan, W. J. 1982. The national recreational fishing benefits of water pollution control. Journal of Environmental and Economic Management. 9:328-354.

Tolley, G. S.; Babcock, L. 1986. Valuation of reductions in human health symptoms and risks. Final report to the Office of Policy Analysis, U.S. Environmental Protection Agency. Chicago, IL: University of Chicago.

U.S. Department of the Interior, National Park Service. 1986. The 1982-1983 Nationwide Recreation Survey. Washington, DC. 95 pp.

Vaughan, W. J.; Russell, C. S. 1982. Valuing a fishing day: an application of a systematic varying parameter model. Land Economics. 58:450-463.

Viscusi, W. K. 1986. The valuation of risks to life and health: guidelines for policy analysis. In: Bentkover, J. D. et al., eds. Benefits assessment: the state of the art. Dordrecht, Holland: D. Reidel Publishing Co.: 193-210.

Viscusi, W. K.; O'Conner, C. 1984. Adaptive responses to chemical labeling: are workers Bayesian decision makers? American Economic Review. 74(5):942-56.

Leisure—The Last Resort: A Comment

Erik Cohen
Department of Sociology and Social Anthropology
The Hebrew University of Jerusalem
Mount Scopus, Jerusalem,
Israel

INTRODUCTION

The conveyors of this volume had some very concrete and practical aims in mind. Chief among them was to demonstrate that leisure has, or may have, some important, non-economic benefits for the individual and society (Driver, Brown and Peterson, this volume). This demonstration, in turn, should make available an important weapon in the struggle to preserve wilderness and other outdoor leisure opportunities (Rolston, this volume), and make available more leisure opportunities in underprivileged urban areas (Jordan, this volume). Less explicit aims were, apparently, to justify demands for more governmental financing for leisure research and to legitimize the recreationist profession or group of professions. Considering the impressive array of empirical data adduced by a variety of eminent professionals, the benefits of leisure seem to have been proved; it is to be hoped that this volume will also help to advance significantly the other aims of the conveyors. However, from the academic perspective of a theoretically oriented sociologist and social anthropologist, the principal question is, do the state-of-knowledge papers in this volume help to formulate or advance an integrated, interdisciplinary theoretical perspective on leisure and its varied benefits? In this respect, the achievements of these papers are less unequivocal. There is little critical examination of the deeper problems in which the specific issue of leisure is embedded in this late modern age, as the world approaches the turn of the millennium. And here, to my mind, an integrated interdisciplinary intellectual effort is necessary, paralleling similar efforts in such problem areas as the environment, energy, and alternative lifestyles.

In this comment I shall first attempt to clarify some theoretically important dimensions of the problem of "benefits of leisure" and then turn to outline some substantive issues related to this clarification.

A fundamental difficulty facing a comprehensive analysis of most of the papers presented in this volume is the extremely broad and vague use of the term "benefits of leisure." There is no commonly agreed concept of either "benefits" or "leisure"; neither do many of the individual contributors define or clarify their own use of these terms. This vagueness is, to my mind, at least in part a consequence of a lack of distinction between two very different sets of problems, or "fronts," faced by leisure researchers.

I wish to thank Boas Shamir for his suggestions on an earlier draft of this comment.

THE TWO FRONTS OF LEISURE IN LATE MODERN SOCIETY

A review of the more than two dozen papers in this volume demonstrates the enormous scope of forms of leisure activities and the wide variety of their consequences on the individual, social, and cultural levels of late modern society. While this demonstration is certainly impressive, the exact nature and status of such consequences remains somewhat obscure. Indeed, the principal deficiency of the papers and of the limited definition of the scope of issues dealt with is the paucity of attempts to relate the alleged benefits of leisure to the broader issue of the relationship between leisure and general social and cultural change. Although some papers (e.g., Orthner and Mancini, this volume) touch upon this issue, they do so only in a partial and specific way. However, as Goodale and Cooper (this volume) have pointed out, leisure has from the days of European antiquity been considered a template of innovative thought and as such, a source of wide-ranging social and cultural change. It is somewhat ironic—and indicative of the quality of much of contemporary mass leisure—that a volume dealing with the contemporary and emergent age of leisure has largely overlooked this aspect. The fact that leisure, as was rightly pointed out, tends to become personalized in our age should not mislead us to think that it therefore has no broader social and cultural implications. Moreover, while certain forms of personalized leisure may be beneficial to the individual, wider social and cultural impacts and consequences may be more problematical (see Haggard and Williams, this volume). Studies of tourism and its impact on the host environment, society, and culture have amply demonstrated this point.

Phenomenologically speaking, leisure activities are not part of the paramount reality of daily life, rather, they constitute a "limited province of meaning" (Schutz 1973, Vol I: 229). Most leisure activities are not "real" in the sense in which everyday activities are "real." Indeed, here lies one of the sources of their enjoyable character. We can enjoy a crime story or a drama partly because, though it resembles reality, it is not real. We can even enjoy vicarious participation in dramatic or even catastrophic events by reading history or seeing a TV documentary because it is not us who are really involved; for those who undergo the real experience the events are decidedly less enjoyable.

It emerges from some of the papers that this unreal character of leisure experiences may be beneficial to the individual in a restorative or therapeutic sense. It is clear, however, that owing to this very character, leisure activities might not have direct "real" consequences for everyday reality: a war game, staged in a playful spirit, is not a war.

But leisure activities certainly can have real impacts, often in an indirect, oblique way; even if pursued in a playful spirit, leisure activities may have serious consequences.

Some ideas developed by the late Victor Turner (1969) on the liminal or liminoid quality of such phenomena as leisure activities can here provide us with important leads. Turner and his followers (Gottlieb 1982, Wagner 1977) pointed to the restitutive or compensatory qualities of liminal phenomena; but Turner also pointed out the creative potential for social and cultural change inherent in them. Turner emphasized the "subjunctive" mode or character of liminal phenomena, a term taken from grammar, where it is contrasted to the "indicative" mode. As such, these phenomena are "potential," fraught with possibilities; hence they are an ideal template for experimentation and trial and error. New ways of thinking, of intellectual and artistic creativity, of perceiving the world and society, and of alternative lifeways and social orders can be worked out in a playful way in such liminal situations.

A pertinent, though perhaps extreme example is offered from my own area of expertise, Thai studies. The sixth king of the present Thai dynasty, King Vajiravudh (Rama VI, reigned 1910-25), was a great lover of literature and theatre. After ascending to the throne, and while he was the absolute ruler of Thailand, Vajiravudh created a toy state, named Dusit Thani, in which he and his courtiers played out imaginary political roles (Vella 1978: 75-76). While often regarded as a bizarre and whimsical form of royal chicanery, Dusit Thani also served as a realm of playful experimentation with alternative forms of democratic government, even at a time when the king ruthlessly subdued any direct threat to his absolute authority. Dusit Thani, in a sense, constituted a liminal precedent to the real political changes following Vajiravudh's rule, which found expression in the introduction of the constitutional monarchy by the revolution of 1932 (Batson 1984). While admittedly far-fetched, this example illustrates the kinds of potentialities for change imminent in leisure situations.

Moreover, not all leisure is playful; there is also serious leisure (Stebbins 1982) to which individuals develop a strong commitment (Shamir 1988). Serious leisure may have direct impacts on the real world, such as amateur pursuits of scientific or artistic activities; indeed, here the boundary between leisure and work activities tends to become fuzzy (Stebbins 1979) and may eventually be completely erased.

While these issues have not been explicitly stated in the majority of the papers in this volume (but see Barnett, this volume), a careful reading of the papers points to a common background against which most evaluations of leisure activities as beneficial for real life are at least tacitly set by their authors. This common background consists of the major personal existential and social problems besetting late modernity. The authors claim that leisure activities, in their varied forms, can in various ways help to resolve or at least ameliorate these problems. Many thus believe in leisure as "a last resort," and the vehemence with which some of the authors (e.g., Jordan, this volume) have spoken of the need for strengthening this field of activity testifies to the strength of their convictions.

What are these common background problems to which most authors in this volume tend to refer? A scrutiny of the contributions indicates that the authors relate the alleged benefits of leisure to two quite different groups of problems, or two distinct "fronts" of late modernity.

Most contributors relate them to the accumulated individual and social stresses generated by the structural features of late modernity; while a minority relate them to the broader problems of the quality of life in the emergent, postmodern society, in which work and occupational concerns cease to be the center of life concern and personal identity for a great number of individuals, and they therefore look for meaning in other spheres of activity.

It has been claimed that leisure activities can be beneficial on both a personal as well as a sociocultural level with regard to both these "fronts," but in somewhat different senses. Thus, in order to introduce some order and system into the multifarious benefits of leisure, I shall first outline a general classificatory model, and then discuss some of the issues implied by it.

THE MODEL

The four-fold model (Table 1), summarizes the salient traits of the various categories of leisure benefits mentioned or alluded to in this volume and illustrates each category with a few salient examples.

Social Problems

This front is primarily past-oriented; leisure activities are of interest primarily because of their remedial or compensatory function—their ability to alleviate the harmful consequences generated by late modern, Western society. The importance of these functions grows the more secularized society becomes because leisure activities under these circumstances take over part of the functions of religion in earlier times. It should be stressed, however, that the compensatory functions of leisure, whatever their importance in specific instances, are limited to dealing only with the consequences, and not the causes, of contemporary social problems. Thus, some leisure activities can help to reduce stresses generated by modern life-patterns (e.g., Levitt; Orthner and Mancini; Ulrich, Dimberg and Driver; Wankel and Berger; this volume), but are largely powerless to influence and change the structural arrangements of modern society which have generated these stresses. Similarly, some leisure activities may help to keep teenagers off the streets and thereby control or reduce the rate of crime in society, but they do not have

Table 1. A classificatory model for benefits of leisure.

Level	Front	
	Social problems	Quality of life
Individual	Physical and mental health improvement Stress reduction Re-creation	Self-actualization Flow and peak experiences Personal growth
Socio-cultural	Crime control Group cohesion Social integration	Social innovation Cultural creativity
Nature of benefit	Compensatory function	Intrinsic meaning
Methods of evaluating benefit	Specific measurements (quantitative)	Diffuse evaluation (qualitative)

any influence upon the deeper factors which bring these teenagers onto the streets (Jordan, this volume). Leisure is thus compensative in the sense that it alleviates existing social problems, but it would be a mistake to ascribe to it a general capacity to resolve them. Moreover, as some of the authors in this volume have pointed out, there exist various forms of negative leisure, such as violent or stressful sports and some individualized electronic games, which, rather than being compensatory, can add to the stresses of late modernity and even generate new social problems.

Owing to these circumstances, rather than talk of leisure activities as a global, undifferentiated category, we have to examine the specific beneficial functions of each kind of leisure activitiy within the social and cultural context in which it is taking place. Many of the papers in this volume list impressive arrays of alleged beneficial consequences of various types of leisure. However, only a few of these papers explicate the specific context within which given kinds of leisure activities yield optimal benefits, or under which conditions some kinds of leisure activities may become harmful. We, therefore, have to conclude that the evaluation of the functions of leisure with regard to the alleviation of social problems cannot be conducted in a general, indiscriminate way. Rather, it is important to develop and apply specific methodologies and measurement techniques which will make it possible to evaluate and compare the specific benefits (and costs) of given kinds of leisure activities in different contexts, and of different kinds of leisure activities in the same context.

Quality of Life

This front is primarily future-oriented; leisure activities are of interest primarily because they will supposedly help to endow the life of late modern man with meaning. Their importance in this respect may become central in the post-modern future as work and the Protestant work-ethic lose their priority in Western societies. Under such circumstances, leisure could indeed become man's last resort, insofar as neither religion nor secular jobs will serve as the ultimate source of meaning for most postmodern men. "Quality of life," as here conceived, does not refer only or even primarily to such issues as health, longevity, or physical well-being, but to deeper personal and spiritual issues such as self-expressional self-actualization (Csikszentmihalyi and Kleiber, this volume) of the individual and the furtherance of "flow" (Csikszentmihalyi 1975) or "peak" (Maslow 1968) experiences. It is further submitted that such personal experiences can help, on the broad societal level, to experiment with and promote innovative social forms of life and, especially, novel forms of cultural creativity.

The value of leisure for the enhancement of the quality of life cannot be easily measured in concrete, specific terms, but must be interpretatively evaluated in broad, diffuse terms. While the compensatory functions of leisure in ameliorating existing social problems are generally susceptible to more or less precise quantitative measurements, qualitative methodologies are necessary for the evaluation of the contribution of leisure to the quality of life in postmodern times.

While most papers in this volume, owing to the practical as well as research concerns of the authors, deal primarily with the compensatory functions of leisure in contemporary society, I shall concentrate here on the principal obstacles in the way of using leisure to improve the quality of life in the post-modern society. I shall deal with this issue in terms of the "paradox of leisure," which, to my mind, confronts contemporary Western society.

THE PARADOX OF LEISURE

As several authors have pointed out, modern affluence and individualism substantially increased the opportunities for leisure of Western man, both in terms of time without obligation as well as in terms of available choices for leisure opportunities; these opportunities will probably increase significantly in the future. But the very culture which created this ambience also blurred the criteria of choice and preference which could help modern man make meaningful and truly beneficial leisure choices. Hence, he finds that freedom of choice is a double-edged predicament. While offering a chance for self-expression and self-actualization in leisure, it also engenders insecurity and confusion. In other words, the lack of institutionalization of the sphere of leisure produces a form of anomie, which threatens to turn man's free time into an empty time of anxiety and boredom. The major problem raised by this paradox of leisure is how the potential inherent in leisure can be realized in a personally, socially, and culturally creative way.

The absence of culturally sanctioned, intrinsic criteria of choice of leisure activities, under conditions of widely available free time and the prevailing capitalist conditions, inevitably leads to a proliferation of commercialized leisure opportunities vying with each other for the consumer's attention. The mass culture which emerged from such commercialization, necessarily tends to cater to the lowest common denominator of its potential customer—even though there is probably more differentiation in the mass leisure market than the most critical commentators of mass culture admit.

Most members of late modern Western societies tend to resolve the paradox of leisure by choosing the most easily available, standardized, commercialized, and widely advertised forms of mass leisure opportunities, ranging from TV watching (see Csikszentmihalyi and Kleiber, this volume), spectator sports, and various hobbies, to organized mass tourism (Cohen 1972); while a minority of cultural rebels tend to actively seek alternative forms of leisure, often embodied in alternative lifestyles or in alternative tourism (Richter 1987).

It seems reasonable to assume that the alternative forms of leisure, being less programmed and permitting greater opportunity for self-direction, will contribute more to the enhancement of the quality of life on both the individual and the sociocultural level.

However, a closer scrutiny of alternative forms of leisure, including tourism, has shown that they are less than an unqualified blessing. In particular, studies of alternative tourism have demonstrated that as such alternative forms of behavior become fashionable, processes of routinization set in, in the wake of which this form of tourism loses much of its uniqueness and often becomes an inexpensive form of routine mass tourism (Cohen 1973). In leisure, as in education and other spheres of modern life, the process of *Vermassung* (i.e., growth on a massive scale) seems to have an independent effect on the quality of the experience, whatever the initial aspirations of the participants.

A realistic policy in the field of leisure for the improvement of the quality of life should not, therefore, be based primarily on the promotion of alternative forms of leisure. Rather, it appears that the principal effort should be devoted to the enhancement of opportunities for self-realization, self-actualization, and creativity within the scope of commercialized forms of mass leisure (Cohen 1987: 16-17). The strategy suggested here for the resolution of the paradox of leisure is, on the one hand, to direct commercialized mass leisure into more promising routes and, on the other hand, to educate the consumers of the mass leisure industry to become more active and discerning in their choices. This is a subject of both theoretical and applied research interest, which until now has not gained sufficient attention on the part of leisure researchers.

CONCLUSION

While leisure activities were shown to help alleviate—if not to resolve—the social problems affecting late modern society, they also appear to contain the potential to become the main vehicle for the enhancement of the quality of life in the future postmodern society. While this potential has yet to be fully proven and comprehended by planners and policymakers, its realization is bedeviled by serious obstacles. These have been conceptualized in terms of a paradox of leisure facing late and postmodern man: an anomic situation in which man lacks criteria for beneficial choices of leisure activities under conditions of growing leisure opportunities. While, as a consequence, people tend to submit to the most easily available commercialized forms of mass leisure, it was argued that rather than fight commercialization in the name of utopian alternative forms of leisure, policymakers should seek to harness commercialized leisure to the goal of an improved quality of life and seek to educate the public to more independence and discernment in making their leisure choices.

LITERATURE CITED

Batson, B. A. 1984. The end of the absolute monarchy in Siam. Singapore: Oxford University Press.

Cohen, E. 1972. Towards a sociology of international tourism. Social Research. 39(1): 164-82.

Cohen, E. 1973. Nomads from affluence: notes on the phenomenon of drifter tourism. International Journal of Comparative Sociology. 14(1-2): 89-103.

Cohen, E. 1987. "Alternative tourism" — a critique. Tourism Recreation Research. 12(2): 13-18.

Csikszentmihalyi, M. 1975. Beyond boredom and anxiety: the experience of play in work and games. San Francisco, CA: Jossey-Bass.

Gottlieb, A. 1982. Americans' vacations. Annals of Tourism Research. 9: 165-187.

Maslow, A. 1968. Towards a psychology of being. New York, NY: Van Nostrand.

Richter, L. K., ed. 1987. The search for appropriate tourism in the third world. Tourism Recreation Research. 12(2): 1-64.

Schutz, A. 1973. Collected papers. The Hague: M. Nijhoff (3 vol.)

Shamir, B. 1988. Commitment and leisure. Sociological Perspective. 31(4): 238-58.

Stebbins, R. A. 1979. Amateurs: on the margin between work and leisure. Beverly Hills, CA: Sage.

Stebbins, R. A. 1982. Serious leisure: a conceptual statement. Pacific Sociological Review. 25(2): 25-72.

Turner, V. W. 1969. The ritual process. London, England: Routledge and Kegan Paul.

Vella, W. F. 1978. Chaiyo! King Vajiravudh and the development of Thai nationalism. Honolulu, HI: University of Hawaii Press.

Wagner, U. 1977. Out of time and place: mass tourism and charter trips. Ethos. 42(1-2): 38-52.

The Construction of Leisure

Elery Hamilton-Smith
Department of Leisure Studies
Phillip Institute of Technology
Bundoora, Victoria
Australia

The literature on leisure abounds with comments on the difficulty inherent in definition of leisure as a term or as an idea. On reviewing the papers in this volume, one can only be struck by the extent to which common agreement on definition is lacking and by the conceptual and mensurational problems which this lack of clarity generates.

I start from the position that leisure is a social construct; it may be constructed in any one of a number of ways and each of these has more or less equal legitimacy. In everyday usage, it is then almost inevitable that the common understanding of the word carries with it fragments of each of a number of logically distinct constructions. This, in turn, often leads to the position that leisure is essentially a very personal matter, so complex and so subject to variation that definitional attempts are bound to end in futility. One of my own students once wrote, "If the time ever arrives when there is a commonly agreed definition of leisure, then leisure as we currently know it will have ceased to exist!"

Now this is probably a useful caution against any attempt to constrain everyday understanding, but for purposes of research, constructs which can be operationalized in research design must be developed. It is not necessary that these should be directly measurable, although those which are will be more readily amenable to current traditions of research. Given the present preeminence of positivism in the common sense view of science, they will also yield much more convincing evidence. However, this does not mean that other approaches to the construction of leisure should be rejected, and in fact, anti-positivism offers rich insights into the sphere of personal and social benefits.

I contend that paying too much attention to measurement and its methodology may divert us from the more important task of developing a satisfactory hermeneutic reconstruction of the phenomena which we are seeking to measure. The hermeneutic tradition implies that we cannot understand without interpretation, and that interpretation is, in itself, part of the path to understanding. So, the endeavor to understand the nature of leisure is important in itself, not just as a means to better measurement.

The hermeneutic perspective on knowledge building also leads to recognition of the inherent ambiguities and contradictions in society. These shift and change with time, so we may never attain finality in our search for truth and understanding—knowledge will always be open and anticipatory. This contrasts markedly with the expectation, upon which sociological positivism was founded—that with sufficient empirical study, we will come to a total understanding of human society. But even physics today generally rejects this sort of naive positivism. It is certainly high time that the social sciences did likewise.

In order to arrive at an improved understanding of any social phenomenon, it also seems important to consider its historical origins. Any phenomenon seen only in the present is imperfectly understood. "We are never completely contemporaneous with our present. History advances in disguise; it appears on stage wearing the mask of the previous scene and we tend to lose the meaning of the play" (Debray 1967). All too often, any discussion of the historical genesis of the leisure idea commences with one of two remarkable simplisms: either real leisure was first described by Aristotle, or leisure commenced with the industrial revolution!

A further difficulty in the contemporary study of leisure is that leisure as a phenomenon is often abstracted from the society in which it occurs. Much of the literature ignores major dimensions of society such as class, gender, and ethnicity; examining the relationship of leisure to processes of domination and submission is similarly totally rejected. As Rojek (1985) has emphasized, the study of leisure has been a sad example of "sociology without society."

A RANGE OF CONSTRUCTS

For present purposes, it seems adequate to deal with four kinds of constructs and to demonstrate their possible implications for benefit measurement. The boundaries of three of these are readily identifiable, and each is accessible to empirical methods. The fourth is essentially personal and subjective, and therefore tends to be more problematic. The four suggested constructs are:

- Leisure as time—generally defined as time which is free from work and survival or other obligatory activities.
- Leisure as action—defined in terms of the behavior and participation in specific activities. Often this is an ad hoc construct, but nevertheless it is widely utilized in research.
- Leisure as action undertaken within specific time/ space—this integrates the two previous constructs, but in doing so, produces a new and distinct construct.
- Leisure as quality of experience—this is the most problematic of the four constructs, and may well be seen as one of the benefits which may arise from any of the others. However, it does represent a major strand in the current literature and must be examined here. It also opens up, perhaps more effectively than other constructs, questions about the constraints which society places upon leisure opportunities for some sections of the population.

Leisure as Time

The use of nonobligated time as the key characteristic of leisure has been advocated because it is seen as being relatively easy to operationalize (Shivers 1985). It is also an important theme in the common sense use of the word (Goodale and Cooper, this volume) although very rarely used in isolation from other definitional elements.

The most familiar research use of this construct is, of course, in time-budget studies (Chapin 1974, Robinson 1977, Szalai 1972). These studies generally demonstrate the "fuzziness" of leisure as a construct—the very notion of being "unobligated" brings with it elements of action and experience. The assumption that time lends itself to naive empiricism soon vanishes, and we face problems of interpretation in any such studies.

Another problem that arises out of the "unobligated" time idea is that it is impossibly broad—it encompasses an immense range of action and experience, much of which would not generally be seen as "true" leisure. Thus, to use this as a construct upon which to base benefit measurement would result mainly in confusion and lack of credibility.

Interestingly, time-budget studies have generally not addressed the issue of benefits. Although they do provide an excellent basis for comparison both between cultures or subcultures and over time, the attribution of benefit to various time patterns has not been considered in other than a very simplistic way. Best (1978) has certainly demonstrated the possibility of options in time use throughout the life cycle and implied benefits which might accrue from some of these. There has also been considerable rhetoric, but all too little research about the effects of flexible workday patterns. One can certainly draw the tentative conclusion that such patterns tend to result in a greater increase of time being spent on family or household obligations than on purely discretionary activities (e.g., Robinson 1977). But there is insufficient evidence to generalize this finding with any confidence, let alone make any inferences of benefit.

In adopting an explicitly interpretive position, one might turn to the question of the way in which time is perceived by individuals or by a culture and the meanings placed upon these varying perceptions. Here we can find various cross-cultural comparisons which vividly demonstrate the differences between so-called "natural time" and "clock time" and the way in which these differing views impact upon the allocation of time (e.g., Cheek and Burch 1976). The perceptual dimension of time certainly also underlies the concept of "time famine" (Lindner 1970), and here one can find at least prima facie evidence that the perception of time as unobligated does in itself convey perceived and probably psychophysiological benefits.

A further problem which demands more exploration amongst leisure scientists is the interrelationship between concepts of time and space. Some, particularly those from France with their notion of "temps sociaux," have commenced exploration of the implications of time/space theory (e.g., Samuel 1986), but none have given adequate attention to its complex ramifications as explored by other disciplines (see Carlstein et al. 1978). I will return below to the issues of both time famine and the time/space relationship.

In summary, although superficially attractive as a more readily operationalized construct, leisure as time is rarely used in its pure form and has not yet proved useful in benefit studies. There may well be value and considerable interest in measuring the benefits which accrue from various options in the arrangement of time. But the necessary scale, and hence cost, of such studies mean that they may well not be undertaken. Even if they were, given the numerous factors which impinge on time use in our society, one can only doubt the extent of their useful applicability.

Leisure as Action

Strangely, few scholars have explicitly claimed this construct as the basis of their work. Yet, when one looks at the detail of research design, it has played an extremely important role. Leisure often is operationalized as defined activities or classes of activity as exemplified in a number of the papers summarized by Driver, Tinsley, and Manfredo or by Wankel and Berger (this volume).

However, the central problem of utilizing this as a means of constructing leisure is that so many activities may not take place only within leisure (however that may be defined)—a large number occur in what we commonly call work as much as in leisure. This problem is, of course, central to the measurement of benefits from physical activity, where the benefits of both work and leisure are interwoven (Froelicher and Froelicher, this volume).

This problem raises the question of whether leisure should be conceptually separated from work. On one hand, from a simple experiential analysis, one can argue that there is no valid clear separation between work and leisure, but rather that they are parts of a continuum of human experience. On the other hand, from a political economy perspective, there is an immense gulf between leisure, however constructed, and most productive employment. To deny or overlook this in our construction of leisure opens our conceptual-political doors to continuing oppression of the underclass.

In summary, although widely used in traditional research, the construction of leisure as participation in specific kinds of action poses considerable problems in benefit measurement simply because it does not confront the complex problems inherent in the work-leisure relationship.

Leisure as Action within Time/Space

When one brings the two previous constructs together, some of the problems inherent in either used alone tend to disappear, and an essentially new idea emerges—namely that of action taking place within a specific time and space context. Essentially, this is the construct which underlies ideas of "leisure service," "recreation service," or perhaps most simply, "recreation." Any agency providing a recreation service to a population sets out to offer the opportunity to participate in action, and often (but not necessarily) locates this in a specific site at a specific time. Most commonly, the time and place context is such as to exclude any possibility of confusion with the productive employment arena, even when the opportunity is developed and provided within the work place (Ellis and Richardson, this volume).

There are a spectrum of ways in which action might occur. At one extreme, it might be almost entirely personalized—an individual takes his own personally constructed fishing tackle to a quiet river and fishes alone. Collective organization by a family or group of friends may result in a picnic; a park service may organize and offer the experience of joining in a conducted nature tour. Or, at the other extreme, an entrepreneur may package a specific recreational opportunity and market this to anybody willing to buy. All of these can be accommodated by the "action within time/space" construct.

I argue that this construct provides one of the most useful and appropriate bases upon which benefit measurement might be developed. Those concerned with the use of benefit measurement (e.g., Siehl and Kostmayer, and Jordan, this volume) are basically interested in the direction of and justification for public expenditure on recreation resources or programs. More importantly, the construct can be readily operationalized in either empirical or interpretive investigational designs. By adopting the terminology "recreation benefits" rather than "leisure benefits" we may also make our intentions somewhat clearer.

This construct readily accommodates studies on activities undertaken within particular programmatic contexts (Ulrich, Dimberg, and Driver; Wankel and Berger; Easley; Driver, Tinsley, and Manfredo; this volume), and on the settings within which activities might be undertaken (Rolston, Hull, Marans and Mohai, this volume). It also provides a more rigorous basis for examining the more diffuse activities and benefits, and avoiding vague statements about "the leisure arena." Undoubtedly, it will be challenged by those who look toward either being all inclusive or taking full account of personal experience. For many other kinds of considerations about leisure, I also would reject it as a construct, but in thinking about benefit measurement, it has considerable potency.

Many of the benefit measurement studies to date have used more or less traditional empirical methods to explore the pattern of benefits which might arise. Most studies have seen qualitative methods as appropriate only for preliminary exploration studies, rather than as important in themselves. Alternatively, qualitative data have been reduced to nomothetic categories in order to simplify analysis. My own (so far unpublished) studies of benefits arising from park visits have relied upon in-depth interviews undertaken from the phenomenological perspective. These demonstrate the importance of an interpretive approach as a basis for deepening our understanding of how people perceive the benefits which accrue to themselves. More importantly, they detail our understanding to the point where, in turn, we can help to detail the physical design and management of parks.

It is appropriate now to return to considering the relationship between time and space. It is often the interaction between these two dimensions which serves to define recreational activity and set it apart from other kinds of activity. More positively, a real understanding of the time/space problem can help us toward better overall management of both resources. Implicitly, it appears that much of the research summarized in this volume is suggesting that the right juxtaposition of time and space may be more beneficial than other suboptimal arrangements. To take up the specific example of time famine, it appears that much of the time famine reported in recent studies is a personal perception of time/space rather than an actual decrease in available time. The ubiquity of that perception is clear, as is the feeling of stress which so often accompanies it. A truly profitable area for research would be to examine the way in which creative management of the time/space relationship might reduce feelings of time famine, and at the same time, reduce any stress which appears to accompany it.

In summary, if we construct leisure as action in time/space, which corresponds with the domain of recreational services, or more simply recreation, then we have a construct which will facilitate useful benefit measurement. It will enable operational design of methodology in either the empirical or interpretive traditions, and the latter of these has probably been inappropriately neglected. Finally, it will help us to consider policy outcomes in terms of enhanced time/space design and management.

Leisure as Experience

By contrast, one might see personally lived experience as the most important construct of leisure. In particular, the work of Czikszentmihalyi (with Kleiber, this volume) has served to draw attention to the importance of experience as a key construct and, again, has highlighted the problem of the leisure-work boundary. Similarly, some of the less tangible concepts dealt with in this volume, such as spiritual benefits (McDonald and Schreyer), mood (Hull), social cohesion (Burch and Hamilton-Smith), and even self-identity (Haggard and Williams) demand at least to some extent, an experiential construct as a basis for research.

If one sets out to map the realm of personal experience, categories such as work and leisure appear to have relatively little meaning in themselves, although some of their concomitants, such as social status and self-esteem, may well prove to be vital stimulators of or constraints upon the quality of experience. This close relationship between work and leisure has also been highlighted by Stebbins (1979) in looking at the roles created and occupied by amateurs. Similar analyses might be extended to a range of other roles, including hobbyists, volunteers, and political activists. However, in pursuing Stebbins' role analysis methodology, one should take care to distinguish between the action in time/space dimension (behavior) where the distinction between work and leisure can be made relatively clear, and the experiential dimension (personal outcomes of behavior) where the distinction becomes more clouded.

Both in everyday usage and in the work of many leisure scholars, leisure is constructed as experience characterized by such qualities as freedom of choice, freedom from external control or constraint, intrinsic satisfaction, and sense of involvement.

Given this construct, leisure is seen as "good" in itself and as a desirable state of being. This then raises conceptual and methodological problems about using an experiential construct as the basis for benefit measurement—it would be simply tautological to measure the benefit of something which is, in itself, defined as good. If, on the other hand, we examine recreation as constructed above—action within time/space—then we can measure the extent and nature of a leisure state of being as a set of the beneficial outcomes.

In everyday language, this is calling for a clear distinction between recreation (action in time/space) and the personal experience which results from that action—which may be of the character many refer to as leisure.

This in turn leads us to a basis for looking at the factors which help to shape the nature and quality of human experience. The same activity in the same time/space may very well result in a different experience for different people.

Those of low social status and low self-confidence might not be able to even avail themselves of the activity; or if they do, may find it a frightening rather than pleasing experience. Examination of leisure (in the quality of experience sense) constraints might then lead us to frame better policies and more effective opportunities.

Perhaps this is also the place to raise the question of what Walvin (1978) has neatly categorized as the "sinful recreations." Simply because the everyday construction of leisure, and even recreation, treat both as good in themselves, leisure scholars have generally ignored the problem of society's moral judgments about such activities as drunkenness, sexual license, taking of illicit drugs, and the like. By placing the question in an historical context, Walvin reminds us that the very definition of sin is subject to fashion just as is any other leisure activity. The taking of what are now generally regarded as illicit drugs was for years sanctioned as the consumption of patent medicines for good health.

More widely, the problem of sinful recreations raises the question of disbenefits. We may recognize the disbenefits to public health of drunkenness, sexual license, or illicit drug-taking, even though these remain amongst our largest leisure "industries." But we probably give all too little attention to other disbenefits from what are otherwise seen as valuable recreational opportunities. Examples which come readily to mind include the excessive injuries resulting from some of the more gladiatorial sports, the strange social values drilled into our children and ourselves by the media (particularly television), the boredom of many suburban environments with its inevitable impact upon mental health and human happiness, and the sad socioeconomic impacts of much international tourism.

CONCLUSION

Essentially, this brief commentary contains a series of exhortations to view leisure research more widely. I have argued for greater consideration of the historical and social context, and for enhancing the quality of research design by considering the various constructions of leisure and critically examining their implications for any given research study. Further, I would hope to see interpretive/qualitative approaches to research taken much more seriously. If we are really to understand the meaning of various phenomena to people, then I see no alternative but to make much more use of the interpretive/qualitative paradigms. I have concluded by arguing for a much more open consideration of disbenefits as well as benefits.

Turning to the logic of benefit measurement research, I believe that the most useful results are likely to arise from an examination of the benefits and disbenefits of recreation (as action in time/space). By subjecting the experience which accrues from this action to detailed analysis as a set of benefits, we will come to more fully understand just what a truly leisured lifestyle might be and what it means to individual people. This can then provide the raw material upon which better policies and programs might be built.

LITERATURE CITED

Best, F. 1978. The time of our lives: the parameters of lifetime distribution of education, work and leisure. Loisir et Societe. 1(1): 95-124.

Carlstein, T.; Parkes, D.; Thrift, N. 1978. Timing space and spacing time. 3 vols. London: Edward Arnold. 150 p., 120 p., 120 p.

Chapin, F. S. 1974. Human activity patterns in the city: things people do in time and space. New York, NY: Wiley. 272 p.

Cheek, N. H., Jr.; Burch, W. R., Jr. 1976. The social organization of leisure in human society. New York, NY: Harper & Row. 283 p.

Debray, R. 1967. Revolution in the revolution. Harmondsworth: Pelican Books. 127 p.

Lindner, S. B. 1970. The harried leisure class. New York, NY: Columbia University Press. 182 p.

Robinson, J. P. 1977. How Americans use time: a social-psychological analysis of human behaviour. New York, NY: Praeger. 210 p.

Rojek, C. 1985. Capitalism and leisure theory. London: Tavistock. 208 p.

Samuel, N. 1986. Evolution de la structure des temps sociaux en France; une transformation des modes de vie. Loisir et Societe. 9(2): 257-278.

Shivers, J. 1985. Leisure constructs: a conceptual reference. World Leisure and Recreation. 27(1): 24-27.

Stebbins, R. A. 1979. Amateurs: on the margin between work and leisure. Beverly Hills, CA: Sage. 280 p.

Szalai, A., ed. 1972. The use of time: daily activities of urban and suburban populations in twelve countries. The Hague: Mouton. 868 p.

Walvin, J. 1978. Leisure and society 1830-1950. London: Longman. 181 p.

Leisure, Justice, and Imagination

Marvin Henberg
Department of Philosophy
University of Idaho
Moscow, Idaho

A THOUGHT EXPERIMENT

Imagine a world of perfect justice—a world without penury in which virtue, talent, and industriousness are properly rewarded. Criminal justice in this world produces no unmerited suffering. The legally guilty are punished swiftly in due degree, whereas the legally innocent never suffer from official corruption or mistaken judgment. All forms of oppression are unknown—the state weighs lightly on its citizens, who enjoy a bounteous liberty compatible with like liberty for all.

Add other features to your own particular taste. Add ethnic diversity and people skilled in music, dance, and philosophy. Add gourmet foods, fast cars, nonpolluting factories. Pick your favorite landscape in which to live, your favorite architecture in which to dwell. People your environs with friends and loved ones. Ban disease and accident; let natural death come late in life, with little pain.

There is, however, one thing you may not have in your imagined world of perfect justice. Though spiced in other respects with your favorite things, this world contains neither fun nor playfulness—the intrinsic goods of leisure. There is no humor, no relief from solemnity. All is compounded of sober devotion to justice. Sensuous gratification is commonplace, a given, such that leisure is never a high holiday of release from pain, torment, or exhaustion.

With the banishing of play, elation, and fun, our colorful imagined world becomes a colorful gray oxymoron. Luster fades from our experiment in thought. We begin to wonder about the coherence of our imagination. What can it mean to speak of a "favorite" landscape or architecture? With fun and elation subtracted, could we have a "favorite" anything? Imagine our experience in such a world: each pleasure a mild throb, too well-mannered to abide for long. Gone would be anticipation and joy, hope and charity, romantic love and selfless devotion. The emotional register of our world of gray justice would be like a musical world confined to a single octave on a tedious instrument like the harmonica.

Imagine now that you possess a magic wand which, when waved, would bring this world of gray justice into existence. All of suffering humanity would fall under its benign jurisdiction. Starvation in Ethiopia, senseless death in the barrios of Los Angeles, corrupt public officials, bloated financiers all swept away, vanished. Replacing these blights on justice would be a population of sober contented creatures leading painless lives of gratifying (ever so *mildly* gratifying) length.

Are you morally obligated to wave the wand? The wretched and deprived beg you to do so—their gain would be immeasurable. The affluent beg you to stay your hand—their loss (though not a *material* loss) would likewise be great.

You are in a quandary. You must decide what degree of suffering, if any, you may continue to impose on some people—perhaps the vast majority of earth's present population—for the sake of preserving playfulness and fun. Or if we imagine less harsh circumstances, how great must injustice grow before you are morally compelled to wave the wand? If only one person suffers unjustly, may you deprive everyone else of playfulness for his or her sake? How about two—a dozen? Is it a numbers game at all? Suppose finally that by waving the wand you can rid the world of injustice while preserving a full emotional register for every other human being. The sole cost is that you alone must sacrifice all future fun. You alone must become a gray person in a world of justice *plus*—for everyone else—playfulness. Are you morally obligated to wave the wand? Do others have the moral right to compel such a sacrifice?

LEISURE AND THE THOUGHT EXPERIMENT

Leisure connects to the preceding thought experiment in several ways, two of which I explore in this essay. The first connection is to the neglect and denigration of leisure bemoaned in this and virtually every other volume of leisure studies. Typically, this neglect is attributed to a work-oriented North American culture in which leisure receives only the scraps fed it when the sober-minded elect to take a break, mainly in the interest of greater efficiency when commencing again to work. Though I accept that our cultural bias against leisure is strong, I shall argue that its roots do not lie solely in sober-minded devotion to work as the antithesis of leisure. The bias is rooted equally in a stern doctrine of justice as the first virtue of social institutions. To the extent we embrace a comparative view of the benefits of leisure, the stern doctrine of justice will, given any degree of distributive inequality, drive us into denigrating leisure, for from a moral point of view there will always be more urgent needs to be met. Our thought experiment is a case in point: conscience tugs at us, however reluctantly, to realize justice for all. Too bad about playfulness; but what can we do? After all, in the scales of justice fun weighs light as a feather. Souls are saved by repentance and serious good deeds. Who ever heard of a clown arriving in heaven for simply being a clown?

I hope further to show that the prospect of a wholescale tradeoff between justice and fun rests on a deep-seated but false dichotomy in our thinking about the goods of leisure. After exposing this false dichotomy, I shall argue that some of the goods of leisure are inherently noncomparative and, as

such, cannot be analyzed as a "benefit" in the sense stipulated by the editors of this volume. If we are to hold out any hope of preserving fun and playfulness against the stern doctrine of justice, our effort must be grounded in an appreciation of the noncomparative, intrinsic goods of leisure. (In making this point, I do not presume to teach leisure scientists something new; rather I offer my remarks as a friendly reminder of truths so familiar that they are easily overlooked.)

Like fun, imagination is a noncomparative good of leisure. This insight opens the way for exploration of a second dimension of our thought experiment. The gray world of perfect justice is, of course, wholly fanciful. To the unimaginative its contemplation may seem a waste: why squander precious time by mentally inhabiting worlds that do not (and probably cannot) exist? Again, if we look only for benefits in a comparative sense, we end in disappointment. Surely there are better and more serious things to be done—e.g., planning to improve the plight of earth's suffering majority. Imagination is squeezed to a vanishing point, victimized by a bias similar to the bias against studying leisure. Only the perception that imagination is a noncomparative good, I shall argue, will save it from banishment in the way Plato (1961) banishes poetry from his ideal Republic. In the course of this argument, I disclose a false assumption in much of our thinking about imagination—namely, that its products are inherently untrue, especially in comparison to the products of reason and sober reflection (the products of *science*, if you will), which always have truth as their object. In denigrating leisure, a stern doctrine of truth is an accomplice of the stern doctrine of justice, and so long as we mistakenly believe that truth and imagination are incompatible, our "leisure science" will be as pallid and uninviting as our gray imagined world of perfect justice.

JUSTICE AND NONCOMPARATIVE GOOD

The stern conception of justice is outlined in the first paragraph of John Rawls' *A Theory of Justice* (1971):

> Justice is the first virtue of social institutions, as truth is of systems of thought. A theory however elegant and economical must be rejected or revised if it is untrue; likewise laws and institutions no matter how efficient and well-arranged must be reformed or abolished if they are unjust. Each person possesses an inviolability founded on justice that even the welfare of society as a whole cannot override.

Though Rawls concedes that this defense of the supremacy of justice is overdrawn, he simultaneously insists that any concession made to the pursuit of goods other than justice must never sully our "refined ideal." Unless we are prepared conceptually to make justice the supreme social good, what point is there in its commendation and defense? When pursuit of some other good dethrones pursuit of justice, watch out—such is the implicit warning of philosophers who advocate the stern doctrine of justice. When justice comes second, pursuit of the alternative supreme good— say, happiness or wealth—yields all too easily to the convenience of unfair distribution. The happiness or wealth of some people is augmented by denying these goods to others. If we are complacent about dethroning justice, what means of redress can we expect when we ourselves happen to fare badly?

Following the spirit of Rawls' "refined ideal," we might conclude that we would be morally obligated to realize the gray world of perfect justice if it lay in our power to do so. But let us think a bit more deeply. From the vantage of fun and playfulness, why do we object to inequities in wealth and income? All too frequently, I think, a tendentious image comes to mind. We think of a pampered elite having fun at the expense of the penurious masses, of aristocratic frivolity prior to the French Revolution, or of Imelda Marcos throwing "refrigeration parties" so that she and her cohorts may wear their furs indoors during a sweltering Philippines summer. Such images enrage more than they enlighten, leading all too quickly to the judgment that fun, playfulness, and other goods of leisure are morally evil.

Two different accounts of leisure and its evils are implicated in the stern doctrine of justice. The first is that fun and playfulness are noncomparative, per se evils, intrinsically bad. The second is that they are comparative evils—morally bad wherever, as is likely to be the case, some people are deprived of leisure while others enjoy it.

Extreme religious and moral ascetics have perhaps held to a belief in the per se evil of leisure, as when *The Rule of Saint Benedict* proclaims, "Idleness is the great enemy of the soul, therefore the monks should always be occupied, either in manual labor or in holy reading" (St. Benedict of Nursia 1905). Refuting ascetic condemnation of fun as a noncomparative evil is, in one sense, a hopeless undertaking. Ascetics behave ascetically out of commitment to a web of belief that few of the rest of us accept. Our arguments are thus pinned to assertions based on reflective judgments which our opponents do not share. Our vision of a robust good life is one which the ascetic reviles, leaving little more to be said. In another sense, however, the doctrine is easy to refute. Consider how few people, whether judging cross-culturally or within a single culture, actually ever attempt to practice asceticism. Consider how many fewer actually practice a *consistent* asceticism. In general, the sober among us tend to disapprove of certain *kinds* of fun rather than of fun per se. If we subject the thesis that fun is a noncomparative, intrinsic evil to a pragmatic rather than a logically demonstrative standard of disproof, it withers in short order. Most people in most cultures most of the time, I believe, regard fun as a noncomparative, intrinsic *good*.

The second view of the evil of leisure holds only in a comparative sense. So long as some people suffer, this view maintains, there is something unseemly—even grotesque— in the spectacle of others enjoying themselves. Leisure is therefore a morally bad thing unless conditions for its realization are equally shared. In its strongest form, this thesis pronounces happiness a moral evil so long as misery and suffering persist anywhere in the world and underwrites a supposed moral obligation for each of us to give away all excess personal wealth until we reach either the same level as the least well-off individual, or some higher level at which our ability to be charitable defeats itself (Singer 1972).

Though there is no questioning the vehemence with which some people adhere to the comparative thesis, it rests ultimately on a false dichotomy. Whatever accompanies an evil, we are tempted to think, is likewise an evil. Thus, in comparing the welfare of two individuals, we may conclude that if it is an evil for one person to be deprived, it is an evil for another to prosper. This judgment holds true, however, only if the one person prospers *at the expense of* the other. If in our comparison there is no connection between the two individuals, we must judge only that *deprivation* of the first is an evil. The relatively higher well-being of the second person remains, morally, a good.

Take food, for instance. If one person has sufficient food and another lacks it, the evil lies in the deprivation of the latter, not in the sufficiency of the former. True, it would be even better morally if both had a sufficiency, but the good of nutrition is noncomparative. It is, quite simply, a good to him who has it irrespective of the amount of food possessed by anyone else. Fun and playfulness, I submit, are goods of exactly this sort—i.e., fundamentally noncomparative. The moral evil in the spectacle of some people playing while others toil or face starvation lies in the suffering of the latter rather than in the positive enjoyment of the former. Envy alone could make us want to reduce the enjoyment of the fortunate if doing so would not improve the lot of those who are deprived.

At this point, of course, an advocate of the stern doctrine of justice claims that this is exactly what we can and must do—improve the lot of suffering humanity by reducing disparities in wealth and privilege. The claim is made that food and fun are noncomparative goods only in a limited respect—namely, insofar as they are enjoyed in moderation.

When it is feast versus famine, exotic pleasure versus extreme misery, how can anyone with a modicum of moral sensibility fail to condemn the excess?

Even at this extreme, however, a comparison between levels of individual welfare does not establish that food and fun beyond a modest level are evils. Rather it establishes that, under conditions of relative economic abundance, deprivation is inexcusable—a worse evil than under conditions of economic scarcity. This point is easily overlooked because it is tempting to slip the doctrine of the noncomparative, per se evil of leisure into the analysis. Exotic food at the table of the gourmand strikes the ascetic as morally bad in apparently the same way that refined leisure on the yachts and in the country estates of the rich strikes the radical egalitarian (Bedau 1967) as morally bad. But there is an important difference. The ascetic would continue to think exotic food bad even if everyone were provided with it. The radical egalitarian, on the other hand, would not think yachts and country homes morally bad if everyone were given them. Perception of injustice in the distribution of economic goods may be comparative where extreme deprivation coexists side-by-side with luxury. Once deprivation is relieved, however, comparison among relative levels of individual well-being has reduced scope in determining the content of justice.

To define a benefit as "… an improvement in condition, or a gain to an individual, to a group, to society, or to another entity" (Driver, Brown and Peterson, this volume) is to embrace an inherently comparative conception of the goods of leisure. I shall illustrate with reference to individual benefit; but the observation extends, with relevant changes, to benefits to a group, society, or nonhuman entity.

The idea that leisure may bring about an improved condition works in one of two main ways: 1) actually, as in a comparison between the preleisure state of the individual and his or her postleisure state; or 2) hypothetically, as in a comparison between an individual's postleisure state and the state he or she would be in without the leisure. Examples will clarify the difference.

Actual comparison.—Call Jones' state prior to a leisure activity J_1. Perhaps she is aggravated about a perceived injustice in her boss's treatment of her. Call Jones' state after a leisure activity J_2—e.g., her state after a round of handball. Her aggravation has subsided and she has become philosophical about the injury done to her. She remembers occasions when she, too, has unfairly criticized others—a thought which disposes her toward forgiveness. Her condition has improved; it is better than it was, and the physiological and psychological effects of playing handball which contributed to the production of J_2 are beneficial based on actual comparison with J_1.

Hypothetical comparison.—Call Smith's state prior to a leisure activity S_1. Suppose Smith is working hard at finishing a draft of an overdue essay. He knows that if he does not rest periodically, he will get a splitting headache. He thus rests. S_2 is his condition after resting. This time, however, save for the temporal difference between S_1 and S_2, the two states are identical. Smith works as hard and as diligently in S_2 as in S_1; he feels physiologically and psychologically the same in both conditions. Nonetheless, we may still declare it a benefit that Smith has rested. We may do so because we compare S_2 to a hypothetical state, S_3, which Smith would have been in had he failed to rest. In S_3, Smith has a splitting headache; he would write poorly, if at all. Vastly preferring S_2 to S_3, Smith thinks of his rest as bringing about an improvement.

One challenge for a reader of this volume is to classify the various benefits of leisure as to whether they presume an actual or hypothetical comparison. Some benefits presume both. A person whose recovery from stress is hastened by observing scenes of nature (Ulrich, Dimberg, and Driver, this volume) is both better off now than when in a state of stress *and* better off than she would have been without having viewed the scene at all. Other leisure activities may be beneficial only on the basis of an actual comparison. Our handball player, for instance, may have benefitted equally from some other leisure activity—e.g., a round of golf serving as well as handball. Thus we cannot say with any certainty that she is better off with the handball playing than without it. Still other activities may be beneficial only in a hypothetically comparative sense—as with the author who takes periodic rest breaks to prevent a headache.

Yet, when all is said and done, when we have classified each and every supposed benefit into actually or hypothetically comparative (or both), we will have missed something important in our evaluation of leisure. We will have missed the noncomparative goods of leisure—fun, freedom, and exhilaration. We will have missed items which are *constituents* rather than *consequences* of leisure. We will have missed the *whole* truth by concentrating in isolation on each individual truth which makes it up. A comparative definition of "benefit" can be misleading to the extent that a leisure activity produces no measurable improvement between an individual's pre- and postleisure states, or between an individual's postleisure state and the state he would have been in without the leisure. Perhaps nothing has been achieved save that an expanse of time has passed in companionship and good cheer. Nothing is gained, nothing restored; there is no resolve to work harder or to be more forgiving—in sum, no improvement. The comparative view compels us to call leisure of this sort indifferent; on a par, perhaps, with sleep or unconsciousness.

Only acknowledgement of noncomparative goods can underwrite the claim that leisure spent without improvement can be, morally speaking, a good thing. If we yield everything to a comparative ideal of the benefits of leisure, we have no means of holding out against the stern doctrine of justice. How can any of us, in conscience, enjoy ourselves when others suffer deprivation and injustice? There is always some comparatively better use of our time than devoting it to leisure (unless, of course, that leisure restores us to the narrow aim of campaigning on behalf of greater justice). To block the stern view of justice we need more than the negative assertion that we do no harm in enjoying ourselves; we need, that is, the stronger claim that we do a positive good, irrespective of whatever improvements result. A noncomparative approach to the goods of leisure keeps us from being ever on the defensive by requiring that whoever would override our claim to fun must have a strong case—a demonstration that our fun comes *at the expense* of others.

None of the preceding implies that leisure and the acquisition of the amenities with which to enjoy it should be considered in isolation from the just distribution of wealth and income. That some may play while others must toil without relief is a basic distributive inequity; but if my analysis holds, the evil lies in some people's having always to work, not in others' having opportunity to play. Indeed, if we do not conclude something along these lines, we cannot make sense of our thought experiment. What fuels our reluctance to embrace the sober world of perfect justice if not the belief that playfulness, fun, and exuberance are goods in their own right which, like other goods, ought to be distributed as equitably as possible? In assuming that these noncomparative benefits of leisure might be traded off in the attainment of justice, we have left out a portion of the good life which the virtue of justice is meant to serve. We may have order and orderliness if all unmerited evil were banished at the cost of eternal sobriety, but the heart of justice would be lacking.

Plato illustrates how justice may be enervated by an excessively ardent pursuit. According to the *Republic,* justice lies in the proper ordering of three elements of the human soul—reason, passion, and high-spirit. Injustice is internal disorder, a rebellion of passion against reason. Leisure— e.g., listening to music in the right mode or practicing gymnastics—maintains proper harmony. Given that the soul's lower faculties of passion and high-spirit have their portion in life, it is the better part of wisdom to divert them with essentially playful activity rather than to risk their incursion into serious affairs—especially into affairs of state. For Plato, leisure well used is an ally of reason in taming and disciplining the restive elements of the soul. On this inherently comparative view, woe to any aspect of leisure which disrupts harmony—imagination serving as a case in point.

POETS, LUNATICS, AND LOVERS

Notoriously, Plato expels poets from his Republic on the grounds that they teach pleasing falsehoods. There is, of course, a terrible irony in his resolve, for few works in history rival the *Republic* in extent of fanciful detail or richness of pleasing speculation. The work is preeminently to be enjoyed, during leisure, as a spur to imagination. We may labor over interpreting it, extracting sober doctrines and arguing about their meaning; but we miss a great deal if we forget that Plato is, among other things, *playing with ideas.*

Simultaneously, however, a stern doctrine of truth leads Plato to disavow the play element inherent in concocting imaginary worlds. Wedded to a mimetic theory, he castigates art that fails to replicate or imitate its objects. Good art is the ally of truth; it copies reality. A statue is good if it resembles the person posing for it—better if it resembles the ideal human form which the great artist, like the great philosopher, knows by power of reason alone. Bad art is the ally of falsehood in that it creates a poor likeness of its original.

Etymologically, we are encouraged to think of the faculty of imagination as manipulation of mental images (Hanfling 1969). In the empiricist tradition, the representational view of perception is used to explicate this connection (Bennett 1971). In seeing, according to most empiricist accounts, we have the object, a copy of that object in the form of a sense impression, and a copy of that copy in the form of a mental image. Imagination is parasitic on memory, which itself is based on image making and image retrieval. Memory is inherently veridical: a false memory is not a memory at all, just as a false diamond is not a diamond. When memory betrays us, when we "remember" what is false, we are likely to say that we only "imagined" the incident or event. We have an image, but the image is a piece of "decaying sense" (Casey 1976); it is mistaken, defective, false.

The foregoing picture leads, among other things, to the dismissal and neglect of imagination in theories of scientific investigation. In the sober world of science, truth is our object; whereas according to the view found both in Plato and empiricists such as Locke and Hume, imagination is linked to falsehood. A stern doctrine of truth surfaces as an ally of the stern doctrine of justice. Imagination is dangerous, leading to uncontrollable fantasies and disordered perception. Some portion of the cultural denigration of leisure may, I think, be traced to this worry, for leisure encourages—indeed thrives upon—imagination. That is why Plato lays down such stringent conditions for the pursuit of leisure among inhabitants of his *Republic*. The only flights of imaginative fancy he allows are "noble lies" conducive to the harmony of the state and individual.

In philosophy of science, the stern doctrine of truth tends toward the view that the essence of scientific investigation lies in the empirical verification of hypotheses. Given this focus, imagination is a quality to be despised—a quality which disrupts hard-headed matching of experimental result to preexperimental expectation. A scientist who does not keep imagination firmly in check is in danger of unconsciously falsifying results.

The preceding view of science exalts the context of verification while ignoring the equally important context of discovery (Hempel 1966). Hypotheses need to come from somewhere, and there are fewer sources more fertile than the unfettered play of imagination. F. A. Kekule, for instance, revolutionized organic chemistry in the wake of a bizarre dream of snakes biting their own tails—a dream which lead him to represent the molecular structure of benzene as a hexagonal ring (Beveridge 1957). Even so, in the workshops devoted to producing this volume imagination was scarcely mentioned, let alone touted, as a desirable quality in a leisure scientist. I suggest that this neglect stems from adherence to the stern doctrine of truth in conjunction with an ideal of science as consisting wholly in experimental verification of hypotheses.

Let me close with an example from Jacob Bronowski (1977) which underscores the intrinsic value of imagination, placing it at the core of scientific inquiry. The example concerns Galileo's argument that a heavy body and a light body dropped from the same height at the same moment will hit the ground at the same time. This argument challenged the authority of Aristotle and St. Thomas Aquinas, both of whom argued "by the light of nature" that the heavier body would reach the ground first.

We have, Bronowski cautions, refashioned the story of Galileo's discovery in the image of our own verificationist inclinations. Popular sentiment goes so far as to place Galileo atop the Leaning Tower of Pisa, dropping balls of different sizes in inspired confirmation of his hypothesis. The truth, however, is richer and deeper than this image allows. Galileo did not drop balls from the Leaning Tower of Pisa. Doing so would have told him little, for his age lacked precision instruments to measure accurately the results of such an experiment. Instead, Galileo relied on imaginative reconstruction of the consequences of not believing in his hypothesis. Let Bronowski take up the story, reconstructed from Galileo's notebooks:

Suppose, said Galileo, that you drop two unequal balls from the tower at the same time. And suppose that Aristotle is right—suppose that the heavy ball falls faster, so that it steadily gains on the light ball, and hits the ground first. Very well. Now imagine the same experiment done again, with only one difference: this time the two unequal balls are joined by a string between them. The heavy ball will again move ahead, but now the light ball holds it back and acts as a drag or brake. So the light ball will be speeded up and the heavy ball will be slowed down; they must reach the ground together because they are tied together, but they cannot reach the ground as quickly as the heavy ball alone. Yet the string between them has turned the two balls into a single mass which is heavier than either ball—and surely (according to Aristotle) this mass should therefore move faster than either ball. Galileo's imaginary experiment has uncovered a contradiction; he says trenchantly, "You see how, from your assumption that a heavier body falls more rapidly than a light one, I infer that a (still) heavier body falls more slowly." There is only one way out of the contradiction: the heavy ball and the light ball must fall at the same rate, so that they go on falling at the same rate when they are tied together.

Nothing about this thought experiment is decisive; Galileo's hypothesis may still benefit from experimental confirmation with the accurate instruments of a later age. Bronowski's point, however, is that Galileo's discovery is a pure product of imagination—a combination and reconfiguration of "images" in his mind. Importantly, Galileo's imagination yields truth—a result contrary to the predictions of the stern doctrine which links imagination with falsehood.

What Bronowski does not mention is that Galileo's notebooks, like the notebooks of any creative scientist, are full of other experiments in thought which do not pan out. Literally speaking, these failed thought experiments are false, representing the world differently from the way it is. At the same time, Galileo's thought experiments, both "true" and "false," are preeminently products of leisure—of a full-blooded, free, and pleasurable playing with ideas. If we confine our evaluation of leisure to an inherently comparative view, if we insist on measuring by "improvements" in state or condition, we must conclude one of two things. We must conclude that only Galileo's productive (i.e., "truthful") thought experiments are beneficial, or we must think of erroneous insights as a cost to be borne for the sake of advancement. Suppose that the creative scientific imagination produces one hundred "false" insights to every "true" insight. The ninety-nine "false" insights, then, are vindicated by the few "true" insights which advance human understanding and human welfare.

We are disposed to the preceding view, I think, because of our modern age's preoccupation with the ideal of progress. Benefit piles on benefit such that each later condition of the individual or society is, in sum, a comparative improvement on earlier conditions. Though I shall not here consider the larger issues raised by this optimistic faith in progress, I shall point to one of its weaknesses in the philosophy of science. If science moves as much by revolutionizing existing paradigms (Kuhn 1970) as by bridging gaps in our understanding of the current paradigm, our evaluation of insights inscribed in the notebook of a creative scientist may prove erroneous. Among the "false" thought experiments may lurk one which is true according to some as yet unconceived and more comprehensive paradigm. Reality may be stranger than we think—strange enough to match up with ideas which we presently dismiss as flights of fancy.

The place of pure thought experiments in moral philosophy, physical science, and leisure studies is, I would urge, a hallowed one. Rather than strain always to point out comparative benefits of leisure, we should rest content with a central core of noncomparative goods—e.g., the fun, the playful, and the imaginative. We do well to keep Shakespeare's words from *A Midsummer Night's Dream* ever before us:

The lunatic, the lover, and the poet
Are of imagination all compact.

Plato warned of the danger of poetry; the rest of us, I trust, can attest to the danger of love and lunacy. Still, we would not want to live without love or an occasional touch of lunacy, nor—Plato's scruples aside—could we do without poetry. Danger must be braved if we are to resist the stern doctrines of justice and truth, thereby fighting off the sober gray world concocted, for the purposes of this paper, in imagination.

LITERATURE CITED

Bedau, H. A. 1967. Radical egalitarianism. In: Pennock, J. R.; Chapman, J. W., eds. Nomos IX: equality. New York, NY: Atherton Press: 3-27.

Bennett, J. 1971. Locke, Berkeley, Hume: central themes. Oxford: University Press. 361 p.

Beveridge, W. I. B. 1957. The art of scientific investigation. 3d ed. New York, NY: Vintage Books. 239 p.

Bronowski, J. 1977. The reach of imagination. In: A sense of the future: essays in natural philosophy. Boston, MA: MIT Press: 272-79.

Casey, E. 1976. Imagining: a phenomenological study. Bloomington, IN: University of Indiana Press. 240 p.

Hanfling, O. 1969. Mental images. Analysis. 29(3): 166-173.

Hempel, C. G. 1966. Philosophy of natural science. Englewood Cliffs, NJ: Prentice-Hall. 116 p.

Kuhn, T. 1970. The structure of scientific revolutions. 2d ed. Chicago, IL: University of Chicago Press. 210 p.

Plato. 1961. The republic. In: Hamilton, E.; Cairns, H., eds. Plato: the collected dialogues. New York, NY: Pantheon Books. 1743 p.

Rawls, J. 1971. A theory of justice. Boston, MA: Harvard University Press. 607 p.

St. Benedict of Nursia. 1905. The rule of St. Benedict. In: Thatcher, O. J.; McNeal, E. H., eds. A source book of medieval history. New York, NY: Charles Scribner's Sons: 435-476.

Singer, P. 1972. Famine, affluence, and morality. Philosophy and Public Affairs. 1(3): 229-243.

IV.

SUMMARY

A Retrospective:
The Benefits of Leisure

Roger C. Mannell
Department of Recreation and Leisure Studies
University of Waterloo
Waterloo, Ontario
Canada

Daniel J. Stynes
Department of Park and Recreation Resources
Michigan State University
East Lansing, Michigan

THE DEVELOPMENT OF A CONSUMERS GUIDE TO WHOLESOME LEISURE?

The idea of this text was to compile an exhaustive catalogue of the benefits of leisure and provide a comprehensive assessment of how well these benefits have been documented by research. The editors in their introductory chapter and several other authors (Jordan, Lewis and Kaiser, Siehl and Kostmayer) argue quite convincingly that well-documented and systematic knowledge of benefits is critical for the creation of leisure opportunities by public and private decisionmakers, and is also of relevance to individual consumers in making wise choices for the use of their free time. So, in assessing the contents of this volume we could ask, "on the basis of the reviews and analyses presented in this book, do we know enough about leisure benefits to develop a *Consumers' Guide to Wholesome Leisure* to inform the choices and planning of consumers and service providers?"

We were invited by the editors to attend the workshop where the papers contained in this volume were initially previewed. Our task was to read each paper, listen to the authors' reflections on their written analyses, participate in the ensuing discussions and then, after sober reflection and the wisdom-enabling passage of time, write a retrospective on the contents of this volume. If you have read this book in a linear, left to right manner before encountering this chapter, you may have some appreciation for how daunting a task we have been foolhardy enough to take on. The leisure benefits identified cover conceptual ground from the physiological to the spiritual. The analyses are framed by perspectives ranging from the philosophical to the bio-medical, and from the provocatively speculative to the thoroughly empirically grounded.

We will attempt to assess the extent to which the authors in this volume have been able to complete the tasks assigned by the editors in their introductory chapter, highlight the recurrent themes and issues that emerge from the various chapters, and take a retrospective look at the utility of the leisure benefit construct, itself, as a strategy for guiding leisure research and the planning of leisure services.

As can be seen from the organization of the book, the benefits have been divided into physiological, psychological, social, and economic and environmental; however, only the physiological, psychological, and social receive detailed attention. The discussion of the economic benefits alerts the reader to research that focuses exclusively on assessing the economic benefits of leisure, particularly outdoor recreation. The idea that there may be environmental benefits of leisure is introduced but not given extensive coverage (Rolston; Roggenbuck, Loomis, and Dagostino).

The *physiological benefits* of certain leisure activities appear to be the most extensively studied. Research on the consequences of leisure for physical health has focused primarily on the effects of physical exercise. These consequences are well-documented. A considerable body of biomedical research finds that physical exercise causes cardiovascular changes associated with lower rates of heart disease and increased lifespan. Medical evidence includes laboratory studies documenting physiological effects of exercise (Froehlicher and Froehlicher) and epidemiological studies establishing a clear association between regular exercise and physical health (Paffenbarger, Hyde and Dow). The literature reviewed by Ellis and Richardson on the health consequences of industrial recreation or organizational wellness programs proclaims many substantial physical health benefits, but these were found to be largely unsubstantiated as a result of poorly designed evaluation studies. Play (Barnett) and sport (Wankel and Berger) also have consequences for physical development and health; however, research in these areas has focused more on the psychological and social benefits stemming from these activities. Research examining the impact of nonexercise forms of leisure on physiological outcomes associated with stress, illness, and so-called lifestyle diseases is clearly lacking.

Benefits receiving the greatest coverage in this volume are those identified as psychological and social. The psychological benefits refer to the positive consequences of leisure involvements for the individual. Social benefits refer to positive impacts on social units of different size. The coverage of the psychological benefits is much more extensive than that of the social benefits. This emphasis is likely a reflection of the tremendous popularity of the psychological and social psychological study of leisure during the last 15 years (Mannell 1984, Mannell and Iso-Ahola 1987), and the relative scarcity of macrosociological analysis and research (Burch and Hamilton-Smith, this volume; Zuzanek 1982.)

The *psychological benefits* identified can be placed into three broad categories. The first, development of the self, includes self-actualization; identity affirmation; the development of interpersonal and leadership skills; cognitive, social, and emotional development in children; and spiritual development. Experiential learning, skill and knowledge acquisition, and environmental attitude change comprise the second category. Flow experiences, mood, and fun comprise a third category of short-term, transient experiential outcomes.

Some of these outcomes such as learning (Roggenbuck, Loomis, and Dagostino; Easley), child development (Barnett), and need satisfaction (Driver, Tinsley, and Manfredo) have been the subject of extensive empirical research and the authors are able to provide comprehensive reviews. Other outcomes such as identity affirmation (Haggard and Williams) have been given only limited research attention and the authors focus primarily on conceptual development. Haggard and Williams devote most of their chapter to developing the argument that recreation activities embody distinct and measurable body images. Participants select activities on the basis of the images they project which are used to create or reinforce the individual's image or self-identity. By linking leisure participation and the development of self-actualization through the mechanism of optimal experiences (flow) Csikszentmihalyi and Kleiber are able to both provide conceptual development and tie the theory into an ongoing research program. The research on the impact of planned therapeutic recreation interventions on these types of outcomes is also at a very rudimentary stage. While Levitt examines only research dealing with psychological disabilities in her chapter, her conclusion regarding the lack of good program evaluations is quite valid for the field as a whole. The most speculative discussion is provided by McDonald and Schreyer dealing with spiritual outcomes.

The authors' assessments of how well the outcomes are "proven," even when well-researched, vary greatly. Barnett discusses the developmental benefits of play for children and finds very little support for beneficial outcomes. She argues that there is a need for research that is much more carefully controlled. Wankel and Berger make the same claim for the extensive research literature on sport. In contrast, Roggenbuck et al. conclude that there is good evidence for the learning benefits of outdoor recreation participation, including learning specific recreation activities and skills, learning about the natural and cultural environment, and developing positive attitudes and behavioral patterns relative to the environment.

There also continue to be challenges for even the most extensive research programs on leisure outcomes. For example, Driver and Tinsley and their associates (Driver, Tinsley, and Manfredo, this volume) have focused on identifying and measuring the psychological outcomes (need-satisfactions) derived from leisure as perceived by the participant. Work is proceeding to discover how various need-satisfactions are linked to leisure activities, settings and experiences and, in turn, how these psychological outcomes contribute to other benefits such as personal growth and life satisfaction (Driver et al. 1987, Mannell 1989, Tinsley and Tinsley 1986).

Much of the discussion concerning *social benefits* is speculative and there are frequent calls for more research (Burch and Hamilton-Smith) and better conceptualizations (Kelly, Cohen). The social benefits discussed range from those that may accrue to a primary group or to society as a whole. These social units include the family, work organizations, communities, and nations. In their chapter, Burch and Hamilton-Smith provide some suggestions for the types of macrosocial benefits we might look at and they argue that there has been little or no research on leisure benefits to large social collectives.

The authors dealing with smaller social units had an easier time identifying research and theory that are at least related to the benefits issue. Orthner and Mancini examine a specific benefit—the impact of leisure on family bonding and satisfaction. They found evidence that leisure provides opportunities to do things together which may affect bonding and satisfaction with the unit. However, even in this highly focused area of inquiry, the authors suggest that much of the discussion of the benefits of family leisure is speculative.

As mentioned earlier, Ellis and Richardson are critical of the quality of the research on the beneficial consequences of organizational wellness or industrial recreation programs. This critique is particularly true of the claims made for benefits such as worker productivity and commitment.

Allen deals with the impact of leisure services on community satisfaction, and Marans and Mohai discuss the beneficial consequences of specially designed leisure environments in new communities. Both chapters demonstrate that benefits of leisure can be examined in terms of community impact. Allen provides some evidence of benefits in terms of perceived quality of life and community development, but indicates that the relationship between recreation services and opportunities on the one hand, and sense of community on the other, has been virtually ignored in the research literature. Marans and Mohai suggest that there is little support for the premise that people in new towns with specially designed leisure environments experience a higher quality of life through greater access to recreation services and resources.

Based on what these authors tell us about leisure benefits, do we currently know enough to create a *consumers' guide* on the benefits of various types of recreation and leisure involvements? The answer to this question seems to be a resounding no! In the introductory chapter Driver, Brown, and Peterson asked the authors of the 21 state-of-knowledge papers to evaluate five aspects of the theory and research from which they derived their discussions of leisure benefits. An assessment of the difficulties authors had in addressing these five issues supports our "no" answer.

"How well-specified in the literature are the beneficial consequence(s) that are discussed in this volume?" The reviews clearly suggest that leisure research generally has not been driven by a quest to discover benefits; however, the

authors of the state of knowledge papers have done an admirable job in corralling research and theory that begins to target some potential areas that warrant further examination. As a whole, the papers cover a good cross-section of the major types of psychological and social outcomes. Additionally, Burch and Hamilton-Smith, and Driver, Tinsley, and Manfredo in their respective discussions of social and psychological benefits provide comprehensive typologies of a wide range of possible benefits that could be examined.

"What is known about the magnitude of the consequence(s) and how adequate are the measures used?" This question of the editors asks not only about the adequacy of the measures of benefits considered, but also about the extent of our knowledge concerning the causes of these benefits, and how much leisure is required to generate a certain magnitude of benefit. First, many of the benefits that have been specified have received little measurement and research attention as suggested by a number of authors having to devote their discussions to primarily definitional, speculative, and conceptual analyses rather than a review of a research literature. Second, in areas where more extensive research is reported, few, if any, of the papers were able to identify research in which the measurement of the benefits or the rigor of the research designs allowed the magnitude of consequences to be precisely determined. The possible exceptions are some of the physiological measures. The crude measurement procedures available to the social scientist and the difficulty of implementing designs in places where leisure typically "happens" has lead to research that at best identifies correlations between some aspect of leisure and benefits.

"What is known about the relative importance or worth of the consequence(s)?" This question assumes that a particular type of benefit has been defined or specified fairly clearly and its magnitude quantified with reasonable reliability and validity. The concern is whether some types of benefits are more meritorious than others. Given the limited state of knowledge for benefit specification and measurement, there is little discussion about the relative importance or worth of various leisure outcomes other than for economic measures of the worth of leisure services (see chapters by Kealy, and Johnson and Brown)—which only index the utility of perceived benefits received. Most other knowledge about value is intuitive and speculative. There is clearly little or no discussion in the literature on how and what individuals or social groups come to see as a beneficial outcome of leisure.

"Identify additional research that is needed" and *"Outline alternative research designs that would further our knowledge of the beneficial consequence(s) under consideration."* Given the general lack of benefits research

identified, the authors as a whole simply argue for more and better controlled research. No special designs were identified, though greater use of experimentation and research strategies that would better allow cause and effect relationships to be established were frequently mentioned, as was the need for more longitudinal studies. Qualitative research was suggested for the exploratory stages of research into benefits that have received little attention, and to aid in better understanding the processes linking leisure and various outcomes.

Finally, we raise one additional question that emerged from our analysis of the 21 reviews. *"How clearly and adequately is the construct of leisure conceptualized as an independent variable or cause in leisure research and theory?"* It is very clear from this collection of papers that the notion of leisure is problematic. Little agreement was found in the literature for the notion of leisure as an independent variable or cause. Although clear specifications are developed by some authors, these vary among authors.

A CLOSER LOOK AT THE ISSUES: A SYSTEMS APPROACH

To stop here, however, would do injustice to the rich source of ideas, concerns, and issues that emerge from a reading of this collection of papers. To facilitate further assessment and a retrospective analysis we will adopt a systems approach—an organizing strategy that has some parallels with the general scheme suggested by our editors. In the introductory chapter Driver, Brown, and Peterson describe a "production process perspective" that they and their associates have adopted in considering leisure benefits which separates the prescriptive part (the consequences) of what is meant by the term *benefits* from the normative part (the worth or value of the consequences to some individual or group). Figure 1 depicts the generalized process by which benefits may derive from leisure.

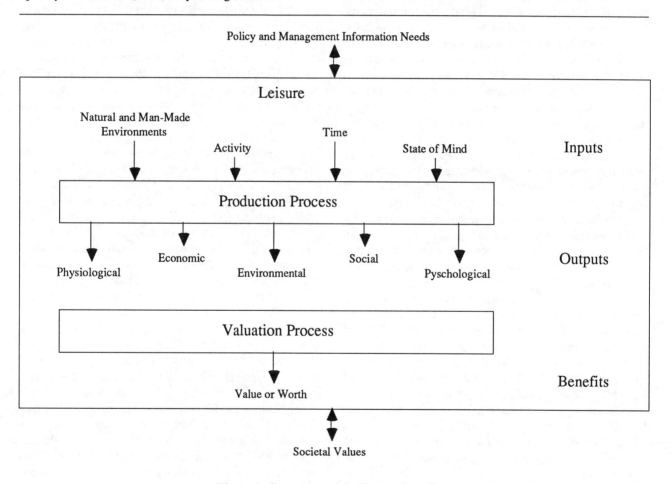

Figure 1. Systems model of leisure benefits.

Our system includes three classes of variables: 1) inputs or stimuli, 2) outputs or consequences, and 3) benefits. The production process is the process by which inputs are translated into outputs (or consequences). Valuation is the process by which outputs (or consequences) are evaluated as being beneficial or not. Within this framework, the approach to understanding leisure benefits is to first understand what consequences are likely to result from participation in recreational activities and settings, or experiences felt to be leisure by the participant. The assumption is that social science can be used to specify the causal links between leisure "stimuli" and subsequent consequences, and further that social science can help determine the worth or value of these consequences, that is, the benefits and nonbenefits of leisure. Using the systems model as our guide, we will discuss eight sets of related issues that surface across the introductory, state-of-knowledge, and disciplinary papers.

Specification of Inputs and Outputs

The need to carefully specify, measure, and value leisure consequences or outputs was clearly laid out in the introductory chapter and is a recurring theme throughout this book. However, to study the consequences and benefits of leisure, we also need theoretical and operational definitions of inputs—definitions that are somewhat more precise than the broad and chameleon-like notion of leisure—as well as of the intervening processes that link leisure and benefits. Burch and Hamilton-Smith, for example, provide a taxonomy of leisure inputs, intervening variables, and benefits as a framework for the study of social benefits. The research described by Driver, Tinsley, and Manfredo has been very much an attempt to link psychological outcomes (need satisfaction) with well-specified leisure settings, activities, and experiences.

Outputs: Outcomes and Consequences

As we have mentioned earlier, the authors as a whole identify a large number of potential consequences of leisure involvements ranging from the thoroughly researched to the highly speculative which have evaded systematic empirical scrutiny. Outcomes such as cognitive and social development (Barnett) and fitness (Froehlicher and Froehlicher) have well-established operational measures, while community satisfaction (Allen) and self-actualization (Csikszentmihalyi and Kleiber) are examples of outcomes that are conceptually and operationally underdeveloped.

To complicate matters further, Henberg challenges us with the argument that certain kinds of intrinsic outcomes such as fun and playfulness are not readily investigated within the general paradigm laid down by the editors. Certainly McDonald and Schreyer challenge the social scientist's ability to measure all leisure outcomes with their discussion of the spiritual consequences of leisure. Rolston's treatment of environmental benefits has a strong spiritual dimension also. He turns our normally anthropocentric view of leisure benefits around, discussing the benefits of man's leisure to the natural environment rather than the benefits the natural environment brings to man. He argues that it is principally during leisure time that man performs works of conservation and preservation benefitting the environment.

Among those authors who were concerned with various psychological outcomes there appears to be a general optimism that psychological benefits can be identified and operationalization of these outputs can occur. Ajzen, for example, feels that a quantitative, positivistic social psychological approach which stresses the development of rigorous operational measures with appropriate psychometric procedures can advance the study of leisure benefits. Certainly, psychological researchers have tackled even the seemingly difficult to operationalize spiritual outcomes of leisure such as those discussed by McDonald and Schreyer. For example, religious experiences in wilderness settings have been studied systematically (see Hood 1977, Rosegrant 1976).

Various authors differ in their views of the possible success of operationalizing social benefits, particularly those accruing to large social units. Burch and Hamilton-Smith present a typology of social benefits that includes role performance, better social awareness, collective release, social bonding, ties between intimates, social integration, and social solidarity. They seem optimistic that we can measure and study these impacts. Allen, who has been attempting to measure the impact of leisure services on community life and development, paints a vivid picture of the difficulties of assessing social outcomes. He argues for the need for a more thorough conceptualization of community and the need to identify appropriate indicators of community life—both individual and global measures.

Other authors feel that there may be limitations to the extent to which benefits to large social systems can be operationalized. Kelly, in his discussion of sociological approaches to the study of leisure benefits, points out that definitions of leisure and benefits change depending on the sociological approach taken. He also seems to feel that it may be impossible to directly measure benefits to large social systems, and argues that we need the systematic accumulation of social indices of social outcomes.

Inputs: Stimuli and Causes

Equally as important as the specification of the outputs or consequences, is the specification of the inputs or stimuli. There was considerable debate at the workshop about the use and meaning of the word "leisure" as a modifier of benefits. The term is certainly too broad and ill-defined to provide obvious operational measures of the input variables or stimuli that are "producing" the consequences examined in the state of knowledge papers. Indeed, it is quite clear that different authors are dealing not only with different outputs, but also with quite different inputs. The stimulus for Froehlicher and Froehlicher is physical exercise, which just happens to occur mostly during leisure time. Rolston; McDonald and Schreyer; and Ulrich, Dimberg, and Driver treat various aspects of the natural or man-made environment as stimuli. Csikszentmihalyi and Kleiber, and Hull directly examine psychological states. It is not always clear whether psychological states are to be treated as inputs, outputs, or characterizations of the production (intervening) process itself.

Chapters by Goodale and Cooper, Godbey and Jung, Burch and Hamilton-Smith, Csikszentmihalyi and Kleiber, and Hamilton-Smith provide background on the history, definition, and cross-cultural dimensions of leisure. The three traditional ways of defining leisure as time, activity, and psychological state were identified. Each definitional approach has significant implications for studying leisure consequences and benefits.

As a *block of time* leisure provides opportunities for increasing the production of many of the beneficial consequences covered in this book. Indeed, as work becomes more sedentary, more stressful, and offers fewer opportunities to produce certain kinds of benefits, leisure time increases in importance. Various chapters particularly note the importance of leisure time for exercise (Paffenbarger et al., Froehlicher and Froehlicher), interaction with the natural environment (Rolston), certain kinds of learning (Roggenbuck et al., Barnett), spiritual activity (McDonald and Schreyer), and family bonding (Orthner and Mancini). Leisure time also has taken on economic functions that far outweigh leisure's traditional role of rest and recuperation from work. The economic importance of leisure time today is primarily as a period for the consumption of goods and services.

Viewing leisure as a block of time, we see one major category of consequences that have been largely overlooked in this collection of papers. These are the consequences of the timing and size of blocks of leisure time. Leisure time in industrial societies tends to be concentrated into two large blocks, one during childhood (Barnett), and the other late in life (McPherson). In between these two periods of ample leisure time, leisure tends to occur in small chunks—coffee breaks, lunch hours, evenings after work, and weekends, with an occasional longer concentration during vacation periods. Without going into the consequences of these patterns of leisure time, let us simply note their wide-ranging consequences for individuals, families, communities, and societies.

However, the time definition of leisure does not capture the uniqueness of leisure relative to other periods of time. Just because an activity is engaged in during free time does not suggest that leisure provides a benefit that could not be obtained during other times. For example, there appears to be no evidence that the physiological effects of physical activity are related to whether the activity is a leisure or nonleisure activity. This may explain why leisure scientists have shown little interest in physiological effects. In terms of physical health, leisure is primarily a block of time or set of activities that offer opportunities for physical exercise. Reduced opportunity for physical exercise during nonleisure time has elevated the importance of leisure time for providing such opportunities.

A number of the papers interpret leisure as specific *activities*. This approach narrows the stimulus or input to something more concrete. Papers discussing physiological consequences (with the exception of Ulrich et al.), focus primarily on physical exercise as the stimulus. Other leisure activities discussed in different chapters include sports (Wankel and Berger), play (Barnett), outdoor adventure activities (Easley), the whole array of community leisure services (Allen), and psychologically involving leisure (Csikszentmihalyi and Kleiber). While probably the most concrete to operationalize, leisure defined as activity tends to obscure the factors that are really responsible for creating outcomes. What factors are present in the activity, the participant, or more likely the interaction of the two that make the activity perform well or poorly in producing consequences? For example, Barnett questions whether it is some intrinsic quality of play or the social interaction that usually accompanies play that produces various benefits claimed for this form of leisure. Would not social interaction in other settings and activities provide the same benefits?

Wankel and Berger make a related point when they argue that it is fruitless to ask whether the outcomes of sport are good or bad. The more appropriate question is, "what are the conditions that are necessary for sport involvement to have beneficial outcomes?" Ajzen, from his social psychological disciplinary perspective, also feels that there is extremely poor conceptualization of leisure as an independent variable and suggests that researchers should ask "what kinds of leisure activities are most likely to produce the benefits under consideration?" and "what are the mechanisms responsible?"

The most popular definition among leisure scholars, but perhaps the least utilized, is the psychological definition of leisure as a certain *state of mind* or *kind of experience*. Neulinger (1974) first translated traditional views of leisure as a state of mind into psychological terms with his well-known typology of leisure and nonleisure states—a typology based on the psychological constructs of perceived freedom and intrinsic motivation. Driver and his associates (e.g., Driver and Tocher 1970) also gave the "recreation experience" a prominent place in theory linking outdoor recreation to psychological outcomes. Csikszentmihalyi's notion of optimal experience which he calls "flow" (see chapter with Kleiber) has been the most influential construct in shaping thinking and research on the actual experiential content of leisure (Mannell and Iso-Ahola 1987).

The chapter by Csikszentmihalyi and Kleiber is really the only attempt to examine the benefits of leisure experientially defined. However, once we approach leisure as a state of mind, not only are some interesting theoretical and research possibilities made available, but we also encounter some conceptual quicksand. Leisure as experience can be a stimulus, a consequence, or the actual intervening process between the leisure setting or activity and certain consequences. Consequently, instead of viewing leisure as an input or consequence, we could conceptualize leisure as a state variable describing the process of producing benefits. These "leisure states" in some cases may have advantages over other states in producing certain consequences. It should be noted that this process has been labeled a "leisure state" by some theorists (e.g., Mannell 1979, Tinsley and Tinsley 1986). However, Csikszentmihalyi prefers to use more neutral terms such as optimal experience or flow, since he and Kleiber argue that these "states" may be derived from nonleisure activities as well, and that not all leisure involvements result in optimal experiences and hence self-actualization opportunities.

Process

This discussion of inputs and outputs has necessarily lead to a consideration of the processes linking leisure and benefits. The issue warrants further discussion. Figure 1 includes two boxes which designate the production of consequences and valuation processes. Our knowledge of the processes represented by these boxes appears to vary from purely *black box models*, where we know certain inputs yield certain outputs but we do not know how or why, to fairly complete models of cause and effect that trace changes in outputs to changes in inputs through a series of intervening variables.

Numerous calls were made for the identification of intervening process-oriented variables and some attempts were made to identify intervening variables that might be of potential interest (Burch and Hamilton-Smith; Driver, Tinsley, and Manfredo). Csikszentmihalyi and Kleiber's analysis illustrates the importance of considering process. They attempt to connect leisure to self-actualization through the vehicle of the "flow" construct and in so doing demonstrate that it is not just leisure per se that contributes to self-actualization but experiences having certain qualities that may also be available in other domains of life.

Other authors identify the need to consider process as well. Hull argues that temporary and transient mood states are benefits of leisure. However, moods are not seen as the primary outcome but more as an intervening variable between leisure and cognition and a variety of social behaviors, such as learning, helping behavior, self-concept, and health. McDonald and Schreyer suggest that spiritual experience can act as an intervening variable that can contribute to the achievement of other types of benefits such as psychological well-being, personal development, community life, social consciousness, sense of wellness, and mental health.

At the more sociological level, McPherson argues that researchers who have been concerned with the link between leisure and aging have not taken into account the mediating influences of population and demographic factors. Older adults are not homogeneous. If we are to determine if leisure benefits differ depending on age and if services and policies should vary for different age groups, there is a need to treat developmental and subgroup differences as mediating variables.

Driver, Tinsley, and Manfredo, and the editors in their introductory chapter, identify the difficulty of sorting out what are ultimate and intervening consequences. They point out that benefits are causally chained and occur in a time context which can lead to conceptual confusion. For example, they suggest that need gratification through leisure experience can best be seen as an intervening variable with the antecedents being leisure experiences and the consequences being such benefits as life satisfaction and physical health. They ask where in the chain of benefits can we most meaningfully measure the benefits of leisure and go on to suggest that researchers need to make theoretical links between the benefits in the causal chain.

Efforts to establish cause-effect relationships and test theories about the intervening processes generally require highly reductionist approaches and experimental designs. A number of the authors in this volume recommend more researchers take this approach. This recommendation is not new and has been frequently repeated during the past 15 years by leisure researchers (e.g., Crandall and Lewko 1976, Iso-Ahola 1980).

Experimental approaches require the isolation and control of the stimulus. We are likely to find that many of the stimuli of interest to us are neither readily isolated nor easily controlled. Leisure researchers have not been inclined to be experimentalists and survey methodologies have predominated. The call by those of us doing leisure research for the use of methodologies that afford greater control is in danger of simply becoming a cliche.

Time

Perhaps one of the most important contributions of a systems perspective is that it directs our attention to the temporal dimension of understanding social and psychological phenomena. Our use of the word "process" implies a structure or set of relationships over time. There are important temporal dimensions to both the production and valuation processes. For example, Hull discusses mood, a relatively transitory consequence of leisure; while Paffenbarger et al. identify longer term effects of exercise on lifespan using epidemiological evidence. Whether consequences of leisure are transitory or more permanent is of considerable importance. Long-term beneficial consequences are generally more highly valued than short-term consequences. Short-term consequences are, however, more easily identified, as long-term effects often involve a host of intervening variables and multiple causes. As we have seen, a number of authors see that short-term outcomes such as spiritual experience and flow, sometimes translate into longer term benefits.

Time is a critical variable in designing research on leisure benefits. Both the timing and duration of the stimuli and the timing and duration of the consequences must be understood. The chapter by Ulrich et al. is the only one that actually plots stimulus-response patterns over time.

Feedback Effects

Temporal processes suggest feedback effects and complex chains of relationships over time. These temporal processes are not readily investigated with the cross-sectional, comparative, and static research approaches which have dominated the field of recreation and leisure studies. Feedback effects can also make the identification of causes and effects somewhat arbitrary. Little discussion is given to feedback effects by the authors. However, feedback effects are prominent in Hull's discussion of the role of mood in linking leisure and consequences. Mood could be described as a state of the psychological system at a given point in time, which changes over time, and is both effected by and affects inputs and outputs. Feedback effects are likely to be important in the analysis of many of the benefits identified in this volume. For example, feedback effects may play a role in the

relationship between recreation activity choice and identity affirmation as discussed by Haggard and Williams. Not only does participation in an activity provide opportunities for identity development and consolidation, but conversely, the choice of an activity itself is likely influenced by the nature of an individual's identity at any point in time. Similarly, the flow experience may not only contribute to self-actualization, but individuals who are more self-actualized may be better able to experience flow in a wider range of situations (Csikszentmihalyi and Csikszentmihalyi 1988, Kleiber and Dirkin 1985).

Relationships Among Outputs

With each of the state of knowledge chapters addressing specific categories of consequences, the contribution the papers are able to make to understanding relationships among consequences is limited. Several chapters including the two dealing with the community impacts of leisure (Allen, Marans and Mohai) do attempt to integrate a wide range of consequences, and both are rather critical of the state of our knowledge.

There seems to be a tendency to handle integration more within the valuation process than the production process. We tend to study the consequences independently and not until attempting to make resource allocation or planning decisions on the basis of what we know about these consequences and their beneficial nature, do we consider their relative contributions and interrelationships. For example, little evidence was presented on how natural environments, mental states, physiological outcomes, and social conditions might interact to modify the types or amounts of leisure consequences.

Scientific progress has relied heavily on reductionist approaches. The use of positivistic science has lead, as mentioned earlier, to the greatest advancement in our knowledge in the area of physiological consequences. Here we have very specific stimuli, amenable to study in relatively controlled laboratory settings, and "hard" evidence of consequences using physiological measures. Yet, most leisure researchers are likely to find these physiological results wanting for the very reasons we have advanced for their success. While both leisure stimuli and consequences have been reduced to operational measures, the end result does not tell us much about "leisure." Only a handful of variables are explored, these do not include many that leisure scientists would choose to study, and the clearest results are obtained in highly controlled laboratory settings that may shed little light on what happens in the "real world." We need both holistic and reductionist approaches that build on one another. This book is an important step in that direction.

Level of Analysis

Analyses and research findings are discussed at the level of the individual, the family, the small social group, the neighborhood, the community, and society at large. Also, Rolston's warnings against limiting our analyses to the human domain raises a parallel set of levels of analysis for different living and nonliving entities.

Levels of analysis are also built into the academic disciplines that provide a home for researchers. Psychologists and physiologists restrict themselves primarily to the individual level. Sociologists and anthropologists work more at the social group and community level. Economists and geographers typically work at aggregate levels.

The ideal explanation of leisure benefits would include how one aggregates or disaggregates outcomes as one moves from one level to another. For example, in the simplest of schemes, family benefits are the sum of individual benefits within the family and community benefits the sum of individual and family benefits, etc. However, many consequences are not defined at all levels and many others are likely not additive. While health may be a characteristic of individuals, families, communities, nations, and the global community, its definition is different at each level.

Research on the physiological consequences of leisure has been almost entirely at the level of the individual. However, Ellis and Richardson's review of studies of organizational wellness programs, particularly where savings in health care costs and the level of worker productivity at the level of the organization are examined, provides another example of where benefits at the individual level not only can but need to be examined at other levels of analysis.

There appears to be considerable merit in clearly identifying levels of analysis and exploring interrelationships between levels. Indeed, Homans (1967) has argued that one of the greatest problems of social science in general has been in linking propositions about individuals to propositions about aggregates.

Worth or Value

Our systems approach implies one can first identify consequences and then in a separate step assign measures of relative worth or value to these consequences. However, in reality there are occasions when these two steps may be inseparable. For example, individuals might value mood changes that are produced by natural environments differently than they value the same mood change induced by a hallucinogenic drug. Physical development is valued differently depending upon whether it is produced by physical exercise or steroids. Thus, in some cases, values may depend

as much on the production process as on the consequences produced. Generally, though, it seems to make sense to separate the production from the valuation process.

If we make this separation, leisure "benefits" research clearly divides into two quite distinct camps. Economists have had almost total claim to the study of the valuation process, while other social scientists have largely confined their investigation of leisure benefits to the production process. To date, the two camps have paid little attention to one another, although both Kealy, and Johnson and Brown identify many links between economic and other social science approaches to leisure benefits.

While there are some advantages to the division of labor, there are also some significant losses. Our understanding of leisure benefits in the broader sense and the valuation process more specifically, is limited by our lack of understanding of how individuals, families, or societies weigh the relative importance of different consequences of leisure in assigning worth to particular experiences, resources, blocks of time, or states of mind.

The success of economists in studying leisure benefits has come from a clear focus on resource allocation problems. By treating the consequences of participation in a leisure activity as part and parcel of the activity itself, economists have been able to obtain measures of the worth or value of recreation experiences or resources without getting into a host of messy problems associated with identifying the benefit production process. Further, these values are comparable to how we generally value alternative activities or uses of these same resources.

While many questions related to public resource allocations can be answered adequately without unbundling the psychological, social, environmental, economic, and physiological consequences of leisure, many others cannot. Economic measures of worth generally rest upon assumptions of consumer sovereignty (the consumer knows best what is good for him or herself) and existing income distributions. Both of these assumptions are often challenged, and particularly so in addressing leisure issues.

Although the primary characteristics of leisure, perceived freedom, and intrinsic motivation would argue in favor of consumer sovereignty as a basis for determining worth or value, society frequently questions the leisure choices that individuals make, attributing greater "value" to socially preferred leisure activities and frequently deploring participation in others such as television watching and gambling.

Gans (1962) has noted how many of the purported benefits of recreation and the outdoors originated in a social reform movement that focused more on social than individual benefits of recreation. Individual leisure choices often do not reflect societal preferences.

Reconciling social and individual leisure choices requires a clearer understanding of the consequences of leisure activities to individuals, families, communities, and societies. Most of these consequences involve nonmarket goods and services. Although most of the field of recreation economics has been focused on nonmarket valuation, the range of nonmarket consequences of leisure that have been examined is quite limited. Kealy discusses how these techniques may be extended to many of the consequences discussed in this book, while also noting the need for economists to collaborate with other social scientists to help identify and measure the values of these consequences.

It became apparent in the discussions at the workshop that many social scientists have difficulty dealing with the notion of worth or value in their research. The intermingling of the terms "benefits" and "consequences" throughout this book is one indication of the difficulty leisure scientists have in separating prescriptive from normative science. A few authors acknowledged that the consequence they were examining was a benefit by virtue of their own, other scientists, or society's value judgements (e.g., Csikszentmihalyi and Kleiber), that what may be a benefit for one person may not be for another (Roggenbuck et al.), and that not all consequences are beneficial (Haggard and Williams). Even the widely accepted benefits of play discussed by Barnett are not seen as benefits by all analysts. The same consequences of play and their application can be seen to "enrich" or "hurry" the child's development—the former outcome beneficial, the latter deleterious.

Cohen puts the issue of the valuation of consequences into a broader context. While he feels that these papers provide practitioners and lobbyists with ammunition to promote the need for resources to support leisure services and programs, he argues that this book with its focus on benefits leads to the side-stepping of some important questions. For Cohen the major problem is the paucity of attempts to relate the benefits of leisure to the wider problem of developing a sociological or cultural perspective on modern society, that is, how leisure relates to the wider social structure and culture. Is leisure a force of good that allows us the space and time to be creative and to experiment and develop innovative approaches to changing our institutions to allow meaningful lifestyles and living arrangements? Is leisure a dark and alienating force with its focus on the consumption of goods and services? One gets the impression that Cohen would have liked to have seen more discussion devoted to this broader valuation issue and consideration given to the appropriate social values necessary to provide a context for individuals and institutions to make "good" leisure choices from among the myriad of alternatives available.

An empirical perspective that is not necessarily in conflict with Cohen's, and which, in fact, might help clarify the valuation issue is suggested by Ajzen. As a social psychologist, he sees consequences judged as benefits to be based on a group norm which becomes internalized by the individual. He argues that social psychologists have been quite successful at studying norm formation, and suggests that leisure researchers can and should subject the process by which consequences become benefits to empirical scrutiny.

System Boundary

Our systems model includes a rough boundary identifying what is included within the system and what is treated as external. We can identify two important parts of the external system: 1) the broader values of society that are used in making choices and valuing various consequences; and 2) the policy, management, and planning uses of leisure benefits information. While not directly part of the system we have described thus far for studying leisure benefits, both parts of the external system influence and are effected by this system. These aspects of the external system most obviously influence the valuation process that we have just discussed. The flow of influences across the system boundary are particularly important in examining strategies for applying knowledge about leisure benefits.

The chapters concerned with applications stress the need for better information about leisure benefits. Within the United States, the driving forces behind most policy and management decisions are presently economic—jobs, income, inflation, interest rates, etc. The preeminence of economists and economic values in the policy arena is not coincidental. Economists have directly addressed the issues of allocation and efficiency. As Siehl and Kostmayer note, the budget process and economic concerns dominate policy in government. The disadvantage that noneconomists see with valuing all goods and services in terms of dollars becomes a significant strength in this arena. Dollar values provide a common denominator to compare programs and make allocation decisions. Given the strength of libertarian, free market values in the United States, we should not be surprised that benefits that are valued in economic terms receive more weight in the policy arena than those that are not.

Economic approaches and measures of benefits were intentionally down-played in this book as they currently dominate the recreation and leisure benefits area. As pointed out earlier, Johnson and Brown note that economists studying leisure benefits have primarily focused on valuation problems by measuring the worth of leisure experiences in terms of an individual's or a society's willingness to pay and have largely ignored the processes for producing consequences. Goods and services are priced according to their ability to be exchanged for other goods and services. As psychological states, community satisfaction, family stability, and many other important leisure consequences are not exchanged, nor are they priced. While resource economics deals extensively with unpriced values (Sinden and Worrell 1979), techniques for valuing nonmarket goods have not been applied to many of the unpriced consequences discussed in this book.

Those who wish to see noneconomic measures of benefits given more attention in the policy arena have two courses of action available. The first is to "buy" into the economic approach and develop dollar measures of value for benefits that have not traditionally been valued in economic terms. Many parks and recreation programs have done so, vying for attention with their own measures of spending, income, jobs, and consumer surplus. These efforts have opened up entirely new areas of application of economic tools. This trend reflects an "if you can't beat 'em, join 'em" strategy.

An advantage of this strategy is the reduced need to document all consequences if they can be valued without all this detail and/or knowledge. Johnson and Brown note that by assessing the willingness to pay through measuring the travel cost to a park, we can arrive at a value of a park without any knowledge of what contribution the park makes to a person's physical, mental, or social well-being. For some policy questions, this is all the policymaker needs. The success of this strategy will depend on success in developing nonmarket economic values for various leisure benefits within a framework that focuses on goods and services.

An alternative strategy is to attempt to change the rules or at least alter the balance between what are loosely termed "economic" and "noneconomic" values. It is largely at the administrative or policy analysis level that economic methods and values tend to dominate. However, most policy decisions are made within a political system where the rules include pressure groups, demonstrations, letters to elected officials, votes, and compromises (Siehl and Kostmayer). It is in this arena that intrinsic values and intangibles, information about noneconomic leisure benefits, may exert as strong an influence as information about dollars and cents.

Social scientists and leisure professionals have not been very effective in directly confronting policymakers. The "softness" of our science and the intangibility and diffuse nature of leisure consequences have been major obstacles. Within the political arena a focus on noneconomic measures of benefits, identified and documented by social science, may prove useful particularly if it allows the benefits to be more clearly and effectively communicated to those lobbying for various causes (Jordan). However, we should also be realistic. Very often policy is more the result of political strategy than science. For example, wilderness areas in the U.S. were not set aside because of cost/benefit analyses or any systematic identification of their leisure consequences. The Wilderness Act was the result of intensive lobbying by many groups and emotional appeals to the intrinsic values of a wilderness system.

SOME FINAL OBSERVATIONS ON THE BENEFITS OF A BENEFITS PERSPECTIVE

Driver and associates, both in this volume and elsewhere (e.g., Schreyer and Driver 1989), have elaborated on the leisure benefits construct and provide an elegant plea for further scholarly work in this area. This volume provides us with a good idea of what the leisure research of the past decade and a half tells us about leisure benefits. That is not to say that everyone is likely to agree with the conclusions of the various authors. For example, Barnett (this volume) does not feel that the developmental benefits of play have been empirically demonstrated. On the other hand, other scholars are more positive (e.g., Johnson et al. 1987). Also the chapters in this book do not provide an exhaustive list and analysis of all the benefits that may accrue from leisure. For example, only one paper deals with the therapeutic benefits of leisure and only one type of problem area is examined. Also a chapter on perceived freedom and control, as a benefit of leisure, would have been instructive. However, the papers comprising this volume as a whole appear to identify the major consequences of leisure that have the potential to be benefits. They also specify the outcomes that have been empirically documented, those outcomes for which there is partial support, and those that are purely speculative at this time.

From the reviews and analyses of the authors it is apparent that there is much to be learned about how leisure produces various behavioral and experiential consequences, and how these consequences come to be evaluated as beneficial. However, pessimissm does not seem to be warranted. In the present chapter we have tried to show that collectively the contributors raise a variety of important issues that are not only of value in our attempts to understand the benefits of leisure, but are of relevance to leisure researchers in general in their attempts to better understand leisure as psychological and social phenomena.

Additionally, it would seem that the benefits construct is a useful heuristic device for encouraging a reflective look at what research, dispersed in time and disciplinary focus, has collectively accomplished. In a sense, a benefits framework is useful for "packaging" and "show-casing" leisure research. We see today the emergence of a number of broader generic constructs being used to organize and provide a conceptual focus for what is often at best loosely connected theory and research on leisure. For example, the leisure *constraints* construct recently has received considerable attention (see Goodale and Witt 1989, Jackson 1988). Some of the same research that was reviewed under the *benefits* rubric for this volume has also been claimed by constraints theorists. These developments are not necessarily bad. In fact, the use of a generic construct is one way to "promote" research in a more meaningful and attractive manner, and draw the attention of practitioners, funding agencies, and researchers themselves, to issues that concern the leisure services field. Such generic approaches are useful strategies as long as they do not come to obscure the distinctiveness of the phenomena under scrutiny and suggest theoretical and conceptual coherence where none exists.

Finally, we note that a full understanding of the beneficial consequences of leisure also requires knowledge about the detrimental consequences. Leisure choices involve both benefits and costs to individuals and society. What may be seen as a benefit to one individual or social group may be a cost to another. One level of exercise may be a benefit, too much a cost. Inherent in our model of the "benefit process" (Fig. 1), is the need for a full and balanced accounting of consequences, followed by a valuation process that determines the worth of an activity based upon both benefits and costs.

LITERATURE CITED

Crandall, R.; Lewko, J. 1976. Leisure research, present and future: who, what, where. Journal of Leisure Research. 8: 150-159.

Csikszemtmihalyi, M.; Csikszentmihalyi, I. S. 1988. Optimal experience: psychological studies of flow in consciousness. New York, NY: Cambridge University Press. 416 p.

Driver, B. L.; Brown, P. J.; Stankey, G. H.; Gregoire, T. G. 1987. The ROS planning system: evolution, basic concepts and research needed. Leisure Sciences. 9: 210-212.

Driver, B. L.; Tocher, S. 1970. Toward a behavioral interpretation of recreational engagements, with implications for planning. In: Driver, B. L., ed. Elements of outdoor recreation planning. Ann Arbor, MI: University of Michigan Press: 9-31.

Gans, H. J. 1962. Outdoor recreation and mental health. In: Trends in American living and outdoor recreation. ORRRC Study Report #22. Outdoor Recreation Resources Review Commission. Washington, DC: US Government Printing Office: 233-242.

Goodale, T. L.; Witt, P. A. 1989. Recreation nonparticipation and barriers to leisure. In: Jackson, E. L.; Burton, T. L., eds. Understanding leisure and recreation: mapping the past, charting the future. State College, PA: Venture Publishing, Inc.: 421-449.

Homans, G. C. 1967. The nature of social science. New York, NY: Harcourt, Brace and World Inc. 109 p.

Hood, R. 1977. Eliciting mystical states of consciousness with semistructured nature experiences. Journal for the Scientific Study of Religion. 16: 155-163.

Iso-Ahola, S. 1980. The social psychology of leisure and recreation. Dubuque, IA: Brown. 436 p.

Jackson, E. L. 1988. Leisure constraints: a survey of past research. Leisure Sciences. 10: 203-215.

Johnson, J. E.; Christie, J. F.; Yawkey, T. D. 1987. Play and early childhood development. Glenview, IL: Scott, Foresman and Company. 269 p.

Kleiber, D.; Dirkin, G. R. 1985. Intrapersonal constraints to leisure. In: Wade, M., ed. Constraints on leisure. Springfield, IL: Charles C. Thomas: 17-42.

Mannell, R. C. 1979. A conceptual and experimental basis for research in the psychology of leisure. Society and Leisure. 2: 179-196.

Mannell, R. C. 1984. A psychology for leisure research. Society and Leisure. 7: 13-21.

Mannell, R. C. 1989. The concept of leisure satisfaction. In: Jackson E. L.; Burton T. L., eds. Understanding leisure and recreation: mapping the past, charting the future. State College, PA: Venture Publishing, Inc.: 281-301.

Mannell, R. C.; Iso-Ahola, S. 1987. Psychological nature of leisure and tourism experience. Annals of Tourism Research. 14: 314-331.

Neulinger, J. 1974. The psychology of leisure. Springfield, IL: Charles C. Thomas. 216 p.

Rosegrant, J. 1976. The impact of set and setting on religious experience in nature. Journal for the Scientific Study of Religion. 15: 301-310.

Schreyer, R.; Driver, B. L. 1989. The benefits of leisure. In: Jackson, E. L.; Burton, T. L., eds. Understanding leisure and recreation: mapping the past, charting the future. State College, PA: Venture Publishing, Inc.: 385-419.

Sinden, J. A.; Worrell, A. C. 1979. Unpriced values: decisions without market prices. New York, NY: John Wiley. 511 p.

Tinsley, H. A.; Tinsley, D. 1986. A theory of the attributes, benefits, and causes of leisure experience. Leisure Sciences. 8: 1-45.

Zuzanek, J. 1982. Leisure research in North America from a socio-historical perspective. In: Ng, D.; Smith, S. L., eds. Perspectives on the nature of leisure research. Waterloo, Canada: University of Waterloo Press: 170-186.

V.

APPENDIX: SUMMARY OF DISCUSSION GROUPS

INTRODUCTION

Preliminary drafts of the chapters in this text were previewed at a meeting of the authors in Snowbird, Utah in May 1989. Since the purpose was to provide feedback to the authors, most of the time at that 3-day workshop was spent in small group discussions.

This appendix summarizes the key issues and recommendations raised by the three discussion groups. The three reports of those discussion groups offer rich insights into the topic of measuring leisure benefits, and they cover some topics not included in the 35 chapters in this text.

Summary of Group 1 Discussion

Elery Hamilton-Smith
Department of Leisure Studies
Phillip Institute of Technology
Bundoora, Victoria
Australia

The first issue addressed by our group related to *content*. Although a need was expressed for a better conceptual and definitional framework of the kinds of potential benefits which might arise from leisure, our group recognized that no one taxonomy or classification of benefits would suffice. There would be contradictions and problems of incommensurability which would have to be considered by any classification scheme.

A key point discussed was that in drawing up such a classification, one could make use of the extent to which philosophy has examined many of the questions involved with human benefits, especially what might be called personal and social "goods." One could start by looking at the values which relate to the cultural, social, and economic contexts concerned. For instance, these might be values of happiness, beauty, knowledge, affluence, or even survival. But with each of these values we must select attributes, identify stimuli, and measure and evaluate the consequences of those stimuli—remembering that it's not just a matter of consequences in isolation; it's a matter of which consequences arising from what and accruing to whom or to what. In other words, we need a discriminatory analysis, not a global one.

The second issue our group looked at was *process*. Discussions focused on the need to develop some sort of operational models of processes and linkages. One of these, christened ISOOFE from the initial letters of the key words involved, is a micro model where one looks at a particular service or program. Within such a model, we can measure the inputs of the program, whatever they may be. They may consist of resources, staff, participants in programs—a whole range of possibilities. We can also measure the immediate outputs, e.g., the feelings of satisfaction that come from taking part in a particular program. But to be really effective

in measuring benefits, we also have to measure long-term outcomes. So, the long-term outcomes—the ultimate benefits that might accrue some months down the line after participation in a program—were seen by our group as quite important in this model. It is a model, without goals; one does not have to specify goals for programs to start with. After assessing the outputs and outcomes and evaluating them (our group distinguished between assessment and evaluation), that information must be fed back not only to the service itself (which might lead to change in inputs in order to make the service more effective), but also to the organizational environment, or social and organizational environment, within which the service is located.

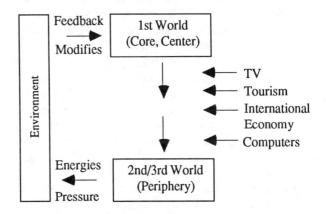

We also considered a second model which relates all of this to world systems. That model suggested that the core—the first world countries (the United States in particular)—generates a series of recreational patterns and benefits and exports them to other countries. This includes things such as televisions, tourism, computers, and impacts on the international economy. The more peripheral societies generate aspirations to enjoy the same sort of things. Regrettably, many of these things are energy hungry and often costly. Thus, as demands for them grow among a much wider population, considerable pressures are also generated that affect the physical and natural environment—pressures of pollution and of energy consumption. These in turn, will eventually result in some feedback to the core or center and hopefully, that feedback will lead to modification of the energy-conservative behavior going on at the center. But perhaps that is a bit optimistic. That is one of the questions we will have to look at if we consider the benefits in a world context. It was noted, too, that although some of the variables may not be directly observable or measurable, they might well be identified through use of measurable indicators.

Our group held the consensus view that if we are to manage programs, i.e., to predict outcomes, we need to understand not just inputs and consequences but the nature

ISOOFE

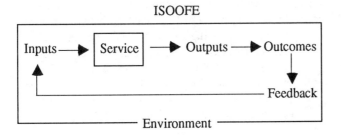

of the process that produces the consequences. In other words, what is it that goes on in the program or the leisure service delivery and use systems that connects those inputs together and leads to some sort of output as a result?

There was considerable agreement that the term leisure may be a problem. It may lead to ignoring the broader context. For instance, to what extent may many of the benefits that accrue from leisure accrue more effectively from work? The term may also distract us from seeing benefits which are not necessarily leisure-related, but instead are side effects of leisure and recreation. Our group felt that we have to think very clearly about the kind of language we use, its implications, and the extent to which it might restrict us. The long-term nature of outcomes pointed to the need for long-term research—longitudinal studies and research which remains stable over a very long time. Paffenbarger's research on the health outcomes of physical activity (see chapter by Paffenbarger, Hyde, and Dow) is a very clear but very rare example of just what is needed.

Finally, in our deliberations on process, the difficulty of nondollar values was noted. We recognize that there are problems in achieving measurement of nondollar values, and there are problems in attaining credibility for the measures once made. But some of those nondollar values are very important. It would indeed be problematic if our measurement of benefits came to focus only on those things that were easily measurable. We may well miss some of the more fundamentally important benefits that do not lend themselves to simple and ready measurement.

A third issue on which we concentrated attention was that of *social justice*, particularly the segmented distribution of benefits. It's easy enough to identify a very wide range of segments of the population who might be advantaged or disadvantaged in respect to particular benefits. This segmentation might be based on age—children, adolescents, middle-aged, aging; on life cycle—students, marrieds, singles, retired; on specific disadvantaged—the disabled or the mentally ill; on gender; on social status—the wealthy, the poor, the unemployed; on cultural divisions—whether these be ethnic, religious or other; on the setting—whether rural or urban and if urban, whether central city or outer suburban, or whatever. And there are many other segmentations that can be made. People making up each of these segments will differ in their personal resources, in their access to social resources, in their opportunity to utilize social resources, in their preferences for utilization of resources, and in the consequences of that utilization. In other words, each segment really needs to be studied quite separately when considering the benefits of leisure. Here again our group emphasized the need for much more discrimination in benefit study: Who gets which benefits? Information

on just that question is currently very inadequate. There may even be quite erroneous beliefs among service providers as to who is getting which benefits and who is not getting particular benefits. We just do not know enough about the distribution of benefits across the population and its many segments. However, it's probably a relatively safe assumption that many benefits are distributed in a way which correlates with the distribution of other social goods. Reduced benefits from recreation probably correlate with reduced benefits from work, with reduced financial resources, and probably with a number of other deprivations.

Our group identified a number of key questions regarding leisure and social justice/equitable distributions of benefits. Can recreational services or activities compensate for other deprivations? If so, is this an adequate basis for policy, or is it simply concealing and hiding the impact of wider social deprivation? In other words, is there a problem in using recreation as a distraction from disadvantage or oppression? One also encounters at this point the general question about universal or selective services. Are selective services that target a specific group likely to diminish the disadvantage of that group or simply perpetuate the difference and to perpetuate their separation?

Another policy question was raised by our group: On what basis should public funds be allocated to services for specific groups? Our group recognized that ideas about social justice depend upon the way in which we define justice. There are a range of definitions, the egalitarian, the libertarian, the welfare definitions, and merit definitions. These different perspectives have been dealt with in the literature and are well known to social policy personnel and to philosophers, but they may not be familiar to most practitioners in the recreation field. In our discussions of leisure opportunities and social justice, we noted that social order expressed by lack of conflict may very well be a sign of a repressive or oppressive society rather than a sign of genuine benefit and satisfaction.

The fourth and last issue addressed was that of *policy*, with a focus on the current challenge in all countries of resource scarcity in the public sector. Policymakers seem to be asking for more convincing evidence that scarce public resources are worth allocating to the leisure and recreation area. Our group felt that this issue hinges on how we define leisure. If we have a clear, common idea about what we mean by leisure, or recreation, then perhaps we can put forward more convincing arguments. One option would be to produce better evidence and argue in terms of the beneficial outcomes of indulging in recreational activity that are measurable in dollar values. Here, leisure would be defined primarily in terms of the goods and services for which people reveal a willingness to pay. Another possibility would be to view leisure as being its own benefit and talk about leisure and other benefits of recreation valued both in dollar and nondollar terms. If we take this line and see leisure itself as a benefit that arises not only out of recreational activities but sometimes out of work activity, our argument then is not just one of dollar values but also one of the intrinsic self-standing values of human society—values about human happiness and satisfaction that cannot be seen just in dollar values but can be seen in terms of desirable lifestyles. It could be argued that the purpose of a society is to provide its citizens with a lifestyle of value.

Alternatively, another position would be to define leisure as all nonjob activity. If we take this truly broad definition, then there are immense and wide-ranging benefits. A great deal of what makes for human society—courtship, marriage, and family life—fall into the leisure arena so defined. So does an immense amount of voluntary activity. Our very city governments, for instance, may depend upon volunteer city fathers or mothers as councilors. All this depends on the leisure arena. So there is this possibility of a broad-scale argument about the benefits of leisure. But it would depend on a broad and common agreement that this perspective is what we are talking about when we speak of leisure. Our group agreed, too, that the present crises in public funding indicates the need for a much more visible public constituency or lobby for recreation and leisure. Also, we felt that recreation practitioners need to become much better at clarifying the relationship between the technical/scientific aspects of an argument and the political aspects and at joining the aspects together much more effectively than they have often done.

We identified a number of areas and problems that have to be overcome in developing an effective public constituency. One is the extent to which so many recreation planners adopt a rationalist, centralist mode of planning and management—an overprofessionalized mode in which the ordinary citizen is frequently excluded. Another problem is that leisure is made far too comprehensive, diffuse, and complex by the leisure professionals. To build a public constituency, there is a need for some simple slogans. The self-evident contrast between the success of major league sports in building a public constituency vis à vis other activities speaks to this very eloquently. There is also a need for better planning and managing processes which will foster knowledge transfer. Additionally, there is the need for a more credible scientific approach. We questioned, too, whether the old dichotomy between basic and applied research is really valid. It seems too simplistic; research is too complex and unpredictable an endeavor to be classified into those two simple categories.

Finally, we leisure scientists probably deify theory too much. We give it too much importance. In doing so and by talking about it in abstruse language, we manage to separate theory and practice rather than maintain a dynamic relationship between the two, where theory is seen as the explanation upon which we base and explain our practice.

Summary of Group 2 Discussion

A. T. Easley
School of Natural Resources
Sir Sandford Fleming College
Lindsay, Ontario

Our small group discussion generated 19 thoughtful and provoking questions. To organize those questions into related topics, the discussion group conducted a "mental factor analysis"—without a 7090 Vector Computer or even an abacus. The 19 questions were loaded, intuitively and with some stress, on 5 factors which were then labeled as Factor Questions. Each Factor Question and its component questions are presented in tabular style.

FACTOR QUESTION 1: How can we convey the benefits of leisure more effectively?

1. What do we really know about the benefits of leisure?

2. What is a better concept or term for describing benefits—social wellness?

3. How can we articulate benefits to decision-makers? Can research be politically effective?

4. What is the appropriate role of government in providing benefits?

5. Why do we need to articulate benefits?

There was consensus that as scientists we must make conditional statements to limit generalizability of conclusions, particularly if there is a difference between an outcome (consequence) and a benefit (improved condition). As scientists, we have a right and indeed a societal obligation to decide if a consequence is a benefit, but we must declare "why" and link it conceptually to higher orders of beneficiaries. Specifically, how does an individual benefit contribute to a societal or community benefit?

Because of the impassioned pleas of Charles Jordan, the legislative insights of George Siehl, and the managerial needs of Darrell Lewis, we were mindful that we need to develop political relevance. There is great need to better transfer our research results and implications to the policymakers and resource allocators and to the folks "making a difference" on the ground and "in the trenches."

FACTOR QUESTION 2: Can we reach a broadly generalizable definition of benefits?

1. Can leisure address the problems of life in the post-industrial state?

2. How will definitions of benefits change with changing social, environmental, and economic conditions?

3. What are benefits versus consequences?

We pursued but did not successfully develop a more general, expedient, or socially acceptable conceptual framework for our "benefits" research efforts. Benefits research as input into the more savvy term "social wellness" was considered. We concede the need for a term that connotes positive leisure outcomes and optimal well-being.

We spent considerable time assessing our abilities to track a moving benefits target, in the context of ever changing social, environmental, and economic conditions. We agreed that there are significant challenges ahead and if the askers of questions are precise and theoretically grounded (and resources are allocated), we, as a scientific community of independent seekers of the truth, can meet the research needs. There are, however, no umbrella agencies at the moment to initiate or support the much needed research on the benefits of leisure.

Clearly, there are rich and productive areas of objective research which can be initiated immediately to triangulate on the portended future. For example, a research protocol to predict future changes followed by efforts to research the implications of these changes may result in a valuable advocacy position for a group such as ours.

FACTOR QUESTION 3: What is the scope of the benefits and consequences of leisure?

1. Have we identified all the consequences of leisure?

2. How can we look beyond individual benefits of leisure?

3. How can we be tolerant of a diversity of definitions?

4. Should we study the negative outcomes of leisure?

We discussed the notion of a holistic analytic or accounting system for benefits research to help ensure conceptual linkages from individual consequences to societal consequences. We were ever mindful of the "Tragedy of the Commons" where, simplistically stated, the sum of individual benefits results in a societal disbenefit or adverse consequence. Our holistic accounting system must, after measuring the magnitude of outcomes, also address the relative worth of such outcomes to societal well-being.

FACTOR QUESTION 4: How can we improve outcomes research?

1. What kinds of questions need longitudinal research?

2. Can research designs be improved?

3. Is there one objective measure of benefits?

4. Can benefits be quantified?

There was consensus that more rigor is required in conceptually or theoretically grounding future research on the benefits of leisure. We need innovative developments in research methodologies which are both process-oriented and outcome-oriented. Graduate students in several areas need to "borrow" more rigorous experimental, quasi-experimental, and qualitative protocols from other disciplines and exercise caution and intuitive good sense when transferring the methodologies to "field" situations.

Research over time is desperately required but longitudinal research of the traditional sort falls short of our needs. Lagged time series and cohort analyses will help reduce both internal and external threats to validity caused by rapidly changing social conditions. Where possible, multiple measures of outcome, or criterion measures, should be used. Acceptability of repeated or replicated important research by journals would be a help in developing a longer term perspective.

FACTOR QUESTION 5: What do we know about what causes benefits from leisure?

1. What types of consequences are caused by different forms of leisure?

2. What is the contribution of natural environments in providing benefits?

3. Are there substitutes for leisure benefits?

We do know some of the tentative causal links with outcomes. There is a definite need, however, for research that addresses the activity, environment, and person (individual differences) interactions. In many instances, the environment or setting may determine the limits of substitutability. With increased urbanization, this potential for substitutability for natural environment activities must become better understood.

Summary of Group 3 Discussion

Dennis K. Orthner
Human Services Research Laboratory
University of North Carolina at Chapel Hill
Chapel Hill, North Carolina

Our group represented a cross section of the leisure professions, including basic and applied researchers and program managers. In the course of reviewing issues surrounding leisure benefits, the group decided to focus on four central themes:

- Differentiation of leisure benefits across society.
- Assessing beneficial consequences of leisure.
- Impact of leisure on societal problems.
- Knowledge of leisure benefits.

The points raised by the group about each of these issues are elaborated below.

Differentiation of Leisure Benefits Across Society

The group posited several assumptions related to the differentiation of leisure benefits across society.

1. Many factors serve to create an unequal distribution of leisure benefits including inequities in the distribution of leisure/recreation opportunities.

2. Conventional market factors do not result in equitable distributions.

3. There appears to be greater disparity in recreation opportunities than ever before.

4. A single perspective should not dominate the leisure delivery system.

5. Many types of differentiations need to be considered including those dealing with economic, racial, rural-urban, regional, and other classifying variables.

An examination of these assumptions raises issues that should be of concern to the recreation-related professions. These include our responsibilities to be more proactive versus reactive in the provision of leisure opportunities.

Conventional response has been market driven (i.e., reactive) to the neglect of proactive strategies that reach out to deliver effective services to different types of populations across the nation. This raises the question of our role as social engineers and whether it is appropriate for the leisure professions to promote or prescribe different leisure patterns than currently exist. Another question is our role in leading in this area versus following other professionals that have had a more traditional focus on working with disadvantaged populations, such as the extension service or social work.

The issue of public recreation for different disadvantaged populations is of growing concern to many recreation professionals. In part, this comes from lack of information about the leisure needs of these groups. It also is of concern to many public park professionals who see some of the destructive aspects of the leisure patterns of economically disadvantaged groups, especially those who vandalize valuable facilities. Our group was quite concerned about the need for more information about the constructive leisure needs of these groups. We were concerned, too, about the need for improved methods for studying potential users and not just current users. Most of our assessment programs tend to be oriented toward current user populations. Better methods for assessing the leisure needs of the entire community including populations who are not currently using available facilities and programs are sorely needed.

Assessing Beneficial Consequences of Leisure

One of the issues discussed by our group was the use of different and often incomparable measures for assessing the consequences of leisure. Some persons argue for more holistic measures that assess the underlying gestalt of the experience, while others suggest that more individual and particularistic measures are needed to better assess the range of specific types of benefits. Of course, inadequacies of our current definitions of leisure benefits create problems for the development of adequate measures of benefits. The measures of benefits must consider such factors as the context of the experience, the level of coparticipation, the specific behaviors associated with the experience, and of course the effect of the experience.

The issue of levels of benefits must also be considered in improved definitions of the consequences of leisure experiences. That is, most leisure research, to date, focuses on the benefits for the individual and specifically on some subdimension of that individual such as cardiac functioning, psychological well-being, or physical strength attributes. We know relatively little about the benefits for groups or organizations such as families, recreation teams, work units, sponsoring organizations, or communities. Little attention has been given to any of these more aggregative units of impact.

Another issue discussed was the need to better understand the long-term benefits of leisure and recreation experiences. There has been little evaluation research on the consequences of recreation programs, and almost no longitudinal studies examining benefits of leisure experiences beyond the immediate or short range. That research is needed and should include both specific and holistic measures and use both quantitative and qualitative methodologies.

There is also an important need to encourage and develop additional funding and for existing agencies to be more actively involved. Traditional sources of funding for individual, family, or organizational research have not supported basic research on leisure experiences. This has hampered development of large-scale longitudinal studies that are badly needed to answer some of the fundamental questions raised by our group.

Impact of Leisure on Societal Problems

To advance the contribution of leisure to the resolution of fundamental social problems, the leisure-related professions must concentrate more resources on the macroenvironment. Two fundamental questions were asked by our group: How does leisure contribute to solving social problems? What is "negative leisure" and how are the associated experiences different in their consequences either for the individual or society? It was clear from our discussion that leisure outcomes by themselves cannot be distinguished as either good or bad. Rather, they lie on a continuum from positive to negative depending on the circumstances of the individual and the consequences for others.

Our group reached consensus that leisure professionals need to understand better the causes of social problems. Even though this has not been a traditional area of interest to those professionals, our failure to join with other disciplines in seeking ways to address social problems results in abdication of our responsibility to improve the quality of life for individuals, families, and communities. Leisure professionals need to know which leisure activities provide a medium for correcting social ills, or at least the contribution that leisure experiences can have for reducing the negative consequences of problems that are experienced by individuals in our society. Clearly, it is of significant importance. It might well be potentially more significant for us to understand how leisure experiences benefit those whose lives are troubled than to assess the benefits to those whose lives are already enriched.

Knowledge of Leisure Benefits

An underlying concern of our group was confusion about the concept of leisure itself. It was clear from our discussion that there is considerable debate about the value of leisure experiences, as well as the definition of leisure itself, both conceptually and operationally. There is also a gap between the potential of leisure experiences, as described in many of the papers, and the reality of leisure, as observed in the lives of leisure participants. For example, a significant current gap is the information needed for people to make appropriate recreation choices. Based on recent reviews, the public appears to be woefully uninformed of what leisure opportunities are available, how leisure experiences can help people, and the means through which they can achieve leisure benefits. A much better marketing job is needed to inform the public about leisure benefits. This will break down some of the negative stereotypes of leisure experiences that still exist in our society and create a more positive atmosphere for the delivery of recreation services.

People in the leisure delivery arena also need to be more aware of leisure benefits. It was suggested that leisure delivery systems shift gears from a passive mode to more of an extension mode and reach out to populations who currently misunderstand the benefits of leisure or who are not receiving leisure services. We need to turn to a greater involvement of volunteers in the delivery of leisure services and the re-education of recreation professionals and away from a skills orientation approach to leisure benefits. Two strategies that were suggested for encouraging improved leisure delivery services included: 1) examining organizational wellness programs as a model for developing community wellness systems, and 2) seeking funding for developing community demonstration models that can test alternative ways of delivering enhanced leisure services.

The final point addressed by our group is the need to disseminate the substance of our deliberations to others. This includes but is not limited to this text on the *Benefits of Leisure*. Pamphlets need to be developed and distributed to community residents, park directors, and other allied social service professionals. Those pamphlets should describe the contributions that leisure experiences can have and elicit public support in building a more effective leisure delivery system. Finally, leisure professionals need to take more proactive measures in public and congressional hearings in which leisure issues and resources are debated. It is time to stop cutting park and recreation resources first in local, state, and federal resource reallocations. Unless policymakers better understand the benefits of leisure experiences and the negative consequences associated with reducing recreation resources, individual, family, and community life will suffer, and many of our programs will continue to be decimated.

BOOKS FROM VENTURE PUBLISHING

Acquiring Parks and Recreation Facilities through Mandatory Dedication: A Comprehensive Guide
 by Ronald A. Kaiser and James D. Mertes

The Activity Gourmet
 by Peggy Powers

Adventure Education
 edited by John C. Miles and Simon Priest

Amenity Resource Valuation: Integrating Economics with Other Disciplines
 edited by George L. Peterson, B.L. Driver and Robin Gregory

Behavior Modification in Therapeutic Recreation: An Introductory Learning Manual
 by John Dattilo and William D. Murphy

Beyond the Bake Sale—A Fund Raising Handbook for Public Agencies
 by Bill Moskin

The Community Tourism Industry Imperative—The Necessity, The Opportunities, Its Potential
 by Uel Blank

Dimensions of Choice: A Qualitative Approach to Recreation, Parks, and Leisure Research
 by Karla A. Henderson

Doing More With Less in the Delivery of Recreation and Park Services: A Book of Case Studies
 by John Crompton

Evaluation of Therapeutic Recreation Through Quality Assurance
 edited by Bob Riley

The Evolution of Leisure: Historical and Philosophical Perspectives
 by Thomas Goodale and Geoffrey Godbey

The Future of Leisure Services: Thriving on Change
 by Geoffrey Godbey

Gifts to Share—A Gifts Catalogue How-To Manual for Public Agencies
 by Lori Harder and Bill Moskin

Great Special Events and Activities
 by Annie Morton, Angie Prosser and Sue Spangler

Leadership and Administration of Outdoor Pursuits
 by Phyllis Ford and James Blanchard

The Leisure Diagnostic Battery: Users Manual and Sample Forms
 by Peter A. Witt and Gary Ellis

Leisure Diagnostic Battery Computer Software
    by Gary Ellis and Peter A. Witt

Leisure Education: A Manual of Activities and Resources
    by Norma J. Stumbo and Steven R. Thompson

Leisure Education: Program Materials for Persons with Developmental Disabilities
    by Kenneth F. Joswiak

Leisure Education Program Planning: A Systematic Approach
    by John Dattilo and William D. Murphy

Leisure in Your Life: An Exploration, Third Edition
    by Geoffrey Godbey

A Leisure of One's Own: A Feminist Perspective on Women's Leisure
    by Karla Henderson, M. Deborah Bialeschki, Susan M. Shaw and Valeria J. Freysinger

Marketing for Parks, Recreation, and Leisure
    by Ellen L. O'Sullivan

Outdoor Recreation Management: Theory and Application, Revised and Enlarged
    by Alan Jubenville, Ben Twight and Robert H. Becker

Planning Parks for People, by John Hultsman
    by Richard L. Cottrell and Wendy Zales Hultsman

Private and Commercial Recreation
    edited by Arlin Epperson

The Process of Recreation Programming Theory and Technique, Third Edition
    by Patricia Farrell and Herberta M. Lundegren

Quality Management: Applications for Therapeutic Recreation
    edited by Bob Riley

Recreation and Leisure: An Introductory Handbook
    edited by Alan Graefe and Stan Parker

Recreation and Leisure: Issues in an Era of Change, Third Edition
    edited by Thomas Goodale and Peter A. Witt

Recreation Economic Decisions: Comparing Benefits and Costs
    by Richard G. Walsh

Recreation Programming And Activities For Older Adults
    by Jerold E. Elliott and Judith A. Sorg-Elliott

Risk Management in Therapeutic Recreation: A Component of Quality Assurance
    by Judith Voelkl

Schole VI: A Journal of Leisure Studies and Recreation Education

A Social History of Leisure Since 1600
by Gary Cross

Sports and Recreation for the Disabled—A Resource Manual
by Michael J. Paciorek and Jeffery A. Jones

A Study Guide for National Certification in Therapeutic Recreation
by Gerald O'Morrow and Ron Reynolds

Therapeutic Recreation Protocol for Treatment of Substance Addictions
by Rozanne W. Faulkner

Understanding Leisure and Recreation: Mapping the Past, Charting the Future
edited by Edgar L. Jackson and Thomas L. Burton

Wilderness in America: Personal Perspectives
edited by Daniel L. Dustin

Venture Publishing, Inc
1999 Cato Avenue
State College, PA 16801
814-234-4561